Ibn Qayyim al-Jawziyya and the Divine Attributes

Islamic Philosophy, Theology and Science

TEXTS AND STUDIES

Edited by

Hans Daiber
Anna Akasoy
Emilie Savage-Smith

VOLUME 104

The titles published in this series are listed at *brill.com/ipts*

Ibn Qayyim al-Jawziyya and the Divine Attributes

Rationalized Traditionalistic Theology

By

Miriam Ovadia

BRILL

LEIDEN | BOSTON

Cover illustration: Design by Shani Ovadia-Soffer

Library of Congress Cataloging-in-Publication Data

Names: Ovadia, Miriam, author.
Title: Ibn Qayyim al-Jawziyya and the divine attributes : rationalized traditionalistic theology / by Miriam Ovadia.
Description: Leiden ; Boston : Brill, [2018] | Series: Islamic philosophy, theology and science ; V. 104 | Includes bibliographical references and index.
Identifiers: LCCN 2018024128 (print) | LCCN 2018024833 (ebook) | ISBN 9789004372511 (e-book) | ISBN 9789004371293 (hardback : alk. paper)
Subjects: LCSH: God (Islam)–Attributes. | Ibn Qayyim al-Jawzīyah, Muḥammad ibn Abī Bakr, 1292-1350. Ṣawāʾiq al-mursalah ʿalá firaq al-Muʿtazilah wa-al-Jahmīyah wa-al-Muʿaṭṭilah.
Classification: LCC BP166.2 (ebook) | LCC BP166.2 .O96 2018 (print) | DDC 297.2/112–dc23
LC record available at https://lccn.loc.gov/2018024128

Typeface for the Latin, Greek, and Cyrillic scripts: "Brill". See and download: brill.com/brill-typeface.

ISSN 0169-8729
ISBN 978-90-04-37129-3 (hardback)
ISBN 978-90-04-37251-1 (e-book)

This book is printed on acid-free paper and produced in a sustainable manner.

Contents

Acknowledgments VII
Note on Transliteration and Translation VIII

Introduction: Ibn al-Qayyim's *al-Ṣawāʿiq*: A Hostile Response to Rationalism 1
Islamic Traditionalistic Theology 11
Ibn Qayyim al-Jawziyya as (an) a (In)dependent Scholar 13
Methodological Lines of the Textual Inquiry 16

1 **The Scholarly Setting of Mamluk Damascus: *al-Ṣawāʿiq*'s Birthplace** 22
1.1 A Stormy Approach: Ibn Taymiyya on the Issue of Divine Attributes 38
1.2 Ibn Taymiyya's View on *taʾwīl* in *Bayān talbīs al-jahmiyya* 44

2 **A Stroke of Lightning: *al-Ṣawāʿiq* in Ibn al-Qayyim's Theological Writing** 53
2.1 Scope of *al-Ṣawāʿiq*: The Text and Related Writings 55
2.2 *Al-Ṣawāʿiq* within Mamluk Intellectual Literature 61
2.3 Appropriating the Taymiyyan Discourse in *al-Ṣawāʿiq*: Ibn al-Qayyim's Systemization 75
2.4 *Al-Ṣawāʿiq* as a *Kalām* Manual: Ibn al-Qayyim's Rationalization 81
2.5 Against *taʾwīl*: *al-Ṣawāʿiq*'s Main Argument 89

3 **First *ṭāghūt* Refutation: The Islamic Scriptures Produce Certain Knowledge** 114
3.1 Ibn al-Qayyim's Rationalized-Traditionalistic Arguments on Epistemology in *al-Ṣawāʿiq* I 118
3.2 Fakhr al-Dīn al-Rāzī on Certain Knowledge: Skepticism 138
3.3 Ibn Taymiyya's Initial Critique against al-Rāzī 145
3.4 Ibn al-Qayyim's Development: Restoring Optimism 159

4 **Second *ṭāghūt* Refutation: Revelation is the Provenance of Knowledge** 175
4.1 Ibn al-Qayyim's Rationalized-Traditionalistic Arguments on Epistemology in *al-Ṣawāʿiq* II 176
4.2 Ibn Taymiyya's Initial Critique against al-Ghazālī (from the View of Ibn al-Qayyim) 178
4.3 Ibn al-Qayyim on the Epistemological Value of Revelation 190

5 Third *ṭāghūt* Refutation: Undermining the Theoretical Basis of *majāz* 199
5.1 Prefatory Remarks: The *ḥaqīqa*/*majāz* Dichotomy and the Origin of Language 201
5.2 Ibn Taymiyya's Critique against *majāz* 207
5.3 Ibn al-Qayyim's Rationalized Hermeneutics 218
5.4 Attacking the Muʿtazilite Heritage 235
5.5 Ibn al-Qayyim's Rational-Traditionalistic Inspiration 243
5.6 Ibn al-Qayyim's Recruitment of Ibn Rushd against *taʾwīl* 252

6 Fourth *ṭāghūt* Refutation: Hadith Literature Produces Certainty 266
6.1 Ibn Taymiyya on the Validity of *ḥadīth al-āḥād* 269
6.2 Ibn al-Qayyim's Ten Arguments on the Value of *ḥadīth al-āḥād* 271
6.3 Structural Aspects of Ibn al-Qayyim's Rationalization: *al-Ṣawāʿiq*'s Literary Symmetry 283

Conclusions 291

Bibliography 297
Index of Names 316
General Index 319

Acknowledgments

This book is the final outcome of a doctoral research project conducted between the years 2012–2017 in Berlin Graduate School Muslim Cultures and Societies (BGSMCS). The doctoral research project was funded by the Excellence Initiative of the German Federal and State Governments (DFG) and by Freie Universität Berlin. In my dissertation, I have significantly extended and reworked parts of my MA thesis entitled "Ibn Qayyim al-Jawziyya's Hermeneutical Approach to God's Attributes and the Anthropomorphic Expressions in the Quran and the Hadith Literature" (2012) which has been carried out in Bar-Ilan University in Ramat-Gan, Israel. Both the thesis and the dissertation were written as part of a project funded by the German-Israeli Foundation for Scientific Research and Development: "Patterns of Argumentation and Rhetorical Devices in the Legal and Theological Works of Ibn Qayyim al-Jawziyya" (GIF 1079–111.4/2009), in which I was privileged to take part as a graduate student and research assistant between 2011 and 2015.

With the completion of this book, I would like to express my gratitude to the Principle Investigators of the GIF projects who were also my supervisors. I thank my first supervisor, Dr. Livnat Holtzman, chair of the Arabic Department in Bar-Ilan University, for her professional and devoted guidance and for sharing her erudite knowledge with me. I thank her for enabling me to take part in her impressive research enterprise and for inspiring me to further advance in the road of academic research. By the same token, I offer my sincerest gratitude to my second supervisor, Prof. Dr. Birgit Krawietz, from the Institute of Islamic Studies in Freie Universität Berlin, for her invaluable, adept professional advice and kind support and encouragement.

This is also a wonderful opportunity to thank my colleagues and friends at BGSMCS, a splendid group which outgrew the strictly professional framework and became a source of mental strength as well as cerebral interaction.

Last but far from least, I wish to thank my family. I am indebted to my parents, Carmela and Mordechai, who long nurtured my instinct of curiosity, for their trust and constant, unconditional support. I am also thankful to my dear sister Shani, for her interest, understanding and support, without which these lines could have never been written.

Note on Transliteration and Translation

Arabic Transliteration follows the Library of Congress conventions, briefly outlined below:

ء	ʾ	خ	kh	ش	sh	غ	gh	م	m
ب	b	د	d	ص	ṣ	ف	f	ن	n
ت	t	ذ	dh	ض	ḍ	ق	q	ه	h
ث	th	ر	r	ط	ṭ	ك	k	و	w
ج	j	ز	z	ظ	ẓ	ل	l	ي	y
ح	ḥ	س	s	ع	ʿ				
		ة	a/t			ال	al-/ʾl-		

◌َ	a	◌ُ	u	◌ِ	i
◌ً	an	◌ٌ	un	◌ٍ	in
آ	ā	◌ُو	ū	◌ِي	ī
◌َا	ā	◌ُوّ	ūw	◌ِيّ	īy
ى	ā	◌َو	aw	◌َي	ay

* Final vocalization is stated in superscript, when needed.

The Chicago Manual of Style (CMS) serves as the basis for all issues of bibliographical style.

Translation of all Quran verses follows: Abdel Haleem, M.A.S., *The Qurʾan: A New Translation*, Oxford World's Classics (Oxford: Oxford University Press, 2008).

INTRODUCTION

Ibn al-Qayyim's *al-Ṣawāʿiq*: A Hostile Response to Rationalism

The theological issue of the divine attributes (*ṣifāt Allāh*) was one of the major bones of contention in the dispute between traditionalist and rationalist Muslim scholars who spent much time and efforts dwelling on this subject since the early centuries of Islam. Striving to attain an appropriate understanding of the various characteristics attributed to God in the texts sacred to Islam, namely the Quran and the literature of Hadith, the traditionalists and the rationalists used differentiated—at times opposing—methods of approaching those texts and deriving their meanings concerning God and the divine. Gaining considerable gravity, the issue of divine attributes grew to be a close-to-compulsory topic of engagement for numerous theologians of Islam. Thought-provoking in this regard is a reference made by the Ḥanbalite scholar of 8th/14th century Damascus, Shams al-Dīn Muḥammad ibn Abī Bakr ibn Qayyim al-Jawziyya (d. 751/1350, henceforth: Ibn al-Qayyim). In the opening part to one of his major works entitled *al-Ṣawāʿiq al-mursala* (The Unleashed Thunderbolts), which in the Islamic scholarship contains *de rigueur* a passage of praise to God, Ibn al-Qayyim quite naturally appropriated the belief in a traditionalistic view of the divine attributes to the customary profession of belief in Allah and the Prophet Muḥammad (*shahāda*):

> I profess that there is no God except Allah alone, who has no associates, who is described with the attributes of glory (*ṣifāt al-jalāl*) and depicted in the depictions of perfection (*nuʿūt al-kamāl*), who is transcendent (*munazzah*) beyond anything that contradicts His perfection, [such as] depriving the essential realities (*ḥaqāʾiq*) of His names and attributes, which requires describing Him with deficiencies and likening Him to the created human beings (*shibh^{i} makhlūqīn*) [...] And I profess that Muḥammad is His worshiper and Messenger ...[1]

1 Ibn Qayyim al-Jawziyya Shams al-Dīn ibn Abī Bakr Muḥammad (d. 751/1350), *al-Ṣawāʿiq al-mursala ʿala ʾl-jahmiyya wal-muʿaṭṭila*, ed. ʿAlī al-Dakhīl Allāh, third edition in 4 vols. (Riyadh: Dār al-ʿĀṣima, 1418/1998), 1:147–148.

 | DOI: 10.1163/9789004372511_002

Not only did Ibn al-Qayyim find the issue of the divine attributes noteworthy at the very beginning of his work, he also took the liberty of integrating it as a part of the *shahāda*, one of the five pillars of Islam (*arkān al-islām al-khamsa*). In this self-adjusted testimony of faith, he actively incorporated his personal idea of the image of the one God and the distinct nature of His attributes within the most basic Islamic tenet. These attributes of God are abundant in the texts of the Quran and the Hadith literature (Sunna, i.e., transmitted virtuous sayings and costumes of the Prophet Muḥammad), a fact which raised a question of belief: how should a Muslim perceive the names (*al-asmāʾ al-ḥusnā*) and attributes (*ṣifāt*) that describe God, and what are the theologically implied meanings? From a philosophical perspective, this question arises out of the inherent tension between the notion of one essence (*al-dhāt*) and that of multiple attributes (*al-ṣifāt*), when speaking about a sole God.[2] The correct manner of understanding the divine attributes has therefore been a cause for dogmatic points of dispute between diverse Muslim scholars affiliated to different theological schools and has gradually evolved into one of the most complex issues in Islamic religious thought.

Setting aside several other apparent theological ideas mentioned in the short passage by Ibn al-Qayyim cited above, this opening certainly illustrates the strong connection between the issue of the divine attributes and the question of anthropomorphism (*tashbīh*, lit., likening or assimilating God to His creation). Such expressions implying the assimilation of God and His created beings also appear in the Quran, for example where verses refer to His face (Q 55:26–27), His eyes (Q 11:37), His hand (Q 48:10) or His seat on His throne (Q 20:5). The literature of the Hadith elaborates on such mundane descriptions by ascribing human-like feelings to God (e.g., cunning (*makr*), laughter or love),[3] which the theologians feared would be understood negatively, thus

2 In early times, God's names were perceived as separated ontological entities (*ashyāʾ*, lit., things) existing inside Him, rather than descriptive semantic signifiers of His attributes. This can be seen in the writings of the early Muʿtazilite scholar Wāṣil ibn ʿAṭāʾ (d. 131/748) from Baṣra, who rejected such an ontological grasp of God's attributes; Nader El-Bizri, "God: Essence and Attributes," in *The Cambridge Companion to Classical Islamic Theology*, ed. Tim Winter (Cambridge: Cambridge University Press, 2008): 121–124; Arent J. Wensinck, *The Muslim Creed: Its Genesis and Historical Development* (Cambridge, London: Frank Cass, 1932), 70–77; Harry Austryn Wolfson, *The Philosophy of the Kalam* (Cambridge: Harvard University Press, 1976), 112–119, 131–132.

3 This topic is questioned and explored in the article: Holtzman, "'Does God Really Laugh?'—Appropriate and Inappropriate Descriptions of God in Islamic Traditionalist Theology," in *Laughter in the Middle Ages and Early Modern Times*, ed. A. Classen (Berlin: de Gruyter, 2010):

diminishing God's absolute perfection. Other Hadith accounts express 'passive-anthropomorphism,' such as the idea that God will be seen as the promised reward for believers on the Day of Judgment (*ruʾyat Allāh*, this also appears in Q 75:22–23). Outwardly, descriptions of this kind collide with the categorical prohibition in Islam of likening God to mankind, as He is perceived as being absolutely transcendent: "there is nothing like Him" (Q 42:11) and "no one is comparable to Him" (Q 112:4).[4] Rather concisely, Ibn al-Qayyim's rendered profession of faith also includes the belief in an utterly transcendent deity, hence reflecting an interesting theological approach of conciliation between the (highly problematic) issues already mentioned. Ibn al-Qayyim captures here at least two vital theological debates in a single thought articulated as a core matter of righteous Islamic belief.

The nuanced *shahāda* cited above opens the prominent work by Ibn al-Qayyim *al-Ṣawāʿiq al-mursala ʿala ʾl-jahmiyya wal-muʿaṭṭia* (The Unleashed Thunderbolts Directed against the Heretics and the Deniers), which stands in the heart of this study. True to the teachings of his mentor, the exceptional scholar Taqi ʾl-Dīn Aḥmad Ibn Taymiyya (d. 728/1328), Ibn al-Qayyim expressed in *al-Ṣawāʿiq* the Taymiyyan concepts on the theological issue of divine attributes.[5] *Al-Ṣawāʿiq* is considered to be a completed monograph comprised of four main parts which originally constituted a voluminous work whose length is estimated in some thousand pages (only the first half of them survived until today, yet the available manuscripts were scientifically com-

---

169. Several anthropomorphic Hadith accounts of God's laughter on doomsday are discussed, while referring to the inter-traditionalistic disagreements between Ḥanbalite and Ashʿarite theologians.

4 Gerhard Böwering, "God and His Attributes," *Encyclopaedia of the Qurʾān*, 2:316–331; El-Bizri, "God: Essence and Attributes," 121–140; Josef van Ess, "Tashbīh wa-Tanzīh," *EI*², 10: 341–344; Daniel Gimaret, "Ṣifa", *EI*², 9:551–552; Cloude Gilliot, "Attributes of God," *The Encyclopaedia of Islam, THREE*. Edited by: Kate Fleet, Gudrun Krämer, Denis Matringe, John Nawas, Everett Rowson. Brill Online. 07 January 2011, URL http://www.brillonline.nl/subscriber/entry?entry=ei3_COM-0163; Livnat Holtzman, "Anthropomorphism," *EI THREE*, 1:48–49; Binyamin Abrahanov, *Islamic Theology: Traditionalism and Rationalism* (Edinburgh: Edinburgh University Press, 1996), 52–53.

5 At the age of 21, Ibn al-Qayyim met the exceptional scholar Ibn Taymiyya who deeply affected his thinking. Consequently, Ibn al-Qayyim became Ibn Taymiyya's most esteemed disciple over the next 15 years; Caterina Bori and Livnat Holtzman, the Introduction to: *A Scholar in the Shadow: Essays in the Legal and Theological Thought of Ibn Qayyim al-Ǧawziyyah*, eds. Caterina Bori and Livnat Holtzman, Oriente Moderno XC/1 (Rome: Istituto per l'Oriente C.A. Nallino, 2010), 17.

piled and supply a very good source for the study of that part).[6] Both modern researchers as well as scholars of Ibn al-Qayyim's time describe *al-Ṣawaʿiq* as one of the most important theological compositions among his abundant and various writings.[7] Although *al-Ṣawāʿiq* is one of Ibn al-Qayyim's most copious works, and given its importance for his combative defiance against the rationalistic thought, so far there has been very little scholarly engagement with this text. Offering comprehensive philological analysis of the work in a close reading while taking into account the historical setting in which it was composed, this study is the first large-scale attempt in modern scholarship to thoroughly read and analyze *al-Ṣawāʿiq*'s challenging text as a unity. In addition to the engagement with *al-Ṣawāʿiq*'s contents, this study also draws a clearer scholarly portrait of its author, Ibn al-Qayyim, and his singular contribution to Islamic theological thought, whose significance has only recently been identified and acknowledged in Western research.

Belonging to the traditionalist Ḥanbalites (also known as: *ahl al-sunna wal-ḥadīth*), Ibn al-Qayyim voiced an uncompromising adherence to the texts of the Quran and the Hadith as the only provenance for all human knowledge. Consequently, he composed *al-Ṣawāʿiq* as a harsh tirade against the Ashʿarite scholars who embraced moderate rationalistic argumentation methods in their theological deliberations, most relevant here is the figurative interpretation of the texts (*taʾwīl*). Ibn al-Qayyim's discussion on the divine attributes in *al-Ṣawāʿiq* reflects the intellectual clash between traditionalism and rationalism in Islamic thought and, even more so, the discrepancy within Sunnite-traditionalistic thought between the ultra-traditionalist Ḥanbalites and the rational-traditionalist Ashʿarites. It is worth mentioning, in the time of the Mamluk sultanate it was Ibn al-Qayyim's famous mentor Taqi 'l-Dīn Aḥmad Ibn Taymiyya (d. 728/1328) who made the most forceful denunciation of the rationalistic theological stances, for example in his major works *Darʾ taʿāruḍ al-ʿaql wal-naql* (Refutation of the Contradiction between Reason and Revelation)

6 Ibn Qayyim al-Jawziyya, *al-Ṣawāʿiq al-mursala* the editor's introduction, 1:82. I will further elaborate on the work's edited version and its abriedgemetnt henceforth, and especially in chapter 2.

7 Most of Ibn al-Qayyim's works were written after the death of his mentor and represent an intellectual development of some 23 years. Holtzman offered a periodization of Ibn al-Qayyim's theological works, dividing them into early, middle and later periods. Her division to middle and later works relied on the fact that "in his later works Ibn Qayyim al-Jawziyyah cites widely from his middle works"; Livnat Holtzman, "Ibn Qayyim al-Jawziyya (1292–1350)," in: *Essays in Arabic Literary Biography 1350–1850*, eds. Joseph E. Lowry and Devin Stewart (Wiesbaden: Harrassowitz Verlag, 2009), 205–206.

and *Bayān talbīs al-jahmiyya* (Exposing the Deceit of Heretics).[8] Transmitting the salient Taymiyyan teachings on the theological issue of divine attributes, Ibn al-Qayyim's intellectual loyalty to his teacher concerning this subject is evident beyond a doubt in *al-Ṣawāʿiq*. In this highly spirited monograph of critique, Ibn al-Qayyim targets his contemporary Ashʿarites who made up the elite group of religious scholars in Mamluk Damascus (the *ʿulamāʾ*). From a larger perspective, however, *al-Ṣawāʿiq* can be seen as a categorical argument against the later Ashʿarite doctrines as a whole and against Islamic rationalism up to the 8th/14th century.

Ibn al-Qayyim's theological engagement with the issue of divine attributes in *al-Ṣawāʿiq* is conveyed as a harangue against four rationalistic fundamental methodologies used by his contemporary Ashʿarites in 8th/14th century Mamluk Damascus with relation to the theological issue of divine attributes. Each of these principle rationalistic methods is derogatorily titled by Ibn al-Qayyim as *ṭāghūt* (lit., false idol; and allegorically, false conviction) that must be refuted. Ashʿarism of that time mostly followed the scholarly heritage of the renowned Fakhr al-Dīn al-Rāzī (d. 606/1209) whose writings on rationalistic dialectical theology made a great impact. Prior to al-Rāzī, a major turning point in Ashʿarite theological thought occurred during the 6th/12th century; this was a result of the activity of the influential theologian Abū Ḥāmid al-Ghazālī (d. 505/1111) and his integration of the philosophical tradition into Islamic theology, thus harmonizing the classical-Ashʿarite teachings and methods with those of the Islamic philosophers (*falsafa*). This introduced the expansion of rationalistic theological discourse, and symbolized a new stage of the dialectical use of Reason (*ʿaql*) in the traditionalistic Ashʿarite doctrine;[9] Rāziyyan Ashʿarism signified further development in the direction of philosophized-theology. Unfolding a rich intellectual debate, the work *al-Ṣawāʿiq* is therefore particularly interesting in the case of the theological dispute between the later Ḥanbalites and the later Ashʿarites, which reflected the societal-political circumstances amid the *ʿulamāʾ* of the Mamluk era.

8 As will be further discussed in chapter 1, Ibn Taymiyya's opposition also stemmed from political tensions and represented the struggle of powers amid the class of religious scholars; Jon Hoover, "Ḥanbalī Theology," in: *Oxford handbook of Islamic Theology*, ed. Sabine Schmidtke (Oxford: Oxford University Press, 2016), 633–634; George Maqdisi, "Hanbalite Islam," in: *Studies on Islam*, ed. M.L. Swartz (New York: Oxford University Press, 1981), 224–226, 238–240, 260–261.

9 Frank Griffel, *Al-Ghazālī's Philosophical Theology* (New York: Oxford University Press, 2009), 7–8.

Apparently not long after *al-Ṣawāʿiq* had been written, a contemporary of Ibn al-Qayyim, Muḥammad ibn Muḥammad Abū ʿAbdallāh Shams al-Dīn Ibn al-Mawṣilī (d. 774/1372), compiled an abridged version of the work (*mukhtaṣar*). Ibn al-Mawṣilī is described in biographical sources an esteemed Shāfiʿite scholar and preacher (*khaṭīb*) in the large Umayyad mosque located in the city of Baalbek. In his quest for knowledge he visited other cultural centers in greater Syria of that period, such as Damascus and Tripoli. He is reported to have held traditionalistic theological view with an admiration for the position taken by Ibn Taymiyya. In addition to authoring a few independent works and poems, he also compiled works of previous scholars, abridged several of them and occasionally added annotations. Ibn al-Mawṣilī was also a book dealer, which is probably how he came across an original copy of Ibn al-Qayyim's *al-Ṣawāʿiq*. Hence, the work's abridgement is considered a reliable source that is largely true to the original work. Nevertheless, *al-Mukhtaṣar* is clearly declared an abridgement, its aim being to summarize *al-Ṣawāʿiq*. Therefore, it deliberately omits considerable sections of the work, and possibly exceedingly vital ones.[10] The existence of such an abridgement, however, definitely points to a considerable amount of interest *al-Ṣawāʿiq* aroused amid the scholarly circles of its time.

A brief—yet meaningful—reference to *al-Ṣawāʿiq* appears in the important centenary biographical collection of the Egyptian Hadith scholar and historian Ibn Ḥajar al-ʿAsqalānī's (d. 853/1449) *al-Durar al-kāmina fī aʿyān al-miʾa al-thāmina* (Hidden Pearls about the Notables of the Eighth [Islamic] Century). *Al-Ṣawāʿiq* is specifically mentioned amongst the works of Ibn al-Qayyim which "were all highly demanded by people of different communities".[11] Despite being a rather general statement, Ibn Ḥajar's positive description of the demand for Ibn al-Qayyim's works provides a good indication for the respectable status of *al-Ṣawāʿiq* in the intellectual environment close to Ibn al-Qayyim about a century after his lifetime. Unfortunately, nowadays we lack substantive knowledge on *al-Ṣawāʿiq*'s reception and circulation in later periods. Still, it is appar-

---

10 Ibn Qayyim al-Jawziyya, *al-Ṣawāʿiq al-mursala*, the editor's introduction, 1:117–125; Ibn Qayyim al-Jawziyya, *Mukhtaṣar al-Ṣawāʿiq* (the abridgement of Ibn al-Mawṣilī), the editor's introduction, 1:32–35, 42–53, 62; Yasir Qadhi, "'The Unleashed Thunderbolts' of Ibn Qayyim al-Jawziyya: An Introductory Essay", in *A Scholar in the Shadow: Essays in the Legal and Theological Thought of Ibn Qayyim al-Ǧawziyyah*, eds. Caterina Bori and Livnat Holtzman, Oriente Moderno XC/1 (Rome: Istituto per l'Oriente C.A. Nallino, 2010), 137–138.

11 Ibn Ḥajar al-ʿAsqalānī, Shihāb al-Dīn Abu 'l-Faḍl Aḥmad ibn ʿAlī, *al-Durar al-kāmina fī aʿyān al-miʾa al-thāmina* ed. Muḥammad ʿAbd al-Muʿīd Ḍān, in 6 vols. (Hyderabad, India: Daʾirat al-Maʿārif al-ʿUthmāniyya, 1392/1972), 5:139.

ent that at least *al-Ṣawāʿiq*'s abridgement written by Ibn al-Mawṣilī was preserved, and has been read—to an unknown degree—until modern times; for years, *Mukhtaṣar al-ṣawāʿiq* was the most widely known version of the *magnum opus*. Throughout the 14th/20th century, the book was edited mostly in an old-fashioned manner and printed in various scholarly centers in Arab countries.[12]

A case in point is *al-Ṣawāʿiq*'s recognition after the awakening of Islamic fundamentalist movements and the appearance of Muḥammad ibn ʿAbd al-Wahhāb (d. 1206/1792), the chief ideologue of the Wahhābi movement in Saudi Arabia of early modern times. Proclaiming to reform Islamic religiosity by evoking the way of the worthy and pious ancestors (*salaf*), the Ḥanbalite theologian heavily relied on the principal legal and theological teachings of Ibn Taymiyya and Ibn al-Qayyim.[13] The approach of Ibn ʿAbd al-Wahhāb was depicted as correspondent to that of Ibn Taymiyya and Ibn al-Qayyim who, in their lifetimes, battled in Jihad against all "idols and evil powers" (*al-jibt wal-ṭāghūt*)[14] which took possession of the community of Muslim believers. Ibn Taymiyya and Ibn al-Qayyim sent thunderbolts (*ṣawāʿiq*) upon their rivals from their 'sky-high of knowledge' (*min samāʾi ʿilmihimā*).[15] In fact, Ibn ʿAbd al-Wahhāb wrote yet

12 Outdated edition of Ibn al-Mawṣilī's abridgement were published, for example, in Mecca in 1348/1929 ([no editor mentioned], al-Maktaba 'l-Salafiyya, in two vols. with multiple typos) and in Cairo in 1380/1960 (ed. Zakariyya ʿAlī Yūsuf, Maktabat al-Mutamabbī, in one vol., reprinted in 1400/1981).

13 Michael Cook, "On the Origins of Wahhābism," *Journal of the Royal Asiatic Society, Third Series*, 2/2 (Jul., 1992), 191–202; Muḥammad Nabīl Mouline, *ʿUlamāʾ al-islām: taʾrīkh wa-bunyat al-muʾasassa al-dīniyya fī 'l-saʿūdiyya bayn^a 'l-qarnayn^i 'l-thāmin ʿashar wal-ḥādī wal-ʿishrīn*, trans. Muḥammad al-Ḥājj Sālim and ʿĀdil ibn ʿAbdallāh, second ed. (Beirut: al-Shabka 'l-ʿArabiyya lil-Abḥāth wal-Nashr, 2013), 37–80. Daniel Lav, *Radical Islam and the Revival of Medieval Theology* (New York: Cambridge University Press, 2012). Elliott A. Bazzano: "Ibn Taymiyya, Radical Polymath, Part 1: Scholarly Perceptions" and "Part 2: Intellectual Contributions," *Religion Compass* 9/4 (2015): 100–116, 117–139 (respectively).

14 The expression is derived from verse Q 4:51.

15 Freely paraphrasing the title of *al-Ṣawāʿiq*, that comment was made by Muḥammad Ḥāmid al-Fiqī (d. 1389/1969), a scholar from al-Azhar and the founder of a pro-Wahhābi organization in Egypt, in his essay on the history of Wahhābism. Muḥammad Ḥāmid al-Fiqī, *Athar al-daʿwa al-wahhābiyya fī 'l-islāḥ al-dīnī wal-ʿumrānī fī jazirat al-ʿarab wa-ghayrihā* (Cairo: Matbaʿat al-Nahda, 1354/[1935]), 17–19; David Commins, "From Wahhabi to Salafi," in: *Saudi Arabia in Transition: Insights on Social, Political, Economic and Religious Change*, eds. Bernard Haykel, Thomas Hegghammer, and Stéphane Lacroix (New York: Cambridge University Press, 2015), 156. Al-Fiqī's references to *al-Ṣawāʿiq* can indicate that he—and plausibly other Azhari graduates in the 14th/20th century—were not only familiar with *al-Ṣawāʿiq* and its contents, but were also deeply motivated by its martial style, as it definitely fitted the mindset of the more extremists thereof.

another (rather sparse) abridgement of *al-Ṣawāʿiq* which was critically edited and published only recently.[16] The fact that Ibn ʿAbd al-Wahhāb dedicated a work of his own to explore Ibn al-Qayyim's ideas in *al-Ṣawāʿiq*—while rendering them to fit his early-modern ideology—points to the work's significance in the eyes of the Islamic reformist, whose impact is very much evident in Wahhābi Muslim communities of the present day.

Due to its complex theological topic, it would be hard to say that *al-Ṣawāʿiq* can be considered a popular reading. However, surely evident is the scholarly interest that modern Muslims intellectuals find in the monograph. Shaykh ʿAlī ibn Muḥammad al-Dakhīl Allāh, today a lecturer in the Department of Theology (*uṣūl al-dīn*) in the Imām Muḥammad ibn Masʿūd University in Saudi Arabia,[17] was the first scholar to systematically study *al-Ṣawāʿiq* when he compiled its first two sections (i.e., first two *ṭawāghīt* of the unabridged work) into a critical scientific edition in his doctoral dissertation in 1418/1998. According to his own presentation in the opening part of his edition, he focused on the compilation of the three manuscripts of the text currently available, whilst enriching it with a vast number of highly useful annotations. Since it only contains some historical background and a summary of the edited manuscripts in its introduction, this edition offers only a partial analysis of the work's contents. Therefore, as of now, even in the most up-to-date critical edition of *al-Ṣawāʿiq* by al-Dakhīl Allāh, we still have an incomplete version of the work. The manuscripts available are lacking in overall scope and, as evaluated by al-Dakhīl Allāh, cover only approximately the first half of the massive original work.[18] Nonetheless, this scientifically edited version of *al-Ṣawāʿiq* containing the first two argumentations refuted by Ibn al-Qayyim is highly valuable source of study.

In order to receive a far more complete presentation of *al-Ṣawāʿiq*, special attention must be drawn to the additional source (already mentioned above):

---

16 As I have only recently learnt about the existence of the book, it was not included in the present study. At any rate, this abridgement seems to concern only the first part *al-Ṣawāʿiq*, namely its two first refutations; Ibn Qayyim al-Jawziyya, *Mukhtaṣar al-ṣawāʿiq al-mursala ʿala 'l-jahmiyya wal-Muʿaṭṭila*, the abridgement of Muḥammad ibn ʿAbd al-Wahhāb, ed. Daghash ibn Shabīb al-ʿAjmī, in 1 vol. (Kuwait: Maktabat Ahl al-Āthār, 2016).

17 http://ar.islamway.net/scholar/389/علي-بن-محمد-الدخيل-الله, webpage last accessed on December 8th, 2014.

18 Al-Dakhīl Allāh states that *al-Ṣawāʿiq*'s first part alone is made up of some 500 manuscript pages in length. In my opinion, as they are believed to comprise the first half of *al-Ṣawāʿiq*, it is reasonable to assume the work was around a thousand pages in length; however, it is clear not all of these pages have survived. Ibn Qayyim al-Jawziyya, *al-Ṣawāʿiq al-mursala* the editor's introduction, 1:82.

the work's abridgement *Mukhtaṣar al-ṣawāʿiq al-murasala* compiled Ibn al-Mawṣilī. On the whole, *al-Mukhtaṣar* condenses all four argumentations in the original *al-Ṣawaʿiq*, including the second part of the work (i.e., the two remaining argumentations). Since the second half of *al-Ṣawaʿiq* is available nowadays in its abridged form alone, Ibn al-Mawṣilī's work is indispensible when aiming to achieve an overall outlook of *al-Ṣawaʿiq*'s text. The most up-to-date scientific edition of *al-Mukhtaṣar* was published in 1425/2004 by al-Ḥasan ibn ʿAbd al-Raḥman al-ʿAlawī as a part of his doctoral dissertation, completed at the Islamic University of Medina in Saudi Arabia.[19] Therefore, out of the primary sources of *al-Ṣawāʿiq* and *Mukhtaṣar al-ṣawāʿiq* available today, both above-mentioned editions are greatly beneficial for examining Ibn al-Qayyim's four argumentations in the most sufficient manner possible.

Ibn al-Qayyim's monograph *al-Ṣawāʿiq* has by no means been fully studied in Western research. To the best of my knowledge only very few studies about the work *al-Ṣawāʿiq* have been published thus far.[20] In Arabic, one can find somewhat descriptive journal articles on *al-Ṣawāʿiq*.[21] However, an inclusive outlook of the work *al-Ṣawāʿiq* in its entirety has yet to be fully realized. Moreover, modern research has yet to investigate many sensitive hermeneutical deliberations that Ibn al-Qayyim employed, including his approach to the anthropomorphic expressions concerning God in the work. This is particularly the case when one considers its relations to—and with—other main works of relevance Ibn al-Qayyim referred to in *al-Ṣawāʿiq*. In addition, very little has been discovered

19 Ibn Qayyim al-Jawziyya, *al-Ṣawāʿiq al-mursala*, the editor's introduction, 1:117–125; Idem, *Mukhtaṣar al-Ṣawāʿiq* (the abridgement of Ibn al-Mawṣilī), the editor's introduction, 1:32–35, 42–53, 62; Qadhi, "'The Unleashed Thunderbolts'," 137–138.

20 In Western research, only two publications concentrating exclusively on *al-Ṣawāʿiq* are available (both were published in the Bori-Holtzman edited volume on Ibn al-Qayyim from 2010): "'The Unleashed Thunderbolts' of Ibn Qayyim al-Jawziyya: An Introductory Essay" by Y. Qadhi, and "Ibn Qayyim al-Ğawziyyah et sa contribution à la rhétorique arabe" by A. Belhaj. Other recent academic publications mention and use parts of *al-Ṣawāʿiq*; however, they mostly concentrate on a very specific subject therein (for example, Hoover analyses Ibn al-Qayyim's conceptual engagement with the idea of the annihilation of Heaven and Hell in two articles from 2009 and 2013, respectively). For further elaboration on this topic in Islamic theology, see footnote 36 in chapter 1.

21 Such as: "*Qawāʿid wa-ḍawābiṭ wa-fawāʾid min kitāb al-Ṣawāʿiq al-mursala li-Ibn al-Qayyim*" (2008?) by Jamal Ahmed Badi of the International Islamic University Malaysia. Another paper in Arabic is "*Jadaliyyat al-taʾwīl wal-majāz ʿind*[a] *Ibn Qayyim al-Jawziyya min khilāl*[i] *kitābih*[i] *al-Ṣawāʿiq al-mursala*" (2010?) by Belgacem Hamam of the University of Ouargla in Algeria.

about *al-Ṣawāʿiq*'s singular place as a part of the feisty theological discussion on divine attributes within the very certain social-intellectual milieu of Mamluk Damascus, and with relation to the political rivalries surrounding the authoring of the work.

The present study, thus, fills a meaningful gap and inspects first and foremost Ibn al-Qayyim's contribution to Islamic theology focusing on the complex debate on the issue of divine attributes in the Quran and Sunna and the related anthropomorphic question, as he conveyed in his work *al-Ṣawāʿiq*. The main goal is to thoroughly examine the refined theoretical approaches constructed by Ibn al-Qayyim in *al-Ṣawāʿiq*—namely, epistemology and hermeneutics—during the course of his theological engagement. This study also is designed to better identify Ibn al-Qayyim as a theologian, a scholar and an author through the prism offered by his sophisticated work *al-Ṣawāʿiq*.[22] Upon careful inspection of Ibn al-Qayyim's theology, it is possible to better qualify his stature within Ḥanbalite traditionalistic theology, and even more so with respect to his great mentor Ibn Taymiyya whose legacy was unmistakably carried on by Ibn al-Qayyim in *al-Ṣawāʿiq*. Shedding more light on the intellectual relation between the two, the vast and mature text of *al-Ṣawāʿiq* demonstrates an advanced stage of Ibn al-Qayyim's authorship skills while tackling a complex theological issue. Hence, exploring Ibn al-Qayyim's scholarly figure as reflected from the text of *al-Ṣawāʿiq*'s makes it possible to better define his allegiance to the Taymiyyan teachings, (or rather, his appropriation of Taymiyyan theology).

Observing a compound text like *al-Ṣawāʿiq* through such a conceptual lens prompts questions such as: How is Ibn al-Qayyim's scholarly image—and even his self-consciousness—reflected in *al-Ṣawāʿiq*? How does the structural form of *al-Ṣawāʿiq* impact the conceptual meaning produced? How was Ibn al-Qayyim's discussion on the theological issue of divine attributes in *al-Ṣawāʿiq* a contributing factor to the conceptual sharpening of this disagreement in Islamic thought?[23] What interior/exterior discourse/s does *al-Ṣawāʿiq* serve and how? What can all of this teach us about Ibn al-Qayyim's writing in *al-*

---

22 In this respect, relevant is the volume edited by Lale Behzadi und Jaakko Hämeen-Anttila, *Concepts of Authorship in Pre-Modern Arabic Texts* (Bamberg: University of Bamberg Press, 2015).

23 Numerous examples can be found for the case of theological polemics in Islam going back-and-forth between different schools over time, consequently resulting in a substantial refinement of ideas debated as well as the methodologies used. See for instance, the theory of causality: Dominik Perler and Ulrich Rudolf, *Occasionalismus: Theorien der Kausalität im arabisch-islamischen und im europäischen Denken*, 3 Folge (Göttingen: Vandenhoeck & Ruprecht 2000).

Ṣawāʿiq? As a whole, this study displays an orderly and coherent picture of Ibn al-Qayyim as a scholar and his work *al-Ṣawāʿiq*.

Islamic Traditionalistic Theology

From the first centuries of Islam, different approaches were formulized concerning the origin of religious knowledge and its derived power of authority. In the everlasting struggle between the epistemic factors of Reason and Tradition, the traditionalist theologians preferred the authority of the textual sources of the Quran and Ḥadith literature to human intellect as the ultimate foundation of knowledge. During the 3rd/9th century, the Quran (namely *kalām Allāh*, i.e., "the speech of God") and the Prophetic traditions, together with the consensus of Muslim believers' community (*ijmāʿ*), were accepted as the most prominent of all modes of attaining religious knowledge, particularly knowledge about the divine. In the light of traditionalistic adherence to the texts, human Reason mostly came second and its legitimacy of use in theological debates was highly controversial. Thus, conflicting viewpoints concerning the application of rationalistic modes of argumentation perceived as alien to authentic Islam are also evident within separate traditionalistic trends of thought.[24] The two schools in Islamic theology most relevant to the present research are the Ḥanbalite and the Ashʿarite of the 8th/14th century, both of which can generally be considered traditionalistic (*ahl al-sunnah wal-ḥadīth*).[25] However, whereas the Ḥanbalite School demanded an inherently traditionalistic understanding of the scriptures, the Ashʿarite School had absorbed certain rationalistic ideas over the course of time, thus permitting the use of more rationalistic argumentations in their overall traditionalistic theological discourse.[26]

---

24 Binyamin Abrahamov, "Scripturalist and Traditionalist Theology," in: ed. Sabine Schmidtke, *The Oxford Handbook of Islamic Theology*, Oxford Handbooks Online (Oxford University Press), last accessed on 2 April 2014, 1, 4–7.

25 In early Islam, "the scholars of the Hadith" (*aṣḥāb al-ḥadīth*) are distinguished from "the scholars of self-opinion" (*aṣḥāb al-raʾy*), who allowed independent thinking in their rulings and ideas; Christopher Melchert, *The Formation of the Sunni Schools of Law, 9th–10th Centuries C.E.* (Lieden: Brill, 1997), 13–26, 69–70, 137, 155; Nimrod Hurvitz, *The Formation of Hanbalism: Piety into Power* (London: Routledge Curzon, 2001).

26 Inevitably, the impact of the Muʿtazilite ultra-rationalistic school must be taken into account. Its influence reached its highest level from the middle of the 2nd/8th century until apparently the beginning of the 4th/10th century. Parts of the rationalistic Muʿtazilite ideas have since profoundly affected the development of theological general views in

In terms of the current state of Western research, it was only at the beginning of the 14th/20th century that Henri Laoust recognized the importance of the Ḥanbalite School within the Islamic intellectual world in his pioneering work, *Essai sur les doctrines sociales et politiques d'Ibn Taimîya (661/1262–728/1328)* (1939).[27] His work has paved the way for other Islamic studies researchers to further explore the ideology of traditionalist scholars in classical and post-classical times. Up until this time, distinguished scholars (e.g., Ignaz Goldziher) tended to play down the importance of the traditionalists, seeing them as little more than simplistic, rigid extremists.[28] Following the lead of Laoust, George Makdisi, for instance, provided significant analysis of the Sunnite schools of law and a remarkable assessment of the transition process of the Ḥanbalite movement from a small traditionalistic stream of thought in ancient times to a far more dominant Islamic modern movement.[29] Notable are also the early works of research focusing on the theological creed in Islam, its progression and the diverse approaches—including the traditionalistic ones—manifested with respect to various theological issues.[30]

Epistemological and hermeneutical differences between traditionalistic theological schools in Islam, including Ḥanbalite and Ashʿarite, were clearly expressed in their theological dispute regarding the issue of divine attributes and the derived anthropomorphic question. Throughout the ages, various Is-

Islam. The Muʿtazilite solution for the problem of anthropomorphism was to implement the figurative interpretation (*taʾwīl*) regarding God's names and attributes; Daniel Gimaret, "Muʿtazilah," *EI*², 7:786–789. A more elaborated reference to the Muʿtazilite though will be made regarding various points along this study.

27 Henri Laoust, *Essai sur les doctrines sociales et politiques d'Ibn Taimîya (661/1262–728/1328)*, (Le Caire: IFAO Institut français d'archéologie orientale, 1939); and also: Idem, "Les premiere professions de foi Ḥanbalites," *Melanges Louis Massignion* 3 (Damascus, 1956–1957):7–35.

28 Ignaz Goldziher, *Vorlesungen über den Islam*, second ed. (Heidelberg, Germany: C. Winter, 1925).

29 George Makdisi, "The Significance of the Sunni Schools of Law in Islamic Religious History," *International Journal of Middle East Studies*, 10/1 (1979), 1–8. Makdisi further sustained the importance of the traditionalists and greatly elaborated on the arguments he developed in his articles: "Ashʿarī and the Ashʿarite in Islamic Religious History" (Part I, 1962; Part II, 1963) and "Ḥanbalite Islam" (1981).

30 Prominent in this regard are: *The Muslim Creed Its Genesis and Historical Development* (1932) by Arent J. Wensinck, *Revelation and Reason in Islam* (1957) by Arthur J. Arberry, *Muslim Theology: A Study of Origins with Reference to the Church Fathers* (1964) by Morris S. Seale and *The Formative Period of Islamic Thought* (1973) by William Montgomery Watt. All of those studies dedicate parts of the discussion to the traditionalistic doctrine.

lamic scholars have unequivocally disagreed in their understanding of the extremely diverse characteristics associated with God in the Quran and Hadith literature. Affirmation (*ithbāt*) of the existence of God and His divine attributes became a key principle of faith in Islamic traditionalistic thought; however, it entailed a hermeneutical challenge. The points of disagreement between Muslim scholars regarding these theological predicaments and the various hermeneutical approaches developed to adequately handle them are the subject of many modern studies, which offer a vital analysis of the theological issues at the center of contemporary research.[31]

Ibn Qayyim al-Jawziyya as (an) a (In)dependent Scholar

Currently, systematic research dealing with the contribution of Ibn al-Qayyim as a thinker in his own right is fairly scarce. Focusing on the role of Ḥanbalite thought within the Sunnite-fundamentalist revival of the late 20th century, Western research of this period settled quite easily with a brief 'name-dropping' of Ibn al-Qayyim in passing, almost instinctively attached to his master Ibn Taymiyya. Whereas the ideas of Ibn Taymiyya were decidedly attractive to the efforts of Western intelligentsia, for various contemporary political reasons, Ibn al-Qayyim remained on the scholarly backburner with little foreseeable chance to play an important role as an actual subject of research. In the field of Islamic theology, Ibn al-Qayyim's abundant work has remained largely—

31 The following studies have deepened our understanding of these issues: "Created in His Image: A Study of Islamic Theology" (1990) and "Some Muslim Discussions on Anthropomorphism" (1990) by W.M. Watt. Also notable are *Islamic Theology: Traditionalism and Rationalism* (1998), *Anthropomorphism and Interpretation of the Qur'ān in the Theology of al-Qāsim ibn Ibrāhīm: Kitab al-Mustarshid* (1996) and "The 'Bi-lā Kayfa' Doctrine and Its Foundations in Islamic Theology" (1995) by Binyamin Abrahamov. Daniel Gimaret, Claude Gilliot, Josef van Ess, Gerhard Böwering and Livnat Holtzman have contributed insightful entries to the *Encyclopaedia of Islam* in its second and third editions. More recent studies provide a more specific approach and focus on the question of anthropomorphism. A case in point is *A Medieval Critique of Anthropomorphism: Ibn al-Jawzī's Kitāb Akhbār al-Ṣifāt* (2008) by Merlin Swartz. Two other studies by Wesley Williams are: "Aspects of the Creed of Imam Aḥmad ibn Ḥanbal: A Study of Anthropomorphism in Early Islamic discourse" and "A Body unlike Bodies: Transcendent Anthropomorphism in Ancient Semitic Tradition and Early Islam" (2009). An important study is "God Created Adam in His Image" (2011) by Christopher Melchert. A recent collection of further significant articles is *The Oxford Handbook of Islamic Theology* (ed. Sabine Schmidtke, 2016; much of it is available online).

somewhat indifferently—overlooked and basically understudied.[32] In recent years, many scholars and PhD candidates in the Arab world—especially in Saudi Arabia—have been producing compilations of Ibn al-Qayyim's works and editing manuscripts for scientific editions, some of them of very high quality. Satisfactory critical research of these edited books has, for the most part, not yet been conducted; however, they are highly useful for studying the thought of Ibn al-Qayyim. In addition, several valuable modern biographies of Ibn al-Qayyim were published in Arabic, incorporating preliminary overviews of his general scholastic work.[33] These studies took initial important steps in researching the ideological approach expressed by Ibn al-Qayyim and his style of authorship. Furthermore, they indicate the growing interest in Ibn al-Qayyim as a profound research subject in modern Muslim societies.

In Western research, it is apparent that Ibn al-Qayyim's scholarly image has long been tightly jointed to his celebrated master Ibn Taymiyya. In this respect, portraying Ibn al-Qayyim's singularity of thought is closely connected to such perception of him as the subordinate party in a pair.[34] Hence, there is a tendency of crediting Ibn al-Qayyim more as an after-effect of his relation

32 An interesting exception: Joseph N. Bell provided the first reference to Ibn al-Qayyim as a theologian in his book *Love Theory in Later Hanbalite Islam* (1979). Alina Kokoschka and Birgit Krawietz, "Appropriating Ibn Taymiyya and Ibn Qayyim al-Jawziyya: Challenging Expectations of Ingenuity," the introduction to *Islamic Theology, Philosophy and Law: Debating Ibn Taymiyya and Ibn Qayyim al-Jawziyya* (Berlin, Boston: De Gruyter, 2013), 4–5, 7–10.

33 Such as *Ibn Qayyim al-Jawziyya: ʿaṣruhᵘ wa-manhaguhᵘ wa-ārāʾuhᵘ fī ʾl-fiqhⁱ wal-ʿaqāʾiqᵃ wal-taṣawwūfⁱ* (1984) by ʿAbd al-ʿAẓīm ʿAbd al-Salām Sharaf al-Dīn. Other studies of great significance are *Al-taqrib li-ʿulūm Ibn al-Qayyim* (1996) and *Ibn Qayyim al-Jawziyya: ḥayātuhᵘ athāruhᵘ mawāriduhᵘ* (2002) by the Saudi scholar Bakr ʿAbdullah Abū Zayd, who has devoted his high-quality academic work to Ibn al-Qayyim's thought. Also worth noting is the discourse with Ibn al-Qayyim's ideology in other books; however, these studies can be viewed as secondary in this regard, such: *Ibn Qayyim al-Jawziyya: minhajuhᵘ, wa-marwīyātuhᵘ ʾl-taʾrikhīya fī ʾl-sīra ʾl-nabawiyya ʾl-sharīfa* (2001) by Yāsīn Ḥaḍīr al-Ḥaddād. Of course, some biographical information is also found in primary sources, for instance, in the biographical composition by Ibn al-Qayyim's well-known disciple, Ibn Rajab, Zayn al-Dīn Abu ʾl-Faraj ʿAbd al-Raḥman ibn Aḥmad (d. 795/1392), *al-Dhayl ʿalā ṭabaqāt al-ḥanābila*, ed. Muḥammad Ḥāmid al-Faqī (Cairo: Maṭbaʿat al-Sunna al-Muḥammadiyya 1372/1952) 2:450.

34 The tendency to speak of Ibn Taymiyya and Ibn al-Qayyim simultaneously can be observed, for example, in the chapters dedicated to the two scholar's legal condemnation of the phenomenon of saints' graves visitations (*ziyārat al-qubūr*) in: Christopher S. Taylor, *In the Vicinity of the Righteous: Ziyāra and the Veneration of Muslim Saints in Late Medieval Egypt* (Leiden: Brill, 1999), 168–218.

with his mentor, rather than illustrating the singular aspects of his thought. Nonetheless, a paradigm change can be seen in recent Western research of the past few years, which has aimed to decouple Ibn al-Qayyim and Ibn Taymiyya. This transformed approach came into being in several important publications which have contributed to the start of candid academic interest in Ibn al-Qayyim's scholarly work and independent convictions. Therefore, it can be stated that the first decade of the 21st century introduced a stimulating shift in Western study towards a much higher appreciation of Ibn al-Qayyim's individual intellectual efforts.[35] Of greater significance than a mere current research trend, Ibn al-Qayyim has been gradually recognized as a scholar of major importance for continuing to develop an understanding of the class of religious scholars (*ʿulamāʾ*), their endeavors as well as social power and impact in Mamluk times. Thanks to the clear increase in the academic study of Ibn al-Qayyim and his works over the past few years—this also includes undergraduate and graduate students' final thesis papers—recent research strongly depicted Ibn al-Qayyim as a prolific and talented scholar in his own right and more than a mere epigone of his celebrated master, Ibn Taymiyya.

The latest published studies have not only presented several of Ibn al-Qayyim's individual perceptions, but have also begun to attentively portray his differentiated methodologies and ways of thinking. In the introduction to their recently edited volume, Alina Kokoschka and Birgit Krawietz convincingly suggest evaluating both Ibn Taymiyya and Ibn al-Qayyim through the lens of

35 An example of early inquiry of Ibn al-Qayyim's theological thought can be seen in Livnat Holtzman's dissertation "Predestination (*al-Qaḍāʾ wal-Qadar*) and Free Will (*al-Ikhtiyār*) as Reflected in the Works of the Neo-Ḥanbalites in the Fourteenth Century" (2003). Another significant study to address the scholar's prolific output is: "Ibn Qayyim al-Jawziyya: His Life and Works" (2006) by Birgit Krawietz. In this article, the author specifically discusses the monographs written by Ibn al-Qayyim according to disciplinary categories or genres. The chronological biography and a list Ibn al-Qayyim's works are presented in Holtzman's article "Ibn Qayyim al-Jawziyya (1292–1350)" (2009). The collection of papers edited by Caterina Bori and Livnat Holtzman, *A Scholar in the Shadow: Essays in the Legal and Theological Thought of Ibn Qayyim al-Jawziyyah* (2010), is the first series of articles dealing exclusively with Ibn al-Qayyim's stand points regarding several juridical and theological issues. An overall description of the volume and its content can be found in my review of the book (under the name Miriam Ben Moshe) in: *Sehepunkte* 13 (2013), Nr. 4 [15.04.2013], URL: http://www.sehepunkte.de/2013/04/22887.html. The most recently published volume to devote significant attention to Ibn al-Qayyim and his thought, called *Islamic Theology, Philosophy and Law: Debating Ibn Taymiyya and Ibn Qayyim al-Jawziyya* (2013), was edited by Birgit Krawietz and Georges Tamer (in collaboration with Alina Kokoschka).

the singular "agency in the production of meaning"; in other words, as separate actors, who represented and promoted different—to a certain degree, even disconnected—agendas.[36] While still giving special consideration to his works as testament to his specific intellectual goals, Ibn al-Qayyim's individual motives of writing become more and more apparent. This approach motivates a more detailed inspection of Ibn al-Qayyim's prolific oeuvre, which can be seen in recent (and ongoing) studies which choose to focus on a single monograph among his works.[37] The accumulative data that is achieved by such concentrated examining of single monographs will offer several additional angles for evaluating Ibn al-Qayyim's thought and the methods he used in order to deliver it. The following study of Ibn al-Qayyim and his *al-Ṣawāʿiq* is yet another step forward in that direction, revealing his interesting mode of authorship in the work as well as the purposes it aimed to serve.

Methodological Lines of the Textual Inquiry

Modern research has been increasingly attempting to attain a better understanding of human ideas and perception as they have evolved throughout the times. However, since such knowledge is often embedded in various and complex surroundings—historical, political, social, cultural, biographical, scholastic—it seems the task of putting conceptual sets of mind into words is quite a challenge. Hence, it has long been difficult to establish the guiding lines of systematic methodologies for engaging in theoretical research on the formation and shaping of concepts.[38] Another difficulty in this regard is the characteri-

36 Kokoschka and Krawietz, "Appropriating Ibn Taymiyya and Ibn Qayyim al-Jawziyya," 4.

37 The recently submitted dissertation of Katja Brinkmann examines Ibn al-Qayyim's *Ighathat al-lahfān min maṣāyīd al-shayṭān* (Assistance for the Grieving from the Snares of the Devil) on moral theology (2015). Another dissertation by Antonia Bosanquet explores *Aḥkām ahl al-dhimma* (Rules on the People of Custody), which concerns Ibn al-Qayyim's legal theory regarding the status of non-Muslims under Islamic rule ('Minding their Place: Space and Religious Difference in Ibn al-Qayyim's *Aḥkam ahl al-dhimma*,' 2016).

38 Riccardo Bavaj, "Intellectual History," Version: 1.0, in: *Docupedia-Zeitgeschichte*, 13.9.2010, URL: http://docupedia.de/zg/Intellectual_History?oldid=106434, 1–5; Victoria E. Bonnell and Lynn Hunt in their introduction to *Beyond the Cultural Turn: New Directions in the Study of Society and Culture* (Berkley, Los Angeles: University of California Press, 1999), 5–11; Peter E. Gordon, "What Is Intellectual History? A Frankly Partisan Introduction to a Frequently Misunderstood Field," internet document, (Harvard University, summer 2013), 1–3. http://projects.iq.harvard.edu/files/history/files/what_is_intell_history_pgordon_mar2012.pdf.

zation of the intellectual (i.e., the cerebral producer and developer of ideas) or, according to postmodern theories, the product of those ideas. Such pondering takes a special turn when the source of inspection and evaluation is a text, which simultaneously serves two functions: the creation and circulation of ideas, and the creation of an author and his image. In a way, the classical literary trio of author-text-reader can be rendered here into author-text-ideas, fusing the element of reader with its perceived conceptions.

Focusing on Ibn al-Qayyim the author, his theological ideas and their conceptualizations in his work *al-Ṣawāʿiq*, the methodological approach taken here comprises a philological close reading and textual analysis of selected culminating parts from the work *al-Ṣawāʿiq*, alongside its contextualization with additional primary sources either cited or used by Ibn al-Qayyim as he generated his discussions. The contextual approach means that supplementary works of relevance created by other significant scholars are examined here in terms of their connection to the text *al-Ṣawāʿiq*. More specific clarifications will be supplied in the suitable place in course of the chapters; however, for the time being, noteworthy scholars to be mentioned are Ibn Taymiyya, Fakhr al-Dīn al-Rāzī, al-Ghazālī (d. 505/1111), Ibn Rushd (Averroes, d. 595/1198) and Ibn Ḥazm (d. 456/1064). This study's methodology merges a close reading of the texts together with their comparative analysis with respect to one another. The objective is to highlight *al-Ṣawāʿiq*, its author and his ideas—as well as the various processes that made them come into being—, at the backdrop of the scholastic and cultural environment in which the text was written.

Furthermore, when contemplating a suitable manner to conduct research explicitly targeting a single monograph, I strongly believe it is worthwhile to follow *al-Ṣawāʿiq*'s text according to the original order in which it had been written and initially structured by Ibn al-Qayyim. In my opinion, the preplanned arrangement of a work carries a significant portion of its author's intention and should therefore be retained, especially when dealing with a highly organized piece such as *al-Ṣawāʿiq*. Taking this approach also expedites a closer preservation of the original mode of discussion that *al-Ṣawāʿiq* was meant to convey. Hence, this study follows the multilayered contents of *al-Ṣawāʿiq* in accordance with the work's original structure, as far as it is possible, trusting that the text's initial arrangement definitely exhibits Ibn al-Qayyim's authorial command. From the literary aspect, walking along the reading line Ibn al-Qayyim dictated for his work will enrich our understanding of his compilation techniques in structuring of a voluminous work such as *al-Ṣawāʿiq*.[39] Likewise, underlining

39 Insights on Ibn al-Qayyim's literary techniques of quoting and compiling materials taken

Ibn al-Qayyim's particular choices of mentioning other texts during his writing, in a specific timing and place, teach us about his authorial motives. Additionally, the contextual reading sheds more light on Ibn al-Qayyim's available library, the texts he knew and made use of as well as his sources of inspiration and critique. Unfolding the prominent parts of the network of references laid out in *al-Ṣawāʿiq* is of great significance to Ibn al-Qayyim's appropriation of earlier ideas. Registering the manner in which he treats familiar works and ideas with relation to the works of other thinkers is of benefit for understanding Ibn al-Qayyim's respective suitable position within the mindset amid the class of religious scholars he was a part of, as well as *al-Ṣawāʿiq*'s status as a singular product of thought.

A supplemental methodological guideline I adopted emphasizes an adequate appropriation of Ibn al-Qayyim through the reading of *al-Ṣawāʿiq*. It regards this study's goal to further inspect Ibn al-Qayyim's intellectual characterization in the light of the Taymiyyan scholarship, derived and developing from the principle thought of his renowned mentor. A useful method to emancipate Ibn al-Qayyim from Ibn Taymiyya's prevailing prominence has been recently proposed by Kokoschka and Krawietz in their essay "Appropriating Ibn Taymiyya and Ibn Qayyim al-Jawziyya: Challenging Expectations of Ingenuity" (2013). They argue the main reason for Ibn al-Qayyim's lack of sufficient appreciation in Western research was that he did not fit to the Romantic perception of the outstanding "original genius" in the ways Ibn Taymiyya did, and was therefore dismissed as a mere epigone. The complimentary model of scholarly ingenuity that they suggest in order to conduct a disinterested examination of the relation between Ibn al-Qayyim and Ibn Taymiyya is that of appropriation: "We understand appropriation as a set of practices that—consciously or unconsciously—occupy meaning. An object, a figure, sign, formulation, topic, narrative, style and so forth is turned into something that, within the logic of personal life practice, is 'made one's own (*proprius*)' and, by this, appropriate".[40] This notion allows to take into account the intellectual singularity—rather than innovation—in Ibn al-Qayyim's writings in which he tends to constantly cite other sources, including his master.

---

from other works and his tendency of transgressing conventional definitions of genre appear in: Kokoschka and Krawietz, "Appropriating Ibn Taymiyya and Ibn Qayyim al-Jawziyya," 27–30.

40 Kokoschka and Krawietz, "Appropriating Ibn Taymiyya and Ibn Qayyim al-Jawziyya," 20–28.

According to the concept of appropriation, a meticulous reading of the text *al-Ṣawāʿiq* assists in revealing Ibn al-Qayyim as an autonomous scholarly figure. In this respect, dissecting Ibn al-Qayyim's way of recording his mentor's teachings will contribute to the ongoing clarification of their intellectual connections. Simultaneously, this approach has its value not only when inspecting Ibn al-Qayyim's singular thought, but also when retrieving the finely intertwined web of intellectual references Ibn al-Qayyim presented in *al-Ṣawāʿiq*. Moreover, stressing the attempt to distinguish Ibn al-Qayyim from his mentor justly advocates for a far more dynamic model of knowledge acquisition, transmission and utilization in a very short and specific timeframe, covering the relation between a teacher and his immediate pupil as well as vice versa. These processes were also affected by historical developments, thus, were not limited to the lifetime of Ibn al-Qayyim and Ibn Taymiyya, as they produced their own path in history.

Scholars and the intellectual output they yield are usually to be understood as products of their surrounding environment. At times it would be unjust to gratuitously detach a specific scholarly activity from the context and situation surrounding it, which both influenced and helped create it. Moreover, a relative comparison to social and historical scenery is part of the reason why certain scholars and their works stand out and become truly remarkable. The case of Ibn al-Qayyim's work *al-Ṣawāʿiq* is not an exception in this respect; *al-Ṣawāʿiq* mirrors important elements of Ibn al-Qayyim's writing which is firmly rooted in the historical setting of 8th/14th century in Mamluk Damascus. Thus, chapter 1 henceforth portrays the background of historical and societal-political occurrences stimulating the writing of *al-Ṣawāʿiq*. Laying the first foundations for the appropriation of Ibn al-Qayyim and *al-Ṣawāʿiq* to the Taymiyyan theological heritage, I will focus on Ibn al-Qayyim's association with his feisty mentor Ibn Taymiyya and the approach the latter articulated on the issue of divine attributes. General overview of the work *al-Ṣawāʿiq* and several of its literary features will be presented in chapter 2, setting the stage for its more detailed inspection in the chapters to come. Additionally, I will outline *al-Ṣawāʿiq*'s thematic framework as it is unfolded from Ibn al-Qayyim's introduction, where he discards the rationalistic use of figurative interpretation (*taʾwīl*) regarding the divine attributes. This is carried out while paying close attention to the greater discourse of theological debates (*munāẓarāt*) that he mastered. Pinpointing the greater discourse that *al-Ṣawāʿiq* was a part of—and simultaneously contributed to its creation—is essential in order to aptly apprehend the variety of claims manifested in the work. Chapter 2 also aims to construe Ibn al-Qayyim's singular intellectual contributions with respect to the target audience of *al-Ṣawāʿiq* amidst the class of Mamluk religious scholars. Given the fact that *al-*

Ṣawāʿiq is a combative work that defies the doctrinal matters of belief shared by the elite of the *ʿulamāʾ*, this is a very interesting matter. Understanding Ibn al-Qayyim's range of reference from *al-Ṣawāʿiq* itself will assist in defining its proper placement within the intellectual and historical context in which it was created.

Corresponding to Ibn al-Qayyim's own division of *al-Ṣawāʿq* into four parts, each of the chapters 3–6 is dedicated to a single *ṭāghūt* refutation of a rationalistic methodology used in theological discussion on the matter of the divine attributes. In a similar manner, chapters 3 and 6 concentrate on Ibn al-Qayyim's conceptual epistemological view; chapters 4 and 5 involve the hermeneutical approach derived therefrom. These chapters predominantly make up the beating heart of *al-Ṣawāʿiq* and cover large parts of its *ṭawāghīt*. For the limited span available, the examination and analysis here target the culmanative sections in Ibn al-Qayyim vast discussion. After carefully detecting the main points and highlights of the debate, I explore their wider intellectual context, therefore striving to achieve a meaningful understanding thereof by the means of comparison to other primary sources of relevance. As mentioned before, the additional primary sources used for the contextualization of *al-Ṣawāʿiq* were chosen according to their relation to the text at hand, and to what extent the text refers to them (as will be shown, some references are more explicit then others). Chapters 3–6 are constructed in a similar manner: respectively, they open with Ibn al-Qayyim's positive conceptualization of stances on either epistemology or hermeneutics. Then, the discussion moves onwards to the rationalistic positions rejected by Ibn al-Qayyim as they appear both in *al-Ṣawāʿiq* and in its complimenting primary sources. From here on, each chapter continues delving further into the roots of the topics Ibn al-Qayyim addresses, more or less following his progression of discussion.

Thereafter, the concluding part of chapter 6 supplies inclusive structural analysis of the text of *al-Ṣawāʿiq*, taking into consideration the findings arising from the previous chapters. Cutting across Ibn al-Qayyim's meticulous systemization of themes and methodologies as demonstrated in *al-Ṣawāʿiq*, I was able to decrypt the text's literary structure and to connect it to previous theological works which concentrated on the issue of divine attributes; thus presenting the intellectual development *al-Ṣawāʿiq* embodied. All put together, the text's arrangement allows for an exploration of the alternative approach for which Ibn al-Qayyim advocates in *al-Ṣawāʿiq* against the later Ashʿarite rationalistic notions, as well as his outspoken defiance against his fellow traditionalists. As a matter of fact, throughout his validation of the Taymiyyan doctrine of divine attributes in *al-Ṣawāʿiq*, Ibn al-Qayyim didactically systemized his teacher's theoretical discourse on theology; hence he offers much more than a blunt duplication (i.e., *taqlīd*) of his mentor's ideas.

As a whole, the *ṭawāghīt* (i.e., the principle rationalistic modes of argumentation) that Ibn al-Qayyim seeks to abolish in *al-Ṣawāʿiq* ultimately exceed the particular issue of divine attributes. Dealing with the highly complex doctrines of epistemology and hermeneutics, Ibn al-Qayyim engages the theoretical subjects that are at the very core of religious treatment of the texts of the Quran and Hadith. Consequently, the alternative theoretical approaches promoted by Ibn al-Qayyim surpass the realm of Islamic theology (*uṣūl al-dīn*) since they represent fundamental lines of reasoning which can be applied on various other fields of the Islamic sciences, such as legal methodology (*uṣūl al-fiqh*), practical jurisprudence (*furūʿ al-fiqh*), the science of Hadith tradition (*ʿilm al-ḥadīth*) or Arabic linguistics (e.g., *ʿilm al-ʿarabiyya, naḥū, taṣrīf, balāgha*).

This study is structured to conduct an overarching study of a scholar via a single work he created, and vice versa, of the monograph via its author. For more thorough insights, a historical perspective is taken in order to capture the interesting interplay between these two cardinal elements.

CHAPTER 1

The Scholarly Setting of Mamluk Damascus: *al-Ṣawāʿiq*'s Birthplace

The scholar Abū ʿAbdallāh Shams al-Dīn Muḥammad ibn Abī Bakr ibn Ayyūb ibn Saʿd ibn Ḥarīz ibn Makkī Zayn al-Dīn al-Zurʿī 'l-Dimashqī, who is mostly known as Ibn Qayyim al-Jawziyya, was born near Damascus on the 7th of *Ṣafar* 691/1292 to a family of a rather humble means from the village al-Zurʿ (one of Ḥurān villages)[1] near Damascus. He was then raised and educated in Damascus. His father, Abū Bakr ibn Saʿd al-Zurʿī, was the superintendent (*qayyim*) of the famous Ḥanbalite *madrasa* (religious college) *al-jawziyya*, founded by ʿAbd al-Raḥman ibn al-Jawzī (d. 597/1200) in Damascus. The father's occupation was the source of the name under which the son was known: Ibn Qayyim al-Jawziyya. Ibn al-Qayyim was the first member of his family to attain the status of an honorable scholar. He mostly taught at *madrasa*s, only gaining a certain degree of professional recognition towards the end of his life as a preacher of sermons and tutor at *al-madrasa 'l-ṣadariyya* and *al-madrasa 'l-jawziyya*. The latter *madrasa* also served as the court of law and the official residence of the Ḥanbalite chief judge (*qāḍi 'l-quḍāt*) of Damascus starting from 664/1266; therefore, it offered official representation of the city's Ḥanbalite population. However, even when it reached its highest point, Ibn al-Qayyim's career was still relatively modest and unassuming.[2] Nonetheless, the tight allegiance Ibn al-Qayyim expressed towards his fiery teacher Ibn Taymiyya not only had a tremendous impact on his own intellectual output, but also the independent position he came to hold among his contemporary elitist social class of religious scholars in Damascus, the *ʿulamāʾ*.

A preliminary acquaintance with various intellectual occurrences in Ibn al-Qayyim's main working environment is required in order to attain a clear

1 The village is better known under the name al-Zarrāʿa (الزرّاعة); Shihāb al-Dīn Abū ʿAbdallāh Yāqūt ibn ʿAbdallāh al-Rūmi 'l-Ḥamawī (d. 626/1229), *Muʿjam al-Buldān*, no editor mentioned, in 5 volumes (Beirut: Dār Ṣādir, 1397/1977), 3:135.

2 Holtzman, "Ibn Qayyim al-Jawziyya (1292–1350)", 207–208; Krawietz, "Ibn Qayyim al-Jawziyya: His Life and Works," *Mamlūk Studies Review*, 10/2 (2006), 21; Laoust, "Ibn Ḳayyim al-Dj̲awziyya," *EI*², 3:821; Abū Zayd, *Ibn Qayyim al-Jawziyya*, 17–20; Bori and Holtzman, the Introduction to: *A Scholar in the Shadows*, 17–18.

 | DOI: 10.1163/9789004372511_003

understanding of his thought, whether in the field of theology or others. Hence, this chapter focuses on placing Ibn al-Qayyim and his writings in a historical context in order to set a firm foundation for a better exploration of his theological notions concerning the issue of divine attributes as they appear in his work *al-Ṣawāʿiq*. In providing this historical outlook, the aim is to deepen previous research's claims and conclusions concerning Ibn al-Qayyim's scholastic figure within the close social class of religious thinkers (*ʿulamāʾ*) of which he was a part.[3] More precisely, I briefly clarify the prominent socio-historical conditions behind Ibn al-Qayyim's theologically centered oeuvre to set the stage for the following core chapters, which will further examine the contents of his work *al-Ṣawāʿiq*, their intellectual relation to other works and their place within the fascinating structure of scholarly interrelations—not only in Mamluk times, but also before this period.

Doing so, it is impossible to avoid addressing the great mark Ibn Taymiyya left on Ibn al-Qayyim as both an honored and cherished mentor and role model. Looking into several complex aspects of the relations between Ibn al-Qayyim and Ibn Taymiyya—including connections between specific works each of them authored—is an important step before delving into the analysis of Ibn al-Qayyim's later, more developed theological works for their own sake and *al-Ṣawāʿiq* in particular. This chapter will therefore also describe Ibn al-Qayim's prime source of inspiration to the standpoint he articulated

3 The social, political, religious and cosmic hierarchies cultivated by the medieval cultural distinction between "high" and "low" was the subject of several important studies of cultural history. However, the topic of the structure of the Damascene society in Mamluk times extends the attention span of the present study and will only be addressed to highlight Ibn al-Qayyim's theological work. Exemplary secondary literature pertaining the socio-historical aspects are: Carlo Ginzburg, "High and Low: The Theme of Forbidden Knowledge in the Sixteenth and Seventeenth Centuries," *Past and Present* 73 (Nov., 1976), 28–41. Further development on the dichotomy between "popular culture" and "elite" as reflecting means of social power in modern times can be found in the work of the critical theorists Theodor W. Adorno (d. 1969) and Max Horkheimer (d. 1973) titled *Dialectic of Enlightenment*, edited by Gunzelin Schmid Noerr and translated by Edmund Jephcott (Stanford: Stanford University Press, 2002). Studies especially relevant to the Mamluk period are, for example: Jonathan P. Berkey, "Popular Culture under the Mamluks: A Historiographical Survey," in: *Mamluk Studies Review* IX/2 (2005), 134–137; idem, *Popular Preaching & Religious Authority in Medieval Islamic Near East* (Seattle and London: University of Washington Press, 2001), 9–12. As already noted by Shoshan, there was an apparent flow of mutual relations among medieval Islamic society in a way of a vivid synthesis, which differs from the much more severe social structure of European society of the time, for example; Boaz Shoshan, "High Culture and Popular Culture in Medieval Islam," in: *Studia Islamica* 73 (1991), 89–90.

in *al-Ṣawāʿiq* regarding the issue of divine attributes, namely the Taymiyyan approach. Most notable with relation to *al-Ṣawāʿiq* are Ibn Taymiyya's political-theology which appear in two of his texts: the iconic treatise *al-Ḥamawiyya 'l-kubrā* and the voluminous work *Bayān talbīs al-jahmiyya*; it will be inquired here in sections 1.1 and 1.2, respectively. Both of these texts definitely demonstrate Ibn Taymiyya's interesting viewpoint within the surrounding scholastic milieu of the *ʿulamāʾ* in Mamluk Damascus, as well as its immediate—at times, uneasy—effect on Ibn al-Qayyim. Altogether, this chapter illuminates key ideas relevant to Ibn al-Qayyim's appropriation of his teacher's thought in *al-Ṣawāʿiq*.

Ibn al-Qayyim's intellectual training in Mamluk Damascus is an interesting example of the general educational prospects the city could offer its *ʿulamāʾ*. Various primary biographies and studies written about Ibn al-Qayyim supply important information regarding his wide-ranged education, his many areas of expertise, his teachers and other significant historical factors, all of which contributed to shaping his scholarship. In the field of practical jurisprudence (*furūʿ al-fiqh*) Ibn al-Qayyim studied the traditional texts of the Ḥanbalite school of thought customary in the region of Syria at the time. These included, for example, the book *al-Mukhtaṣar* [Abridgement of Aḥmad ibn Ḥanbal's opinions] by the jurist Abu 'l-Qāsim al-Khiraqī (d. 334/946), which was the first Ḥanbalite text to deal clearly with jurisprudence and was used in Ḥanbalite teaching for generations to come. Ibn al-Qayyim studied inheritance law with his father as well as with Ibn Taymiyya. With Ibn Taymiyya, he also studied the book *al-Muḥarrar fi 'l-fiqh ʿalā madhhab al-imām Aḥmad ibn Ḥanbal* written by Majd al-Dīn Abu 'l-Barakāt (d. 652/1254, Ibn Taymiyya's grandfather), another text which was considered mandatory for the Ḥanbalite school of law. In addition, one of Ibn Taymiyya's brothers, Sharaf al-Dīn (d. 727/1327), was also mentioned as a jurisprudence teacher of Ibn al-Qayyim. As far as the field of Islamic law is concerned, it seems Ibn al-Qayyim was acquainted with several scholars from Ibn Taymiyya's family.[4]

However, in the field of legal methodology and hermeneutics (*uṣūl al-fiqh*) Ibn al-Qayyim was also very familiar with the thought of scholars who did not belong to the Ḥanbalite school. He studied parts of the book *Rawḍat al-nāẓir wa-jannat al-munāẓir* of the Ḥanbalite scholar Ibn Qudāma (d. 631/1223) on jurisprudence methodology. Together with Ibn Taymiyya, he studied the book of the Ashʿarite-Shāfiʿite thinker Fakr al-Dīn al-Rāzī (d. 607/1210), *al-Maḥṣūl fī ʿilm uṣūl al-fiqh*, which at the time was considered an important source of

4 Bori and Holtzman, the Introduction to: *A Scholar in the Shadows*, 17–18.

training for jurists affiliated with all four schools of Islamic law.[5] Furthermore, Ibn al-Qayyim also studied a book entitled *Kitāb al-aḥkām fī uṣūl al-aḥkām* by another Ashʿarite-Shāfiʿite scholar, Sayf al-Dīn al-Āmidī (d. 631/1233); this book represented a rationalistic approach of juridical theory. Under the guidance of Ibn Taymiyya, who saw himself as an independent jurist (*mujtahid*) unconfined to any individual school's legal measures, Ibn al-Qayyim was introduced to various methodological aspects of comprehending and practicing the discipline of Islamic jurisprudence.[6]

In the field of theology and principles of religion (*uṣūl al-dīn*), Ibn al-Qayyim's education was most obviously based on the rationalistic Ashʿarite methods of speculative theology (*Kalām*), particularly the keen perception of Fakhr al-Dīn al-Rāzī's notions. In fact, Ibn al-Qayyim's first theology instructor was one of Ibn Taymiyya's dissidents and an avid supporter of the Ashʿarite thought, Ṣafī 'l-Dīn al-Hindī (d. 715/1315), who taught him sections of al-Rāzī's works *Kitāb al-arbaʿīn fī uṣūl al-dīn* (The Book of Forty, on the Principles of Religion) and *Muḥaṣṣal afkār al-mutaqaddimīn wal-mutaʾakhkhirīn min al-ʿulamāʾ wal-ḥukamāʾ wal-mutakallimīn* (A Compendium of the Opinions of Ancient and Later Scholars, Philosophers and Speculative Theologians).[7] Interestingly enough, later on Ibn al-Qayyim studied parts of these books with Ibn Taymiyya as well. Hence, under the influence of two radically different teachers, Ibn al-Qayyim probed into al-Rāzī's theological conceptions in full detail. Moreover, unlike in the field of jurisprudence, Ibn al-Qayyim also read and studied theology from the writings of Ibn Taymiyya himself. Another special impact reflected in Ibn al-Qayyim's works is that of classical Greek philosophy, also in reference to philosophy and medicine, e.g., in his books *Kitāb al-rūḥ* (Book of the Spirit) or *al-Tibb al-nabawī* (Prophetic Medicine). Ibn al-Qayyim's biographies do not seem to mention Greek writings as sources used during the course of his education.[8] Nonetheless, given the rationalistic scholarly surroundings of Mamluk

5 Highly relevant in this respect is the indication this book gives us of the penetration of Fakhr al-Din al-Rāzī's scholarship in Mamluk Damascus. Y. Tzvi Langermann provided some interesting insights on Ibn al-Qayyim's appreciation of al-Rāzī and his works in his article "The Naturalization of Science in Ibn Qayyim al-Ǧawziyyah's *Kitāb al-Rūḥ*," in Bori and Holtzman (eds.), *A Scholar in the Shadows*, 211–228.

6 Bori and Holtzman, the Introduction to: *A Scholar in the Shadows*, 18.

7 These two works' major centrality with regard to Ibn al-Qayyim's work *al-Ṣawāʿiq* will be elaborately discussed in chapter 3. Additional important insights about Ibn Taymiyya and Ibn al-Qayyim's perception of Rāzī's theological teachings and their response to it will be shortly discussed in section 1.1.

8 Bori and Holtzman, the introduction to: *A Scholar in the Shadows*, 18–19; Avivit Cohen,

Damascus, it is highly plausible he came across different aspects of Greek Philosophy and gained at least vicarious acquaintance with material of that kind.[9]

All in all, Ibn al-Qayyim's intellectual training appears to have been basically Ḥanbalite, largely leaning towards Ibn Taymiyya's revolutionary approach and his outstanding manner for contemplating religious principles. At the age of 21, Ibn al-Qayyim met this impressive and exceptional scholar who deeply affected his thinking. Consequently, Ibn al-Qayyim became Ibn Taymiyya's most esteemed disciple over the next 15 years. Without a doubt, their individual characters were fundamentally different: Ibn al-Qayyim is depicted in the biographical sources as mild-natured and slightly insecure (even after having establishing his scholarly status), whereas Ibn Taymiyya's sayings and acts portray him as a far more aggressive, loud and hot-tempered person.[10] Furthermore, Ibn Taymiyya is famous for the many rivalries he had managed to create with other religious scholars of the time due to uncompromising polemics as well as doctrinal and legal controversies, which led to his involvement in the political arena and the somewhat hostile attitude on the side of Mamluk authorities.[11]

A short clarification of the structure of Damascene society in Ibn al-Qayyim's lifetime, its political system and religious establishment can assist in evaluating Ibn al-Qayyim's stature amid the religious scholars in Damascus, and more so the clash between the two. Studies conducted on Muslim society in Mamluk times—in its two centers of Cairo and Damascus—tend to depict it as a highly heterogeneous community in a somewhat threefold dissection: the ruling military caste, a civilian administrative elite and the laymen. The administrative elite can in itself be divided into a majority group constituting the religious establishment (i.e., *ʿulamāʾ*), and a minority group that contained other notables. More than anything else, public social activity was dependent on patterns of organization led by the *ʿulamāʾ*, carrying out the religious practices in all levels of the community's life and providing spiritual guidance to the masses. They are considered a "class", as in a distinct part of the society whose members shared a more or less similar socio-cultural characteristics and functions.

Between "the Garden of Lovers" and "the Censure of Profance Love": A Comparative Study of Ibn Qayyim al-Jawziyya and Ibn al-Jawzi's Theory of Love, unpublished MA thesis (Ramat-Gan: Bar-Ilan University, 2010), 11.

9 See further elaboration on Ibn al-Qayyim's possible deployment of his familiarity with Hellenistic philosophy and methods of argumentation in *al-Ṣawāʿiq* in section 3.4 to come.

10 Bori and Holtzman, the Introduction to: *A Scholar in the Shadows*, 17; Holtzman, "Ibn Qayyim al-Jawziyya (1292–1350)," 209, 211.

11 Henri Laoust, "Ibn Taymiyya," *EI*^{2}, 3:952–953.

In their relations with the ruling Mamluks, the class of *ʿulamāʾ* usually strove to protect its independence and to distance itself from the "corruptive power of government". Yet, due to the synthesis of religion and politics, the class of *ʿulamāʾ* came to adopt one of two parallel approaches: either estrangement from the state or cooperation with it.[12]

In fact, the members of the *ʿulamāʾ* in Damascus were granted the role of guardians of the Sacred Law (*sharīʿa*) and, henceforth, the practice of religious norms. Consequently, the *ʿulamāʾ* class held a special role within the society of the Mamluk sultanate similar to other societies under Islamic rule. Their authority was expected to be equally accepted by the common people as well as the rulers; for the latter, mainly as a means of additionally legitimizing their sovereignty.[13] By and large, Sunnite *ʿulamāʾ* were characterized by a common course of juristic and theological training and their adherence to a text-based approach. Nevertheless, the *ʿulamāʾ* were far from being unanimously united under a single banner; rather, they were separately affiliated into one of the four schools of Islamic law (*madhhab*, pl. *madhāhib*) and had different political interests regarding the Mamluk state and its rulers. A number of historical accounts confirm that, under the Mamluks, most of the *ʿulamāʾ* were rather satisfied with their status, both personally and as pious Muslims. It probably comes as no surprise that Ibn Taymiyya was an exception to the rule.[14]

The *ʿulamāʾ* of the Ḥanbalite school are mostly considered to have had the clearest features of social cohesion and solidarity. However, Ibn Taymiyya's

---

12 Rethinking the work of previous modern scholars, Yaacov Lev pointed out the nuanced relations between the *ʿulamāʾ* and the Mamluk rulers, historically depicting a broad system of corporations and frictions which shaped the role of *ʿulamāʾ* as much more than a mediating class between the subjects and the regime; Lev, "Symbiotic Relations: Ulama and the Mamluk Sultans," *Mamlūk Studies Review* XIII (1) 2009, 1–26.

13 Noteworthy is the relatively deteriorated political autonomy the *ʿulamāʾ* held during the Mamluk era in comparison to earlier Islamic regimes. Due to the militarization processes of the Mamluk ruling system, which was a result of the need to defend their government against exterior attacks (especially from the Mongols), the *ʿulamāʾ* became more and more dependent on the ruler's patronage and support; Zuhair Ghazzal, "The ʿUlamāʾ: Status and Function," in: ed. Youssef M. Choueiri, *A Companion to the History of the Middle East* (Malden, MA: Blackwellm 2005), 75.

14 Michael Winter, "ʿUlamāʾ Between the State and the Society in Pre-Modern Sunni Islam," in: Meir Hanita (ed.), *Guardians of Faith in Modern Times: ʿUlamāʾ in the Middle East* (Leiden: Brill, 2009), 22–24, 30–33; Amalia Levanoni, "Who Were the 'Salt of the Earth' in Fifteenth-Century Egypt?," *Mamlūk Studies Review*, 14/1 (2010): 63, 77–81; Gustave E. Von Grunebaum, *Medieval Islam: A Study in Cultural Orientation*, second edition (Chicago, London: The University of Chicago Press, 1969), 186.

immediate association with the typical traditionalistic nature of Ḥanbalite school has already been convincingly challenged in modern research. This is due to his conspicuous nonconformist attitude towards scholars and notions not only of other law or theological schools, but also of those which were generally accepted as authoritative figures amongst the majority of traditionalist Ḥanbalites. Among Ḥanbalite representative scholars, there were several instances of disapproval concerning Ibn Taymiyya's preoccupation with "sterile polemics" rather than dealing with cardinal juristic and theological issues. Another matter of reproach was Ibn Taymiyya's arrogance and his pretentious attitude towards his fellow Ḥanbalites, not to mention his ideological rivals from other schools. Historical accounts of this kind demonstrate the criticism within Ḥanbalite circles towards Ibn Taymiyya and clearly show he did not fit the Sunnite—and, more precisely Ḥanbalite—scholastic consensus.[15]

The lack of clear, wide-ranged appreciation did not prevent Ibn Taymiyya from accumulating a highly devoted circle of close disciples in a similar manner to other prominent scholars. This close circle is referred to in historical sources as *al-jamāʿa* (lit., the group), in this case meaning an exclusive and elitist assembly of disciples and supporters who shared Ibn Taymiyya's call for an activist style, and considered him the most authoritative Shaykh, viz. religious leader. Moreover, the members of Ibn Taymiyya's *jamāʿa* also assisted in spreading and publicizing their master's way of thinking, his ideas as well as multiple writings. It seems that in these scholars' eyes, the exclusive bond with the *jamāʿa* often exceeded their affiliation to a certain legal *madhhab* in importance, presumably as a consequence of the somewhat restricted elitist nature of that circle. Given this background, Ibn al-Qayyim's great loyalty to Ibn Taymiyya can be more feasibly understood as being a part of a closely connected scholarly circle which was vastly criticized from the outside, thus creating a more substantial need for belonging and acceptance within the circle itself.[16]

As much evidence reveals, not only was Ibn al-Qayyim a member of Ibn Taymiyya's *jamāʿa*, he was also its most avid supporter and a true Taymiyyan scholar. The remarkable closeness between the two scholars had major consequences for Ibn al-Qayyim, which were as concrete as they were intellectual. In the year 726/1326, Ibn al-Qayyim was the only disciple of Ibn Taymiyya to be imprisoned with him in the fortress of Damascus—*qalʿa*, the fortress had also

---

15 Caterina Bori, "A New Source for the Biography of Ibn Taymiyya," *Bulletin of the School of Oriental and African Studies, University of London*, 67/3 (2004), 326–328.

16 Caterina Bori, "Ibn Taymiyya *wa-jamāʿatuhu*: Authority, Conflict and Consensus in Ibn Taymiyya's Circle," in: *Ibn Taymiyya and His Times*, ed. Yossef Rapoport and Shahab Ahmed (Karachi: Oxford University Press, 2010), 25–36, 42–43.

been used as a municipal prison—for his public support of his teacher. The immediate reason of Ibn Taymiyya's initial arrest was a ruling (*fatwā*) he issued against visiting the tombs of saints (*ziyārat al-qubūr*), which he perceived a forbidden, un-Islamic ritual. Shortly afterwards, Ibn al-Qayyim delivered a sermon in Jerusalem, in which he stated his agreement with Ibn Taymiyya's juristic stand on the matter, including visitations to the Prophet Muḥammad's grave in Medina. On another occasion, Ibn al-Qayyim supported Ibn Taymiyya's rule concerning the issue of divorce (*ṭalāq*), which was contradictory to the legal opinion of most of Damascene Shāfiʿite jurisprudents.[17] For this opinion, Ibn al-Qayyim was publicly beaten and led by a donkey in a humiliating excursion in the streets of Damascus to prison, where he had been sentence to serve two years.[18]

This was not the first time in which the mentor, Ibn Taymiyya, had been detained by the authorities for his ideological stances and rulings. In 705/1306, twenty years earlier, Ibn Taymiyya has been summoned to trial several times where he was accused of anthropomorphism (*tashbīh*, lit., 'likening', i.e., inappropriately ascribing human attributes to God). In the first trial, held in Damascus, he was acquitted on all counts; however, in Cairo he later was found guilty and imprisoned in the fortress of Damascus for seven years. These initial trials marked the start of a period of many accusations made by the authorities against Ibn Taymiyya on the basis of his theological thought and creed (*ʿaqīda*). These intense times lasted until the end of his life, when, together with Ibn al-Qayyim, he was sent to prison for a second time in Damascus; he died there while imprisoned in 728/1328. In fact, Ibn Taymiyya's trials signified a milestone not only in his own life, but also in the ongoing conflict between traditionalism and rationalism in Islamic thought.[19]

The background behind the ideological accusations against Ibn Taymiyya is of much relevance to achieve proper understanding of the mindset at the time—and even more so, of the period in which Ibn al-Qayyim was writing—as far as it concerns the strife between the theological schools in Damascus.

---

17 An interesting analysis of Ibn Taymiyya's view on the primarily legal matter of divorce oaths and its social context appears in the study: Yossef Rapoport, "Ibn Taymiyya on Divorce Oaths," in: eds. Michael Winter and Amalia Levanoni, *The Mamluks in Egyptian and Syrian Politics and Society* (Leiden, Boston: Brill, 2004), 191–217.

18 Holtzman, "Ibn Qayyim al-Jawziyya (1292–1350)," 210–211; Bori and Holtzman, the introduction to: *A Scholar in the Shadows*, 19; Taylor, *In the Vicinity of the Righteous*, 171–194; Avivit Cohen, *Between "the Garden of Lovers" and "the Censure of Profane Love,"* 13.

19 Sherman A. Jackson, "Ibn Taymiyyah on Trial in Damascus," *Journal of Semitic Studies* 39/1 (Spring 1994), 41; Henri Laoust, "Ibn Taymiyya," *EI*², 3:951–952.

With relation to the issue of divine attributes, a quarrel that occurred around Ibn Taymiyya's treatise *al-ʿAqīda ʾl-wāsiṭiyya* is an exquisite example of the theological polemics which took place at that time. In *al-Wāsiṭiyya*, Ibn Taymiyya referred to the five major theological questions on which diverse Islamic theological schools had fundamentally differed,[20] including the question of divine attributes. Ibn Taymiyya described the Sunnite principles of belief (*ʿaqīda*, creed) according to his understanding, claiming that they are the ones which express an "intermediary faith" (*wasaṭ*) between two extremes. On the issue of divine attributes, Ibn Taymiyya writes:

> Belief in God includes the belief in the attributes He has used to describe Himself in His book [i.e., the Quran] and the attributes His Messenger Muḥammad used to describe Him, without falsification (*taḥrīf*), without negation (*taʿṭīl*), without ascribing modality (*takyīf*) and without assimilation (*tamthīl*).[21]

Hence, Ibn Taymiyya states the correct Islamic belief is between those who negate the divine attributes, meaning the ultra-rationalistic Muʿtazilite and the rational-traditionalistic Ashʿarite schools, and those who accept anthropomorphism, meaning *al-mujassima* (lit., the corporealists).[22]

Al-Wāsiṭiyya was the central treatise towards which Ibn Taymiyya had drawn attention during his trials; however, another theological treatise he wrote, *al-Ḥamawiyya ʾl-kubrā* (the Grand [Response Written] for the People of Hamat), was the direct reason why he had initially been charged with theological delinquency.[23] During Ibn Taymiyya's trial in Damascus, the Shāfiʿite-Ashʿarite schol-

20 As Ibn Taymiyya lists them in his treatise, those points of disagreement are: God's attributes (*bāb ṣifāt Allāh*), God's actions (*bāb al-afʿāl*), the Godly threat (*bāb waʿīd Allāh*), the belief and religion (*bāb asmāʾ al-īmān wal-dīn*), and the Prophet's companions (*aṣḥāb rsūl Allāh*); Henri Laoust, *La profession de foi d'Ibn Taymiyya: texte, traduction et commentaire de la Wāsiṭiyya* (Paris: Geuther, 1986), 14–15.

21 Laoust, *la Wāsiṭiyya*, 1; the term *taʿṭīl* is a part of the Islamic theological discourse of polemics regarding the issue of the divine attributes. There are terms with a positive connotation, such as *tanzīh* (perceiving God as transcendent) and *ithbāt* (affirmation of the divine attributes). On the other hand, negative associations are connected to the terms *tashbīh* (anthropomorphism) and *taʿṭīl* ([accusation on] negating/denying the divine attributes); van Ess, "Tas͟hbīh wa-Tanzīh," *EI*², 10: 341–342.

22 Livnat Holtzman "Predestination (*al-Qaḍāʾ wal-Qadar*) and Free Will (*al-Ikhtiyār*) as Reflected in the Works of the Neo-Ḥanbalites in the Fourteenth Century," unpublished PhD dissertation (Ramat-Gan, Israel: Bar-Ilan University, 2003), 13.

23 See further elaboration on the treatise in section 1.1.

ar Ṣafi 'l-Dīn al-Hindī[24] added another allegation to the accusation of anthropomorphism: he argued that, at the theological level, *al-Ḥamawiyya 'l-kubrā* is not in accordance with the Quran and the Sunna. An additional allegation that was raised against the treatise had to do with some previous suspicions of Ibn Taymiyya's involvement in political activity in favor of the Mongol invaders and against the Mamluk regime in Cairo and Damascus. Demanding to publicly reply to the allegation of political infidelity as well as refute it, Ibn Taymiyya alluded to his treatise *al-Wāsiṭiyya*, named after the city of Wāsiṭ in Iraq, which fell into Mongol hands around the same time and some of its occupiers had converted to Islam. Ibn Taymiyya realized his detractors meant to accuse him of intentionally writing *al-Wāsiṭiyya* in order to convert the Mongols to Islam for his own cause, allegedly against the Mamluk rulers. To counter this allegation, Ibn Taymiyya stressed that he wrote *al-Wāsiṭiyya* at the request of an anonymous man from Wāsiṭ seven years before, which was prior to the Mongol invasion. For him, the Damascus trials were an opportunity to overtly disprove the charges of masking dangerous political intentions in his theological writing.[25]

Ibn Taymiyya gave an account of his impressions of his trials, apparently written several years after they took place.[26] Ibn Taymiyya's writing about the Damascus trials reflects his impression that the primary aim of these trials was his humiliation, undermining his position among the *ʿulamāʾ* class and the wider public. In order to achieve this objective, Ibn Taymiyya's adversaries utilized the theological debate between the traditional stance, represented by

24 Around the year 705/1306 Damascus, the Shāfiʿite legal school enjoyed a considerable hegemony; therefore, Shāfiʿite scholars were Ibn Taymiyya's initial prosecutors. Ibn Taymiyya's brother, Sharaf al-Dīn, had listed the people who attended the trial's hearings concerning *al-ʿAqīda 'l-wāsiṭiyya* in a letter he sent to their other brother, Zayn al-Dīn, in which he asked to disprove the many rumors around the ongoing trial. Among the trial's attendants, Sharaf al-Dīn also named several officials who held very high judicial positions, such as the Shāfiʿite-Ashʿarite scholar Ṣafi 'l-Dīn al-Hindī. As previously mentioned, he was one of Ibn Qayyim al-Jawziyya's teachers in the field of law; Laoust, *la Wāsiṭiyya*, 14–17; Jackson, "Ibn Taymiyyah on Trial in Damascus," 43–45.

25 Jackson, "Ibn Taymiyyah on Trial in Damascus," 49–51; Jon Hoover, *Ibn Taymiyya's Theodicy of Perpetual Optimism* (Leiden: Brill, 2007), 54–56.

26 Sherman Jackson provides an English translation of a part of Ibn Taymiyya's memoirs as they appear in two primary sources: 1. Ibn Taymiyya's records of the theological debate (*munāẓara*), which took place in the first trial in Damascus and can be found in his *Majmūʿat al-fatāwā*; 2. Writings of one of Ibn Taymiyya's disciples, the Ḥanbalite scholar Muḥammad ibn Aḥmad ibn ʿAbd al-Hādī (d. 744/1343), *al-ʿUqūd al-durriyya min manāqib shaykh al-islām Aḥmad ibn Taymiyya*; Jackson, "Ibn Taymiyyah on Trial in Damascus," 43.

Ibn Taymiyya, and the Ashʿarite stance, which was held by numerous scholars among the city's hegemonic scholastic elite. The main argument that Ibn Taymiyya's ideological rivals presented as grounds for charging him with a crime of belief was that the usage of a figurative interpretation (*taʾwīl*) with regard to the divine attributes—to which Ibn Taymiyya opposed—is theologically legitimate. As they stated, without the usage of the allegorical interpretation, certain Quranic verses or Hadith accounts necessarily lead to an undesirable anthropomorphic perception of God. Ibn Taymiyya firmly guarded his stance, mentioning once again that the righteous predecessors of the Muslim community (*salaf*) were never engaged in *taʾwīl* as claimed by his Ashʿarite rivals but, rather, this was a later development introduced by the speculative theologians (*mutakallimūn*) and their alien methods.[27]

Nonetheless, Ibn Taymiyya's opponents, who enjoyed significantly greater political power, managed to prevail. During the following years, Ibn Taymiyya was the focus of numerous theological clashes and debates; he was even put on trial and imprisoned once again in the year 726/1326, this time accompanied by his supporters. Notable is that the reasons for this longer imprisonment were not a dispute over anthropomorphism, but Ibn Taymiyya's overall stance, which was seen as dangerously radical in the eyes of the religious establishment. Ibn al-Qayyim's imprisonment alongside his mentor was an event which had drastic consequences on the disciple's life. During that period of time, the two devoted their highest efforts to writing books and letters. Supplying the most detailed account of the time of imprisonment, Ibn al-Qayyim's biography—written by Ibn Rajab—even mentions Ibn al-Qayyim having a Ṣūfī-mystical experience, which stimulated him to further concentrate on studying the Quran. Ibn al-Qayyim was released from prison one month after Ibn Taymiyya's death in 728/1328. Now he faced the challenge of reinstating his eminence as a proficient scholar in his own right.[28]

By the age of 36, Ibn al-Qayyim attained a highly respected position as an independent teacher. Wishing to preserve the Taymiyyan legacy, he gradually began passing on Ibn Taymiyya's doctrine to his pupils. Ibn al-Qayyim carried out the pilgrimage to Mecca while writing several books. When he returned to Damascus, he dedicated much of his time to establishing himself as a *muftī* (i.e., a legal expert issuing rulings). Regaining confidence and higher position, Ibn al-Qayyim began tackling more convoluted subjects, thus commencing to write theological works in an attempt to contest and refute scholastic approaches he

27 Jackson, "Ibn Taymiyyah on Trial in Damascus," 42, 51–52.

28 Holtzman, "Ibn Qayyim al-Jawziyya (1292–1350)," 210–211.

found dubious. Much like Ibn Taymiyya, one of the issues that preoccupied his mind was the theological issue of divine attributes; part of his goal was to subvert the principles of the Muʿtazilite and Ashʿarite approaches. Unmistakable in this respect is how Ibn al-Qayyim uses theological issues and inner-Islamic polemics as a vessel for expressing his disagreement with the religious establishment and the scholastic elite of the *ʿulamāʾ*.[29]

The highest position of Damascus' religious establishment was the city's Chief Judge (*qāḍi 'l-quḍāt*)—appointed by the Mamluk authorities—which was held by the Shāfiʿite scholar Taqi 'l-Dīn al-Subkī (d. 756/1355). In the light of Ibn al-Qayyim's enduring loyalty to Ibn Taymiyya's views even after the teacher's death, al-Subkī found him to be both a substantial hazard and a threat. This brought about a major confrontation between al-Subkī and Ibn al-Qayyim, which lasted from the years 745–749/1345–1349 until Ibn al-Qayyim's death in 750/1350. The first incident, initiating the confrontation, occurred in 741/1341, when the Mamluk emir al-Fakhrī (d. 742/1343) attempted to retrieve several of Ibn Taymiyya's books which had remained locked and inaccessible since the days of his imprisonment. Historical accounts reveal that al-Subkī actively interfered and blocked access to these writings. Only after the emir al-Fakhrī threatened his high-ranking position and even his life, did al-Subkī back down, and the books were sent afterward to Ibn al-Qayyim and to one of Ibn Taymiyya's brothers. As a result, al-Subkī experienced major humiliation.[30]

Ibn al-Qayyim's stances in his rulings with regard to two matters of jurisprudence soured his dealings with al-Subkī even further. First, al-Subkī confronted Ibn al-Qayyim several times for the latter's approach in the case of divorce (*ṭalāq*).[31] The two differed, for example, in the issue of conditional divorce (*al-*

29 Holtzman, "Ibn Qayyim al-Jawziyya (1292–1350)," 211–215; Cohen, *Between "the Garden of Lovers" and "the Censure of Profance Love,"* 14.

30 Bori and Holtzman, the introduction to: *A Scholar in the Shadows*, 22.

31 Al-Subkī referred to Ibn Taymiyya's rulings in the issue of divorce first hand in *Kitāb al-ṭalāq* in his *fatwā*'s collection. According to his own statements there, al-Subkī openly disagreed with the Taymiyyan view expressed in the work *al-Ijmāʿ wal-iftirāq fī masāʾil al-imān wal-ṭalāq* (Connection and Separation: the Issues of Oath and Divorce). He dedicates a chapter to address and disprove Ibn Taymiyya's position on the matter. Moreover, al-Subkī mentions two treatises he had written as a counter-reply to Ibn Taymiyya's rulings: *al-Taḥqīq fī masʾalat al-taʿlīq* (Determining the Issue of Conditional Repudiation [i.e., *taʿlīq al-ṭalāq*]) and *Kitāb rafʿal-shiqāq ʿan masʾalat al-ṭalāq* (Book of Solving the Disunity on the Issue of Divorce); Taqi 'l-Dīn al-Subkī, Abu 'l-Ḥasan ʿAlī ibn ʿAbd al-Kāfī (d. 756/1355), no editor mentioned, *Fatāwā 'l-Subkī* (Beirut: Dār al-Maʿrifa, [1410]/[1990]), 2:303–309.

ḥilf bil-iṭlāq). To be precise, this kind of divorce is the result of an oath taken by the husband that if "so and so happens" the wife shall be let go. Whereas al-Subkī accepted this kind of divorce—as did many jurisprudents at the time—Ibn al-Qayyim supported Ibn Taymiyya's opinion, which rejected it.[32] Second, from a legal point of view, al-Subkī did not see anything wrong with the use of judicial trickeries (*ḥiyāl*) in order to allow gambling or different kinds of races (*musābaqāt*), while Ibn al-Qayyim condemned them, once again advocating in favor of previous Taymiyyan rulings.[33]

Additional significant sources for acquiring a better understanding of the hostile attitude towards Ibn al-Qayyim are two treatises written by al-Subkī, in which he rebuked Ibn al-Qayyim for his position regarding theological issues. These two writings are generally included within the six treatises al-Subkī had set down against Ibn Taymiyya when the latter was still alive. The main subjects to be discussed therein with respect to Ibn Taymiyya are for the most part legal ones, such as the divorce issue or the prohibition of visits of sacred tombs.[34] On the other hand, al-Subkī's decision on debasing Ibn al-Qayyim's views in the theological foci comes as not much of surprise, given the fact that at that period of time (ca. 745/1345) Ibn al-Qayyim has written several of his most developed theological works. Among these were, for example, *Shifāʾ al-ʿalīl fī masāʾil al-qaḍāʾ wal-qadr wal-ḥikma wal-taʿlīl* (Healing the Person Afflicted [with Wrong Conceptions] about Predetermination, Wisdom and Causality) and the mentioned *al-Ṣawāʿiq al-mursala ʿala ʾl-Jahmiyya wal-Muʿaṭṭila* (Unleashed Thunderbolts Directed against the Heretics and the Deniers [of the divine Attributes]). It most definitely seems that al-Subkī considered those works as a manifested attempt to carry on Ibn Taymiyya's line of

32 See footnote 17 in this chapter. In addition, Yossef Rpoport indicates that Ibn al-Qayyim's legal stance on the matter highly supports and goes along the same lines as the Taymiyyan one, as he stated in his work on the methodology of jurisprudence *Iʿlām al-muwaqqiʿīn ʿan Rabb al-ʿālamīn* (Informing the Legal Officials [of All There Is to Know] on the Authority of the Lord of All Beings); Rapoport, "Ibn Taymiyya on Divorce Oaths," 192, 199–200.

33 Bori and Holtzman, the introduction to: *A Scholar in the Shadows*, 22; Holtzman, "Ibn Qayyim al-Jawziyya (1292–1350)," 220.

34 Evidently, al-Subkī feared the pragmatic approach of jurisprudence introduced by Ibn Taymiyya because of the possibility the common people would embrace it. The six writings appear in their entirety in the book *al-Rasāʾil al-Subkiyya fi ʾl-radd ʿalā Ibn Taymiyya wa-tilmidhihi Ibn Qayyim al-Jawziyya* (al-Subkī's Treatises [of Rejection] in Reply to Ibn Taymiyya and His Pupil Ibn Qayyim al-Jawziyya), alongside with a comprehensive introduction by Kamāl Abu ʾl-Munā (Beirut: ʿĀlam al-Kutub, 1403/1983).

scholarship, therefore treating them and their author with an increasing sense of resentment.[35]

Al-Subkī's first treatise likely to be understood as countering Ibn al-Qayyim is called *al-Iʿtibār bi-baqāʾ al-janna wal-nār* (Acknowledging the Ever-Lasting [Nature of] Heaven and Hell). As inferred by its title, in this text al-Subkī expressed his condemnation of the eschatological idea that Heaven and Hell would ever cease to exist.[36] Although in the treatise al-Subkī did not mention by name any specific ideological rival, he might have directed it towards Ibn Taymiyya, who dedicated his last work to this matter. However, since the treatise is dated from 748/1348—some twenty years after Ibn Taymiyya's death—it is more than plausible it was directed against Ibn al-Qayyim, since he was the prominent follower of the Taymiyyan thought. Furthermore, the subject of the duration of Heaven and Hell appears in several of Ibn al-Qayyim's later works (including *al-Ṣawāʿiq al-mursala*).[37]

---

35 Taqi 'l-Dīn al-Subkī, *al-Rasāʾil al-Subkiyya*, 77–80; Bori and Holtzman, the introduction to: *A Scholar in the Shadows*, 22–24.

36 The fundamental idea of the annihilation of Hell and Heaven (*fanāʾ al-nār wal-janna*) was widely discussed by Muslim theologians throughout the ages. The subject received its first Western academic treatment in the article of Binyamin Abrahamov, "The Creation and Duration of Paradise and Hell in Islamic Theology," *Der Islam* 79/1 (2002): 87–102. Abrahmaov's conclusion about Ibn al-Qayyim's view was polished by Jon Hoover in a more recent paper, in which he further explored this notion, paying special attention to Ibn al-Qayyim's position. Jon Hoover explains that, according to the common Sunnite perception derived from the Quran accepted by the Islamic consensus (*ijmāʿ*), the retribution of those who believe in the one and only true God is entering Heaven, whereas the punishment promised to the heretics or to those who connect God with other deities (*mushrikūn*) is an eternity in the fires of Hell. Nonetheless, in the course of the theological debate, one of the questions emerged was: Is it not a far too severe punishment to be inflicted upon human beings, even if they are heretics? (This was, for example, Fakhr al-Dīn al-Rāzī's opinion in his Quran commentary). Hoover presents Ibn al-Qayyim's view, who claimed that Hell is connected to a limited time of existence; at the end, not only will the heretics' punishment be carried out to the fullest degree, their souls will also go through a process of purification, bringing salvation to all of mankind; Hoover, "Islamic Universalism: Ibn Qayyim al-Jawziyya's Salafī Deliberations on the Duration of Hell-Fire," *The Muslim World* 99 (2009), 181–182; Hoover, "Against Islamic Universalism: ʿAlī al-Ḥarbīs 1990 Attempt to Prove That Ibn Taymiyya and Ibn Qayyim al-Jawziyya Affirm the Eternity of Hell-Fire," in: G. Tamer and B. Krawietz (eds.), *Islamic Theology, Philosophy and Law. Debating Ibn Taymiyya and Ibn Qayyim al-Jawziyya*, (Berlin: de Gruyter, 2013), 377–399.

37 In this respect, the disagreement in recent modern research regarding the person to whom al-Subkī addressed his treatise is noteworthy: on the one hand, Hoover states it was directed at Ibn Taymiyya; Hoover, "Against Islamic Universalism," 398. However, on

The second relevant treatise of al-Subkī against Ibn al-Qayyim's conceptions was also written in 748/1348, and is noticeably longer than the previous one. It is entitled *al-Sayf al-ṣaqīl fi 'l-radd ʿalā Ibn Zafīl* (The Polished Sward in Response to Ibn Zafīl [viz. one of Ibn al-Qayyim's designations]), and attacks Ibn al-Qayyim's work *al-Kāfiya 'l-shāfiya fi 'l-intiṣār lil-firqa 'l-nājiya* (The Suffice and Healing [Poem] on the victory of the Vindicated Sect, also known as *al-Qaṣīda 'l-nūniyya*). *Al-Kāfiya* is a long didactical poem which is, in fact, a polemic theological piece against the Ashʿarites.[38] In this work, Ibn al-Qayyim most definitely expanded several of the Taymiyyan theological perceptions. In this case, al-Subkī purposely cited sections of *al-Kāfiya* and also referred to Ibn Taymiyya. Al-Subkī strove to disqualify the derogatory designations used by Ibn al-Qayyim when he referred the Ashʿarites and other trends of thought, such as Jahmiyya, Muʿaṭṭila, Muʿtazīla etc.[39] Moreover, al-Subkī explored several theological aspects concerning God's entity and His attributes in terms of figurative interpretation (*taʾwīl*) and also deals with eschatological issues. Writing this treatise as a response to *al-Kāfiya* is highly instructive, and illustrates al-Subkī's great distress about the ongoing—and even increasing—circulation of Ibn Taymiyya's writings, as well as the fact that Ibn al-Qayyim was widely seen as their promoter and developer.[40]

Indeed, the treatises penned by al-Subkī corroborate Bori and Holtzman's assumption that Ibn al-Qayyim was gaining popularity; his works were impossible to overlook, which meant Ibn Taymiyya's ideology was also spreading. Obviously aware of this, al-Subkī feared the exhilaration surrounding these works would eventually destroy the legal consensus, which was one of the main Taymiyyan principles: Ibn Taymiyya had rejected any religious authority, as well as the general legal consensus (*ijmāʿ*) of his own generation, as a valid source of

---

the other hand, Bori and Holtzman sustain that it was addressed to Ibn al-Qayyim. Personally, I tend to agree with the latter view because of the historical context of when the treatise was penned; Bori and Holtzman, the introduction to: *A Scholar in the Shadows*, 24; Taqī 'l-Dīn al-Subkī, *al-Rasāʾil al-Subkiyya*, 12, 193–208.

38 More detailed information on *al-Kāfiya* can be found in Holtzman's study, "Insult, Fury, and Frustration: The Martyrological Narrative of Ibn Qayyim al-Jawzīyah's *al-Kāfiyah al-Shāfiyah*," *Mamlūk Studies Review* 17 (2013), 155–198; idem, "Accused of Anthropomorphism: Ibn Taymiyya's *Miḥan* as Reflected in Ibn Qayyim al-Jawziyya's *al-Kāfiya al-Shāfiya*," *The Muslim World* 106:3 (July, 2016), 561–587.

39 The meaning of these groups' designation mentioned above will be explained in section 2.2, subsection: The Title of *al-Ṣawāʿiq* in page 63.

40 Taqi 'l-Dīn al-Subkī, *al-Rasāʾil al-Subkiyya*, 11, 81–147; Bori and Holtzman, the introduction to: *A Scholar in the Shadows*, 25.

jurisprudence. In his work *I'lām al-muwaqqi'īn*, where he elaborately listed the reasons behind Ibn Taymiyya's trials, Ibn al-Qayyim also mentioned al-Subkī's state of alarm. Al-Subkī's main reason for this—as stated by Ibn al-Qayyim—was his great fear of possibly transgressing the *ijmā'* boundaries, especially on the issue of divorce. According to Ibn al-Qayyim, al-Subkī considered it a threat looming over the entire judicial system, on which both the *'ulamā'* and the Mamluk Sultanate were dependent.[41]

As we can see, in the final years of Ibn al-Qayyim's life he was continuously harassed by al-Subkī as a part of the latter's effort to strike down the remaining Taymiyyan legacy. Because he was constantly watched by the authorities for his loyalty to his master's thought, this background shaped the layout of Ibn al-Qayyim's later and more matured theological writing. For this reason, Ibn al-Qayyim found himself in the middle of several political and scholarly conflicts (e.g., the imprisonment together with his teacher), yet these did not stop his prolific intellectual activities. In 742/1342 Ibn Taymiyya's books were found and delivered to Ibn al-Qayyim, much to al-Subkī's clear dismay. In the same year, Ibn al-Qayyim was publicly active to a certain extent in his tutoring position in *al-madrasa 'l-ṣadriyya*. Additionally, as has already been stated, from 745/1345 onwards Ibn al-Qayyim wrote several of his major theological works where he expanded and distilled a number of Taymiyyan ideas.[42]

It is vital to highlight the significant role doctrinal disagreements played in the scholastic atmosphere of that time, which was saturated in political rivalries. More than the different legal controversies, highly relevant to the current

---

41 Bori and Holtzman, the introduction to: *A Scholar in the Shadows*, 26; Rapoport, "Ibn Taymiyya on Divorce Oaths," 207–2014.

42 Bori and Holtzman, the introduction to: *A Scholar in the Shadows*, 26; Bori, "The Collection and Edition of Ibn Taymīyah's Works: Concerns of a Disciple," *Mamlūk Studies Review* 13/2 (2009): 55. Noteworthy in this respect are several studies which scrutinized and characterized the "Taymiyyan scholarship", such as Henri Laoust's monumental book *La profession de foi d'Ibn Taymiyya* (1986), Daniel Gimaret's article on the human act in Ḥanbalite thought: "Théories de l'acte humain dans l'école hanbalite," *Bulletin d'études orientales* 29 (1977), 156–178, Yossef Rapoport and Shahab Ahmed's introduction to their edited volume *Ibn Taymiyya and His Times* (2010), two interesting articles in the same volume are: Walid A. Saleh, "Ibn Taymiyya and the Rise of Radical Hermeneutics: an Analysis of *an Introduction to the Foundations of Qur'āic Exgesis*," 123–162, and Khalid El-Rouayheb, "From Ibn Hajar al-Haytami (d. 1566) to Khayr al-Dīn al-Ālūsī (d. 1899): Changing Views of Ibn Taymiyya amongst Sunni Islamic Scholars," 269–318, Yahya Michot's book: *Against Extremism: Texts Translated & Introduction* ([Beirut]: Albouraq Editions, 2012), and Mohamed Yunis Ali's study on Sunnite legal theorists: *Medieval Islamic Pragmatism: Sunni Legal Theorists' Models of Textual Communication* (Richmond, Surrey: Routledge, 2000).

study are the theological controversies which are undoubtedly represented in the process of Ibn al-Qayyim's scholarly writing. The theological issue of divine attributes had special urgency: even though at first glance it seemed mainly theoretical, it had concrete implications over power struggles and the political order amid the *ʿulamāʾ* of Mamluk Damascus. These aftermaths are best reflected in Ibn Taymiyya's trials and afterwards in al-Subkī's persecutions. Within this fascinating array of forces, Ibn al-Qayyim rigidly defended the Taymiyyan views and clearly and overtly expressed them in his writing with eloquence and a sufficiently loud voice, turning him into a true representative of the Taymiyyan theological tradition.

1.1 A Stormy Approach: Ibn Taymiyya on the Issue of Divine Attributes

According to the historical evidence, Ibn Taymiyya was a rigorous and active participant in public debates and disputes (*jadal, mujādala, munāẓara*) in his attempt to define the correct form of Islamic belief as he saw it.[43] His categorical promotion of extreme Ḥanbalite doctrine was a cause of constant friction with *ʿulamāʾ* who belonged to the other theological schools and most evidently with the rational-traditionalistic Ashʿarites. Since the most important of the

43 The social hierarchies of power among the social civil elite (*aʿyān*) of the *ʿulamāʾ* were structured by the gain of prestige and fame, which was earned by winning public debates in certain fields of knowledge. Of tremendous social importance, these debates were perceived not only as contests to determine who was right, but also who established personal honor among the *ʿulamāʾ*, which at times led to an official position under the Mamluks (*mansib*). The most commonly used arena for such intellectual debates to take place was the *majlis*, the name for the forum or session where an assembly of the *ʿulamāʾ* practiced their everyday scholarly activities, including their theological debates; Michael Chamberlain, *Knowledge and Social Practice in Medieval Damascus, 1190–1350* (Cambridge: Cambridge University Press, 1994), 24–25, 108–110, 152–156, 164–165; Hava Lazarus-Yafeh, the Preface to the volume: Lazarus-Yafeh, Hava; Cohen, Mark R.; Somekh, Sasson; Griffith, Sydney H. (eds.), *The Majlis: Interreligious Encounters in Medieval Islam* (Wiesbaden: Harrassowitz, 1999), 7–8. Another relevant article from the same edited volume is: Sarah Stroumsa, "Ibn al-Rāwandī's *sūʾ adab al-mujādala*: the Role of Bad manners in Medieval Disputations", 66–85. The developments in the Islamic dialectic and argumentative tradition on the topics of law and theology are examined in the study of Abdessamad Belhaj, *Argumantation et dialectique en islam: Formes et séquences de la munazara* (Brussels: Presses universitaires de Louvain, 2010). The best description of Ibn Taymiyya's social activity is (still) Laoust's book *La profession de foi d'Ibn Taymiyya*. Ibn Taymiyya's struggle against the popular rites and visitation of graves is described there in detail.

widespread *ʿulamāʾ* affiliated to the Ashʿarites, they were the ones to set the norms of the religious discourse and promoted the rationalistic speculative theology, i.e., *Kalām*. To be more precise, they most dominantly indorsed the *Kalām*ic form as conceived by the renowned Ashʿarite scholar Fakhr al-Dīn al-Rāzī (d. 606/1209). Ibn Taymiyya advocated for his version of Ḥanbalism and openly denounced the Rāziyyan scholarship, thereby confronting the most powerful among his contemporary *ʿulamāʾ* and rattling the socio-political conditions in the city. In fact, the Ḥanbalites of Damascus were sometimes considered outsiders in the eyes of the Ashʿarite-Shafiʿite elite, since they mostly arrived to the city as migrants fleeing from Mongol and crusader invasions to Jazīra and Palestine, respectively. Moreover, Ibn Taymiyya's harsh doctrinal approach also marginalized him to a certain degree among the Damascene ultra-traditionalistic Ḥanbalite circle itself. In his adamant public expression of Ḥanbalite theological stances, he was perceived as drawing hostile attention to the traditionalists as a whole.[44] At any rate, the public trials Ibn Taymiyya endured (described in the previous section) indeed reflected the long-lasting public disputes in the spirit of the *munaẓarāt* among the *ʿulamāʾ* social class under the Mamluk Sultanate. It all took place at the core of the elitist social stratum of Damascus during that particular period.

A highly intriguing piece of evidence that demonstrates Ibn Taymiyya's unique participation in the public practice of theological debates can be seen in his penning of polemical didactic poems, such as his response to a question on predetermination poetically expressed in verse (*suʾāl ʿan al-qadar*). Given the description of the circumstances of its composition as depicted in the primary sources, in which Ibn Taymiyya immediately recited (or hastily wrote) his poem of response in the course of the public debate, this example stands out as quite remarkable. Aside from illustrating Ibn Taymiyya's intellectual character as one of a truly capable scholar with an excellent command in the Arabic language and its poetic mysteries; the example of the versified public response to an intricate theological question conveys the prestigious fashion in which Ibn Taymiyya acted in the public sphere of the scholastic elite. He was in close scholarly relationship with the other *ʿulamāʾ* of his environment in Damascus and also Cairo, including those he disagreed with; they were all familiar to a certain extent with each other's literary yield and even evaluated and ranked each other by their ability in poetic composition. This kind of mutual connec-

44 Michael Chamberlain, *Knowledge and Social Practice*, 167–172; Livnat Holtzman, *Anthropomorphism in Islam: The Challenge of Traditionalism, 700–1550* (Edinburgh: Edinburgh University Press, 2018), 316–317.

tions cultivated a vibrant dynamic among the *ʿulamāʾ*, who competed with one another by assessing the stylistic quality of their literary output, while simultaneously dealing with complex theological issues. The contents of such poems within the discourse of *munāẓarāt* involved highly theorized theology and were apparently not intended for a laymen audience; however, they were written as mnemonic poems, which made them easier to grasp. Ibn Taymiyya's involvement in broadening the genre of medieval *munāẓarāt*—more commonly written in prose—along with the great appreciation he received from his contemporary peers is yet another indication for his well-earned status among the Mamluk elite.[45]

Hence, and despite the turmoil caused in the Damascene scholastic scene, Ibn Taymiyya gained a very solid scholarly status. At first, since he belonged to a well-respected family and had positive connections with the Mamluk army and the Sultan, he enjoyed a stable position.[46] During the course of time, Ibn Taymiyya established himself as someone with an uncompromising personality, whose credibility could not be simply discarded by the more entrenched—and somewhat patronizing—*ʿulamāʾ* of Damascus. Rather, Ibn Taymiyya's fellow *ʿulamāʾ* who faced his intellectual challenge responded to his ideological allegations, therefore accepting him into their elitist milieu in due course. Amid the *ʿulamāʾ* themselves, Ibn Taymiyya still had his devoted company of close scholars, known as *al-jamāʿa*, who followed him. Simultaneously, the Taymiyyan scholarship enjoyed a widespread reception from laymen not only within his hometown of Damascus, but also among Muslims living in more remote areas, such as Iraq or the area of Ḥarran.[47] Furthermore, Ibn Taymiyya nurtured a well-established connection with the masses, delivering his teachings with enthusiastic zeal and widely spreading his doctrinal ideology. Within this socio-political narrative of that time and amid the numerous topics Ibn Taymiyya wrote about, the theological dispute on divine attributes was of heavy weight.

---

45 This specific poem and Ibn Taymiyya's response to it are discussed as a case study for the broader intellectual phenomenon of poetic-theological composition in Mamluk times in: Livnat Holtzman, "The Dhimmi's Question on Predetermination and the Ulama's Six Responses: The Dynamics of Composing Polemical Didactic Poems in Mamluk Cairo and Damascus," *Manlūk Studies Review* 16 (2012), 1–4, 20–24, 30–32.

46 Caterina Bori, *Ibn Taymiyya: una vita esemplare. Analisi delle fonti classiche della sua biografia*, Supplemento monografico n. 1 alla Rivista di Studi Orientali, LXXVI (Pisa-Roma: Istituti Poligrafici Internazionali, 2003), 117–130.

47 Berkey, *Popular Preaching & Religious Authority in Medieval Islamic Near East*, 18, 43–47, 95–96; Bori, "A New Source for the Biography of Ibn Taymiyya," 326.

Written upon the request of the people of the city of Ḥamat in northern Syria, Ibn Taymiyya's iconic treatise *al-Ḥamawiyya 'l-kubrā* (already mentioned above) was the foremost reason for which he was persecuted, accused of anthropomorphism and consequently brought in front of a law court. Ibn Taymiyya dictated *al-Ḥamawiyya 'l-kubrā* as a legal response (*fatwā*) to the people of Ḥamat who had asked him for his opinion about the meaning of Quran verses and Hadith accounts which describe God with human-like characteristics (i.e., *āyāt al-ṣifāt* and *aḥādīth al-ṣifāt*), such as His seat on His throne (Q 20:5) or the *ḥadīth*: "the hearts of the human beings are [held] between two of the All-Merciful's fingers". Replying to a seemingly modest informative question, Ibn Taymiyya composed a political proclamation against his dogmatic rivals of the Ashʿarite elite and their adherence to the Rāzziyan form of *Kalām*. Ibn Taymiyya was actually highly conversant with the writings of Fakhr al-Dīn al-Rāzī and his doctrinal views; hence he attacked them cleverly and effectively. A shiny status symbol in the eyes of the Ashʿarite elitists, al-Rāzi's convoluted *kalām*ic discourse was considered the fashionable mode of engagement with the so-called rationalism of the time. The traditionalists, on the other hand, were condescendingly perceived as simple and 'ignorant'. Expressing an extreme ultra-traditionalistic stance on the issue of divine attributes, Ibn Taymiyya issued *al-Ḥamawiyya 'l-kubrā* in a highly accessible writing style for a wide public audience of educated and lay traditionalists alike. In the text, Ibn Taymiyya was warning the traditionalists not to follow the Ashʿarite scholars—i.e., the elite of the religious establishment—and their heretic ways.[48] Instigating further animosity, he implicitly indicted the Ashʿarite officials for purposely distorting the true meaning of the Islamic texts of the Quran and Hadith literature.

Molded in clear opposition to the Ashʿarite stances of his political rivals, *al-Ḥamawiyya 'l-kubrā* expressed Ibn Taymiyya's comprehensive creed on the theological issue of divine attributes in the Islamic scriptures, namely *āyāt al-ṣifāt* and *aḥādīth al-ṣifāt* (the Quranic verses and Hadith accounts which contain anthropomorphic descriptions of God). Closely studying the text of *al-Ḥamawiyya 'l-kubrā*, Livnat Holtzman describes Ibn Taymiyya's approach as a unique understanding of the originally traditionalistic formula of *bi-lā kayfa*.[49]

---

48 Holtzman, *Anthropomorphism in Islam*, 316–318.

49 The formula of *bi-lā kayfa* is the traditionalistic hermeneutical method which called for an affirmation and acceptance (*ithbāt*) of all divine attributes, including those which may infer on anthropomorphic features, "without asking how" those could be realized and with no attempt of interpreting their modality. This formula was widely adopted by traditionalists as a contra-method to the figurative interpretation of *ta'wīl* embraced by the

Referring to Jon Hoover who had already presented Ibn Taymiyya's stance on the matter as a combination of four elements,[50] Holtzman lists them following the text of *al-Ḥamawiyya 'l-kubrā*:

> The first element is the traditionalistic method of reading the anthropomorphic descriptions without asking how God performed any act. The second element was unique to Ibn Taymiyya: while rejecting the device of *ta'wīl*, Ibn Taymiyya insisted that the divine attributes and anthropomorphic descriptions deserved linguistic inquiry which would lead to an understanding compatible with the appropriate discourse about God. Thus, he investigated the meaning of the attributes. The third element was developed by Ibn Taymiyya's predecessors, for example Ibn Khuzayma [d. 311/932, an important Hadith scholar. She refers here to his work *Kitāb al-tawḥīd*]: Ibn Taymiyya recognized that the divine attributes in general and the anthropomorphic descriptions in particular referred to an actual reality in God. The fourth element was borrowed from the traditionalistic scholars with rationalistic tendencies like Ibn Qutayba [d. 276/889, a grammarian], and it appeared also in the thought of Ibn Fūrak [d. 406/1015, an early Ash'arite and one of the formalizers of the Ash'arite thought]: Ibn Taymiyya defined the divine attributes and the anthropomorphic descriptions as representations of God's perfection [i.e., *kamāl*].[51]

In the text of *al-Ḥamawiyya 'l-kubrā* Ibn Taymiyya accused his contemporary Ash'arites of straying away from the way of the pious and worthy ancestors (*salaf*) by applying false rationalistic methods on the texts of Quran and not

---

purely rationalists (e.g., the ultra-rationalists of the early Mu'tazilite school). The traditionalists themselves differed in their understanding and use of the *bi-lā kayfa* formula. Whereas the ultra-traditionalists perceived it as "affirmation with no interpretation whatsoever", the Ash'arite rational-traditionalists perceived it as "affirmation without assuming a modality (*kayfiyya*)", thus partly permitting figurative interpretation; Binyamin Abrahamov, "The "Bi-lā Kayfa" Doctrine and Its Foundations in Islamic Theology," *Arabica* 42, 1–3 (Nov., 1995): 366–370, 378; van Ess, "Tashbīh wa-Tanzīh," 10: 341–344; Wensinck, *The Muslim Creed*, 68–73; Holtzman, "Anthropomorphism," *EI THREE*, 1:46–55; Seale, *Muslim Theology*, 53–56; Abrahamov, "Scripturalist and Traditionalist Theology," *Oxford Handbooks Online* (Oxford University Press, March 2014).

50 Jon Hoover, "Ḥanbalī Theology," in: *Oxford handbook of Islamic Theology*, ed. Sabine Schmidtke (Oxford: Oxford University Press, 2016), 637–639.

51 Holtzman, *Anthropomorphism in Islam*, 318–320.

believing in the Hadith material (*al-kufr bil-samʿ*). As Holtzmann explains, "the rationalists applied this method [i.e., ultra-traditionalistic *bi-lā kayfa*] to *āyāt al-ṣifāt*, while they rejected the lion's share of *aḥādīth al-ṣifāt*. Of the minute amount of *aḥādīth al-ṣifāt* that they did accept, the rationalists deployed *taʾwīl*."[52] Moreover, Ibn Taymiyya explicitly mentions Fakhr al-Dīn al-Rāzī's work *Asās al-taqdīs* (Foundations of the Sanctification; also entitled *Taʾsīs al-taqdīs*)[53] as one of the dangerous books written by respectable scholars who revive ultra-rationalistic Muʿtazilite ideology (the only other scholar mentioned by name is Ibn Fūrak). Indeed, *Asās al-taqdīs* was circulated and studied on a vast scale by Ashʿarites of that period, promoting al-Rāzī's philosophized Ashʿarite *Kalām* and one of its most solid Muʿtazilite features—*taʾwīl*, that is, a metaphorical interpretation of God's allegedly corporeal attributes. Discrediting the Rāzziyan theology, Ibn Taymiyya positioned himself in clear opposition to the religious establishment, a step that had immediate consequences; *al-Ḥamawiyya ʾl-kubrā*—the text which signified him as a political opponent—was publically banned. In the longer run, *al-Ḥamawiyya ʾl-kubrā* stood as the backdrop of Ibn Taymiyya's prosecutions by his political enemies, including his trials.[54]

To all intents and purposes, Ibn Taymiyya's *al-Ḥamawiyya ʾl-kubrā* represented a new traditionalistic approach to the divine attributes, especially in its treatment of *aḥādīth al-ṣifāt*. Strongly adhering to the Islamic textual sources, Ibn Taymiyya rebuked the rationalistic rejection of *aḥādīth al-ṣifāt*, which he considered indivisible from the canonical body of the Hadith literature. In addition, Ibn Taymiyya also approved the use of physical gestures to allude to God's direction or spatiality, such as pointing with a finger or raising the hands (*al-ishāra bil-sabbāba* and *rafʿ al-yadaynⁱ*) towards the sky. Citing textual evidence from the Hadith literature, Ibn Taymiyya corroborated his claim with descriptions of the Prophet himself raising his hands during his personal supplication. According to the Ashʿarite view, however, gesturing upwards and suggesting God is confined to a certain direction was an expression of sheer corporealism and anthropomorphism. Even more so, they scorned Ibn Taymiyya using the highly derogatory label of *ḥashwī* (pl. *ḥashwiyya*), meaning a vulgar anthropomorphist in the most loathed manner of the uneducated and uncultured. Ibn Taymiyya did acknowledge the tendency of the masses to naïve

52 Holtzman, *Anthropomorphism in Islam*, 320.

53 *Asās al-taqdīs* will be further discussed in section 1.2 and with direct relation to Ibn al-Qayyim's *al-Ṣawāʿiq* in section 3.2 and in chapter 6 henceforth.

54 Holtzman, *Anthropomorphism in Islam*, 320–321.

anthropomorphic belief. One could say his encouragement of the use of gestures to demonstrate God's spatiality induced the proliferation of his approach on the veridical reality (*ḥaqīqa*) of the divine attributes in the public sphere. Due to the popularity of Ibn Taymiyya and the vast reception of his creed among the laymen, the highbrow religious establishment perceived his notions as a threat to the hegemony of Ashʿarite theology in the Mamluk sultanate. Keeping the background of Ibn Taymiyya's prosecutions in mind, I will now turn to another source closely related to *al-Ḥamawiyya 'l-kubrā*.[55]

1.2 Ibn Taymiyya's View on *ta'wīl* in *Bayān talbīs al-jahmiyya*

Accessibly expressed also for the common people in the treatise *al-Ḥamawiyya 'l-kubrā*, Ibn Taymiyya's approach on the issue of divine attributes was more eruditely articulated in his substantial work *Bayān talbīs al-jahmiyya fī ta'sīs bidaʿihim al-kalāmiyya* (Exposing the Deceit of the Heretics in their Establishment of *Kalām*ic Undesired-Innovations; also known as *Naqḍ ta'sīs al-jahmiyya*, Criticizing the Foundations of the Jahmites).[56] To the best of my knowledge, the work has yet to be thoroughly studied or analyzed in modern research; however it offers highly instructive insights concerning Ibn Taymiyya's doctrinal view regarding the issue of divine attributes, as will be shown shortly. Ibn Taymiyya wrote *Bayān talbīs al-jahmiyya* as a straight response to al-Rāzī's above-mentioned theological work *Asās al-taqdīs* which was dedicated entirely to the expanded statement of the rationalistic method of *ta'wīl*.[57] In

55 As useful weapons to attack the Rāziyyan doctrine, Ibn Taymiyya listed in *al-Ḥamawiyya 'l-kubrā* 24 books written by early traditionalists, among which was Ibn Kuhzayma's *Kitāb al-tawḥīd* (Book of Monotheism, or [God's] Unity). Mainly a compilation of *aḥādīth al-ṣifāt*, the book was composed in the tenth century and was of large demand in Baghdad of the eleventh century, where it played a massive role in the political conflict between ultra-traditionalists and Muʿtazilite ultra-rationalists. Presenting a fiery traditionalistic approach to the issue of divine attributes, *Kitāb al-tawḥīd* was the book against which Fakhr al-Dīn al-Rāzī authored his work *Asās al-taqdīs*; Holtzman, *Anthropomorphism in Islam*, 271–272, 278–283, 326–329, 324–339.

56 Ibn Taymiyya, *Bayān talbīs al-jahmiyya fī ta'sīs bidaʿihim al-kalāmiyya*, eds. Yaḥya b. Muḥammad al-Hunaydī et. al., in 10 vols. (Madina: Majmaʿ al-Malik Fahd li-Ṭibāʿat al-Muṣḥaf al-Sharīf, 1426/ [2005]). The work will also be discussed in section 3.3 of this study.

57 Fakhr al-Dīn al-Rāzī, *Asās al-taqdīs*, ed. Aḥmad Ḥijāzī al-Saqā (Cairo: Maktabat al-Kuliyyāt al-Azhariyya, 1406/1986). Al-Rāzī dedicated the book the powerful Ayyūbid ruler al-Mālik al-ʿĀdil (r. 596–615/1200–1218; Ṣalāḥ al-Dīn's brother) in its preface (p. 10); Ibn Taymiyya, *Bayān talbīs al-jahmiyya*, the editor's introduction 1:13–16; Frank Griffel, "On Fakhr al-Dīn

fact, Ibn Taymiyya asserts *Bayān al-talbīs* is intended to negate al-Rāzī's *Asās al-taqdīs*, since—according to his argument—it concluded the Ashʿarite objections raised against the treatise *al-Ḥamawiyya 'l-kubrā*, for which he was put to trial in Cairo.[58] As al-Rāzī puts it in the opening part of *Asās al-taqdīs*, one of his declared wishes is to force his adversaries to acknowledge their mere dependence on sensational or imaginary decrees even before involving themselves with the actual proofs. Promptly designating those ideological adversaries, al-Rāzī mentions two sects by name: "*al-karrāmiyya wal-hanābila*".[59] Therefore, *Asās al-taqdīs* should be understood as being more than a simple Rāziyyan tutorial writing in favor of *ta'wīl* methodology. Rather, given al-Rāzī's own declaration of intentions in his preface, *Asās al-taqdīs* is also a manifestation of his battle of wits against his contemporary ideological opponents, most conspicuously the Ḥanbalite scholars.[60] About a century later, al-Rāzī's allegations against the Ḥanbalites in *Asās al-taqdīs* were actively adopted by the elitist Ashʿarite *ʿulamā'* of Damascus, to which the enthusiastic polemicist Ibn Taymiyya could seemingly not have remained indifferent. In the following section I will concentrate on a highpoint from Ibn Taymiyya's reproof of the figurative interpretation method of *ta'wīl* in *Bayān talbīs al-jahmiyya*, as he replies back to al-Rāzī.

Presenting his expertise with al-Rāzī's text, Ibn Taymiyya addresses the second part (out of four in total) in *Asās al-taqdīs* entitled "on the figurative interpretation of the ambiguous traditions and verses (*fī ta'wīl al-mutashābihāt min[a] 'l-akhbār wal-āyāt*)".[61] Ibn Taymiyya explains al-Rāzī means Quran verses

---

al-Rāzī's Life and the Patronage He Received," *Journal of Islamic Studies* 18:3 (2007), 339; Tariq Jaffer, "Muʿtazilite Aspects of Faḫr al-Dīn al-Rāzī's Thought," *Arabica* 59 (2012), 511; Hoover, "Ḥanbalī Theology," 634; Holtzman, *Anthropomorphism in Islam*, 317.

58 Ibn Taymiyya repeats his assertion on the connection between *Bayān al-talbīs* and *al-Ḥamawiyya* at least three times along *Bayān al-talbīs*; Ibn Taymiyya, *Bayān talbīs al-jahmiyya*, 1:8, 5:457; 8:537.

59 Fakhr al-Dīn al-Rāzī, *Asās al-taqdīs*, 15, 19–21; *al-Karrāmiyya* (or the Karrāmite) was an Islamic sect mainly in eastern Iran (Nishapur) from the 3/9 century until the period of the Mongol invasions (7/13 century). Sunni opponents of the sect rejected its conceptions concerning God's attributes and even accused it of anthropomorphism. For instance, *al-karrāmiyya* saw God as a bodily substance (*jawhar, jism*); Clifford E. Bosworth, "Karrāmiyya," *EI*², 4:667–669.

60 Jaffer, "Muʿtazilite Aspects of Fakhr al-Dīn al-Rāzī's Thought," 514–517.

61 Q 3:7 "it is He who has sent this Scripture down to you [Prophet]. Some of its verses are definite in meaning—these are the cornerstone of the Scripture—and others are ambiguous." Quran commentators explained this verse, maintaining that the Quran largely contains clear verses (*muḥkamāt*) and ambiguous ones (*mutashābihāt*). Some of them divided the

in which God described Himself and Prophetic traditions in which God's Messenger described Him, namely the textual sources which contain the divine attributes. Then, he explains al-Rāzī's principle stance which obliges to negate (*al-nafī*) all of the attributes these verses and traditions indicate, and also to include them all amongst the "ambiguous verses" which are not intended to be understood in the limited human mind. Ibn Taymiyya does agree that several of those textual sources can be qualified as ambiguous; however al-Rāzī's all-encompassing view is too generalized and hence wrongful. This generalizing claim illustrates al-Rāzī's opinion alone, who acts like many of the *mutakallimūn*, easily averting meaningful portions of the Quran and Hadith which do not match their doctrines by announcing they are 'ambiguous'. The same goes for various rationalistic streams of thought, such as the Muʿtazilites, the Jahmites (derogatorily denoting the Ashʿarites),[62] several Shiʿite-Ismāʿīlite groups (e.g., Qarāmaṭīs and other Shiʿī-extremists)[63] and the Arab philosophers.[64] To Ibn Taymiyya, such fastidious treatment of the texts of the Quran

ambiguous verses into three groups: those which are in incomprehensible, those which are comprehensive, and those which only the experts (*al-rāsikhūn fi 'l-dīn*) are able to comprehend; Leah Kinberg, "Ambiguous," *Encyclopaedia of the Qur'ān*, 1:71–72; Joseph van Ess, *Theologie und Gesellschaft im 2. und 3. Jahrhundert Hidschra: eine Geschichte des religiosen Denkens im fruhen Islam*, 6 Bände (Berlin: de Gruyter, 1990): 4:647.

62 The term Jahmites (*jahmiyya*) refers to an early and obscure Islamic sect whose alleged founder is Jahm ibn Ṣafwān Abū Muḥarraz (d. 128/746). Besides him, it is not known which scholars were affiliated with this sect. Moreover, Jahm ibn Ṣafwān's own relation to the Jahmiyya is quite vague, as he was executed some 70 years before the sect was first referred to in Islamic writing. In any case, Ḥanbalite scholars often used this term to denote their adversaries, as did Ibn Taymiyya and Ibn Qayyim al-Jawziyya with regard to the rationalistic Ashʿarite school and other rival groups; William Montgomery Watt, "D̲jahm b. Ṣafwān," *EI*², 2:388; Idem, "D̲Jahmiyya," *EI*², 2:388.

63 The Qarāmaṭīs and other Shiʿī-extremists belonged to the Shiʿite-Ismāʿīlite stream, which adhered to the doctrine that raised the esoteric (*bāin*) meaning of the Islamic texts above its literal exoteric wording (*ẓāhir*). Several names are often used in order to denote this sect, for instance: *Mulāḥida, Ismāʿīliyya, Qarāmiṭa, Bāṭiniyya, Khurramiyya, Muḥammara*, and *Nusayriyya*. The designation *al-bāṭina* was also used as a pejorative name for the Shiʿite-Ismāʿīlites. Noteworthy is Ibn Taymiyya's solid familiarity with Shiʿite and Ismā'ilite tenet evident, for example, in his work *Minhāj al-sunna al-nabawiyya*, in which he attacked the Shiʿite theologian al-ʿAllāma al-Ḥillī (d. 726/1325). Ibn Taymiyya's polemics in this respect are discussed in the paper: Tariq al-Jamil, "Ibn Taymiyya and Ibn al-Muṭahhar al-Ḥillī: Shiʿī Polemics and the Struggle for Religious Authority in Medieval Islam," in: (eds.) Rapoport, Yossef; Ahmed, Shahab, *Ibn Taymiyya and His Times* (Karachi: Oxford University Press, 2010), 229–246.

64 Ibn Taymiyya, *Bayān talbīs al-jahmiyya*, 5:447–450.

and Hadith is unthinkable, and more so, it deters the reader from attaining the original intention of the Islamic sources.

Consequently, Ibn Taymiyya cites the heading of the short introduction to the second part of *Asās al-taqdīs*, in which al-Rāzī "asserts that all of the Islamic sects are united [in the opinion that] it is inevitable to apply figurative interpretation on some of the apparent [expressions] (*ẓawāhir*) of the Quran and Hadith." As Ibn Taymiyya concisely describes al-Rāzī's general argument and its structure, he states that al-Rāzī actually claims there is an overall consensus among all Muslim (i.e., *ijmāʿ*) on the matter of using *taʾwīl*, and whoever denies it does so contrarily to that commonly accepted doctrinal view. Diligently paraphrasing al-Rāzī, Ibn Taymiyya clarifies the act of *taʾwīl* in accordance with al-Rāzī's terminology and explains that it means "to divert an expression away from its apparent indication to another [meaning] by an indicative proof". This technical definition (*iṣṭilāḥ*) of *taʾwīl*, says Ibn Taymiyya, is arbitrary and was artificially designed by the later rationalists (*mutaʾakhirū al-mutakallimīn*) who entwined it into their conventional terminology. This kind of *taʾwīl* is very specific and utterly differs from the meaning of the expression as it appears in the Quran, the Hadith, the teachings of the pious ancestors of the Muslim community (*salaf*) and the sayings of the earlier exegetists of the Quran. The previous Muslim scholars specialized in the fields of Islamic jurisprudence, Hadith recitation and transmission, and Quranic exegesis, understood the expression *taʾwīl* as a synonym of *tafsīr*, i.e., interpretation according to the apparent meaning of the words (*al-maʿnā al-ẓāhir*).[65] In the Quran, *taʾwīl* indicates the actual meaning (*ḥaqīqat al-maʿnā*) or its first denotation, which exists

---

65 A known term from the scholarly branch of Quranic exegesis, *tafsīr* entails interpretation, exegesis, explanation (from the Arabic root *f.s.r*; equivalent to the Arabic word *sharḥ*). The word also connotes an actual commentary corpus, especially on the Quran, but in can also refer to other subjects: poetry, philology, grammar, sciences etc. Etymologically, the verb *fassara* could be borrowed from Aramaic, where it denotes "to discover something hidden". The circumstances in which the word *tafsīr* converted into a technical term in Quranic sciences are unclear. The term *taʾwīl* initially denoted interpretation, exegesis, since its literal sense relates to the notion of "returning a thing to the beginning, to its first and primary state" (from the Arabic root *a.w.l*). This is the second technical term in the semantic field of interpretation. The original meaning of the verb *taʾawwala*, signifying the person who performs *taʾwīl*, means "to understand a verse according to a given situation", viz. a simple act of interpretation. Only later on was the meaning of allegorical interpretation via the use of metaphors ascribed to the term *taʾwīl*, by the rationalistic schools of thought; Claude Gilliot, "Exegesis of the Qurʾān: Classical and Medieval," *Encyclopaedia of the Qurʾān*, 2:99–100; Kess Versteegh, *Arabic Grammar and Qurʾanic Exegesis in Early Islam* (Leiden: Brill, 1993), 63–64; Al-Tahānawī, Muḥammad Aʿlā ibn ʿAlī ibn Muḥammad Ḥāmid

outside of the text, such as in verse 7:53 "What are they waiting for but the fulfillment (*taʾwīluh*^{u}) of [the Scripture's final prophecy]? On the Day it is fulfilled (*taʾwīluh*^{u}), those who had ignored it will say, 'Our Lord's messenger spoke the truth …'"[66]

Ibn Taymiyya continues as he further elaborates on the cognitive subtleties connected to the understanding of an expression as it appears in a text (*lafẓ al-ẓāhir*) and its meaning (*maʿnāh*^{u}). Notable to him is that the 'apparent' (*al-ẓāhir*) may refer to the expression itself (*lafẓ*) as it is heard or understood in a person's heart, it may also refer to the expression's meaning (*maʿnā*), and it may refer to them both. In the end, it is known that the apparent and the concealed are relative matters; a person or a group of people may find something apparent, whereas others may fail to notice it at all. The reasons thereof can be various, changing from the speech itself, to the speaker, to the listener etc. Another important idea Ibn Taymiyya emphasizes is that the apparent meaning of an expression does not only have to be a result of a particular linguistic imposition (*waḍʿ al-lugha*; i.e., assigning certain meanings to certain expressions).[67] Meaning can also a result of the individual reality perception, be it linguistic, conventional or religious. Moreover, a meaning can even convey a metaphor (*majāz*) which relates to the expression in a specific context, for those who denote that as a 'metaphor'.[68] It is also known, Ibn Taymiyya proceeds, that the assigned meaning of a certain expression tends to change, depending on whether it comes as a single word or combined within a set phrase, and most of the times this change is substantial. Therefore, the saying of numerous people, namely the rationalists, that 'the apparent' of the Quran and Hadith (*ẓāhir al-qurʾān wal-akhbār*, i.e., the texts, both expressions and meanings) is to be figuratively interpreted by *taʾwīl*—equally, whether it complies with the texts or contradicts it—is false. In Ibn Taymiyya's view, that is an important subject which many sects misunderstood, and thus strayed away from the righteous path of the Quran, leading their followers with them towards deception.[69]

(year of death is unknown), *Mawsūʿat iṣṭilāḥāt al-ʿulūm al-islāmiyya (al-maʿrūf fi kashshāf iṣṭilāḥāt al-funūn)*, in 6 volumes (Beirut: Khayat, 1385/1966), 1:89.

66 Ibn Taymiyya, *Bayān talbīs al-jahmiyya*, 5:451–453.

67 Weiss. "Waḍʿ al-Luġa," *Encyclopedia of Arabic Language and Linguistics*, online source, 1. The grammatical issue of the origin of language in Islam will be more elaborately discussed in the first section of chapter 5, concentrating on hermeneutics in Ibn al-Qayyim's *al-Ṣawāʿiq* and the special input Ibn Taymiyya had on the matter.

68 In Ibn Taymiyya's opinion, there is no such thing as a metaphor (*majāz*) in the language; see section 5.2 henceforth.

69 Ibn Taymiyya, *Bayān talbīs al-jahmiyya*, 5:454–456.

Furthermore, harshly criticizing al-Rāzī's call for *taʾwīl*, Ibn Taymiyya rhetorically asks: when you proclaim the apparent text does not convey what the speaker intended to, are you saying that God did not eloquently clarify His intention in His Book and in the speech of His Messenger, or that it is necessary to clarify the texts? If it is the first option, then the entire Quran cannot be taken as providing guidance and clarity to people, nor can the Prophetic traditions. If it is the second option, then the intention is to be grasped by the means of a different discourse (*khiṭāb*) on which all of the religious scholars agree. Thus, clarifying the problematic verses and traditions must rely on the Islamic scriptures, on the speech of God and His messenger, which is attainable and trustworthy because people must believe in the Quran as a whole and not only in parts thereof while disbelieving others. That is also the opinion of the Imam Aḥmad ibn Ḥanbal (d. 241/855), the eponym and role model of the Ḥanbalite school, states Ibn Taymiyya. Without identifying its title, Ibn Taymiyya mentions that ibn Ḥanbal composed "a prominent treatise" on the matter, in which he replied to those who clung to some of the apparent expressions in the Quran and Hadith but refrained from other interpretations of the verses and traditions that contain the divine attributes.[70] It is highly plausible that Ibn Taymiyya proposes here the polemic treatise ascribed to Aḥmad ibn Ḥanbal: *al-Radd ʿala ʾl-zanādiqa wal-jahmiyya* (Reply against the Heretical Sects).[71]

In this treatise Aḥmad ibn Ḥanbal (allegedly) attacks arguments of sects he considers heretic, with a special emphasis placed on the ultra-rationalistic Muʿtazilite school; by doing so, he formulated several basic principles of the Islamic creed. Generally, Aḥmad ibn Ḥanbal used Quranic verses in order to reprove his rivals; however, he also employed rationalistic argumentation techniques. The treatise was commonly adopted by later Ḥanbalite and traditionalistic scholars throughout the era, who tended to quote it extensively as a source

70 Ibn Taymiyya, *Bayān talbīs al-jahmiyya*, 5:456–457.

71 The treatise is directed against two sects considered to be heretical: 1. *zanādiqa*—(from Persian, lit.: "fire sparks"). In recent years, research has come to realize the Persian noun *zindīq* is derived from the Aramaic word *ṣaddiq*, a derogatory name denoting believers of Manichaeism and dualism between good vs. evil. As time went by, the name also included heretical groups, atheists, or sects considered to be religious innovators, such as the Muʿtazilite school. In this case, it is plausible that Ibn Ḥanbal meant a sect that claimed the Quran contains inherent contradictions and therefore doubted its authority; 2. *jahmiyya*—a name which denotes groups of heretics, especially the Muʿtazila; Livnat Holtzman, "Aḥmad b. Ḥanbal," *EI—THREE*, 1:20; Aḥmad b. Ḥanbal, *al-Radd ʿala ʾl-zanādiqa wal-jahmiyya*, in: *ʿAqāʾid al-salaf*, the editor's preface, 20–21, 40–41; François C. De Blois, "Zindīḳ," *EI*^{2}, 11:511; Joseph van Ess, *The Flowering of Muslim Theology*, translated by Jane Marie Todd (Cambridge: Harvard University Press, 2006), 24–27.

of a high religious authority.[72] The position taken by Ibn Taymiyya on *taʾwīl* in *Bayān talbīs al-jahmiyya* does seem to rely on Aḥmad ibn Ḥanbal in *al-Radd ʿala ʾl-zanādiqa wal-jahmiyya*. Aḥmad ibn Ḥanbal presents the enduring remnant scholars (*baqāyā min ahl*[i] *ʾl-ʿilm*), who protect the Quran in each and every generation; he praised their scholarly activity, which is in sharp contrast to the acts of the *mutakallimūn*, who use the ambiguous verses during their theological debates:

> Praise be to Allah who in every age and *fatra* [i.e. an interval of prophetic succession] raises up a remnant of learned men, who bearing ill-use patiently, recall the lost to guidance; revive the dead and give sight to blind eyes by means of Allah's book and His light … They bar from Allah's book the corruptions of the extravagant (*taḥrīf al-ghālīn*, i.e. the Shiʿites), the false professions of the strippers (*intiḥāl al-mubṭilīn*, i.e. the Muʿtazilites), and the interpretations of the ignorant (*taʾwīl al-jāhilīn*). All such as fly the flag of heresy and let loose rebellion; Allah's book they dispute over, contradict and unanimously set aside; they speak of Allah and say about Him and His book they know not what; they discuss what is ambiguous with *Kalām* and device the ignorant with their impositions. To Allah we fly for refuge from the guile of the seducers![73]

In the passage above, the issue of *taʾwīl* is mentioned with clear reference to the ambiguous verses of the Quran, which contain anthropomorphic expressions. Aḥmad ibn Ḥanbal condones here the Muʿtazilite school for exploiting

72 A number of modern researchers question the attribution of this work to Ibn Ḥanbal himself, for two reasons: first, Ibn Ḥanbal usually utilized Quranic verses in his argumentations, yet the treatise is abundant with a use of rationalistic techniques. Second, the use of the *bi-lā kayfa* formula might indicate a certain anachronism, since it was more commonly employed in later stages. The first scholar to have doubt the treatise's authenticity was the Shafiʿī-Ashʿarī historian, Sahms al-Dīn al-Dhahabī (d. 748/1374). An attempt to discern the veracity of the work *al-Radd ʿala ʾl-zanādiqa wal-jahmiyya* was made in Saud Saleh Al-Sarhan's doctoral dissertation "Early Muslim Traditionalism: A Critical Study of the Works and Political Theology of Aḥmad Ibn Ḥanbal," carried out under the supervision of Robert Gleave (Exeter: University of Exeter, September 2011), 48–53; Jon Hoover, "Ḥanbalī Theology," in: ed. Sabine Schmidtke, *the Oxford Handbook of Islamic Theology* (Oxford: Oxford University Press, 2016), 627–628; Holtzman, "Aḥmad b. Ḥanbal," *EI—THREE*, 1:20; Holtzman, "Ḥanbalīs," *Oxford Bibliographies Online*, 8.

73 Aḥmad ibn Ḥanbal, *al-Radd ʿala ʾl-zanādiqa wal-jahmiyya*, 14–15, 39–40; the English translation is taken from: Morris S. Seale, *Muslim Theology: A Study of Origins with Reference to the Church Fathers* (London: Luzac, 1964), 96–97.

the ambiguous verses—which are not to be interpreted—in order to reinforce their claims about God's characteristics.[74] According to the hermeneutical view of Aḥmad ibn Ḥanbal, an adequate interpretation does not question the texts and does not insert any external ideological innovations in addition to them. As opposed to the Muʿtazilite figurative interpretation, Aḥmad ibn Ḥanbal adopts the reception of the literal meaning of anthropomorphic expressions as they appear in the Islamic holy texts, saying that: "God is to be described exactly how He described Himself."[75] Ibn Taymiyya's allusion to Aḥmad ibn Ḥanbal's "prominent treatise" seems to serve him well in sustaining his claims against the use of *taʾwīl*, as well as in covertly pointing out Muʿtazilite elements in the hermeneutics of the later Ashʿarites, and more so in the thought of Fakhr al-Dīn al-Rāzī.

As Ibn Taymiyya goes on in *Bayān talbīs al-jahmiyya*, he refers the readers to his other writings for elaboration on the falsehood of *taʾwīl*, and among which he especially states the treatise *al-Ḥamawiyya 'l-kubrā*. Framing his current discussion, Ibn Taymiyya declares his objective is to follow al-Rāzī's argumentation in *Asās al-taqdīs* and to highlight his false judgment of the matter of the texts' apparent expressions (*ẓāhir al-lafẓ*).[76] Ibn Taymiyya's detailed discussion advances, as he slashes al-Rāzī's convictions using an abundance of examples from the Quran and Hadith as well as from the teachings of previous scholars he finds reliable. Already in the sections discussed above from *Bayān talbīs al-jahmiyya*, undoubtedly detectable are the four prominent elements of Ibn Taymiyya's approach to the divine attributes and the anthropomorphic descriptions of God, as they were listed beforehand: he accepts them with no hesitation as integral part of the texts of Islamic Revelation (*bi-lā kayfa*), he invests time and effort in a linguistic inquiry opting for a meaningful understanding of the attributes, he believes in the reality the attributes convey, and—perhaps not as explicitly in this example—he perceives them as evidence for God's perfection.

Fully devoted to Ibn Taymiyya's theological teachings, this is the formative approach Ibn al-Qayyim expresses and considerably expands in his work *al-Ṣawāʿiq*.[77] Therefore, the stances Ibn Taymiyya articulated are to be borne in

---

74 Seale, *Muslim Theology*, 53–56; van Ess, *Theologie und Gesellschaft*, 4:688–692.

75 Holtzman, "Aḥmad b. Ḥanbal," *EI—THREE*, 1:22.

76 Ibn Taymiyya, *Bayān talbīs al-jahmiyya*, 5:456–458.

77 Interestingly enough, Ibn al-Qayyim quotes the position of Aḥmad ibn Ḥanbal from the treatise ascribed to him *al-Radd ʿala 'l-zanādiqa wal-jahmiyya* with respect to *taʾwīl* in the former's work *Ijtimāʿ al-juyūsh al-islāmiyya ʿalā ghazw al-muʿaṭṭila wal-jahmiyya* (Mustering the Islamic Armies to Attack the *Muʿaṭṭila* and the *Jahmiyya*). Ibn Qayyim al-Jawziyya,

mind while reading through Ibn al-Qayyim's text, since our main goal is to study the monograph and thereby Ibn al-Qayyim's appropriation of the Taymiyyan scholarship. Of course, I will refer to Ibn Taymiyya and his works again in due time and with special significance to Ibn al-Qayyim's writing in *al-Ṣawāʿiq*. Altogether, this chapter has laid out succinctly the foundational theological ideas in Ibn Taymiyya's thought for the following inspection of Ibn al-Qayyim's theology in *al-Ṣawāʿiq*.

Ijtimāʿ al-juyūsh al-islāmiyya ʿalā ghazw al-muʿaṭṭila wal-jahmiyya, ed. ʿAwwād ʿAbdallāh al-Muʿtiq, in two volumes (Riyadh: Maṭābīʿ al-Farazdaq al-Tijāriyya, 1408/1988), 2:211–213. This work *Ijtimāʿ al-juyūsh* is of special relevance to *al-Ṣawāʿiq*, as will be explained in section 2.1.

CHAPTER 2

A Stroke of Lightning: *al-Ṣawāʿiq* in Ibn al-Qayyim's Theological Writing

It has already been established that, among other ideological and political tensions, theological controversies played a highly significant role in the scholastic circles of 8th/14th century Mamluk Damascus. Lauded with mutual wrangling and rivalry, this intellectually dense environment was the arena in which both traditionalist Ḥanbalite and rational-traditionalist Shafiʿite-Ashʿarite scholars manifested their own theological principles in writing. As a result, systematic study of theological texts composed during the Mamluk period has a lot to contribute to our ongoing understanding of the intellectual thought in medieval Islam. Significant in this respect is Caterina Bori's diagnosis in her article "Theology, Politics, Society: The Missing Link" in which she addresses several dilemmas and missing elements on the intellectual doctrinal output of the Mamluk period and its connection to society in current Western research. In her own words:

> For the Mamluk period we lack a comprehensive and reliable overview of which books were mostly studied; what were the most widespread theological themes and discussions; to what extant *kalām* [i.e. rationalistic speculative theology] was taught in *madrasah*s, as it seems to have been in the Ayyūbid period; and which intellectual solutions were provided for the various debated matters. The impressions that manuals and modern histories of Islamic theology convey is that theological production after al-Ghāzālī and Fakhr al-Dīn al-Rāzī was marginal, hence not worth of being considered. Accordingly, a great deal of attention has been dedicated to Muʿtazilī *kalām* and Ashʿarī rationalist theology up to the early 13th century, to the exclusion of what comes afterwards, both in the form of *kalām* and not [...]
>
> The later Mamluk period (second half of 14th century to early 16th century) also deserves to be investigated together with any changes that this specific time lap will carry with itself.[1]

1 Caterina Bori, "Theology, Politics, Society: The Missing Link. Studying Religion in the Mamlūk Period," in: *Ubi sumus? Quo vademus? Mamluk Studies—State of the Art*, ed. Stephan Conermann (Göttingen: Vandenhoeck & Ruprecht, 2013), 62, 65.

 | DOI: 10.1163/9789004372511_004

As Bori points out here, a crucial void is discernible in academic study today when it comes to paying adequate attention to Ibn al-Qayyim and Ibn Taymiyya's period of activity; therefore, many of their dogmatic teachings remained untouched. What is more, whereas Ibn Taymiyya's thought has received academic consideration over the past two decades or so, the importance of Ibn al-Qayyim's works on matters of tenets and belief is just now beginning to be broadly discovered and appreciated. Therefore, a close reading of the theological text of *al-Ṣawāʿiq*—as the main primary text analyzed—together with its contextualization in the following chapters will surely shed more light on the intellectual state of mind in Ibn al-Qayyim's surroundings and, more so, on his singular theological authorship.

Thus, this chapter introduces the work *al-Ṣawāʿiq* along general lines, giving special consideration to the work's main themes and its cross-cutting concerns. Section 2.1 briefly depicts the position of *al-Ṣawāʿiq* within Ibn al-Qayyim's theological output pertinent to the issue of divine attributes and therefore to the text's investigation to come. Sections 2.2 examines *al-Ṣawāʿiq* against the backdrop of Mamluk intellectual literature, exploring possible functional ends Ibn al-Qayyim could have intended *al-Ṣawāʿiq* to serve in his immediate scholastic environment. Section 2.3 focuses on Ibn al-Qayyim's appropriation of the Taymiyyan discourse in *al-Ṣawāʿiq*, prominently illustrating its methodological systemization. Section 2.4 concentrates on the rationalized-traditionalistic mode of discourse of *al-Ṣawāʿiq* and its *Kalām*ic character. Section 2.5 surveys Ibn al-Qayyim's focal argument in *al-Ṣawāʿiq* as he discredits the Ashʿarite practice of *taʾwīl* in the introduction to the work. Notable at this point is that the literary structure of *al-Ṣawāʿiq* became apparent towards my final reading of the text, and only then was I able to fully unravel its stylistic arrangement and aesthetics. However, analyzing here the work's structural formation beyond its general presentation would be premature. Since I believe it would be wiser to first grasp the text's contents and their relation to previous works before addressing its structural-stylistic aspects, this topic will be further explored in chapter 6 which decrypts the literary structure of the work.[2] Altogether, this chapter supplies a combined conceptual lens, leading to *al-Ṣawāʿiq*'s content analysis conducted in the following chapters

2 See section 6.3 Structural Aspects of Ibn al-Qayyim's Rationalization: *al-Ṣawāʿiq*'s Literary Symmetry.

2.1 Scope of *al-Ṣawāʿiq*: The Text and Related Writings

The work *al-Ṣawāʿiq*, along with its more popular abridgement (*mukhtaṣar*),[3] is a large-scaled piece of highly systemized dialectical theology, which is widely perceived as one of Ibn al-Qayyim's most important and mature works. It is dated from the last years of Ibn al-Qayyim's life,[4] therefore its substantial importance as one of the last and comprehensive works that he ever wrote. In *al-Ṣawāʿiq* he articulates radical criticism—originated in the Taymiyyan teachings—against the Muʿtazilite and Ashʿarite approaches to the issue of divine attributes and the anthropomorphic question.[5] Ibn al-Qayyim's prime objective in this work is to refute four fundamentals of the rationalistic epistemological views and hermeneutical techniques which were commonly applied in other theological debates as well. Ibn al-Qayyim designates these four rationalistic fundamentals with the Arabic word *ṭawāghīt* (singular: *ṭāghūt*), which, according to the terminology used in his other works, means a false and destructive principle, conviction or a way of thinking that leads to heresy.[6] Attacking the later Ashʿarite theoretical modus operandi, Ibn al-Qayyim didactically unfolds his positive epistemological and hermeneutical alternative approaches

3 Ibn Qayyim al-Jawziyya, *Mukhtaṣar al-Ṣawāʿiq al-mursala ʿala ʾl-jahmiyya wal-muʿaṭṭila*, the abridgement of Ibn al-Mawṣilī, Shams al-Dīn Abū ʿAbdallāh Muḥammad ibn Muḥammad (d. 774/1372), ed. Al-Ḥasan ibn ʿAbd al-Raḥman al-ʿAlawī, in 4 volumes (Riyadh: Aḍwāʾ al-Salaf, 1425/2004).

4 In *al-Ṣawāʿiq*, Ibn al-Qayyim mentions his other work *Ḥādī ʾl-arwāḥ ilā bilād al-afrāḥ* which is dated in his manuscripts to the year 745/1344. The monograph's main outline is described in the article of Yassir Qadhi, "'The Unleashed Thunderbolts' of Ibn Qayyim al-Jawziyya: An Introductory Essay," in *A Scholar in the Shadow: Essays in the Legal and Theological Thought of Ibn Qayyim al-Ǧawziyyiah*, ed. Caterina Bori and Livnat Holtzman, *Oriente Moderno 90/1* (2010): 135–149; Krawietz, "Ibn Qayyim al-Jawzīyah: His Life and Works," 31.

5 Notable is that Ibn al-Qayyim referred the Ashʿarites with the derogatory term *jahmiyya* for the stance they took on the theological question of predetermination, but not for the disagreement on the issue of the divine attributes. He used this denunciation slightly earlier in his work *Shifāʾ al-ʿalīl*. Holtzman "Predestination (*al-Qaḍāʾ wal-Qadar*) and Free Will (*al-Ikhtiyār*)," 169–174; Ibn Qayyim al-Jawziyya, *al-Ṣawāʿiq*, the editor's introduction, 75–78, 84; Qadhi, "'The Unleashed Thunderbolts'," 135–136.

6 Henceforth, the Arabic term *ṭāghūt* will be used to designate each of the four rationalistic methodological principles discussed in *al-Ṣawāʿiq*. In my opinion, following Ibn al-Qayyim's own terminology in this respect provides a more convenient manner of expressing the rather complex and uncommon meaning Ibn al-Qayyim conveys with the term, which can be either reduced or overly long when translated into English. For a more elaborated discussion of the terminology used in *al-Ṣawāʿiq*, see page 65.

to the issue of divine attributes. In fact, as will be elucidated along this chapter—and throughout this study—, Ibn al-Qayyim authored *al-Ṣawāʿiq* in a distinctive rationalized-traditionalistic fashion which fits into the *Kalām*ic discourse. From a broad textual outlook, *al-Ṣawāʿiq* is a systemized projection of the Taymiyyan theological ideas, manner of literary composition and rather aggressive oratory. Given the historical context of the epoch in which Ibn al-Qayyim lived, it is of much plausibility that he made use of *al-Ṣawāʿiq* to shrewdly transfix his rationalist contemporaries, with whom he was in direct contact, i.e., the Ashʿarite Damascene *ʿulamāʾ*. It is notable that Ibn al-Qayyim claimed his theology to be identical to the that of the traditionalists (*ahl al-sunna* or *ahl al-ḥadīth*); however, meticulous reading of his works reveals that, like his master Ibn Taymiyya before him, his approach to a number of theological issues, including the issue of divine attributes and anthropomorphic expressions, is much more complex and nuanced than the approach of his Ḥanbalite predecessors.

In the historical sources, *al-Ṣawāʿiq* is listed amongst Ibn al-Qayyim works in the biographical dictionary *al-Dhayl ʿalā ṭabaqāt al-ḥanābila* (Addition to the Biographical Book of the Ḥanbalites), which was composed by one of his most distinguished pupils, Ibn Rajab (d. 798/1392). Naturally, Ibn Rajab dedicates a comparatively large amount of space (some six pages) to his teacher, carefully recording Ibn al-Qayyim's writings.[7] A noteworthy point is the incredibly large abundance of sources that Ibn al-Qayyim either mentioned or cited in *al-Ṣawāʿiq*. In his introduction to the work's critical edition, Al-Dakhīl Allāh states that in the two parts of *al-Ṣawāʿiq* together (i.e., both in his edition and in *Mukhtaṣar al-ṣawāʿiq*) some 150 books are recorded, 43 of which are noted in *Mukhtaṣar al-ṣawāʿiq*. Amongst those sources, a reference is clearly made to Ibn Taymiyya's work *Darʾ taʿāruḍ al-ʿaql wal-naql* (Rejecting the Contradiction between Reason and Tradition).[8] Moreover, in many places in *al-Ṣawāʿiq* Ibn al-Qayyim quotes from the works of prominent rationalist scholars who employed methodologies of speculative theology (*mutakallimūn*), such as: Ibn Sīnā (Avicenna, d. 482/1037), al-Ghazālī (d. 505/1111), Ibn Rushd (Averroes, d. 595/1198), Sayf al-Dīn al-Āmidī (d. 631/1233) and Fakhr al-Dīn al-Rāzī (d. 606/1209). Al-Dakhīl Allāh registers a detailed list of the names of the works and authors Ibn

7 Ibn Rajab, Zayn al-Dīn Abu 'l-Faraj ʿAbd al-Raḥman ibn Aḥmad (d. 795/1392), *al-Dhayl ʿalā ṭabaqāt al-ḥanābila*, ed. Muḥammad Ḥāmid al-Faqīy (Cairo: Maṭbaʿat al-Sunna al-Muḥammadiyya, 1952/1372), 2:450.

8 Binyamin Abrahamov, "Ibn Taymiyya on the Agreement of Reason with Tradition," in: *The Muslim World* 82/3–4 (1992), 257, 272; Qadhi, "'The Unleashed Thunderbolts'," 143–144.

al-Qayyim referred to in *al-Ṣawāʿiq*. Similarly, a meticulous list is found in al-ʿAlawī's introduction to *Mukhtaṣar al-ṣawāʿiq*, where he mentions 159 books. These two most comprehensive lists definitely indicate the immense intellectual richness on which Ibn al-Qayyim relied and demonstrated in his writing.[9]

The following table describes the overall structure of the work *al-Ṣawāʿiq* in a schematic manner, referring to two modern editions of *al-Ṣawāʿiq* by al-Dakhīl Allāh and *Mukhtaṣar al-Ṣawāʿiq* by al-ʿAlawī:[10]

The part of the work	*al-Ṣawāʿiq*	*Mukhtaṣar al-ṣawāʿiq*
Preface	Elaborated (1:147–174)	Abridged (1:3–16)
Introduction—against *taʾwīl*	24 chapters	11 full chapters, 7 abridged
1. Refutation of the First *ṭāghūt*	Vols. 1–2	(In vol. 1, brief)
2. Refutation of the Second *ṭāghūt*	Vols. 3–4	(In vols. 1–2, abridged)
3. Refutation of the Third *ṭāghūt*	–	Vols. 2–4
4. Refutation of the Fourth *ṭāghūt*	–	Vol. 4

As can be clearly seen, the largest part of *al-Ṣawāʿiq* contains the refutation of the four rationalistic principles Ibn al-Qayyim wished to attack, all of which revolve around the single theological issue of divine attributes and the rationalistic approaches that either negate the literal/actual meaning of the attributes or nullify their meaning altogether. In addition, as a preliminary step towards his forthcoming refutation of the four rationalistic arguments, Ibn al-Qayyim preceded a separate discussion in his introduction on *taʾwīl* which he perceives as more than the allegorical method of interpretation of the rationalists, but as a signifier of a wide intellectual phenomenon that distorts the meanings conveyed in the texts of the Quran and Hadith (see section 2.5 henceforth). Looking at the work in a general view, it is safe to say its thematic theological concern is very much solid and uniform.

9 Ibn Qayyim al-Jawziyya, *al-Ṣawāʿiq*, the editor's introduction, 1:84–92; Idem, *Mukhtaṣar al-Ṣawāʿiq* (the abridgement of Ibn al-Mawṣilī), the editor's introduction, 1:64–73.

10 The table relies on the full comparison made by al-Dakhīl Allāh between the two parts of *al-Ṣawāʿiq* according to the principles' order which appears in the 11th section of his introduction (in al-ʿAlawī's edition of *al-Mukhtaṣar* there is a slight difference); Ibn Qayyim al-Jawziyya, *al-Ṣawāʿiq*, the editor's introduction, 1:117–125. I have used al-ʿAlawī's edition to complete the parts that are not mentioned by al-Dakhīl Allāh (arguments 3 and 4).

Roughly drawing the four *ṭawāghīt*, i.e., the rationalistic convictions Ibn al-Qayyim starkly criticized in *al-Ṣawāʿiq*, one can make use of the following outline:[11]

	ṭāghūt
1	The texts of the Qur'an and the Hadith contain verbal evidence (*adilla lafẓiyya*), which do not produce certain knowledge (*ʿilm yaqīn*)
2	In case of conflict, Reason (*ʿaql*) is prior to Revelation (*naql*)
3	Anthropomorphic expressions are metaphors (*majāzāt*) of no reality (*ḥaqīqa*)
4	Prophetical tradition with a limited number of chains of transmissions (e.g., *ḥadīth al-āḥād*) cannot produce certain knowledge

Ibn al-Qayyim perceived these four principles as the major methodological false-pillars of the rationalistic approach to the scriptures of the Quran and the Hadith literature. A more elaborated examination of selected sections of those *ṭawāghīt* refutations will be carried out in the course of the following chapters. It is important to state that, due to the limited attention span of this study, the particular sections chosen for the upcoming discussions represent the pinnacles of the four *ṭawāghīt* refutations, to the best of my understanding. In that manner, I aim to capture the viewpoint expressed in the entire work and to depict the polemical atmosphere illustrated in *al-Ṣawāʿiq*. As the next chapters will unfold, there is no doubt Ibn al-Qayyim authored *al-Ṣawāʿiq* for the purpose of confronting the religious worldview practiced by the rationalist *ulamā'* of his close environment.

The hostile ground of theological debates in Mamluk times concerning the issue of divine attributes and the anthropomorphic question is also evident in Ibn al-Qayyim's several other theological writings. Since one of this study's aims is to explore Ibn al-Qayyim as both a theologian and a scholar, it must inevitably refer to some of his other significant theological works which are similar to *al-Ṣawāʿiq* in terms of thematic orientation. Thus, Ibn al-Qayyim's key theological works on the divine attributes will be surveyed and *al-Ṣawāʿiq* will be aptly placed within his vast oeuvre. Still, we should first outline the reference range of this particular study: the following investigation will mainly concentrate on Ibn al-Qayyim's relatively late work *al-Ṣawāʿiq*. Two additional

11 Ibn Qayyim al-Jawziyya, *al-Ṣawā'iq*, 2:632.

theological works will be presented, as they are of particular relevance to Ibn al-Qayyim's discussion on divine attributes. Highly notable is the fact that, despite their common thematic theological tendencies, the differences between all of these three texts in terms of rhetorical styles and literary genres are quite clear. Their distinguished literary characteristics shall therefore be presented as well. Additionally, another important work with relation to the discussion in *al-Ṣawāʿiq* will be presented; however, its main concern is not theology but, rather, Arabic grammar. Hence the following section describes three supplementary texts written by Ibn al-Qayyim that are highly significant to the main text of *al-Ṣawāʿiq*.

The first theological work to be described—written prior to *al-Ṣawāʿiq*—is titled *Ijtimāʿ al-juyūsh al-islāmiyya ʿalā ghazw al-Muʿaṭṭila wal-Jahmiyya* (Mustering the Islamic Armies to Attack the Muʿaṭṭila and the Jahmiyya).[12] This theological work can be largely described as having a very dry and traditionalistic nature. *Ijtimāʿ al-juyūsh* consists mainly of quotations from the Qur'an, the Hadith literature, and the sayings of the *salaf* (the righteous ancestors of the Islamic community), with no eminent use of rationalistic arguments. Here, Ibn al-Qayyim presented his technique of defying the ideological view held by his Ashʿarite opponents by means of a rather typical traditionalistic writing. In this respect, *al-Ṣawāʿiq* can be seen as an innovative, more developed version of *Ijtimāʿ al-juyūsh* in that it further explores Ibn al-Qayyim's arguments against the rationalistic approach on the issue of divine attributes, in terms of both content and style.[13] *Ijtimāʿ al-juyūsh* is therefore mostly a work of citations, and yet it includes many interesting references to major works of several different scholars highly pertinent to this study's exploration of *al-Ṣawāʿiq*.

The second theological work of the current presentation is titled *al-Kāfiya 'l-shāfiya fī 'l-intiṣār lil-firqa 'l-nājiya* (The Sufficient and Healing [Poem] on the Victory of the Saved Sect; or *al-Qaṣīda 'l-nūniyya*).[14] This work is in fact a long didactic poem (*qaṣīda*) and can be seen as a sign of Ibn al-Qayyim's growing intellectual self-confidence, resulting from the experience he gained in theological debates (*munāẓarāt*). In previous research, *al-Kāfiya* was considered to be Ibn al-Qayyim's first work on dogmatic theology as well as a denunciation

---

12 Ibn Qayyim al-Jawziyya, *Ijtimāʿ al-juyūsh al-islāmiyya ʿalā ghazw al-muʿaṭṭila wal-jahmiyya*, ed. ʿAwwād ʿAbdallāh al-Muʿtiq, in two volumes (Riyadh: Maṭābiʿ al-Farazdaq al-Tijāriyya, 1408/1988).

13 Holtzman, "Ibn Qayyim al-Jawziyya (1292–1350)," 202, 214–215, 217; Krawietz, "Ibn Qayyim al-Jawzīyah: His Life and Works," 30–33.

14 Ibn Qayyim al-Jawziyya, *al-Kāfiya 'l-shāfiya fī 'l-intiṣār lil-firqa 'l-nājiyya*, ed. ʿAbd Allāh ibn Muḥammad al-ʿUmayr (Riyadh: Dār Ibn Khuzayma, 1416/1996).

of the rationalistic doctrine in that it sought to refute Muʿtazilite and Ashʿarite tenets, including rationalistic views concerning the divine attributes.[15] This remarkably extensive poem addresses other complex subjects as well, such as predetermination and eschatological matters. *Al-Kāfiya* may have been composed gradually, meaning that it reflects an ongoing process of Ibn al-Qayyim's intellectual efforts which may have continued until his later, more mature writing period. In fact, *al-Ṣawāʿiq*—one of Ibn al-Qayyim's iatest works—is mentioned in *al-Kāfiya*, therefore predating it. Moreover, after long being considered a mere polemical treatise or a Taymiyyan creed, *al-Kāfiya* was recently proven to be "a political treatise, which directly responds to the accusations raised against Ibn Taymiyya by the Ashʿarite *ʿulamāʾ* of his times."[16] This manifold work represents Ibn al-Qayyim's attempt to defend not only the honor of his teacher, but also his theological creeds on the issue of divine attributes. Additionally, Ibn al-Qayyim made a clever use of poetic rhetorical means in order to conceal his sharp political criticism against his scholarly rivals. Looking at the work from a wider angle, *al-Kāfiya* is a statement of defense in favor of the Taymiyyan creed and scholarship that was written in order to cunningly reply to its detractors. This could be an additional source to consult when studying *al-Ṣawāʿiq*.

Ibn al-Qayyim's third work relevant to *al-Ṣawāʿiq*—though not entirely theological—is called *Badāʾiʿ al-fawāʾid* (The Amazing Benefits). It was apparently written after 732/1331 and probably preceded *al-Ṣawāʿiq*. This is a major work of grammar in which Ibn al-Qayyim delves into linguistic questions in order to 'benefit' and gain from them a clearer understanding of the Quran and Hadith literature. In this framework Ibn al-Qayyim also explains doctrinal matters (*ʿaqīda*) and jurisprudence (*fiqh*). The famous scholar Jalāl al-Dīn al-Suyūṭī (d. 911/1505)[17] has mentioned that "it is a large compendium (*jāmiʿ*) ... most of which concentrates on grammatical issues (*naḥū*)." Nevertheless, one of *Badāʾiʿ al-fawāʾid*'s modern editors ʿAlī ibn Muḥammad al-ʿImrān states that the work mainly focuses on Islamic law, and only then on various linguistic subjects

15 Holtzman, "Ibn Qayyim al-Jawziyya (1292–1350)," 214; Birgit Krawietz, "Ibn Qayyim al-Jawzīyah: His Life and Works," 32–33.

16 For the chronological relation between *al-Ṣawāʿiq* and *al-Kāfiya*, see: Livnat Holtzman, "Accused of Anthropomorphism: Ibn Taymiyya's *Miḥan* as Reflected in Ibn Qayyim al-Jawziyya's *al-Kāfiya al-Shāfiya*," footnote 118; idem, "Insult, Fury, and Frustration."

17 Al-Suyūṭī, Abu 'l-Faḍl ʿAbd al-Raḥmān ibn Abī Bakr Jalāl al-Dīn al-Khuḍayrī, was a prominent Egyptian scholar of an outstanding and prolific literary output in a diverse variety of medieval sciences. He is often considered to have followed the prophetic Sunna, following in the footsteps of Ibn Taymiyya; E. Geoffroy, "al-Suyūṭī," *EI*², 9:913–915.

(*naḥū, balāgha*), Quranic exegesis (*tafsīr*), Hadith interpretations, etc. *Badāʾiʿ al-fawāʾid* represents much of Ibn al-Qayyim's linguistic approach, through which he strove to better discern matters of legal theoretical methodology (*uṣūl al-fiqh*).[18] Since significant parts of *al-Ṣawaʿiq* involve Ibn al-Qayyim's hermeneutical approach to an adequate understanding of the Islamic scriptures with respect to the divine attributes, there is no doubt that his linguistic view as captured in *Badāʾiʿ al-fawāʾid* can be of assistance while reading and assessing *al-Ṣawāʿiq*'s contents.

It is highly notable that each of those four works, *Ijtimāʿ al-juyūsh*, *al-Kāfiya 'l-shāfiya*, *Badāʾiʿ al-fawāʾid* and *al-Ṣawāʿiq*, diverges from the others in terms of literary characteristics; in fact, each belongs to a different literary genre. I do take those literary dissimilarities into account as I primarily investigate Ibn al-Qayyim's methodology employed in *al-Ṣawāʿiq*. However, due to the amazingly broad magnitude of *al-Ṣawāʿiq*, the three other works mentioned above will be referred to only in case of special relevance to its contents rather than be systematically examined. The main subject matter for investigation remains the theological issue of the divine attributes.

2.2 *Al-Ṣawāʿiq* within Mamluk Intellectual Literature

In spite of its rather impressive thematic scope and systemized structure, the work *al-Ṣawāʿiq* has yet to be thoroughly studied. Apart from its complexity and massive size, this may also be a result of the generally dismissive attitude modern research has shown towards Mamluk intellectual literature. Until recently, Western research has regarded the collected works produced in the Mamluk era as signifying its literary and intellectual decline. For example, in his article "Mamluk Literature" from 2003, Robert Irwin seemed to have reached the conclusion that, despite its impressive versatility and high level of erudition, generally speaking the literary output of the Mamluk period showed little innovation. In a similar vein, when he mentions Ibn Taymiyya and Ibn al-Qayyim, Irwin mostly refers to them as signifiers of "a literature of piety and rigorism," which deals with spirituality, distinguishing it from the more "vulgar entertainment" (i.e., popular poetry or stories about drinking wine, love, sexuality

18 Ibn Qayyim al-Jawziyya, *Badāʾiʿ al-fawāʾid*, edited by ʿAlī ibn Muḥammad al-ʿImrān and Bakr ibn ʿAbdallāh Abū Zayd, in 5 volumes (Mecca: Dār ʿĀlam al-Fawāʾid lil-Nashr wal-Tawzīʿ, [1424]/2003), the editor's preface, 1:13, 21–32. Krawietz, "Ibn Qayyim al-Jawzīyah: His Life and Works," 38; Holtzman, "Ibn Qayyim al-Jawziyya (1292–1350)," 203.

or romance).[19] Contrariwise, according to the view of Thomas Bauer, statements of such dismissive nature do not at all suffice when describing major amounts of literature which has barely been studied, as he explained in detail in his paper "Mamluk Literature: Misunderstandings and New Approaches" from 2005. For Bauer, Mamluk literature is by no means stale; rather, its academic study is the key through which modern research can reach new literary, cultural, social, and historical insights on the Islamic Middle Ages.[20]

Composed in the vibrant intellectual setting of Mamluk Damascus, the work *al-Ṣawāʿiq*'s polemical tone and its diverse rhetorical features definitely merit closer literary inspection. Thus, this section will shortly review several interesting rhetorical devices Ibn al-Qayyim employs in *al-Ṣawāʿiq* in an attempt to explore the more aesthetic aspects of the monograph as an intellectual literary text written mainly in prose (although it also contains sporadic sections of poetry as well).[21] The enquiry will launch into the fierce, combative figures of speech as they appear in the work's title, then move on to the designated *ṭāghūt* used for its four main sections; last, it will reflect on the text's critical tendency. A careful examination of these three rhetorical layers can surely contribute to the overall view of *al-Ṣawāʿiq* as an output of intellectual activity in Mamluk times. A literary point of view may also assist in evaluating for what purposes *al-Ṣawāʿiq* was composed or, more precisely, how did the literary means of theological writing in prose serve Ibn al-Qayyim's objectives in his refutation of the four rationalistic methods of argumentation in *al-Ṣawāʿiq*. In this respect, it should be noted that this section will also provide an initial step towards a better understanding of the scholarly works of prose produced by Mamluk *ʿulamāʾ* as religious literary texts.[22]

---

19 Robert Irwin, "Mamlūk Literature," *Mamlūk Studies Review* 5/1, 2003: 22–24, 27, 29.

20 Thomas Bauer, "Mamluk Literature: Misunderstandings and New Approaches," *Mamlūk Studies Review* 9/2, 2005: 107, 129–130.

21 A noteworthy reference to the study of Ibn al-Qayyim's theological output in the form of poetry is Holtzman's literary analysis of his theological-political poetic work *al-Kāfiya 'l-shāfiya* in her article: "Insult, Fury, and Frustration: The Martyrological Narrative of Ibn Qayyim al-Jawzīyah's *Al-Kāfiyah al-Shāfiyah*" (2013).

22 An overall study of the literary style of Arabic prose texts of the post classical period goes beyond the scope of the following section. However, the volume *The Cambridge History of Arabic Literature: Arabic Literature in the Post Classical Period* edited by Roger Allen and D.S. Richards (Cambridge: Cambridge University Press, 2006) includes several studies of relevance to the matter at hand. Noteworthy is also Julie S. Meisami's entry "Artistic Prose" in *The Routledge Encyclopedia of Arabic Literature*, First Edition (London: Routledge, 2010), 105–106. Additionally, this section draws on Bauer's article "Mamlūk Literature as a Means of Communication" (2013), which mainly focuses on the literary aspect.

The Title of al-Ṣawāʿiq

It almost goes without saying that a text's title presents crucial stylistic elements, which express not only its author's subjective intentions, but also aim to arouse curiosity and attract potential readers.[23] Ibn al-Qayyim's choice of title for his work surely fits these two aspects in that it intriguingly suggests the forces of nature: *al-Ṣawāʿiq al-mursala ʿala 'l-jahmiyya wal-muʿaṭṭila* (The Unleashed Thunderbolts Directed against the Jahmiyya and the Muʿaṭṭila). The title originates in the Quranic verse 13:13 "He sends thunderbolts to strike whoever He will. Yet still they dispute about God—He has mighty plans." Ibn al-Qayyim discloses here the sheer wrath that motivated and accompanied his writing as well as his utter condemnation of his ideological rivals, who are denounced with specific derogatory labels. The two groups referred to by the Muʿaṭṭila and the Jahmiyya are, respectively, the ultra-rationalistic Muʿtaziltes, who denied the divine attributes by practicing *taʿṭīl*,[24] and the rational-traditionalist Ashʿarites, who are often described with loathing in Ibn al-Qayyim's writings.[25]

Such a hostile tone appears to have been commonly used in the theological debates (*munaẓarāt*) in Ibn al-Qayyim's milieu. Since the scholastic debates in which the *ʿulamāʾ* participated were perceived as intellectual competitions—or, even more so, as combats—the use of militant language was quite common. As Michael Chamberlain brilliantly puts it, "the scholars of a certain field of knowledge were its 'horsemen' (*fārisūn*) or 'armies' (*juyūsh*), and their words were 'the swords of books'."[26] More specifically, books of refutation (usually opening with the word *radd*, i.e., 'reply [back to ...]') were abundant with mil-

---

An interesting study, for instance—from the field of historiography, however—is Konrad Hirschler's *Arabic Medieval Historiography: Authors as Actors* (London; New York: Routledge, 2006). Hirschler combines research approaches taken from the two disciplines of social history and literary studies, while looking at medieval Arab authors and their formation of a historical narrative.

23 Gerard Genette and Marie Maclean, *Introduction to the Paratext, New Literary History*, 22/2 (Spring, 1991), 262–265; Marie Maclean, *Pretexts and Paratexts: The Art of the Peripheral, New Literary History*, 22/2 (Spring, 1991), 275–277.

24 The term *taʿṭīl* is a part of the Islamic theological discourse of polemics regarding the issue of the divine attributes, literally meaning "stripping God from His attributes". See footnote 21 in chapter 1.

25 For elaboration on the term Jahmiyya, see footnote 62 in chapter 1.

26 Chamberlain, *Knowledge and Social Practice*, 153–154. This use of the word *juyūsh* (i.e., armies) is also found in Ibn al-Qayyim's work *Ijtimaʿ al-juyūsh al-islāmiyya*, which was described above and is closely related in its theological theme in *al-Ṣawāʿiq*.

itary metaphors.[27] As a text of refutation, the forceful title given to *al-Ṣawāʿiq* does not come as a complete surprise. In fact, this martially inspired title fits well to the conventional linguistic norms depicting the debate and dispute culture of Mamluk Damascus.

Nevertheless, Ibn al-Qayyim's title does entail a distinction from the literary conventional use of titles, as the combat conveyed there is of an unmistakably different nature. Straight away it becomes clear from the title that Ibn al-Qayyim's state of mind fully earnest and his intention hostile; he aims to literally strike down his adversaries, reducing them to ashes. Following the well-known Arabic literary convention of phrasing a title in the form of rhymed prose (*sajʿ*), the title conforms to the typical style of linking two nominal phrases by a preposition (*ʿalā*). The first word of the title '*Ṣawāʿiq*' (sing. *ṣāʿiqa*) is most conveniently translated as 'thunderbolts', and refers to the divine sphere as a fire sent from the sky by God. In certain cases, it can also carry the meaning of any destructive punishment or cause of death.[28] Furthermore, the use of the preposition *ʿalā* after the adjective *mursala* is derived from the expression *arsala ʿalā*, which in its Quranic use conveys a harsh and negative connotation of God punishing the heretics.[29] Altogether, the literal meaning of the work's title reveals that Ibn al-Qayyim composed it as a manifestation of a highly violent rebuke towards his rationalist Ashʿarite contemporaries.

Placing special emphasis on Ibn al-Qayyim's martial terminology, Abdessamad Belhaj points out that, as far as Ibn al-Qayyim is concerned, Mamluk culture of dispute is a fight which can be considered *jihād* (i.e., a religious struggle of power). Belhaj finds several justifications from Ibn al-Qayyim's works for this claim, one of which appears in *al-Ṣawāʿiq*. Taking into consideration Ibn al-Qayyim's manner of speech in his other writings, this is one of the more militant rhetorical features he uses: "God watched these [deviant ones among]

---

27 As stated before in chapter 1 (page 36), one of al-Subkī's treatises against Ibn al-Qayyim himself was titled *al-Sayf al-ṣaqīl fī 'l-radd ʿalā Ibn Zafīl* (The Polished Sword in Response to Ibn Zafīl [viz. one of Ibn al-Qayyim's designations]); Chamberlain, *Knowledge and Social Practice*, 166–167.

28 Edward William Lane, *Arabic-English Lexicon* (New York: F. Ungar Pub. Co., [1955–1956]), 4:1690.

29 According to Lane's dictionary, the meaning of the expression in Q. 19:83 *arsalnā 'l-shayāṭīn ʿala 'l-kāfirīn* ("We [= God] sent evil ones on the disbelievers") can be seen as equivalent to that of the expression in Q. 43:36 *nuqayyiḍ lahu shayṭān^{an}* ("We [= God] assign an evil one as a comrade for whoever [turns away from the revelation of the Lord of Mercy]"). As stated by Lane, the preferred explanation thereof is: 'We have sent the devils *against* the unbelievers'. Lane, *Arabic-English Lexicon*, 3:1082.

humankind [i.e., the rationalists], and established soldiers to assault their kings with swords and spears [*bil-sayf*ⁱ *wal-sinān*ⁱ], and other soldiers to assault their scholars with argumentations and demonstrations [*bil-ḥujja*ᵗⁱ *wal-burhān*ⁱ]."[30] It is quite obvious that Ibn al-Qayyim includes himself as one of 'God's scholarly soldiers', whose objective is to intellectually defeat the misleading scholars. In this case, God is the one who calls into being the 'soldiers' to make a raid against the heretics.

Since the battle referred to in this title is not an ordinary battle of flesh and blood scholars, in the title of *al-Ṣawāʿiq*, Ibn al-Qayyim appears to have stretched this fierce terminology and extended its boundaries. This battle involves the heavens, the thunderbolts, the forces of nature, and the divine power which governs them. In this manner, Ibn al-Qayyim takes a daring step forward, in that he relates his work to the deistic realm and assumes the position of a priest who is able to summon up godly punishment, such as lighting strike against whoever he considers to be unbelievers. While still bearing in mind the common literary use of martial language in Ibn al-Qayyim's environment, viewing 'The Unleashed Thunderbolts' from this perspective suggests this title is rather exceptional in comparison to the mundane combats of the titles of other works. The reader faced with the text of *al-Ṣawāʿiq* must then decide whether to join Ibn al-Qayyim and conform to his theological tenets, or choose to join the opposing side, thus risking the threat of godly punishment.

Division of Sections in al-Ṣawāʿiq

It has been established that, in terms of its title, *al-Ṣawāʿiq* can be literarily seen as a manifestation of war between the one true God and the false idols that dare to hazard the true God's indisputable sovereignty. In this scenario, Ibn al-Qayyim facilitates the position of the earthly representative of the one true deity, whose objective is to defeat the idols and their heresy. This literary tendency to depict a divine warzone is intensified to a greater extent when viewing the guiding phrases[31] used for each of the four sections of the work, each dedicated to refute a single rationalistic principle—*ṭāghūt* (pl. *ṭawāghīt*; from the root *ṭ.gh.w/y*). Literally, the term's meaning is "one that is exorbitant with pride,

30 Ibn Qayyim al-Jawziyya, *al-Ṣawāʿiq*, 4:1079; Abdessamad Belhaj, "Disputation is a Fighting Sport: *munāẓara* according to Ibn Qayyim al-Jawziyya," *Mamlūk Studies Review*, 18/1 (2016): 3.

31 In his study, Hirschler explains that "guiding phrases", along with a work's title and its division into section, were "markers of the mode of emtplotment and were intended to prepare the reader for the following narrative structure." This model can be clearly seen in *al-Ṣawāʿiq*; Hirschler, *Arabic Medieval Historiography*, 66–67.

corruptness, disbelief or disobedience, of the *jinn* [i.e., a devil]."[32] It is known from the pre-Islamic era, describing the Arab idols of *al-Lāt* in the city of Ṭā'if and *Manāt* in Mecca. After the emergence of the Islam, it was used to denote false idols or other anti-Islamic forces, such as devils or warlocks. The term is also mentioned in the Quran 2:256 "whoever rejects false gods [*ṭawāghīt*] and believes in God ..."[33]

At this point, the manner in which Ibn Taymiyya made use of the phrase *ṭāghūt* in his writing should be noted. Put simply, Ibn Taymiyya considers *ṭāghūt* to be "anything or anyone which exalts oneself without Godly obedience, whether it is a person, a devil, or an idol." Accordingly, a person who holds a belief that contradicts the Quran and the Sunna or issues judicial rulings in opposition is also considered *ṭāghūt*.[34] Ibn Taymiyya unequivocally mentions the *mutakallimūn* and the Muʿatazilites, as he writes: "If a man speaks contradictory to the truth and relies on the faulty knowledge of Reason alone, he diverts others rather than directs them. He guides his followers from light to darkness, like a *ṭāghūt*; as said in the Quran [2:257] 'close to the unbelievers are their false gods, who take them from the light into the depth of darkness'..."[35] Moreover, Ibn Taymiyya included the *mutafalsifa* and similar rationalistic scholars in the groups of hypocrites (*munāfiqūn*) who do not believe in the Quran but, rather, in evil idols (i.e., *ṭawāghīt*). Linguistically, he explains, it is the measure *faʿlūt* of the word *ṭuryān*, which means exorbitance, foul or heresy. Hence, *ṭāghūt* denotes a false idol, and, in the same vein, also people who offer a false belief. In his opinion, these are the groups that distort the Quran and Sunna: Jews, Christians, Zoroastrians, those who worship other gods in addition to Allah (*mushrikūn*) as well as the rationalistic streams of thought (e.g., *falāsifa*).[36] With respect to the issue of divine attributes, Ibn Taymiyya uses the term *ṭāghūt* in his "Book of Names and Attributes" (*Kitāb al-asmāʾ wal-ṣifāt*). There he attacks the *mutakallimūn*, claiming they force their rationalistic arguments on God's speech, thereby negating His attributes. In his eyes, the *mutakallimūn* resemble those who "turn to unjust tyrants [*ṭawāghīt*] for judgment, although they have been ordered to reject them" (Q. 4:60): they say they

32 Lane, *Arabic-English Lexicon*, 5:1857.

33 T. Fahd and F.H. Stewart, "Ṭāghūt," *EI*^{2}, 10: 93–94.

34 Ibn Taymiyya, *Jāmiʿ al-rasāʾil*, ed. Muḥammad Rashād Sālim (Riyadh: Dār al-ʿAṭāʾ, 1422/2001), 2:373–374.

35 Ibn Taymiyya, *Darʾ taʿāruḍ al-ʿaql wal-naql*, ed. Muḥammad Rashād Sālim (Riyadh: Jāmiʿat al-Imām Muḥammad ibn Saʿūd al-Islāmiyya, 1411/1991), 5:213–214.

36 Ibn Taymiyya, *Majmūʿat al-fatāwā*, eds. ʿĀmir al-Jazzār and Anwar al-Bāz (Riyadh: Dār al-Wafāʾ, 1419/1998), 28: 112–114.

have good intentions and wish to make a compromise between Reason and Scriptural evidence; however, in reality their proofs are highly questionable.[37]

Along the lines of the Taymiyyan view, Ibn al-Qayyim clearly uses the term *ṭāghūt* in a similar negative fashion. However, he seems to have significantly expanded its meaning beyond this immediate sense and loaded it with an abstract meaning of ungodly rule or an argument that diverts man from God's path. He discusses this in his work *Iʿlām al-muwaqqiʿīn ʿan rabb al-ʿālamīn* (Notifying those who are Authorized to sign [on juridical documents] on behalf of the World's Governor), which concentrated on the methodology of jurisprudence. Here, Ibn al-Qayyim explains *ṭāghūt* is "anything that a jurist judges according to which, that is not God and His Messenger, or that a man worships beside God, or that a man follows without knowledge from God thereof." Clarifying his intention, Ibn al-Qayyim writes: "Any opinion (*raʾy*), syllogism (*qiyās*), blindly following an Imām (*taqlīd imām*), dream (*manām*), discovery (*kushūf*), inspiration (*ilhām*), persuasion (*ḥadīth al-qalb*), preference (*istiḥsān*), reasonability (*maʿqūl*), court's ruling (*sharīʿat al-dīwān*), kings' policy (*siyāsat al-mulūk*), or common customs that are not a part of Islamic jurisprudence (*ʿawāʾid al-nās*)—all of which are *ṭawāghīt*, and are forbidden to be followed in the process of ruling; the only authority to be followed are the sacred texts."[38]

Clearly Ibn al-Qayyim also uses the phrase *ṭāghūt* in his polemic poem *al-Kāfiya al-shāfiya* in the section titled "breaking the *ṭāghūt* which was used to negate the attributes of [He who owns the] sovereignty and greatness", where he writes:

> (3758) Despicable is that *ṭāghūt*, may it be damned/ the *ṭāghūt* of the heretic who negates the attributes
> (3579) How many prisoners and even casualties/ have been caused by this *ṭāghūt* as time passed by [...]
> (3767) You have set this *ṭāghūt*/ and then negated with it the obligatory meaning of the Quran [...]
> (3775) This catapult and *ṭāghūt* demolished/ your houses to the ground.[39]

37 Ibn Taymiyya, *Majmūʿat al-fatāwā*, 5:15–16.

38 Ibn Qayyim al-Jawziyya, *Iʿlām al-muwaqqiʿīn ʿan rabb al-ʿālamīn*, ed. Muḥammad ʿAbd al-Salām Ibrāhīm, in 4 volumes (Beirut: Dār al-Kutub al-ʿIlmiyyah, 1411/1991), 1: 39–40, 186.

39 Ibn Qayyim al-Jawziyya, *al-Kāfiya al-shāfiya fī 'l-intiṣār lil-firqa 'l-nājiya: al-qaṣīda 'l-nūniyya*, ed. ʿAbdallāh ibn Muḥammad al-ʿAmīr (Riyadh: Dār Ibn Khuzayma, 1417/[1996]), 275–276.

These verses explicitly mention the theological issue of the divine attributes. In this particular context, it appears that Ibn al-Qayyim refers to a leading principle or a certain idea of severely catastrophic outcomes. Therefore, a plausible denotation of the phrase *ṭāghūt* as shown here would be a mode of thinking that leads towards heresy.

Returning to the *ṭāghūt* as a leading phrase in the work *al-Ṣawāʿiq*, it is evident that Ibn al-Qayyim's perception of the term here is based on Ibn Taymiyya's teachings in which he mentions a false idol worshipped apart from God or a person that turns to a misbelief (i.e., the Muʿtazilites and the Ashʿarites). However, Ibn al-Qayyim introduces an interesting development in this definition of the term *ṭāghūt* as a guiding phrase in *al-Ṣawāʿiq*. Using the phrase *ṭāghūt* to designate each of the four rationalistic principles he condemns, Ibn al-Qayyim ascribes an intangible meaning to the term as an unlawful and destructive thinking method. Following the lines of this far more abstract definition of the *ṭāghūt*, the four *ṭawāghīt* Ibn al-Qayyim aims to disprove are to be seen as rules or arguments of an ungodly source, whose goal is to twist the original meaning of God's speech, thereby leading humanity away from the righteous path.[40] Figuratively depicting a scenario of a battle between the one true God and four fraud combatants of the intellect, Ibn al-Qayyim reinforces his construction of a narrative of the uncompromising war of minds against the elitist rationalistic Damascene scholars.

Al-Ṣawāʿiq*'s Textual Tendency*

Given its stern martial title and the derogatory definitions of *ṭawāghīt* in its four sections, one cannot help but evaluate the text of *al-Ṣawāʿiq* in a literary prism. Ibn al-Qayyim's use of such a harsh literary tone throughout the entire text of *al-Ṣawāʿiq* conveys inexplicit extrapolations concerning the work's nature and intention. First, a martial textual tendency reflects an employment of a particular structured narrative. In other words, Ibn al-Qayyim's well-thought-out use of numerous martial rhetorical elements reveals his deliberate choice of promoting a narrative where it is both entwined in the text and simultaneously mirrors its purpose.[41] In the article "Insult, Fury, and Frustration: The Marty-

40 Qadhi, "'The Unleashed Thunderbolts'," 140–141. Throughout this study, the term *ṭāghūt/ṭawāghīt* will not be translated into English, due to the obvious difficulty of finding an adequate translation which will convey its complex meaning as described in this section. Rather, I will use the Arabic transliteration, adding explanation when necessary.

41 Hirschler, *Arabic Medieval Historiography*, 67, 72. Due to a vast use of all-inclusive language as a rhetorical strategy of communication, this topic brings to mind the narrative

rological Narrative of Ibn Qayyim al-Jawzīyah's *al-Kāfiyah al-Shāfiyah*" (2013), Holtzman has already delved into the characterization of the narrative echoed in Ibn al-Qayyim's work *al-Kāfiya*. As mentioned before, both *al-Ṣawāʿiq* and *al-Kāfiya* are concerned with the doctrinal and political disagreements between the Taymiyyan view and the rationalistic one stemming from the theological dispute regarding divine attributes. Consequently, it is highly likely these two texts also share a continuous leading narrative which validated the formation of the Taymiyyan circle of followers and conceptualized their self-perception after the mentor's death. Principally, the 'martyrological narrative' identified by Holtzman in the poem *al-Kāfiya* is most certainly relevant to the prose of *al-Ṣawāʿiq*. Putting aside the poetic aspect, I specifically refer to Holtzman's diagnosis on the harsh rhetoric used in *al-Kāfiya*, which definitely corresponds with the martial text of *al-Ṣawāʿiq*:

> *Al-Kāfiyah al-Shāfiyah* is a raging poem: its militant atmosphere, occasional foul language, and determined attacks on the Ashʿarīs all combine to create a piece that is much more than a versified creed or a mere polemical treatise. The "emotional baggage"—if we may borrow a contemporary term—invested in *Al-Kāfiyah al-Shāfiyah* is tremendous. Ibn al-Qayyim, who had his share of *miḥan* [i.e., inquisitions, ordeals] (of which the listeners were well aware), weaves the martyological narrative from three basic emotions: insult, fury, and frustration. Alongside these, he emphasizes the importance of perseverance, acceptance—a state accomplished after completing a process of rationalization—and self-pride.[42]

Indeed, *al-Ṣawāʿiq*'s prose expresses this highly emotional narrative of self-victimization, but its main focus is more pragmatic: to critically disvalue four rationalistic methodologies. To be more precise, whereas the two texts of *al-Kāfiya* and *al-Ṣawāʿiq* do foster a common narrative, their textual tendencies differ significantly. *Al-Kāfiya* was composed as a voluminous poem and enabled Ibn al-Qayyim to wisely conceal his political denunciation of his Ashʿarite rivals, which was meant to answer the emotional and social needs of the scholars and laymen who followed Ibn Taymiyya's path.[43] In contrast, *al-Ṣawāʿiq*—a

elements of the Islamic sermon (*khuṭba*); Linda Jones, *The Power of Oratory in Medieval Muslim World* (New York: Cambridge University Press, 2012), 101–103.

42 Holtzman, "Insult, Fury, and Frustration: The Martyrological Narrative of Ibn Qayyim al-Jawzīyah's *al-Kāfiyah al-Shāfiyah*," *Mamlūk Studies Review* 17 (2013), 182.

43 Holtzman, "Insult, Fury, and Frustration," 162–163.

prose text that is far less constrained by stylistic conventions—had a different set of purposes, which had much more to do with the intellectual domain and the class of *ʿulamāʾ*.

Since *al-Ṣawāʿiq* dialectically engages the highly theoretical subjects of epistemology and hermeneutics, it becomes evident that the text was directed at the very specific audience who was acquainted with that kind of theoretical knowledge. Ibn al-Qayyim's *al-Ṣawāʿiq* appears to address the *ʿulamāʾ*, the religious scholars, along with the higher and more educated social class (*al-aʿyān, al-khāṣṣa*) to a greater extent than would sermons preached in front of the laymen (*al-ʿāmma*). In the post classical times—including the Mamluk period—the status of texts written in prose was considered noble as a means of articulation used by the elitist chanceries. Although the *ʿulamāʾ* were distinguished from other professional functionaries in this respect, the prose they contributed to the Islamic sciences was of fine literary quality.[44] *Al-Ṣawāʿiq*'s text is yet another example of Ibn al-Qayyim's well-known tendency towards didactical writing, whose goal is to systematically organize familiar—and, in this case, complex—knowledge in order for the reader to easily grasp its meaning. It may very well be that *al-Ṣawāʿiq*'s didactical trait served Ibn al-Qayyim's ongoing endeavor of sponsoring the Tayymiyan circle's narrative. Likewise, it must have been intended to supply the intellectual needs of the Taymiyyan circle of scholars, equipping them with the scholarly stratagems needed to outsmart their Ashʿarite ideological opponents.

As *al-Ṣawāʿiq* reproaches the harms of *taʾwīl* as a simulacrum of the later Ashʿarite worldview, it also introduces the positive paradigms to counter it and, hence, constructs an alternative model to Islamic theoretical reasoning. The contextual reading of *al-Ṣawāʿiq* taken in the course of this study unveils the interplay of relations between the primary text under inspection and its author's exterior literary sources of reference in a twofold manner: first, composing a work of fierce refutations against the rationalistic *taʾwīl* as an all-encompassing intellectual phenomenon lethal to Islam, Ibn al-Qayyim reprimanded his Ashʿarite contemporaries, thus directing the lion's share of his criticism against the renowned later Ashʿarites Fakhr al-Dīn al-Rāzī, al-Ghazālī, and their respective relevant works. Since he perceived the theoretical views and methodologies of Ashʿarite school to stem from—and perpetuate—the Muʿtazilite ultra-rationalistic heritage, Ibn al-Qayyim also condemned Muʿtazi-

44 Muhsin al-Musawi, "Pre-modern Belletristic Prose," in: Roger Allen and D.S. Richards (eds.) *The Cambridge History of Arabic Literature: Arabic Literature in the Post Classical Period* (Cambridge: Cambridge University Press, 2006), 99–111.

lite scholars. Second, and in sharp contrast to the former aspect, Ibn al-Qayyim draws his inspiration from the Islamic sacred texts, in accordance of course with the decisive teachings of Ibn Taymiyya. More intriguingly, Ibn al-Qayyim favorably refers to relatively early scholars with vibrant rationalistic tendencies, such as Ashʿarite luminary Abū Isḥāq al-Isfarāyīnī (d. 418/1027), the Ḥanbalite polymath Ibn ʿAqīl (d. 513/1119), and even the celebrated philosopher Ibn Rushd (Averroes, d. 595/1198). Ibn al-Qayyim establishes his reproach against his Ashʿarite contemporaries as he depends on scholars who sponsored the use of Reason (*ʿaql*) as a central human faculty for an adequate apprehension of the Revelation. Ibn al-Qayyim's sources of validation in *al-Ṣawāʿiq* indicate a stark rationalized leaning, which is inherently different to that of his contemporary rationalists (who preferred later Ashʿarism). Taking into account the various scholastic stimuli unfolded in *al-Ṣawāʿiq*, Ibn al-Qayyim's singular systemization of the Taymiyyan theoretical grounds appears to be ultimately designed in order to equip the reader with a global and far-reaching intellectual alternative to the Ashʿarite thought of Mamluk time.

In the light of his authorship in the work *al-Ṣawāʿiq*, Ibn al-Qayyim emerges as an "outsider theologian" who attempted to redefine the Sunnism of his lifetime, which was largely hegemonized by Rāziyyan Ashʿarism. A theologian of necessity, he treated doctrinal matters as a part of his endeavor to amend the religious and social order of that time period, in which the intellectual elite of Ashʿarite scholars went out of their way in persecuting Ibn Taymiyya's circle of followers, including himself. Nevertheless, Ibn al-Qayyim's position as an outsider did not diminish his great intellectual capacity of authoring a systemized—and even highly martial—work against his powerful adversaries. The "outsider's theology" served Ibn al-Qayyim as a means of communication with the rest of the Taymiyyan group of scholars, as can be seen in the case of his vast political poem *al-Kāfiya ʾl-shāfiya*. Thematically close to *al-Ṣawāʿiq*, the work *al-Kāfiya* nourished the narrative of martyrdom promoted by Ibn al-Qayyim, pointing to the emotional and social needs of the persecuted followers of Ibn Taymiyya.[45] In *al-Ṣawāʿiq* one can clearly notice Ibn al-Qayyim's ongoing predisposition towards this narrative, yet it is expressed from a slightly different angle; the narrative of martyrdom was not only rigidly defended, but may even have fueled the unleashed rage expressed in Ibn al-Qayyim's writing in *al-Ṣawāʿiq*. According to my understanding of the text at hand, Ibn al-Qayyim's wrath and general emotional turmoil could have simulated him to recruit additional intellectual armory to accompany his huge arsenal of schol-

45 Holtzman, "Insult, Fury, and Frustration," 176–177.

arly knowledge. This extra weapon was the *Kalām*ic systemized and rationalized authorship, which was used in the highly developed *al-Ṣawāʿiq* to shield the martyrized 'saved sect' of the followers of Ibn Taymiyya, as well as strike the ultimate blow on the rival Ashʿarite entrenched elite, thus further bonding and reinforcing the smaller Taymiyyan circle.

Examining *al-Ṣawāʿiq* from a different point of view, the text's aggressive tone can very plausibly infer that Ibn al-Qayyim intended his work to be also read by others besides the *ʿulamāʾ* of the Taymiyyan circle; indeed, he may have intended it for the entire scholarly elite of his time, rationalists and traditionalists alike. Aimed against the potential readers from the entire spectrum of the *ʿulamāʾ* class, *al-Ṣawāʿiq*'s dialectical manner of composition and militant tendency is largely another aspect of its compound layout, which is an integral part of the discourse of theological debates (*munāẓarāt*). In their written (rather than oral) form, the *munāẓarāt* culture created a literary stylistic structure to those texts of argumentation, expressing "the struggle for precedence".[46] As Josef van Ess remarked with regard to Islamic theological writing: "it is the art of dialogue we are taught here, the dialectic method of speech ... Every defensive argument is noted [...] and refuted with final and complacent apodictic certitude."[47] In *al-Ṣawāʿiq*, Ibn al-Qayyim clearly presents extensive discussions of such dialectical theological writing drawn from his impressive command in the practice of *munāẓarāt* against his Ashʿarite contemporaries. *Al-Ṣawāʿiq*'s dialectical style contributes to the general nature of as a text of persuasion; its entire objective is to convince the reader in the arguments presented against the four *ṭawāghīt*, while making abundant use of argumentative rhetoric.[48] Furthermore, Ibn al-Qayyim strives not only to exhibit persuasive arguments, but also to provide extensive positive—and equally persuasive—alternatives to replace the four *ṭawāghīt*. Ibn al-Qayyim might have quite ambitiously wished a wide range of exposure and reception for his work.

Evaluating *al-Ṣawāʿiq* with relation to its immediate historical setting, it becomes apparent that Ibn al-Qayyim inclusion of a new form of dialecti-

---

46 E. Wagner, "Munāẓara," *EI*², 7:565–566.

47 Josef van Ess, "The Logical Structure of Islamic Theology," in: G.E. von Grunebaum (ed.) *Logic in Classical Islamic Culture* (First Giorgio Levi Della Vida Biennial Conference: Wiesbaden 1970), 23.

48 Interestingly, this observation comes to terms once again with the persuasive nature of the sermon (*khuṭba*) in the face of the audience for which it was intended. An interesting description in this regard is Linda Jones' third chapter of *The Power of Oratory in Medieval Muslim World* titled "Rhetorical and Discursive Strategies of Persuasion in the *Khuṭba*," 87–110.

cal knowledge also served a socio-intellectual end in terms of his communication with the Taymiyyan reference group of alliance, as stated above. Ibn al-Qayyim's *Kalām*ic authorship possibly embeds two additional levels of communication: the first thereof intended to reach out to the Ashʿarite scholastic elite itself as an audience for his work, as a reference group of rivalry. Harnessing the rationalized mode of dialectical discourse as well as contents of familiar works of *Kalām*, Ibn al-Qayyim adjusted his writing to the cultural capital of the Ashʿarites surrounding him and employed their own set of shared ideas—while at the same time disputing them—in *al-Ṣawāʿiq*; hence, he vicariously included them as a reference group for the theological discussions he generated.[49] In this respect, Ibn al-Qayyim's active embracement of dialectical-*Kalām*ic authorship could have enlarged his potential audience of readers in a considerable manner; he was speaking the scholarly lingua franca of the Ashʿarite elite—so to say—and thus most likely aspired to earn the prestige of being a more reputable scholar, even if a combative one. Such a pragmatic approach is corroborated by the rhetorical devices of Ibn Taymiyya already detected in modern research, being a scholar who did not discard the option of addressing disparate groups on their own terms. This does not signify a mere tolerance of acceptance, but rather an unembellished pragmatic respect for the Ashʿarite rivals.[50] A carrier of the Taymiyyan way, Ibn al-Qayyim motivation to attack *Kalām* by the means of *Kalām* is very likely to have stemmed from a deep and candid religious belief that rationalism as practiced by his contemporaries was morally wrong[51] and, therefore, he demanded its reform by offering his alternative. Ibn al-Qayyim's indirectly responded that in a passage about the alleged repentance of four Ash'arites and his presentation of the victory of the traditionalists.[52]

49 From the perspective of the sociology of knowledge, this kind of use of shared ideas—or rather, in this particular case, a shared discourse—is a common feature of an intellectual's scholarly interaction via networks of alliance or rivalry, thus affiliating oneself with (while simultaneously differentiating oneself from) a certain group in which one aims to gain higher status. An interesting study on the importance of reference groups and their shared ideas in the context of Islamic social and intellectual history is: Mohammad Gharaibeh, "The Buldāniyyāt of as-Saḫāwī (d. 902/1496): A Case Study on Knowledge Specialization and Knowledge Brokerage in the Field of Ḥadīṯ Collections," *Annemarie Schimmel Kolleg Working Paper* 18 (Bonn, October 2014), 1–16.

50 Hoover, *Ibn Taymiyya's Theodicy*, 19–24.

51 Hoover, *Ibn Taymiyya's Theodicy*, 24; Hoover discusses the significance of the moral aspect in Ibn Taymiyya's approach.

52 This passage is discussed in page 181, as part of section 4.2 Ibn Taymiyya's Initial Critique against al-Ghazālī (from the View of Ibn al-Qayyim).

Evenly significant is the second probable level of communication Ibn al-Qayyim's militant authorship in *al-Ṣawāʿiq* is very likely to have targeted. This somewhat inferred level comprises the traditionalist *ʿulamāʾ* as a reference group which can be characterized as a mix of 'rivalry-alliance' (or 'alliance-rivalry'). By all accounts, the Damascene traditionalists belonged to the same ideological cluster as did Ibn al-Qayyim (and also Ibn Taymiyya and the rest of the Ḥanbalites). Albeit, the traditionalist *ʿulamāʾ* who were active in Ibn al-Qayyim's surrounding failed to form a meaningful opposition in their writings—socio-political and intellectual alike—to the established Ashʿarite elite. Preferring to remain within the boundaries of their scholarly 'comfort-zone', the traditionalist *ʿulamāʾ* refrained from facing the challenge imposed by the late Ashʿarite scholars. Even amid the traditionalist scholars who belonged to the Taymiyyan circle of immediate disciples, such as Shams al-Dīn al-Dhahabī (d. 748/1347), Ibn Kathīr (d. 774/1373) and Ibn Rajab (d. 795/1392), it is difficult to find voices of straightforward criticism expressed towards the predominant echelons of the Ashʿarite *ʿulamāʾ*. *Al-Ṣawāʿiq* and its dialectical manner of composition can therefore be taken as a growl of defiance directed towards Ibn al-Qayyim's fellow-traditionalists and their writing, which abstained from answering back to the rationalistic elite. Sustaining his competence of authoring a work of *Kalām*, the persecuted Ibn al-Qayyim could have proven his ability to openly express his disagreement with the elites and possibly also to get the better of them. Ibn al-Qayyim's rationalized-traditionalistic authorship presented in *al-Ṣawāʿiq* can also signify his wish to revolutionize the religious discourse of his time.

Looking at the broader historical picture encompassing Ibn al-Qayyim and the writing of *al-Ṣawāʿiq*, political aspirations should not be underestimated. The tight connection of Mamluk *ulamāʾ* to the practical implementation of the correct Islamic model in state's affairs could have been a contributing factor to Ibn al-Qayyim's *Kalām*ic authorship. The rationalized mode of discourse provided him with a suitable common ground in order to be more noticeable in the in the public arena, as he sought to widen the exposure of Taymiyyan theoretical teachings. This tendency can be seen in Ibn al-Qayyim's effort to proliferate Ibn Taymiyya's works and doctrine after the mentor's death. In the specific case of the highly erudite *al-Ṣawāʿiq*, the target audience is more likely to have been that of the educated and politically engaged elite—be they Taymiyyan, Ḥanbalite or Ashʿarite—more so than the laymen; however, given Ibn al-Qayyim's known didactical character, it is also probable that the work was intended for all seekers of knowledge.[53] Notwithstanding, as a representa-

53 Perho describes the possible audience of anther theological work by Ibn al-Qayyim *Shifāʾ*

tive of the Taymiyyan group, who gained much of its support from the lower social class of Damascus, the socio-political interests of the common people surely had a place in the eyes of Ibn al-Qayyim. In fact, Ibn al-Qayyim's *Kalām*ic authorship and *al-Ṣawāʿiq* could signify his entrance ticket to the public realm. According to Anjum's study of Taymiyyan political thought, the real target of later Ashʿarite *Kalām* in the Mamluk period was political, as it was one of the means by which ruling elite justified the existing hierarchy of powers: claiming to be the only ones who are able to attain certain knowledge of the divine—relying on the epistemic pessimism of al-Ghazālī and Fakhr al-Dīn al-Rāzī—, the later Ashʿarites proclaimed themselves to be the sole guardians of all apodictic truth. Ibn Taymiyya thus promoted an optimistic theoretical alternative, according to which, apodictic truth is attainable from the Islamic sacred texts thanks to the natural disposition (*fiṭra*) of all Muslims led by the scholarly adequate.[54] Striving to widely distribute the Taymiyyan theories of epistemology and hermeneutics concerning the sacred texts, Ibn al-Qayyim actually propagated in favor of a political alternative and against the Ashʿarite secluded hegemony. His *Kalām*ic authorship as expressed in *al-Ṣawāʿiq* must have made Ibn al-Qayyim's political defiance more visible to the surrounding Ashʿarite *ʿulamāʾ*, and placed him in political opposition to them. Fundamentally, the textual tendencies manifested in *al-Ṣawāʿiq* assist the ultimate combined objective of discrediting rationalistic principles while revalidating the Taymiyyan intellectual worldview.

2.3 Appropriating the Taymiyyan Discourse in *al-Ṣawāʿiq*: Ibn al-Qayyim's Systemization

A principal objective of this study is to attain a better understanding of Ibn al-Qayyim's appropriation of the scholarly legacy of his master Ibn Taymiyya via an investigation of the theological discussion in the former's work *al-Ṣawāʿiq*. A

al-ʿalīl fī masāʾil al-qaḍāʾ wal-qadar wal-ḥikma wal-taʿlīl in a similar way: "Man Chooses his Destiny: Ibn Qayyim al-Jawziyya's views on predestination," *Islam and Christian–Muslim Relations* 12/1 (2001), 62–63.

54 Ovamir Anjum, *Politics, Law, and Community in Islamic Thought: The Taymiyyan Moment*, Cambridge studies in Islamic civilization (Cambridge, New York: Cambridge University Press, 2012), 157–158; Holtzman, "The Politics of Fiṭra: On Ibn Taymiyya's Epistemological Optimism," An Essay Review on Politics, Law, and Community in Islamic Thought: The Taymiyyan Moment, by Ovamir Anjum, *Ilahiyat Studies: A Journal on Islamic and Religious Studies* 5 (2), 244.

vital conclusion rising from the discussion in chapter 1 was that Ibn Taymiyya played the interesting role of a popular preacher speaking to the masses and enjoying substantial public support, while simultaneously belonging to the scholastic and social elite of Mamluk Damascus. This unique societal-scholarly position was a contributing factor to the construction of a mode of discourse that transgressed the formal Ḥanbalite ultra-traditionalistic writing methods (i.e., mostly compiling citations of previous authoritative thinkers); therefore, it signifies a distinguishable intellectual Taymiyyan trend of scholarship. One can identify an author's compliance with this scholarship by the means of adequately qualifying the extent in which their output upholds the Taymiyyan ideology and mode of discourse. As for the matter at hand, it is vital to point out Ibn al-Qayyim's appropriation of the—at times, overshadowing—Taymiyyan intellectual legacy in *al-Ṣawāʿiq*.

Wael Hallaq's initially explored "Ibn Taymiyya's discourse" in the introduction to his book *Ibn Taymiyya against the Greek Logicians*, in which he translated Ibn Taymiyya's work *al-Radd ʿala 'l-manṭiqiyyīn* (Refutation of the Logicians).[55] He has already shown that Ibn Taymiyya formed a manner of discourse which was not at all confined to the formal Islamic writing methods known and used before him. His style differed from the then common practice of writing in that his main intention was to criticize his ideological adversaries, thereby guiding the reader towards the correct belief. His mission was not to simply display and deliver knowledge to his readers, but rather to convince them of the falsity of his opponents' credos. Therefore, Hallaq lists three main features of Taymiyyan discourse which should be taken into consideration while approaching his voluminous writings (or while comparing it with that of others). First, Taymiyyan discourse is highly digressive and easily shifts from one topic to another. In an attempt to recapture Ibn Taymiyya's complete view on a single matter, the modern reader often must consult dozens of his treatises, if not more. Second, due to its digressiveness, Taymiyyan discourse is abundant with repetitions. This feature fits the general persuasive nature of Ibn Taymiyya's writing, aiming to prevent stray souls from falling into the trap of disbelief. Third, Ibn Taymiyya seemed to be mostly preoccupied with articulating criticism and discontent regarding the issues at hand, instead of positively providing solutions for these predicaments. In this aspect, Taymiyyan discourse used by its originator is far from representing systemized and orderly notions;

55 Parts of Ibn Taymiyya's work *al-Radd ʿala 'l-manṭiqiyyīn* will be questioned in chapter 4; however, I rely here on Hallaq's inductors as stated in his preface to the translation: Wael Hallaq, *Ibn Taymiyya against the Greek Logicians* (Oxford: Oxford University Press, 1993).

logic and the systemization of ideas were not at all his main concern. In addition, Ibn Taymiyya did his best to accumulate and present as many arguments as possible in order to corroborate his disapproval of his rivals' claims. In this aspect, he seemed to prefer the quantity of reasoning elements to their logical structure.[56]

Previous studies conducted both on Ibn Taymiyya and Ibn al-Qayyim aptly illustrate the co-relation between the two scholars and demonstrate Ibn al-Qayyim's intellectual appropriation of Ibn Taymiyya. The main difference between the two scholars has more to do with style than doctrinal ideas or, as Irmeli Perho put it:

> Ibn Qayyim is known as the popularizer of Ibn Taymiyya's ideas and his views do not differ from those of his teacher. It is mainly in style that one finds the difference between the two scholars. Ibn Taymiyya wrote very sparse prose and expressed his doctrinal views with a minimum of elaboration. In contrast, Ibn Qayyim's prose is more didactic and he makes an effort to make his arguments understandable by illustrating them with examples and approaching them from different angles. His style approaches that of sermons, when he addresses the audience directly [...] His style makes his texts suitable to be read aloud, a quality that was indispensable for an author who wanted to spread his ideas in a society where only very few could afford to own books and many could not even read. Ibn Qayyim did not come with significant doctrinal developments or revolutionary new ideas, but his role was important in making his teacher's views accessible to a wider audience.[57]

In many cases, reading Ibn al-Qayyim's writings as complimentary sources is therefore highly useful while seeking a proper apprehension of Ibn Taymiyya's original ideas. Furthermore, it appears that Ibn al-Qayyim had absorbed his master's teachings and scholarly practices, some of which he later progressively developed into a careful systemization of Taymiyyan theories. Aiming at demonstrating Ibn al-Qayyim's systematic and rationalized appropriation of the theological texts written by Ibn Taymiyya on human free will and the concept of *fiṭra* (i.e., human natural predisposition), Livnat Holtzman argued that:

---

56 Hallaq, *Ibn Taimiyya against the Greek Logicians*, l–lii.

57 Irmeli Perho, "Man Chooses his Destiny", 61–70. Additional notes with a similar take can be found in several places in Jon Hoover's introduction to his book: *Ibn Taymiyya's Theodicy of Perpetual Optimism*, 3–8.

> Ibn Qayyim al-Jawziyya's role here is twofold: first, he offers an almost necessary elucidation of the unwieldy Taymiyyan style, which on its own requires a high degree of cautious reading. A parallel text by Ibn Qayyim al-Jawziyya almost always clarifies the meaning of Ibn Taymiyya's texts. Second, apart from being an editor and interpreter of Ibn Taymiyya, Ibn Qayyim al-Jawziyya takes Ibn Taymiyya's interpretation of the *fiṭra* tradition a step forwards, and he offers not only a refinement of Ibn Taymiyya's approach, but also a novel contribution of his own.[58]

Supported by the conclusions of this previous research, Ibn al-Qayyim's authorship in his vast *al-Ṣawaʿiq* definitely represents his adoption—as well as adaptation—of the Taymiyyan scholarly approach and manner of discourse. More than anything else, the text of *al-Ṣawaʿiq* confirms that Ibn al-Qayyim is an important exporter agent of Taymiyyan theological-theoretical ideas, actively adopting his mentor's ideological as well as practical scholarship. Unmistakable is the polemic tone taken by Ibn al-Qayyim in *al-Ṣawāʿiq* and the harsh criticism directed against his Ashʿarite intellectual opponents. Equally noticeable is Ibn al-Qayyim persuasive style of writing, in which he strives to compel his readers to agree with his ideas and reject those of his rivals. In addition, Ibn al-Qayyim also displays a use of abundant argumentations in *al-Ṣawāʿiq*, stressing the necessity of backing up his claims with numerous, accumulative sources. Another distinctive feature of the resemblance to the Taymiyyan approach—corroborated by prior research—is Ibn al-Qayyim's open-mindedness towards teachings of the speculative theological schools and his willingness to study and accept such teachings when he found them to be correct and fitting to the fundamental approach of the Quran and Sunna.[59] Ibn al-Qayyim does not hesitate to include early Ashʿarites or philosophers in his discussions in *al-Ṣawāʿiq* and, even more so, seems to highly appreciate their erudite contributions to the theological deliberation, as long as they can be combined with his particular traditionalistic purposes.

Another important aspect which illustrates Ibn al-Qayyim conforming to the Taymiyyan discourse in *al-Ṣawāʿiq* is upholding the mentor's interesting

58 Holtzman, "Human Choice, Divine Guidance and the Fiṭra Tradition: The Use of Ḥadīth in Theological Treatises by Ibn Taymiyya and Ibn Qayyim al-Jawziyya," in: eds. Yossef Rapoport and Shahab Ahmed, *Ibn Taymiyya and His Times* (Karachi: Oxford University Press, 2010), 165–166.

59 Irmeli Perho made a similar observation in the study: "Man Chooses his Destiny: Ibn Qayyim al-Jawziyya's views on predestination," *Islam and Christian–Muslim Relations* 12/1 (2001), 61–62.

tendency to supply the reader with a historical orientation. In *al-Ṣawāʿiq*, Ibn al-Qayyim strives to present his theological arguments in the light of an accurate historical context as it was known to him. This tendency is apparent, for example, in Ibn al-Qayyim's first *ṭāghūt* refutation where he discredits Fakhr al-Dīn al-Rāzī's epistemological principle of the 'universal rule' which was commonly practiced in the Mamluk *ʿulamāʾ* surroundings (see chapter 3); more so, this can be seen in the attack of the second *ṭāghūt* refutation on al-Ghazālī's 'universal rule of interpretation', justly recognized as the source from which the Rāziyyan version evolved (see chapter 4). Another instance for Ibn al-Qayyim's effort to place his theological discussion within historically precise boundaries is evident in his third *ṭāghūt* refutation, in which he extensively refers to the early Muʿtazilte provenance of the hermeneutical tool of *majāz*, later employed by the Ashʿarites (see chapter 5). As a whole, authoring an enormous work like *al-Ṣawāʿiq* against the principal Rāziyyan later Ashʿarite doctrines prevalent in his own time of activity demonstrates Ibn al-Qayyim attentiveness to concept of temporality in his writing.

Apart from the important axis of Ibn al-Qayyim's correspondence to the Taymiyyan discourse, one can indicate a number of major scholarly tendencies more singular to Ibn al-Qayyim than to his teacher; these can be seen in his deviations from the Taymiyyan discourse and, hence, in this appropriated and independent authorship. Several of Ibn al-Qayyim's argumentation techniques—also evident in *al-Ṣawāiq*—were already detected and discussed in previous studies, such as his inclination to incorporate massive bulks of citations taken from other works in his writing and his re-compilation of the sources brought into his discussions.[60] In one way or another, this tendency has to do with his attempt to accumulate evidence and spiritedly raising as many arguments as possible out of his broad literary arsenal. Ibn al-Qayyim can be distinguished from his mentor also in his positive reference to the subject matter and his conceptualization of a suitable alternative, to some degree. However, Ibn al-Qayyim's is especially differentiated from Ibn Taymiyya thanks to his highly ordered, systematic and didactical manner of writing.

As the next chapters illustrate, a crucial dimension of Ibn al-Qayyim's contribution to the Taymiyyan discourse is most dominantly his methodological systemization of the theoretical doctrines of his teacher in the fields of epistemology and hermeneutics. Standing out as a main element in the formation of logical reasoning, Ibn al-Qayyim's construction of *al-Ṣawāʿiq* in a distinct struc-

60 See footnote 39 in the introduction; Kokoschka and Krawietz, "Appropriating Ibn Taymiyya and Ibn Qayyim al-Jawziyya," 27–30.

ture (explained hereinafter in section 6.3) not only exemplifies his remarkable abilities for managing knowledge, it also represents his ability to didactically transmit knowledge to his readers. Moreover, since its systematic organization creates a more clearly defined array of textual units, i.e., the work's introduction and its four *ṭawāghīt*, as well as an overall cohesive textual unity, *al-Ṣawāʿiq*'s structural formation greatly impacts its produced conceptual contents. Such an orderly arrangement also cultivates the interplay of mutual relations between textual units, which can be more conveniently followed and, therefore, grasped. Unlike his teacher, Ibn al-Qayyim's high sensitivity to literary aesthetics in *al-Ṣawāʿiq* assisted him in maximizing the advantages of the formal writing structure for a systemization of contents.

The systemization displayed in *al-Ṣawāʿiq* definitely reflects Ibn al-Qayyim's scholarly image and makes him shine as a sophisticated scholar, including in ways that Ibn Taymiyya did not. As already pointed out by Wael Hallaq, Ibn Taymiyya inclined towards digressiveness of writing and tended to depart from the subject matter.[61] Later, Ovamir Anjum supported Hallaq's view, stating that: "[Ibn Taymiyya] was far from being a system builder; in this lay his greatest strength as well as the limit of all his thought."[62] Therefore, Ibn al-Qayyim's systematic construction of the Taymiyyan epistemological and hermeneutical theories in *al-Ṣawāʿiq* can be observed as an advanced representation of the Taymiyyan discourse, in terms of themes, methodology and structure. As a result, *al-Ṣawāʿiq* emerges as a text representing a remarkable development of Taymiyyan theoretical foundations and methodology.

Supplementary indication of Ibn al-Qayyims systemization tendency in *al-Ṣawāʿiq* becomes apparent when we look at the work in the light of *Ijtimāʿ al-juyūsh al-islāmiyya* and *al-Kāfiya al-shāfiya*,[63] his other theological writing on the issue of the divine attributes. Whereas all three works convey Taymiyyan theological teachings and are directed against the Ashʿarite contemporaries of Mamluk Damascus, they greatly diverge in terms of literary genres and rhetorical devices (i.e., each of the texts is profoundly different). One of the most prominent ways in which *al-Ṣawāʿiq* varies from the other two works is indeed its inherent involvement with the theoretical foundations of Taymiyyan thought, which also shapes it in a systematical fashion. Leaving aside the massive, politically oriented poem *al-Kāfiya al-shāfiya*, *al-Ṣawāʿiq*'s uniqueness is

61 This claim is raised in the introduction to Hallaq's book *Ibn-Taymiyya against the Greek Logicians* (Oxford: Oxford University Press, 1993).

62 Anjum, *Politics, Law, and Community in Islamic Thought: The Taymiyyan Moment*, 183–184.

63 Both works were presented in section 2.1 above.

more clearly set out when contrasted with the formally structured traditionalistic composition *Ijtimāʿ al-juyūsh*, which has already been considered a premature version of *al-Ṣawāʿiq* in modern research.[64] Assuming that the sources at Ibn al-Qayyim's disposal in the course of writing the two works were more or less the same, he produced two very different types of works despite their thematic closeness. The dissimilarity between Ibn al-Qayyim's structure of writing in these two works can be illustrated in numerous cases in which he integrates in *al-Ṣawāʿiq*'s text more minor sections from his previous *Ijtimāʿ al-juyūsh*.[65] Given the structure of *al-Ṣawāʿiq*, this difference seems to be more than a simple case of elaboration vs. abbreviation, but rather a difference of structural function. In *Ijtimāʿ al-juyūsh* the aim was to accumulate a critical mass of arguments (e.g., in favor of the essential reality of the divine attribute of aboveness), perhaps for the traditionalistic circles of learning; however, in *al-Ṣawāʿiq* the aim was to substantiate the much larger and more radical claim of seeing *taʾwīl* as a widespread destructive phenomenon that distorts the entire meaning of sacred Islamic texts; hence, this is a distortion of the connection between God and His creation. Ibn al-Qayyim's techniques and goals of writing seem to have substantially progressed by the time he authored *al-Ṣawāʿiq*. His knowledge arrangement tendency grew from serving the purpose of accumulating a critical mass of textual evidence, and transformed into a systemization of the theoretical foundations standing at the very core of the theological knowledge discussed to support objectives of far more dialectical nature—reaffirming the key, primary place of the Islamic sources of Revelation.

2.4 *Al-Ṣawāʿiq* as a *Kalām* Manual: Ibn al-Qayyim's Rationalization

Previous studies concentrating on Ibn al-Qayyim's literary oeuvre classified *al-Ṣawāʿiq* in different ways, using diverse labels in their taxonomy of Ibn al-Qayyim's works. For instance, in his book on Ibn al-Qayyim's place within Islamic thought, ʿAwḍ Allāh Ḥijāzī brought up *al-Ṣawāʿiq*—mentioned only

64 Holtzman, "Ibn Qayyim al-Jawziyya (1292–1350)," 202, 214–215, 217; Krawietz, "Ibn Qayyim al-Jawzīyah: His Life and Works," 30–33.

65 For example: the bulk of citation taken from Ibn Rushd's work *al-Kashf an manāhij al-adilla fī ʿaqāʾid al-milla* that Ibn al-Qayyim incorporated in *al-Ṣawāʿiq* (which is explored in section 5.6 henceforth) appears in *Ijtimāʿ al-juyūsh* in a considerably shortened and somewhat simplified version; Ibn Qayyim al-Jawziyya, *Ijtimāʿ al-juyūsh al-islāmiyya*, 2:322–326; Holtzman and Ovadia, "On Divine Aboveness (*al-Fawqiyya*): The Development of Rationalized Ḥadīth-Based Argumentations in Islamic Theology," (forthcoming, 2018), 43–46.

in a few words—as an example of works of speculative theology and philosophy (*fī ʿilm al-kalām wal-falsafa*).[66] Birgit Krawietz mostly described *al-Ṣawāʿiq* as a "voluminous opus of inner-Islamic religious polemics", stressing Ibn al-Qayyim's adherence to his short-tempered teacher Ibn Taymiyya.[67] Livnat Holtzman chose to emphasize *al-Ṣawāʿiq* as a "mature work of dogmatic theology", in which Ibn al-Qayyim had contested dubious doctrines according to his own opinion.[68] Largely outlining *al-Ṣawāʿiq*'s themes and structure, Yasir Qadhi designated it as "one of the most exhaustive treatises of theology that Ibn al-Qayyim authored".[69] Although principally remaining in the realm of intellectual and theological debates, the semantic nuances expressed in such varied prior studies exemplify an undeniable difficulty in firmly placing the text *al-Ṣawāʿiq* into a single thematic or theoretical framework.

Since *al-Ṣawāʿiq* is considered to be Ibn al-Qayyim's magnum opus in which he expressed a notable diversion of intellectual concerns, discerning *al-Ṣawāʿiq*'s framework is by far more than a semantic quibble. Assessing it from a wide angle, *al-Ṣawāʿiq* indeed discusses the theological questions of the divine attributes and anthropomorphism; however, the majority of the text deals with other theoretical topics, mainly hermeneutics and epistemology. Clearly, the theological deliberations expressed in *al-Ṣawāʿiq* fulfill the functional purpose of delivering his political criticism against his Ashʿarite contemporaries. It is therefore vital to examine the multiple theological aspects echoed in *al-Ṣawāʿiq* beyond the somewhat overly generalized descriptions of it as a work of Islamic theology or polemics. For these reasons, I would like to offer a more precise definition of the—thus far—slightly perplexing framework of *al-Ṣawāʿiq* in order to deepen our understanding of the intellectual prospects Ibn al-Qayyim pursued while writing this extremely complex work; in other words, better exploring the theological orientation Ibn al-Qayyim demonstrated in *al-Ṣawāʿiq*. Although it is uniformly dedicated to the issue of divine attributes, the theological dimension of *al-Ṣawāʿiq* is of a considerably broad character; in fact, it can be seen as the thematic encompassing umbrella under which Ibn al-Qayyim voiced the Taymiyyan criticism against the rationalistic argumenta-

66 ʿAwḍallāh Ḥijāzī, *Ibn al-Qayyim wa-mawqifuh^u min al-tafkīr al-islāmī* ([Cairo]: Majmaʿ al-Buḥūth al-Islāmiyya, 1392/1972), 47.

67 Birgit Krawietz, "Ibn Qayyim al-Jawzīyah: His Life and Works," 30–31.

68 Livnat Holtzman, "Ibn Qayyim al-Jawziyya (1292–1350)," 214, 217.

69 Yasir Qadhi, "'The Unleashed Thunderbolts' of Ibn Qayyim al-Jawziyya: An Introductory Essay," in *A Scholar in the Shadow: Essays in the Legal and Theological Thought of Ibn Qayyim al-Ğawziyyiah*, ed. Caterina Bori and Livnat Holtzman, *Oriente Moderno 90/1* (2010), 136.

tion methods in the theoretical fields of epistemology and hermeneutics. The following table will illustrate the matter:[70]

Ṭāghūt	**Rationalistic principle to be refuted**	**Theoretical subject**
1	The texts of the Qur'an and Hadith contain verbal evidence (*adilla lafẓiyya*) which do not produce certain knowledge (*ʿilm yaqīn*)	Epistemology
2	In case of conflict, Reason (*ʿaql*) is prior to Revelation (*naql*)	Epistemology / Hermeneutics
3	Anthropomorphic expressions are allegories (*majazāt*) of no reality (*ḥaqīqa*)	Hermeneutics
4	Prophetic tradition with a limited number of chains of transmissions (e.g., *ḥadīth al-āḥād*) cannot produce certain knowledge	Epistemology

Advancing the known Taymiyyan theological creed, Ibn al-Qayyim's *al-Ṣawāʿiq* targeted admonishing the very core of rationalistic epistemological and hermeneutical theories and their skeptical approach to the texts of the Quran and the Hadith literature. As the examination on the following chapters will shortly illustrate, Ibn al-Qayyim applies a very logical, dialectic and systemized writing fashion, substantially remote from any sort of traditionalistic writing presented in his time, even the Taymiyyan one. Thus, under the thematic scope of the theological issue of divine attributes in *al-Ṣawāʿiq*, Ibn al-Qayyim attacks four major rationalistic modes of argumentation, while systematically engaging with their underlying theories of epistemology and hermeneutics. Ibn al-Qayyim actually composed a work of a highly developed traditionalistic writing mode which I designate as 'rationalized-traditionalism'.

A work of advanced theological discourse that cultivates the Taymiyyan creed, I argue *al-Ṣawāʿiq* represents a stark rationalized tendency, and therefore can be considered a traditionalistic *Kalām* manual. The dialectical nature of *al-Ṣawāʿiq* is evident both in the sense of its discursive style of theological argumentation and in a thematic sense, for its coverage of further theoretical

70 Ibn Qayyim al-Jawziyya, *al-Ṣawāʾiq*, 2:632.

fields of knowledge other than theology alone.[71] In other words, *al-Ṣawāʿiq* is a traditionalistic work of the literary genre of *Kalām*, i.e., a work of dialectical and speculative reasoning which promotes traditionalistic theological tenets as an alternative model to the later Ashʿarite ones. In order to repudiate his rationalistic adversaries, it seems Ibn al-Qayyim—whether consciously or not—puts into practice their own discourse of dialecticism. Perhaps vanquishing one's powerful opponents in their own arena amplifies and sweetens to an even greater extent the scale of victory. However, to the best of my understanding, Ibn al-Qayyim did not express any deliberate objective to experiment with *Kalām*-like writing in *al-Ṣawāʿiq*, let alone to compose an exclusively *Kalām*ic work. Furthermore, as will be demonstrated along the reading of the text in the course of the following chapters, almost every even minor reference to the rationalistic methodologies and concepts is accompanied by a derogatory title of some kind. And yet, a careful inspection of both the stylistic and the thematic characteristics of *al-Ṣawāʿiq* points to the conclusion that it is indeed a work of *Kalām*, or at least a highly rationalized-traditionalistic composition.

Unfortunately, the subject of Ḥanbalite engagement with *Kalām* has yet to be addressed in detail in modern research;[72] even when it discussed Ibn

71 The term *Kalām* is used to describe two close yet different meanings in Islamic thought: 1. *kalām* is first off a rhetorical or stylistic manner of theological argumentation, usually in a logical and speculative manner; 2. *Kalām* (often written with a capital *K*, meaning *ʿilm al-Kalām*) is one branch of the two main trends in Islamic theology in general, while the second the is traditionalistic theology (*ʿilm uṣūl al-dīn*, the science of religious principles). *Kalām* in this sense refers to Islamic theology which is articulated by the means of the stylistic *kalām*. In addition, *Kalām* as a 'science of rationality' may also include other areas of examination apart from theology (e.g., epistemology or physics); Alexander Treiger, "Origins of *Kalām*," *the Oxford Handbook of Islamic Theology*, p. 3; Livnat Holtzman, "Islamic Theology," in: *Handbook of medieval studies: terms—methods—trends*, 3 volumes, ed. Albrecht Classen (Berlin: De Gruyter, 2010), 1:56–57; Richard M. Frank, "The Science of Kalām," *Arabic Sciences and Philosophy*, vol. 2 (1992), 15–16.

72 A.J. Wensinck has already pointed out in his book *The Muslim Creed* (1932) to an "intellectualizing process" of traditionalistic Islam and "increasing systematizing tendencies", mostly concerning Ashʿarite theology; ibid, 254 footnote 1, 248, 270; Alas, as noted by G. Makdisi in 1997, "for Wensinck, as for scholars generally, at the time, a Hanbali religious intellectual such as Ibn Taymiyya 'stood aloof from the main current of Muslim thought'." Makdisi, *Ibn ʿAqil*, 76; A more positive—yet still early—reference to the significance of the Taymiyyan discourse in this respect can be found in A.J. Arberry's series of lectures from 1965, where he wrote that Ibn Taymiyya "displays in his polemical broadsides a superb mastery of the method of dialectical reasoning." Arberry, *Revelation and Reason in Islam*, 18–19. Another important study of the process of rationalization in Islamic religious thought is: Watt, *The Formative Period of Islamic Thought* (1973).

Taymiyya's 'rational tendency,' it neglected Ibn al-Qayyim.[73] Expanding the horizons of secondary literature on the topic of *Kalām* amid the Ḥanbalites, the following investigation unfolds Ibn al-Qayyim's singular mode of rationalization of the traditionalistic argumentation methods along the text of *al-Ṣawāʿiq*. Moreover, Ibn al-Qayyim's *al-Ṣawāʿiq* is an example of the dissemination of methodologies and means of expression and argumentation between traditionalism and rationalism, clearly indicating the traditionalistic party as the more receptive end of the two. Ibn al-Qayyim's turn towards the deployment of *Kalām*ic discourse may come as a surprise given his modest personal characteristics as a humble scholar; however, such a permeable outlook was in fact not uncommon among Muslim scholars with either a traditionalistic or rationalistic affiliation. In fact, my argument here about Ibn al-Qayyim's absorbance of *Kalām*ic authorship to criticize rationalistic theology resembles in its gist to an interesting argument made by Anke von Kügelgen recently with respect to Ibn Taymiyya. Exploring his condemnation Aristotelian philosophy, von Kügelgen explored Ibn Taymiyya's approach in his work *al-Radd ʿala 'l-manṭiqiyyīn* (Refutation of the Logicians) and his use of philosophical tools of logic in order to contradict it.[74] The teacher's example could have been a source of inspiration for Ibn al-Qayyim (*al-Radd ʿala 'l-manṭiqiyyīn* will be addressed with direct relation to the epistemological discuaaion in *al-Ṣawāʿiq* in chapter 3). Notwithstanding, especially in the view of formally fashioned traditionalistic works, Ibn al-Qayyim's *al-Ṣawāʿiq* represents a highly developed demonstration not only of the Taymiyyan discourse, but also the process of rationalization of Ḥanbalite-traditionalistic thought in Islam.

According to George Makdisi, for example, by the 5th/11th century the evolution of the Islamic dogmatic thought resulted with the formation of "three kinds of theologies" throughout history: *Kalām* (i.e., Muʿtazilite—then Ashʿarite—speculative rationalistic theology), *uṣūl al-fiqh* (i.e., legal methodology based on theological conceptions), and *uṣūl al-dīn* (i.e., theology as the discussion on religious principles of belief). The ambiguity between these 'three

73 For example: Özervarli, "The Qur'ānic Rational Theology of Ibn Taymiyya and His Criticism of the Mutakallimūn" (2010); Anjum, *Politics, Law, and Community in Islamic Thought: The Taymiyyan Moment* (2012), 183–184; more recently published are two articles from 2016: Abrahamov "Scripturalist and Traditionalist Theology," and Hoover, "Ḥanbalī Theology."

74 Anke von Kügelgen, "The Poison of Philosophy: Ibn Taymiyya's Struggle For and Against Reason," in: *Islamic Theology, Philosophy and Law: Debating Ibn Taymiyya and Ibn Qayyim al-Jawziyya*, eds. Birgit Krawietz and Georges Tamer, Studien zur Geschichte und Kultur des islamischen Orients Neue Folge 27 (Berlin, Boston: De Gruyter, 2013), 253–328.

theologies' is inevitable, Makdisi said: "The surest way to tell whether a work on theology was Traditionalist or Rationalist is to examine the contents; for *uṣūl al-dīn* could contain one or the other or the two other theologies, depending on the author."[75] More specifically connected to the intellectual growth towards rationalized-traditionalism in Ibn al-Qayyim's time is the traditionalistic attitude towards *Kalām*, or as Makdisi put it: "Traditionalist orthodoxy condemned *kalām* as unorthodox, but made use of it for its apologetic function. *Kalām* was kept out of the process for determining orthodoxy—excluded from its contents, but kept for the purpose of defending Islam against heretical doctrines, including those of non-Islamic origin."[76]

In fact, studies convincingly show that there was never a definite separation between traditionalistic scholars and the rationalistic ones, but rather a fluid intellectual diffusion between the two streams of Islamic thought. Scholars at both ends of the spectrum shared the same education and yielded similar intellectual products.[77] Focusing on the Ḥanbalite theological school, Makdisi has already observed and carefully explained the complexity of rationalistic inclinations within the traditionalistic theological thought. Makdisi stresses that despite the modest significance of Ḥanbalism as a legal school, its position as a theological force within the general traditionalistic movement was of special significance. The Ḥanbalites became "the mouthpiece of the traditionalistic movement (*ahl al-sunna wal-ḥadīth*)," although they most definitely were not a monolithic school: it had its share of inner antagonisms reflected in rivalries between the more rigid Ḥanbalite scholars, who adhered to the purely traditionalistic teachings relying on the Quran, Hadith and the sayings if the *salaf*, and other Ḥanbalite scholars, who demonstrated what was perceived as 'rationalistic' tendencies in their work.[78] The early diffusion of rationalistic argumentation methods into the traditionalistic movement is highly valuable

---

75 Makdisi, *Ibn ʿAqil: Religion and Culture in Classical Islam* (Edinburgh: Edinburgh University Press, 1997), 73–75.

76 Makdisi, *Ibn ʿAqil*, 73.

77 Makdisi, "Ḥanbalite Islam", 240–242, 263–264; a case study of this phenomenon with relation to the theological issue of the divine attributes is examined in: Holtzman and Ovadia, "On God's Aboveness" (forthcoming 2018).

78 Makdisi notes several Ḥanbalite scholars who authored works of refutation against their predecessor scholars of the same school, for example: Ibn Qudāma (d. 622/1225) wrote a work against what he believed to be Ibn ʿAqīl's "rationalistic Ashʿarite" tendencies. Another example given is Ibn al-Jawzī (d. 597/1201), who wrote a work refuting the ideas of the Ḥanbalite scholars Ibn Ḥamīd (d. 403/1012), Abū Yaʿlā Ibn al-Farrāʾ (d. 458/1066) and Abu 'l-Ḥasan ibn al-Zāghūnī (d. 527/1132); Makdisi, "Ḥanbalite Islam," 238–242.

and should be kept in mind when one intends to read an abundant amount of theological texts written in Mamluk times and, more specifically, Ibn al-Qayyim's *al-Ṣawāʿiq*.

The typological classification of *al-Ṣawāʿiq* as a *Kalām* manual is further confirmed in view of its foremost theoretical content involving epistemology and hermeneutics, since it largely fits the formal constitution of many rationalistic works of *Kalām*. In his article "The Science of *Kalām*", R.M. Frank designates the nature of the science of *Kalām* deployed by the Muʿtazilites and Ashʿarites as "the rational science", that is: formal, conceptualized or speculative reasoning; similar to the practices of *naẓr* or *ta'ammul* (contemplating, cogitating or reflecting) which are meant to establish true knowledge on the metaphysical. Noteworthy is his distinction between the above-mentioned lexical use of the term *Kalām* as "the science of the basic doctrines in Islam" (*ʿilm uṣūl al-dīn*) and the use of the term *Kalām* as an equivalent to the terms *jadal* or *munāẓara* (disputing or debating), which more broadly denote dialectical scholastic disputations on varied topics, also other than the basic religious theories. Speaking of *Kalām* as the science of speculative reasoning on doctrinal matters, Frank claims that the contents under scrutiny in the text also indicate its *Kalām*ic orientation, and sketches a general pattern of topics and their order of appearance in most works of *Kalām*. Described in general, these are: (1) Justified knowledge (2) God's existence and His attributes (3) The Prophet and the meaning of prophecy to human souls. The first section on knowledge and theoretical reasoning has to do with the sources of knowledge and "establishing the principles of scientific reasoning both in general and for other sciences;" viz. the common exposition of *Kalām* compendia includes the involvement with epistemological topics relevant to all disciplines of religious thought. The two main parts thereafter appear to vary in their inner subjects and structure, and yet elaborately address metaphysics including supplying explanations and validations of "the cognitive meaning of the symbolic language in which belief is originally achieved and is actively transmitted;" viz. hermeneutics, or clarification of the cognitive meaning of the sacred texts according to the theological viewpoint of the author. Merging these theoretical discussions together, works of *Kalām* set forth an all-embracing theological dogma.[79]

79 Frank, "The Science of *Kalām*," 7–37; Frank explicitly excludes the Ḥanbalite *ʿulamāʾ* from having used *Kalām*, ibid, 24–25, 37. However, when taking works such as Ibn al-Qayyim's *al-Ṣawāʿiq* into account, Frank's attitude towards Ḥanbalism seems to be somewhat of an over-generalization. Then again, this is not particularly surprising given the fact that, due to his commitment to the underlying teachings of Ibn Taymiyya, both of them representing rationalized traditionalism in the post-classical period, Ibn al-Qayyim is a not typical

Observing the contents of *al-Ṣawāʿiq* in a linear reading, the monograph can be considered a developed representation not only of the *munāẓarāt* discourse (religious debates), but also the debates of the scholars of *Kalām* in the rationalized form of *jadal al-mutakallimīn*. In effect, Ibn al-Qayyim dressed his traditionalism in rationalistic or '*Kalām*-like' attire; hence, rationalizing Ibn Taymiyya's extreme traditionalistic stances, in both themes and argumentation methods, as an alternative model to the later Ashʿarite ones. The interior order of contents of the text of *al-Ṣawāʿiq* appears to closely resemble the guidelines of the *Kalām*'s rationalized theology, as depicted by Frank. This order consists of an exhaustive discussion on epistemology and the theoretical definitions of certain knowledge (first, second and fourth *ṭawāghīt* refutations in *al-Ṣawāʿiq*), then continues to an advanced deliberation on hermeneutics and interpretation devices on the subject of the divine attributes (third *ṭāghūt* refutation). Hence, the order of the rationalistic fundamental thinking methods Ibn al-Qayyim chooses to attack virtually follows the lines of many works of the fields of *Kalām*. Striking in this regard is Ibn al-Qayyim's reversed use of the *Kalām*ic techniques, overturning the function of the so-called 'purely' rationalistic discourse for his individual dialectic purposes. In fact, he composed a solid monograph which articulates the Taymiyyan-traditionalistic stances, creating a mirror image of the Ashʿarite-rationalistic *Kalām*ic discourse; thus, Ibn al-Qayyim uses the platform of *Kalām* to refute it. Basically, *al-Ṣawāʿiq* converts the framework of *Kalām* from "the rational science" in its classical sense to a cleverly modified form of traditionalism, or "rationalized-traditionalism," intertwining compound discussions on epistemology and hermeneutics together with uncompromising traditionalistic theological standpoints.

Ibn al-Qayyim's manifestation of dialectical rationalized-traditionalistic writing in *al-Ṣawāʿiq* may be a result of his general course of education which allowed him to develop close familiarity with Ashʿarite rationalistic argumen-

---

example of Ḥanbalite thought. However, even in the classical period, one can name both Abū Yaʿlā (d. 458/1066) and Ibn ʿAqīl (d. 513/1119) together with Ibn al-Jawzi (d. 597/1201) as exemplary exceptions to Frank's resounding assentation, which approved of rationalistic theology.

Mustafa Shah discusses the evolution of Islamic theological thought and the attention it received from Western research in a highly instructive article. He notes there the disagreement between Makdisi and Frank on the matter of rationalization inclinations in Islamic traditionalistic thought, and even on the originality of the rationalistic tendency of the Ashʿarite school's eponym, Abu 'l-Ḥasan al-Ashʿarī (d. 324/935); Shah, "Trajectories in the Development of Islamic Theological Thought: the Synthesis of *Kalām*," *Religion Compass* 1/4 (2007): 441–444.

tation techniques.[80] Indeed, this fact can explain his impressive expertise of practicing such rationalistic kinds of argumentation methods. Another feature gaining Ibn al-Qayyim deeper familiarity with dialectical argumentation methodologies was most likely his active participation in theological and intellectual debates in the public sphere (i.e., *munāẓarāt*). This can also clarify the much harsher polemical tone of writing in Ibn al-Qayyim's relatively late-period of activity after his release from prison in Damascus and the death of Ibn Taymiyya. Consequently, it would be reasonable to consider *al-Ṣawāʿiq* and its dialectical approach as Ibn al-Qayyim's independent appropriation of *Kalām* as well as an instrumental measure for his own use while discussing the topics of epistemology and hermeneutics. Therefore, Ibn al-Qayyim's writing of *Kalām*—i.e., rationalized speculative theology—in *al-Ṣawāʿiq* is to be seen through this lens, reflecting a rationalistic argumentation method of articulating so-called traditionalistic theological positions. The text of *al-Ṣawāʿiq* is thus a projected embodiment of the *Kalām* discourse culture of Ibn al-Qayyim's times.

2.5 Against *taʾwīl*: *al-Ṣawāʿiq*'s Main Argument

Al-Ṣawāʿiq's introduction contains Ibn al-Qayyim's first theological discussion, in which he generally disputes the rationalistic hermeneutical technique of *taʾwīl* applied on the divine attributes which, according to him, distorts the original meaning of the texts sacred to Islam. Since Ibn al-Qayyim deliberately renounces it, focusing on the introduction of *al-Ṣawāʿiq* will enable a better understanding of the perception of *taʾwīl* held by Ibn al-Qayyim throughout the entire work.[81] Ibn al-Qayyim's introduction to *al-Ṣawāʿiq* opens with

---

80 Holtzman and Bori provide an interesting survey of the thus far little known details concerning Ibn al-Qayyim's educational period in their introduction to the book: *A Scholar in the Shadow: Essays in the Legal and Theological Thought of Ibn Qayyim al-Ǧawziyyiah*, ed. Caterina Bori and Livnat Holtzman, *Oriente Moderno* 90/1 (2010), 17–19. I also referred to that in chapter 1.

81 Ibn al-Qayyim's introduction to his work appears in: Ibn al-Qayyim, *al-Ṣawāʿiq al-mursala*, 1:169–2:545. It is noteworthy that the sections dealing with the meaning of the term *taʾwīl* were omitted in Ibn al-Mawṣilī's abridgement, and were only mentioned briefly in the summary of his introduction. Al-Dakhīl Allāh lists those sections, mentioning that out of the 24 sections: 11 appear in full version in the abridgement, 7 appear only partially, and the remaining 6 were completely omitted; Ibn al-Qayyim, *al-Ṣawāʿiq al-mursala*, 1:94, 118, 161–170; Yasir Qadhi, "'The Unleashed Thunderbolts'," 139.

his depiction of his contemporary scholastic atmosphere of severe intellectual tensions within the traditionalistic stream of Islamic thought, as a result of multiplying rationalistic influences. At the beginning of the introduction, Ibn al-Qayyim describes the prominence of the messengers and prophets sent by God—particularly the Prophet Muḥammad—with regards to transmitting divine knowledge to the whole of mankind so as to acknowledge the monotheistic faith in the sole God and His attributes. Ibn al-Qayyim argues it would be absurd to presume the Prophet Muḥammad transmitted knowledge to mankind about the most corporeal matters, such as customs of eating, drinking or intercourse, yet denied it from learning the very precious knowledge on "what is to be expressed by their tongues, and believed in their hearts with regard to the Lord"; after all, that is the most sublime knowledge of all. Likewise, he continues, it would be an absurd to presume the Prophet explained heresy without informing people about the obscene *taʾwīl* and *majāz* as well as the appropriate way to use their Reason and mind.[82]

Ibn al-Qayyim criticizes the rationalists (*khalaf*, i.e., later-scholars)—who relied on Greek philosophy—for their poor understanding of the theological issue of divine attributes, which he saw as a consequence of their departure from the guiding path of their righteous Muslim predecessors (*salaf*). The rationalists were mistaken in their belief that the early Muslim scholars recited the texts of the Quran and Hadith with no deep intellectual capacity for understanding them. Without any reasonable justification, the rationalists undertook the responsibility of extracting the "true" meaning from the texts of Islam, for which they used over-complicated linguistic devices. Their prime methodology for this task was the *taʾwīl*, viz. a re-interpretation of the texts for which they relied exclusively on Reason, abandoning their predecessor's thought.[83]

Al-Dakhīl Allah, the editor of the work, states that Ibn al-Qayyim does not mention a direct reason for writing *al-Ṣawāʿiq*. He adds that it might be possible that the work was composed as a reply to a rhetorical question posed by Ibn Taymiyya in his theological treatise *al-Ḥamawiyya ʾl-kubrā*,[84] which Ibn al-Qayyim cited early in his introduction:

82 It is noteworthy that this argument is not unique to Ibn al-Qayyim, as it had already appeared in a work of the Ḥanbalite scholar Abū Bakr al-Ājurī (d. 360/971), who was well known to Ibn al-Qayyim; Ibn al-Qayyim, *al-Ṣawāʿiq al-mursala*, 1:93–94, 157–158; Ibn al-Mawṣilī, *Mukhtaṣar al-Ṣawāʾiq*, 1:7–9; Yasir Qadhi, "'The Unleashed Thunderbolts'," 139; Livnat Holtzman, "Anthropomorphism," *EI—THREE*, 1:50.

83 Ibn al-Qayyim, *al-Ṣawāʿiq al-mursala*, 1:161–170.

84 *Al-Ḥamawiyya ʾl-kubrā* was previously mentioned in chapter 1, as it was the main writing for which Ibn Taymiyya had been put to trial. The passage cited appears in: Ibn Taymiyya,

> Our Shaykh said: How can these debarred from good, deficient, embarrassed people be more knowledgeable of God, His attributes, His names, and His verses than the first and previous *muhājirīn* [i.e. the Meccans who emigrated with the Prophet Muḥammad to Medina], *al-anṣār* [i.e. Muḥammad's supporters in Medina], and those who followed them in good deeds? … And how can those young chicks of *al-mutafalsifa* [i.e. the 'so-called' philosophers],[85] the followers of the Indians and the Greeks, the followers of the legacy of the Zoroastrians and of *al-mushrikīn* [i.e. those who shared the believe in God with other copartners], those straying juniors and their kind, be more knowledgeable of God than [the adherents of] the legacy of the Prophets and the people of Quran and belief?[86]

This passage ultimately reflects the martial Taymiyyan spirit of an ideological attack against the newly presented thinking methods considered foreign to the 'authentic' Islamic tradition. In this respect, since it conveys the well-known traditionalistic fideistic approach of firmly adhering to the Islamic textual sources, the polemic idea is of no real novelty when one is seeking comprehensive theoretical traces. Moreover, given the very high level of discourse expressed in *al-Ṣawāʿiq*, it is hardly believable that the reason for its whole creation stemmed from a quite standard rhetorical question such as this one. Hence, Al-Dakhīl Allah's first suggestion—that Ibn al-Qayyim's introduction to *al-Ṣawāʿiq* lacks clearly stated objectives—seems accurate. Such objectives must therefore be embedded in the introduction, in its content and in Ibn al-Qayyim's engagement with the notion of *taʾwīl*.

The discussion on *taʾwīl* in the introduction of *al-Ṣawāʿiq* covers 24 sections, in which Ibn al-Qayyim presents his underlying conceptions regarding the proper act of interpretation when dealing with the Islamic sacred texts of the Quran and Hadith. Noteworthy is the very organized thematic interrogation held by Ibn al-Qayyim, discussing the term *taʾwīl* from several trajectories: firs, he discusses the *taʾwīl* as a linguistic phenomenon within the field of Arabic language. As he does so, Ibn al-Qayyim incorporates a large verity of theological arguments and substantiations, mainly while criticizing his adversaries (sec-

---

Taqi 'l-Dīn Aḥmad (d. 728/1328), *al-Fatwā 'l-Ḥamawiya 'l-kubrā*, ed. Ḥamad ʿAbd al-Muḥsin al-Tuwayjirī (Riyadh: Dār al-Ṣamīʿī, 1425/2004), 197–200.

85 *Afrākh al-mutafalsifa* is a term used by Ibn Taymiyya that refers with obvious discontent to Arabs who embraced the Hellenistic sciences; See in the footnote above.

86 Ibn al-Qayyim, *al-Ṣawāʿiq al-mursala*, the editor's preface, 1: 84, and also in *al-Ṣawāʿiq* itself, 1:169–170.

tions 1–14). Second, Ibn al-Qayyim treats *ta'wīl* as an intellectual phenomenon with perilous repercussions on the whole realm of Islamic thought (sections 15–24). Ibn al-Qayyim's introduction on *ta'wīl* will be surveyed hereinafter in a close-reading, with the aim of identifying the main objectives of this discussion. Furthermore, as has already been stated, this introduction lacks clearly proclaimed targets or stated reasons for writing *al-Ṣawāʿiq*. Determining the main objectives of the introduction will shed more light on the theoretical framework in which *al-Ṣawāʿiq* was composed.

Ta'wīl *as Linguistic Phenomenon*

1 Defining the Act of *ta'wīl* (Sections 1–5)

In line with the definition presented by Ibn al-Qayyim in the introduction's first section, *ta'wīl* is primarily a linguistic term whose meaning corresponds to *tafsīr*, (i.e., to return to a word's original meaning); therefore, the act of *ta'wīl* is defined as the act of interpreting or explaining the original meaning of a word. This is the manner in which the term *ta'wīl* is used in the Quran and Hadith: *ḥaqīqat al-maʿnā*, meaning the essence of the word, or its first denotation. Such use of the term *ta'wīl* is also apparent among early interpreters (*ahl al-tafsīr*), referring to jurisprudence and Hadith: interpretation for a knowledgeable perception of a meaning. Supplying evidence for this understanding, Ibn al-Qayyim quotes Aḥmad ibn Ḥanbal's from *al-Radd ʿala 'l-zanādiqa wal-jahmiyya* saying: some apply (false) *ta'wīl* on the Quran *ʿalā ghayr^{i} ta'wīlih^{i}*, i.e., in a way which differs from its (true) *ta'wīl*. Ibn al-Qayyim maintains that the *mutakallimūn* utilize the term *ta'wīl* in a contradictory manner to its initial virtuous linguistic meaning of *tafsīr*. In their view, *ta'wīl* is an interpretation which contradicts the real origin of an expression as apparent in the text, imposing a figurative meaning on it that requires an indicative proof (*dalīl*).[87] Subsequently, Ibn al-Qayyim distinguishes between a correct (*ṣaḥīḥ*) and false and inappropriate (*bāṭil*) usage of the term *ta'wīl*. In his opinion, a permissible interpretation is that which conforms to the Quran and Hadith. Any other interpretation altering the meaning as it conveyed in the text is seen as faulty and, hence, invalid.[88]

Additionally, Ibn al-Qayyim defines the term *ta'wīl* within the boundaries of Arabic linguistic discourse. According to his definition, *ta'wīl* is an utterance which describes the speaker's intention in an informative manner (*ikhbār*),

87 The term *dalīl* is broadly deliberated in: van Ess, *Theologie und Gesellschaft*, 4:639–640.

88 Ibn al-Qayyim, *al-Ṣawāʿiq al-mursala*, 1:175–180, 187, 215; Yasir Qadhi, "'The Unleashed Thunderbolts'," 139.

and not in a performative manner (*inshāʾ*);[89] in other words, interpretation produces an utterance which assists in understanding the speaker's communicative intention, utilizing his own words in a factual-declarative description of his speech and its meaning. This definition relies on the postulation that the speaker uses expressions (*alfāẓ*, linguistic signs) of clear and apparent (*ẓāhir*) semantic-grammatical meaning in the syntactic function imposed by the speaker (*waḍʿ*).[90] In a case of tropical or metaphorical utterance (*majāz*), for instance, the original speech is burdened by a signification (*dalāla*) which is not essentially and explicitly mentioned. Thus, Ibn al-Qayyim maintains that every interpretation which changes the semantic meaning, as expressed by an intelligent speaker, creates a false utterance.[91]

Ibn al-Qayyim further expounds on the linguistic implications of *taʾwīl* as he distincts between 'distorting interpretation' (*taʾwīl al-taḥrīf*) and 'explanatory interpretation' (*taʾwīl al-tafsīr*). In his view, a distorting interpretation is forbidden both with regard to informative theoretical knowledge (*ʿilm khabarī*) as well as practical knowledge (*ʿilm ṭalabī*). On the other hand, an explanatory interpretation is permissible, for it clarifies and elucidates the meaning embodied within these two kinds of knowledge.[92] Evidently, Ibn al-Qayyim faithfully represents here the approach of his mentor Ibn Taymiyya to *taʾwīl*, as it is articulated in the work *Darʾ taʿāruḍ al-ʿaql wal-naql* (Repulsion of the Contradiction between Reason and Tradition). Ibn Taymiyya elaborately engaged with this issue, distinguishing between the two kinds of knowledge found in the Quran: practical knowledge (*ilm ʿamalī* or *kalām ṭalabī*) that defines religious practices and theoretical knowledge (*ʿilm khabarī naẓarī*) that includes knowledge delivered by God on His essence, His messengers, His book etc. The major difference between the two is that theoretical knowledge describes self-standing truths (*thābit bi-dhātihi*), which are not dependent on the understanding of a reader or his interpretation of them. It is truth itself, even though a human being is unable to imagine or interpret its mode of existence. Human beings must acknowledge the reality of such truth according to its literal meaning;

89 In the Arabic linguistic field of "the science of meanings" (*ʿilm al-maʿānī*) it is customary to clearly distinguish between informative utterances that express a fact or a statement (*khabar*) and performative utterances (*inshāʾ*) that indicate a wish, will, hope etc.; Philip Halldén, "What Is Arab Islamic Rhetoric? Rethinking the History of Muslim Oratory Art and Homiletics," *International Journal of Middle East Studies* 37/1 (Feb. 2005), 22.

90 Author not specified, "Lafḏ," *Encyclopedia of Arabic Language and Linguistics*, 1–3; Bernard Weiss. "Waḍʿ al-Luġa," *Encyclopedia of Arabic Language and Linguistics*, Brill Online, 1.

91 Ibn al-Qayyim, *al-Ṣawāʿiq al-mursala*, 1:202–205.

92 Ibn al-Qayyim, *al-Ṣawāʿiq al-mursala*, 1:215–219.

however, they cannot postulate what it actually is. This is the manner in which Ibn Taymiyya distinguishes between permissible interpretation (*taʾwīl maqbūl*) and text-distorting interpretation (*taḥrīf*).[93]

Similar to his teacher, Ibn al-Qayyim also applies the distinction between the two kinds of knowledge—*khabar* vs. *ṭalab*—as he draws the limitations of the interpretive act. He claims that the purpose of the interpretation of theoretical knowledge (*taʾwīl al-khabar*) is to acknowledge the truths it bears and accept them without any questioning. Contrarily, an interpretation of the practical knowledge is an appropriate and necessary act, since every person who follows and obeys Islamic religious practices is obliged to understand their meaning in order to fulfill them correctly. Ibn al-Qayyim even points disagreements among the Prophet's companions concerning various cases of interpreting Quranic verses of practical content. However, there was never even a single dispute between the Prophet's companions and their followers about the verses on the divine attributes (*ayāt al-ṣifāt*), which are a part of the theoretical knowledge. They all agreed on their acknowledgement of the veracities of these verses, transmitting them to their pupils and affirming their truthfulness (*ithbāt*). In addition, Ibn al-Qayyim notes the verses containing the divine attributes are among the Quranic verses which must never be interpreted (*mutashābihāt al-qurʾān*).[94]

In his work *Darʾ al-taʿāruḍ*, Ibn Taymiyya outlined once more a similar linguistic analysis of the term *taʾwīl*, according to how it had been used by the *salaf*. He concluded the only acceptable meaning of the term is as an 'explanatory interpretation', in the most basic sense of the word, for defining an expression used in the text (*tafsīr al-kalām* or *bayān maʿnāhu*). Any other sort of interpretation—particularly the entangled figurative interpretation employed by rationalistic scholars—was perceived by Ibn Taymiyya as manipulating the text to fit the meaning desired by the interpreter (*maʿnā marghūb*), which does not correspond with God's intention.[95] Furthermore, Ibn Taymiyya rejected the use of *taʾwīl* as allegorical interpretation, arguing that there are no decisive criteria for its use; in addition, there is no set directive rule (*qānūn*) determining

93 Binyamin Abrahamov, "Ibn Taymiyya on the Agreement of Reason with Tradition," *The Muslim World* 82, 3–4 (1992): 264–266; Nadjet Zouggar, "Interprétation autorisée et interprétation proscrite: selon le 'Livre du rejet de la contradiction entre raison et Écriture' de Taqī al-Dīn Aḥmad b. Taymiyya," *Annales Islamologiques* 44 (2010): 204.

94 Ibn al-Qayyim, *al-Ṣawāʿiq al-mursala*, 1:206–214; see footnote 61 in chapter 1.

95 Nadjet Zouggar, "Interprétation autorisée et interprétation proscrite: selon le 'Livre du rejet de la contradiction entre raison et Écriture' de Taqī al-Dīn Aḥmad b. Taymiyya," 202–204.

when and how it should be used. Ibn Taymiyya views figurative interpretation as an arbitrary means which is employed randomly and inconsistently.[96]

The following table reviews the variance in the approaches of Ibn Taymiyya and Ibn al-Qayyim concerning *taʾwīl*, as described above:

	Ibn Taymiyya	**Ibn al-Qayyim**
taʾwīl al-taḥrīf	Forbidden interpretation, for it distorts meaning; this also includes allegorical interpretation.	Forbidden interpretation both for theoretical (*khabarī*) and practical (*ṭalabī*) knowledge; distorting meaning
taʾwīl al-tafsīr	Explanatory interpretation (*tafsīr al-kalām* or *bayān maʿnāhu*). It is the only permissible kind of interpretation (*taʾwīl maqbūl*).	*taʾwīl al-khabar* = acceptance without interpretation. *taʾwīl al-ṭalab* = appropriate and necessary for religious practices.

For the most part, Ibn al-Qayyim's definition of *taʾwīl* resembles the one formulated beforehand by Ibn Taymiyya. However, Ibn al-Qayyim creates another distinction between two kinds of permissible *taʾwīl*, one of which involves no interpretation at all but, rather, acceptance without interpretation.

2 Proponents of *taʾwīl* (Sections 6–9)

After defining the elementary ideas in the basis of both permissible and inappropriate acts of interpretation, Ibn al-Qayyim turns to the scholars perceived as the proponents of *taʾwīl*. He expresses his criticism directed against the *mutaʾawwilūn* (i.e.; the rationalist distorting interpreters) who differentiate between which of the divine attributes are in need of interpretation and which are not. Ibn al-Qayyim asks: in the Quran, God described Himself, His actions and His Messenger with a variety of names and traits; how then can these be interpreted in a manner different to the way in which they explicitly appear (*ʿalā khilāf[i] ẓāhirih[i]*)? How can the divine speech be understood inessentially (*ḥaqīqatih[i]*)? The texts state divine qualities such as seeing, hearing, knowl-

96 Binyamin Abrahamov, "Ibn Taymiyya on the Agreement of Reason with Tradition," 258, 261, 266–267.

edge, ability, wishing, life, love, anger, mercy, joy, laughter, face, hands, and so on. Since all the stated qualities are not exclusive to human nature, accepting the essentiality (*ḥaqīqa*) of these attributes does not necessarily infer anthropomorphism of God (*tashbīh*) and His corporeality (*tajsīm*). Rather, these are attributes that exist within the described object (*aʿrāḍ qāʾima bil-mawṣūf*), which are not the same kind as the attributes of the created beings (*laysᵃ min ṣifāt al-makhlūqīn*). Hence, such attributes must not be negated with respect to God. However, the proponents of inappropriate interpretation find certain attributes of God to be sustainable by the mean of Reason (*mā dallᵃ ʾl-ʿaql ʿalā thubūtihⁱ*) and, therefore, there is no need to interpret them (for instance: knowledge, life or ability). Alternatively, other descriptions of God (for instance: His face, hands, laughter or anger) are perceived as rationally unsustainable, therefore requiring interpretation. Ibn al-Qayyim discards such distinction between attributes which stand in need of interpretation and those which "are acceptable by pure Reason". In his opinion, Reason alone can neither affirm nor negate the divine attributes; rather, one must additionally rely on the hermeneutic tradition of the preceding scholars. According to Ibn al-Qayyim, the reliance on exterior hermeneutical elements caused the problematic situation in which each religious sect or ideological group chooses to interpret certain attributes that do not conform to the particular set of principles they determined for themselves.[97]

Noteworthy is the fact that the approach of repudiating a partial affirmation of the divine attributes, as expressed here by Ibn al-Qayyim, openly emerges from the ideas articulated by his mentor Ibn Taymiyya. In one of his treatises, Ibn Taymiyya refers to the dispute between the traditionalistic Islamic stream of thought, which affirms the divine attributes, and the rationalistic ones including the Muʿtazilite school, which negate many of them. The hypothesis driving them to negate attributes such as God's descent from heavens, His sitting on His throne, or His laughter, was that God must be described only with attributes that express absolute perfection (*ṣifāt kamāl*). In their opinion, attributing God with qualities such as love (*maḥabba*), anger (*ghaḍab*), or laughter (*ḍiḥk*) suggest an imperfection, since they involve a considerable lack of self-control. Ibn Taymiyya resolutely responded to this claim, asserting that all divine attributes must be affirmed with no reservation because, when it comes to a perfect essence such as God, every attribute ascribed to it in the sacred texts is just as perfect. Additionally, any quality of appropriate measure and correct timing expresses perfection, and all the more so concerning God.

97 Ibn al-Qayyim, *al-Ṣawāʿiq al-mursala*, 1:220–233.

In fact, Ibn Taymiyya's intensely developed discussion on the matter allowed Ibn al-Qayyim to thrust aside *taʾwīl* as a figurative interpretation regarding all of the divine attributes.[98]

Ibn al-Qayyim carries on rebuking the exponents of *taʾwīl* in his introduction, arguing that their falsified "interpreted meaning" eventually forced them to return to the undesired meaning from which they had tried to escape. Ibn al-Qayyim accuses them of a contemptuous treatment of the sacred texts, as well as of denying the essential realities (*ḥaqāʾiq*) therein. Maintaining his claim, Ibn al-Qayyim suggests several examples, such as the following: in order to avoid ascribing God a restricted physical place (*taḥayyuz, ḥaṣr*), the early Jahmites (i.e., the early Ashʿarites) interpreted the verses in which God is sitting on His throne saying that the essence of God is everywhere—in houses, wells, potteries, and any other tangible place they wished. As their pupils grasped the falseness of this interpretation, they also rejected it, claiming God is in no place whatsoever (i.e., He does not exist at all). This is a completely impossible situation as well; hence, they decided to ascribe God the initial place they had previously diminished: His divine throne. Ibn al-Qayyim strives to explain the mistake of the proponents of *taʾwīl*, as they misunderstand the sacred texts and wrongly interpret them with untruthful meanings. They even simultaneously integrate *tashbīh* (likening God to the creation, anthropomorphism) and *taʿṭīl* (denying the divine attributes via stressing His absolute transcendence). In Ibn al-Qayyim's view, this is an astonishing exertion because, in this manner, they deprive the texts of their true meaning and intention. As a result, they ultimately show their mistrust of the sacred texts, dispossessing them from their essentialities (*ḥaqāʾiqihā*) which are the core of perfection because of their sacred contents.[99]

Therefore, Ibn al-Qayyim lists four required actions of a proponent of *taʾwīl*, only by which his interpretation can be accepted.[100] The principle Ibn al-Qayyim endeavors to reinforce is a strictly linguistic one, according to which the origin of the semantic meaning of utterances is known from their literal form as it appears in the text (*al-ḥaqīqa wal-ẓāhir*). Any deviation from the textual source requires a proof of four stages: a. at the linguistic level, the interpreter must show that the expression (*lafẓ*) is adequate to hold a new semantic

98 Livnat Holtzman, "'Does God Really Laugh?'—Appropriate and Inappropriate Descriptions of God in Islamic Traditionalist Theology," in *Laughter in the Middle Ages and Early Modern Times*, ed. A. Classen (Berlin: de Gruyter, 2010), 195–198, 200.

99 Ibn al-Qayyim, *al-Ṣawāʿiq al-mursala*, 1:234–238.

100 According to the editor's note, Ibn al-Qayyim also briefly mentioned these four acts in his work *Al-kāfiyya 'l-shāfiyya*; Ibn al-Qayyim, *al-Ṣawāʿiq al-mursala*, 1:288.

meaning (*maʿna*); b. the interpreter must substantiate his specific selection of meaning with an indicative proof (*dalīl*); c. this proof must demonstrate the linguistic expression indeed semantically diverts from its apparent form (*dalīl ṣārf*); d. the interpreter must supply a sufficient answer to whoever opposes him, sides with the real apparent form of the expression and relies on a rational proof, including a proof that originates from the sacred texts (*al-dalīl al-ʿaqlī wal-samʿī*).[101] In fact, the rationalists who employed *taʾwīl* are criticized on the issue of the *samʿiyyāt* (i.e., indications that are derived from the sacred texts alone) more than once in Ibn al-Qayyim's discussion, as emphasizes here their importance with respect to any theological deliberation. Such principal ideas of creed could be known to humankind only because they were transmitted in the Revelation of the sacred texts. The interference of rationalistic thinking concerning the *samʿiyyāt* is approved only in order to resolve special cases of incompatibility between Quranic verses. The *samʿiyyāt* comprise, amongst others, the *ilāhiyyāt*, which deal with the existence of God (*wujūd Allāh*), His attributes (excluding the attributes of seeing, hearing, and speech), and His actions (*afʿāluh^u tʿālā*) and demand a verified textual basis. Contrasted with the *samʿiyyāt* are the *ʿaqaliyyāt*—ideas acquired by means of human Reason, such as the *Kalām*ic theological theories.[102] On his behalf, Ibn al-Qayyim does not consider rationalistic ideas alone as proper substantiations, all the more so when it comes to the divine subject of *ilāhiyyāt*. In this aspect, Ibn al-Qayyim articulates the common traditionalistic stance.

3 Object of *taʾwīl*: The Text and Its Speaker

Ibn al-Qayyim turns the attention to the special character of the texts sacred to Islam and their status in the eyes of the proponents of *taʾwīl*. He accuses the proponents of *taʾwīl* of disrespecting the texts and violating their sanctity, which result in them being led astray from the righteous path. Ibn al-Qayyim refers to God as the speaker in the sacred texts as well as the goals He wishes to achieve thereby: providing guidance to the listeners, explaining them the meaning of scriptures and supplying the Islamic spiritual practices. To that aim, two conditions must be met: first, the speaker must express himself with clarity and eloquence (*bayān*); second, the listener must possess the capacity of understanding those expressions. In case the speaker intended that his speech

---

101 Ibn al-Qayyim, *al-Ṣawāʿiq al-mursala*, 1:288–295.

102 Central themes included among the *samʿiyyāt* are, for instance: prophecy, eschatology, and the religious commands and prohibitions; Louis Gardet, "ʿAḳliyyāt," *EI*², 1:342; idem, "Allāh," *EI*², 1:411.

not be taken at face value (*khilāf ẓāhirih*[i] *wa-ḥaqīqatih*[i]), the intentions of clarification and guidance would be contradicted. Since, to Ibn al-Qayyim, there is no doubt God wishes to guide His human creations, He knows exactly the message He wishes to deliver and He is the most eloquent of all things, employing an interpretation of *taʾwīl* such as that of the *mutakallimūn* is superfluous in every case.[103] Notable here is Ibn al-Qayyim's logical and gradual process of argumentation, while still adhering to the traditionalistic claim in favor of complete adherence to textual sources.

The characteristic of *taysīr al-Qurʾān lil-dhikr* is raised as another inherent quality of the Quranic text which deprives it from unnecessary interpretation. Literally meaning: "easily memorable", this textual quality entails the mnemonic nature traditionally ascribed to the Quran, assisting to its understanding and following of the religious commands therein. Ibn al-Qayyim sees this feature as clashing with any need of interpreting the text of the Quran; since God mercifully sent the Quran as a remedy for the hearts of the believers and as a means of guidance, the meanings borne in the Quranic text are the noblest ones and its linguistic expressions are the most eloquent and glorious. As evidence, Ibn al-Qayyim cites and clarifies the verse (Q 25:33) "They cannot put any argument to you without Our bringing you the truth and the best explanation": 'the truth' (*ḥaqq*) refers to the semantic meanings and the intention of the Quran, while 'the best explanation' (*al-tafsīr al-aḥsan*) refers to the expressions denoting that truth, as in instructive interpretation. Thus, it is impossible to find any better explanatory words for the Quran other than in God's speech in the Quran itself. In disobedience, the fantasies of the scholars of *Kalām* have blackened their hearts as well as their writing sheets of interpretation (*wa-qad sawwadū bihā* [i.e., *bil-khiyālāt*] *al-qulūb wal-awrāq*), for their way utterly contradicts the way of the Quran.[104]

Thereafter, Ibn al-Qayyim positively defines the cases in which *taʾwīl* is acceptable.[105] Utilizing a *Kalām*ic argumentation mode, designated as *taqsīm* (or *qisma*),[106] he first differentiates between three categories of speech (*kalām*):

---

103 Ibn al-Qayyim, *al-Ṣawāʿiq al-mursala*, 1: 296–311, 320, 324; Yasir Qadhi, "'The Unleashed Thunderbolts'," 140.

104 Ibn al-Qayyim, *al-Ṣawāʿiq al-mursala*, 1:330–331, 336.

105 Since its content deals with a linguistic aspect of the *taʾwīl*, I chose to place here the 16th section despite the diversion from the sequential order of the sections in the introduction.

106 Basically, he implements here a mode of argumentation set on the logical form of exclusive disjunction (i.e., either α or β, but not both). This hypothetical reasoning allows him to establish a contrast between several alternative cases, thereby excluding those that are

1. definite statement in the text that corresponds to the intention of the speaker; 2. utterance that appears in the speakers' intention, yet it is possible the intention refers to something different; 3. indefinite utterance in the text which is also unclear in the intention of the speaker, but is rather a general statement requiring an explanation. As for the first category—to this, no sensible mind would employ *taʾwīl*. This category includes the texts of the Quran and Hadith containing verses on the divine attributes, for instance: God is one, He commands and prohibits, He sits on His throne, all-knowing and all-powerful, the angles obey Him, He strolls in the world, and He will bring its annihilation in the Day of Judgment. As for the second category—*taʾwīl* is acceptable in this respect only if it does not alter the literal meaning inferred by the linguistic sign as it appears in the text. For instance: the verb *istawā*—viz. to firmly sit on something—appears in most of the verses describing God sitting on His throne. According to Ibn al-Qayyim, interpreting God sitting on the throne as the act of "ruling", similarly to the denotation of the verb *istawlā* (as done by Muʿtazilite interpreters) is a mistake because it alters the linguistic sign of the expression in the text. As for the third category, *taʾwīl* is acceptable there, only as it comprises explanatory clarification. For instance: it has been argued that God speaking to Mūsā in the verse (Q 4:164) *wa-kallam^{a} Allah^{u} Mūsā* ***taklīm^{an}*** ("to Moses God spoke directly") is a figurative utterance (*majāz*). However, Ibn al-Qayyim explains all speakers of the Arabic language agree this is a grammatical form of emphasis (*mafʿūl muṭlaq lil-taʾkīd*); thus, this is an utterance of essential reality (*ḥaqīqa*).[107] In fact, all of the given examples indicate a use of *taʾwīl* in accordance with the formula of *bi-lā kayfa*,[108] forged in the *Kalām*ic argumentation mode of *taqsīm*.

It seems that Ibn al-Qayyim finalizes his linguistically centered discussion on *taʾwīl* as he raises the general claim that the wrong use of *taʾwīl* terminates the primordial aim for which God created the human language. As humankind is made up of "cultured beings within the creation", language was created for it

---

found improbable. This form of argumentation is not uncommon in Ibn al-Qayyim's writing, as we shall see; Van Ess, "The Logical Structure of Islamic Theology," 40.

107 Ibn al-Qayyim, *al-Ṣawāʿiq al-mursala*, 1:382–389.

108 In other words, the traditionalistic hermeneutical method which calls for an affirmation and acceptance of all divine attributes, including those which may infer on anthropomorphic features, "without asking how" those could be realized (without assuming a modality), with no interpretation whatsoever. This formula was widely adopted by traditionalistic scholars as a contra-method to the figurative interpretation of *taʾwīl* embraced by the purely rationalistic ones; Binyamin Abrahamov, "The "Bi-lā Kayfa" Doctrine and Its Foundations in Islamic Theology," *Arabica* 42, 1–3 (Nov., 1995): 366–370, 378.

not only as a verbal means of communication, but also for using physical gestures, voices and sounds. In this manner humans are able to express their covert feelings, as well as comprehend those of others. *Ta'wīl*, as a form of interpretation that changes the semantic meaning of language and its essentialities as imposed by God, stands in contrast to the benefit that humankind is supposed to derive from language as a concept.[109] Interestingly, Ibn al-Qayyim touches here on a grammatical topic of a clear theological derivation known as the original imposition of language (*waḍʿ al-lugha*) and, most evidently, he upholds the traditionalistic stance that God assigned verbal expressions to their respective semantic meanings (a theory known as *tawqīf*). This stance stems from the traditionalistic understanding of the Quranic verse (Q 2:31) "He taught Adam all the names [of things]". The rationalists—namely the Muʿtazilites—understood the verse in a manner that inferred God gave human beings the ability to decide and name things on their own; hence, language is a human invention subjected to the human conventions of speech (a theory known as *iṣṭilāḥ*).[110] In this respect, Ibn al-Qayyim message is clear: God provided His human creation with language by *tawqīf*; therefore, using *ta'wīl* transforms God's promise of benefit into *takdhīb* (i.e., a false statement). Thus, Ibn al-Qayyim concludes *ta'wīl* opens the door to heresy and assists the enemies of Islamic religion in their attempt to undermine it.[111]

Ta'wīl *as Intellectual Phenomenon*

During the next sections of *al-Ṣawaʿiq*'s introduction (15, 17–23), Ibn al-Qayyim asserts a harsh social-religious critique directed at his contemporary scholarly class of the *ʿulamā'*—more precisely, his contemporary Ashʿarites. His treatment of *ta'wīl* in these sections exceeds the practical aspects of a single *Kalām*ic methodology, having much more to do with the repercussions of using *ta'wīl* in the Islamic intellectual sphere and the immense internal disputes it aroused between different Muslim groups. Ever since its inception, Ibn al-Qayyim found *ta'wīl* to have caused a highly severe crisis within the Islamic world of thought, disrupting the cognitive relation between God and mankind by damaging the linguistics and semantics that appear in the revealed text of the Quran and Hadith literature. Ibn al-Qayyim describes at length the crimes (*jināyāt*)—as

109 Ibn al-Qayyim, *al-Ṣawāʿiq al-mursala*, 1:342–347.

110 Weiss. "Waḍʿ al-Luġa," *Encyclopedia of Arabic Language and Linguistics*, 1. The grammatical issue of the origin of language will be more elaborately discussed in the first section of chapter 5, concentrating on hermeneutics.

111 Ibn al-Qayyim, *al-Ṣawāʿiq al-mursala*, 1:342–347; Yasir Qadhi, "'The Unleashed Thunderbolts'," 140.

he puts it—inflicted by the use of *taʾwīl* amid the religions formed by former messengers and prophets (*rusul*). In his view, it is nothing less than a demolition and eradication imposed on the world as well as faith. To him, the inter-Islamic split is a consequence of ever-shifting interpretations of the Quran and Hadith made from personal interests, which brings about undesired religious innovations and deviations from the righteous path. Different groups, who interpret the sources of Revelation according to their own views while utilizing *taʾwīl*, hurry to accept answers provided by the weak means of Reason, even though they depart from the message delivered by the prophets of God. Ibn al-Qayyim uses a vivid illustration as he depicts this situation: "The devil of *taʾwīl* has raised his head, exposed his molar teeth, and flied the flag of *taʾwīl*, towards which hastened hordes and individuals as one" (*aṭlaʿā shayṭān*^{u} *'l-taʾwīl*^{i} *raʾsah*^{u} *wa-abdā lahum ʿan nājidhayh*^{i} *wa-rafaʿ*^{a} *lahum ʿalam*^{an} *min*^{a} *'l-taʾwīl*^{i} *ṭārū ilayh*^{i} *zarāfāt*^{un} *wa-waḥdān*^{un}). In this manner, *taʾwīl* was transformed into a weapon on a battlefield. This is how the Jews split into 71 groups, the Christians into 72 groups, and the Muslims into 73 groups.[112]

Moreover, Ibn al-Qayyim regards *taʾwīl* as corruptive towards all fields of human sciences and knowledge. In accordance with his claim, *taʾwīl* as a thinking method amplifies scholastic reliance on the speculative theology of the *Kalām*; thus, it is implausible people would take this deceitful science into such great consideration. Naturally, people of knowledge aspire to gain a clear and profound grasp of the intention conveyed in the compositions they read; however, when *taʾwīl* is employed on a text, the original meaning is distorted. Ibn al-Qayyim mentions, for example, the scientific fields of medicine, mathematics and grammar as fields of knowledge requiring precision and absolute clarity; if *taʾwīl* takes them over, they will become false and vague. Thus, the texts of religious law (*sharʿ*) and those which contain the divine attributes must be protected.[113] The responsibility of a person who interprets the holy text and distributes his interpretation to others is perceived by Ibn al-Qayyim as that of a medical expert who prepares a remedy for all of the humanity. The first to sabotage the 'remedy' of faith were the sect of the *khawārij*; the Muʿtazilite

---

112 The renowned orientalist Goldziher has referred to this tradition, claiming it was misunderstood by Muslim theologians. According to him, it spoke of 73 virtues appropriated to Islam, as opposed to 72 to Christianity and 71 to Judaism. These 73 virtues were mistakenly understood as "branches" and, in relation to this, also the number of various Islamic sects initially listed; Ignatz Goldziher, *Vorlesungen über den Islam*, Hebrew translation by Yosef Yoel Rivlin, ed. Meir Martin Plessner (Jerusalem: Bialik Institute, 1951), 137; Ibn al-Qayyim, *al-Ṣawāʿiq al-mursala*, 1:348–355.

113 Ibn al-Qayyim, *al-Ṣawāʿiq al-mursala*, 2:399–400.

and Ashʿarite schools soon followed, contributing their share of damage. Even the famous Ashʿarite scholar Abū Ḥāmid Muḥammad al-Ghazālī (d. 505/1111) is mentioned by Ibn al-Qayyim as he lists several prominent rationalistic scholars who struck a blow against the religious science.[114]

In my opinion, it is highly plausible the historical circumstances in the background of this extreme intellectual crisis—as Ibn al-Qayyim depicts it—have to do with several formative events in the history of Islamic thought, during which rationalism and traditionalism have clashed. First of all, one should keep in mind the *miḥna*, the religious persecutions that took place under the regime of the Abbasid Caliph al-Maʾmūn (in 218/833); during these persecutions the ultra-rationalistic Muʿtazilite school took advantage of its gain of political power and imposed its ideology as the only legitimate dogma against the traditionalistic conventions of faith (*al-taqlīd fi ʾl-dīn*).[115] The Muʿtazilites considered this an imperative mission for civilization; however, in the end they failed to permanently implement it. Another historical process of relevance in this context is the rise of the rationalistic schools of Islamic thought later on, after the time in which the Muʿtazilite were active.[116] Notable is the direct reference to the emergence of the later-Ashʿarite school in Ibn al-Qayyim's passage mentioned above, as it is represented in the influential figure of al-Ghazālī.

Ibn al-Qayyim lists five types of scholars and their different views concerning the texts of Revelation and the issue of divine attributes: 1. People of *taʾwīl*

114 Ibn al-Qayyin relies heavily here on the great Muslim philosopher Ibn Rushd (Averroes, d. 595/1198), citing from the latter's theological work *al-Kashf ʿan manāhij al-adilla*; Ibn al-Qayyim, *al-Ṣawāʿiq al-mursala*, 2:414–417. See further scrutiny of Ibn al-Qayyim's reference to Ibn Rushd in section 5.6 to follow, and also in: Majid Fakhry, *Averroes (Ibn Rushd): His Life, Works and Influence* (Oxford: Oneworld, 2001), 78–79.

115 These persecutions have mainly revolved around another theological question, centering the creation of the Quran vs. its eternality (*khalq al-qurʾān*). Al-Maʾmūn ordered religious scholars to reassert the Muʿtazilite view which maintained that the Quran was created by God and, therefore, was not eternal like Him. The approach espouses by *ahl al-sunna wal-jamāʿa*—the proto-orthodoxy—opined that the Quran was created, hence shared God's eternal quality. This approach was perceived as heretical, and was even condemned as anthropomorphistic (*tashbīh*) for the assimilation of God with His creation. This was the reason for which the accusation of an anthropomorphic belief had also been a part of al-Maʾmūn's inquisition, as it was considered to be a threat upon his regime; Michael Cooperson, *Classical Arabic Biography: the Heirs of the Prophets in the Age of al-Maʾmūn* (Cambridge: Cambridge University Press, 2000), 33–39.

116 Joseph van Ess, *The Flowering of Muslim Theology*, translated by Jane Marie Todd (Cambridge: Harvard University Press, 2006), 142–144; idem, *Theologie und Gesellschaft im 2. Und 3. Jahrhundert Hidschra*, 4:451, 458, 617, 689–692.

(i.e., the rationalists) who employ the most puzzling and mistaken approach; 2. People of illusion (*aṣḥāb al-taḥyīl*) who are incapable to understand the complete prophecy, therefore holding onto what they find to be sensible and possible to grasp;[117] 3. Instructors of ignorance (*aṣḥāb al-tajhīl*), who treat the expressions on the divine attributes as utterly incomprehensible (*mutashābihāt*);[118] 4. Anthropomorphists (*aṣḥāb al-tashbīh wal-tamthīl*), who compare God to His creation in an inappropriate manner; 5. People of the correct path (*aṣḥāb siwāʾ al-sabīl*, including the traditionalists and Ibn al-Qayyim himself), whom God guided to separate from the other groups by affirming the essential reality of His attributes and names while negating any similarity between Him and the created beings.[119]

Continuing along this line of thought, Ibn al-Qayyim delves into the reasons for which the ignorant souls (*al-nufūs al-jāhila*) are easily attracted to accept *taʾwīl*, although it breaks the principle of clarity (*bayān*) which God created for mankind to acknowledge. The formative principle of *fiṭra* (i.e., the natural disposition of humankind by God)[120] is stressed here as an inherent feature of human creation which stands in contrast to the practice of *taʾwīl*; therefore, this means Ibn al-Qayyim identifies *taʾwīl* as an abnormal and ungodly practice. He explains the 'mentally weak' are those inclined to be tempted by frauds decorated with glorified expressions, even though they are wrong. In addition, the true meaning—seeking to be damaged by *taʾwīl*—is presented in an obscene and ugly fashion, which intimidates the human heart. The proponent of *taʾwīl* even ascribes his innovative interpretation to respected sources, such as previous religious scholars or family members of the Prophet Muḥam-

---

117 By this denotation, it seems Ibn al-Qayyim is addressing an early rationalistic group which described God using negative utterances (*aphairesis*) under the influence of the Greek philosopher Albinus. In the basis of this idea stands the recognition that God is inconceivable by the human mind, hence He is to be described only in a manner of negating known attributes (e.g., invisible, amorphous, and so on); Harry A. Wolfson, "Albinus and Plotinus on Divine Attributes," *Studies in the History of Philosophy and Religion*, by Harry A. Wolfson, ed. Isadore Twersky and George H. Williams (Cambridge: Harvard University Press, 1973–1977), 1: 119–125, 129–130.

118 This denotation refers to the Karrāmites, which were an early rationalistic Islamic sect chiefly in Eastern Iran (Nishapur) from the 3rd/9th century until the time of the Mongol invasions of the 10th/13th century. Its Sunnite rivals rejected its corporealistic ideas regarding the divine attributes, and accused it of anthropomorphism; Clifford E. Bosworth, "Karrāmiyya," *EI*^{2}, 4:667–668.

119 Ibn al-Qayyim, *al-Ṣawāʿiq al-mursala*, 2:418–427.

120 The concept of *fiṭra* in Ibn al-Qayyim's thought is discussed in the article: Holtzman, "Human Choice, Divine Guidance and the *Fiṭra* Tradition," 163–188.

mad. Another reason may be an acceptance of *taʾwīl* by a famous and distinguished person of one of the higher scientific fields (mathematics, engineering, music, geography, etc.). This provides further permission for *taʾwīl* in the eyes of laymen and invites them to embrace it.[121] With "the ignorant souls" (*al-nufūs al-jāhila*), Ibn al-Qayyim uses quite ambiguous wording, making it more difficult to understand which exact group in his contemporary Islamic society he is addressing—the so called 'ignorant' Ashʿarites or the less (or even un-)educated commoners (*al-ʿamma*)? Or perhaps all socio-political groups refusing to follow the Taymiyyan scholastic path? At any rate, by referring to scholars of disciplines other than religion alone as a mean of influence, in my opinion it is plausible Ibn al-Qayyim is being deliberately vague when describing the social groups taken by *taʾwīl*. In this manner, he is able to better sustain his claim of the pre-structured illogicality between the concepts of natural Islamic *fiṭra* and unnatural *taʾwīl*.

Ibn al-Qayyim goes on and scolds the proponents of *taʾwīl* for their incompetence in supplying indicative proofs derived from the sacred texts during theological debates where they confronted their adversaries: they will never be able to supply *dalīl samʿī*. According to his claim, since it demonstrates a thinking method of obvious preference of Reason to the Islamic textual sources, this is one of the most destructive harms *taʾwīl* inflicted on Islam. In fact, a definite preference of this kind abolishes all proofs given by God Himself, as He delivered them in the Quran. Moreover, this methodology does not reflect the way of the righteous ancestors (*salaf*) who remained loyal to the texts holy to Islam in their traditionalistic practice of supplying proofs.[122] Therefore, Ibn al-Qayyim declares *taʾwīl* dismisses the authoritative predominance of the sacred texts and replaces them with dishonest ideas and mere human opinions (*ārāʾ*). In his view, whoever argues for an incongruity between Reason and Revelation does so out of a sheer absence of knowledge and proper understanding of the intention of the speaker in the scriptures. On the contrary, the Quran is the embodiment of conjunction between scriptural indicative proofs (*al-dalīl al-samʿī*) and rational indicative proofs (*al-dalīl al-ʿaqlī*).[123]

---

121 Ibn al-Qayyim, *al-Ṣawāʿiq al-mursala*, 2:435–444.

122 Interestingly enough, the rhetorical method of reference to an authoritative source as a persuasive mean was designated by the great Greek philosopher Aristotle as "providing evidence" using citations. Thus, the traditionalistic method of quoting evidence from the Quran and Hadith literature is actually parallel to the persuasive rhetorical methodology of the Aristotelian systematic thought; Harry A. Wolfson, *The Philosophy of the Kalam* (Cambridge: Harvard University Press, 1976), 32–33.

123 Ibn al-Qayyim, *al-Ṣawāʿiq al-mursala*, 2:452–460.

Furthering his intellectual analysis, Ibn al-Qayyim states four reasons which may lead to false *taʾwīl*. The first two concern the speaker (*mutakallim*): either his speech lacks clarity or his intention is poor and faulty. The other two concern the listener: either one does not understand the speech or his own intention is impure. The principal idea here is that mutual communication is based upon the speaker's intention and the listener's apprehension joining together and forming a single lucid meaning. When such a combination fails to occur, the result is a vague—even harmful—meaning. Ibn al-Qayyim gives the example of the companions of the Prophet (*ṣaḥāba*), whose just intention allowed them to comprehend the Quran in the most adequate fashion, so that they did not argue over the interpretation of issues such as acknowledging God, His attributes, His names and His actions. In contrast, at later times the intentions and capacities of scholars were tarnished, producing the obscene and false interpretation of 'reduced' schools of thought, such as the later-Ashʿarites.[124]

Ibn al-Qayyim also addresses several kinds of divergences or disagreements (*ikhtilāfāt*) regarding the Quran, which result from the act of *taʾwīl*. While he sees some of these divergences as condemned and undesirable (*ikhtilāf madhmūm*), he finds others to be legitimate (*ikhtilāf maḥmūd*). He consistently stresses that the condemned divergences are those which involve Quran interpretation, particularly by the means of *taʾwīl*. God has explicitly forbidden them in the Quran, since they cause separation and disparity between different groups within the Muslim community of believers. On the other hand, there are divergences that may be legitimate and fair: whoever achieves true understanding, this is in his favor and he deserves all praise; whoever misses it using his intellectual effort (*ijtihād*)—is described as "condemned", yet he is worthy of praise for his candid attempt and his mistake will be forgiven. However, if his mistake is a result of disobedience and a transgressed attitude, he is to be condemned altogether. In a very realistic manner, Ibn al-Qayyim sees no refuge from disagreements between people, as it is only natural for each person to perceive things in their own way. Nonetheless, when a divergence inflicts troublesome splits within the Muslim community, it is considered as a sin against God.[125]

Sequentially, Ibn al-Qayyim treats the whys and wherefores of the divergence among the Sunnite Muslim scholars after they had already agreed on a sole source of conclusive religious authority, viz. the Quran and the Sunna. He presents the position of the scholar Ibn Ḥazm (d. 456/1064),[126] whose teach-

124 Ibn al-Qayyim, *al-Ṣawāʿiq al-mursala*, 2:500–513.

125 Ibn al-Qayyim, *al-Ṣawāʿiq al-mursala*, 2:514–519.

126 Abū Muḥammad ʿAlī ibn Ḥazm al-Ẓāhirī was a prominent thinker, poet, historian, philoso-

ings were greatly valued by Ibn al-Qayyim. In fact, Ibn al-Qayyim has read many of Ibn Ḥazm's works first hand and found them inspiring for his doctrinal writing.[127] Ibn al-Qayyim cites a bulky segment from Ibn Ḥazm's work on legal methodology *al-Iḥkām fī uṣūl al-aḥkām*, depicting the latter's view on the reasons for scholarly disagreements: it is habitual for all human beings to err, forget what they have said as well as come up with a legal ruling that contradict their previous ones; these are all honest mistakes. In addition, different scholars among the *tābiʿūn* (i.e., the generations following the immediate companions of the Prophet Muḥammad) reached different geographical regions and were continuously affected by the changing cultural atmosphere around them; therefore, their rulings were not necessarily according to the correct Hadith accounts used in the preceding legal tradition (*taqlīd*). Ibn al-Qayyim further clarifies the issue, supplying Ibn Taymiyya's reasons for abandoning the textual sources: first, for a lack of belief that the Prophet indeed said a certain Hadith account; second, for an assumption that the account was said with regard to a question different than the one at stake; or third, for a presumption that a specific ruling was abrogated by another (*mansūkh*). All of these have brought about an unjust distancing from the Holy Scriptures.[128] Despite the somewhat tolerant explanation provided for the occurrence of disagreements among scholars, Ibn al-Qayyim seems to convey his criticism against scholars who neglect their duty of inspecting the amount of credibility of the sources they use in the course of their debates. Nevertheless, Ibn al-Qayyim demonstrates a realistic historical view, relying on two of his scholarly role-figures.

According to the inspection of the arguments put forward in Ibn al-Qayyim's introduction to *al-Ṣawāʿiq* thus far, the introductive sections handling the term *taʾwīl* do not consist of a mere sequence of textual proofs quoted from the sacred sources, as might have been expected from a typical traditionalistic scholar (although the use of textually-based argumentations is of course abundant). Undeniably, Ibn al-Qayyim's arguments reflect a highly profound analy-

---

pher theologian and jurisprudent of Andalusian origin. Among other activities, he amalgamated the thought of the *ẓāhiriyya*, which applied an approach of a literal understanding of the sacred texts according to their apparent textual meaning (*ẓāhir*). He was renowned for employing this approach in the Quranic science; José Miguel Puerta Vílchez, "Abū Muḥammad ʿAlī Ibn Ḥazm: A Biographical Sketch", in: Adang, Camilla; Fierro, Ma. Isabel; Schmidtke, Sabine (eds.), *Ibn Ḥazm of Cordoba: The life and works of a controversial thinker* (Leiden, Boston: Brill, 2013), 3–24; Roger Arnaldez, "Ibn Ḥazm," *EI*², 3:790.

127 Holtzman, "Elements of Acceptance and Rejection in Ibn Qayyim al-Jawziyya's Systematic Reading of Ibn Ḥazm," in *Ibn Ḥazm of Cordoba*, 606–608, 640–641.

128 Ibn al-Qayyim, *al-Ṣawāʿiq al-mursala*, 2:520–521, 533–542.

sis of the issue of *ta'wīl*, as well as an interesting notional progression: he opens by explaining the linguistic meaning of the term *ta'wīl*—the action itself, its employers and its effect on the text. Then, he continues by illustrating a direct line of 'cause and effect' between the flaws he spots in the act of *ta'wīl* and the intellectual maladies he finds within his contemporary scholastic environment. Moreover, the introduction is thoroughly arrayed in sections and subsections, which cultivates an internal logical order for the presentation of the arguments. Thus, it is more than plausible Ibn al-Qayyim chose to display such a string of argumentation out of a systematical approach of drawing his conclusions from a single argument onto the following one. The 24th and concluding section of the introduction represents the pinnacle of Ibn al-Qayyim's opening to *al-Ṣawāʿiq*, and can largely be seen as the last part of his discussion on *ta'wīl* as a destructive intellectual phenomenon. At the same time, this section is also the logical link between *al-Ṣawāʿiq*'s introduction and its body; in other words, the bridging unit between the author's 'statement of intentions' for his work and the work's actual content.

In the 24th section Ibn al-Qayyim lists what he identifies as the four most central rationalistic fundamentals which are at the core of the dangerous intellectual deterioration of the entire Islamic community as a direct consequence of the vast use of *ta'wīl*. He uses the harsh term *ṭāghūt* (pl. *ṭawāghīt*) to signify the abstract notion of 'harmful thinking method'. As he puts it, "the people of the false *ta'wīl* abolished by [these *ṭawāghīt*] the fortresses of religion, inflicted sacrilege upon the Quran, and eliminated the traces of faith."[129] Immediately afterwards, Ibn al-Qayyim specifies the rationalistic claims he aims to contest and refute in *al-Ṣawāʿiq*:

1. Their claim that God's speech [i.e. the Quran] and the sayings of His messenger [i.e., the Hadith] are merely verbal evidence (*adilla lafẓiyya*), that do not produce any knowledge (*ʿilm*) nor certainty (*al-yaqīn*).
2. Their claim that the Quranic verses and the prophetic sayings (*aḥādīth*) about the divine attributes are metaphorical expressions of no reality (*majāzāt lā ḥaqīqa lahā*).
3. Their claim that the Hadith accounts of the Messenger of God, which are considered reliable (*akhbār rasūl Allāh al-ṣaḥīḥa*) and are accepted and transmitted by trustful witnesses of the community of believers, do not produce knowledge (*ʿilm*), but a presumption (*ẓann*) at the most.

129 Ibn al-Qayyim, *al-Ṣawāʿiq al-mursala*, 2:632.

4. Their claim that in case of conflict between human Reason (*ʿaql*) and the texts of the Revelation (*nuṣūṣ al-waḥy*), Reason is to be preferred to the Revelation.[130]

Ibn al-Qayyim considers these four claims detrimental to Islam; hence, they must be countered one after the other. In his own words: "These four *ṭawāghīt* are those which deleted the commands of the Islam, invalided its signs, ruined its foundations, removed the sanctity of the scriptures from the hearts, and led to their slander by any heretic or unbeliever (*zindīq wa-mulḥid*). In every instance a piece of evidence is cited either from the Quran or the Hadith, the opponent refuses to accept it, seeks a refuge in these principles and obeys them. However, God Himself, in His power, strength, grace, and praise, had already broken these *ṭawāghīt* one by one, by the means of the successors of His Messenger and the heirs of His prophets (i.e., authoritative religious scholars). We shall do this as well, smashing one *ṭāghūt* after another."[131] In effect, these principles—or in Ibn al-Qayyim's terminology, *ṭawāghīt*—are rationalistic arguments or philosophical methods used by the speculative theologians of the *Kalām*. To be precise, they were used in an attempt to set down textual references towards God in the Islamic tradition, which—using the general *Kalām*ic rationalistic approach—were professed to be inadequate or inconsistent. Ibn al-Qayyim presents far more than a polemic writing against specific theological concepts, but rather he dialectically attacks the postulations forming those concepts and the methodological devices deployed by Ashʿarite scholars as the rationalistic substitute to a strict and sole loyalty to the literal understanding of the texts of Revelation.

In light of the scholarly depth Ibn al-Qayyim presents in his well-arrayed introduction to his immense work *al-Ṣawāʿiq*, I could not refrain from pondering what motivated him to begin his deluge of accusations against fundamental rationalistic argumentation methods with an upfront attack on the specific device of *taʾwīl*, as in allegorical interpretation. At first glance, *taʾwīl* is only a minor theoretical tool in comparison to the much more formidable four *ṭawāghīt*. Also, since the author surely could have included the act of *taʾwīl* as

130 Ibn al-Qayyim, *al-Ṣawāʿiq al-mursala*, 2:632; It must be noted that the order in which Ibn al-Qayyim presents the four claims in the passage quoted above is not the order of their appearance in the work itself, meaning that the order in *al-Ṣawāʿiq* is: 1, 4, 2, 3 (according to the stated numbering). In the following chapters hereinafter I will regard the order of the claims as they appear in the work, not like in this passage.

131 Ibn al-Qayyim, *al-Ṣawāʿiq al-mursala*, 2:632–633; Yasir Qadhi, "'The Unleashed Thunderbolts'," 141.

a 'harmful thinking method' along with the four other *ṭawāghīt*, why did he decide to separate it from them? Furthermore, why then did he deliberately choose to attack *taʾwīl* as the preference to his whole work? As I have already stated, the answer to these questions is revealed by taking a focused look at the introduction to *al-Ṣawāʿiq*. The close reading taken above reveals Ibn al-Qayyim's vision with regards to *taʾwīl*: It is evident that, for him, *taʾwīl* holds much more than a hermeneutical practice or a particular rationalistic tool. Rather, *taʾwīl* is discussed as a signifier—or symptom—of a wide overarching phenomenon consisting of three gradual levels:

Methodologically: Ibn al-Qayyim considers *taʾwīl* to be a misleading hermeneutical device massively employed by the Ashʿarites in a wrongful manner. This critical initial aspect is evident in the first thematic part of *al-Ṣawāʿiq*'s introduction, where *taʾwīl* is analyzed as a linguistic phenomenon consisting of the act itself, its employers, and the object upon which it is executed. In this level, *taʾwīl* is to be regarded as the basic and foremost sense of figurative interpretation of the divine attributes. Highly relevant in this respect is the penetration of the methods structured by Fakhr al-Dīn al-Rāzī to the discussions of the later Ashʿarites (less so in their writings). Despite al-Rāzī's well-known opposition to Muʿtazilite ultra-rationalism, many of its creeds and argumentation modes were incorporated in his thought, among which the method of *taʾwīl*. Drawing heavily on the Rāziyyan ideas and hermeneutical methodologies, the Ashʿarite contemporaries of Ibn al-Qayyim made a vast use of *taʾwīl*. In this respect, *al-Ṣawāʿiq* tails the Taymiyyan way and stands in opposition to al-Rāzī's work discussed before *Asās al-taqdīs*.

Ideologically: Substantially expanding the primal meaning of the term, Ibn al-Qayyim retains that *taʾwīl* also stands for an unfathomable intellectual dilemma. In this manner, *taʾwīl* is extricated from the purely linguistic realm and transformed into a prominent signifier of the Islamic rationalistic worldview. In Ibn al-Qayyim's terminology, the word *taʾwīl* denotes an unmistakable self-manifestation of the all-embracing rationalistic theology and ideology. Once again, one can point out the apparent infiltration of Rāziyyan thought to the theological discourse of the Ashʿarites of Mamluk Damascus and Cairo.[132]

132 Several previous studies point out to the penetration of the Rāziyyan thought to the theological discourse of the Ashʿarites of the Mamluk period: Holtzman, "Debating the Doctrine of *Jabr* (Compulsion): Ibn Qayyim al-Jawziyya Reads Fakhr al-Dīn al-Rāzī," in: G. Tamer and B. Krawietz (eds.), *Islamic Theology, Philosophy and Law. Debating Ibn Taymiyya and Ibn Qayyim al-Jawziyya*, (Berlin: de Gruyter, 2013), 91–93; Y. Tzvi Langerman, "The Naturalization of Science in Ibn Qayyim al-Ğawziyyah's *Kitāb al-Rūḥ*," in *A Scholar in the Shadow: Essays in the Legal and Theological Thought of Ibn Qayyim al-Ğawziyyiah*,

The spreading of this distinctive type of rationalistic discourse amid Ibn al-Qayyim's intellectual adversaries was evidently perceived as an ideological epidemic, which collided with his stern traditionalistic adherence. Hence, in the context of Ibn al-Qayyim's introduction to *al-Ṣawāʿiq*, the meaning of the term *taʾwīl* takes a much larger magnitude and virtually represents the entire rationalistic stream of thought.

Historically: Tightly related to the former ideological level, Ibn al-Qayyim perceived *taʾwīl* as an indicator of a separate stage within the historical developments of Islamic thought, starting directly with the Muʿtazilite activity of the 2nd/8th century. This level emphasizes the consequences of the methodological and ideological use of *taʾwīl*, which have namely to do with the divergences of the Islamic community and the inner religious quarrels amongst its intelligentsia. Focusing on the specific locus of Ibn al-Qayyim's activity in Mamluk Damascus, such theological debates affected the political struggle of powers as well as the public sphere. In this respect, it is unavoidable to mention the trials Ibn Taymiyya endured on the basis of his view on the divine attributes, which led to both his and Ibn al-Qayyim's imprisonment.[133] From a broader perspective, it can be argued that Ibn al-Qayyim's introduction on *taʾwīl* conveys an impressive historical consciousness, as he strives to properly place the specific theological discussion regarding divine attributes within the course of the historical developments of Islamic thought.

Ibn al-Qayyim's approach towards *taʾwīl* as a multi-layered intellectual phenomenon is by all means far removed from what would have been expected of a typical Ḥanbalite traditionalistic view. Even more so, Ibn al-Qayyim's approach here maintains a permanent contextual logic, which is no less than the use of logic conducted by principally rationalistic scholars. It is striking that Ibn al-Qayyim constructs his theologically traditionalistic arguments in a systemized fashion, while prudently entwining logical arguments within those in favor of relying on the texts of the Quran and Hadith (a thorough analysis and exploration of this authorial tendency throughout *al-Ṣawāʿiq* will accompany the discussions in the following chapters). Evidently, Ibn al-Qayyim's entangled discussion on *taʾwīl* and the divine attributes is derived from his preoccupation with his contemporary intellectual surroundings. From a larger perspective, his introduction to the work surveys a crisis of thought stemming from a rationalistic mishandling of the Islamic sacred texts utilizing malicious methodologies

---

ed. Caterina Bori and Livnat Holtzman, *Oriente Moderno* 90/1 (2010): 220–228; Holtzman and Ovadia, "On Divine Aboveness (*al-Fawqiyya*)," 5, 32, 54.

133 This topic has been described in chapter 1. For further details, see: Sherman A. Jackson, "Ibn Taymiyyah on Trial in Damascus," *Journal of Semitic Studies* 39/1 (Spring 1994): 41–85.

which inflict injurious outcomes on the Islamic religious world. The dimension of critique Ibn al-Qayyim expressed against his contemporary scholastic elite—mainly consisted of Shafiʿite-Ashʿarite rationalists—is loudly and clearly expressed. In Ibn al-Qayyim's introduction, *taʾwīl* stands out as the practical representation of the rationalistic use of the four *ṭawāghīt* which Ibn al-Qayyim wishes to eradicate. As a matter of fact, a stark opposition is unveiled between the theology represented by Ibn al-Qayyim—following in the footsteps of Ibn Taymiyya—and the Ashʿarite theology namely in its Rāziyyan form. Whereas in his advanced stages Fakhr al-Dīn al-Rāzī synthesized the rationalistic theology of the *Kalām* together with Greek philosophy (*falsafa*) in Islamic thought,[134] the theology of Ibn Taymiyya and Ibn al-Qayyim strove to stand as a fierce alternative, constructing a progressive model of Islamic rationalized-traditionalistic thought.

Returning to the discussion on *taʾwīl* and the introduction to *al-Ṣawāʿiq*: in its final section, Ibn al-Qayyim provides a brief presentation of the four arguments he is about to refute. However, he states their connection to *taʾwīl* only in the very broad context of being the main argumentation methodologies of the rationalistic worldview. He does not mention more precisely the grounds on which he decided to object specifically to these four methods. As will be presented in the following chapters, the answer to this question is hidden within embroiled deliberations between rationalistic and traditionalistic—either Ḥanbalite, or in this case, Taymiyyan—scholars, which are not at all easily understood (the final answer for *al-Ṣawāʿiq*'s structure will be unraveled in the end of chapter 5). In the following chapters, it is my aim to identify as closely as possible the scholars Ibn al-Qayyim chose to oppose by the means of contextualization of selected culminative parts of his arguments in *al-Ṣawāʿiq*. In this manner, we will be able to detect networks of intellectual connections that spread throughout a considerable period of time prior to his authoring of *al-Ṣawāʿiq*. In a parallel axle to this chronology, we can also find the ideological arguments and counter-arguments which led to these deliberations. Of course, this is a widely comprehensive task which is almost impossible to be fully achieved in the limited course of this study. Rather, I would like to

134 Additional relevant information on the Rāziyyan thought with relation to Ibn al-Qayyim's *al-Ṣawāʿiq* will be provided shortly, particularly in chapter 3. Ayman Shihadeh, "From al-Ghazālī to al-Rāzī: 6th/12th Century Developments in Muslim Philosophical Theology," *Arabic Sciences and Philosophy*, vol. 15 (2015), 141–179; Frank Griffel, "On Fakhr al-Dīn al-Rāzī's Life and the Patronage He Received," *Journal of Islamic Studies* 18:3 (2007), 321–324; William Montgomery Watt, *Islamic Philosophy and Theology: An Extended Survey*, 2nd edition (Edinburgh: Edinburgh University Press, 1985), 94–95.

sketch the most critical parts of this network, thereby further exploring both the scholastic figure of Ibn al-Qayyim and his monograph *al-Ṣawāʿiq*. The next chapters 3–6 will hence survey Ibn al-Qayyim's four *ṭawāghīt* refutations in a close reading of the primary material, thus delving into the core content of *al-Ṣawāʿiq*. Striving to more accurately discern the manners in which Ibn al-Qayyim's *al-Ṣawāʿiq* fits the scholarly discourse of the *Kalām*, I will note salient aspects of the process of rationalization taken by Ibn al-Qayyim in his writing.

CHAPTER 3

First *ṭāghūt* Refutation: The Islamic Scriptures Produce Certain Knowledge

Theological deliberations of any kind demand a sustainable basis of proof which each side relies on to spread its ideological doctrine in an attempt to convince its opponents its beliefs are true. Muslim theologians have long differed in their epistemological perception on the elementary question of the definition of the necessary knowledge (*ilm ḍarūrī*) which can be used as a theological argument.[1] Another issue of importance in this respect has to do with the set of characteristics which qualifies a piece of knowledge (i.e., single evidence or an indicator, *dalīl*) to be an acceptable supplier of certain knowledge (*ʿilm yaqīn*), which is required in the course of a theological debate. Such discussions about classification and the definition of different sorts of knowledge can be traced back to the first intellectual activities of the scholars of *Kalām*, which took place even before the Ashʿarite school emerged in the early 3rd/9th century.[2] Discussions on knowledge assessments were not as common among the more traditionalistic theological schools of that early period; however, they were most certainly not entirely absent. From the 5th/11th century onwards several important Ḥanbalite scholars accepted parts of the *Kalām*ic views and, thus, were actively engaged with the theoretical issue of the foundations of knowledge. For instance, the Ḥanbalite scholar Abū Yaʿlā Ibn al-Farrāʾ (d. 458/1066) composed the first known Ḥanbalite-*Kalām*ic manual called *al-Muʿtamad fī uṣūl al-dīn* ([The Book of] Foundation on the Principles of Religion).[3] Another noteworthy example is that of the Ḥanbalite theologian and legal expert, Abu

1 Josef van Ess mentions the dynamics of theological disputations of "attack and defense" as he elaborately discusses the argumentation methods of the *Kalām*ic discourse in his article "The Logical Structure of Islamic Theology," 21–50; Binyamin Abrahamov, "Necessary Knowledge in Islamic Theology," *British Journal of Middle Eastern Studies*, 20/1 (1993), 20–25.

2 Franz Rosenthal, *Knowledge Triumphant: The Concept of Knowledge in Medieval Islam* (Leiden: Brill, 2007), 46–47; a relevant and noteworthy study is: Aron Zysow, *The Economy of Certainty: An Introduction to the Typology of Islamic Legal Theory*, Resources in Arabic and Islamic Studies (Atlanta, Georgia: Lockwood Press, 2013).

3 Ibn al-Farrāʾ Abī Yaʿlā Muḥammad ibn al-Ḥusayn al-Ḥanbali ʾl-Baghdādī was one of the most prestigious Ḥanbalite scholars in 5th/11th century Bagdad, holding the high position of the *qāḍī* (judge) in the caliph's palace. His important work *al-Muʿtamad* contains an introduction concentrating on the theory of knowledge; Ibn al-Farrāʾ, *Kitāb al-muʿtamad fī uṣūl al-dīn*, ed.

 | DOI: 10.1163/9789004372511_005

'l-Wafā' ibn 'Aqīl (d. 513/1119), who employed parts of the Mu'tazilite doctrines of *Kalām* in the thoughts articulated in his work *Kitāb al-jadal* (The Book of Dialectics).[4]

A remarkable development of the rationalistic knowledge assessments continued from the 6th/12th century onwards, with the dialectical theological work and output of scholars such as al-Ghazālī (d. 505/1111),[5] Fakhr al-Dīn al-Rāzī (d. 606/1209)[6] or Sayf al-Dīn al-Āmidī (d. 631/1233).[7] By that time, a detailed discussion on the definition of knowledge was considered an indispensable preface to every book involving speculative theology. In this type of literature, one can distinctly see the influential role of Greek philosophy—more precisely, Aristotelian or Stoic logic—on the emerging Islamic philosophical and

Wadīʿ Nirān Ḥaddād (Beirut: Dār al-Mashriq, [1393]/1974), 19–30; Jon Hoover, "Ḥanbalī Theology," 630–361. Lauost, "Ibn al-Farrā'," *EI*², 3:765–766.

4 Abu 'l-Wafā' 'Alī ibn 'Aqīl al-Bghdādī was a significant Ḥanbalite jurist and theologian. The abovementioned Abū Ya'lā Ibn al-Farrā' was one of his teachers; George Makdisi, "Ḥanbalite Islam," in: ed. M.L. Swartz, *Studies on Islam* (New York: Oxford University Press, 1981), 238, 241, 270; idem, "Ibn 'Aqīl," *EI*², 3:699–700. The impact both of these scholars had upon Ibn al-Qayyim's hermeneutics in *al-Ṣawā'iq* will be discussed in section 5.5 of this study.

5 Abū Ḥāmid Muḥammad ibn Muḥammad al-Ṭūsī al-Ghazālī—"reviver of the religion" (*muḥyyi 'l-dīn*)—was an outstanding scholar and is considered the reformer of the Ash'arite Islam. His works deal with theology, jurisprudence and mysticism. The mix between Hellenistic science and Ash'arite *Kalām* is apparent in the introduction to his work on legal theory *al-Mustaṣfā*, which deals with the branches of knowledge; al-Ghazālī, *al-Mustaṣfā min 'ulūm al-dīn*, ed. Ḥamza ibn Zuhayr Ḥāfiẓ, in 4 vols. (Medina: Dār al-Nashr Shirkat al-Madīna 'l-Munawwara lil-Ṭibā'a, [1413]/[1993]), 1:1–6, 12–17; W.M. Watt, "al-Ghazālī," *EI*², 2:1038–1041. Further discussion about his epistemological work and its relation to Ibn al-Qayyim's *al-Ṣawā'iq* will be presented in chapter 4 of this study.

6 Muḥammad ibn 'Umar Fakhr al-Dīn al-Rāzī was the great promoter of Islamic Ash'arite theology and philosophy after the era of al-Ghazālī, who impressively fused *Kalām* with Aristotelian philosophy. One of his hallmark works in this respect is *Muḥaṣṣal afkār al-mutaqaddimīn wal-muta'akhkhirīn*, which will be discussed henceforth on page 140 of this chapter; Frank Griffel, "Fakhr al-Dīn al-Rāzī," *Encyclopedia of Medieval Philosophy*, ed. Henrik Lagerlund (Springer: Dordrecht, 2011), 1:341. For their major relevance to Ibn al-Qayyim's theological writing, al-Rāzī's views on epistemology will soon be explored; see section 3.2 hereinafter.

7 'Alī ibn Abī 'Alī Sayf al-Dīn al-Āmidī was a rationalistic jurist and theologian who mainly acted at the service of the Ayyūbid rulers of his lifetime. He wrote about theology, dialectics and philosophy; Dominique Sourdel, "al-Āmidī," *EI*², 1:434. Notable is al-Āmidī's important theological work *Ghāyat al-marām fī 'ilm al-kalām* and his jurisprudencial treatise *al-Iḥkām fī uṣūl al-aḥkām*, ed. 'Abd al-Razzāq 'Afīfī, in 4 vols. (Riyadh: Dār al-Ṣamī'ī lil-Nashr wal-Tanzī', 1424/2003).

theological thought. Logic was perceived as "the science that produced certain knowledge"; hence, logical arguments were vastly used in the rationalistic speculative theology of *Kalām* as a means for attaining the truth about God.[8] Such adaptation of systemized Greek logic can be seen as part of what has been described as the "naturalization of [Greek] sciences" in Islamic thought.[9] Notwithstanding, substantial foundations for rationalistic methods of argumentation could also be found within the Islamic intellectual capital itself in the field of dialectical science (*ʿilm al-jadal*).[10] Hence, far from remaining indifferent to the intellectual developments occurring in the methodologies of the rationalistic theological schools, traditionalistic institutions of knowledge gradually absorbed and made use of several rationalistic methods; for example, the use of reasoning by analogy (*qiyās*) within the discipline of legal theory (*uṣūl al-fiqh*).[11] A factor of much greater prominence to the current

8 Rosenthal, *Knowledge Triumphant*, 47–51, 195–196; in addition, van Ess registers prominent elements from the Greek philosophy in the *Kalām*ic context. Van Ess, "The Logical Structure of Islamic Theology," 30–32.

9 An example of particular relevance to our specific discussion is Langermann's analysis of the process of penetration of Hellenistic sciences into Ibn al-Qayyim's own thought in his work *Kitab al-rūḥ*, by the means of interrogating the use and meaning of the term *rūḥ* (spirit or soul) with respect to the Greek philosophical idea of psyche or pneuma; Y. Tzvi Langermann, "The Naturalization of Science in Ibn Qayyim al-Ǧawziyyah's *Kitāb al-Rūḥ*," in *A Scholar in the Shadow: Essays in the Legal and Theological Thought of Ibn Qayyim al-Ǧawziyyiah*, ed. Caterina Bori and Livnat Holtzman, *Oriente Moderno 90/1* (2010): 211–214. Langermann based his argument on the approach articulated by the late Abdelhamid I. Sabra in his article: "The Appropriation and Subsequent Naturalization of Greek Science in Medieval Islam: A Preliminary Statement," *History of Science*, 25 (1987), 223–243 (several additional reprints are available).

10 Relevant in this respect is Josef van Ess's early observation concerning the use of the ambiguous term 'logic', which from the very beginning was related to *adab al-kalām* or *adab al-jadal*. Van Ess, "The Logical Structure of Islamic Theology," 22. In a recent paper, Belhaj expressed his disagreement with the notion of the "naturalization of the sciences" coined by Langermann, preferring the inherently Islamic *jadal*; Belhaj, "Disputation is a Fighting Sport," 7.

11 The entire conceptualization of epistemological perceptions is also of important significance to the field of Islamic legal theory and methhodology (*uṣūl al-fiqh*). In this regard, several comprehensive studies are highly relevant, for example: Bernard G. Weiss, *The Search for God's Law: Islamic Jurisprudence in the Writings of Sayf al-Dīn al-Āmidī* (Salt Lake City: University of Utah Press, revised edition 2010). Weiss analyzes al-Āmidī's writings from a dialectic point of view, providing a profound examination of the scholar's methodologies for understanding the sacred law. A more general overview of the assessment of knowledge for legal purposes can be found in the studies of Wael b. Hallaq: *A History of*

matter of knowledge assessment in the field of theology (*uṣūl al-dīn*) was the incorporation of the science of dialectics (*jadal*) in the traditionalistic theological curriculum.[12] Consequently, traditionalistic scholars were familiar with the various basic elements of dialectical argumentations from a relatively early stage (ca. 5th–6th/11th–12th centuries), which more or less overlapped the time period in which major developments in rationalistic theological thought occurred. These intellectual developments took shape with an emphasis placed on human Reason and the use of rationalistic methods—namely as formulated in the teachings of al-Ghazālī and Fakhr al-Dīn al-Rāzī—, which implied the rise of later-Ashʿarism.[13] It is essential to keep in mind this intellectual-historical background of interwoven connections and correlations between traditionalism and rationalism in Islamic thought when exploring the later epistemological deliberations in Ibn al-Qayyim's *al-Ṣawāʿiq*.

This chapter analyzes a number of key ideas that appear in ibn al-Qayyim's first *ṭāghūt* refutation in *al-Ṣawāʿiq al-mursala*, discussing the rationalistic-traditionalistic incongruity concerning the degree of certainty that can be ascribed to evidential knowledge derived from the textual sources of the Islamic Revelation. In terms of structure, I believe the best way to continue this survey is through a close reading of Ibn al-Qayyim's positive approach in a short overall presentation of the relevant text *al-Ṣawāʿiq*. Thereafter, in order to expand the horizons of inspection, I contextualize Ibn al-Qayyim's text from *al-Ṣawāʿiq* by referring to additional prominent players in the intellectual network whose importance became more apparent and continue the process of providing a close reading of the primary text. Such 'players' were indeed the scholars preceding Ibn al-Qayyim; their ideas stimulated his advanced theoretical writing concerning the theological issue of divine attributes, as it is demonstrated in *al-Ṣawāʿiq*. Whether they be rationalists or traditionalists, the scholars referred to by Ibn al-Qayyim are at times concealed in his writing rather than explicitly mentioned. Comparing these other scholars' claims as articulated in their own works to those same claims as communicated by Ibn al-Qayyim, I strive to achieve a more accurate account of the rationalistic arguments Ibn al-Qayyim so harshly opposed. In addition, this line of inspection

---

Islamic Legal Theories: An Introduction to Sunni Uṣūl al-Fiqh (Cambridge: Cambridge University Press, 1997), and *The Origins and Evolution of Islamic Law* (Cambridge: Cambridge University Press, 2005).

12 Makdisi, "Ḥanbalite Islam," 238.

13 The historical course of these methodological developments in the Ashʿarite school are instructfully described in: George Makdisi, "Ashʿarī and the Ashʿarites in Islamic Religious History," *Studia Islamica* (1962–1963) 17:37–80 and 18:19–39.

also allows the retrieval of the historical-intellectual background of Ibn al-Qayyim's epistemological view in *al-Ṣawāʿiq*. Altogether, this chapter covers the first epistemological discussion found in *al-Ṣawāʿiq* and, therefore, provides an initial illustration in favor of the claim raised in the previous chapter: *al-Ṣawāʿiq* unfolds Ibn al-Qayyim's scholastic character as a *Kalām* writer who took an active part in the theological discourse of *munāẓarāt*.

3.1 Ibn al-Qayyim's Rationalized-Traditionalistic Arguments on Epistemology in *al-Ṣawāʿiq* I

In order to aptly pinpoint the location of Ibn al-Qayyim's positive approach—which will be the main focus in this section—I would like to schematically sketch the general structure of Ibn al-Qayyim's 73-sections-long refutation of the first *ṭāghūt* in *al-Ṣawāʿiq*. As it is consisted of a progressive thematic line, this *ṭāghūt* can be divided according to the following headings:

1. Fakhr al-Dīn al-Rāzī's ten conditions for attaining certain knowledge, which constitute al-Rāzī's "Universal Rule" (*al-qānūn al-kullī*)[14]
2. Ibn Taymiyya's rejection of al-Rāzī's skeptical stance
3. Ibn al-Qayyim's general refutation of al-Rāzī's stance (by logical deduction)
4. Ibn al-Qayyim's specific refutation of each of al-Rāzī's ten conditions
5. Ibn al-Qayyim's positive confirmation of the Revelation's supreme value in producing 'certain knowledge'—restoring epistemological optimism
6. Devastating repercussions of the rationalistic perception of 'certain knowledge'

Noticeable is the fact that Ibn al-Qayyim's positive proclamation of the utmost certainty achieved by adhering to the Islamic sources actually appears towards the end of his refutation of the first *ṭāghūt* in *al-Ṣawāʿiq*. Ibn al-Qayyim first assembles a wide variety of arguments in order to refute the rationalistic view, according to which, "the texts of the Revelation (*nuṣūṣ^u 'l-waḥī*, namely the Qur'an and the Hadith) are verbal indicative evidence (*adilla lafẓiyya*),[15] that do

14 I will further elaborate on this subject in section 3.2 of this chapter.

15 From now on, I will translate the term *dalīl* as 'indicator' or 'indicative evidence', for its theological context. As a term used greatly in the realm of Islamic legal theory (*uṣūl al-fiqh*), *dalīl* can be translated interchangeably as 'an indicator', 'an argument', or 'a signifier [of meaning]'. A useful study on numerous legal terminological and theoretical issues

not produce certain knowledge (*ʿilm yaqīn*)."[16] This rationalistic notion undermines the basic traditionalistic idea of reliance on verbally or orally transmitted religious knowledge. Ibn al-Qayyim systematically examines this argument and strives to tear it apart, while at the same time defending the Islamic texts and promoting their supreme value as suppliers of proof of apodictic certainty in the course of a theological discussion. Only after excruciatingly draining the first *ṭāghūt* of any possible form of potency does he turn to explaining his more positive approach, providing his rationalized-traditionalistic solution as the most suitable alternative and one that any Muslim believer must follow. For the sake of the further discussion, I have slightly altered the order of sections (*wajh*; pl. *wujūh*) in Ibn al-Qayyim's discussion and have also omitted several of them due to their redundancy.

Ibn al-Qayyim first expresses his well-known approach in favor of firm adherence to the literality of the scriptures as the sole affirmative source for any kind of knowledge, asserting their much higher level of clarity (*bayān*) and apparent manifestation (*ẓuhūr*) compared to those which dubiously seems to be derived from 'Reason':

> The cogent indicators [of a signification of meaning, *adilla qāṭiʿa*] are based on the veracity of all that the Messenger had delivered. Their [i.e., the cogent indicators'] signification of his veracity are of more clarity and evidence than the signification of those rational sophistic arguments (*al-shaba 'l-ʿaqliyya*), contrary to what has been declared by the rationalists (*al-ʿuqalāʾ*). No one doubts this, unless their brains (*ʿaql*) are dirty and their hearts and natural dispositions (*fiṭra*) are damaged.
>
> Where are the sophistic arguments that reject God's aboveness (*ʿulū*) over His creation, His uttering His pre-eternal will (*takallum^ihi^ bi-ma-*

is: Mohamed M. Yunis Ali, *Medieval Islamic Pragmatics: Sunni Legal Theorists' Models of Textual Communication* (Routledge: Richmond, Surrey, 2000). The author dedicates a separate inquiry of "Ibn Taymiyya's contextual theory of interpretation", and distinguishes his '*Salafī*' approach from mainstream Muslim thinkers in the field of legal theory or general philosophy (chapter four in that book). Ibn al-Qayyim is portrayed as the only true follower of the Taymiyyan scholarship once again, and is referred to many times in this chapter.

On a more general note, the terms *dalīl*, *madlūl*, and *istidlāl* are closely connected to the Stoic logical system of proofs; Van Ess, "The Logical Structure of Islamic Theology," 26–28.

16 Ibn Qayyim al-Jawziyya, *al-Ṣawāʿiq al-mursala*, 2:633. The full *ṭāghūt* appears therein, pages 2:633–3:796.

> *shīʾa*[tihi]) and His speaking to His creation? [Where are the sophistic arguments that reject] His attributes of perfection, the actual beatific vision of Him in the hereafter, His actions—existing in Him—that created the proofs (*barāhīn*), which are more than a thousand and immensely various? How, then, does one discard these rational necessary proves (*al-barāhīn*[a] *'l-ʿaqliyya*[ta] *'l-ḍarūriyya*[ta]) with an imaginary [and an already] contradicted doubt, unless they are of the most wrongful people, both in terms of Reason and thought (*ʿaql*[an] *wa-naẓr*[an])? Is it not the kind of doubt which expressed skepticism about the sensations and intuitive instincts (*tashkīk al-ḥissiyāt wal-badīhiyyāt*)? In this respect, even though many people are incapable of being free from them [i.e., their sensations and instincts], they still recognize that they discard what they have perceived in their senses necessarily. Those who are capable to be detached from their senses—they cannot judge that which is sensorial.[17]

This passage expresses Ibn al-Qayyim's initial grounds for his positive conceptualization of the human capacity of acquiring certain knowledge about the divine. In his view, human perception of the 'truth' and 'certainty' of God is a crucial part of the foundational idea of the *fiṭra* (i.e., the believer's corporal natural disposition)[18] which is effectively designed in order to instinctively perceive and accept knowledge about God, His Messenger and the Revelation. As a consequence, human perception of this type of knowledge is achieved by grasping the physical sensations and their process as laid out in the mind by Reason. Highly interesting at this point is Ibn al-Qayyim's dismissive reference to the Sophistic philosophical thought of ancient Greece, which evoked sheer doubt with regard to human sensations and intuition as a means to attain truths. For example, the Sophist philosopher Protagoras (ca. 485–415 BCE) is known to have claimed: "Of all things the measure is Man", meaning that "everything is relative to individual experience, judgment, and interpretation".[19] The Sophists expressed an overall doubt—if not a complete denial—regarding the

---

17 Ibn Qayyim al-Jawziyya, *al-Ṣawāʿiq al-mursala*, 2:729–730 (*al-wajh al-arbaʿūn*).

18 A good discussion on the concept of *fiṭra* in Ibn Taymiyya's thought—which Ibn al-Qayyim followed—appears in: Ovamir Anjum, *Politics, Law, and Community in Islamic Thought: The Taymiyyan Moment*, 215–265.

19 Joshua J. Mark, "Protagoras," *Ancient History Encyclopedia*, online source, last modified September 02, 2009, http://www.ancient.eu/protagoras/. In Arabic the Sophists are designated as *al-Sūfisṭāʾiyyūn*. I have detected the expression *al-ḥissiyāt wal-badīhiyyāt* in a similar context in: al-Isfarāʾinī, ʿIṣām al-Dīn Ibrāhīm ibn Muḥammad, *Sharḥ al-ʿaqāʾid* ([Istanbul]: [n.p.], [1833]/1249), 49–50.

very existence of God (either a god or gods), as it promoted the idea of a philosophical relativism of the human experience, including the 'sensations and instincts'. The Sophists deduced that human perception—sensorial and mental alike—is subjective and cannot infer of the existence of God.[20] Not only does Ibn al-Qayyim oppose this conclusion in the passage cited, he also depicts a differentiated model of an utterly intuitive belief in which one must follow his/hers inner natural instincts. Knowledge about this kind of belief is described as almost tangible, since it is perceived by human sensorial faculties.[21] Once a human being is created with accordance to the *fiṭra* idea and is connected to his "sensations and instincts", he/she will unavoidably perceive the apparent knowledge about the righteous belief as it is manifested in the Islamic scriptures. Therefore, attaining knowledge about God, Ibn al-Qayyim claims, is dependent on the created being's sensorial awareness and his willingness to perceive the 'cogent indicators' (*adilla qāṭiʿa*) of the Revelation.[22]

Following this line of argument, Ibn al-Qayyim backs up his view on the instinctive nature of the Islamic belief by providing evidence from the Quran (13:27–28): [27]"The disbelievers say, 'Why has no miracle been sent down to him

20 The Sophist movement was one of the earliest known advocators of philosophical relativism. The Sophistical skepticism was also noted with connection to epistemology in the work *Talbīs Iblīs* by Ibn al-Jawzī (d. 597/1200); I.R. Netton, "al-Sūfisṭāʾiyyūn", *EI*², 9:765. G.B. Kerferd, *The Sophistic Movement* (Cambridge; New York: Cambridge University Press, 1981), 165–167.

21 As a matter of fact, it is very plausible that the idea of human relativism was not at all alien to Ibn al-Qayyim: In his study, Mohamed M. Yunis Ali describes "Ibn Taymiyya's theory of cognitive relativism," according to which mental abilities are different from one individual to another, hence they have an effect on the human capacities for change in terms of the acquisition of knowledge. Ali, *Medieval Islamic Pragmatics*, 94–95; nonetheless, the conclusions derived from the shared relativistic view by the Sophists on one hand, and Ibn Taymiyya and Ibn al-Qayyim on the other, obviously contradict each other. This can suggest the duo's inclination towards the early *Kalām*, which was based on Stoic logic, since the Stoics "had to guard against the attacks of their skeptic adversaries." Van Ess, "The Logic Structure of Islamic Theology," 45; Abrahamov, "Necessary Knowledge in Islamic Theology," 21–22.

22 Highly notable is the similarity between the instinctive approach delivered by Ibn al-Qayyim and Ibn Ḥazm's ideas concerning attaining truth, which appear in the preface to his work *al-Faṣl* under the title "all the proofs that lead to true knowledge" (*al-brāhin al-jāmiʿa al-muwaṣṣila ilā maʿrifat al-ḥaqq*). For the limited span of the current study, I was unable to delve further into the topic, but will refer to future similarities in footnotes and more generally in the end of this section; Ibn Ḥazm, *al-Faṣl fī 'l-milal wal-ahwāʾ wal-niḥal*, eds. Muḥammad Ibrāhīm Naṣīr and ʿAbd al-Raḥmān ʿAmīra, second edition in 5 vols. (Beirut: Dār al-Jīl, 1416/1996), 1:38–42. Also, see footnote 126 in chapter 2.

from His Lord?' [Prophet], say, 'God leaves whoever He will to stray, and guides to Himself those who turn towards Him, [28]those who have faith and whose hearts find peace (*taṭma'inn*^{u} *qulūbuhum*) in the remembrance of God—truly it is in the remembrance of God that hearts find peace'." Observing yet another bodily aspect of religious faith, Ibn al-Qayyim points out that the Quran contains the utmost truth (*al-ḥaqq*) which soothes the hearts of the believers and reassures their souls. With relation to the previous passage, which concentrated on the human physical means for the perception of divine knowledge, Ibn al-Qayyim does not neglect the appeasing psychological effect this type of knowledge has on the believers and their spirits. If the Revelation was false, he explains, believers would feel nothing but doubt and skepticism (*shakk*^{an} *wa-rayb*^{an}); falseness creates a disturbance of mind whereas truthfulness pacifies it. Therefore, if the verbal expressions of the Quran (*kalimātuh*^{u} *wa-alfāẓuh*^{u}) did not produce certain knowledge in their indicated meaning (*tufīd*^{u} *'l-yaqin*^{a} *bi-madlūlihā*), then the hearts of the believers would not find them to be pacifying and trustworthy. Such a high degree of mental assurance can only result from the reliance on certain knowledge and, more so, only with sheer certainty (*al-yaqīn*^{u} *bi-ʿayn*^{ihi}).[23] Ibn al-Qayyim establishes both a physical and psychological connection between the believer and the certainty of knowledge produced by texts of Revelation. In this respect, his ability to combine the physical with the spiritual and the mundane with the divine is remarkable, as each aspect illuminates and compliments the other. To be more precise, even when he mentions traditionalistic concepts per se (e.g., the veracity of the Prophet, the *fiṭra*, citation of Quranic verses), Ibn al-Qayyim does so while strongly setting them in a rationalized, realistic and tangible mode of discourse, using them as legitimate arguments in his discussion.

Notwithstanding, arguments of proper traditionalistic fideism are not at all missing from Ibn al-Qayyim's positive writing on epistemology in *al-Ṣawāʿiq*. While still depicting the physical-mental aspects of the human consumption of certain knowledge, he specifically points to the Prophet Muḥammad and his exceptional capacities in this regard: "The Reason (*ʿaql*, lit., brain) of the Messenger of God is outright the most perfect one of all the mundane people. Was his Reason (*ʿaql*) weighed against all of the others together, it would *outweigh* (*rajjaḥa*) them all." In the first sentence Ibn al-Qayyim remarkably echoes the theory of "the perfect man" (*al-insān al-kāmil*) conceived by the famous and controversial Ṣūfī thinker Muḥyi 'l-Dīn ibn al-ʿArabī (d. 638/1240). According to this theory, humankind is the embodiment of the highest divine creation

23 Ibn Qayyim al-Jawziyya, *al-Ṣawāʿiq al-mursala*, 2:741 (*al-wajh al-thāmin wal-arbaʿūn*).

as a microcosm gifted with consciousness, and the Prophet Muḥammad is the most perfect of all created humans.[24] The second sentence in the above citation is a double entendre, intertwining the Prophet's cognitive perfection in the former sentence with the Hadith tradition. Ibn al-Qayyim uses the verb *rajjaḥa* (literally: to tip the scales) which has a double function in this context: in the legal discourse, *tarjīḥ* entails "the exercise of preference," or deciding which legal opinion or concept outweighs another. However, in the way Ibn al-Qayyim uses the verb *rajjaḥa* here, he assimilates a cognitive weighing to a physical one derived from the Prophetical biography (*sīra*), where Muḥammad's heart was put on the scales and outweighed the hearts of all the community of believers (*umma*).[25] In the citation above, the actual brain of the Prophet is out on the scales and outweighs the brains of all the Muslims, including the brains of all the rationalists (like al-Rāzī) whom Ibn al-Qayyim opposes.

Immediately thereafter, Ibn al-Qayyim presents an interpretation of a Quranic verse cited as evidence to the traditional narrative: before God provided Muḥammad with the Revelation, he had not known of the righteous belief or the Book (42:52) "So We have revealed a spirit to you [Prophet] by Our command: you knew neither the Scripture nor the faith, but We made it a light,

24 This concept appears in Ibn al-ʿArabī's text *Fuṣūṣ al-ḥikam* (The Bezels of Wisdom) with close connection to the theological issue of the divine attributes. Ibn al-ʿArabī claims the entire cosmos is in its essence a created manifestation of the divine virtuous attributes and names, in which man is a polished microcosmic being. Extensive engagement with Ibn al-ʿArabī's theory of *al-insān al-kāmil* is found in numerous modern studies, such as: Rom Landau, *The Philosophy of Ibn al-ʿArabī* (London: George Allen & Unwin Ltd, 1959), 67–68, 70–75; Masataka Takeshita, *Ibn ʿArabī's Theory of the Perfect Man and its Place in the History of Islamic Thought*, PhD dissertation (Tokyo: Institute for the study of Languages and Cultures of Asia and Africa, Tokyo University of Foreign Studies, 1987); William C. Chittick, "Microcosm, Macrocosm, and Perfect Man in the View of Ibn al-ʿArabī", *Islamic Culture* 63/1–2 (January–April 1989), 1–12.

25 According to the Islamic narrative, part of Muḥammad's initiation to prophethood is denoted as *shaqq al-ṣadr* ("the splitting of the chest"), when angels sent by God opened Muḥammad's chest and removed and purified his heart in preparation for receiving the Quran (according to other Hadith accounts this was in Muḥammad's childhood and/or before Muḥammad's ascendance to the skies, *miʿrāj*). At times, the *ḥadīth* is considered to refer to verse 94:1 in the Quran "Did We not relieve your heart for you?"; Muḥammad ibn Ismāʿīl Abū ʿAbdallāh al-Bukhāri 'l-Juʿfi (d. 256/870), *Ṣaḥīḥ al-Bukhārī*, ed. Muḥammad Zuhayr Nāṣir al-Nāṣir, in 9 vols. (Beirut: Dār Ṭawq al-Najāh, 1422/[2001]), 1: 78 (*ḥadīth* 349), 2:156 (*ḥadīth* 1636), 4:135 (*ḥadīth* 3342); Muslim ibn al-Ḥajjāj Abu 'l-Ḥasan al-Qushayri 'l-Nīsābūrī (d. 261/874), *Ṣaḥīḥ Muslim*, ed. Muḥammad Fu'ād ʿAbd al-Bāqī, in 5 vols. (Beirut: Dār Iḥyā' al-Turāth al-ʿArabī, [1374]/[1954]), 1:148 (*ḥadīth* 263).

guiding with it whoever We will of Our servants." This verse assists Ibn al-Qayyim in his interpretation of the following verse Q 93:6–7 "[6]Did He not find you an orphan and shelter you, [7]find you lost and guide you [...]?" Hence, as the Revelation itself provided guidance to God's Messenger, he is the most perfectly God-created man of Reason (*aʿqal^{a} khalq^{i} Allāh^{i}*). According to Ibn al-Qayyim, this notion reconciles with God's words in verse Q 34:50 "Say, 'If I go astray, that is my loss, and if I am rightly guided, it is thorough what my Lord has revealed to me'." Clearly being ironic, Ibn al-Qayyim asks: how then—given the scriptural evidence—can those men of foolish Reason (*sufahāʾ al-ʿuqūl*), deprived of dreams and visions (*akhfāʾ al-aḥlām*) and fickle-hearted (*farāsh al-albāb*), achieve the truths of faith using their Reason alone without the texts of the prophets (*nuṣūṣ al-anbiyāʾ*)? Ibn al-Qayyim then cites the verses Q 19:89–90 [89]"How terrible is this thing you assert: [90]it almost causes the heavens to be torn apart, the earth to split in thunder, the mountains to crumble to pieces."[26] This means, compared to the Prophet's most complete mental capacity of retaining Reason resulting from a direct divine guidance, rationalistic scholars do not stand even the slightest chance to attain certain knowledge on faith. Ibn al-Qayyim constructs his argument here utilizing Quranic verses and the traditionalistic exegetical method of *al-tafsīr al-qurʾān bil-qurʾān*; "exegesis of the Quran by the Quran", in other words, interpreting a verse (here, 42:52) by the means of evidence taken from the Quran itself (here, verse 93:6–7).[27] However, the interpretation offered by Ibn al-Qayyim reflects to a great extent his own point of view and is constructed to support his claim against rationalism. Ibn al-Qayyim deploys here an interpretation mode that closely adheres to the textual sources.

The next subject in Ibn al-Qayyim's epistemological discussion—after focusing on the human factors—is the unique linguistic merit of the sacred textual sources, which requires the knowledge they produce to be of full certainty. In this respect, Ibn al-Qayyim's use of linguistic assertions become highly apparent and, therefore, the arguments taken from the grammatical field of knowledge in favor of his anti-rationalistic view; in this case, Ibn al-Qayyim's interpretation better fits the rationalistic *tafsīr bil-rayʾ* "exegesis of opinion" (i.e., an interpretation that articulates the scholar's personal opinion while not necessarily making use of the canonical textual materials). Ibn al-Qayyim thus presents a varied technique which intertwines traditionalism and rationalism.

26 Ibn Qayyim al-Jawziyya, *al-Ṣawāʿiq al-mursala*, 2:734–735 (*al-wajh al-rābiʿ wal-arbaʿūn*).

27 A comprehensive survey of the topic of Quran interpretation can be found in: Claude Gilliot, "Exegesis of the Qurʾān: Classical and Medieval," *Encyclopedia of the Qurʾān*, 2:99–124.

First, he stresses the believer's obligation (*ḥujja*) to abide by the texts of the Quran and Sunna, including verbal indicative evidence (*adilla lafẓiyya*) which produce certainty of knowledge.[28] Apparent here is his view of fideism, according to which, religious faith is itself the very basis of truth.[29] Shortly afterwards, Ibn al-Qayyim describes the Quranic textual qualities—both in terms of content and style—and their sheer benefits for forming an impeccable clarity of meaning. Evidently, Ibn al-Qayyim relies on the exegetical genre of *maʿāni ʾl-Qurʾān* (i.e., "the meanings of the Quran" or "the qualities of the Quran")[30] which once again lends his discourse the feel of being an adaptation of rationalistic argumentation methods. As Ibn al-Qayyim's linguistically-inspired arguments seem to be somewhat repetitive, I will illustrate here his general line of discussion while also referring to several interesting exemplary cases of his bold tendency to rationalize the Taymiyyan traditional arguments.

Ibn al-Qayyim's positive conceptualization of the linguistic aspects of the certainty of knowledge produced by the holy sources follows what has been depicted as "the contextual approach to meaning and interpretation" initiated by Ibn Taymiyya.[31] Ibn al-Qayyim further establishes this view as he begins with a universal statement on the most basic nature of any human language, and then specifies the locus and status of the sacred scriptures:

---

28 Ibn Qayyim al-Jawziyya, *al-Ṣawāʿiq al-mursala*, 2:735–737 (*al-wajh al-khāmis wal-arbaʿūn*).

29 Relevant in this aspect is that Henri Laoust designated Aḥmad ibn Ḥanbal's (d. 241/855, the renowned traditionist of Baghdad who became the eponym of the Ḥanbalite school, and played an important role in Sunni scholarship, also in its later stages) approach concerning the theological issue of the divine attributes as "fideism"; Laoust, "Aḥmad b. Ḥanbal," *EI*², 1:275; Maqdisi, "Ḥanbalite Islam," 216.

30 This branch in Quranic sciences was developed via the introduction of grammar and the linguistic sciences to the exegetical theories namely associated with early rationalistic schools such as the Muʿtazilite school (ca. 3rd/9th century). This encounter aided in making Quranic exegesis appear as a "sure science", backed up with the sureness of grammar. However, many jurists, theologians, and exegetes were reluctant to see the Quranic text used as a subject of grammar; in their opinion, the only "sure science" was the traditions of the Prophet. Despite the later more traditionalistic inclination in the field of Quranic exegesis, the dialectic *Kalām*ic theology found ways to insert linguistics into the exegetical field; Claude Gilliot, "Exegesis of the Qurʾān," 2:109–110.

31 Several prominent aspects of Ibn Taymiyya's contextual theory are discussed in this study, particularly in relation to his and Ibn al-Qayyim's rejection of the *ḥaqīqa-majāz* dichotomy. Of most relevance to this subject is Ibn al-Qayyim's refutation of the third *ṭāghūt*, which will be examined later in chapter 5. Also, see footnote 15 in this chapter.

His[32] saying that 'knowing the thing indicated by verbal indicator [or: expression] is dependent on the existence of many meanings [to one word; *naql*, polysemy][33] in the language' (*inn*^{a} *'l-ilm*^{a} *bi-madlūl*^{i} *'l-addila*^{ti} *'l-lafẓiyya*^{ti} *mauqūf*^{un} *ʿalā naql*^{i} *'l-lugha*^{ti}) is false.

That is because the indication of the Quran and the Sunna on the meanings therein is of the same kind as any indication [of meaning] in any people's language, based on what they know and are accustomed to use in that language. This is not special to the Arabs alone, but a matter that occurs necessarily amongst all human beings. Their knowledge of the thing indicated by their language is dependent on their mastery over that language in which the exchange of words occurs. For this reason, God sent a Messenger who speaks the language of his people, so that [the message] is clear to them, and thus the evident proof (*ḥujja*) is furnished for them through the verbal message that he [i.e., the Messenger] transmitted to them, a message that they understand.

Therefore, the indication/signification of the word (*fa-dalāla*^{ta} *'l-lafẓ*^{i}) is to know the speaker's intention (*qaṣd*).

A signification (*dalāla*) contains two matters: 1. Transmission of the signified thing (*naql*^{u} *'l-dāll*^{i}), 2. Comprehensibility of the expression (*kawn*^{u} *'l-lafẓ*^{i} *bi-ḥayth*^{i} *yufham*^{u} *maʿnā*^{an}). For this reason, it is said: one signified a signification with his speech, and that the speech signified a signification, so that the speaker signifies by his speech and his speech signifies by its arrangement.

We know this from the speaker's habitual use of his expressions (*ʿāda*^{ti} *'l-mutakallim*^{i} *fī alfāẓih*^{i}). When it is his habit to propose by an expression a specific meaning, then we know that this is his intention when he uses it, for two reasons:

*First, the signification of the expression (*dalāla*^{tu} *'l-lafẓ*^{i}) is founded upon the speaker's habit, which is observed in his words and upon the rationale behind his language in which he habitually speaks. If the hearer knows the meaning of the expression and knows that it is the speaker's habit to use that expression in its meaning, he will then know for cer-

32 Ibn al-Qayyim refers here to the Ashʿarite scholar Fakhr al-Dīn al-Rāzī, whose epistemological stance on the matter will be examined later in section 3.2.

33 The theoretical translation of the word *naql* in this linguistic context is "the process of assigning a new meaning to an old expression … the process of *transferring* an expression from its original meaning to a new one." Thus, the technical term usually used in order to translate the word *naql* in this context is "polysemy" (from Greek, 'of many meanings'); Ali, *Medieval Islamic Pragmatics*, 107, 138.

> tain (*qaṭʿ*^{an}) that that meaning is the speaker's intention. Otherwise no speaker's intention can ever be known, which is impossible.
>
> Second, if the goal of the speaker is to make his utterance understood by the hearer, and the addressee […] knows via the speaker's character and the way he speaks (*ṭarīqa*^{tihi} *wa-ṣifa*^{tihi}) that the speaker wants to make his intention manifest and not to deceive him, the addressee will, given he obtains the knowledge of both the above matters [i.e., he knows the meaning of the expression and knows that it is the speaker's habit to make his intention manifest], be fully certain (*afāda*^{hu} … *'l-yaqīn*^{a}) of the speaker's intention and never to doubt it. If, by contrast, he fails to recover the speaker's intention, it would mean that there is something wrong either with his knowledge of the meaning of the expression or with his knowledge of the speaker's way of speaking (*ʿibāra*^{ti} *'l-mutakallim*^{i}), his character (*ṣifāt*^{ihi}) and his goal (*qaṣd*^{ihi}).*[34]

Common knowledge of language and its particles of speech is presented here as the conventional and, indeed, sufficient means of attaining full confidence in the speaker's intention. Ibn al-Qayyim replies to a later Ashʿarite claim that, at times, an expression (i.e., a verbal indicator) can have more than a single conclusive meaning—that is, it may have several differentiated meanings—and therefore is not able to produce certain knowledge. In turn, Ibn al-Qayyim discards this claim and says that every language has its habitual conventions (*ʿādāt*) of using a singular expression for a particular intention (*murād*). When the listener strives to follow the speaker's habitual norms of speech and knows the speaker's aim is to be understood, then there should be no doubt regarding the delivered meaning, which is crystal clear and, therefore, certain. In addition, this claim is even more strongly validated when the speakers are God and His Messenger, as the certainty of speech they produce soars above any other speaker (*ifāda*^{tu} *kalām*^{i} *Allāh*^{i} *wa-rasūlih*^{i} *lil-yaqīn*^{i} *fawq*^{a} *istafāda*^{ti} *dhālik*^{a} *min kalām*^{i} *kull*^{i} *mutakallim*^{in}). The more the listener is familiar with the speaker, his characteristics, his goal, his clarity and his habitual use of the language, the more complete will be his grasp of the speaker's intention.[35]

---

34 Ibn Qayyim al-Jawziyya, *al-Ṣawāʿiq al-mursala*, 2:742–744 (*al-wajh al-tāsiʿ wal-arbaʿūn*). The translation for the section between the asterisks is taken from: Ali, *Medieval Islamic Pragmatics*, 134; the author refers there to the equivalent section as it appears if *al-Ṣawāʿiq*'s abridgement of Ibn al-Mawṣilī; however, it remains faithful to the original text with no major alterations. *Mukhtaṣar al-ṣawāʿiq*, 1:222–223. The Arabic terminology used in the text was inserted into the translation by me.

35 Ibn Qayyim al-Jawziyya, *al-Ṣawāʿiq al-mursala*, 2:744.

The linguistic reasoning presented by Ibn al-Qayyim further develops as he depicts the special textual nature of the Quran and its exceptional process of transmission. Ibn al-Qayyim claims the verbal expressions of the Quran are *nuṣūṣ ṣarīḥa* (i.e., expressions that manifest unequivocal meaning),[36] thus producing a cogent certainty of knowledge (*al-yaqīn al-qaṭʿī*).[37] Afterward, Ibn al-Qayyim once again opposes the later Ashʿarite claim that "understanding the meaning of verbal indicators is dependent on the [correct] transmission of their grammatical inflection and morphological structure (*al-naḥū wal-taṣrīf*)." When it comes to the text of the Quran, Ibn al-Qayyim claims its inflections (*iʿrāb*) were massively transmitted—just as its expressions and their meanings were—in *tawātur*, in other words, by multiple trustworthy chains of transmission, a method which guarantees their authenticity.[38] Moreover, the transmission of the Quran—together with all its linguistic features—is the most correct version to be found on earth in that the rules of grammar and morphology are discerned by the Quranic text, as well as other significant principles, such as those of all legal affairs. In this respect Ibn al-Qayyim puts into practice Ibn Taymiyya's "contextual theory of definition" on the Quranic text: an expression's meaning is conceptualized by a defining context, based on the observation that "the relationship between the expression and the meaning is conventional."[39] This time, the Quran and Hadith themselves are taken as the defining "bed" and, hence, the ultimate context of the expressions therein. Taken here even further, the Quran and Hadith are seen as operating in a dimension of absolute certainty of meaning, in which the speakers are God and His Messenger. Since it is the sacred speech of God and his Messenger transmitted by *tawātur*, it is no ordinary habitual use of a language, but rather that of the divine. As a result, the verbal indicative expressions found in these texts are defined with the utmost certainty possible, thus producing certain knowledge.

Next, and with an obvious mocking tone, Ibn al-Qayyim rebukes "the exponents of that rule", maintaining that:

> They say: 'the most explicit expression (*aẓhar al-alfāẓ*) is *Allāh*,' and yet they have forcefully differed from one another about its understanding.

36 The commonly used translation of the word *naṣṣ* is 'text', yet here it is used as a technical term better translated as 'unequivocal meaning'; Ali, *Medieval Islamic Pragmatics*, 128.

37 Ibn Qayyim al-Jawziyya, *al-Ṣawāʿiq al-mursala*, 2:745 (*al-wajh al-thānī wal-khamsūn*).

38 A.J. Wensinck, [W.F. Heinrichs], "Mutawātir," *EI*², 7:781–782; G.H.A. Juynboll, "Tawātur," *EI*², 10:381–382. Muslim traditionalists upheld the notion that *tawātur* produces necessary knowledge; Abrahamov, "Necessary Knowledge", 21–22.

39 Ali, *Medieval Islamic Pragmatics*, 95–96.

> Is it a form derived from another word (*mushtaqq*^{un}) or not? And if so, is it derived from *al-taʾalluh* [root *ʾ-l-h*,][40] from *al-walah* [root *w-l-y*][41] or from *lāh* [root *l-y-h*]?[42] The same applies to the word *ṣalāt* [i.e. prayer]—there is disagreement [on its derivation]. Is it derived from [the meaning of] 'humbly asking for God's bestowing' (*duʿāʾ*), or from 'to follow with respect of actions' (*ittibāʿ*), or from the movement of the hindquarters (*taḥrīk*^{i} *ʾl-ṣalwayn*^{i}) [which reminds the movement of one who performs the Muslim prayer]? If this is 'the most explicit expression', why do they suspect it of being something else?
>
> Behold of this error and deception, this uncertainty and deceit: all of the people in the world, both learned men and ignorant, whether they know [theoretical] derivations or not, either Arab or not, they all know that '*Allāh*' designates the Lord of the world, the creator of the skies and earth who gives life and puts to death, the Lord and govern of all things. They have no disagreements about the signified intention of this noun. It is the most explicit for them, the most celebrated, and the most famous of all names, in terms of assigning a name with its meaning (*waḍʿ*). Even if people are arguing about its derivation, this is not an argument concerning its meaning. The case of the word *ṣalāt* is the same [...] It is only a disagreement about an aspect (*wajh*) of the indication of an expression (*dalālat*^{i} *ʾl-lafẓ*^{i}) on that meaning, as they agree on that single meaning [...] thus, this expression provides the listener with certainty (*al-yaqīn*) in its intention (*musammā*, nominatum).[43]

As this passage shows, grammar is seen as an important means of attaining a correct understanding of verbal indicative evidence from the sacred texts in order to obtain certainty of knowledge. However, in Ibn al-Qayyim's view, the Quranic habitual context of expressions and their common use in language came before fixed grammatical theory. Whether scholars deliberate on a verbal expression's root (e.g., as represented by the example of the expression *Allāh*) or on its derivation of meaning (e.g., the expression *ṣalāt*)[44] in

40 In other words, to be perplexed, "since minds are confused by His greatness or majesty, or because He is the object of resource of protection"; Lane, *Arabic-English Lexicon*, 1:83.

41 In other words, to hold authority, to govern; Lane, *Arabic-English Lexicon*, supplements: 3060.

42 In other words, another possible origin for the Arabic word 'God'; *Lane, Arabic-English Lexicon*, supplements, 3015.

43 Ibn Qayyim al-Jawziyya, *al-Ṣawāʿiq al-mursala*, 2:749–751.

44 In fact, the word *ṣalāt* comes from Aramaic (Syriac); G. Monnot, "Ṣalāt," *EI*^{2}, 3:925.

both cases, the singular intended meaning is clear to all those taking part in Islamic discourse. Grammatical lengthy debates are valid, and yet they do not affect the conclusive meaning of the expression.[45] Ibn al-Qayyim reveals his extensive knowledge of the rationalistic arguments of grammar, their subdivisions and instances, while at the same convincingly responding to them so far as to ridicule the entire initial claim. Indeed, as he makes use of the linguistic approach to reaffirm his traditionalistic view, he expertly 'reconstructs' a grammatical counter-argument: verbal indicative evidence supply certainty of knowledge also when examining the matter through a 'rationalistic'-linguistic lens. To Ibn al-Qayyim, the meaning originated in those expressions is the one and only, and can be easily perceived when one is aware of the common conventions of the language used in the Islamic holy texts.

Ibn al-Qayyim's linguistic reasoning reflects another aspect of Ibn Taymiyya's contextual view of the language, upholding the basic notion that in order for an expression to have a clear meaning, it must be read and understood within a defining context. In other words, a single expression which stands on its own—isolated and without context—is deprived of conveying meaning and cannot be considered a meaningful part of a language.[46] The epistemological implications of this stance are clarified by Ibn al-Qayyim when he negates the rationalistic skeptical approach, according to which an expression may convey more than a single meaning and, therefore, does not produce certainty. Ibn al-Qayyim answers:

> It is known that the scholars of linguistics (*ahl al-lugha*) do not permit the speaker to speak on his intention in a way that contradicts its apparent [meaning] (*khilāf^{a} ẓāhir^{ihi}*), unless [he provides] a context that clarifies his intention. A metaphor (*majāz*) indicates [a meaning] only when it appears in a context (*qarīna*) [that signifies a meaning] other than the

45 The resemblance to Ibn Ḥazm's grammatical theories is striking, and it is possible Ibn al-Qayyim draws on the former's teachings to a certain extent. Ibn Ḥazm held a negative view of the speculative approach to language. Instead, "in his *Rasā'il* he clearly encourages the study of Arabic language in its two main areas, grammar and lexicon, but, and that is important, within limits". The idea is that full knowledge of religion cannot be acquired without basic linguistic knowledge; Salvador Peña, "Which Curiosity? Ibn Ḥazm's Suspicion of Grammarians," in: Adang, Camilla; Fierro, Ma. Isabel; Schmidtke, Sabine (eds.), *Ibn Ḥazm of Cordoba: The life and works of a controversial thinker* (Leiden, Boston: Brill, 2013), 235–236, 240, 244–245.

46 Ali, *Medieval Islamic Pragmatics*, 98–100.

> literal one (*ḥaqīqa*); then it indicates an abstract meaning (*tajarrud*). In a similar manner, omission [of an expression] (*ḥadhf*) or an implication [of a meaning] (*iḍmār*) are forbidden, unless the speech contains an indicator for them. This is also the case of a specification (*takhṣīṣ*); one is forbidden to use it, unless they provide a context that indicates it.[47]

As we can see, Ibn al-Qayyim perceives the context in which an expression appears as the prime provider of its meaning. Setting forth a grammatical explanation on which he elaborates, Ibn al-Qayyim lists different cases of possible ambiguity in the language (in another section he also mentions the case of a homonym; *ishtirāk*), and solves all of them with the conception of contextual cohesion. Stressing the point even further, Ibn al-Qayyim argues that, since it is articulated with apparent expressions (*min*[a] *'l-qarā'in*[i] *mā yajib*[u] *an yakūn*[a] *lafẓiy*[yan]), when a context exists, it is impossible to overlook. Therefore, knowledge produced from an expression together with its context is determinative and conclusively understood and, hence, certain.

Ibn al-Qayyim further develops his linguistic discussion on the Quranic expressions, as he depicts another rationalistic argument regarding several of its peculiarities of expression: since the Quran introduced numerous words/nouns (*asmāʾ*) into the Arabic language previously unknown to Arabs until their Revelation, they are potential reasons for obscuring meaning; thus, they do not produce certainty. These nouns denote the religious obligations (*al-asmāʾ al-sharʿiyya*), such as *ṣalāt, zakāt, ṣiyām* (prayer, religious donation, fasting) etc.; the religious faith (*al-asmāʾ al-dīniyya*), such as *islām, imān, kufr* (devotion to God, belief, heresy) etc.; collective nouns (*asmāʾ mujmala*), such as *al-sāriq/al-sāriqa, al-zānī/al-zāniya* (a thief, an adulterer of either sex, in legal matters) etc.; or homonyms (*asmāʾ mushtaraka*), such as *qarʾ* (which has two contradictory meanings: menstruation, or a state of purity from menstrual discharge) or the verb *ʿasʿas*[a] (which also has two contradictory meanings: [darkness] either coming or ending, Q 81:17) etc. After carefully explaining this, Ibn al Qayyim provides a systematically arrayed answer to the alleged predicament, maintaining these nouns exist in the Quran with three kinds of clarifications (*anwāʿ al-bayān*):

1. Attached clarification (*bayān muqtarin*)—the noun appears together with clarification. Together they produce certainty of the noun's intention.

---

47 Ibn Qayyim al-Jawziyya, *al-Ṣawāʿiq al-mursala*, 2:752 (*al-wajh al-sādis wal-khamsūn*).

2. Separated clarification (*bayān munfaṣil*)—the clarification for the noun appears in another Quranic verse. Combining the two together produces certainty of the noun's intention.
3. Clarification of reliance on the Prophet Muḥammad (*bayān mawkūl*)—the noun is clarified by the sayings of the Prophet; together they produce certainty of the noun's intention.[48]

Evidently, the solution Ibn al-Qayyim suggests originates from the traditionalistic hermeneutical methods of *tafsīr al-qur'ān bil-qur'ān* (the first and second clarifications) and *tafsīr bil-ma'thūr* (the third one).[49] Once again, Ibn al-Qayyim employs the contextual theoretical approach and identifies the Islamic texts themselves—whether the Quran or the Prophet's Sunna—as the clarifying means for an expression that could be perceived as indicating a vague meaning. Ibn al-Qayyim stresses that certainty of knowledge is achieved in all three cases mentioned above, even when the clarifying text is placed far from the ambiguous noun. In this manner, the speech of God and His Messenger never lose their authoritative position as producers of certain knowledge.[50]

In the following phase, Ibn al-Qayyim further illustrates his positive conceptualization of the Islamic Scriptures as the most authoritative source of certain knowledge. In Arabic, such indications are called *adilla samʿiyya* (revelational proofs), and refer to knowledge that can only be found in divine Revelation. In this context, the expression can be translated as "informative indicators", implying knowledge originating in the religious scriptures.[51] In the words of Ibn al-Qayyim: "obtaining certainty by the means of the indication of informative indicators, and knowledge of the speaker's intention while using them, is more prosperous and apparent (*aysar^{u} wa-aẓhar^{u}*) than by means of the indication of rational indications (*al-adilla^{ti} al-ʿaqliyya^{ti}*)." To support this view, Ibn al-Qayyim uses as an example an infant's basic understanding of communication: the first actions they take result from their intuitive grasp of understand-

48 Ibn Qayyim al-Jawziyya, *al-Ṣawāʿiq al-mursala*, 2:753–754 (*al-wajh al-sābiʿ wal-khamsūn*).

49 As explained on page 124 above.

50 Ibn Qayyim al-Jawziyya, *al-Ṣawāʿiq al-mursala*, 2:757.

51 "samʿ," *EI*^{2}*: Glossary and Index of Terms*. Last accessed on July 6, 2015 http://referenceworks.brillonline.com/entries/encyclopaedia-of-islam-2-Glossary-and-Index-of-Terms/sam-SIM_gi_04106; Several English translations are used for the notion of *samʿ*, namely "authoritarian; scriptural or traditional authority." Mostly capturing the gist of the term's implicated meaning, this translation insufficiently transfer relation to the more basic meaning as "information" or "knowledge" (achieved by hearing). Here I adapt the latter, found in: Ali, *Medieval Islamic Pragmatics*, 45.

ing their parents' intentions by listening to what their parents are saying (*bi-khiṭābihimā*). This is a simple fact of life occurring long before children become acquainted with rational indications. Even more so, a person who wishes to teach someone the required meaning of a rational indicator (*muqtadā 'l-dalīl*^{i} *'l-ʿaqlī*) cannot do so until they fully inform the pupil of the intended meaning of the verbal expressions, which literally form that specific rational indicator. Thus, the teacher must first clarify the meaning of the informative indicators, which is required to understanding the rational indictor. According to Ibn al-Qayyim, this is the natural alignment of the different layers of information within the human mind, which in its final stage produces knowledge. Moreover, according to Ibn al-Qayyim, no human being can do without informative indicators; how can they, when God taught Adam—their "father"—the principles of informative indicators? These are all names (*asmāʾ*), words and their meanings, as well as knowledge of the Revelation (*waḥī*) that cannot be known by Reason alone. This is also the case of all the prophets who delivered knowledge with informative indicators, which they could have not obtain by their Reason; since it is God's message (*khiṭāb Allāh*), their prophecy conveys certainty. God guided the prophets and their followers using informative indicators, not rational indicators.[52]

Ibn al-Qayyim develops his view further, seeking to re-establish the conception that the prophecy contains informative messages revealed to the prophet (*ann*^{a} *'l-nubuwwa*^{ta} *khiṭāb*^{un} *samʿī*^{un}). Thus, Ibn al-Qayyim demonstrates his familiarity with the Aristotelian philosophical approach regarding prophecy, to which he dismissively answers:

> [Prophecy ...] is not only knowing the truths by the power of holiness which separates [the prophet] from others, by the power of imagination which enables conceptualization and fine observation, and by the power of influence which enables to manage freely among the different groups of people in the world, as the *mutafalsifa* say. They also say that the information (*maʿārif*) of the prophet is attained only by the mediation of rational syllogism (*bi-wisāṭa*^{ti} *'l-qyās*^{i} *'l-ʿaqlī*) similar to all other human beings, but his perception is quicker and more complete (*huw*^{a} *asraʿ*^{u} *wa-akmal*^{u} *idrāk*^{an}) than that of all other average people and God knows this. They also argue that certainty and knowledge are to be produced only from rational indicators, not from scriptural-informative

52 Ibn Qayyim al-Jawziyya, *al-Ṣawāʿiq al-mursala*, 2:757–759 (*al-wajh al-thāmin wal-khamsūn*). The topic of the origin of language will be examined in detail in section 5.1 hereafter.

> indicators [...] This is one of the principles of philosophy (*aḥad*[u] *uṣūl*[i] *'l-falsafa*), atheism (*ilḥād*) and heresy (*zanadiqa*), which includes the forsaking of the prophecies and informative indicators God's messengers delivered, as well as the enthroning of the logical doctrines and the philosophical views. The later Jahmites [i.e., Ibn al-Qayyim's contemporary Ashʿarites] adopted this principle and used it to assault 'the people of the Book and the Sunna' [i.e., the traditionalists]. Their predecessors [i.e., the early Ashʿarites] neither declared it nor stressed it; however, the later ones openly revealed this struggle, stripped off the mantles of religion (*alqaw jilbāb*[a] *'l-dīn*[i]), and declared on their disposal of the way of Revelation.
>
> Muslim believers, and all of people of faith (*ahl*[u] *'l-milal*[i]), know the most complete teaching is that of God who taught Adam all of the names, the most complete speech is that of God to Mūsā [*kalīm*[u] *Allāh* is known as Moses' epithet, meaning 'the prophet who talked with God'], and the kinds of knowledge (*ʿulūm*, pl. of *ʿilm*) of most superiority and greatness as producers of certainty are those that God introduced to His prophets in the mediation of *samʿ* [i.e., scriptural authoritative indications].[53]

In this passage Ibn al-Qayyim criticizes the Muslim philosophers' approach in which they prefer to rely on rational indicators alone in the attempt to reach certainty of knowledge, instead of putting their faith in the Quran and Hadith. Moreover, due to their willingness to give in to the philosophical version of the use of Reason, the Ashʿarite scholars constituting Ibn al-Qayyim's intellectual milieu are considered to be the philosopher's accomplices. As Ibn al-Qayyim illustrates above as well as in his discussion thus far, the righteous alternative favors the exact meaning as found in the textual sources. Interestingly enough, this brings into mind the Stoic logical system which engaged with dialectics and the epistemology of language. They developed the idea of "the inference from *signs*"; translated to Arabic as *dalāʾil*.[54] On the whole, Ibn al-Qayyim obvi-

53 Ibn Qayyim al-Jawziyya, *al-Ṣawāʿiq al-mursala*, 2:759–760 (*al-wajh al-tāsiʿ wal-khamsūn*).

54 S. van den Bergh, "Dalīl," *EI*², 2:101–102. We have already seen another element of resemblance to the Stoic logical thought in Ibn al-Qayyim's positive conceptualization of the human ability to reach certainty of knowledge about God through the senses. The Stoics also held a somewhat similar optimistic view about the possibility of obtaining stated truths by means of the human experience of "cognitive impressions" (i.e., sensations grasped by the human mind). This epistemic notion was criticized by members of the New Academy, who were highly skeptical; how can one accurately recognize having such an experience? Dirk Baltzly, "Stoicism", *The Stanford Encyclopedia of Philosophy* (spring 2014 Edition), Edward N. Zalta (ed.). URL page was last viewed on July 17th 2015. http://

ously sides here with optimistic fideism, once again promoting the informative indicators found in texts holy to Islam as providing cast-iron certainty.

Yet another emphasis appears directly after this passage in the form of a comparison used to illustrate the gap of value between knowledge achieved by the informative indicators—which were revealed to the prophets—and truthful knowledge (*al-ʿulūm*^{i} *'l-ṣaḥīḥa*^{ti}) achieved by the thoughts of the rationalists. Ibn al-Qayyim compares the dissimilarity between these two kinds of valid knowledge to that which distinguishes a grain of mustard to an enormous mountain. How, then, the relation (*nisba*) between the certain and informative kinds of knowledge (*al-ʿulūm*^{i} *'l-samʿiyya*^{ti} *'l-yaqīna*^{ti}) of the prophets and the imaginary views (*al-shibh*^{i} *'l-khyāliyya*^{ti})—which resemble those of the Sophistic philosophers—can ever realize?[55] Once more, Ibn al-Qayyim refers here to the Sophistic thought, which is famous for its highly skeptical epistemological assessment, and scorns it as being utterly absurd. In Ibn al-Qayyim's opinion, scriptural informative indications (*adilla samʿiyya*) are thus perceived as producers of certainty. This kind of verbal indicative evidence (*adilla lafẓiyya*) attains its authority by the power of traditionalistic fideism; however, Ibn al-Qayyim's logical deduction achieved by making a comparison to Sophistic philosophical thought can be seen as an additional dialectical argument supporting his claim. In other words, when Ibn al-Qayyim carefully explains his preference for traditionalistic thought in a comparative manner, he most obviously employs a dialectical type of argumentation represented in the *Kalām*ic discourse.[56]

Ibn al-Qayyim's overall positive conceptualization of the epistemological benefits of the Islamic textual sources as illustrated above suitably demonstrates the general approach taken towards the first *ṭāghūt* in *al-Ṣawāʿiq*. Therefore, at this point I would like to depart from the description of Ibn al-Qayyim's discussion and make several observations to conclude it. These observations

---

plato.stanford.edu/archives/spr2014/entries/stoicism. I would prefer to refrain from an over-generalization of these few points of similarity; by no means do I aim to present Ibn al-Qayyim as an advocate of stoicism. Albeit, I would say that the guise of the epistemological-theological disputations between these ancient Greek philosophical schools is, to a certain extent, echoed in the texts of *al-Ṣawāʿiq*, as well as the Islamic traditionalistic-rationalistic deliberations on the matter. However, this question deserves to be explored and analyzed as the subject of another study.

55 Ibn Qayyim al-Jawziyya, *al-Ṣawāʿiq al-mursala*, 2:761.

56 The resemblance to Ibn Ḥazm is not coincidental, as has been mentioned in footnotes 22 and 45 above. However, Ibn Ḥazm's literalist approach is rationally articulated by Ibn al-Qayyim.

will lead us forward to the next section with a more detailed contextualization of the epistemological ideas Ibn al-Qayyim delivers in *al-Ṣawāʿiq*, as described above. In a broader sense, we will also be able to more accurately appropriate the place of Ibn al-Qayyim's work within the intellectual network of connections and interrelations among the scholastic milieu of his epoch (and possibly even earlier). For the time being, however, let us pinpoint several prominent remarks concerning the singular discussion on the certainty of knowledge:

First, it is essential to properly place Ibn al-Qayyim's refutation of the first *ṭāghūt* within the general framework of the text of *al-Ṣawāʿiq*, as well as discern the relation between *al-Ṣawāʿiq* and its abridgement. As previously mentioned, the first *ṭāghūt* appears both in Al-Dakhil Allah's critical edition of *al-Ṣawāʿiq* from 1998 and in al-ʿAlawī's critical edition of the abridged *Mukhtaṣar al-ṣawāʿiq* (of Ibn al-Mawṣilī) from 2004. Nonetheless, the difference between these two available sources is highly significant for the aim of this current inspection: Al-Dakhil Allāh mentions that the refutation in *al-Mukhtaṣar* contains only 18 out of the 73 sections (*wajh*; pl. *wujūh*) discussed in Ibn al-Qayyim's original work—starting with the 40th section onwards and omitting all previous 39 sections.[57] Supporting this report, al-ʿAlawī states that many of the various proofs and examples presented by Ibn al-Qayyim in *al-Ṣawāʿiq* were completely omitted, summed up or reedited into different segments. As a whole, al-ʿAlawī counts only 17 sections from *al-Ṣawāʿiq*'s first refutation remaining in *al-Mukhtaṣar*.[58] This means Ibn al-Mawṣilī considerably shortened Ibn al-Qayyim's original refutation, while totally neglecting the opening parts. In this regard, I can see the rationale behind Ibn al-Mawṣilī's choice to abridge Ibn al-Qayyim's epistemological deliberation. Categorically, the first 39 sections are of a more polemical nature and mostly express Ibn al-Qayyim's criticism of rationalistic arguments. The 40th section onwards, however, expresses the same critical ideology with a tendency towards being far more positive and didactical. Indeed, during my own inquiry of Ibn al-Qayyim's refutation of the first *ṭāghūt*, I also noticed these nuances (as well as some repetitions). Thus, I also decided to delve into the positive conceptualization Ibn al-Qayyim offers, rather than on the argumentative and combative opening sections.[59]

57 Ibn Qayyim al-Jawziyya, *al-Ṣawāʿiq al-mursala*, the editor's introduction, 1:120–121; Al-Dakhil Allāh also provides a detailed table, which compares the sections appearing in *al-Ṣawāʿiq* with those of *al-Mukhtaṣar*, and exactly identifies the numbers of the sections that do appear in *al-Mukhtaṣar* with respect to the sections in *al-Ṣawāʿiq*.

58 Ibn Qayyim al-Jawziyya, *Mukhtaṣar al-ṣawāʿiq al-mursala*, the editor's introduction, 1:75.

59 Still, since it is the more complete version of the text available, I have principally relied on

Second, as has already been shown, Ibn al-Qayyim's stance concerning the first *ṭāghūt* eventually reaffirms the value of the transmitted sources of Revelation as the cradle of all knowledge, together with the theological knowledge of certainty. Ibn al-Qayyim's developed deliberation so far provides the evidential infrastructure of his theological and ideological claims on the matter of the divine attributes. In this respect, highly notable is the fact that Ibn al-Qayyim's discussion here does not deal with theology per se but, rather, emphasizes epistemology and the theoretical aspects of knowledge acquisition.[60] The broad theological issue of divine attributes supplies the intellectual foundation for his discussion. Indeed, epistemology is the cardinal theme of interest for Ibn al-Qayyim as he examines the first *ṭāghūt*, while the theological issue of divine attributes is the thematic umbrella overarching *al-Ṣawāʿiq* as a whole.

Third, the fact that Ibn al-Qayyim's positive epistemological view mainly draws on the ideology of Ibn Taymiyya, perceiving the Islamic sources of Revelation as the premier producers of both worldly and supernatural knowledge, is evident. Within the intellectual environment of Mamluk Damascus of 8th/14th century, it was Ibn Taymiyya who articulated a clear opposition to the later Ashʿarite rationalistic approach of seeking knowledge about God by utilizing rationalistic methods, such as *Kalām* or philosophy. Ibn Taymiyya's theological thought stemmed from the Islamic notion of the complete dissimilation between God and man; thus, he concluded the human rational process of thinking can never supply knowledge concerning God. Ibn Taymiyya sharply criticized the rationalistic theological approach presented by al-Ghazālī or Fakhr al-Dīn al-Rāzī, for instance, in his work *al-Radd ʿalā al-manṭiqiyyīn* (The Refutation of the Logicians).[61]

In addition, the resemblance between the positive epistemic evaluation of the Islamic texts articulated by Ibn al-Qayyim and the teachings of another ear-

---

the discussion in *al-Ṣawāʿiq*. The abridged version of this text in *al-Mukhtaṣar* was referred to only in cases of particular relevance.

60 The same can also be said on the fourth rationalistic method Ibn al-Qayyim disproves, that "prophetical tradition with a limited number of chains of transmissions (e.g. *ḥadīth al-āḥād*) cannot produce certain knowledge". The tsubject is analyzed in chapter 6 hereinafter.

61 William Montgomery Watt, *Islamic Philosophy and Theology: An Extended Survey* (Edinburgh: Edinburgh University Press, 1985), p. 144; Georges Tamer, "The Curse of Philosophy: Ibn Taymiyya as a Philosopher in Contemporary Islamic Thought" in: G. Tamer and B. Krawietz (eds.), *Islamic Theology, Philosophy and Law: Debating Ibn Taymiyya and Ibn Qayyim al-Jawziyya*, (Berlin: de Gruyter, 2013), 330, 334. The work *al-Radd ʿalā al-manṭiqiyyīn* will be taken as a point of special reference to Ibn Taymiyya's epistemology in section 3.3 hereinafter.

lier scholar, Ibn Ḥazm, is striking, especially in the introduction to his work *al-Faṣl fī 'l-milal wal-ahwāʾ wal-niḥal*. According to the copious list of works Ibn al-Qayyim explicitly mentions in *al-Ṣawāʿiq* (made by its editor al-Dakhīl Allāh), Ibn Ḥazm's work is not recorded amongst the exterior sources stated or used by Ibn al-Qayyim in *al-Ṣawāʿiq*;[62] I also was not able to track any direct citation from *al-Faṣl*. Be that as it may, and given Ibn al-Qayyim's close familiarity with the literary output of Ibn Ḥazm, it is very much plausible that fractions of the Ẓāhirī-literalistic ideology penetrated Ibn al-Qayyim's construction of the discussion on epistemology in *al-Ṣawāʿiq*. Furthermore, *al-Faṣl* is a vast encyclopedic work that deals with theology, heresiography and philosophy, and thus seems to fit the overall thematic context of *al-Ṣawāʿiq*.[63] Nonetheless, in addition to the resemblance to Ibn Ḥazm's opinion on the supremacy of the Islamic texts and the inferiority of linguistic arguments as a means to reach certain knowledge, it is my impression that there is also a difference. Whereas Ibn Ḥazm accepts the use of linguistics at its very basic level, Ibn al-Qayyim actively uses far more intricate linguistic and grammatical issues (more so in his third *ṭāghūt* refutation, see chapter 5). Ibn al-Qayyim's preference for textual sources does not withdraw him from becoming involved in the field of linguistics; rather, it pushes him to partake in it, even in its highly speculative mode. Ibn al-Qayyim's rationalized discussion draws more on the dialectics of the Taymiyyan discourse than on Ibn Ḥazm's scripturalism. At any rate, the close similarity of the ideas Ibn al-Qayyim expresses to the grammatical theory of Ibn Ḥazm is indeed remarkable.

3.2 Fakhr al-Dīn al-Rāzī on Certain Knowledge: Skepticism

Given the centrality of al-Rāzī's thought in Ibn al-Qayyim's refutation of the first argument in *al-Ṣawāʿiq*, one should take into consideration Ibn al-Qayyim's previous significant educational experiences with Fakhr al-Dīn al-Rāzī's writings when investigating his expounded discussion on 'certain knowledge'. Ibn al-Qayyim's focus on al-Rāzī's epistemological thought as the point of departure for his refutation of the first *ṭāghūt*—followed by his confirmation of the

62 Ibn Qayyim al-Jawziyya, *al-Ṣawāʿiq al-mursala*, the editor's introduction, 1:84–92.

63 Ibn al-Qayyim cites from *al-Faṣl* in his two theological works *Kitāb al-rūḥ* and *al-Kāfiya al-shāfiya*, as discussed in: Holtzman, "Elements of Acceptance and Rejection in Ibn Qayyim al-Jawziyya's Systematic Reading of Ibn Ḥazm," in: Adang, Camilla; Fierro, Ma. Isabel; Schmidtke, Sabine (eds.), *Ibn Ḥazm of Cordoba: The life and works of a controversial thinker* (Leiden, Boston: Brill, 2013), 614–629.

superior value of the sources of Revelation—points out to Ibn al-Qayyim's profound familiarity with al-Rāzī's conceptual theory concerning certainty of knowledge. Ibn al-Qayyim's emphasis on al-Rāzī's thought can also hint at the major acceptance of al-Rāzī's approach within the rationalistic scholastic circles of Damascus during Ibn al-Qayyim's time.[64] However, it is possible that, together with this reasoning, Ibn al-Qayyim's heavy reference to al-Rāzī[65] stems from a narrow understanding of al-Rāzī's arguments only in the way rationalistic scholars of Ibn al-Qayyim's era perceived al-Rāzī's thought (i.e., without paying attention to the larger context of al-Rāzī's writings). Such an approach may be indicative of Ibn al-Qayyim's somewhat constricted methodological capacity. The puzzling question of the modus in which the Rāziyyan ideas are used by Ibn al-Qayyim should be kept in mind while critically reading his *al-Ṣawāʿiq*. Especially in light of the previous section, even if Ibn al-Qayyim's comprehension of the Rāziyyan thought was partial, incomplete and perhaps rather selective, I personally believe his work still exhibits a progressive intellectual tendency. Not only did he not ignore the Rāziyyan-Ashʿarism as it was commonly perceived in his lifetime, he also responded to it and dared to criticize it. The same cannot be said for the large majority of the traditionalists in his close Taymiyyan circle or elsewhere. Ibn al-Qayyim's advanced conceptualization of the epistemological matter of the possibility of attaining certainty of knowledge—as it is expressed in *al-Ṣawāʿiq*—surely sustains this claim.

As the previous section focused on Ibn al-Qayyim's positive approach, the present section will touches on the more polemical portion of his writing. Ibn al-Qayyim's refutation of the first *ṭāghūt* starts with a citation of a saying of

64 Several biographical sources report that he studied al-Rāzī's *Muḥaṣṣal* and *Kitāb al arbaʿīn*, and was generally very influenced by Rāziyyan theological thought. Both Ibn al-Qayyim and Ibn Taymiyya saw al-Rāzī as an appreciated ideological rival. In addition, an illuminating example of Ibn al-Qayyim's and Ibn Taymiyya's familiarity with Rāziyyan thought can be found in their discussion on the doctrine of compulsion (*jabr*), in which they adopted and even combined a considerable share of al-Rāzī's arguments on the idea of free will (*ikhtiyār*) in the traditionalistic perception of predetermination (*al-qaḍāʾ wal-qadar*); Holtzman, Livnat, "Debating the Doctrine of *Jabr* (Compulsion): Ibn Qayyim al-Jawziyya Reads Fakhr al-Dīn al-Rāzī," in: Tamer and Krawietz (eds.), *Islamic Theology, Philosophy and Law*, 61–93.

65 Ibn al-Qayyim's second attack in *al-Ṣawāʿiq* is directed against *al-qānūn al-kullī* ("The Universal Rule") initially posed by al-Ghazālī and fully systemized by al-Rāzī. This principle argues that in case of conflict, human Reason (*ʿaql*) is prior to Revelation (*naql*); see further elaboration in chapter 4 hereinafter. This means a sizable part of at last two out of the four rationalistic arguments confronted in *al-Ṣawāʿiq* is drawn directly from later Ashʿarite thought, with special emphasis placed on the Rāzīyyan one.

"their *Kalām* scholar" (*mutakallimuhum*) without mentioning his name; however, giving the accurate references to al-Rāzī's writings, Ibn al-Qayyim is no doubt referring to him:

> A piece of verbal indicative evidence (*al-dalīl al-lafẓī*) does not produce certainty [of knowledge] (*al-yaqīn*), unless ten conditions are ascertained: (1) Infallibility of all the transmitters in the chain of narration (*ruwāh*) in the wording of those expressions (*al-alfāẓ*), (2) in their inflection (*iʿrāb*), and in their morphology (*taṣrīf*); (3) the expression must not be a homonym (*ishtirāk*), (4) a metaphor (*majāz*), (5) a polysemy (*naql*), (6) or any specification of individuals or time (*takhṣīṣ*); (7) there must not occur any implication (*iḍmār*), (8) re-ordering of the sentence's original components (*al-taqdīm wal-taʾkhīr*; hysteron proteron), (9) or abrogation of Qurʾanic verses (*naskh*); (10) there is no rational opposed [proof] (*al-muʿāriḍ al-ʿaqlī*) which is of greater weight. Since preferring the Revelation to the human Reason demands the rejection of Reason, it is necessarily required to reject the Revelation, for the Revelation requires the Reason. In case this result ever was assumable, what would you think of it?![66]

Those ten conditional requirements cited by Ibn al-Qayyim appear in three of al-Rāzī's works: *Asās al-taqdīs* (which was already mentioned), *Muḥaṣṣal afkār al-mutaqaddimīn wal-mutaʾakhkhirīn min al-ʿulamāʾ wal-ḥukamāʾ wal-mutakallimīn* (A Compendium of the Opinions of Ancient and Later Scholars, Philosophers and *Mutakallimīn*), and with slight alterations in *Kitāb al-Arbaʿīn fī uṣūl al-dīn* (The Book of Forty, on the Principles of Religion).[67] Recent study on al-Rāzī's life and output shows that there is only little convincing evidence for generating a proven chronology of his works. Despite this fact, some modern studies do indicate a relative order in which his major works were written.[68]

66 Ibn Qayyim al-Jawziyya, *al-Ṣawāʿiq al-mursala*, 2:633–634; al-Rāzī, Fakhr al-Dīn Abū ʿAbdallāh Muḥammad ibn ʿUmar (d. 606/1209), *Muḥaṣṣal afkār al-mutaqaddimīn wal-mutaʾakhkhirīn*, with the commentary *Talkhīṣ al-Muḥaṣṣal* by Nṣīr al-Dīn Abū Jaʿfar Muḥammad ibn Muḥammad ibn al-Ḥasan al-Ṭūsī (d. 672/1274), ed. by Ṭaha ʿAbd al-Ruʾūf Saʿd (Cairo: Maktabat al-Kulliyyāt al-Azhariyya, n.d.), 51.

67 Al-Rāzī, *Kitāb al-Arbaʿīn fī uṣūl al-dīn*, ed. by Aḥmad Ḥijazī al-Saqqā, in two volumes (Cairo: Maktabat al-Kulliyyāt al-Azhariyya, [1409/1989]), 2:251–254.

68 Suggestions regarding this chronology from some earlier studies—such as: Paul Kraus, "Les 'Conreverses' de Fakhr al-Dīn al-Rāzī", *Bulletin d'Institut d'Egypte* 19 (1937), 187–214, or Josef van Ess, *Die Erkenntnislehre des ʿAḍuddadīn al-Īcī: Übersetzung und Kommentar*

In consulting these studies, it is highly remarkable that al-Rāzī's three works mentioned above are considered to have been composed in his later stage of involvement in philosophical theology, which can be distinguished from his previous classical Ashʿarite *Kalām*-oriented works. *Al-Muḥaṣṣal*, for example, is a vastly eclectic piece in its contents combining ideas and arguments of both a *Kalām*ic and philosophical nature. Simultaneously, the basic framework of the work is *Kalām*ic overall, and yet its structure is somewhat modified along the lines of the eclectic thematic style. Ayman Shihadeh identifies this transgressed fashion in al-Rāzī's writing as a factor of major contribution to his unique synthesis between *Kalām* and *falsafa* in Muslim thought.[69] *Kitāb al-Arbaʿīn*, which was ostensibly written after *al-Muḥaṣṣal*, is likely to represent a work of a similar and continuous trend of thought of al-Rāzī's 'Islamic philosophy'.[70] *Asās al-taqdīs* was most probably written around the same time (between 1199 and 1210).[71] It follows that the passage of al-Rāzī cited by Ibn al-Qayyim in his aforementioned passage is very much linked to the wider context of the more advanced stage in the Rāziyyan theological perception.

In both *al-Muḥaṣṣal* and *Kitāb al-Arbaʿīn*, al-Rāzī's ten conditions for certain knowledge are included in his theoretical discussion on the possible kinds of indications (*adilla*) and the different types of knowledge which can be derived from each and every one of them (in *Asās al-taqdīs* the context is slightly different, as the ten conditions appear within a discussion on "the way to know whether a Quranic verse is clear or ambiguous" in order to figuratively interpret it in *taʾwīl*).[72] Furthermore, in his *Muḥaṣṣal* these ten conditions appear in the

des ersten Buches seiner Mawaqif (Weisbaden: Steiner, 1966)—have been revised and rethought by later scholars, who seem to have reached some more accurate conclusions, for example: Daniel Gimaret, *Théories de l'acte humain en théologie musulmane* (Paris: Vrin, 1980); Ayman Shihadeh, "From al-Ghazālī to al-Rāzī: 6th/12th Century Developments in Muslim Philosophical Theology," *Arabic Sciences and Philosophy*, vol. 15 (2015), 141–179; Frank Griffel, "On Fakhr al-Dīn al-Rāzī's Life and the Patronage He Received," *Journal of Islamic Studies* 18:3 (2007), 313–344.

69 Shihadeh, "From al-Ghazālī to al-Rāzī," 171–172; Griffel, "On Fakhr al-Dīn al-Rāzī's Life," 321, 323–324; William Montgomery Watt, *Islamic Philosophy and Theology: An Extended Survey*, 2nd edition (Edinburgh: Edinburgh University Press, 1985), 94–95.

70 Shihadeh, "From al-Ghazālī to al-Rāzī," 178; Idem, *The Teleological Ethics of Fakhr al-Dīn al-Rāzī: Islamic Philosophy, Theology and Science* (Leiden: Brill, 2006), 7–9; in his appendix to the article "On Fakhr al-Dīn al-Rāzī's Life," Griffel offers "a tentative provisional chronology of Fakr al-Dīn al-Rāzī's major theological works" (p. 344).

71 Tariq Jaffer, "Muʿtazilite Aspects of Fakhr al-Dīn al-Rāzī's Thought," *Arabica* 59 (2012), 514–515, footnote 19.

72 Al-Rāzī, *Asās al-taqdīs*, 234–235.

context of al-Rāzī's four pillars of the whole science of *Kalām* (*arkānᵘ ʿilmⁱ 'l-kalām*). The first *rukn* consists of three introductions, with the ten conditions mentioned present in the third introduction thereof. In a concise manner, the following table organizes the conclusions of al-Rāzī's discussion derived from his three works mentioned above:

Indicative evidence / Resulted knowledge	***dalīl ʿaqlī*** **indicator of Reason**	***dalīl naqlī*** **(*dalīl samʿī*) transmitted indicator from the sources of Revelation**	***dalīl murtakab*** **= *ʿaqlī* + *naqlī* (most common) combined indicator**
yaqīn = certain	If most of its premises are certain or true (*ḥaqq*), then the result is *certain knowledge*	–	If all of the above mentioned ten conditions are met, then the result is certain knowledge *
ẓann = presumption	1. If most of its premises are a presumption or 2. if some are certain and some are a presumption Than the result is a *presumption*	–	Since each of the ten conditions is a premise of presumption, then even when they are met, the result is necessarily a *presumption*
muḥāl bāṭil = false absurd	–	If most of its premises are based on the sources of Revelation (Quran and Hadith), then the result is an *absurd*	–

The table sums up al-Rāzī's harshly skeptical approach with regard to the human prospects of achieving any kind of knowledge, which in the vast majority of cases will only result in a presumption (*ẓann*). According to al-Rāzī, the key source to all knowledge comprehension is human Reason; *al-ʿaql^{i} huw^{a} aṣl^{u} ʾl-naql^{i}*.[73] It is obvious that, by following the strict classification al-Rāzī provides in many of his later works, the possibility of attaining certainty of knowledge in absolute terms has only very little probability. In al-Rāzī's mind, because of the limited abilities of the human rational capacity as a created and mundane being, this task is impossible to accomplish by means of either *Kalām*ic or philosophical methods of argumentation. Al-Rāzī's unprecedented pessimistic inclination is articulated even more forcefully when addressing metaphysical or theological knowledge, meaning knowledge about God and the divine. This skeptical tendency has already been observed by Ayman Shihadeh, who designates it as "epistemological pessimism".[74]

Al-Rāzī's pessimistic epistemic approach is a result of his inclination towards the Muʿtazilite views, which he incorporated into his advanced philosophized version of Ashʿarite ideology. In fact, and as argued by Tariq Jaffer, "al-Rāzī sees the exegetical problem of *taʾwīl* through the lens of epistemology."[75] Thus, the criteria postulated by al-Rāzī for the human possibility of attaining certainty of knowledge were a part of his effort to build a methodology for interpreting the divine attributes (i.e., performing Muʿtazilite *taʾwīl*). Within the Rāziyyan epistemic system, the two suppliers of decisive evidence were either the rational indicator (*dalīl ʿaqlī*) or the verbal indicator (*dalīl lafẓī*). By referring to verbal indicators transmitted by the means of *tawātur* (i.e., massively transmit-

---

73 Further clarifications on this formula's origin will be provided in the opening of chapter 4 henceforth.

74 Shihadeh, *The Teleological Ethics of Fakhr al-Dīn al-Rāzī*, 181–199; According to al-Rāzī, the way to overcome this existential pessimism is "the way of the Quran" (*ṭarīqat al-qurʾān*), which is discussed in Shihadeh's study. The term "pessimism" has to do with human agency (not with epistemology), meaning the limited ability of humans to act according to their free-will (*ikhtiyār*); this is because all actions are decreed by God through predetermination and, thus, are forced upon the created beings (*jabr*). Hence, al-Rāzī's pessimistic approach is first a derivative of his opinion on human agency; however, it is also appropriate to his view on the prospects of achieving certain knowledge. Furthermore, al-Razi's epistemological view is elitist, while Ibn al-Qayyim suggests that certain knowledge is accessible to anyone who accepts the scriptures. The social aspects of the issue in al-Rāzī's thought are dealt with by Shihadeh as well. Another relevant erticle by Shihadeh is "The Mystic and the Sceptic in Fakhr al-Dīn al-Rāzī" in: ed. Ayman Shihadeh, *Sufism and Theology* (Edinburgh: Edinburgh University Press, 2007), 101–122.

75 Jaffer, "Muʿtazilite Aspects of Faḫr al-Dīn al-Rāzī's Thought," 531.

ted Hadith accounts), al-Rāzī is revealed to be following the path of the more radical Muʿtazilite view of strong and rigid skepticism. According to this view, the textual materials massively transmitted in *tawātur* are a fertile subject for errors, be they grammatical, linguistic, or simply unintentional human error; hence, it was severely criticized. The only possible knowledge to be achieved by verbal indicators from the transmitted textual sources can be—at best—a presumption, yet never certain knowledge. This is to a great extent the epistemology promoted by the highly rationalistic scholars of the Muʿtazilite school, nullifying the epistemic value of the Quran and Hadith.[76] Given this remarkable observation, Ibn al-Qayyim's aims to confront al-Rāzī's epistemological pessimism and connect it to early Muʿtazilite notions illustrate his profound understanding of the Rāziyyan claims within their thematic theological context.

In addition, Ibn al-Qayyim's reference to al-Rāzī's thought in *al-Muḥaṣṣal* and *Kitāb al-Arbaʿīn* is far from arbitrary; in fact, it is closely connected to Ibn al-Qayyim's role as a significant systemizer of the doctrinal ideas of his mentor Ibn Taymiyya. Despite Ibn al-Qayyim's declared objective of undermining the *Kalām*ic fundamentals, he is indicated in the—fairly scarce—biographical sources, which depict him as a thinker who received an Ashʿarī-based education, mainly through the Tayymiyan scholarly lens, but also independently and before the two met. Al-Rāzī's two writings mentioned above—*al-Muḥaṣṣal* and *Kitāb al-Arbaʿīn*—are particularly mentioned as sources which had been read, and probably also memorized, during Ibn al-Qayyim's general theological training.[77] Therefore, Ibn al-Qayyim's quote from these Rāziyyan theological writings in *al-Ṣawāʿiq* is more than understandable due to his close familiarity with their contents. Ibn al-Qayyim's use of these writings is even less surprising when one considers the heritage of Ibn Taymiyya's teachings (including several lost writings we no longer possess), which will be addressed shortly.

In his discussion in *al-Ṣawāʿiq*, Ibn al-Qayyim illuminates the harsh and definitive critique voiced by Ibn Taymiyya on the ten conditional requirements immediately after quoting al-Rāzī's ten conditions for obtaining certain knowledge. According to Ibn al-Qayyim, Ibn Taymiyya refused to accept the Rāziyyan postulation of such extremely pessimistic epistemological view concerning the human ability to achieve certain knowledge, assigning special treatment to the epistemological involvement with theological subjects. As a result, Ibn

---

76 Tariq Jaffer, "Muʿtazilite Aspects of Faḫr al-Dīn al-Rāzī's Thought," 527–535.

77 Holtzman, "Debating the Doctrine of *Jabr* (Compulsion): Ibn Qayyim al-Jawziyya Reads Fakhr al-Dīn al-Rāzī," 91–92.

Taymiyya utterly discredited al-Rāzī's ten conditions for certainty of knowledge. Before exploring in detail Ibn Taymiyya's criticism against al-Rāzī, it is important to point out Ibn al-Qayyim's contribution to the issue in question. Ibn al-Qayyim's capacity as a prominent systemizer of the theoretical teachings of his mentor Ibn Taymiyya is strikingly revealed in the opening part of his refutation of the first *ṭāghūt* in *al-Ṣawāʿiq*. This part of the work seems to preserve several prominent ideas from Ibn Taymiyya's extinct works. It is not improbable that Ibn Taymiyya had expressed this view in one or two of his lost works: *Sharḥ awwal al-muḥaṣṣal lil-imām Fakhr al-Dīn* (A Commentary on the First [Section] of 'The Compendium' by the Imām Fakhr al-Dīn), or *Sharḥ biḍʿat ʿashr masʾala min al-arbaʿīn lil-Rāzī* (A Commentary on a Portion of Ten Issues from 'The Forty' of al-Rāzī). These two works are mentioned in several biographical sources as works composed by Ibn Taymiyya.[78]

For the obvious lack of sufficient sources, it is very difficult—if not completely impossible—to accurately judge to which extent Ibn al-Qayyim's particular discussion in *al-Ṣawāʿiq* indeed preserves the material originated in either of Ibn Taymiyya's two lost works. Even so, in the light of Ibn al-Qayyim strong tendency of relying on his master's writings and sayings as a stepping-stone to his own discussions, one may assume that, at least to a certain degree, Ibn al-Qayyim did incorporate Ibn Taymiyya's critique against al-Rāzī into *al-Ṣawāʿiq* as it had appeared in one (or both) of those missing works. Moreover, in view of the fact that Ibn al-Qayyim was a direct pupil of Ibn Taymiyya, it is also possible that, in *al-Ṣawāʿiq*, the student integrated some of the teacher's oral transmissions given during public lectures or even private tutoring sessions. This is a splendid example of Ibn al-Qayyim's contribution to the systemization of the Taymiyyan doctrine, not only in general thematic terms, but also giving access to some of Ibn Taymiyya's lost writings and, to a certain extent, almost keeping them alive.

3.3 Ibn Taymiyya's Initial Critique against al-Rāzī

In order to more properly determine and characterize Ibn al-Qayyim's role as a "systemizer of the Taymiyyan theoretical doctrine," one should first attempt

78 Biographical sources such as: *Al-Wāfī bil-wafyāt* and *Aʿyān al-ʿaṣr wa-aʿwān al-naṣr* by al-Ṣafadī, and *Al-Dhayl ʿalā ṭabqāt al-ḥanābila* by Ibn Rajab; Muḥammad ʿAzīz Shams and ʿAlī ibn Muḥammad al-ʿImrān (eds.), *Al-Jāmiʿ li-sīrat shaykh al-Islām Ibn Taymiyya khilāl[a] sabʿat qurūn*, with an introduction by Bakr ibn ʿAbdallh Abū Zayd, 3rd edition (Mecca: Dār ʿĀlam al-Fawāʾid, 1422/2001), 354, 377, 482.

to take a closer look at these Taymiyyan ideas to understand their apparent worth and search for evidence of links between their two lines of arguments against al-Rāzī's epistemological pessimism. Apart from raising the assumption regarding a possible link between Ibn al-Qayyim's *al-Ṣawāʿiq* and several of Ibn Taymiyya's missing works, I have managed to detect a remarkable section of some 60 relevant pages in a still available—yet, to the best of my knowledge, little studied—work by Ibn Taymiyya titled *Bayān talbīs al-jahmiyya*, which has already been mentioned and read from in section 1.2 above. The work can be of significant use and evaluation when tracking some of the possible Taymiyyan provenances of Ibn al-Qayyim's claims in *al-Ṣawāʿiq* also when it comes to epistemology. As noted before, Ibn Taymiyya composed *Bayān talbīs al-jahmiyya* in order to rebuke al-Rāzī's work *Asās al-taqdīs* and especially his deployment of the Muʿtazilite *taʾwīl*, viz. figurative interpretation of God's attributes. And so, since in *Asās al-taqdīs*, al-Rāzī once more brings up his ten conditions for achieving *ʿilm yaqīn*,[79] Ibn Taymiyya criticized them himself in *Bayān talbīs al-jahmiyya*.[80]

In al-Rāzī's *Asās al-taqdīs*, which has a similar overall context to his two previously described works (*al-Muḥaṣṣal* and *Kitāb al-Arbaʿīn*), his ten conditions for *ʿilm yaqīn* are located in a core part of the work titled "An Account on the Way of the Pious Ancestors" (*taqrīr madhhab al-salaf*, the third part out of four in the entire work).[81] However, those ten conditions are only mentioned shortly and are lacking in the beginning part of the work—the introductions themselves deal with the different possible kinds of proofs. This could mean that the two more detailed versions in *al-Muḥaṣṣal* and *Kitāb al-Arbaʿīn* were composed prior to *Asās al-taqdīs*; therefore, there was no need to redundantly repeat the extended explicative versions. Perhaps by the time *Asās al-taqdīs* was written, the "ten epistemic conditions" were, to a certain degree, already commonly known (however, according to Griffel's tentative chronology of al-Rāzī's works, all three works were written around the same time, with only a span of several years separating one them from another).[82] At any rate, al-Rāzī finds it appropriate to mention time and again his ten conditions for the attainment of certain knowledge, maintaining that it is impossible for verbal evidential

79 Fakhr al-Dīn al-Rāzī, *Asās al-taqdīs*, 234–235.

80 Ibn Taymiyya, *Bayān talbīs al-jahmiyya*, 8:470–530. For the aim of my current examination, I will thus concentrate mainly on the most relevant parts therein for the following epistemic discussion.

81 The four parts of the work's content are briefly described in: Jaffer, "Muʿtazilite Aspects of Fakhr al-Dīn al-Rāzī's Thought," 516.

82 Griffel, "On Fakhr al-Dīn al-Rāzī's Life," 344.

indicator to be of a conclusive nature (*fa-thubit*^{a} *ann*^{a} *shay*^{ʾan} *min*^{a} *ʾl-dalāʾil*^{i} *ʾl-lafẓiyya*^{ti} *lā yumkin*^{u} *an yakūn*^{a} *qaṭʿiyy*^{an}).[83] Tariq Jaffer describes the different sections of *Asās al-taqdīs*, explaining al-Rāzī's advanced methodology, which firmly relies on the speculative Muʿtazilite grounds with respect to the theological "*taʾwīl*-issue". As has already been shown in section 3.2, in the Rāziyyan opinion, knowledge derived from the Quran and Sunna can supply extremely limited epistemic value and, as a result, is virtually useless when dealing with *taʾwīl* and the divine attributes.[84]

On the other side of the fence, and about a century later, Ibn Taymiyya's promoted his critique in *Bayān talbīs al-jahmiyya* against al-Rāzī's glorification of the *taʾwīl* rationalistic theological methodology with regard to the divine attributes. This is the general framework in which Ibn Taymiyya condemns Al-Rāzī's decisive and very pessimistic claim of the "ten conditions" towards certainty of knowledge. In the work *Bayān talbīs al-jahmiyya*, Ibn Taymiyya first explicitly cites al-Rāzī's ten conditions for *ilm yaqīn*, which he instantly rejects and then explains his rejection in several somewhat muddled arguments (*wujūh*). By doing so, he ultimately—yet tortuously—discloses bits and pieces of his epistemological approach and its cerebral foundations. *Bayān talbīs al-jahmiyya* is therefore an important source to examine when one wishes to understand Ibn Taymiyya's views concerning epistemology and, of more relevance to this study, Ibn al-Qayyim's representation of these Taymiyyan views in his refutation of the first *ṭāghūt* in *al-Ṣawāʿiq*. For this reason, I will succinctly describe Ibn Taymiyya's main arguments countering al-Rāzī's ten conditions.

In *Bayān talbīs al-jahmiyya*, Ibn Taymiyya first refers to the very basic and natural human action as suppliers of common knowledge. Hence, it is necessary that knowledge of the speaker's intention (*al-ʿilm bi-murād*^{i} *ʾl-mutakallim*) is commonly known (*amr maʿlūm*), since speaking—like every other voluntary action (*afʿāl ikhtiyāriyya*)—conveys its actor's goal (*qaṣd*); for instance, when a person chooses to eat and drink, he/she usually does so in order to satisfy his hunger and appetite. In the same manner, other sounds or voices naturally produced by a person, either voluntarily or not, such as breathing, coughing, sneezing or laughing, convey perfectly clear and understandable knowledge on one's intention. At times, though, it is possible that these actions convey a different intention; however, this is not the standard meaning of the specific action (for example, crying "crocodile tears", as in fake tears).[85]

---

83 Fakhr al-Dīn al-Rāzī, *Asās al-taqdīs*, 234–235.

84 Jaffer, "Muʿtazilite Aspects of Fakhr al-Dīn al-Rāzī's Thought," 516–533.

85 Ibn Taymiyya, *Bayān talbīs al-jahmiyya*, 8:470–471.

The traditionalistic principle of absolute reliance on knowledge transmission from the Prophet Muḥammad onwards is the second argument in Ibn Taymiyya's criticism against al-Rāzī's skepticism. According to Ibn Taymiyya, the people who testified their belief in Allah in front of the Prophet had heard his direct speech (*kalāmah*^{u}) on the fundamental commandments in Islam, as he specifically clarified to them his intention (*murād*) by explaining the precise definition of his expressions (*bayyan*^{a} *lahum musammā hādhih*^{i} *'l-alfāẓ*). Therefore, the first Muslim believers necessarily understood the Prophet's intention and transmitted it onwards to others in a manner which produced certainty of knowledge (*naql*^{an} *yufīd*^{u} *'l-yaqīn*). Ibn Taymiyya states, in this way the transmitted knowledge is even of much greater certainty (*al-ʿilm aʿẓam min*^{a} *'l-yaqīn*), for this kind of knowledge is superior to the mere expressions which encompass it (*al-ʿilm* [...] *aʿẓam min alfāẓih*^{i}).[86]

Aligning with the critique above, the following three arguments presented must have been connected to the linguistic and grammar part of al-Rāzī's ten conditions. Once again, they provide an indication of Ibn Taymiyya's reluctance to be constrained by meager rules of language, along with his well-known tendency towards general pragmatism. The first and foremost linguistic component, Ibn Taymiyya declares, is the meaning (*maʿnā*), which can be conveyed in numerous and various verbal expressions (*alfāẓ*). In the Quran, for instance, God spoke of the early prophets and their peoples who strayed from the righteous path; however, not even a single one of the expressions was revealed in their own language. Rather, only the meaning of their speech was transmitted in Arabic, following the coherent stylistic arrangement of the Quran (*naẓm al-qur'ān*). Another example is brought with regard to the Hadith: Ibn Taymiyya claims when one understands a Hadith account, he/she is allowed to tell its meaning to the crowd without sticking to the exact verbal expression—*al-ʿilm fil-maʿnā*, (i.e., knowledge exists in the meaning).[87] Moreover, "the knowledgeable people" on the Quran and the Hadith (*ahl al-ʿilm*) transmitted the Prophet's exact language alone; hence, the scholars of religion have no need for any assistance from linguistic scholars or grammarians in order to comprehend the Quran and Hadith, except in some very specific cases, such as the obscure expressions therein (*gharīb 'l-qur'ān wal-ḥadīth wal-fiqh*). All in

86 Ibn Taymiyya, *Bayān talbīs al-jahmiyya*, 8:471–472, 479.

87 Ibn Taymiyya's claim here does not seem to represent wide-spread agreement on this issue, for he also states that "those who prevent [telling a Hadith account by its meaning alone], do so as a result of mere fear ..." In addition, the editor provides various opinions of anonymous contrarians on the matter in his footnote; Ibn Taymiyya, *Bayān talbīs al-jahmiyya*, 8:473, note. 4.

all, states Ibn Taymiyya, al-Rāzī's linguistic restrictions are simply worthlessly excessive (*takthīr bi-lā fā'ida*).[88] This tendency corroborates Ibn Taymiyya's well-known endeavor to ensure ultimate pragmatism as well as his preference for practical solutions.

Ibn Taymiyya addresses al-Rāzī's tenth and last condition, according to which a verbal indicator could produce cogent certainty only if there is no opposed proof, either rationalistic/linguistic or textual (*al-muʿāriḍ 'l-ʿaqlī wal-samʿī*). Adhering to his epistemic ground rule in favor of the intended meaning, Ibn Taymiyya explains that when the intention (*murād*) of the texts is cogently understood (*ʿulim^a qaṭʿ^an*), no other indicator (*dalīl*) can contradict this understanding.[89] This argument finalizes Ibn Taymiyya's treatment with each of al-Rāzī's ten conditions for certain knowledge, allowing him to conclude with an utter rejection of al-Rāzī's allegation, stating:

> The claim made by this alleger (i.e. al-Rāzī), that the use of verbal indicative evidence as intended by the speaker (*al-dalīl 'l-lafẓī ʿalā murād^i 'l-mutakallim*) is dependent upon ten premises, is absolutely false. Even of more falsehood is the claim that every single premise is a presumption (*muqaddima ẓanniyya*). All of these premises—upon which the understanding and the speaker's intention are dependent—can be cogent (*qaṭʿiyya*) in most cases for whoever contemplates them.
>
> So, if it is said: when the intention was clarified by the speaker by another expression and it was transmitted consecutively (in *tawātur*), there is no use for the expression. As for the transmission, this should be answered with: the intention was transmitted, which is the expression's intention (*wa-huw^a 'l-murād^u bil-lafẓ^i*) so that the expression indicates it. This is how the obligation of pilgrimage was transmitted, which is the intention of the verse [Q 3:97] "Pilgrimage to the House is a duty owed to God by people who are able to undertake it"; the intention of this expression refers to the obligation to make a pilgrimage to the Mosque [*bayt*] in Mecca. The same goes for the verse [Q 2:185] "It was the month of Ramadan" [about the obligation to fast], verse [Q 2: 43] "Keep up the

88 Ibn Taymiyya, *Bayān talbīs al-jahmiyya*, 8:476–479.

89 This is the wording used by Ibn Taymiyya, where he includes a scriptural opposed proof derived from the Quran, (i.e., *al-muʿāriḍ 'l-samʿī*). It should be noted this is an addition that does not appear in the original tenth condition put forth by al-Rāzī, referring only to rationalistic opposed proof, in other words, *al-muʿāriḍ al-ʿaqlī* (mentioned previously in section 3.2 Fakhr al-Dīn al-Rāzī on Certain Knowledge: Skepticism); Ibn Taymiyya, *Bayān talbīs al-jahmiyya*, 8:479.

prayer, pay the prescribed alms", and so forth. When those expressions are heard, it is cogently understood that the speaker intends a specific meaning, in the same way it is understood that this is the meaning intended by the Messenger of God—peace be upon him; both of the matters are known cogently (*maʿlūm*^{un} *qaṭʿ*^{an}). Even if someone said: "I am obliged to perform the pilgrimage and to fast during the month of Ramadan, since this is transmitted consecutively", I say the intention of the fasting of Ramadan is to last 30 successive days, and the intention of the pilgrimage to the House is to visit the houses of knowledge and wisdom, and the intention of the prayer is the [public] prayer of Friday; this is known necessarily.

In addition, when what I intend to say is initially understood in terms of its expression, but someone does not understand it and asks for clarification, it must be interpreted according to the commonly understood meaning that was transmitted by the Prophet. Thus, it will be remembered and followed [...]. We do not deny that a person's understanding could be dependent at times on [the ten conditions that al-Rāzī] mentioned. Rather, what is denied is the generality and predominance [of those ten conditions]. For most people, most of the verses of the Quran are not dependent on [al-Rāzī's] ten conditions. That is the most apparent falsehood! Even in case of the meager verses that one could be dependent on [al-Rāzī's] ten conditions, that is a result of his ignorance and his remoteness from any knowledge on the Prophet and his prophecy, as if that person was newly acquainted with Islam, or has just arrived from a desert far away from the lands of knowledge and belief, so he does not know that God exalted obliged [His believers with] pilgrimage, fasting, prayer or the prohibition of wine drinking. This cannot be the general-rule concerning the majority of Muslims. In the same vein, if it was decreed for one to be unable to attain knowledge of the meaning of some verses, but only with the dependence on indicators of presumption (*adilla ẓanniyya*), it is not required that he will not attain any knowledge about them and about most of the Quranic verses other than them. And, if it was decreed for that one not to attain [knowledge], it is not allowed to say that [attaining knowledge on] the intention is impossible. This is what [al-Rāzī] says, that a verbal indicator cannot [produce] cogent [knowledge].

[By this claim, al-Rāzī] rejects the possibility of any expression to be cogent. This is even faultier than saying: 'an indication of Reason (*shay' min*^{a} *'l-adilla 'l-ʿaqliyya*) cannot be cogent', since knowledge of the speaker's intention is the most apparent and obvious one. It does not matter if an indicator is rational (*ʿaqlī*) or a textual (*samʿī*) [for it to be] cogent,

> but the point is that the indicator signifies the speaker's intention. Then, the speaker himself is known as one whose intention is the truth. They [i.e., the speakers of the transmitted knowledge] are deliberately infallible (*maʿṣūmūn*[a] *ʿamd*[an]) of any lie or mistake in their transmission [of knowledge] on God exalted, as they received it, in the exact meaning He desired. In this case, we cogently understand that this [knowledge] is the truth on that matter. If the speaker was not like that, in other words, he could have made a mistake, we would cogently understand his intention, but not if it was correct and truthful.[90]

Even more strikingly than articulating his harsh rejection of al-Rāzī's ten conditions, Ibn Taymiyya expresses in this passage several key principles of his own epistemological view. His absolute reliance on the traditionalist chain of narration of the Islamic sacred texts of Revelation reassures his complete confidence in those transmitted sources as valid evidence of certain religious knowledge. Notwithstanding, this basic fideistic starting point by no means leads to a typical Ḥanbalite-traditionalistic epistemological approach; Ibn Taymiyya arises additional imminently entwined elements to be queried before accepting the transmitted sources as conclusive evidence. Ibn Taymiyya expresses his full confidence in the natural understanding of the listener, through which certainty of knowledge of the speaker's intention is instinctively achieved; the scriptures of Islam are inherently understandable. This observation fits the anti-elitist epistemological approach generally held by Ibn Taymiyya—cogent knowledge is available to all.[91] In response to the examples in the passage above concerning the fundamental commands of Islamic belief, Ibn Taymiyya bluntly mocks Fakhr al-Dīn al-Rāzī and his skepticism; al-Rāzī himself, as the representative of later Ashʿarites, is depicted as "he who was decreed not to attain certainty." Furthermore, Ibn Taymiyya does not ignore the respectable position of human Reason in his epistemological view, as he discusses the apodictic value of both transmitted and rational evidence simultaneously, though he clearly prefers the first kind to the latter. The main point is that the intended meaning conveyed in the scriptures can definitely be understood by the community of Muslim believers; therefore, there is no need for any supplementary tools outside of the texts.

---

90 Ibn Taymiyya, *Bayān talbīs al-jahmiyya*, 8:480–483.

91 Ovamir Anjum, *Politics, Law, and Community in Islamic Thought: The Taymiyyan Moment*, 228–229.

In this manner, in *Bayān talbīs al-jahmiyya* Ibn Taymiyya presents a combined epistemological approach, which firmly rests on the transmitted sources of Revelation without separating it from the human capacity of reasonable thinking. This notion is articulated in his claim that human Reason has a significant part in the process of attaining knowledge from the scriptural informative indicators (*al-adilla 'l-samʿiyya*). At times the textual sources provide informative utterances of knowledge alone (*mujarrad al-khabar*; i.e., statements) which depict inevitably factual truth,[92] whereas at other times they may be considered indicators of Reason (*al-adilla 'l-ʿaqliyya*) which hold information God provided about Himself, His traits and His actions. Noteworthy is Ibn Taymiyya's particular conceptualization of these "indicators of Reason" in this regard, as it seems to convey a different meaning than that of "rational indicators" in the *Kalām*ic use of the phrase. Using the Taymiyyan terminology, indicators of Reason also include the signs of creation that all humans regularly experience (*al-āyāt al-makhlūqa 'l-ʿiyāniyya*). The created world and its variety of evident phenomena are perceived as indicators of Reason, as a reasonable person understands the divine omnipotence or the divine will, for instance, by observing the world around him/her and using his/her common sense.[93] The cogent epistemological value of this kind of indications is equivalent to those which are demonstrated by the textual indicators found in the Islamic scripture (*al-āyāt al-munzala 'l-masmūʿa 'l-qurʾāniyya*, or *al-āyāt 'l-qawliyya*), as the textual indicators infer the openly evident signs of creation, and both

---

92 See a linguistic explanation of the term *khabar* in footnote 89 in chapter 2.

93 With relation to divine will, Ibn Taymiyya implicitly expresses here his differentiation between the term *mashīʾa*, which denotes a divine predetermined decree of the existence of either good or bad (*amr kawnī/qadrī*), and the more positive terms *riḍāʾ/ḥubb* (desire, love), which denotes a divine predetermined decree of what is religious (*amr dīnī/sharʿī*). The verb *arād*[d] encompasses these two kinds of divine will, and can be seen as being overall neutral concerning that matter. The use of distinctive verbs to designate the outcome of divine will is namely connected to the theological issue of predestination and human free will. In the disagreement between the Ashʿarite and the Ḥanbalite views on the issue of predestination, Ibn Taymiyya—and Ibn al-Qayyim—insisted on segregating the Arabic verbs that denote divine will according to its created outcome, since it is implausible that God would desire or love immoral things, although he created them with His will; Holtzman, *Predestination (al-Qaḍāʾ wa-l-Qadar) and Free Will (al-Ikhtiyār) as Reflected in the Works of the Neo-Ḥanbalites in the Fourteenth Century* (PhD dissertation, Bar-Ilan University Israel, 2003), 219–225. Ibn Taymiyya's passage above shows that, epistemologically, the knowledge provided about all outcomes both morally good and bad is certain, whether it is scriptural or based on Reason.

are perceived by human Reason (*bi-mujarrad al-ʿaql*). Verbal textual evidence directs the reasonable person towards *al-adilla ʾl-ʿaqliyya* and inform him/her of them. Ibn Taymiyya then continues this line of argumentation, further contrasting his understanding of "indicators of Reason" with the rationalistic ones of the scholars of *Kalām* and *falāsifa*, whom he accuses of heresy.[94] Such epistemic conceptualization of the "indicators of Reason" goes hand in hand with the Taymiyyan idea of *fiṭra* (i.e., the natural disposition of humankind leading to Islamic belief) according to which certainty of knowledge is equally attainable for all Muslim believers.

Supplementary epistemological trajectory is clearly manifested in another immensely important work by Ibn Taymiyya in this context, *al-Radd ʿala ʾl-manṭiqiyyīn* (Refutation of the Logicians).[95] In this work, Ibn Taymiyya criticized two of the central principles of Greek Aristotelian logic (definition—*ḥadd*, and deduction by syllogism—*qiyās*) in an attempt to disown it entirely and demolish the validity of any logical treatment of metaphysical and theological issues. Cleverly amassing already known arguments—both Greek and Islamic—against logic, Ibn Taymiyya composed a work of highly expounded criticism against rationalism. This work has long been neglected in research, but secondary literature offers several (though still very few) publications who have addressed it and conducted research on the clues to Taymiyyan epistemological approach as apparent in the work.[96] Ibn Taymiyya's deliberations in *al-Radd ʿala ʾl-manṭiqiyyīn* are a source of great importance for a more elaborate understanding of Taymiyyan theory of knowledge and, more so, of the place dedicated to human Reason and cognition therein. According to my examination of the work, despite the numerous cases in which he refers explicitly and in detail to al-Rāzī and his thought, in *al-Radd* Ibn Taymiyya does not men-

94 Ibn Taymiyya, *Bayān talbīs al-jahmiyya*, 8:483–487.

95 Ibn Taymiyya, *al-Radd ʿala ʾl-manṭiqiyyīn*, in one volume, no editor mentioned (Beirut: Dār al-Maʿrifa, n.d.). This work was composed in the same period of time as his *Darʾ taʿāruḍ al-ʿaql wal-naql*, and should be examined and seen as linked to this enormous master piece. Anke von Kügelgen suggests that these two works "have much in common and supplement each other"; von Kügelgen, "The Poison of Philosophy," 265–267, 279.

96 von Kügelgen, "The Poison of Philosophy", 266–271; von Kügelgen, "Ibn Taymīyas Kritik an der Aristotelischen Logik und sein Gegenentwurf," *Logik und Theologie: das Organon im arabischen und im lateinischen Mittelalter*, ed. Dominik Perler and Ulrich Rudolph (Leiden: Brill, 2005), 171–177; Wael b. Hallaq dedicated a book to a scrutiny of the abridgement of *al-Radd ʿala ʾl-manṭiqiyyīn*, written by the important scholar Jalāl al-Dīn al-Suyūṭī (d. 911/1505), titled *Kitāb Jahd al-qarīḥa fī tajrīd al-naṣīḥa—Ibn Taymiyya against the Greek Logicians* (Oxford: Oxford University Press, 1993), xiv–xv.

tion the Rāziyyan ten debated conditions required for achieving certainty of knowledge. Nonetheless, some of Ibn Taymiyya's chief conceptual perceptions concerning the issue of attaining certainty of knowledge are intertwined with his vast epistemic arguments against the use of rationalistic logic—with special emphasis placed on matters of metaphysics—by Muslim scholars who either preceded him or were active during his own time.

In a recently published study of *al-Radd*, Anke von Kügelgen discusses the term *ṣarīḥ al-ʿaql* as reflected through the Taymiyyan epistemological prism. Rather than translating it as 'clear Reason' or 'common sense', she chooses to call it 'uncontaminated Reason', thus contrasting it with the reasoning of Ibn Taymiyya's ideological adversaries. She argues, in his opinion, Reason as it was deployed by rationalistic schools of thought was contaminated by the elements of this superfluous logic. Moreover, von Kügelgen shows that the Taymiyyan consideration of 'human Reason' for the aim of achieving necessary and certain knowledge is based on two key epistemological assumptions: First, the innate natural intelligence of the *fiṭra*, which in *al-Radd* could be seen as "the predisposition and the faculty to correctly and immediately grasp true knowledge and reject false knowledge." *Fiṭra* is a relativistic trait which is manifested differently among people, according to each and every human being's different cognitive and corporal aptitudes of perception. Second, Ibn Taymiyya makes a distinction between two modes of knowledge:

1. Necessary (*ḍarūrī*) or evident (*badīhī*) knowledge, meaning an immediate and certain (*yaqīnī*) epistemic mode.
2. Acquired (*kasbī/muktasab*) or speculative (*naẓarī*) knowledge, that is, a secondary epistemic mode of probability alone (*ẓannī*).[97]

In accordance with the Taymiyyan epistemological theory unfolded in *al-Radd*, the sensorial and mental abilities of a person play the biggest role in the process of knowledge consumption. Therefore, the first mode of evident knowledge—including: concepts (*taṣawwurāt*), judgments (*taṣdīqāt*), sensory perceptions (*ḥissī*), experiences, widespread dispositions (*mashhūrāt*) etc.—provides immediately understood and, hence, certain knowledge. The special incorporation of the specifically discussed idea of *fiṭra* together with the idea of immediate and sensorially evident knowledge considerably expands Ibn Taymiyya's perception with regard to the theoretical possibility of attaining certainty of

97 Von Kügelgen, "The Poison of Philosophy," 297–300.

knowledge; with comparison to the much more doubtful epistemic approach presented by the philosophers and some of the later *Kalām* theologians.[98] This observation corroborates beyond a doubt the previous description of the Rāziyyan highly pessimistic understanding of the scarce theoretical plausibility of gaining any knowledge of certainty (see section 3.2). Furthermore, this view is thoughtfully explained by Ibn al-Qayyim as he conceptualized the positive approach concerning certainty of knowledge in *al-Ṣawāʿiq*, as shown in section 3.1 above.

In terms of methodologies, Ibn Taymiyya's overall alternative epistemological outlook also offers a wide and universal spectrum of human opportunities for achieving certain knowledge. Von Kügelgen concludes by listing three kinds of "rational inferences" Ibn Taymiyya "considered capable of leading to true knowledge within and beyond the scope of Revelation":[99]

1. Inference by signs, or "God's method of indication by signs" (*istidlāluh*[u] *taʿālā bil-āyāt*[i]): this is immediate *fiṭrī* knowledge, for example the rise of the sun or the stars, which imply God's creation of all of nature. The 'signs of the Quran' (*āyāt al-Qurʾān*, i.e., the Quranic verses) are also included in this category.[100]
2. Inference by *a fortiori* argument, or by *qiyās al-awlā*: this inference deals with knowledge about God alone. As Jon Hover showed, Ibn Taymiyya used this clever argument to affirm the contrast between God and His creation, claiming all human characteristics apply even more so to God as the single and most perfect source of any mundane creation.[101]
3. Inference based on analogy, or a "common factor" (Aristotelian categorical syllogism; *qiyās* as it is utilized in Islamic jurisprudence): here Ibn Taymiyya follows a 'middle way' of accepting knowledge derived by analogy, while still stressing it is not to be perceived as limited to Greek logic.

For Ibn Taymiyya, all three methods of inference of true and, therefore, certain knowledge originated and are mentioned in the Quran. Consequently, Ibn

98 Von Kügelgen, "The Poison of Philosophy," 300–305; idem, "Ibn Taymīyas Kritik an der Aristotelischen Logik und sein Gegenentwurf," 192–198; Anjum, *Politics, Law, and Community in Islamic Thought*, 210–213.

99 Von Kügelgen, "The Poison of Philosophy," 328.

100 Ibn Taymiyya also mentioned this kind of worldly inferences in his account in *Bayān talbīs al-jahmiyya*, which was discussed above (*al-āyāt al-makhlūqa 'l-ʿiyāniyya*), see page 152.

101 For instance, in: Hoover, *Ibn Taymiyya Theodicy*, 56–61.

Taymiyya understands the Quran and the Revelation as the undeniable origin authority cultivating these rationalized methods of reaching knowledge.[102]

In a similar vein, another study by Ovamir Anjum depicts the alternative epistemological view Ibn Taymiyya posed in *al-Radd* in the face of the *Kalām*ic one, and follows the Taymiyyan rendering of the Quranic concept of *fiṭra* into a "theory of human psychology and epistemology." Anjum attempts to distinguish and define Ibn Taymiyya's designations of *fiṭra* and Reason/intellect (*ʿaql*), stressing *fiṭra* is to be understood as an inborn inclination towards the truth, whereas Reason is the cognitive tool with which a person inclined-to-the-truth perceives it. According to this model of human cognitive capacity, if the *fiṭra* is corrupted, Reason loses its lead towards righteousness, turning instead to doubt and heresy; therefore, Reason is dependent on the *fiṭra*.[103] This definition of mutual relations—while still maintaining separate roles—between *fiṭra* and Reason, combined together with Von Kügelgen's conclusions, points to the highly developed stage of Ibn Taymiyya's criticism against the prevalent rationalistic epistemology. In an impressive intellectual endeavor, he theorized on a substitute system of human knowledge, drawing directly from the familiar Quranic tenets.

Ibn Taymiyya's work against the rationalistic use of logic, *al-Radd ʿala 'l-manṭiqiyyīn*, discloses once again his sophisticated attitude towards traditionalistic use of Reason and its possible implications in all Islamic fields of knowledge, although our attention is of course concentrated on the fields of theology and metaphysics. Therefore, the epistemological approach arising in the works *Bayān talbīs al-jahmiyya* and *al-Radd ʿalā 'l-manṭiqiyyīn* should most definitely be taken as plausible sources of inspiration for Ibn al-Qayyim's later discussions in *al-Ṣawāʿiq*.[104] More generally, and in accordance with the scrutiny of the available primary sources as depicted thus far, it can be presumed that Ibn al-Qayyim's demonstration of Ibn Taymiyya's initial critique against al-Rāzī could have also been a consequence of the teacher's oral lectures or lost works. At

102 Von Kügelgen, "The Poison of Philosophy," 322–328; idem, "Ibn Taymīyas Kritik an der Aristotelischen Logik und sein Gegenentwurf," 212–214.

103 Anjum, *Politics, Law, and Community in Islamic Thought*, 215, 220–223.

104 In spite of the fact that the scope of the immediate reception of Ibn Taymiyya's works against rationalism is largely unknown, it is evident Ibn al-Qayyim utilized his teacher's main lines of thought in several of his own works, including *al-Ṣawāʿiq*. Von Kügelgen mentions in particular Ibn Taymiyya's *Darʾ taʿāruḍ al-ʿaql wal-naql*; however, the impact of several other writings is possible as well; Von Kügelgen, "The Poison of Philosophy," 280–281.

any rate, it can be safely said that Ibn al-Qayyim's arguments as they appear in *al-Ṣawāʿiq* draw heavily on Taymiyyan opinions and, to a great extent, systematically gather them into a single unified text.

In order to broadly display the discussion in sections 3.2 and 3.3, I would like to outline the chronological and thematic interrelations between the different writings mentioned so far:

Time period	Author	Writings and significance	
Ca. 1200	Fakhr al-Dīn al-Rāzī	*al-Muḥaṣṣal, Kitāb al-arbaʿīn*	philosophical-*Kalām*ic theology
		Asās al-taqdīs	promoting *taʾwīl*; against contemporary Ḥanbalite scholars
Ca. 1300	Ibn Taymiyya	[*Sharḥ awwal al-muḥaṣṣal*], [*Sharḥ biḍʿat ʿashr masʾala min al-arbaʿīn lil-Rāzī*]	missing writings, answering back directly to two of al-Rāzī's theological writings
		Bayān talbīs al-jahmiyya	answering back directly to al-Rāzī's *Asās al-taqdīs*; against *taʾwīl*
		al-Radd ʿalā ʾl-munṭiqiyyīn	criticizing fundamental principles of Greek logic, in an attempt to demolish any validity of logical treatment of metaphysical topics
Ca. 1350	Ibn al-Qayyim	*al-Ṣawāʿiq al-mursala*	utilizing and expanding the Tayymiyan critique to attack contemporary Ashʿarite scholars for their promotion of Rāziyyan ideas

Spread over a time span of almost two centuries, this table portrays but a miniscule section of the interesting scholastic yield stimulated by the ideological conflict between the Rāziyyan later Ashʿarite thought and the Taymiyyan worldview. In this context, Ibn al-Qayyim's *al-Ṣawāʿiq* represents another step in the progression of that intellectual combat.

A significant interim conclusion arising from the examination of the concept of 'certain knowledge' in the writings of al-Rāzī and Ibn Taymiyya is that both agree that, indeed, such knowledge cannot to be attained by purely rationalistic methods (i.e., either Greek philosophy or *ʿilm al-Kalām*). On the other hand, the two scholars most discernibly differ in the solution they offer for this predicament, which—to the best of my understanding—relates to the way they perceive two main elements: traditionally transmitted knowledge (*naql*) and the Muʿtazilite device of *taʾwīl*. For Ibn Taymiyya, the answer lays in the Islamic Revelation, the Quran and Hadith, and in his total confidence in the concept of *naql*, namely the narration of the Prophetic knowledge through reliable chains of transmitters. Another factor in favor of Revelation, as has already been discussed, is *al-ʿaql al-ṣarīḥ* and its inherent rationalism. For al-Rāzī, however, the sources of the Revelation produce mere verbal indications and proofs, which are retained by insufficient chain of transmission or by blind *taqlīd*, thus producing no knowledge whatsoever. Al-Rāzī's alternative way is the "way of the Quran", which in his mind is not a form of *naql* since it has to do with a divinely transmitted knowledge.[105] This approach relies greatly on Muʿtazilite principles.

Another point that should be noted at this stage is that, in *al-Radd ʿalā 'l-munṭiqiyyīn* for example, Ibn Taymiyya adopts the terminology used by al-Rāzī and 'the later *mutakallimūn*' (i.e., later Ashʿarites) while replying to their arguments. Ibn Taymiyya's vast use of terms such as *ʿilm yaqīn* or *ẓann* changes them into key terms in his conceptualization of traditionalistic ideas. It can be said that Ibn Taymiyya not only channels Aristotelian notions for sustaining his point of view, as von Kügelgen rightfully shows, he also mobilizes *Kalām*ic rationalistic terminology for his own specific use, adapting those notions and terms to his ideas by redefining them according to his own worldview. This can be taken as another aspect of the 'naturalization of sciences' that Langermann speaks of and the penetration of philosophical ideas to Muslim thought.[106] In *al-Radd ʿalā 'l-manṭiqiyyīn*, Ibn Taymiyya aims at disprove Aristotelian logic by means of Aristotelian logic itself. His sophisticated counter-methodology left its mark on Ibn al-Qayyim, as the latter formulated his argumentations

105 For additional details on the important role of epistemic transmission for al-Rāzī, see: Jaffer, "Muʿtazilite Aspects of Faḫr al-Dīn al-Rāzī's Thought," 532–535.

106 See footnotes 9 and 10 in page 116 of this chapter.

in *al-Ṣawāʿiq* in a manner that amalgamates rationalism together with traditionalism. To the best of my understanding, the two approaches—the first, describing an Islamic adaptation of an exterior Greek methodology; and the second, describing a utilization of methodology embedded in Islamic rhetorical tradition—do not contradict one another. On the contrary, in my opinion it is most likely that each of these two factors had its own role in shaping dialectical argumentation methods in Islamic theological thought, whether amongst the more rationalistic movement or the traditionalistic one. The following section's exploration of Ibn al-Qayyim's epistemological approach in *al-Ṣawāʿiq* is but a single example of such a merge between "naturalized science" and Islamic dialectics.

3.4 Ibn al-Qayyim's Development: Restoring Optimism

Returning to the work *al-Ṣawāʿiq al-mursala* which stands at the core of the present study, and to our discussion on epistemology, it seems Ibn al-Qayyim's selective choice of the material cited on behalf of his teacher Ibn Taymiyya largely reflects his own ideas on the matter of attaining certainty of religious knowledge. Ibn al-Qayyim first displays his valuable method of arranging the Taymiyyan materials known to him, dividing his teacher's critique concerning al-Rāzī's pessimistic epistemological notions into two key levels: a general critique followed by specific refutations of each of the ten conditions set by al-Rāzī. Given the somewhat repetitive nature of these parts of *al-Ṣawāʿiq*, I will only briefly demonstrate this kind of systemization before moving on to the final section of the first *ṭāghūt*'s refutation, in which a more meaningful development of argumentations is presented. Notwithstanding, I believe Ibn al-Qayyim's systemization is a vital feature of his participation in the *Kalām*ic discourse, not only as it captures the Taymiyyan scholarly activities, but also since it further presents Ibn al-Qayyim's rationalization of the traditionalistic thought. Due to lack of sufficient research, it is currently beyond our knowledge to soundly discern whether any other scholars of Ibn al-Qayyim's time who perceived themselves to be members of the Taymiyyan circle made such an attempt to articulate the mentor's ideology in this *Kalām*ic manner.[107] In terms of genre and rhetoric style, however, it does seem that traditionalism prevailed, at times also within Ibn al-Qayyim's oeuvre itself (e.g., in his work preceding *al-*

107 Bori, "Theology, Politics, Society: The Missing Link," 67–68, 77–78.

Ṣawāʿiq—Ijtimāʿ ʾl-juyāsh ʾl-islāmiyya).[108] Albeit, *al-Ṣawāʿiq* surely epitomizes Ibn al-Qayyim's intelligible construction of dialectical argumentations, as he systemized the theoretical foundations for his teacher's theological thought and sought to widely distribute it, also reaching out towards the Ashʿarite elite beyond the traditionalistic milieu. Liable to the Taymiyyan non-elitist attitude, Ibn al-Qayyim's combination of systemized theology and didactical style was sensibly meant to deliver theological ideas also to the ordinary people and laymen (*ʿāmma*).[109]

Evidence for the goal of the proliferation of the Taymiyyan ideology can be seen in numerous places in *al-Ṣawāʿiq*. Ibn al-Qayyim's immediate reference to the sayings of Ibn Taymiyya, which he immediately presents after Fakhr al-Dīn al-Rāzī's ten conditions for certain knowledge, is relevant to Ibn al-Qayyim's deliberations regarding the first *ṭāghūt*. Ibn al-Qayyim expresses Ibn Taymiyya's—whom he refers to in the text as "*shaykh al-islām*"[110]—primary rejection, apparently as it was orally expressed or in one of the teacher's lost works:[111]

> We do not accept [the premise] that [certainty] is dependent on these ten premises. On the contrary, we say it is not dependent on [the rhetoric features] by which the speaker's intention is perceived. Saying that 'verbal indications (*al-adilla ʾl-lafẓiyya*) do not produce certain knowledge', he [i.e., al-Rāzī] means that they do not supply knowledge on the speaker's intention. As for [his claim] that the speaker's intention [should be] in accordance with the truth, this depends on substantiating his truthfulness and knowledge. But this is what they mean. Had they meant only this—without the first [argument] of dependence on substantiating the

108 See section 2.1 above, which discusses *al-Ṣawāʿiq*'s relation to Ibn al-Qayyim's previous theological works.

109 From a social perspective, the Taymiyyan approach of increasing the laymen's accessibility to tangled theological knowledge stands in contrast to the elitism of the Ashʿrite one, especially since the times of al-Ghazālī. However, the elitist later Ashʿarite tendency was also highly present in Mamluk times, in the activity of Taqi ʾl-Dīn al-Subkī for instance, as a means of protecting their high social status and political authority; Bori, "Theology, Politics, Society: The Missing Link," 79–83.

110 This epithet was ascribed in the Muslim world to the most eminent and honorable *ʿulamāʾ*, expressing the great measure of respect they received from their community. Ibn al-Qayyim commonly uses this title when referring to his master Ibn Taymiyya.

111 According to the editor's footnote, he was unable to detect the passage in any of Ibn Taymiyya's printed works, therefore it is most likely to have appeared in his missing work *Sharḥ awwal al-muḥaṣṣal*; see the table in page 157 above.

> speaker's infallibility and knowing his honesty—then whoever acknowledges that the Messenger of God intended this meaning and that he spoke the truth, attains certain knowledge.
>
> Secondly, as a matter of belief, everyone who declares that Muḥammad is the Prophet of God recognizes that [this statement] is information [produced from verbal indicative evidence] that matches the one who informed about it. Therefore, it is impossible that he [i.e., Muḥammad] informed of something which did match its informer.[112]

All in all, this argument reflects the traditionalistic perception regarding necessary and certain knowledge, which—according to Ibn Taymiyya—is supposed to be homogenous among the religious scholars.[113] Ibn al-Qayyim carefully explains his master's above-mentioned claim, maintaining previous scholars have agreed the debated rationalistic argument contains two elements of certainty: certainty about the speaker's intention (*al-yaqīn bi-murādⁱ 'l-mutakallim*), and certainty that the speaker's intention conveys truth (*al-yaqīn bi-mā arādahᵘ huwᵃ 'l-ḥaqq*). Therefore, al-Rāzī's argument—that "the speech of God and His Messenger do not produce certain knowledge"—is understood in three possible ways:

1. Certain knowledge is not produced by the speakers' intention and, even if it were so, there is no certainty that his intention conveys the truth.
2. If certain knowledge is produced by the speaker's intention, then his intention conveys the truth.
3. If certain knowledge is produced by the speaker's intention, there is no certainty that the intention conveys the truth.

Describing Ibn Taymiyya's opinion, Ibn al-Qayyim sustains that the first and third options are absolutely false; therefore the only reasonable possibility is the second one.[114] Highly evident is the similarity to criticism against al-Rāzī expressed by Ibn Taymiyya in *Bayān al-talbīs*, where the importance of attaining certainty of the speaker's intention (*murād*) is greatly stressed.[115] Ibn al-Qayyim delivers Ibn Taymiyya's analytical examination of al-Rāzī's argument while targeting its disposal on the basis of rationality.

---

112 Ibn Qayyim al-Jawziyya, *al-Ṣawāʿiq al-mursala*, 2:634.

113 Abrahamov, "Necessary Knowledge in Islamic Theology," 20–21.

114 Ibn Qayyim al-Jawziyya, *al-Ṣawāʿiq al-mursala*, 2:634–635.

115 See in section 3.3 Ibn Taymiyya's Initial Critique against al-Rāzī above.

Another means used in order to validate Ibn Taymiyya's line of attack is affirming the favorable alternative—in his view—to al-Rāzī's argument: relying on the consecutively and massively transmitted texts of the Revelation (*al-naql al-mutawātir*), meaning the Quran and Hadith literature. Ibn al-Qayyim repeats here Ibn Taymiyya's well-known position from *Darʾ al-taʿāruḍ* (for instance), according to which, there is no sense in preferring Reason (*ʿaql*) to the transmitted textual sources (*naql*) whenever these texts reputedly contradict human Reason. There is no use shunning the Revelation and firmly diverting attention away from it in the issue of reflecting and attaining knowledge about God, His names, His attributes and His actions. Knowledge on the speaker's intention is achieved by the transmitted texts of Revelation, just as it is achieved by the speaker's use in particular expressions (*lafẓ*) in them. This is the case of all of the Quranic verses which were consecutively transmitted on behalf of the Prophet Muḥammad. Since the texts were transmitted with perfect precision from God the His Messenger to the rest of the Muslim community, the Islamic sources give us cogent (*qaṭʿ*) knowledge of their speaker's intention (*murād*), on the verbal expressions used therein (*alfāẓ al-qurʾān*) as well as of their meaning (*maʿāni ʾl-qurʾān*). Moreover, Ibn al-Qayyim states that the Prophet took more interest in informing the community about the meanings of the Quran than informing them of its verbal expressions; thus, knowledge of the meanings reached even those who did not retain its verbal expression. Therefore, the transmission of the meanings conveyed in the sources of Revelation is necessarily stronger, so that the retention of meaning is easier than that of verbal expression. Many people know and retain the meaning (*ṣūrat al-maʿnā*) but do not memorize the verbal expressions. Those who did transmit the religion on the basis of verbal expression know its intention cogently, due to their exact recitation of the expressions.[116] This view closely resembles—and to some extent paraphrases—the teachings of Ibn Taymiyya in *Bayān al-tablīs*, where he maintains that "the transmission of the meaning comes first" (*naql al-maʿnā awlā*). Ibn Taymiyya relies here on a saying attributed to Aḥmad ibn Ḥanbal: "knowing the Hadith and its understanding is more beloved than its recitation".[117]

Further supporting Ibn Taymiyya's opinion as it appears in *Bayān al-tablīs*, Ibn al-Qayyim clarifies the absolute quality of verbal informative indicators derived from the Islamic texts alone (*al-adilla ʾl-samʿiyya ʾl-lafẓiyya*). Gener-

116 Ibn Qayyim al-Jawziyya, *al-Ṣawāʿiq al-mursala*, 2:635–636.

117 Ibn Taymiyya, *Bayān talbīs al-jahmiyya*, 8:475–476; See in addition Ibn Taymiyya's discussion described in page 148.

ally, he explains, there are two apodictic premises at the basis of all verbal indicative evidence of this kind. First, that each and every one of their transmitters understood their speaker's intention (*murād al-mutakallim*); and second, that they transferred this intention to us, along with the verbal expression that conveys it. Ibn Taymiyya argues that these two premises must be known and confirmed, since it is known that the people who heard the Prophet Muḥammad when he delivered the Qur'anic Revelation understood his intention in every single expression (*lafẓ*). This trend has continued with every generation of transmitters, passing over the verbal expressions attached to the knowledge of their intended meaning. Among these two elements (i.e., verbal expression and intended meaning) the element of meaning is of course far more important, while the verbal expression is the vehicle of transfer which conveys the intended meaning (*wasīla ilayh^{i}*). And yet, there is no doubt that they were both transmitted with utmost certainty. When considered by a reasonable person (*al-ʿāqil*), this is the only convincingly conclusive way for transmitting knowledge (*ṭarīqa qāṭiʿa*).[118]

Moreover, Ibn al-Qayyim further continues by stating a reasonable person knows that whoever attacks the possibility of attaining knowledge by the Quran's meanings alone (*maʿāni 'l-qur'ān*) is worse than those who attack the possibility of attaining knowledge by the Quran's transmitted expressions (*alfāẓih^{i}*). Two sects are mentioned as heretical groups for following either of these two approaches. The first sect is *al-rāfiḍa* (i.e., the Shīʿites), which refused to transmit some of the expressions of the Quran. The second sect is *al-bāṭina wal-mulāḥida* (i.e., the Ismāʿilite Shīʿites) which denied the possibility of achieving knowledge from the Quran's meanings.[119] The Shiʿite-Ismāʿīlite sect did agree that the Prophet's companions transmitted the verbal expressions uttered by the Prophet and that the Quran was transmitted according to them; however, they interpreted those expressions allegorically using the rationalistic tool of *ta'wīl* and preached for the esoteric meanings of those texts, which differ from the meanings known "by all Muslims" (i.e., the Sunnites).[120]

---

118 Ibn Qayyim al-Jawziyya, *al-Ṣawāʿiq al-mursala*, 2:637–638.

119 The designation *al-bāṭina* was used as a pejorative name for the Shiʿite-Ismāʿīlite stream. In addition, see footnote 63 in chapter 1. The editor of *al-Ṣawāʿiq* also refers to this affiliation in a footnote in its first volume, p. 303; Paul E. Walker, "Bāṭiniyya", *EI*^{3}, online-source; Yaron Friedman, *The Nuṣayrī-ʿAlawīs: An Introduction to the Religion, History, and Identity of the Leading Minority in Syria*, 189–190.

120 Ibn Qayyim al-Jawziyya, *al-Ṣawāʿiq al-mursala*, 2:638.

As a matter of fact, Ibn al-Qayyim's systemization of Ibn Taymiyya's stances as they appear in *Bayān al-talbīs* (and possibly also in the missing work *Sharḥ awwal al-muḥaṣṣal*) can be mostly summed down to a rejection of any Muslim group's methodology for comprehending the Islamic textual sources and their indications of meaning about God, which does not strictly adhere to the literal meaning of the text. As previously illustrated, the central linguistic elements of this approach are the speaker and his truthful intention that is articulated within a specific context, which in turn, produces expressions indicating a certain meaning. When all of these are massively transmitted by the means of *tawātur*, there is no reason to doubt the certainty of meaning delivered by the texts sacred to Islam.[121] In this aspect Ibn al-Qayyim manifestly shares the standpoint of his mentor, who displayed a meticulously rationalized treatment of al-Rāzī's epistemic system as he rejected it.[122] For this reason, it is a rather perplexing task to make a clear-cut distinction between Ibn al-Qayyim's reliance on Ibn Taymiyya's arguments and his own independent writing. Nonetheless, it seems that the section finalizing Ibn al-Qayyim's refutation of the first *ṭāghūt* bears much of Ibn al-Qayyim's singular voice. Ibn al-Qayyim dedicates this section to a survey of what he identifies as the devastating repercussions of the rationalistic perception of certain knowledge.[123] It is very plausible that the teacher's critique still has its resonance in this highly spirited ending, and yet Ibn al-Qayyim transgresses namely the linguistic reasoning offered by Ibn Taymiyya to the already linguistic-grammatical ten conditions for certainty of knowledge that al-Rāzī had set. Rather, the final *ṭāghūt* refutation on that issue concentrates on criticizing rationalistic intellectual discernments—Ibn al-Qayyim even sees them as illnesses—which were the long term results of the massive reception of Rāziyyan Ashʿarism among rationalistic Muslim scholars and their vast deployment of his epistemological pessimistic approach on theological matters. In this manner Ibn al-Qayyim

121 Ibn Taymiyya expresses this view in his *Darʾ al-taʿāruḍ* as well; Abrahamov, "Ibn Taymiyya on the Agreement of Reason with Tradition," 261.

122 Supplementary confirmation of Ibn al-Qayyim's and Ibn Taymiyya's rationalized attitude towards knowledge assessments, which can be obtained by textual significations, is also apparent in the field of Islamic jurisprudence. Baber Johanson describes these Neo-Ḥanbalite rationalized tendencies concerning the notion of satisfactory proof in his article: "Signs as Evidence: The Doctrine of Ibn Taymiyya (1263–1328) and Ibn Qayyim al-Jawziyya (d. 1351) on Proof," *Islamic Law and Society* 9/2 (2002), 179–183, 187–189,192–193.

123 For a general outline of Ibn al-Qayyim's array of the first *ṭāghūt* refutation, see page 118. More specifically, I refer to sections (*wujūh*) 61–73 of the first *ṭāghūt*; Ibn Qayyim al-Jawziyya, *al-Ṣawāʿiq al-mursala*, 2:766–794.

takes a step forwards in his critique, as he exhibits a developed and systemized phase in the rationalization of the traditionalistic opposition to the Ashʿarite epistemological theory of his time and calls for a restored optimism.

The most obvious repercussion Ibn al-Qayyim condemns is the departure of the rationalists from the textual sources of the Quran and the Hadith which, in his opinion, stands as a conscious declaration of disbelief and fallacy. It is an absolute absurdity, Ibn al-Qayyim says, that all other books' compilers (*muṣannifūn*[a]) in all disciplines of knowledge (*fī jamīʿ*[i] *'l-ʿulūm*) had clarified their intention and their readers attained knowledge of it with sheer certainty, whether that knowledge was true or false, whereas the intention of God and His Messenger articulated by their own speech is still unclear to the people of their religion (*al-umma*) who still remained incredulous to that very day. This can only be said by the most oblivious person who knows nothing of God, His Messenger and His speech. Indeed, there are scholars among "the lords of rationalism" (*arbāb al-maʿqūlāt*) who are so remote from knowing God to the point that they lack any trust in Him, think wickedly of Him and consider His speech to be a message of no proof (*khiṭāba*[tan] *lā burhān*[a]). They imagine Him as a fantasy in their minds, which became obscured by their rationalistic preoccupations, so that they depict God in tangible imageries (*wa-akhrajuhā fī 'l-ṣuwar*[i] *'l-maḥsūsat*[i]). The rationalists behave as if the Quran is but a message sent to the ignorant Arabs, who are the most ignorant of all people in their knowledge and understanding of truths; thus, the only way for their call of faith to appear is as a fictional message and not as a path of wisdom and rational evidence.[124] Ibn al-Qayyim's accusations continue, as he scolds the rationalists for upholding the perception that the way of knowledge and evidence is alien to the philosophers, the logicians, the fools that assign idols to God (*al-ṣābiʾa*) and

124 Notable is Ibn al-Qayyim's presentation of later Ashʿarite *Kalām* as an expression of the condescending views that the Persian scholars—the protagonists of Ashʿarite rationalism—held towards the Arabs (especially Ḥanbalite) scholars and the masses alike. This state of mind is described in numerous historical accounts, including that of the violent riots (*fitna*, pl. *fitan*) that broke out between the students of the Ashʿarite scholar Ibn al-Qushayrī (d. 514/1120) and their Ḥanbalite opposers in Baghdad in 469/1077. Ibn al-Qayyim's passage above seems to draw directly on the way these riots were recorded by the Ashʿarite-Shafiʿite scholar Ibn ʿAsākir (d. 571/1176) in a work titled *Tabyīn kidhb al-muftarī fīmā nusib*[a] *ilā 'l-Imām Abi 'l-Ḥasan al-Ashʿarī* (Damascus: Maktabat al-Tawfīq, 1347/1928); Holtzman, "The *miḥna* of Ibn ʿAqīl (d. 513/1119) and the *fitnat* Ibn al-Qushayrī (d. 514/1120)", in: ed. Sabine Schmidtke, *Oxford Handbook of Islamic Theology* (Oxford: Oxford University Press, 2016), [Online Publication Date: Jun 2014], 1, 7–18. Ibn al-Qayyim cited from Ibn ʿAsākir's work *Tabyīn kidhb al-muftarī* in his second *ṭāghūt* refutation in *al-Ṣawāʿiq*, 4:1264, 1281, and also in *Ijtimāʿ la-juyūsh al-islāmiyya*, 2:133, 286.

their followers. There is no doubt then that they do not find certainty in the Quran, as God said Q 41:44 "Say, 'for those who have faith it is guidance and healing, but the ears of the disbelievers are heavy, they are blind to it, [as if] they are being called from a distant place.'" Meaning, the disbelievers cannot acquire certainty from the Islamic texts, since they arrogantly favor mere mundane matters which they are able to perceive (*al-umūr al-wujdāniyya 'l-ḥāṣila lahum*).[125] Putting it very bluntly, Ibn al-Qayyim charges the rationalists with a denial of the divine message (*jaḥd al-risāla*), namely *takfīr*.[126]

Enhancing his criticism, Ibn al-Qayyim raises several examples of disagreement amid differentiated rationalistic trends and their variety of contradictory opinions on the knowledge attained from the scriptures of Islam:

> Every so often the upholders of this 'rule' change their minds about it, turning away from [the truth] to falsehood (*yu'fak*[u] *'anh*[u] *man ufik*[a]).[127] At times they say: "while we know what a total rejection of the apparent text is (*intifā' al-ẓāhir*[i] *qaṭ'*[an]), and this is not what we mean." In other times they say: "the Messenger delivered to the people a collective message (*khiṭāb*[an] *jumhūrī*[yan])", which meets the knowledge they already possess and were already familiar with [i.e., the *Kalām*]. Had he [i.e., the Prophet] addressed them confirming the existence of an existent which exists not inside this world nor outside of it, [an existent which] does not speak and is not spoken to, [an existent which] cannot be seen with the eyes nor can be pointed at—they would have said: these are attributes of an absent rather than of an existent (*hādhih*[i] *ṣifāt*[u] *ma'dūm*[in] *lā mawjūd*[in]),[128] and

125 Ibn Qayyim al-Jawziyya, *al-Ṣawā'iq al-mursala*, 2:766–768 (*al-wajh al-ḥādī wal-sitūn*).

126 Ibn Qayyim al-Jawziyya, *al-Ṣawā'iq al-mursala*, 2:769 (*al-wajh al-thālith wal-sitūn*).

127 The Arabic expression in brackets appears in the Quran, verse 51:9. Also, the use of the verb *afak*[a] echoes the story from a traditional report known as *ḥadīthat al-ifk* ('the affair of falsehood'), when a group from the hypocrites (*munāfiqūn*) falsely accused the Prophet Muḥammad's favorite wife 'Ā'isha of committing adultery with his companion (*ṣaḥābī*) Ṣafwān ibn al-Mu'aṭṭal; G.H.A. Juynboll, "Ṣafwān ibn al-Mu'aṭṭal", *EI*², 8:820. This allegation is believed to have been later refuted by the Quranic verse (24:11) "It was a group from among you who brought the false accusation—do not consider it a bad thing for you [people]; it was a good thing—and every one of them will be charged with the sin he has earned. He who took the greatest part in it will have a painful torment."

128 See footnote 117 in chapter 2. It seems that Ibn al-Qayyim is referring to an early rationalistic group which described God using negative utterances (*aphairesis*) under the influence of the Greek philosopher Albinus. On the basis of this idea stands the recognition that God is inconceivable by the human mind, hence He is to be described only in a man-

> thus they would have fallen back to negating the divine attributes (*taʿṭīl*). It would have been much better for them had he brought them expressions that indicate whatever it is that fits their own wrongly ascribed [attributes] and their own writings, so that they would achieve the negation [of the divine attributes].[129]

The above passage illustrates Ibn al-Qayyim's advanced criticism against the rationalists, as he allows himself to run rampant and express his independent opinion on their mishandling of the texts of the Quran and Hadith. In spite of the fact that the term is not specifically mentioned, Ibn al-Qayyim uses here a rationalistic mode of argumentation similar to the *ilzām* technique, as he accuses his ideological rivals of holding a belief which makes no sense; he lists the rationalistic views he opposes and pinpoints the contradictions he finds therein.[130] Using hypothetical sentences, Ibn al-Qayyim scorns the Ashʿarite way of thinking and shows just how ridiculous the Prophetic message would have been had it been formulated in *Kalām*ic terminology. The blunt tone of irony carries on in the next passage:

> How, then, can this claim meet their saying: "[we do] not intend the apparent [text]"? If they intend the apparent [text], their saying—that the apparent [text] is not the issue—is false; and if they intend the allegorical interpretation (*taʾwīl*), their saying—that they intend what they believe, and thereby can affirm the Creator (*ithbāt al-ṣāniʿ*) and be liberated from negation (*taʿṭīl*)—is false. What contradiction is greater than that?! If you [i.e., the Ashʿarites] mean the apparent text, you have a false understanding, which is indicated by its [very] expression; and if you do not mean the apparent text, but rather the allegorical interpretation, the objective that you have mentioned is not attained, you are not freed of negation [of the divine attributes], and that does not [serve you as] a trickery in order to rebut it.[131]

---

ner of negating known attributes (e.g., invisible, amorphous, and so on); Wolfson, "Albinus and Plotinus on Divine Attributes," 1: 119–125, 129–130.

129 Ibn Qayyim al-Jawziyya, *al-Ṣawāʿiq al-mursala*, 2:771 (*al-wajh al-rābiʿ wal-sitūn*).

130 This line of argumentation goes further on with an apparent speculative affinity, using time and again the well-known *Kalām*ic formula of 'if you [i.e., the adversaries] say …, we reply …' (*in qultum … qulnā/qīl*[a] …). Van Ess, "The Logical Structure of Islamic Theology," 23–24.

131 Ibn Qayyim al-Jawziyya, *al-Ṣawāʿiq al-mursala*, 2:771.

It is clear that in Ibn al-Qayyim's opinion, the rationalists twist themselves into countless intellectual entanglements that, at the end of the day, all result in the absurd conclusion of the negation of divine attributes. As he examines the rationalistic argument, Ibn al-Qayyim points to a logical contradiction, aiming at proving that the issue at hand is in fact the figurative interpretation. Ibn al-Qayyim continues:

> Both of these ways are false and contradict the meaning of the Prophetic message (*qaṣd al-risāla*): those would fantasize things that benefit them, even if there is no truth therein;[132] and the proponents of the figurative interpretation (*aṣḥāb al-taʾwīl*) would interpret [the text] as the exact opposite of what is indicated in His speech and His text. At times they say that they intend to allegorically interpret the holy texts, whereas at other times they say that they intend to leave the texts to the discretion of God (*tafwīḍ*). God and His Messenger transcend beyond intending false meanings or diminishing the clarification of their intention [...] This is a cogent indicator of the transcendence of God and His Messenger beyond all of this: God cannot be bared with any imaginary deceitful doubt.[133]

Quite forcefully, Ibn al-Qayyim depicts the rationalistic epistemological discourse as a statement of reduction of the indicative verbal evidence in the Islamic textual sources to the degree of complete dismissing their sanctity. Ibn al-Qayyim stresses the irony conveyed in the theological concept of *tafwīḍ* regarding the ability to understand these texts.[134] In this context, his use of the pronoun "they" in the cited passage can refer to the Muʿtazilites, and so: leaving the meaning of the texts to their own discretion (according to the rationalistic method of *taʾwīl*); and equally, it can refer to the Ashʿarites, as in leaving the texts to God and avoid any kind of interpretation (according to the traditionalistic formula of *bi-lā kayfa*). Either way, Ibn al-Qayyim stresses the irony in a situation, in which the understanding of the textual sources provided to humankind is to be left to God's discretion.

---

132 In other words: the rationalistic group mentioned above which described God using negative utterances, or the rationalists in general, who apply figurative interpretation on the divine attributes, turning them into non-actual, vague descriptions.

133 Ibn Qayyim al-Jawziyya, *al-Ṣawāʿiq al-mursala*, 2:771–772.

134 A good discussion on *tafwīḍ* in Islamic theology can be found in: van Ess, *Theologie und Gesellschaft*, 5: 34. The term is also used in Islamic legal theory mostly as a delegation of power.

A considerably more logical manner of argumentation can be easily found as well in Ibn al-Qayyim's assessments, for instance, as he rationally analyzes the premises (*muqaddimāt*) upon which al-Rāzī's ten conditions for certainty of knowledge are based:

> They who conceive the speech of the upholders of this principle rest on three presumptions:
>
> 1. Knowledge of the speaker's intention is dependent on attaining knowledge of whatever indicates his intention;
> 2. There is no way to attain knowledge [of the speaker's] intention apart from banishing (*intifāʾ*) those ten conditions;
> 3. There is no way to attain knowledge of their banishing.
>
> The first presumption is true, whereas the other two are false. As for the first one, it is correct. Knowledge of the speaker's intention is often necessary knowledge (*ilm*^{an} *iḍṭirāriy*^{yan}), like knowledge of the massively transmitted prophetic traditions (*al-akhbār al-mutawātira*). Therefore, when one hears a transmitter (*mukhbir*) reporting on a matter he understands, he thinks (*ẓann*^{a}) and then consolidates it with [a report of] another transmitter in order for it to become necessary knowledge. Similarly, when one hears a speaker's speech (*kalām al-mutakallim*), he might already identify the intention as necessary [knowledge] or might think of it. Then he repeats the speech—what the speaker said or what he heard[135] him say. When he indicates the [original] intention, his knowledge becomes necessary.
>
> A speech that conveys the intention might be a speculative indication (*istidlāl*^{an} *naẓariy*^{yan}). In this case, [the speech] is to be made dependent on one condition, or two, or more, taking into consideration the listener's need, his power to understand, his quickness or slowness of perception, his little or voluminous [knowledge] acquisition, his intellectuality, and also the complete clearance of the speaker or his [lack of clarity]. Therefore, the declaration that every verbal indication must meet ten conditions is determinately false.[136]

---

135 *Samāʿ* is one of the eight technical terms used in the science of Hadith in order to denote a form of Hadith instruction; here it designates an indirect hearing of the traditions; Muḥammad Zubair Siddiqi, *Ḥadīth Literature: Its Origin, Development and Special Features*, 2nd ed. (Cambridge: Islamic Texts Society, 1993), 86.

136 Ibn Qayyim al-Jawziyya, *al-Ṣawāʿiq al-mursala*, 2:779–780 (*al-wajh al-sabʿūn*).

This passage illustrates a striking merge of Ibn al-Qayyim's systemization of Ibn Taymiyya's ideas together with his rationalized argumentation style. First, he unfolds what he perceives to be the basic logical foundations behind al-Rāzī's ten conditions, demonstrating a high level of use in Reason. Second, Ibn al-Qayyim puts those foundations to test, as he investigates them one after another and concludes that only one of them actually holds water. Then, he provides the Taymiyyan explanation of the only true premise; this fits to a great extent Ibn Taymiyya's view on the two possible modes of knowledge, as articulated in his work *al-Radd ʿalā ʾl-manṭiqiyyīn*.[137] Ibn al-Qayyim contributes his own designations, when he sustains the evidence in the Quran—that the rationalists refer to as 'verbal indicators'—are of two kinds: informative (*samʿī/ḍarūrī*) and rational (*ʿaqlī*).[138] In addition, the passage above repeats the notion of relativism and difference of mental capacities between different people, with a strong stress on the human intellectual ability to perceive knowledge, as was previously shown in Ibn al-Qayyim's discussion in *al-Ṣawāʿiq*.[139] This logical manner of argumentation goes further, as Ibn al-Qayyim attacks the tenth among al-Rāzī's conditions:

> Even falser is the condition which states that the intention [in a piece of knowledge] cannot be known unless it has been banished of having an indicator that points to its opposite. This is conclusively wrong, since it is known that knowledge which affirms one of two opposites disproves any knowledge which affirms the other one. So, this knowledge on an intention disproves any possibility (*iḥtimāl*) to contradict it.
>
> Hence, concerning the claim of eliminating any rational or informative contradictory indicator (*nafī ʾl-muʿāriḍⁱ ʾl-ʿaqlī wal-samʿī*), when knowledge on an intention is cogent (*ilm qaṭʿī*), it will not be eliminated by any other indicator, either rational or informative, as they contradict it.
>
> When one thing is confirmed as truth, its opposite is banished. Then, this principle is turned against them [i.e., the rationalists], as we say: knowledge on the indications of the speech of God and His Messenger [i.e., the Quran and Hadith] is cogent certain knowledge which has no possible contradiction. Therefore, we establish the indication on the fallacy of anything that contradicts them, by the means of affirming the knowledge of them [...] This fundamental principle (*aṣl*) is of greater

---

137 See in section 3.3 of this chapter, page 154.

138 Ibn Qayyim al-Jawziyya, *al-Ṣawāʿiq al-mursala*, 2:793.

139 See page 121.

> truth than their principle and it is closer to Reason, faith and the verification of prophecy. The speech of God and His Messenger shows its truthfulness and clarifies anything which appears therein.[140]

Eloquently articulating his criticism in the passage above, Ibn al-Qayyim reconstructs the final condition among the ten requirements set by al-Rāzī. While getting to the bottom of the logical factors of this rationalistic principle and rearranging them in order to conform them to his own viewpoint, Ibn al-Qayyim reveals not only his singular attitude, but also his impressive skill of rationalized authorship. In fact, in a performance of 'reconstruction' Ibn al-Qayyim exhibits several interesting aspects of his methodological input. First of all, he accomplishes laying a meaningful intellectual opposition to his later Ashʿarite rivals. The means in which he does so are purely rationalistic and rely on simple Aristotelian logic, although the content is of downright traditionalistic nature. Moreover, Ibn al-Qayyim treats the tenth condition by al-Rāzī as the central core of the entire set of requirements posed. Whilst the other nine conditions mainly touch upon grammar and linguistics, the tenth focuses on rationality alone—there should be no other "rational opposed indication (*muʿāriḍ ʿaqlī*) of a greater weight," which contradicts the verbal indicator.[141] This condition is perceived by Ibn al-Qayyim here as the final conclusion of the model of the ten conditions to the degree of encompassing all possible situations; in Ibn al-Qayyim's words, every statement has its negative. Separating the wheat from the chaff, Ibn al-Qayyim does not fail to detect the value concealed in this last condition and, by making a witty use of it, he actually disarms it. Once again, Ibn al-Qayyim strives to reveal the absurdity of his opponent's claim, as it is well illustrated in the passage cited.

Towards the end of his discussion on the first *ṭāghūt*, Ibn al-Qayyim provides a harsh castigation not only against his contemporary rationalist scholars, but also against the rationalistic and philosophical trends as a whole. He sustains that by adhering to al-Rāzī's ten conditions, the rationalists cannot enjoy the certain knowledge contained in the Islamic sources. As a result, they are intellectually troubled in a severe manner, moving back and forth between different theological schools. The *falāsifa* are mostly affected by this approach, says Ibn al-Qayyim, as he refers the reader to their claims recorded in two important works. The first one is the well-known work by the Ashʿarite school's eponym Abu 'l-Ḥasan al-Ashʿarī (d. 324/935–936; first a Muʿtazilite, but then

---

140 Ibn Qayyim al-Jawziyya, *al-Ṣawāʿiq al-mursala*, 2:780–781.

141 See the 'ten conditions' in page 140.

a traditionalist)[142] *Maqālāt al-islāmiyyīn* (Dogmatic teachings of the Islamic Sects). The second—and more surprising—work is *al-Ārāʾ wal-diyānāt* (Convictions and Faiths) by the Shiʿite-Muʿtazilite al-Ḥasan ibn Mūsa ʾl-Nawbakhtī (d. ca. 300/912).[143] In Ibn al-Qayyim's opinion, every philosopher and *Kalām* scholar announces he possesses pure Reason (*ṣarīḥ al-ʿaql*) and that anyone who disagrees with him deviates from it. Ibn al-Qayyim says with sarcasm:

> We say then that they are all correct, and thereby eliminate the Reason of one group with the Reason of the other. Then we say to them all: by the means of which Reason of yours [can] the speech of God and His Messenger be weighed? [...] Which one is of your Reasons is that of the ten conditions, on which the speech of God and His Messenger are dependent, in order to produce certain knowledge—by not contradicting it?[144]

Ibn al-Qayyim clearly mentions here the 'contrary rational indicator' (*muʿāriḍ ʿaqlī*) from al-Rāzī's tenth condition, mocking the differences of opinions—different rationalities, as he sees them—within the rationalistic streams of thought. Listing some 30 different scholars and religious sects—starting with the ancient Greek philosophers to scholars relatively closer to his lifetime—Ibn al-Qayyim preserves a fine track of the prominent scholars with rationalistic tendencies, to whom he objects.[145] In fact, it is not only the rationalists he rejects, but any group that diverges from a literal understanding of the texts of the Quran and Hadith, such as the esoteric meanings suggested by several Shiʿite sects. Moreover, Ibn al-Qayyim argues, there is no uniform cohesion among the rationalists themselves, since each of them promoted an individual systematic approach for the use of Reason, resulting in multiple rationali-

---

142 ʾAlī ibn Ismāʿīl ibn Isḥāq Abu ʾl-Ḥasan al-Ashʿarī was a famous theologian who permitted the penetration of rationalistic ideas to the traditionalistic dogma, resulting in the formation of the Ashʿarite theological school in Islam. He was first a Muʿtazilite, but thereafter joined *ahl al-sunna*. Therefore, he was well acquainted with both the rationalistic and traditionalistic creeds, which he described in his three works on the theology of different Islamic sects; W. Montgomery Watt, "Abū ʾl-Ḥasan al-Ashʿarī", *EI*², 1:694.

143 Abū Muḥammad al-Ḥasan ibn Mūsā ibn al-Ḥasan al-Nawbakhtī was a theologian and a philosopher of Shiʿite affiliations. It is also reported that the Muʿtazilites described him as one of their own. The work *al-Ārāʾ wal-diyānāt* has only partly survived. The Ḥanbalite scholar Ibn al-Jawzī (d. 597/1200) has preserved parts of al-Nawbakhtī's *al-Ārāʾ* in the latter's *Talbīs Iblīs* (Deceit of Satan); Josef van Ess, *Der Eine und das Andere: Beobachtungen an islamischen häresiographischen Texten*, in 2 vols. (Berlin: de Gruyter, 2010), 1:220–222.

144 Ibn Qayyim al-Jawziyya, *al-Ṣawāʿiq al-mursala*, 2:781–783 (*al-wajh al-ḥādī wa-sabʿūn*).

145 Ibn Qayyim al-Jawziyya, *al-Ṣawāʿiq al-mursala*, 2:783–790.

ties distinguished from one another. Ibn al-Qayyim rebukes the ever-changing nature of the rationalistic discourse, to the point where he describes it as completely randomized. His critique against the "later scholars", referring to the later Ashʿarites following the age of al-Ghazālī, depicts a state of even greater intellectual inadequacy, in which the rationalists allowed themselves to break all former conventions known in their own intellectual circle, preferring their own independent—hence, unstable, contradictory and confused—opinions. In Ibn al-Qayyim eyes, al-Rāzī's rationalistic conditions for certain knowledge were chosen in the same arbitrary manner and are not adequate for evaluating the texts of Revelation, which the rationalists degrade even further to a level of mere 'verbal indicators' (*adilla lafẓiyya*).[146] As will be shown in the next chapter, Ibn al-Qayyim's denial of the notion of *muʿāriḍ ʿaqlī* (i.e., rational opposed indication) is further discussed in his refutation of the second *ṭāghūt*.

The developed stage of rationalized discourse is apparent in Ibn al-Qayyim's closure of the first *ṭāghūt* refutation. His familiarity with preceding rationalists and their intellectual effect on the epistemological issue at stake is indeed impressive. Then again, another question arises: how familiar was Ibn al-Qayyim with the teachings of these scholars? Was he simply name-dropping (he did mention Alexander the Great in a same breath as that of the greatest Hellenic-Greek thinkers) or was he more deeply engaged with particular parts of rationalistic or early philosophical thought? It is hard to believe that Ibn al-Qayyim knew the Hellenistic philosophical teachings at first hand, since he openly expressed his clear opposition to foreign influences upon Islam—as did his master Ibn Taymiyya. In addition, Ibn al-Qayyim's interest concerning Hellenistic philosophy was theologically motivated, especially in the case of *al-Ṣawāʿiq*. Nevertheless, Ibn al-Qayyim could have easily been exposed to Greek philosophy as it had its presence in the rationalistic scholastic environment around him. It was also argued by Langermann that the scholarly atmosphere in Mamluk Damascus already absorbed much of the philosophical forms of discourse and argumentation.[147] More so, Muslim intellectuals are known to have used Ancient Greek wisdom literature as a scholastic tool very early on.[148]

146 Ibn Qayyim al-Jawziyya, *al-Ṣawāʿiq al-mursala*, 2:791. Ibn al-Qayyim's main lines of argument against al-Rāzī were presented in section 3.1 Ibn al-Qayyim's Rationalized-Traditionalistic Arguments on Epistemology in *al-Ṣawāʿiq* I.

147 Langermann, "The Naturalization of Science in Ibn Qayyim al-Ǧawziyyah's *Kitāb al-rūḥ*," 212–213. This argument is corroborated to some extent by Dimitri Gutas' observations in *Greek Thought, Arabic Culture* (London: Routledge, 1998), 169–171.

148 Notable is Gutas' study on the prominence of the social functions of Ancient Greek wisdom literature (*ḥikma*) in classical Arabic literature: Muslim intellectuals widely deployed

With relation to scientific and medical knowledge, for instance, Ibn al-Qayyim has been described as a carrier of Hellenistic thought in his works *Kitāb al-rūḥ* (Book of the Spirit) and *Zād al-maʿād fī hadī khayr al-ʿibād Muḥammad* (Provisions for the Hereafter, on the guidance of the best of servants, Muḥammad).[149] Although it is difficult to offer a conclusive claim on the matter here, it does seem that Ibn al-Qayyim was lured by different aspects of thought originated in the Hellenistic philosophy, at least concerning theological matters as reflected in his discussion on epistemology in *al-Ṣawāʿiq*.

Returning to the main argument of this chapter on Ibn al-Qayyim's first *ṭāghūt* refutation in *al-Ṣawāʿiq*, the erudite criticism dialectically articulated by Ibn al-Qayyim here goes beyond the typical traditionalistic model and could perfectly fit into the *munāẓarāt* and *Kalām* discourse. At a time in which the Taymiyyan circle and the Ashʿarite elite were at sword's point, Ibn al-Qayyim armored his stances as an equal to the rationalists, attacking them while employing their own *Kalām*ic methodology. This interesting rationalized tone further continues in the next parts of *al-Ṣawāʿiq*, as presented in the following chapters.

---

maxims in their discourse and arguments as a means of presenting an authoritative form of knowledge; Gutas, "Classical Arabic Wisdom Literature: Nature and Scope", *Journal of the American Oriental Society* 101/1, Oriental Wisdom (Jan.–Mar., 1981), 67–69.

149 The last section of *Zād al-maʿād* belongs to the genre of Prophetic medicine and, as demonstrated by Irmeli Perho, Ibn al-Qayyim attempted to combine the knowledge derived from the Islamic tradition with the teachings of physicians such as Hippocrates and Galen; Perho, "Ibn Qayyim al-Ǧawziyyah's contribution to the Prophet Medicine", in: (eds.) Bori and Holtzman, *A Scholar in the Shadow*, 193–196, 198–199, 202.

CHAPTER 4

Second *ṭāghūt* Refutation: Revelation is the Provenance of Knowledge

The epistemological issue regarding the level of certainty one can hope to gain from the texts of Islamic Revelation is the opening part of Ibn al-Qayyim's examination on the theory of knowledge in *al-Ṣawāʿiq*. In the following part of the work, Ibn al-Qayyim repudiates the second rationalistic *ṭāghūt*, as he seems to more profoundly delve into the realm of epistemically sensitive concerns. The next focus of interrogation is the question of the origin of knowledge, or what source of knowledge is to be named as primary and, therefore, of greater authoritative power in a case of contradiction: Reason or Revelation? The tangled co-relations between these two key elements have been the decisive topic for an immense number of debates in Islamic thought throughout history, as well as important studies in the Western academic world.[1] There is hardly any *Kalām* manual or treatise that does not dedicate an opening chapter of this kind to the sources of knowledge. Following this pattern, Ibn al-Qayyim's choice of voicing his opinion on the matter of *ʿaql* vs. *naql* is a part of his attempt to strike down his contemporary rationalists together with their employed methodological principles. Although Ibn al-Qayyim's discussion reflects the traditionalistic worldview, he attacks the topic from different angles, thus providing a surprising contribution to the subject matter. Section 4.1 here provides, therefore, a contextualized reading of the preliminary data from Ibn al-Qayyim's second *ṭāghūt* refutation in *al-Ṣawāʿiq*. In the following

1 It is almost impossible to refrain from addressing the issue of tense between *ʿaql* and *naql*, whether in the field of Islamic theology or on many other (sometimes overlapping) fields, such as Islamic jurisprudence, Quranic studies and exegesis, Islamic mysticism, Islamic philosophy, etc. Among the many studies, exemplary ones of direct relevance as of now would be: Binyamin Abrahamov, *Islamic Theology: Traditionalism and Rationalism* (Edinburgh: Edinburgh University Press, 1998); Idem, "Ibn Taymiyya on the Agreement of Reason with Tradition," *The Muslim World* 82, 3–4 (1992): 256–273; Richard M. Frank, "Knowledge and *Taqlīd*: The Foundations of Religious Belief in Classical Ashʿarism," *Journal of the American Oriental Society*, 109/1 (Jan.–Mar., 1989), 37–62; Idem, "The Science of *Kalām*," *Arabic Sciences and Philosophy*, 2 (1992): 7–37; William M. Watt, *The Formative Period of Islamic Thought* (Edinburgh: Edinburgh University Press, 1973); Arthur J. Arberry, *Revelation and Reason in Islam* (London: Allen and Urwin Ltd., 1965).

 | DOI: 10.1163/9789004372511_006

discussion, I strive to pinpoint the locus of Ibn al-Qayyim's specific, culminative deliberations here within the scholastic web of thought preceding him, hence examining his appropriation of additional epistemic ideas which were wide-spread and common in his intellectual surrounding of Mamluk times. A proceeding guidance to Ibn al-Qayyim's writing against the later Ashʿarite dogma, the initial critique expressed by Ibn Taymiyya about the issue is portrayed in section 4.2. Section 4.3 thereafter is dedicated to a more thorough examination of Ibn al-Qayyim's extension of positive epistemological conceptualizations.

4.1 Ibn al-Qayyim's Rationalized-Traditionalistic Arguments on Epistemology in *al-Ṣawāʿiq* II

The traditionalistic gist, according to which the textual sources are the words of God as they were revealed to His Messenger, saw no remote possibility of contradiction between Revelation and Reason. Since human Reason is itself created by God in accordance with the notion of *fiṭra* (i.e., the believer's natural disposition towards faith) and, thus, is subjected to His will, it cannot compete with the texts of Revelation; rather, the use of Reason is supposed to compliment them and lead to mutual coherence. If a contradiction does occur, it is only due to the inability of the created and mundane human mind to correctly understand the texts of Revelation. In sharp contrast, by expressing skeptical approaches, the rationalistic counter position mainly maintains the contradictions between Reason and Islamic textual sources. These contradictions, however, could and should be solved in a way that respects the human intellectual capacity. A chief rationalistic solution suggested by the early Muʿtazilite school of the 3rd/9th century was figurative interpretation (*taʾwīl*), for example, regarding the theological issue of divine attributes which may imply anthropomorphic characteristics of God. The emergence of the Ashʿarite school about a century later signified the beginning of the diffusion of rationalistic notions and methodologies into traditionalism; thus, while securing the dominance of Revelation, the Ashʿarites took a more tolerant approach towards rationalistic understanding of the textual sources. Later Ashʿarites like al-Ghazālī or Fakhr al-Dīn al-Rāzī—whose ten conditions for certain knowledge were examined in the previous section—articulated more radical stances in favor of human Reason and asserted its utter predominance to Revelation.[2]

---

2 Abrahamov, "Ibn Taymiyya on the Agreement of Reason with Tradition," 256–257, 271–272; Watt, *The Formative Period of Islamic Thought*, 48–50, 65–68, 92–95.

In the light of this short history of intellectual development, as well as some two centuries later, the principal approach Ibn al-Qayyim articulatedy, like Ibn Taymiyya before him, follows the lines of traditionalism. Ibn al-Qayyim opens his second *ṭāghūt* refutation in *al-Ṣawāʿiq* with a rejection of "their [i.e., the rationalists'] saying", to which he refers as "the brother of that [previous] principle" (*akhū dhālik*[a] *'l-qānūn*, referring to the previous *ṭāghūt*):

> Contradiction (*taʿāruḍ*) between Reason and Revelation obliges giving priority to Reason, because it is impossible to combine the two together, to dismiss them both, or to give priority to Revelation. This is because Reason is the foundation of Revelation. If priority were given to Revelation, Reason would be dismissed, and as it is the foundation of Revelation, Revelation would be dismissed too. Thus, giving priority to Revelation would oblige the dismissal of both Reason and Revelation. Therefore, the fourth option is the required one: giving priority to Reason.[3]

As a matter of fact, this passage is a more detailed version of the tenth and final condition of the first *ṭāghūt* regarding *muʿāriḍ ʿaqlī* (i.e., contradictory rational indicator) which, as noted before, was formulated by al-Rāzī. Putting flesh on the rather dry bone of the nine linguistically-centered conditions, Reason is illustrated here as the ultimate and most apt means not only for attaining certain knowledge, but also for resolving any misunderstandings that might occur while reading the Islamic scriptures; Reason's position of power is hence considerably amplified. Ibn al-Qayyim's discussion of the second *ṭāghūt* is therefore dedicated specifically to the derivation of the first *ṭāghūt*.

Duly crediting his mentor, Ibn al-Qayyim mentions that Ibn Taymiyya "has already relieved us [from doubt] on the subject matter" (*wa-qad ashfā shaykh*[u] *'l-islām fī hādha 'l-bāb*[i]), as he demolished this *ṭāghūt* in his "great book", meaning his teacher's monumental *Darʾ taʿāruḍ al-ʿaql wal-naql* (Rejecting the Contradiction between Reason and Revelation).[4] As he notifies the reader that he will discuss the arguments raised in his teacher's work, Ibn al-Qayyim humbly adds that his discussion is "a mere drop in his ocean". Along the same lines as the refutation of first *ṭāghūt*, the epistemological discussion begins after his

3 Ibn Qayyim al-Jawziyya, *al-Ṣawāʿiq al-mursala*, 3:796–797. This passage is parallel to Ibn Taymiyya's presentation of al-Rāzī's principle that appears in: Ibn Taymiyya, *Darʾ taʿāruḍ al-ʿaql wal-naql*, ed. Muḥammad Rashād Sālim, in 10 vols. (Riyadh: Jāmiʿat al-Imām Muḥammad ibn Saʿūd al-Islāmiyya, 1411/1991), 1:4–5, 78–79.

4 A detailed survey of this important work, its themes and structure appears in: Anjum, *Politics, Law, and Community in Islamic Thought*, 196–227.

declared opposition to the rationalistic principle, followed by Ibn Taymiyya's rejection of it. This time—as is evident from Ibn Taymiyya's opening of his *Darʾ al-taʿāruḍ*—the principle discussed is the "Universal Rule" (*al-qānūn al-kullī*) established by al-Rāzī, who presented it in several of his works (including the previously mentioned *Muḥaṣṣal afkār al-mutaqaddimīn wal-mutaʾakhkhirīn*[5] and *Asās al-taqdīs*).[6] Furthermore, Ibn Taymiyya shrewdly recognized al-Rāzī's account of the "universal rule" can be traced back to al-Ghazālī's "universal rule of interpretation" (*al-qānūn al-kullī fī ʾl-taʾwīl*). This means that the celebrated "universal rule" is the Rāziyyan version of the original one formulated by al-Ghazālī.[7] Thus, following the clues for contextualization provided by Ibn Taymiyya himself, a profounder examination of the intellectual interconnections prior to Ibn al-Qayyim will shed more light on Ibn al-Qayyim's refutation of the second *ṭāghūt* in *al-Ṣawāʿiq*.

4.2 Ibn Taymiyya's Initial Critique against al-Ghazālī (From the View of Ibn al-Qayyim)

Al-Ghazālī's ground-rule appears in a short epistle that he composed around 490/1097 known under the title *al-Qānūn al-kullī fī ʾl-taʾwīl* (The Universal Rule of Allegorically Interpreting Revelation). In this epistle, al-Ghazālī replied to an inquiry concerning a particular Hadith account, promising to equip the inquirer with a "universal rule" which would be at one's service at all times to reconcile between the apparent text (*ẓāhir*) and Reason (*ʿaql*). While doing so, al-Ghazālī pointed out his highly rationalistic preference of allegorical interpretation in case of conflict between Reason and Revelation. Al-Ghazālī, as stated before, considered Reason equal to Revelation and, more so, he saw it the vehicle leading one to the truth of Revelation. Reason—according to al-Ghazālī—is never wrong; it leads to the certainty of Revelation, which contains knowledge on the subjects that are beyond Reason (the divine attributes is one

---

5 Al-Rāzī, *Muḥaṣṣal afkār al-mutaqaddimīn wal-mutaʾakhkhirīn*, 51: "… *wa-ʿadam … al-muʿāriḍ al-ʿaqlī*." For details on the work, see page 140.

6 Here, al-Rāzī provides a more detailed version of the rule; al-Rāzī, *Asās al-taqdīs*, 220–221. For details on the work, see footnotes 55 and 57 in chapter 1 and section in 3.2 starting on page 138.

7 Abrahamov, "Ibn Taymiyya on the Agreement of Reason with Tradition," 257; Frank Griffel, "Al-Ghazālī at His Most Rationalist: The Universal Rule for Allegorically Interpreting Revelation (*al-Qānūn al-Kullī fī t-Taʾwīl*)," in: (ed.) Georges Tamer, *Islam and Rationality* (Leiden: Brill, 2015), 90–91; Anjum, *Politics, Law, and Community in Islamic Thought*, 147–149.

such subject).[8] Hence, the "universal rule" postulated by al-Ghazālī sustains that there is no contradiction between Reason and Revelation; rather, both are considered the foundations (*uṣūl*) of knowledge. In practical terms, especially for the later Ashʿarites, this is a call to implement the figurative interpretation (*taʾwīl*) in areas in which Revelation surpasses Reason. Given the explanation of al-Ghazālī's origin of "the universal rule", Ibn Taymiyya's claim that al-Ghazālī and al-Rāzī saw Reason as the foundation of Revelation is evidently only partial. However, according to al-Ghazālī, "one who calls Reason wrong also calls Revelation wrong, because it is through Reason that the truth of Revelation is known." This is apparently the position rejected by Ibn Taymiyya in his *Darʾ al-taʿāruḍ*: the idea that human Reason is the foundation, as in the 'verifying factor', of Revelation.[9] Highly notable is the similarity of the two supposedly opposing claims of al-Ghazālī and Ibn Taymiyya, in other words, that there is no contradiction between Reason and Revelation. Nonetheless, for Ibn Taymiyya, human Reason is inferior to divine Revelation and the two can never be considered equal, let alone Revelation dependent on Reason. Therefore, in Ibn Taymiyya's opinion, the later Ashʿarite conclusion promoting figurative interpretation (*taʾwīl*) was unacceptable.

In the second *ṭāghūt* refutation in *al-Ṣawāʿiq*, Ibn al-Qayyim threads his way through Ibn Taymiyya's notions in *Darʾ al-taʿāruḍ* and generates a compound discussion on al-Ghāzālī and his ideology. Ibn al-Qayyim only briefly mentions al-Ghazālī; however, his delicate treatment of al-Ghazālī's rationalistic design points to his familiarity with al-Ghazālī's thought and his accurate assessment of the latter's stature among the later Ashʿarites as the thinker who reformulated the school's major theological methodologies. This can be exemplified with a short yet meaningful passage by Ibn al-Qayyim:

> Those who disclaim the scriptural informative indicators (*adilla samʿiyya*) remain with two possible ways [of attaining knowledge]: either the way of contemplation (*ṭarīq al-naẓār*[10]), which is that of rational syllogistic indi-

8 The same approach appears in al-Ghazālī's engagement with another theological issue, concentrating on the verification of prophecy, for example, in his work of refutation (*radd*) *Tahāfut al-falāsifa* (The Incoherence of the Philosophers); Griffel, "Al-Ghazālī's Concept of Prophecy: The Introduction of Avicennan Psychology into Ašʿarite Theology," *Arabic Sciences and Philosophy*, vol. 14 (2004): 117–118; Griffel, *Al-Ghazālī's Philosophical Theology* (New York: Oxford University Press, 2009), 111–112.

9 Griffel, "Al-Ghazālī at His Most Rationalist," 97, 108, 115–120.

10 This is the spelling as it appears in the critically edited text of al-Dakhīl Allah; however, it is my understanding that the correct spelling was supposed to be *al-naẓar* (this is also

cators (*al-adilla 'l-qiyāsiyya 'l-ʿaqiyya*), or the way of illuminative investigation (*ṭarīq al-kashf*),[11] of what is perceived by a disciplinary exercise (*riyāḍa*), and of clarifying the esoteric (*ṣafāʾ al-bāṭin*). Each of these two ways is false. They involve contradiction, collision, and corruption that only God can comprehend. Therefore, most of those who went in the first way are highly embarrassed and doubtful, and most of those who took the other way are 'shaking in ecstasy'.[12] Hence, most members of the first [group] do not confirm what is true, whereas the members of the other group confirm what is untrue; the state of the priors resembles that of those who "incur anger" and the state of the latter is that of those who "have gone astray"; the former end up denying and negating [the divine attributes], and the latter end up professing heresy (*ilḥād*), God's unity (*waḥda*) and monism (*ittiḥād*).[13] Thus, when the most skillful among them walked in the way of contemplation until its end, and realized that it teems with demons and harmful things, they understood that his road does not lead to the desired healthy aim. Therefore, they returned to the way of Revelation and the Prophetic traditions, as announced by al-Rāzī, Ibn Abi 'l-Ḥadīd (d. 655/1257 or 656/1258),[14] Abū Ḥāmid [al-Ghazālī],

---

the way in which the term is used in another place in this section). In the specific context of this passage, I would say that the term transcripted above is lapsus linguae, and should have appeared with a short vowel.

11 Lit.: "to unveil"; the technical *kashf* term frequently refers to Sūfī mysticism in the sense of "making the realities of the world—which are behind a veil—apparent and complete," aspiring epiphany. The opposing correlative in this regard is *satr* (veiling or occultation). Another usage of the term *kashf* is connected to Shiʿite—mostly Ismāʿīlite—theology, as in: "the apprehension of the 'hidden meaning' (*bāṭin*) of reality," as opposed to *ẓāhir* (i.e., the apparent meaning); L. Gardet, "Kas͟hf," *EI*², 4:696–698.

12 Ibn al-Qayyim conveys a pun: *shaṭḥ* = lit. Movement, shaking or agitation, but also imagination; in addition, *shaṭḥ* denotes the Ṣūfī practice of using an ecstatic expression for mystical sayings; C. Ernst, "S͟haṭḥ," *EI*², 9:361.

13 Ibn al-Qayyim evidently enters a fight against Ṣūfī thought as postulated by the great Andalusian thinker Muḥyī al-Dīn Abū ʿAbdallāh Muḥammad Ibn al-ʿArabī (d. 638/1240), accentuating the core ideas of the Unity of God (*tawḥīd*) and The Oneness of Being (*waḥdat al-wujūd*). In this context, notable is Ibn al-ʿArabī's vast encyclopedic work *al-Futūḥāt al-Makkiyya* (Meccan Illuminations) which covers a wide variety of theological and legal themes in detail; William Chittick, *The Sufi Path of Knowledge: Ibn al-ʿArabi's Metaphysics of Imagination* (Albany, N.Y.: State University of New York Press, 1989), x–xvi, 3–12, 33–59.

14 Ibn Abu 'l-Ḥadīd was a prolific scholar whose wide range of intellectual interests included Arab language, poetry, rhetoric and *Kalām*. He is often considered to have had Muʿtazilite

Abu 'l-Maʿālī (d. 478/1085)[15] and others. At the end of the day they recognized that all of the ways are directed to the Revelation and the narrated Tradition.[16]

Reproving several theological groups in a single passage, Ibn al-Qayyim depicts here two main methodological approaches of attaining true knowledge about the divine, both of which he observes to be improper: the first is the speculative theology of *Kalām* deployed first by the Muʿtazilites and then by the Ashʿarites; whereas the second is the investigation of hidden esoteric knowledge, respectively deployed by Ṣūfī and Shiʿite-Ismāʿilite scholars. Despite the differences between the two, these approaches are perceived as correspondingly mistaken and leading to heresy. Notable is Ibn al-Qayyim's style of rhetoric, as he paraphrases Quranic verses 1:6–7 "[6]Guide us to the straight path: [7]the path of those You have blessed, those who incur no anger and who have not gone astray." Widely understood as referring to Jews and Christians, these verses receive an uncommon, particular interpretation by Ibn al-Qayyim who utilizes the Quranic text in order to criticize Muslim scholars he disagrees with.[17] This kind of use of scriptural evidence considerably departs from known traditionalistic methodologies. Moreover, it stands as a sign of Ibn al-Qayyim's confidence to express his traditionalistic opposition in an advanced manner, harnessing the scriptures not only for accumulating a critical mass of textual evidence, but also for his singular articulation of opinions.

Evident in the passage above is also the topic of religious repentance, which is illustrated by mentioning the four Ashʿarite scholars: al-Rāzī, Ibn Abu 'l-Ḥadīd, al-Ghazālī and Abu 'l-Maʿālī. Each of these leading figures has reportedly

---

tendencies. At the same time, he was also Shiʿite, and composed the important work *Sharḥ nahj al-balāgha*; L. Veccia Vaglieri, "Ibn Abi 'l-Ḥadīd", *EI*², 3:684–685.

15 It seems that this refers to al-Juwaynī, Abu 'l-Maʿālī Abd al-Mālik, the son of Imām al-Ḥaramayn. He was studying *uṣūl al-fiqh* and the science of *Kalām*, representing the middle stage between the early Ashʿarites and the later ones. He was also one of the teachers of al-Ghazālī.; C. Brockelmann, L. Gardet, "al-Djuwaynī," *EI*², 2:605–606. Al-Juwaynī's alteration of opinions on the theological issue of determinism is discussed in: Holtzman, *Predestination (al-Qaḍā' wa-l-Qadar) and Free Will (al-Ikhtiyār)*, 267–265.

16 Ibn Qayyim al-Jawziyya, *al-Ṣawāʿiq al-mursala*, 4:1165–1166 (*al-wajh al-thāmin ʿashr[a] baʿd al-miʾa*).

17 For additional particular (as opposed to universal) readings of the opening *sūra* of the Quran and with relation to mysticism, for example, see (in Hebrew): Avraham Elqayam, "al-Fatihah: The Mystery of Opening in Jewish and Islamic Mysticism," in: Haviva Pedaya (ed.), *The East Write Itself* (Tel Aviv: Gama, 2015) 157–249. Elqayam refers to verses 1:6–7 in pages 169–174.

gone through a respective phase of repentance—or re-evaluation of the path of their faith—that resulted in a shift in theological opinions, among other life changes. Ibn al-Qayyim clearly reflects the traditionalistic fondness towards such stories of "returning to the way of Revelation," as they infer the advantage of the traditionalistic theological stances. The passage cited essentially presents Ibn al-Qayyim's attempt to demonstrate the victory of traditionalism over rationalism, as he lists an almost consecutive array of Ashʿarites (at least in the case of Abu 'l-Maʿālī and his direct pupil al-Ghazālī), who expressed serious doubts about their religious way. This is a major point for Ibn al-Qayyim, who time and again advocated in favor of the coherence of the traditionalistic worldview. Looking at Ibn al-Qayyim's deliberation on epistemology from this perspective, it appears that dominantly noting al-Ghazālī serves a twofold function. At the fundamental level, as already stated, al-Ghazālī is the instigator of the 'universal rule of allegorical interpretation of Revelation', from which Fakhr al-Dīn al-Rāzī developed his 'universal rule'; that thus connects the first *ṭāghūt* refutation to the second one both thematically and structurally. At a deeper—perhaps implicit—level, al-Ghazālī is mentioned to exemplify the motif of repentance and self-reflection, which is even further accentuated since it is carried out by one of the most prominent Ashʿarite thinkers. These two aspects ultimately complement one another, supporting the Taymiyyan-traditionalistic claim for intellectual supremacy.

An elaborate reference to al-Ghāzālī and his most significant work *Iḥyāʾ ʿulūm al-dīn* (Revival of the Religious Sciences) appears in Ibn al-Qayyim's discussion as well. The *Iḥyāʾ* was al-Ghāzālī's manifestation of his deep feeling of frustration with the religious scholars of his time, which he converted into a teaching book on ethics and all religious practices and intellectual activities needed for the believer in order to reach salvation in the afterlife.[18] Ibn al-Qayyim provides an intriguing image of his understanding of the depicted confrontation between Ibn Taymiyya's *Darʾ al-taʿāruḍ* and the Ghazāliyyan positions in a section describing the way in which "the Imams of Islam and kings of Sunna" (i.e., the early authoritative scholars, i.e., the *salaf*) expressed their repugnance of the dangerous and harmful ways of the *mutakallimūn*. He begins with generally accusing the rationalists to be unbelievers, quoting the saying of the *salaf* that: "whoever seeks the religion by using *Kalām* reneges on faith" (*man ṭalab[a] 'l-dīn[a] bil-kalām tazandaq[a]*), or on behalf of al-Shāfiʿī, who

18 The massive work is divided into four 'quarters': *ʿibādāt* (religious practices), *ʿādāt* (social customs), *muhlikāt* (vices, or faults of character leading to perdition), *munjiyāt* (virtues, or qualities leading to salvation). Each quarter is thematically arrayed in ten 'books'; Watt, "al-Ghazālī," *EI*^{2}, 2:1040–1041.

said that "anything one does which was prohibited by God, apart from adjoining other god/s to Him (*shirk*), is better engaging in *Kalām*. The people of *Kalām* had introduced what I would have never expected from a Muslim."[19] Then Ibn al-Qayyim cites a portion of Ibn Taymiyya's (*shaykhunā*) reproach against the *Kalām* in *Darʾ al-taʿāruḍ*, maintaining that the early righteous ancestors of the Muslim community and its leaders (*salaf*[u] *ʾl-umma wa-aʾimmatuhā*) agreed that the scholars of the *Kalām* are condemned for their ignorance, lies and injustice, which they forced on the texts of the Quran and Hadith and the uncontaminated clarity of Reason (*ṣarīḥ al-maʿqūl*). Ibn Taymiyya's view continues, as he particularly mentions al-Ghāzālī's work *al-Iḥyāʾ*, from which he cites al-Ghāzālī's unfavorable perception of the *Kalām*:

> He said there [al-Ghazālī in *al-Iḥyāʾ*]: if you say that the science of *Kalām* and the study of argumentation (*jadal*) is as blameworthy (*madhmūm*) as astrology[20] or that it is permissible (*mubāḥ*) or recommended (*mandūb*), you should know that people exceed and exaggerate [in their opinions on] that matter from both sides. So, there are those who say it [i.e., *Kalām*] is innovation (*bidʿa*) and unlawful (*ḥarām*) and that anything else—apart from adjoining gods to God—would be better, and there are those who say [*Kalām*] is obligatory (*wājib*), either as a personal or a communal commitment [i.e., either *farḍ ʿayn* or *farḍ kifāya*], and that [*Kalām*] is indeed a [human] act [according to the laws of *sharīʿa*] and the most pious deed, and that [*Kalām*] verifies the knowledge of [God's] unity, and is a defense of God's religion.
>
> Among those who prohibited *Kalām* were al-Shāfiʿī, [Anas ibn] al-Mālik, Aḥmad ibn Ḥanbal, Sufyān [al-Thawrī] (d. 161/778),[21] and all of the early traditionalists (*ahl al-ḥadīth min*[a] *ʾl-salaf*) [...] they prove their claim arguing that if [*Kalām*] was [integral to] religion, it would have been commanded to the Prophet—may God bless him—it would have been learnt and his followers would repeat it. [The Prophet] informed them of the

19 Ibn Qayyim al-Jawziyya, *al-Ṣawāʿiq al-mursala*, 4:1263–1264. These quotations already appear in al-Ghazālī's *al-Iḥyāʾ*, see footnote 24 in this chapter.

20 Ibn al-Qayyim's reference to the field of astrology in this passage is interesting, as he discussed it at length in his work *Miftaḥ dār al-saʿāda*, denouncing it together with alchemy; John W. Livingston, "Ibn Qayyim al-Jawziyyah: A Fourteenth Century Defense against Astrological Divination and Alchemical Transmutation," *Journal of the American Oriental Society*, 91/1 (Jan.–Mar., 1971), 96–103.

21 Sufyān ibn Saʿīd ibn Masrūq Abū ʿAbd Allāh was a prominent traditionist and a representative of early Islam; H.P. Raddatz, "Sufyān al-Thawrī," *EI*², 9:771.

rules of cleaning oneself after defecating (*istinjā'*), urged them to follow the commands, [but] forbade them the *Kalām*. His teachings were kept by the Prophet's companions (*ṣaḥāba*) to the letter. To add to what a teacher set forth is disloyal and unjust; they are the leading teachers and we are the following pupils [...]

As for its benefit, it is assumed that the value [of *Kalām*] is to reveal realities and discover their [foundations]; however, the *Kalām* does not fulfill this honorable task. In case you hear this from a traditionalist (*muḥaddith*) or a *ḥashwī*,[22] bear in mind that people are hostile towards things they are ignorant about. So, hear this from he who had learnt *Kalām* and then left it after true learning and after immersing in it until reaching the level of the *mutakallimīn*—the one who abandoned *Kalām* in order to immerse himself in other sciences apart from *Kalām*, only to realize that the road leading to the truths of knowledge in this direction is blocked.

Upon my life, *Kalām* will reveal, unfold or clarify a few things, but only rarely and mostly on matters[23] that you can nearly better understand before employing *Kalām*. The only benefit [of *Kalām*] is guarding the creed and preserving it [for the laymen] from the confusions of the innovators and from different kinds of disputes. As for the layman (*'āmmī*),

22 *Ḥashwiyya* was used as a derogatory name by the scholars of *Kalām* or the Islamic philosophers, referring to other scholars who negated *Kalām*, especially the traditionalists; A.S. Halkin, "The Ḥashwiyya," *Journal of the American Oriental Society* 1 (Mar., 1934), 12–15, 20–28; Anjum, *Politics, Law, and Community in Islamic Thought*, 157–158. Anjum discussed the same passage there (with his translation) in his effort to stress the sociopolitical aspects of al-Ghazālī's objection to *Kalām*.

23 In the text *al-Ṣawā'iq* it is said *fī umūr^{in} jalīla^{tin}*; however, the correct wording in *al-Iḥyā'* is rather *fī umūr^{in} jaliya^{tin}*, meaning "on apparent/clear matters." The English translation of the text by N.A. Faris mentions "simple and clear matters which are readily understood." In my opinion, the option of *jaliya* sounds more fitting in the current sentence; al-Ghazālī, *The Foundations of the Articles of Faith*, 28. Notable in this respect is the specific differentiation between *'ulūm jalīla* (major and important knowledge) and *'ulūm daqīqa* (subtle or trivial knowledge) in the Ghazāliyyan theological terminology, as well as the separate differentiation between *'ulūm jaliya* (clear and significant knowledge) and *'ulūm khafiya* (hidden and obscure knowledge). Al-Ghazālī discusses these kinds of religious knowledge (i.e., 'matters'), for instance, in the first book of *al-Iḥyā* titled *Kitāb al-'ilm*; al-Ghazālī, *Iḥyā' 'ulūm 'l-dīn lil-Imām Abī Ḥāmid al-Ghazālī* (Cairo: Dār al-Sha'b [n.d.]), no editor mentioned, 16 volumes, 1:52; al-Ghazālī, *The Book of Knowledge: Being a translation of the Kitāb al-'Ilm of al-Ghazālī's "Iḥyā' 'Ulūm al-Dīn,"* translated by Nabih Amin Faris (Lahore: Sh. Muhammad Ashraf, 1962), 70.

> he is only shaken by [the innovator's argument] although it may be false; and to confront a false statement with another refutes it ... [*Kalām*] brings damage as it honors doubts, changes credos, and deprives them from apodictic judgment and resolution.[24]

Originally, all of the sections above appear in the first 'quarter' of *al-Iḥyā'* on religious practices (*'ibādāt*) in the second book called *Qawā'id al-'aqā'id* (Foundations of Beliefs), in which al-Ghāzālī surveys the history of the main schools of Islamic dogmatic theology.[25] Al-Ghazālī replies here to a hypothetical question posed in order to explain his opinion on the *Kalām*. Embedded in his own intellectual experience, al-Ghāzālī articulates his personal conclusion as a rationalist who intentionally renounced worldly life at the peak of his academic career in *al-Niẓāmiyya*, the leading *madrasa* in Baghdad of that time. Consequently, he also departed from Ash'arism in a candid attempt to find solace in an intellectually secluded life of celibacy and asceticism.[26] Given this context, it remains unclear whether Ibn Taymiyya and Ibn al-Qayyim were aware of the personal setting behind al-Ghazālī's composition of his work *al-Iḥyā'*; notwithstanding, it would not do much justice to either Ibn Taymiyya or Ibn al-Qayyim if it were presumed they were merely ignorant of this, since al-Ghazālī declared that he had left *Kalām* in the cited passage itself.[27] Very plausible is that Ibn al-Qayyim

---

24 Ibn Qayyim al-Jawziyya, *al-Ṣawā'iq al-mursala*, 4:1268–1272. The complete sections quoted by Ibn al-Qayyim are found in: al-Ghazālī, *Iḥyā' 'ulūm 'l-dīn*, 1:163–168. For the translation of the passage cited above, I have occasionally made use of the book: *The Foundations of the Articles of Faith: Being a translation of the Kitāb Qawā'id al-'Aqā'id of al-Ghazālī's "Iḥyā' 'Ulūm al-Dīn,"* translated by Nabih Amin Faris (Lahore: Sh. Muhammad Ashraf, 1963, reprinted 1999), 16–30.

25 The cited passages are a part the second section (*faṣl*) thereof, "on the gradual advance towards spiritual guidance and the arrangement of stages of belief" (*fī wajh[i] 'l-tadrīj[i] ila 'l-irshād[i] wa-tartīb[i] darajāt[i] 'l-i'tiqād*). Once again, the elitist attitude of later Ash'rite thought is well demonstrated in al-Ghazālī's writing, speaking of "stages of belief" and thus separating the academic religious elite from the common people.

26 These experiences are elaborately described in al-Ghazālī's modern biography which appears in: Griffel, *Al-Ghazālī's Philosophical Theology*, 31–49. Another valuable source is the introduction to the book (in Hebrew): al-Ghazālī, *Ha-podeh min ha-te'iyyah ve-ha-ta'ut* הפודה מן התעייה והטעות*: Modern Hebrew translation of al-Ghazālī's 'Deliverer from Error'* (*al-Munqidh min al-dalal*), ed. Hava Lazarus-Yafeh (Tel Aviv: Dvir, 1965), 9–17.

27 In addition, both Ibn Taymiyya and Ibn al-Qayyim were quite familiar with the celebrated biographical dictionary *Tā'rīkh Dimashq* (History of Damascus) written by the historian 'Alī Ibn 'Asākir (d. 571/1176), which contains a detailed biography of al-Ghazālī; Ibn 'Asākir, Abu 'l-Qāsim 'Alī ibn Abī Muḥammad al-Ḥasan, *Tā'rīkh Dimashq*, ed. 'Amr ibn Gharāma

recognized the particular historical and personal circumstances surrounding al-Ghazālī's statement against *Kalām* in this text. However, it is evident that Ibn al-Qayyim's use of al-Ghazālī's materials is selective and perhaps even slightly narrow, picking on this short passage from the vast corpus of *al-Iḥyā'* seemingly based on the mediation of his mentor. Still, even if limited, his selective choice of citations is highly beneficial and accurately serves his objective of abolishing the late Ashʿarite notion that promoted Reason's predominance to Revelation.

Ibn al-Qayyim extends this discussion in *al-Ṣawāʿiq* and explicitly shares his opinion about al-Ghazālī's critical view on *Kalām*. In Ibn al-Qayyim's eyes, a scholar of al-Ghazālī's magnitude with deep knowledge of the *Kalām* who rejected it and claimed it departed from the Islamic tenets is the best evidence for the inferiority of *Kalām* and the rationalistic set of methodologies. Therefore, rationalistic *Kalām* (*Kalām ʿaqlī maqbūl*) cannot be held as a contradictory indicator to the Quran and Sunna. Ibn al-Qayyim insists Al-Ghazālī's denunciation of the *Kalām* and its proponents is central, considering its dangers and damages and also the *salaf*'s cited view against it. Ibn al-Qayyim further elaborates, that as a matter of fact, the Prophet's message itself is to be seen as a rule against *Kalām* and *falsafa*, as he did not inform his community of them. Since the Prophet did not mention *Kalām*, one must conclude that *Kalām* was not true (*ḥaqq*^{an}) in itself, including its entire components, namely its issues (*qaḍāyāh*^{u}) and presumptions (*muqaddamātuh*^{u}) were not truthful (*ṣādiqa*^{tan}) and its informative signs (*maʿlūmātuh*^{u}) were not truthful as well.[28] Ibn al-Qayyim then mentions the approach of the righteous *salaf* towards *Kalām*. The tendency to return to the *salaf* and reconstruct (or reshape) their opinions is cardinal in the discourse produced by Ibn al-Qayyim, as well as in that of Ibn Taymiyya. This can be demonstrated in the following passage:

> As to the *salaf*, they did not reproach *Kalām* only for the sake of it, or only because it comprises conventional and technical expressions (*alfāẓ iṣṭilāḥiyya*) if their meanings are truthful. [The *salaf*] did not forbid the [attainment of] knowledge by an indicator on the Creator, His

---

al-ʿAmrawī, in 80 vols. (Beirut: Dār al-Fikr, 1415/1995), 55:200–204. According to historical reports, one of Ibn al-Qayyim's teachers was al-Bahāʾ ibn ʿAsākir (d. 600/1203) who was the son of the mentioned ʿAlī ibn ʿAsākīr and very possibly taught his father's books; al-Ṣafadī, Ṣalāḥ al-Dīn Khalīl ibn Aybak (d. 764/1362), *Aʿyān al-ʿaṣr wa-aʿwān al-naṣr*, ed, ʿAlī Abū Zayd et al., in 5 vols. (Beirut: Dār al-Fikr al-Muʿāṣir, 1418/1998), 4:366; idem, *al-Wāfī bil-wafayāt*, eds. Aḥmad al-Arnāʾūṭ and Turkī Muṣṭafā, in 29 vols. (Beirut: Dār Iḥyāʾ al-Turāth, 1420/2000), 2:195.

28 Ibn Qayyim al-Jawziyya, *al-Ṣawāʿiq al-mursala*, 4:1273.

> attributes, and His actions—they were the most knowledgeable people in this respect. They also did not forbid truthful contemplation (*naẓar*) on a truthful indicator which instructs beneficial knowledge, nor a debate (*munaẓāra*) on these matters, either for guiding the rightful follower or for ceasing the liar—they were the best of all people in their contemplation skills, their seeking of proofs by indications and their search for evidence (*naẓar^an wa-istidlāl^an wa-iʿtibār^an*). They contemplated upon the most truthful and credible indicators, as they contemplated the best, most just and most noble [thing], that is most indicative of the truth and is most reaching to the intended meaning in the closest ways—the speech of God (*kalām Allāh*, i.e., the Quran). They were contemplating the verses [lit. signs] of God, the faraway ones as well as those of the self (*al-ufqiyya wal-nafsiyya*); so that they *saw* indicators which indicate that the Quran is true. Hence, [the *salaf*] *saw* the informative scriptural indications (*samʿ*) and Reason (*ʿaql*) as corresponding to one another, and so does Revelation (*waḥī*) and human natural disposition (*fiṭra*). As God said in verse (Q 41:53) "We *shall show* them Our signs on the far horizons and in themselves, until it becomes clear to them that it is the Truth", or (Q 34:6) "[Prophet], those who have been given knowledge *can see* that what has been sent to you from your Lord is the truth".[29]

The *salaf* are portrayed in Ibn al-Qayyim's inspection above as if they were shaped precisely to fit the circles of *Kalām* scholars with an upfront implementation of the speculative methodologies. A parallel line is implicitly drawn between the Quranic uses of words relating to sight and the rationalistic term *naẓar* (lit.: view, look) designating the intellectual means of speculative contemplation. In his endeavor to devalue Reason's priority to Revelation, Ibn al-Qayyim ties al-Ghazālī's initial account against *Kalām* together with his rendered vision of the *salaf*, and reaches all the way back to the Quranic text.

Such 'rational' characterization of the *salaf* might appear puzzling at first glance; however, Ibn al-Qayyim's attitude here is perfectly suited to the Taymiyyan worldview and reflects his mentor's uncompromising commitment to Reason or, rather, to "uncontaminated Reason."[30] As carefully analyzed by Ovamir Anjum, one of Ibn Taymiyya's goals was to refute al-Ghazālī's claim that the *salaf* had abandoned sophistication of rationalistic arguments, becoming trapped in crude scriptural adherence. In *Darʾ al-taʿāruḍ* Ibn Taymiyya pro-

---

29 Ibn Qayyim al-Jawziyya, *al-Ṣawāʿiq al-mursala*, 4:1274.

30 See elaboration on Ibn Taymiyya's concept of 'uncontaminated Reason' in page 154 above.

fessed that al-Ghazālī and his fellow "masters of *Kalām*" had failed to understand the *salaf*'s teachings (just like many of the traditionalists who categorically forbade any use of Reason), when this was not at all the case—not only did the *salaf* permit rational debate in order to contest a wrongful claim, they also abundantly involved themselves in it. The philosophized-scholars (*mutafalsifa*, 'self-proclaimed' philosophers) and rationalists distorted the Reason received from God on the one hand, whereas the traditionalists over-simplified the scripture's value to the extent of redundancy, on the other.[31] Following the Taymiyyan pursuit, in *al-Ṣawāʿiq* Ibn al-Qayyim fiercely reclaims the terms commonly used by the rationalists by attaching them to the earliest Islamic teachings possible, and thus neutralizing their rationalistic contents and connotations. This clever reconstruction of the image of the *salaf* as the original upholders of true Reason discloses beyond doubt Ibn al-Qayyim's devotion to the Taymiyyan narrative of the formative Islamic community; just as likely, it also infers Ibn al-Qayyim's high command in re-authoring this narrative based on his close familiarity with the balance of powers exposed in his mentor's *Darʾ al-taʿāruḍ*.

For a scholar highly acquainted with traditionalistic methodologies of knowledge management—if I may borrow this modern terminology—which are chiefly based on the citation of textual sources, Ibn al-Qayyim is revealed here as a polymath at his best. As the traditionalistic intellectual heritage of an hierarchical citation of the *naql*, viz. Quran, Hadith, the four great Imam's, their followers (*tābiʿūn*) and the followers' followers (*attibāʿ^{u} 'l-tābiʿīn*) and so on, Ibn al-Qayyim's discussion here does not entirely skip this stage; however, in a way it begins on the next level with a utilization of large excerpts of text from Ibn Taymiyya's *Darʾ al-taʿāruḍ* more than anything else, but also from numerous other works, such as al-Ghazālī's *Iḥyāʾ ʿulūm^{i} 'l-dīn* (Reviving the Sciences of Religion) as well as his earlier work *Tahāfut al-falāsifa* (The Incoherence of the Philosophers). Curious in this respect is the fact that *Tahāfut al-falāsifa* aimed to refute twenty of the Muslim philosophers' teachings, including parts of their epistemology, for which al-Ghazālī harshly condemned them as unbelievers.[32] Ibn al-Qayyim seems to be indifferent towards—or simply unaware of—this Ghazāliyyan inclination; he tends to generalize the discourse and talk in a single breath of several rationalistic theological schools in Islam, without making the necessary distinction between *falsafa*, Muʿtazilism, or early/later Ashʿarism. In the relatively small section (some eight pages) cited from *al-*

---

31 Anjum, *Politics, Law, and Community in Islamic Thought*, 178–181, 185.

32 Griffel, *Al-Ghazālī's Philosophical Theology*, 5; Griffel, "Al-Ghazālī's Concept of Prophecy," 120.

Tahāfut, Ibn al-Qayyim criticizes both the philosophers and al-Ghazālī together for their "renunciation of the Creator" (*inkār al-ṣāni*ʿ, i.e., God), while using al-Ghazālī's text in question.[33] Albeit, Ibn al-Qayyim's mentioning of al-Ghazālī and his work does not seem coincidental given the contextual background illustrated thus far, as well as the revealed network of relations between Ibn Taymiyya (in *Darʾal-taʿāruḍ*) al-Ghazālī (more than anything else, in his fundamental *al-qānūn al-kullī fī ʾl-taʾwīl*) and Ibn al-Qayyim. Highly motivated by *Darʾal-taʿāruḍ*, he launches the refutation of the second *ṭāghūt* in *al-Ṣawāʿiq* with yet another immediate respond to a later Ashʿarite scholar, which is inspired by Ibn Taymiyya's previous critique.[34]

In order to keep a clear track of the primary sources mentioned in this section, the following table organizes them and schematically sketches the thematic and chronological relations between them:

Time period	Author	Writings and significance	
488/1095	Al-Ghazālī	*Tahāfut al-falāsifa*	Refutation of main Muslim philosophers' teachings; epistemology
Ca. 490/1097		*al-Qānūn al-kullī fī ʾl-taʾwīl*	Universal rule of allegorically interpreting Revelation, promoting *taʾwīl* as the ultimate solution for contradictions between Reason and Revelation. * This is the origin for al-Rāzī's "universal rule", viz.: Reason > Revelation
After (?) 490/1097		*Iḥyāʾ ʿulūm al-dīn*	Ethics; *Qawāʿid al-ʿaqāʾid* (Principles of Beliefs) therefrom describes the historical progress towards virtuous Islamic belief

33 Ibn Qayyim al-Jawziyya, *al-Ṣawāʿiq al-mursala*, 3:963–971.

34 In this respect, according to the editor's tables of comparison between the two works, it is worth noting that Ibn al-Qayyim's two above-mentioned references to al-Ghazālī were not included in *al-Ṣawāʿiq*'s abridged version (*al-Mukhtaṣar*); Ibn Qayyim al-Jawziyya, *al-Ṣawāʿiq al-mursala*, the editor's introduction, 1:122–123. This fact can point out that,

(cont.)

Time period	Author	Writings and significance	
Ca. 715/1315	Ibn Taymiyya	*Darʾ taʿāruḍ al-ʿaql wal-naql*	Refutation of rationalistic Islamic theology and confirmation of the inherent consolidation between Reason and Revelation; answers back to both al-Ghazālī and Fakhr al-Dīn al-Rāzī
Ca. 1350	Ibn al-Qayyim	*al-Ṣawāʿiq al-mursala*	Expanding the Tayymiyan epistemological theory to invalidate contemporary Ashʿarite scholars' reliance on rationalism

Much like the approach taken in the first *tāghūt* refutation, Ibn al-Qayyim turns once again to the systemization of the Taymiyyan theoretical doctrines and substantially advances them. The next section largely portrays Ibn al-Qayyim's positive epistemic conceptualization of Revelation as the prime source of all truth and knowledge, as it is expressed in his second *ṭāghūt* refutation. As already stated, the second *ṭāghūt* in fact originated from the first one and, hence, it represents Ibn al-Qayyim's enhanced and deepened discussion on the alleged epistemological tension between Reason and Revelation. Such a focused prism of close engagement with the kernel of the later Ashʿarite rationalistic stance is thus another step forwards in Ibn al-Qayyim's attempt to uproot the paradigms standing at the very basis of the rationalistic epistemological theory of his times.

4.3 Ibn al-Qayyim on the Epistemological Value of Revelation

When one takes into account the main sources of stimulation for the authoring of *al-Ṣawāʿiq* as a work embedded in the Taymiyyan theories, Ibn al-Qayyim's

---

although Ibn al-Mawṣilī is considered to have summarized the original text in an overall satisfactory manner, the cuts he made left out significant parts of the work. This has perhaps less of an impact on the overall contents; however, for the modern reader, the ability to appropriately contextualize the materials is considerably reduced when relying on the abridgement alone.

clear propensity for an optimistic epistemological view is revealed as more than sensible. Nonetheless, it is somewhat more difficult to detect Ibn al-Qayyim's positive articulation of this epistemological optimism concerning the second *ṭāghūt*, unlike the refutation of the first one which was organized according to deductive reasoning. The tone taken in the course of the second refutation is considerably more polemical and argumentative, most likely as a result of it still being a continual part of the more extensive first *ṭāghūt*, the concluding sections of which repudiate the Rāziyyan version of the 'universal rule'.[35] Only after explaining the intellectual cradle of this 'universal rule'—which is the Ghazāliyyan 'universal rule of allegorical interpretation'—is the motive for the increasingly hostile tone fully understood: Ibn al-Qayyim has reached the very heart of the matter, and now it is an all-out war. Ibn al-Qayyim fires his arguments, utilizing his massive arsenal of textual evidence, which in turn comprises much more than mere citations from the Islamic scriptures. In fact, Ibn al-Qayyim considerably broadens the meaning of the typical traditionalistic use in 'textual evidence', as will shortly be shown. Hence, the following section will concisely present the optimistic epistemological approach conceptualized by Ibn al-Qayyim through the lens of one of his fiercer theological polemics.[36]

Despite the apparent disorganized manner of writing, the numerous and divergent arguments constructing the second *ṭāghūt* refutation can be largely divided into three main topics:

1. Comprehensive rationalized-traditionalistic repudiation of 'the universal rule'
2. Assertion of the mutual relation of necessity between Reason and Revelation
3. Reaffirmation of the verification of the divine attributes (*thubut al-ṣifat*)

35 In the very general overview of their contents found in his introduction, Al-Dakhīl Allah, the editor of *al-Ṣawāʿiq*, expresses a similar opinion about the relation between the first and second *ṭawāghīt*; Ibn Qayyim al-Jawziyya, *al-Ṣawāʿiq al-mursala*, 1:97–98.

36 Worth mentioning is the fact that *al-Ṣawāʿiq*'s second refutation is rather lengthy (Ibn al-Qayyim lists some 241 aspects of examination, *wujūh*). Therefore, it contains several additional issues that are quite tempting for further critical examination. Unfortunately, this goes beyond the limited scope available in this study. One example of such an issue—which has been referred to in recent research—is Ibn al-Qayyim's elaborate reply regarding the eschatological question of the duration of hell-fire; Jon Hoover, "Islamic Universalism: Ibn Qayyim al-Jawziyya's Salafī Deliberations on the Duration of Hell-Fire," *The Islamic World* 99 (2009), 193–201.

Henceforth I will exemplify each of these topics by closely capturing several of the diverse arguments Ibn al-Qayyim puts forward, which I will mainly apply to the first and, even more so, the second. The discussion on the third topic will be further developed in the next chapter of this study, which deals with Ibn al-Qayyim's third *ṭāghūt* refutation.

As expected, Ibn al-Qayyim first addresses the above-mentioned 'universal rule', calling for its complete elimination: Ibn al-Qayyim introduces the rationalistic principle—with priority given to Reason rather than Revelation—and analyzes it while listing three initial premises on which it is dependent:

1. Validation that there is indeed a contradiction between Reason and Revelation
2. Limitation of the possible options to the following four: Reason comes first, Reason and Revelation are combined, they are both dismissed, or Revelation comes first.
3. Invalidation of the other three options, so that only the one with Reason as a priority remains.

Indirectly answering this, Ibn al-Qayyim invalidates the principal rationalistic idea of separating Reason and Revelation. Rather, he presents the correct alternative according to his opinion: should there be a contradiction between two revelational indicators (*dlīlān*^{i} *samʿiyyān*^{i}), two rational indicators (*dalīlān*^{i} *ʿaqliyyān*^{i}), or a revelational one and a rational one (*samʿi*^{yun} *wa-ʿaqli*^{yun}), then three possibilities arise:

1. If both of them are cogent (*qaṭʿiyān*^{i}) there cannot occur a contradiction, for a cogent indicator necessarily signifies its indication. If they are contradictory, it would be required to integrate two opposites (*al-jamʿ bayn*^{a} *'l-naqīḍayn*^{i}); no reasonable person doubts this.
2. If one of them is cogent (*qaṭʿi*^{yyan}) and the other is a presumption (*ẓanni*^{yyan}) the cogent indicator is prior, equally whether it is revelational or rational.
3. If both of them are a presumption (*ẓanniyayn*^{i}), we must turn to the exercise of preference (*tarjīḥ*)[37] whereby the outweighing indicator is the predominant one, may it be revelational or rational.[38]

37 The term is mostly used in the practical realm of Islamic jurisprudence, designating the *muftī*'s process of evaluating (lit. weighing) the available evidence and ruling accordingly in a legal matter; N. Calder and M.B. Hooker, "Sharīʿa," *EI*^{2}, 9:324–325.

38 Ibn Qayyim al-Jawziyya, *al-Ṣawāʿiq al-mursala*, 4:796.

Ibn al-Qayyim uses a well-known *Kalām*ic argumentation mode, designated as *taqsīm* (or *qisma*), as he reshapes the rationalistic claim that he mentioned before. Basically, he implements here a mode of argumentation set on the logical form of exclusive disjunction (i.e., either α or β, but not both). This hypothetical reasoning allows him to establish a contrast between several alternative cases, thereby excluding those that are found improbable.[39] Most evident here is Ibn al-Qayyim's use of logic, which enables him to offer a rationalized-traditionalistic alternative to the late Ashʿarite stance concerning the ultimate predominance of Reason. As he does so, he interlinks the already accepted and commonly used means of evidence evaluation derived from the Islamic legal doctrine. In addition, as portrayed by Ibn al-Qayyim, the peculiarities the rationalists rely on when they speak of the predominance of Reason to Revelation are inaccurate; the certain and apodictic nature of an indicator plays a greater role in its acceptance as predominant than whether it is revelational or rational. Thus, the conclusion Ibn al-Qayyim aims for is clear: the rationalists and their 'universal rule' are wrong; not only do they promote a concept that fails to pay the appropriate respect to the texts of Revelation; neither do they meet their so-called 'rationalistic' standards. Moreover, Ibn al-Qayyim seals his argument stating once again that all reasonable people (*ʿuqalāʾ*, i.e., people of common sense) agree on this disjunction.

As Ibn al-Qayyim proceeds, many other rationalized arguments are set forth in order to repudiate 'the universal rule'. For example, he asserts the absurdity in a situation in which whoever has professed the verification of the Prophet Muḥammad would ever retain a notion contrary to the Revelation; therefore, such a contradictory indicator can never occur. In a similar vein, in the assumption about the existence of such a contradictory indicator itself, Ibn al-Qayyim sees what God warned of in the texts of Revelation (*ʿayn al-maḥdhūr*). Furthermore, Ibn al-Qayyim presses on, ensuring his reader that even if a contradiction between Reason and Revelation were plausible, it would be Revelation that prevails and comes first, not Reason. Revelation is incredibly far-reaching and contains what Reason alone does not comprehend. In addition, Reason can be wrong—and more than once. Ibn al-Qayyim raises an image from everyday life to illustrate the affinity between Reason and Revelation: Reason with Revelation is like a layman who devotedly follows faith with the assistance of a knowledgeable Muftī (*kal-ʿāmmi ʾl-muqallid maʿa ʾl-muftī ʾl-ʿālim*). At any rate, Ibn al-Qayyim declares that an indicator signifying truthfulness is not

39 Van Ess, "The Logical Structure of Islamic Theology," 40. For additional example of Ibn al-Qayyim's utilization of this kind of argument, see footnote 106 in chapter 2.

obliged to have a foundation (*aṣl*).[40] Ibn al-Qayyim's second *ṭāghūt* refutation is abundant with additional claims of a similar fideistic spirit, some of which have already appeared in Ibn Taymiyya's *Darʾ al-taʿāruḍ*. Ibn al-Qayyim's repudiation of 'the universal rule' is hence loyal to his mentor's ideology and his rationalized-traditionalistic discourse.

A more positively articulated discussion can be found in the sections where Ibn al-Qayyim turns to a careful conceptualization of the relation of mutual necessity between Reason and Revelation. Reason is necessary (*malzūm*) for attaining religious knowledge (*sharʿ*) but, at the same time, cannot be separated from it (*lāzim*^{un} *lah*^{u}). The existence of one part is dependent on the other, therefore denying one will require the denial of the other. Ibn al-Qayyim thus offers his alternative to the rationalistic claim: rather than accepting Reason as the foundation of Revelation, whereby the truthfulness of Revelation is acknowledged, as the rationalists argue, Ibn al-Qayyim polishes their position, maintaining that Reason is actually the foundation of the truthfulness of our knowledge regarding Revelation. According to him, Reason is an indicator for us, which points to Revelation's truth (*dalīl*^{un} *lanā ʿalā ṣiḥatih*^{i} [i.e., *al-samʿ*]). This is similar to all other kinds of created beings (*maḥlūqāt*), for they are signs and indicators (*āyāt wa-dalāʾil*) validating the Creator; their reality necessarily displays His reality (*thubūt*), yet their absence does not denote God's absence and His existence does not require their existence. The same goes for indications concerning the prophecy of God's Messenger. There is no means of attaining knowledge on Revelation other than Reason; the two necessarily require one another (*mutālazimān*^{i}). Albeit, Ibn al-Qayyim sustains that the truthful nature of Revelation on a certain matter is more powerful than the truth of a rational indicator on it.[41] Evidently he does not call for the predominance of Revelation to Reason, but rather refines the differentiation of definitions between the two at a very basic level. Reason is a highly necessary vessel, but it is created and, therefore, mundane. It allows the created humankind to perceive the truth of knowledge on Revelation, which is divine and remarkably more far-reaching than them both. Accordingly, the respective epistemological value of Reason and Revelation is to be set apart; Reason assists in the evaluation of knowledge, whereas Revelation contains truthful knowledge.

Ibn al-Qayyim's conceptualization of the absolute epistemological value progresses as he tightly fastens together the notions of Reason and Revelation.

---

40 Ibn Qayyim al-Jawziyya, *al-Ṣawāʿiq al-mursala*, 4:802–803, 807–809.

41 Ibn Qayyim al-Jawziyya, *al-Ṣawāʿiq al-mursala*, 4:1091–1095.

Interestingly, he describes all messengers of God as persons of the highest rational capacity (*aʿqal al-ḥalq*), who possessed the most complete Reason (*akmal*ᵘ *'l-ʿuqūl*). Therefore, they were able to deliver a message which was above all human Reason (*fawq*ᵃ *ʿuqūl*ⁱ *'l-bashar*). This also made them capable of performing good, which was impossible for anyone but them, and capable of pacifying different states of hearts and souls, reviving them with peace and purifying them with knowledge and deeds, both in this world and the afterlife. Praising the messengers sent by God, Ibn al-Qayyim sustains that if incoherence (*tafāwut*) occurred between their reasons and those of the rest of the people on matters relating to wishes, actions, love and hatred, it was not incoherence of knowledge or information (*al-ʿulūm wal-maʿārif*), nor was it incoherence of anything related to knowing God, His names and His attributes. In other words, Ibn al-Qayyim limits any disagreement between the messengers sent by God and the rest of the believers to personal affairs or a difference of opinions, proclaiming that Islamic doctrinal and theological issues were never a cause of incongruity. Ibn al-Qayyim expresses here an infuriated attitude:

> Oh God, what a wonder! How the claim of those who [state in their alleged 'chain of knowledge narration']: "my reason told me, on behalf of Ibn Sīnā (Avicenna, d. 428/1037),[42] al-Fārābī (d. 339/950),[43] Aristotle" and so forth, or "on behalf of Abu 'l-Hudhayl al-ʿAllāf (d. 226/840–235/849–850),[44] al-Shaḥḥām (d. after 257/871),[45] al-Naẓẓām (d. 220/835–230/845)[46]" and alike, or on behalf of whoever had met them—can be preferred to the statement of whoever says: "the arch-angel Jibrīl [Gabriel] told me on behalf of the Lord of the world"? [God's] Messenger stated: "my Lord told me," and that opposer says: "my reason told me or Aristotle" or such![47]

42 Abū ʿAli 'l-Ḥusayn ibn ʿAbdallāh ibn Sīnā is known to have been one of the most famous Muslim philosophers following the ancient Greek ideas. He was also a remarkably celebrated physician; A.M. Goichon, "Ibn Sīnā," *EI*², 3:941.

43 Abū Naṣr, Muḥammah ibn Muḥammad ibn Ṭarkhān, also known as Alfarabius or Avennasar, was one of the most famous and most significant Muslim philosophers; R. Walzer, "al-Fārābī," *EI*², 2:778.

44 Abu 'l-Hudhayl, Muḥammad ibn Hudhayl al-ʿAbdī, is considered to have been the first speculative theologian of the Muʿtazilite school. He formulated a most abstract and transcendent notion of God; H.S. Nyberg, "Abu 'l-Hudhayl al-ʿAllāf," *EI*², 1:128.

45 Abū Yaʿqūb Yusūf ibn ʿAbdallāh, was a Muʿtazilite theologian, a disciple of Abu 'l-Hudhayl; D. Gimaret, "al-Shaḥḥām," *EI*², 9:202.

46 Abū Isḥāq Ibrāhīm ibn Sayyār was another Muʿtazilite theologian and a disciple of Abu 'l-Hudhayl. He was also a poet; J. van Ess, "al-Naẓẓām," *EI*², 7:1057.

47 Ibn Qayyim al-Jawziyya, *al-Ṣawāʿiq al-mursala*, 4:1350–1351.

This little passage aptly reflects Ibn al-Qayyim's approach described thus far: as shown before, he fires away irritably while listing varied prominent rationalist scholars—Greek philosophers, Muslim philosophers, early Muʿtazilites and their followers—all in a single breath (although orderly separated); all of them stand in sharp contrast to the messengers sent by God, as mentioned in the Quran and Hadith literature. Reliance on previous rationalist scholars is depicted here as a silly and unreasonable manner of corroborating one's view, whose value can never be associated with the value of knowledge derived from the true Revelation.

In another section Ibn al-Qayyim further elaborates on the above-mentioned concept of *al-aʿqal*, that is to say, the special groups of people whom he perceived as having the most copious rational capacity. A strong traditionalistic inclination drives him once again to reclaim the very definition of Reason back from the hands of the rationalists, fusing it into Islamic Revelation alone. According to Ibn al-Qayyim:

> The persons of utmost highest rational capacity (*aʿqal al-ḥalq^{i} ʿala 'l-iṭlāq^{i}*) are the Messengers. Their followers are the people of most Reason among the religions (*aʿqal al-umam*). Among them, the "people of the book and the divine laws" [*ahl al-kitāb wal-shawāriʿ*, i.e., other religious communities who received a prophetic Revelation in write, as Jews, Christians and Zoroastrians] are of the most Reason; and amid them, the Muslims are of most Reason. Among the Muslims, the persons of most Reason are the companions of the Prophet—peace be upon him—and their followers (*tābiʿūn*) [who perform] good deeds. After them, the people of the Sunna and Hadith [i.e., the traditionalists] are of most Reason definitely. The evidence (*burhān*) for this is that the Messengers had manifested beneficial knowledge, virtuous deeds and good means for this world and the afterlife, which were not seen before, not even close, not even partly, from the side of any person of Reason beside them [...]
>
> On the other hand, their rivals and opponents have manifested the deficiency of their Reasons (*nuqṣān ʿuqūlihim*), [to the degree of] the Reason of a brute animal. [Yet, their lack of Reason] does not approach its destruction. The opponents of the Messengers and their followers fall down [and get tangled] in the cords of their destruction like moths drawn to fire. The deficiency of their Reason is apparent in their branches of knowledge and information, just as it is apparent in their actions. Every person of light and perception, when he witnesses the righteous Reason (*al-ʿaql al-ṣaḥīḥ*) and faultless predisposition (*wal-fiṭra 'l-salīma*) that the Messengers brought—and who does not maliciously speak of denial and

> negation (*al-nafāta 'l-muʿaṭṭilatu*) concerning God exalted—recognizes that the difference between the two [Reasons] is greater than the difference between the feet and the head.[48]

In Ibn al-Qayyim's mind, it is completely absurd that scholars who consider themselves as dependent on rationality are blind to the supreme Reason of the Messengers sent by God and, hence, to the Reason delivered by Him. Fideism is definitely a prominent keynote of Ibn al-Qayyim's positive conceptualization of the absolute epistemological value of Revelation. However, in the spirit of the rationalized-traditionalistic authorship he introduces in his refutations in *al-Ṣawāʿiq*, Ibn al-Qayyim binds together Reason and Revelation claiming that Reason—in its true and righteous version—is under the control of the traditionalists, the real *ʿuqalāʾ*, not the self-proclaimed rationalists. In this respect, it is worth noting that Revelation's epistemic hegemony is supported by the authoritative nature of the scriptural sources as the word of God. Still, Ibn al-Qayyim manages to redeem Reason from the rationalistic scholarship quite successfully, as he employs a sophisticated rationalized-traditionalistic mode of argumentation.

Although seemingly trivial and only little used in Ibn al-Qayyim's overall terminology, this superlative form of *al-aʿqal* (and its derivations, such as, *aʿqal al-khalq*, *aʿqal al-umam*, *aʿqaluhum*, etc.) appears to me to be one of the comparatively scarce positive significations he provides in his epistemological discussion at hand. To put it differently, while Ibn al-Qayyim diligently develops a polemic deliberation in the course of his second *ṭāghūt* refutation, a positive conceptualization of his statements can be found in a considerably diminished fashion. Ibn al-Qayyim's restructuring and active reclaiming of the concept of Reason is a striking example of the—still minor—positive discussion.

Remarkably, and as was shown, the second *ṭāghūt* refutation is targeted—much like the first refutation—against the later Ashʿarite promotion of figurative or allegorical interpretation as a legitimate technique to be applied onto the Islamic textual sources. Likewise, this insight elucidates the introduction of *al-Ṣawāʿiq*, in which Ibn al-Qayyim addresses specifically the phenomenon of *taʾwīl* and examines it thoroughly. Indeed, rebuking the practical implementation of *taʾwīl* is the link that can be traced through all four refutations of *ṭawāghīt* in *al-Ṣawāʿiq*, even as they mainly dissect theoretical subjects in the field of epistemology (i.e., the first and second refutations explored so far). The next chapter thus examines Ibn al-Qayyim's third *ṭāghūt* refutation,

48 Ibn Qayyim al-Jawziyya, *al-Ṣawāʿiq al-mursala*, 4:1514–1515.

which more explicitly delves into the subject matter of *majāz* (metaphor) from a grammatical lens, thereby aiming to refute a central tool required for the performance of rationalistic *ta'wīl*. Yet again, the third *ṭāghūt* is founded on a theoretical infrastructure, this time of hermeneutics.

CHAPTER 5

Third *ṭāghūt* Refutation: Undermining the Theoretical Basis of *majāz*

After discerning satisfactory kinds of knowledge to be used in theological deliberations, another significant question arises: what is the correct manner for reaching their adequate understanding? The numerous possible answers have crucial implications on the hermeneutical subtleties enfolding within complex doctrinal matters; in this respect, the issue of divine attributes in Islamic thought is no exception. Entering the theoretical realm of hermeneutics, including Arabic linguistics and grammar, Ibn al-Qayyim devotes his third *ṭāghūt* refutation in *al-Ṣawāʿiq* to a vast and highly systemized discussion against a key rationalistic device used to figuratively interpret the divine attributes appearing in the texts of Revelation—*majāz* (trope or a metaphor).[1] Consisting of two main areas of discussion, this refutation is the largest in *al-Ṣawāʿiq* and make up the lion's share of Ibn al-Qayyim's criticism of *taʾwīl*. The first part of the refutation concentrates on the theoretical invalidity of the concept *majāz* from a linguistic-grammatical prism.[2] In the second area of discussion, Ibn al-Qayyim examines ten particular divine attributes that were considered to be *majāz* by rationalistic scholars, asserting their essential reality (*ḥaqīqa*); the choice of these specific attributes seems intentional, as they can convey a strong anthropomorphic meaning. These are: God's advent (*ṣifat al-majīʾ*), God's name (*ismuh^{u}*), God's seat on His throne (*sifat al-istiwāʾ*), God's two hands (*ṣifat al-yadayn^{i}*), God's face (*ṣifat al-wajh*), God's light (*ṣifat al-nūr*), God's aboveness (*ṣifat al-fawqiyya*), God's descent (*nuzūl al-rabb*), God's simultaneity (*maʿiyya*, lit. being with His creation) and closeness (*qurb*) and God's proclamation and speech (*nidāʾuh^{u} wa-taklīmuh^{u}*).[3] Throughout the entire third *ṭāghūt* refutation, Ibn al-Qayyim intricately weaves various rhetorical elements and didactical features into a rich discussion, through which he deprecates the rationalistic method of allegorical interpretation applied on the

1 As noted before, this part can only be found in the abridged version of *al-Ṣawāʿiq*. However, it is still the most extensive refutation therein; see section in 2.1 (page 57).

2 Ibn Qayyim al-Jawziyya, *Mukhtaṣar al-Ṣawāʿiq* (the abridgement of Ibn al-Mawṣilī), 2:690–856.

3 Ibn Qayyim al-Jawziyya, *Mukhtaṣar al-Ṣawāʿiq* (the abridgement of Ibn al-Mawṣilī), 2:856–3:1400.

 | DOI: 10.1163/9789004372511_007

divine attributes, rendering their literal meanings into figurative ones in the form of metaphors (*majāzāt*). Furthermore, his declared aim is to prove that all of the divine attributes in the Revelation designate different aspects of God's reality and are veridical expressions (*ḥaqiqa*) denoting ontological and transcendental truth.[4]

The following chapter focuses on selected segments from Ibn al-Qayyim's massive third *ṭāghūt* refutation, emphasizing the alternative hermeneutical model he sets forth in an attempt to positively delineate the hermeneutics to be applied on the divine attributes. As Ibn al-Qayyim generates a discussion which penetrates the scientific fields of Arabic linguistics and grammar, section 1 henceforth depicts the concept of *majāz* in these areas in order to set the ground for the investigation in this chapter. Section 2 focuses on Ibn al-Qayyim's immediate inspiration for constructing his opinion—the hermeneutical approach taken by his teacher Ibn Taymiyya, who voiced a radical critique against the use of *majāz*. Section 3 portrays the positive hermeneutical approach constructed and promoted by Ibn al-Qayyim in *al-Ṣawāʿiq*. Closer consideration is given to several fairly early scholars whom Ibn al-Qayyim mentions in his writing, either as ideological opponents or intellectual role models. Section 4 concerns Ibn al-Qayyim's attack against Muʿtazilite doctrines, whereas section 5 depicts his advancement of early rational-traditionalistic ideology. The topic of earlier traditionalistic motivation is a particularly interesting point for the contextualization of Ibn al-Qayyim's discussion, since these scholars had already demonstrated an initial stage of rationalized-traditionalism. Finally, section 6 pays particular attention to Ibn al-Qayyim's understanding of the philosophical-theology of the renowned thinker Ibn Rushd (Averroes, d. 595/1198) as yet another means of rejecting rationalistic hermeneutics.

---

4 Udo Simon, "Majāz," *Encyclopedia of Arabic Language and Linguistics—Brill Reference Online*, http://referenceworks.brillonline.com.proxy1.athensams.net/entries/encyclopedia-of-arabiclanguage-and-linguistics/majaz-EALL_SIM_vol3_0082, last accessed in March 2016. The term *ḥaqīqa* presented here will be elaborately explained henceforth, illustrating the nuanced meanings it carries in the theological context. Thus, the English translation of *ḥaqīqa* used in this chapter aims to reflect this theological sense. Nonetheless, at times this meaning was slightly modified to "essential/actual reality"—especially when directly translated from Arabic—in order to represent the specific mindset that appears in the primary texts.

5.1 Prefatory Remarks: The *ḥaqīqa/majāz* Dichotomy and the Origin of Language

Ibn al-Qayyim's fierce rejection of the insertion of the concept of *majāz* to the theological discussion on divine attributes is historically rooted in a basic hermeneutical disagreement between traditionalism and rationalism (which, in turn, reflects the epistemological one investigated in chapters 3 and 4). *Majāz* is a term that initially belongs to the discipline of Arabic linguistics, which grew to denote an expansion (*ittisāʿ*) of the original meaning (*aṣl*) to form a figurative speech. Therefore, the historical development of the meaning of *majāz* also entails the theologically-concerned issue of the origin of language (*aṣl al-lugha*).[5] Since Ibn al-Qayyim mentions this issue in his refutation of *majāz*, it is very important to present an introductory explanation of the term not only from a theological perspective, but also with relation to the linguistic theories on the origin of language. Thus, in order to prepare the ground for a closer inspection of Ibn al-Qayyim's critique in his third *ṭāghūt* refutation in *al-Ṣawāʿiq*, this section concisely depicts the historical findings on the theological concept of *majāz* and its relation to the theories on the origin of language.

From a historical perspective, the development of the idea of *majāz* represents an intellectual mix of Arabic linguistics and rhetoric (*ʿilm al-bayān*, as systemized in ca. 6th/12th–7th/13th century) and theological and legal thought in medieval Islam. Muslim thinkers considered Arabic lexicography, grammar and morphology pivotal elements for understanding the texts of Revelation (*sharʿ*), and thus created differentiated approaches for the practical application of linguistic sciences for the sake of gaining legal or theological benefits (for instance, in the disciplines of *uṣūl al-fiqh* and *uṣūl al-dīn*).[6] Dealing specifically with the *Kalām*ic discourse on the theological issue of divine attributes, linguistic theories were used in the endeavor of aptly apprehending the descriptions of God in the Quran and Hadith. At this stage stated rather schematically, we can say that, while the traditionalists preferred adhering to the literal meanings of Revelation and minimizing the interference of exterior notions, the rationalists were much more enthusiastic supporters of linguistic conceptions in their

5 The special connection between linguistics and theology in medieval Islam is profoundly discussed in the study: Kees Versteeg, "Linguistic Attitudes and the Origin of Speech in the Arab World," in: A. Elgibali, (ed.), *Understanding Arabic: Essays in Contemporary Arabic Linguistics in Honor of El-Said Badawi*, (Cairo: American University in Cairo Press, 1996), 15–31.

6 Bernard G. Weiss, "Language and Tradition in Medieval Islam: The Question of *al-Ṭarīq ilā maʿrifat al-lugha*," *Miszellen* 61 (1984), 91–93; Versteeg, "Linguistic Attitudes and the Origin of Speech in the Arab World," 21.

hermeneutical methodologies. Subsequently, a discourse of dichotomy developed about the two counter-terms of *ḥaqīqa* and *majāz*. Both terms designate formal units of expression (*lafẓ*) that transfer (by *naql*) corresponding meaning (*maʿnā*); however, it is the quality of that meaning which contrasts them with one another. Whereas *ḥaqīqa* grew to signify an ontologically veridical meaning, *majāz*—originally a linguistic term—grew closer to *istiʿāra*, which is the more distinct denotation of a metaphor delivering a figurative meaning.[7]

According to modern research conducted in the field of the Arabic Language, in the rationalistic thought, the somewhat technical division of language into expressions of *ḥaqīqa* (i.e., actual meaning) and *majāz* (i.e., figurative meaning) was initially created as a theological instrumental means for the hermeneutical issue of the divine attributes in the Islamic texts. Among others, Wolfhart Heinrichs and Kees Versteegh articulated this conclusion in several of their studies. Heinrichs claims that in the 4th/10th century, many disciplines of knowledge in the Islamic intellectual sphere came of age and established themselves as independent fields of science (*ʿulūm*) with theoretical principles (*uṣūl*) and various practical aspects (*furūʿ*), such as: literature, exegesis, theology, jurisprudence, grammar, language and translation. It was only in the 5th/11th century when, most openly by al-Ghazālī and with a considerable amount of success, attempts were made to bring the best of the different sciences together and weld them into a unified Islamic ideal. This was a result of the 4th/10th scholarly tendency to restructure the past, reflecting back onto the 'first early scholars' (*awāʾil*) and the formative notions they used when striving to establish their own field. In fact, in this particular period the interactive exchange of ideas between disciplines was much more common. This was also the case with the term *majāz*; early references show it had not yet gained the meaning of a 'metaphor' or a 'trope', as is was defined in later literature.[8]

The term *majāz* first appeared in relation to two contexts: either philological-hermeneutical or theological; it is unclear which one was the primary origin. At any rate, the motivating force for the use of *majāz* was the need to extract correct linguistic meanings—from which legal or other meanings were derived—out of the texts of the Quran and Hadith literature. Therefore, the approach taken towards the texts until the 4th/10th century was nearly always

7 Simon, "Majāz," *Encyclopedia of Arabic Language and Linguistics*, online source.

8 Heinrichs, "Contacts between Scriptural Hermeneutics and Literary Theory in Islam: The Case of *Majāz*," in: *Zeitschrift für Geschichte der arabisch islamischen Wissenschaften* 7 (1991/92): 253–255; Kees Versteegh, *Arabic Grammar and Qurʾanic Exegesis in Early Islam* (Leiden: Brill, 1993), 122.

only explanatory, as a means of attaining a proper understanding of the scriptures. One of the earliest recorded use of the term was in a book called *Majāz al-qur'ān* by philologist and exegete Abū ʿUbayda (d. 210/825); here, *majāz* referred to "what is allowed to be signified by the rules of language" (lit. *majāz*). The difficulty of understanding figurative utterances soon occurred, as they are abundant in the Islamic texts and are not always easily grasped. In this manner, the term *majāz* was gradually associated with understanding metaphorical expressions. During later medieval times, the use of the term *majāz* was narrowed down to the areas of legal theory and methodology (*uṣūl al-fiqh*) and rhetoric (*ʿilm al-bayān*). Thus, the meaning of the technical term *majāz* resulted from mutual exchanges between the different disciplines, and was only understood as a 'metaphor' at a relatively later time. From a theological standpoint, the early Muʿtazilite discourse on the issue of divine attributes had already radically shaped the designation of the term *majāz* as a metaphor in the 3rd/9th century. Evidence strongly suggests that the theory of division between *ḥaqīqa* and *majāz* was conceived as a hermeneutical-theological device among the Muʿtazilites and early *Kalām*ic circles of Basra and Kufa. Using the principal view that the Islamic texts cannot always be taken literally, but rather are merely allegories, Muʿtazilite scholars strove to strip God of any possible sign of anthropomorphism or comparison to His creation.[9]

Such perception of metaphorical *majāz* stems from the theories of the linguists and grammarians who were active in the early Muʿtazilite milieu. Important representatives of these scholars were the grammarian Ibn Qutayba (d. 276/889) and the renowned linguist and poet al-Jāḥiẓ (d. 255/868–869), who demonstrated a stark affinity towards using the term *majāz* for figurative expressions, particularly metaphors and figures of speech (*istiʿārāt*). The Ashʿarite grammarian ʿAbd al-Qāhir al-Jurjānī (d. 471/1078) further crystallized the terminological distinction between *ḥaqīqa* and *majāz* in his work *Asrar al-balāgha* (Secrets of Rhetoric) that concentrates on the science of meanings (*ilm al-maʿānī* or *ilm al-bayān*). In this work, the term *majāz* is a trope formed by a single word, a clause or a sentence used in a sense other than their conventional meaning, therefore creating new fields of associations. Al-Jurjānī also makes a distinction between expressions which denote reality with

9 Heinrichs, "On the Genesis of the *Ḥaqīqa-Majāz* Dichotomy," 111–117; Gilliot, "Exegesis of the Qur'ān: Classical and Medieval," 108–109; Hossein Modarressi, "Some Recent Analyses of the Concept of Majāz in Islamic Jurisprudence," *Journal of the American Oriental Society* 106/4 (Oct.–Dec., 1986): 787; Miriam Goldstein, "Abū l-Faraj Hārūn (Jerusalem, 11th c.) on *majāz*, between *uṣūl al-naḥw, uṣūl al-fiqh* and *iʿjāz al-Qur'ān*," *Der Islam* 90/2, 2013, 378–381; Aḥmad Māhir al-Baqrī, *Ibn al-Qayyim al-lughawī*, 215–216.

sensuous perceptibility and a metaphor in conceptual perceptibility (*ḥaqīqa fī 'l-maḥsūsāt wa-majāz fī 'l-ma'qūlāt*).[10] In addition, he also interpreted Quranic verses of the acts of God, maintaining that they cannot be understood in their apparent meaning for the similarity to human-acts, and thus must be understood as *majāz*.[11] This kind of ideas began flourishing from the 4th/10th century onwards among linguistic as well as theology scholars, and was of course preserved in the terminology of the later scholars of *Kalām*.[12] Highly relevant in this regard is the contribution of Fakhr al-Dīn al-Rāzī (d. 606/1209) to the theory of *majāz* in his work *Nihāyat al-ījāz fī dirāyat al-iʿjāz* (Final Confirmation on the Knowledge of [the Quran's] Inimitability), where he introduced philosophical notions from logic and combined them with the tradition of rhetoric as advocated by al-Jurjānī. In his very influential work on the Principles of Religion *al-Maḥṣūl fī 'ilm al-uṣūl*, al-Rāzī further formulated methodological aspects of the theory of *majāz*, expanding his discussion to semantics and linguistics, which followed earlier Muʿtazilite teachings.[13] Therefore, the meaning of the term *majāz* was not always immediately associated with "metaphors" but, rather, progressively evolved into this definition. As a consequence of the mutual interchange between the scholars of *uṣūl al-fiqh* (such as the legal expert Abū Bakr al-Jaṣṣāṣ, d. 370/981) and the linguists and grammarians, this denotation penetrated Islamic theological terminology only in the course of the 4th/10th century. This allowed the rationalist theologians to adopt *majāz* as metaphor and as a hermeneutical device in their deliberations on the theological issue of the divine attributes.[14]

A related linguistic topic referred to in the course of Ibn al-Qayyim's third *ṭāghūt* refutation is another debated issue concerning the origin of language (*aṣl al-lugha*, or *mabda' al-lugha*) in the Islamic narrative, which in fact con-

10 Al-Jurjānī, Abu 'l-Bakr 'Abd al-Qāhir ibn Abd al-Raḥman (d. 471/1078), *Asrar al-balāgha fī 'ilm al-bayān*, ed. Muḥammad 'Abduh and Muḥammad Rashīd Riḍā (Beirut: Dār al-Maʿrifa, [1398]/1978), 203; Simon, "Majāz," *Encyclopedia of Arabic Language and Linguistics*, online source.

11 Abdessamad Belhaj, "Ibn Qayyim al-Ğawziyyah et sa contribution à la rhétorique arabe," in: ed. Bori and Holtzman, *Essays in the Legal and Theological Thought of Ibn Qayyim al-Ğawziyyah* (Rome, Istituto per l'Oriente C.A. Nallino, 2010), 152.

12 Heinrichs, "On the Genesis of the *Ḥaqīqa-Majāz* Dichotomy," 137–140; Heinrichs, "Contacts between Scriptural Hermeneutics and Literary Theory in Islam: The Case of *Majāz*," 256–258, 282–283.

13 Simon, "Majāz," *Encyclopedia of Arabic Language and Linguistics*, online source.

14 A comprehensive evaluation of this process is found in: Heinrichs, "Contacts between Scriptural Hermeneutics and Literary Theory in Islam: The Case of *Majāz*," 258–284.

tains significant paradigms of relevance to the concept of *majaz*.[15] In this respect, the main question is that of agency with relation to the Islamic concept of the imposition of language (or "positing", assignment, *waḍʿ*):[16] who assigned expressions (*alfāẓ*) to their meanings (*maʿānī*)—God or human society? For most Muslims, the point of departure for the discussion was the Quranic verse 2:31 "He [i.e., God] taught Adam all the names [of things]." Muslim scholars of the classical period endorsed two principal views on the topic of the origin of language: on the one hand, there was the revelationist theory (*waḥy, tawqīf*) of the traditionalists, according to which language was pre-imposed by God; words were assigned with meanings by Him, while the human creation was necessarily disposed with the intuitive knowledge thereof (as a part of the idea of *fiṭra*). This was the approach embrace by, for example, the traditionalist scholar Ibn Fāris (d. 395/1005). On the other hand, the conventionalist theory (*iṣṭilāḥ*) of the Muʿtazilie ultra-rationalists hypothesized that language and meanings were established (or assigned, *mawḍūʿa*) by humankind itself through the habitual conventions of speech; according to this theory, the choice of names is basically arbitrary. In the course of time and the evolution of scholarship in Islam from the 4th/10th century onward, the early controversy between the Muʿtazilites and the traditionalists declined.

---

15 Bernard G. Weiss closely addressed the matter, for example, in his articles: "Medieval Muslim Discussions of the Origin of Language" (1974), "Language and Tradition in Medieval Islam: The Question of *al-Ṭarīq ilā maʿrifat al-lugha*" (1984), or the more recent contribution to the *Encyclopedia of Arabic Language and Linguistics*, "Waḍʿ al-Luġa" (first appeared online in 2011). In addition, publications of relevance by Weiss are: "A Theory of the Parts of Speech in Arabic (Noun, Verb and Particle): A Study in *ʿilm al-waḍʿ*" (1976), "Language and Law: The Linguistic Premises of Islamic Legal Science" (1984), and the book *The Search for God's Law: Islamic Jurisprudence in the Writings of Sayf Al-Din Al-Amidi* (2010). Worthy of mentioning as well are the publications by Kees Versteegh, such as the article "Linguistic Attitudes and the Origin of Speech in the Arab World" (1996) and the book *Landmarks in Linguistic Thought III: The Arabic Linguistic Tradition* (1997). An earlier important study by Versteegh is: "La «grande étymologie» d'Ibn Ǧinnī" (1985). The article by Mustafa Shah, "Classical Islamic Discourse on the Origins of Language: Cultural Memory and the Defense of Orthodoxy" (2011) is yet another important contribution available.

16 The Arabic term *waḍʿ* is more or less equivalent to the Greek notion of *thésis* (i.e., institution/establishment of language, law or customs by divine or human agency) used by the Greek philosophers as an attempt to determine to which extent words reflect reality. The counter notion of *phúsis* denotes nature or inexorable power ruling the visible world; Vivien Law, "Language and its Students: the History of Linguistics," in: N.E. Collinge (ed.), *An Encyclopaedia of Language* (London & New York: Routledge, 1990), 788–789; Versteeg, "Linguistic Attitudes and the Origin of Speech in the Arab World," 22.

This was due to the rise of Ashʿarite scholarly activity at that time—such as al-Bāqillānī's (d. 403/1013)—which accepted both doctrines as evenly plausible, thereby resolving the question which had been raised. Still, separately and respectively, each theory contributed to shaping a range of derived theological debates, including the hermeneutical dispute on the quality of the divine attributes.[17]

The concept of *majāz* as a figurative expression could have been notionally justified by retaining the conventionalist theory (*iṣṭilāḥ*) with respect to the origin of language; on the other hand, it might have been deemed invalid by the revelationalist theory (*tawqīf*). The employment of these linguistic theories is evident in Ibn al-Qayyim's discussion on hermeneutics in *al-Ṣawāʿiq*, as will be shown shortly. Conceptualizing his hermeneutics in *al-Ṣawāʿiq* on the basis of the teachings of Ibn Taymiyya, Ibn al-Qayyim joins the idea of *tawqīf* to the refutation of *majāz*. Ibn Taymiyya had revitalized the rather marginal issue of the origin of language for his attack against the rationalists who promoted the concept of *majāz* concerning the issue of divine attributes. For this aim, he denounced the theory of *iṣṭilāḥ* as a detrimental innovation (*bidʿa*) and accused the rationalistic resort to metaphor as an attempt to spread heretical doctrines. Countering his ideological adversaries, Ibn Taymiyya invigorated the doctrine of *tawqīf*—fusing it with the principal of adhering to the conventional use of Arabic language—as a means of defying the theological use of *majāz*. Nevertheless, in his *Kitāb al-īmān* (Book of Belief) Ibn Taymiyya displayed a highly flexible rendering of the rigid *tawqīf* by thoroughly connecting it to the known linguistic conventions. Ibn al-Qayyim follows his mentor's lead and appears to have carefully taken into account the technical-grammatical argumentations together with their theological significances. Therefore, both Ibn Taymiyya and Ibn al-Qayyim manifest a well-developed understanding—as well as critique—of an earlier historical progression of thought concerning the linguistic-theological topic of the origin of language.[18]

---

17 Weiss, "Waḍʿ al-Luġa," online source; Weiss, "Medieval Muslim Discussions of the Origin of Language," *Zeitschrift der Deutschen Morgenländischen Gesellschaft* 124/1 (1974), 33–41; Versteeg, "Linguistic Attitudes and the Origin of Speech in the Arab World," 27–28; Mustafa Shah, "Classical Islamic Discourse on the Origins of Language: Cultural Memory and the Defense of Orthodoxy," 315–316.

18 Mustafa Shah, "Classical Islamic Discourse on the Origins of Language: Cultural Memory and the Defense of Orthodoxy," 334–339. It is necessary to note several modern studies conducted in Arabic on his linguistic approach. Although little in number, the contribution of this research is substantial, especially while concentrating on the topic of *majāz* in the thought of Ibn al-Qayyim. Valuable publications for the following's chap-

5.2 Ibn Taymiyya's Critique against *majāz*

Much like in the case of *al-Ṣawāʿiq*'s previous refutations, Ibn al-Qayyim devotion to the doctrinal teachings of Ibn Taymiyya is highly evident throughout the third *ṭāghūt* refutation against the theoretical existence of *majāz*. Similar to his teachings in many other fields, Ibn Taymiyya introduced an innovative point of view in his deliberations on the theological implications derived from the anthropomorphic descriptions of God in the Islamic textual sources. Despite his self-identification as a Ḥanabalite as well as member of the traditionalistic milieu (*ahl al-sunna wal-jamāʿa*), it is hard to say Ibn Taymiyya's opinion on the matter at hand truly reflected typical traditionalism. Previous traditionalists accepted those expressions about God as they reconciled themselves to the approach that they pose no religious requirement, so there is no need to fully realize their meaning in order to believe in them. Ibn Taymiyya did not find this convincing. For him, the divine attributes must contain a concrete and comprehensible meaning; moreover, a correct grasp of the anthropomorphic expressions should retain a complete transcendence of the one and only God and, at the same time, His imminence. Ibn Taymiyya employed rationalistic arguments to enforce his claim: he explained God's descriptions that could have suggested His affinity to the created humans as entirely abstract and metaphysical things, which do not exist in reality. That is to say, even though they shared denotations (living, knowing, hearing seeing, etc.), the meaning of divine attributes is not equal to the attributes used to describe a human being. Ibn Taymiyya corroborated this statement by a complex hermeneutical reading of the Islamic texts, incorporated with argumentations derived from logic and Reason. In a number of cases he justifies his point saying that "this is demonstrated by the Quran,

ter's investigation are: *Ibn Qayyim al-Jawziyya: juhūduh[u] fī 'l-dars al-lughawī* (Ibn Qayyim al-Jawziyya: His Endeavour in the Study of Linguistics; 1976) by Ṭāhir Sulaymān Ḥamūda, *Ibn Qayyim al-lughawī* (Ibn al-Qayyim the Linguist; 1978) by Aḥmad Māhir al-Baqarī, *Ibn Qayyim al-Jawziyya: ʿaṣruh[u] wa-manhaguh[u] wa-ārāʾuh[u] fī 'l-fiqh wal-ʿaqāʾiq wal-taṣawwūf* (Ibn Qayyim al-Jawziyya: His Era, Method, and Approach on Law, Theology, and Islamic Mysticism; 1984) by ʿAbd al-ʿAẓīm Sharaf al-Dīn, and *Ibn Qayyim al-Jawziyya wa-ārāʾuh[u] 'l-naḥwiyya* (Ibn Qayyim al-Jawziyya and his Grammatical Approach; 1995) by Ayman ʿAbd al-Razzāq al-Shawwā. A couple of more recent articles with direct relevance to the work *al-Ṣawāʿiq* are: "*Qawāʿid wa-ḍawābiṭ wa-fawāʾid min kitāb al-Ṣawāʿiq al-mursala li-Ibn al-Qayyim*" (Principles, Percepts and Benefits from *al-Ṣawāʿiq* of Ibn al-Qayyim, 2008?) by Jamal Ahmed Badi and "*Jadaliyyat al-taʾwīl wal-majāz ʿind[a] Ibn Qayyim al-Jawziyya min khilāl[i] kitābih[i] al-Ṣawāʿiq al-mursala*" (The Controversy of *taʾwīl* and *majāz* in Ibn al-Qayyim's *al-Ṣawāʿiq al-mursala*, 2010?) by Belgacem Hammam.

the Sunna and human Reason."[19] Nevertheless, and as was depicted in chapter 1, several of Ibn Taymiyya's ideological adversaries publicly accused him of siding with an extreme and decidedly simplistic form of anthropomorphism, also known as *ḥashwiyya*.[20] However, the stance voiced by Ibn Taymiyya was expressed in his elucidatory claim, in which he writes: "there is nothing like [God], neither in His essence, nor in His attributes, nor in His actions."[21]

Ibn Taymiyya addressed the *majāz* topic in a number of works, which surely were at Ibn al-Qayyim's disposal and some of them were used in *al-Ṣawāʿiq*. Noticeable is that Ibn Taymiyya's negation of the concept of *majāz* in his work *Kitāb al-īmān* was the point of origin for Ibn al-Qayyim's arguments against *majāz* in *al-Ṣawāʿiq*; the resemblance between the texts is unmistakable, and it seems that Ibn al-Qayyim quoted this teacher almost verbatim. Wolfhart Heinrichs studied the passage in which Ibn Taymiyya discussed the concept of *majāz* in *Kitāb al-imān*, translating parts of it into English in his article: "On the Genesis of the *Ḥaqīqa-Majāz* Dichotomy"; the following discussion will thus rest on Ibn Taymiyya's arguments as analyzed by Heinrichs.[22] Whereas in many other cases of reliance on his mentor Ibn al-Qayyim refers to Ibn Taymiyya by specifically stating that his Shaykh said this or that (using phrases such as: *qāla*[a]

---

19 Jackson, "Ibn Taymiyyah on Trial in Damascus," 53–55; Holtzman, "'Does God Really Laugh?'," 195; Ibrāhīm ibn Manṣūr al-Turkī, *Inkār al-majāz ʿind*[a] *Ibn Taymiyya: bayn*[a] *al-dars al-balāghī wal-lughawī* (Riyadh: Dār al-Miʿrāj al-Dawliyya, 1999), 51–60.

20 This is a derogatory name used to denote heretic anthropomorphic groups, literally meaning "scholars of the unfertile debate." Similar denunciations are *mujassima* (corporealistic), *mumaththila* (likening), or *nābita* (mob). Notable is the inconsistency of use with regard to these names, as all kinds of theological streams of thought used them interchangeably to refer to one another as wrong and heretical. Among others, the Muʿtazilites called traditionalistic schools *mushabbiha* (anthropomorphists), whereas Ashʿarite scholars made the accusations against the Muʿtazilites. Ibn Taymiyya himself accused the Muʿtazilites of comparing God to the human creation while promoting their principle of divine justice (*ʿadl*). Ibn Taymiyya considered this to be a false analogy to the human concepts of right vs. wrong and, hence, a defiance against God's dissimilation to His creation; Holtzman, "Anthropomorphism," 1:47; Hoover, *Ibn Taymiyya's Theodicy of Perpetual Optimism*, 212–215.

21 Hoover, *Ibn Taymiyya's Theodicy of Perpetual Optimism*, 47–49, 55–56.

22 Heinrichs, "On the Genesis of the *Ḥaqīqa-Majāz* Dichotomy," 115–117. The passage from *Kitāb al-īmān* analyzed by Heinrichs appears with only minor changes in *Mukhtaṣar al-Ṣawāʿiq* of Ibn al-Qayyim; Ibn Qayyim al-Jawziyya, *Mukhtaṣar al-Ṣawāʿiq* (the abridgement of Ibn al-Mawṣilī), 2:691–694, 706. See Ibn al-Qayyim's text in section 5.3 in this chapter; Abdessamad Belhaj, "Ibn Qayyim al-Ǧawziyyah et sa contribution à la rhétorique arabe," 153.

shaykhunā or *qāl^a Aḥmad*), the relevant passage in *al-Ṣawāʿiq* makes no direct mention of his mentor, although it seems to be a close to direct citation.[23] At any rate, Ibn al-Qayyim certainly advocates for the Ibn Taymiyya's approach in which he opposes the concept of *majāz* and the division of language into 'essential/veridical' vs. 'metaphors', maintaining that *majāz* was introduced to theological debate by the Muʿtazilites after the first three centuries of Islam (i.e., the 4th/10th century), from then onwards being continuously nurtured by the early rationalists and the scholars of *Kalām* that followed.

In *Kitāb al-īmān* Ibn Taymiyya addressed the issue of *majāz* as part of his discussion about the principles for proper Islamic belief. In the part of the work which concentrates on the belief in and affirmation of the divine attributes, Ibn Taymiyya had already spotted the inception of *majāz* as a Muʿtazilite theological device used in the rationalistic argumentations involving the issue of divine attributes. In addition, while specifying the formidability of good religious practices (*aʿmāl*) as an indispensable part of the belief, Ibn Taymiyya referred to a rationalistic claim which suggested that, since the nominatum 'belief' includes these deeds, it should be considered a case of *majāz* (*dukhūl al-ʿamāl fī musamma 'l-imān majāz^an*).[24] Ibn Taymiyya sternly discards this opinion and, while doing so, describes a series of historical processes which—as he sees it—led to creating the hermeneutical method of deploying *majāz* in theological deliberations. Since neither the Prophet's companions, the four great Imams, nor the early Arab grammarians mentioned it, he believed the dichotomy of *ḥaqīqa/majāz* arose only after the first three centuries of Islam. Ibn Taymiyya also points to Abū ʿUbayda's book *Majāz al-Qurʾān*, amplifying the letter's understanding of the term that denotes the appropriate linguistic manner in which the text of the Quran is expressed. The Muʿtazilites were those who authorized a synthetic dichotomy between the concepts of *ḥaqīqa* and *majāz* without sufficient knowledge and with the false support of the theory of *iṣṭilāḥ* (i.e., that language is the product of arbitrary human conventions). Aḥmad Ibn Ḥanbal had indeed stated the term *majāz* in his (alleged) work *al-Radd ʿalā 'l-zanādiqa wal-jahmiyya*,[25] but only in the meaning of "what

23 This is not the only case in which Ibn al-Qayyim copies parts of Ibn Taymiyya's writings without stating their source. A prominent example of this literary tendency can be seen in Ibn al-Qayyim's discussion in his work *Shifāʾ al-ʿalīl*, as examined in the paper: Holtzman, "Human Choice, Divine Guidance and the *Fiṭra* Tradition: The Use of Ḥadīth in Theological Treatises by Ibn Taymiyya and Ibn Qayyim al-Jawziyya," 165.

24 Al-Turkī, *Inkār al-majāz ʿind^a Ibn Taymiyya*, 61.

25 This work was apparently not composed by Ibn Ḥanbal and is only ascribed to him. See footnoes 72 in chapter 1.

is permissible according to the rules of language" (*min majāz^{i} 'l-lugha^{ti}*). Ibn Taymiyya lists other scholars who share his view, the Ẓāhirite school among these.[26] Furthermore, Ibn Taymiyya brings up a group of scholars that repudiated the existence of *majāz* not only in the Quran, but in the entire language,[27] such as the important early Ashʿarite scholar Abū Isḥāq Ibrāhīm ibn Muḥammad al-Isfarāyīnī (d. 418/1027).[28] This approach provides staunch evidence of Ibn Taymiyya's general attitude to the *majāz* in relation to his theology, and is also echoed most confidently in Ibn al-Qayyim's discussion in *al-Ṣawāʿiq*. Nevertheless, Ibn Taymiyya grapples with the subject as a rather casual manner as something accompanying his issue of main interest. Whereas Ibn Taymiyya pays attention to *majāz* in the course of his discussion on belief, Ibn al-Qayyim offers an independent treatment of the idea of *majāz* in a profound manner. This shows Ibn al-Qayyim's tendency of systemizing and developing his master's ideologies from a place of deep understanding and knowledge of his teachings.[29]

Ibn Taymiyya's engagement with the hermeneutical concept of *majāz* was not limited to the work *Kitāb al-imān*. Due Ibn al-Qayyim's view in *al-Ṣawāʿiq* expressing a great affinity to the ideas of his teacher as described above, one ought to explore Ibn Taymiyya's stance in additional relevant sources. Henceforth I will turn to three treatises composed by Ibn Taymiyya which are relevant to the issue. The first two are: *al-Risāla al-madaniyya* and *Risālat al-ḥaqīqa wal-majāz*, both of which appear in the vast compilation namely dedicated to his legal writings *Majmūʿt al-fatāwā*. In addition, I will inspect prominent sections

26 The Ẓāhirite was a theologico-juridical school in medieval Islam, whose name is derived from the Arabic word *ẓāhir*, i.e.: the apparent—and hence literal—meaning of the text, signifying the school's preference for adhering to the literallity of Revelation to other jurisprudential measures (such as independent opinion—*ray'*, or analogy—*qiyās*); Abdel-Magid Turki, "al-Ẓāhiriyya," *EI*^{2}, 11:394.

27 Heinrichs, "On the Genesis of the *Ḥaqīqa-Majāz* Dichotomy," 115–118; Zysow, *The Economy of Certainty*, 95–96.

28 Al-Isfarāyīnī is known to have contributed considerably to the formation of Ashʿarite theology, as he expended topics which remained untouched by his teacher, Abū Ḥasan al-Ashʿarī, the school's eponym. On the matter of anthropomorphism, he held the view of an abstract God closer to the Muʿtazilite one, opposing Karrāmite rationalistic corporealism. None of his works on dogmatic theology has survived, but he is quoted by later scholars; Wilferd Madelung, "al-Isfarāyīnī," *EI*^{2}, 4:108.

29 Ali, *Medieval Islamic Pragmatics*, 87–89; Belhaj, "Ibn Taimiyya et la négation de la métaphore," in: (eds.) D'hulster K., Van Steenbergen J., *Continuity and Change in the Realms of Islam: Studies in Honour of Professor Urbain Vermeulen* (Leuven: Uitgeverij Peeters, 2008), 65–68.

from Ibn Taymiyya's iconic treatise *al-Ḥamawiyya 'l-kubrā* for which he was publicly put on trial where he was accused of anthropomorphism.[30] The objective is to demonstrate the general Taymiyyan approach through these three primary sources as the underlying backdrop of Ibn al-Qayyim's hermeneutical deliberation in *al-Ṣawāʿiq*.

Al-Risāla 'l-madaniyya fi 'l-ḥaqīqa wal-majāz fi 'l-ṣifāt (Treatise [to the People of] Medina on *ḥaqīqa* and *majāz* concerning the [Divine] Attributes) is found in the second part of Ibn Taymiyya's composition titled *al-Asmāʾ wal-ṣifāt* ([God's] Names and Attributes).[31] Exhibiting his opinion concerning the interpretation method applied by the scholars of *Kalām* onto the Quranic verses and *ḥadīth*s in which the divine attributes are stated, Ibn Taymiyya expresses his agreement with the Great Imam al-Shāfiʿī (d. 204/820) who said that every Muslim must believe in God and "what was delivered by God according to God's intention (*ʿalā murādⁱ Allāhⁱ*)" and in God's Messenger and "what was delivered by God's Messenger according to God's Messenger's intention"—i.e., Muslims are required to believe in God and His Messenger in the exact way in which they are described in the authoritative texts of the Quran and Hadith and in accordance to their own intention. Moreover, Ibn Taymiyya adds that the figurative interpretation (*taʾwīl*) embraced by the rationalists is faulty (*bāṭil*), whereas the traditionalists (*ahl al-ḥadīth*) possess the truth "both outside and inside" of the texts (*ẓāhir^{an} wa-bāṭin^{an}*).[32] It is worth noting that, in modern linguistics, it is customary to distinguish the speech-act (or: the expressed utterance, locution) from the manner in which the speaker intended when producing that utterance (illocutionary force, such as statement—*khabar*, command—*amr*, prohibition—*nahy*, and so on). Thus, Ibn Taymiyya emphasizes here the status of illocutionary force of the divine discourse, sustaining that those who listen to the divine speech must grasp the intended meaning of it following the lines of the inclusive context together with the speaker's known habit of speech.[33]

---

30 The importance of the treatise was discussed in detail in section 1.2.

31 Ibn Taymiyya, *Majmūʿat al-fatāwā*, eds. ʿAmir al-Jazzār and Anwar al-Bāz, in 37 vols. (Riyadh: Dār al-Wafāʾ lil-Ṭibāʿa wal-Nashr wal-Tawzīʿ, 1494/1998), 6:211–319.

32 Ibn Taymiyya, *Majmūʿat al-fatāwā*, 6:212–213. In another treatise titled *Risāla fi ʿilm al-bāṭin wal-ẓāhir*, Ibn Tayimyya explains the two terms as simply as possible, insisting that *bāṭin* is the basic explained and clarified meaning of an expression, whereas *ẓāhir* is the literal expression "which is spoken and written" (*yutakallam^{u} bih^{i} wa-yuktab^{u}*). He does not enter the esoteric/exoteric terminology employed in the field of mysticism; Ibid, 13:233.

33 This model of hermeneutics constructed by Ibn Taymiyya critically challenges al-Ghazālī's theory for the interpretation of the Islamic texts, which follows the rationalistic supremacy granted to the use of human Reason; Paul A. Hardy, "Epistemology and Divine Dis-

Ibn Taymiyya continues by listing three main questions about which the traditionalists and the later Ashʿarites disagreed: the description of God's aboveness on His throne (*waṣf Allāh*[i] *bil-ʿulū ʿala 'l-ʿarsh*[i]), the question of the Quran as the speech of God (*mas'alat al-qur'ān*) and the figurative interpretation of the divine attributes (*mas'alat ta'wīl al-ṣifāt*). He explains that the righteous ancestors of the three first centuries of Islam (*salaf*) and their devout followers (*khalaf*) claimed that these descriptions of God must be accepted and transmitted as they appear in the texts (*tamurr*[u] *kamā ja'at*). The early scholars' consensus (*ijmāʿ*) was to approve the divine attributes, while negating their modality as well as refrain from likening God to His creation (*ma*[ʿa] *nafi 'l-kayfiyya*[ti] *wal-tashbīh*[i]). Ibn Taymiyya stresses that this approach is an affirmation of the essence or the existence of the attributes (*ithbāt al-dhāt* or *ithbāt al-wujūd*), not an affirmation of their modality or attempting to interpret their meanings (*lā ithbāt al-kayfiyya*). In this manner, God has a hand and He can hear; however, the hand must not be interpreted metaphorically as "ability" (*qudra*) and hearing must not be interpreted as "knowledge" (*ʿilm*).[34] This approach follows the traditionalistic formula of *bi-lā kayfa*.

Clarifying the correct practice of understanding the speech as it appears in the texts (*ẓāhir al-kalām*), Ibn Taymiyya claims that words like "hand" or "anger" are indeed used in order to describe a body-part or quality of a created human but, when they refer to God, they signify an entirely different meaning; nothing is like God, neither in its essence, its attributes, nor its actions. The apparent meaning is in fact the instinctive understanding of the speech by the common sense of a person who speaks a particular language. No mundane human-like attributes would be instinctively comprehended in the mind of a believer concerning God, as He cannot be perceived in descriptions of this kind. The divine attributes are sanctified and fit to the essence of the deity that they depict. Ibn Taymiyya states that, therefore, the divine attributes of knowledge or face represent a special essence within God (*ṣifa dhātiyya*). The created mind is unable to speculate or understand their meaning, for they do not resemble in any way the created essences which humans can understand. The only one who knows what the divine attributes are and how they come into expression or realization is God Himself. Even though the believers cannot comprehend these attributes, they are ordered to believe in them. Ibn Taymiyya therefore rejects any attempt of interpreting the divine attributes that appear in the Quran and

course," in ed. Tim Winter, *The Cambridge Companion to Classical Islamic Theology* (Cambridge: Cambridge University Press, 2008), 288–289.

34 Ibn Taymiyya, *Majmūʿat al-fatāwā*, 6:213.

Hadith, including the Muʿtazilite or Ashʿarite allegorical method of interpretation. In his view, the rationalistic approach distorts the original intention of the texts and burdens them with superfluous forced meanings. The rationalists actually create new attributes which either increase or decrease the meanings that the texts contain (*ṣifāt ḥāditha, aw iḍāfiyya aw ʿadamiyya*).[35]

A similar vein of argumentation can be found in another of Ibn Taymiyya's treatise titled *Risālat al-ḥaqīqa wal-majāz*. Ibn Taymiyya opens his treatise with an explanation of a conviction made by the later Ashʿarite theologian (who had formerly been Ḥanbalite) Sayf al-Dīn al-Āmidī (d. 631/1233), which he made in his major work on the principles of Islamic jurisprudence *Iḥkām al-ḥukm fī uṣūl al-aḥkām*.[36] It was al-Āmidī's contention that the theologians specializing in the principles of religious law (*al-uṣūliyyūn*) disagreed whether the Arabic language contains metaphorical nouns (*asmāʾ majāziyya*) or not.[37] As for himself, al-Āmidī pointed out, like most scholars, he sides with the position which recognizes the existence of figurative expressions. Ibn Taymiyya replies to this claim, dividing his answer into two sections: first, he wishes to clarify al-Āmidī's meaning of the term *uṣūliyyūn*; second, he aims at inspecting the arguments of both sides (i.e., the supporters of *majāz* and its objectors).

Regarding the term *uṣūliyyūn*, Ibn Taymiyya argues that, among these scholars, al-Āmidī simultaneously includes both the *salaf* and the *khalaf* (i.e., the early righteous scholars and those who came afterwards). In Ibn Taymiyya's opinion, this is an improper use of the term since the previous scholars were more adequately trained and capable of attaining legal rulings from the indications found in the Islamic sacred texts (*dalālat adilla sharʿiyya ʿalā al-aḥkām*) in accordance with the correct consecutive steps of consulting the Quran, Hadith, the community's consensus (*ijmāʿ*) and, only thereafter, the scholar's independent opinion (*al-ijtihād wal-raʾy*). In fact, states Ibn Taymiyya, every

35 Ibn Taymiyya, *Majmūʿat al-fatāwā*, 6:213–215.

36 Sayf al-Dīn ʿAlī ibn Abī ʿAli ʾl-Āmidī was a renowned scholar of speculative theology and theoretical law, who is known to have written his works in a highly dialectical manner. He gained much appreciation from his contemporaries as well as later scholars for his vast knowledge and his high quality writing; Bernard G. Weiss, "al-Āmidī, Sayf al-Dīn," *Encyclopaedia of Islam*, THREE, url address http://referenceworks.brillonline.com/entries/encyclopaedia-of-islam-3/al-amidi-sayf-al-din-COM_24214; Dominique Sourdel, "al-Āmidī," *EI²*, 1:434. Weiss, *The Search for God's Law: Islamic Jurisprudence in the Writings of Sayf Al-Din Al-Amidi* (Salt Lake City; Herndon, Va: University of Utah Press, 2010), 7–10.

37 Al-Āmidī's approach towards the significance of linguistic knowledge to be held in the hands of legal experts before interpreting or deducing law was examined in Weiss' article: "Language and Law: The Linguistic Premises of Islamic Legal Science" (1984), 15–21.

mujtahid (i.e., a scholar who rules according to his own judgment on the basis of an optimal familiarity with the textual sources) is an *uṣūlī*. Moreover, the term *uṣūliyyūn* denotes the four greatest Imams of the Islamic legal schools, whose rulings are the most virtuous, and therefore cannot be dismissed. Ibn Taymiyya recalls al-Shāfiʿī, stating it is widely known he was the first to use abstract speech (*jard al-kalām*) or expanded speech (by *tawassuʿ*) in the field of *uṣūl al-fiqh*; however, he still did not divide the language into literal-veridical meaning (*ḥaqīqa*) and metaphorical meaning (*majāz*). Thus, whoever believes the early *mujtahidūn*, the four Imams and the *salaf*, separated expressions into literal as opposed to metaphorical ones does so for the lack of sufficient knowledge. This is the case of several scholars of *Kalām* in the discipline of *uṣūl al-fiqh*. Ibn Taymiyya specifically notes al-Āmidī and Fakhr al-Dīn al-Rāzī, who—in his view—were not satisfactorily erudite in the teachings of the four Imams, as well as the Muʿtazilites and Ashʿarites, who employed rationalistic modes of argumentation. Summing up the point, Ibn Taymiyya stresses that, indeed, most of the scholars agree on dividing language into the literal-veridical and metaphorical; however, none of them is sufficiently knowledgeable in the different fields of Islamic sciences (*funūn al-islām*), such as Quranic exegesis, Hadith, jurisprudence, linguistics or grammar.[38]

In the second part of his answer, Ibn Taymiyya examines the arguments of the scholars who supported the dichotomy between *ḥaqīqa* and *majāz*. For example, they considered the use of allegorical speech to expand and loosen (by *iṭlāq*) the meaning of a certain expression; therefore, the word "lion" can stand for a brave man, although in its essence (*ḥaqīqa*) it indicates a predatory animal. Or the word "donkey" can stand for a stupid man although in its essence (*ḥaqīqa*) it indicates only an animal. In other examples the meaning of a whole phrase is extended, so that the expression 'so-and-so went on the wing of travel' (*fulānᵘⁿ ʿalā janāḥⁱ ʾl-safarⁱ*) means the person embarked on a long journey, or the expression "the curls of night turned white" (*shābat limmaᵗᵘ ʾl-laylⁱ*) means a long and dark night. Contrarily, Ibn Taymiyya states the expansion of meaning is not a result of speech being a metaphor but, rather, is due to the use of the expressions in a certain context (or associative indication, *qarīna*). As far as Ibn Taymiyya is concerned, if the figurative meaning of *majāz* is consequential to its dependence on the context and literal expression (*lafẓ*), it does not have any meaning on its own. Hence, the entire expression must be seen as veridical *ḥaqīqa* (*al-ḥaqīqa ṣifa lil-majmūʿ*). This is exactly the same case as that of

38 Ibn Taymiyya, *Majmūʿat al-fatāwā*, 20:220–222.

the use of a homonym (*ishtirāk*) or an etymologically derivative (*ishtiqāq*), as similar words can infer different meanings when they appear in different contexts.[39]

It once more becomes clear that the elementary fundamental for Ibn Taymiyya's disavowal of the use of *majāz* emphasizes that the audience to which the divine speech of the Quran is directed must understand the text as it was intended to be understood by God. Therefore, every expression (*lafẓ*) is dependent on the context of meaning therein (*al-qarāʾin al-maʿnawiyya*). The wise speaker chose to use certain expressions in a certain place and in a certain meaning; hence the reader/listener of the speech about God must accept it as an utterance with a preordained meaning, as an expression which signifies a specific use (*istiʿmāl al-lafẓ*). The expression itself is based upon the habitual discourse of the speaker (*ʿādat al-mutakallim*) in the Islamic texts. In this manner, the meaning of the expressions stems from their usage in the text (*istiʿmāl*). The context of meaning—perceived by Reason—discerns the one and only way in which an expression was intended to be used. It follows that the general context and the intention of the speaker grant the expression its meaning; not the device of *majāz*. As a result, the dichotomy between *ḥaqīqa* and *majāz* is refuted.[40] This indicates that the most prominent linguistic principle in Ibn Taymiyya's theoretical negation of the concept of *majāz* is contextualization (i.e., emphasizing the position of the containing context as the factor through which expressions gain their meanings). The basic approach formulized here by Ibn Taymiyya with relation to *majāz* and *taʾwīl* is that meaning is reliant on the actual context. The context is an inseparable part of the overall produced intention of the speaker, therefore it determines the meaning of the expressions. In other words, the relationship between expressions and their meanings in a particular context serves here a vital cohesive function in the text.[41] These ideas reflect the pragmatic approach that Ibn Taymiyya upheld concerning linguistic discourse, in which he voices a contextual approach of textual communication.[42]

---

39 Ibn Taymiyya, *Majmūʿat al-fatāwā*, 20:222–223, 227–230; Belhaj, "Ibn Qayyim al-Ǧawziyyah et sa contribution à la rhétorique arabe," 153–154; idem, "Ibn Taimiyya et la négation de la métaphore," 70–72.

40 Ibn Taymiyya, *Majmūʿat al-fatāwā*, 20:249–250; Hardy, "Epistemology and Divine Discourse," 289, 293–295; Ali, *Medieval Islamic Pragmatics*, 34–37, 110–111.

41 Esam N. Khalil, "Cohesion," *Encyclopedia of Arabic Language and Linguistics*, online source.

42 Ali, *Medieval Islamic Pragmatics*, 90–91; Al-Turkī, *Inkār al-majāz ʿind*[a] *Ibn Taymiyya*, 162–175.

Ibn Taymiyya's hermeneutical approach depicted so far gains considerable momentum in his polemical writing against the rationalistic figurative method of interpretation in one of his most famous treatises of faith (*ʿaqīda*) titled *al-Ḥamawiyya 'l-kubrā*. Forcefully maintaining that the indications of Revelation contradict the denial of divine attributes, Ibn Taymiyya blames the rationalists for their departure from the text (*naṣṣ*) provided by God and the apparent expressions thereof (*ẓāhir*) as delivered by the Prophet. Moreover, he accuses them of diminishing the teachings of the most notable scholars of the early Islamic community (*khayr al-umma*), in other words, the Prophet's companions, thus neglecting the traditionalistic chain of knowledge transmission. Not only do the scholars of *Kalām* ignore the Islamic sources of righteous knowledge, they endorse and actively follow a foreign set of beliefs, imitating that of the Persians, Hellenists, Jews, Christians, the philosophers (including the Indian ones) and the polytheists. In accordance with Ibn Taymiyya's view of the historical concatenation, the Ashʿarite hermeneutics of *ta'wīl* known in his times is a remnant of the ultra-rationalistic Muʿtazilism which, in turn, was formed as a result of the blending of alien ideologies into Islam after the third/ninth century.[43] Apart from the impressive—yet eclectic—historical perspective, it is also worth mentioning the terminology Ibn Taymiyya uses when he refers to Revelation and how it should be understood. He repeatedly uses the two terms *naṣṣ* and *ẓāhir* together, inferring the tight correlation between them; the sacred texts were manifested in apparent expressions, hence deviating from the apparent expressions is also a deviation from Revelation. In this fashion, the texts of Revelation are viewed as a sealed unit of reference, which constitutes a singular context for its apparent expressions to be grasped as veridical.

Using an analogy to the human spirit (*rūḥ*), Ibn Taymiyya explains the meaning of *ḥaqīqa* concerning the divine attributes in the following passage:[44]

> The 'spirit' which is inside human beings—a reasonable person knows that people are preoccupied with [its understanding]; but the texts (*nuṣūṣ*) refrain from clarifying its modality (*kayfiyya*). Why then do [people] not say about the spirit what they say about God's modality? Even when we know that the spirit is inside the body, and that it will leave it and

43 Ibn Taymiyya, *Majmūʿat al-fatāwā*, 5:14–19.

44 An important study in this regard is: Duncan B. Macdonald, "The Development of the Idea of the Spirit in Islam," *Acta Orientalia*, 9 (1931), 307–351. Langermann referred to the subject in the thought of Ibn al-Qayyim and Ibn Taymiyya in his article: "The Naturalization of Science in Ibn Qayyim al-Ǧawziyyah's *Kitāb al-rūḥ*," 214–215.

> ascent to the sky, gently removed from [the body], as mentioned in the truthful texts—we do not exaggerate in abstracting it (*tajrīdihā*), as done by the philosophers and their followers, by denying its [attributes of] ascending or descending, and its connection to the body and its departure from it. They struggle about [the spirit] since they do not see it as [a part] of the human body and its descriptions. But, assimilating (*tamthīl*) the spirit to the body does not deny the veracity of its descriptions. Nevertheless, they do not interpret (*yufassirū*) [the meaning] according to the texts, and so they use mistaken expressions!
>
> We do not say [that the spirit] is a mere part of the body like blood or odor are, for instance, or a physical attribute. It changes [from one body to another], but equal in its definition (*ḥadd*) and reality (*ḥaqīqa*), like some of the people of *Kalām* argue. Moreover, we know for certain (*natayaqqan*[u]) that the spirit itself does not exist in the body, it is not assimilated in it, and it is described as articulated in the texts veridically and not metaphorically (*ḥaqīqa*[tan] *lā majāz*[an]). When this is our understanding of the essential reality (*ḥaqīqa*) of the spirit and its descriptions—between denial and assimilation—how can we presume anything on the attributes of the Lord of the worlds?![45]

Positioning his hermeneutical approach "between that of the deniers of the divine attributes (*muʿaṭṭila*, i.e., rationalism) and the assimilators (*mumththila*, i.e., corporealism)", Ibn Taymiyya argues to represent the reasonable middle road for understanding the texts of Revelation (this was also the case in his *al-ʿAqīda 'l-wasiṭiyya*). His view in the passage above demonstrates a considerably simplified version of a vast and highly complex discussion on the perception of the human spirit, which is separated from the topic of *ḥaqīqa*/*majāz* and goes beyond the aims of the current study.[46] Nevertheless, Ibn Taymiyya evidently

45 Ibn Taymiyya, *Majmūʿat al-fatāwā*, 5:75–76.

46 Since *al-Ḥamawiyya 'l-kubrā* was written in response to a question that arrived from the people of the Syrian city Hama, its approachable and explanatory tone makes a lot of sense. A similar—yet far more developed—discussion comparing the understanding of the spirit to the *ḥaqīqa* meaning of the divine attributes can be found in Ibn Taymiyya's polemical work against the rationalists *Bayān al-talbīs*. Siding with an ontological perception of the divine attributes, in *Bayān al-talbīs*, Ibn Taymiyya discredits al-Ghazālī's conceptions, which disconnected the human spirit from the physical realm (*ʿālam al-ajsām*) and considered it to be a part of the metaphysical realm (*ʿālam al-amr, lays*[a] *min ʿālam al-khalq*). See for example in: Ibn Taymiyya, *Bayān talbīs al-jahmiyya*, 6:557–558, 564–566.

expresses a stern ontological perception of the divine attributes as veridical realities concerning God, which does not contradict the fact that their modality (*kayfiyya*) cannot be grasped in the human mind. In this respect, Ibn Taymiyya cleverly deploys the traditionalistic formula of *bi-lā kayf*^{a} in order to reject the rationalistic *taʾwīl*, eliminate the use of *majāz*, and fortify the concept of *ḥaqīqa* as actual essence from a theological point of view.

5.3 Ibn al-Qayyim's Rationalized Hermeneutics

In *al-Ṣawāʿiq*, Ibn al-Qayyim starts his third refutation *ṭāghūt* with a general rejection of the later Ashʿarite use of *majāz* as a tedious and redundant instrument used to negate the divine attributes which appear in the textual sources. Moreover, he militantly accuses the rationalists: "they seek refuge in this *ṭāghūt* and turned it into a shield, with which they protect themselves from the shooting arrows [of the attackers] and thrust the veridical-realities (*ḥaqāʾiq*) of the clear Revelation." The aggressive tone of a combatant cannot be mistaken, as it illustrates a roaring battlefield where the *majāz* is a defensive weapon. This time, the task of quickly and correctly identifying the scholar/s Ibn al-Qayyim opposes is slightly trickier than it was in the previous two *ṭawāghīt* refutations. Rather than focusing on the opinion of a single scholar, Ibn al-Qayyim presents several rationalistic definitions to the two chief terms of the following refutation, *ḥaqīqa* and *majāz*:

> Some of them say: *ḥaqīqa* is the commonly used expression (*al-lafẓ*^{u} *'l-mustaʿmal*^{u}) namely the [expression] that was assigned to it originally (*fīmā wuḍiʿ*^{a} *lah*^{u} *awwal*^{an}). Others say, *ḥaqīqa* is the meaning (*maʿnā*) that was assigned to the expression firstly, and *majāz* is the use of an expression in a [meaning] that was assigned to it secondly. So, here we have three matters—expression (*lafẓ*), meaning (*maʿnā*) and usage (*istiʿmāl*). Several of them consider the principle of separation (*taqsīm*; also: classification) to be the first [matter], some consider it to be the second, and others consider it to be the third. Then others say: the *ḥaqīqa* of an expression is 'so and so', and its *majāz* is 'so and so', turning [the two terms] to be of an anomalously accidental meaning. They say, for example: the *ḥaqīqa* of 'lion' is a predator animal and its *majāz* is a brave man, ascribing the *ḥaqīqa* and the *majāz* to the meanings, not to the expressions. When they say that this usage is *ḥaqīqa* and that usage is *majāz*, they refer to the [meaning and the expression] as the [secondary] consequences of the usage (*min tawābiʿ*^{i} *'l-istiʿmāl*^{i}). When they say that this expression

> is *ḥaqīqa* and that expression is *majāz*, they turn them into accidental expressions. And so on and so forth …[47]

Ibn al-Qayyim sets off into the sphere of Arabic linguistics, philology and grammar, which—in the perspective of theological debates (as well as the rest of the religious sciences)—is usually the intellectual comfort zone of the rationalists. This makes no difference for Ibn al-Qayyim, who very roughly sketches a rationalistic diversity of confused and shifting opinions concerning the principal definition of *ḥaqīqa* and *majāz*. He proves his familiarity with the theoretical discussions from Arabic rhetoric regarding the functional connections between expressions, their meanings and usage.[48] With the stroke of a pen, Ibn al-Qayyim manages to heap scorn onto the rationalistic approaches regarding the *ḥaqīqa*/*majāz* dichotomy. Furthermore, in the context of the passage above, the Arabic word *taqsīm* (lit. separating, dividing into parts) relates to the *Kalām*ic logical method of exclusive disjunction,[49] showing Ibn al-Qayyim's blunt mockery towards *Kalām*ic terminology. He clarifies that, for the most part, all rationalists separated evenly between the expression and its signified meaning, or its signified use, in an attempt to achieve three suppositions:

1. Particularizing the primary idea of separation.
2. Establishing the correctness of this separation by showing the similarities and differences between the particles.
3. Showing that the separation requires including all possible aspects; otherwise it is a false separation.

After exhibiting his analytical understanding of the rationalistic viewpoint and ridiculing them, Ibn al-Qayyim criticizes it as a whole. He replies that the rationalistic separation of expressions, their meanings and their use with relation to the forced dichotomy of *ḥaqīqa* and *majāz*—may it be rational (*ʿaqlī*^{yan}), scriptural (*sharʿī*^{yan}), linguistic (*lughawī*^{yan}) or terminological (*iṣṭilāḥī*^{yan})—is false, as are the three suppositions listed above. On the whole, Ibn al-Qayyim

---

47 Ibn Qayyim al-Jawziyya, *Mukhtaṣar al-Ṣawāʿiq* (the abridgement of Ibn al-Mawṣilī), 2:690–691.

48 Further information on the mutual connection between expressions and meanings in these theories is found in several entries in Brill Reference Online—*Encyclopedia of Arabic Language and Linguistics*, such as: "Maʿnā" (by Kouloughli) and "Lafḍ" (author not specified); Aḥmad Māhir al-Baqrī, *Ibn al-Qayyim al-lughawī*, 189–190.

49 For a previous example of Ibn al-Qayyim's utilization of *taqsīm* argumentation, see page 99 in chapter 2 above.

opened his third *ṭāghūt* refutation with an attack on the entire rationalistic array of argumentations—even the entire rationalistic worldview—in a manner that prominently features his capacity of clearly describing the position that he faces.[50]

According to Ibn al-Qayyim, Reason has no role in the assignment of words to their meanings; were it a rational matter, there would be no disagreements concerning it and everyone would know the exact meanings of all expressions. Revelation did not indicate any separation of the language to *ḥaqīqa* or *majāz*. Also, the early Arab linguists (*ahl al-lugha*), such as: the renowned al-Khalīl (d. 173/789), Sibawayh (d. 180/796), or al-Farrā' (d. 207/822) etc., never declared any kind of dichotomy between *ḥaqīqa* and *majāz*. It cannot be found in the sayings of any of the Prophet's companions, their followers or the followers' followers, or in the sayings of any of the four great Imams. Like Ibn Taymiyya before him, Ibn al-Qayyim identifies the philologist Abū ʿUbayda ibn al-Muthannā (d. 209/824–825) as the first to introduce the expression *majāz* to Islam in his work *Majāz al-qur'ān*.[51] Notable is that modern research indeed describes Abū ʿUbayda's *Majāz al-qur'ān* as the first known work of Quran interpretation, containing short notes on the literal meanings of certain words or expressions, which are arranged in accordance with the Sūras' order.[52] Given Ibn Taymiyya's mention of the work in his own denunciation of *majāz*,[53] it may be possible that Ibn al-Qayyim got to know the work via his teacher; however, he might have come across it on his own. At any rate, the main point raised by Ibn al-Qayyim is that rationalistic separation is unknown in the Islamic tradition as well as the Arab linguistic tradition, hence the division between *ḥaqīqa* and *majāz* lacks a sufficient authoritative base. Ibn al-Qayyim constitutes a historical perspective of early Islamic scholarly tradition and confronts it with the later rationalistic development of *majāz* in a declared effort to deprive its legitimacy.

50 Ibn Qayyim al-Jawziyya, *Mukhtaṣar al-Ṣawāʿiq* (the abridgement of Ibn al-Mawṣilī), 2:691–692.

51 Ibn Qayyim al-Jawziyya, *Mukhtaṣar al-Ṣawāʿiq* (the abridgement of Ibn al-Mawṣilī), 2:692–694.

52 Among the scholars who studied the work and the meaning of the term *majāz* therein, one can point out John Wansbrough, Ella Almagor and Wolfhart Heinrichs; H.A.R. Gibb, "Abū ʿUbayda," *EI*^{2}, 1:158; Heinrichs, "Contacts between Scriptural Hermeneutics and Literary Theory in Islam: The Case of *Majāz*," 255; Gilliot, "Exegesis of the Qur'ān: Classical and Medieval," 108.

53 See in page 209 above.

In order to further reinforce this stance, Ibn al-Qayyim turns to the Imam Aḥmad ibn Ḥanbal, providing his opinion on *majāz* as it appears in the work attributed to him titled *al-Radd ʿala ʾl-zanādiqa wal-jahmiyya*.[54] On one occasion, Ibn Ḥanbal explains the co-relation between two Quranic verses said by God to Moses, and shows how they fall into place and supplement one another. The first verse is Q 26:15 "We shall *be with you*." This sentence, phrased according to the rules of the [Arabic] language, or according to what is conventional usage in the language—*min majāz*^{i} *ʾl-lugha*^{ti}; a person may say to his friend: you will receive your reward, I am devoted to you. The second verse is Q 20:46 "I *am with you both*, hearing and seeing everything." Again, Ibn Ḥanbal states that the expression 'to be with someone' bares the meaning of taking care of that person, and it is allowed to be used by the language (*jāʾiz fī ʾl-lugha*). Relying on this account, Ibn al-Qayyim stresses Ibn Ḥanbal intended to what is permitted and not prevented (*lā min*^{a} *ʾl-mumtanaʿ*), and did not mention the *majāz* that is allegedly opposed to *ḥaqīqa*. Rather, like Abū ʿUbayda in *Majāz al-Qurʾān*, he meant literal interpretation in order to ensure the Quranic expressions will be used as they were set by the language, and that they will only be understood according to their literal meaning—*ḥaqīqa*—as they signify veridical reality.[55] Ibn al-Qayyim claims that many Ḥanbalite scholars, such as Abū Yaʿlā[56] and his disciple Ibn ʿAqīl[57] (but also Mālikites and others), expressed this negative attitude towards *majāz*. Moreover, Ibn al-Qayyim maps the two ends of the spectrum of reference to *majāz*, noting there are scholars who have already utterly denied the linguistic existence of *majāz*, such as the early Ashʿarite theologian Abū Isḥāq al-Isfarāyīnī.[58] Ibn al-Qayyim asserts many of the later scholars failed to comprehend the depth of his statement, as they considered this to be a mere linguistic debate. Ibn al-Qayyim ensures that al-Isfarāyīnī's way is the most truthful one in terms of Reason (*asadd*^{u} *wa-aṣaḥḥ*^{u} *ʿaql*^{an}) and it is an approach that was arrived at within the school of the proponents of *majāz* (i.e., the Ashʿarites). At the other extreme, other scholars—Ibn al-Qayyim hints at the Muʿtazilite school—exaggerated their support of *majāz* to the point of

54 Jon Hoover, "Ḥanbalī Theology," *The Oxford Handbook of Islamic Theology*, ed. Sabine Schmidtke (Oxford: Oxford University Press, 2016), online version pp. 3–4; See footnote 72 in chapter 1 above.

55 Aḥmad ibn Ḥanbal, *al-Radd ʿala ʾl-zanādiqa wal-jahmiyya*, 49; Heinrichs, "Contacts between Scriptural Hermeneutics and Literary Theory in Islam: The Case of *Majāz*," 116–117.

56 See footnote 3 in chapter 3 above.

57 See footnote 4 in chapter 3 above.

58 See footnote 28 in this chapter.

announcing that most of the language is *majāz*, indeed, even all of it. In Ibn al-Qayyim's eyes, their tactics is utterly repugnant and shameful.[59]

Presenting the support the discussed comprehension of the word *majāz* received, Ibn al-Qayyim concludes that dividing the expressions into two separate kinds of meaning—veridical-literal (*ḥaqīqa*) vs. metaphorical (*majāz*)—is not grounded in Reason of either religious tradition or linguistics. Thus, he discerns *majāz* as a figurative utterance is merely a technical term, or 'just a term' (*iṣṭilāḥ*^un^ *maḥḍ*^un^),[60] that appeared after the third century of Islam. It originated from the Muʿtazilite school, its rationalistic carriers (*jahmiyya*) and the scholars of *Kalām*.[61] From this point onwards, Ibn al-Qayyim endeavors to admonish the rationalistic vast employment of allegorical interpretation by *majāz* in their hermeneutical treatment of the Islamic sources, with special consideration given to the theological issue of the divine attributes. He lists more than 50 aspects (*wujūh*) of refutation, all of which target the rebuke of *majāz* and its advocates; this polemical discussion comprises the entire first bulk of the third *ṭāghūt* refutation.

Meticulous screening of these materials enables us to detect Ibn al-Qayyim's positive conceptualization of the suitable hermeneutics to be applied to the divine attributes as they appear in the scriptures of Islam. The first hermeneutical element Ibn al-Qayyim touches on is the habitual linguistic conventions of the Arabic language (*ʿurf*, or *kalām al-ʿArab*—the language of the Bedouin), which should be followed in order to correctly understand the Quran and Hadith.[62] The customary use of grammar and semantics is to be followed out of the belief that human language originated in Revelation. In this respect, Ibn

59 Ibn Qayyim al-Jawziyya, *Mukhtaṣar al-Ṣawāʿiq* (the abridgement of Ibn al-Mawṣilī), 2:694–699.

60 Ibn Taymiyya and Ibn al-Qayyim often use the word *maḥḍ* (lit. pure, clear) to disparage the *Kalām*ic terminology. See for example, in: Ibn Taymiyya, *al-Radd ʿala 'l-manṭiqiyyīn*, 1:176 (where Ibn Taymiyya scorns the rationalistic use of syllogism, *qiyās*), or in: Ibn Qayyim al-Jawziyya, *al-Ṣawāʿiq al-mursala*, 1:228, 230 (where Ibn al-Qayyim rejects the denial of the divine attributes, *taʿṭīl*).

61 Ibn Qayyim al-Jawziyya, *Mukhtaṣar al-Ṣawāʿiq* (the abridgement of Ibn al-Mawṣilī), 2:700; Belgacem Hammam, "Jadaliyyat al-ta'wīl wal-majāz ʿind^a^ Ibn Qayyim al-Jawziyya min khilāl^i^ kitābih^i^ al-Ṣawāʿiq al-mursala," *Fikr wa-Ibdāʿ* (2010?), 245–249, 259–260; Aḥmad Māhir al-Baqrī, *Ibn al-Qayyim al-lughawī*, 191–195.

62 Arab grammarians considered the customary use of Arabic as spoken by the Bedouin tribes even in pre-Islamic times to be a role model for eloquence. This is the language of the Quran and poetry; Versteegh, "Linguistic Attitudes and the Origin of Speech in the Arab World," 15–17. Nevertheless, Ibn al-Qayyim evenly speaks of the 'language of the Arabs' and 'all other languages'; ibid, 2:757.

al-Qayyim reveals his close familiarity with the rationalistic approach as he depicts 'their most famous canon', saying that "*ḥaqīqa* is the used expression in its originally assigned meaning," while some of the rationalists added to this definition "according to the convention of discourse" (*fī 'l-'urf^i 'l-ladhī waqa'^a bih^i 'l-takhāṭub^u*). In this manner, three kinds of *ḥaqīqa*—or three kinds of literal-veridical meanings—appear: linguistic (*lughawiyya*), revelational (*shar'iyya*, also: legally binding) and conventional (*'urfiyya*). Exploiting this rationalistic definition to his dialectical benefit, Ibn al-Qayyim questions the concept of the imposition of language (*waḍ'*) and contests the theory of *iṣṭilāḥ* as a whole, more specifically with respect to the concept of *majāz*. Identifying the Mu'tazilite provenance of later Ash'arite stances, Ibn al-Qayyim opposes the view held and promoted by the Mu'tazilite scholar Abū Hishām al-Jubbā'ī (d. 321/933)[63] and his followers in favor of the establishment of language by humankind. In fact, Ibn al-Qayyim says, the assignment of meanings to expressions becomes so arbitrary that the theoretical discussion on the linguistics behind it loses its credibility; all the more so when it comes to an assignment of figurative meanings, as proclaimed by *majāz*. The habitual usage of the Arabic language is perceived as a theoretical guideline in itself, preceding both theories of *tawqīf* and *iṣṭilāḥ* and evenly overpowering both of them. Shifting the meanings of commonly used expressions is forbidden regarding the created things (*ḥarām fī ḥaqq^i 'l-makhlūq^i*), so how can it be applied regarding the speech of God and His Messenger, (i.e., Revelation)? Ibn al-Qayyim sees the veracity of Revelation as the validating means of the already recognized usage of language, hence neutralizing the discussion on the origin of languages from being an argument to justify *majāz*.[64] Once again, Ibn al-Qayyim strives to prove the rationalists wrong as he thoroughly examines the argument at hand and discovers possible logical weaknesses therein. The principal he stresses is of course that of fideism and reliance on Revelation as the foundation of all

---

63 Abū Hāshim 'Abd al-Salām [ibn] al-Jubbā'ī was Mu'tazilite scholar with a Sunnite tendency (son of the famous Mu'tazilite of the same name al-Jubbā'ī, d. in 303/915–916). He was known for his theory of modes (*aḥwāl*) concerning the divine attributes, which was conceptualized to support the Mu'tazilite idea of *ta'ṭīl*, as in "negating the actual reality/essence of the attributes." According to this theory, the attributes are turned into simple terms or words, which represent the intermediate state "between existence and non-existence." This approach evolved its way into the ideas of many Islamic philosophers, rationalists and scholars of *Kalām*; L. Gardet, "al-Djubbā'ī," *EI*², 2:569–570; idem, "al-Asmā' al-Ḥusnā," *EI*², 1:714.

64 Ibn Qayyim al-Jawziyya, *Mukhtaṣar al-Ṣawā'iq* (the abridgement of Ibn al-Mawṣilī), 2:701–702.

human knowledge, including linguistics; a thesis known in Islamic tradition as *tawqīf*.[65] He finds flaws in the manner in which the supporters of *majāz* deploy the notions of linguistic *waḍʿ* (the a priori predetermined assignment of meaning to an expression) and *isitiʿmāl* (the speaker's intended usage of the expression);[66] in fact, he remarks on a principle phenomenon that is known to have already caused intellectual difficulties among Muslim linguistic theorists themselves concerning *majāz* and its relation to the concept of *waḍʿ*.[67] At any rate, Ibn al-Qayyim's intention is obvious—the commonly known use of the language, its expressions and meanings prevail when they are confronted with any other random or sporadic figure of speech such as *majāz*.

Another element of importance in the positive hermeneutical conceptualization suggested by Ibn al-Qayyim is the semantic context (*al-qarina/qarāʾin al-maʿnawiyya*) in which an expression appears. As an alternative to the idea of *majāz* as a generator of a figurative meaning, Ibn al-Qayyim recaps the known terms *iṭlāq* (lit. loosening) and *taqyīd* (lit. tying, restricting), which are observed as an inseparable part of the existing context of an expression and its connection with other elements in a sentence; this idea can be translated as the dichotomy of unqualified/qualified meaning.[68] Thus, the usage of an expression can take place either in an expanded manner which loosens and broadens its meaning (by *iṭlāq*) and creates an unqualified meaning, or in a restricted manner which limits it (by *tqyīd*) and creates a qualified meaning. One way or another, the expression describes a veridical reality (*ḥaqīqa*) and is to be literally understood in line with the linguistic and grammatical structure in which it is constructed (*al-qayd bil-tarkīb*). Already available in the framework of Arabic linguistics, this explanation annuls the legitimacy of *majāz* as a semantic case. Ibn al-Qayyim carefully develops this opinion, stating that the natural and obvious understanding (*mā yutādabir^u ila ʾl-dhihn^i*) of the expression within the sentence is the correct one and is only *ḥaqīqa*. An expression without qualification (*qayd*) and grammatical construction (*tarkīb*) is "in the status of cried

65 Shah, "Classical Islamic Discourse on the Origins of Language," 314–320, 325–326.

66 Simon, "Majāz," *Encyclopedia of Arabic Language and Linguistics*, online source; in addition, these two terms appear and are applied in the vast corpus of Islamic legal theory (*uṣūl al-fiqh*, principles of law). A helpful study on their respective roles in Islamic textual communication is found in: Ali, *Medieval Islamic Pragmatics*, 15–36. Relevant is the fact that the majority of sources discussed in Ali's chapter are written by Ashʿarite scholars.

67 Ali, *Medieval Islamic Pragmatics*, 17; Weiss, "Medieval Muslim Discussions of the Origin of Language," 34–39.

68 Ali, *Medieval Islamic Pragmatics*, 118–119; Belgacem Hammam, "Jadaliyyat al-taʾwīl wal-majāz ʿind^a Ibn Qayyim al-Jawziyya min khilāl^i kitābih^i al-Ṣawāʿiq al-mursala," 261–263.

voices which produce no meaning."[69] In fact, Ibn al-Qayyim replies directly to the opinion of the Ash'arite scholar al-Āmidī in his work *Iḥkām al-ḥukm fī uṣūl al-aḥkām*.[70] In a lengthy discussion there, al-Āmidī articulates his support of the differentiation between *ḥaqīqa* and *majāz*, arguing that an abstract and unqualified expression isolated from a context (*min iṭlāq*ⁱ *'l-lafẓ min ghayr*ⁱ *qarīna*ᵗⁱⁿ) is separated from other expressions, so that the obvious understanding thereof is *ḥaqīqa* and the other one is *majāz*.[71]

Ibn al-Qayyim unequivocally announces: expressions must appear in a context in order to convey a valuable meaning and, when they do, they describe veridical reality (*ḥaqīqa*). As far as he is concerned, this determined contextual approach of hermeneutics is not up for compromise. Below Ibn al-Qayyim illustrates this guideline relying on examples derived from typical traditionalistic materials of the Islamic texts and Arab tradition:

> The same goes for the expression 'belief'—when it is unqualified (*'ind*ᵃ *'l-iṭlāq*), it includes the religious deeds. Like in the saying of the Prophet, peace be upon him: Belief is 77 [deeds], the superior of which is the announcement 'there is no god but God', and the lowest of which is removing harms out of the way. Life is but a portion of the belief. Concerning the religious deeds (*a'māl*), his signified meaning was the verification in the heart (*al-taṣdīq bil-qalb*), as said [in the Quran, 103:3] "believe, do good deeds." So, the signified meaning of [the expression 'belief'] has changed in these two instances by its expansion and qualification (*bil-iṭlāq*ⁱ *wal-taqyīd*ⁱ), and it describes reality (*ḥaqīqa*) in both cases.
>
> In a similar manner, the expressions 'poor man' (*faqīr*) and 'unfortunate man' (*maskīn*)—one is included in the other, when they are expanded/unqualified. But when they are put together, one's nominatum (*musammā*) is not included in the other's [...]
>
> Of further specification is when an expression is used only in a qualified manner (*muqayyad*ᵃⁿ), such as 'head', 'injuries', or 'hand' etc.; the Arabs did not use these expressions in an unqualified manner, but only [in an annexation], like 'head of a man', 'head of a bird', 'head of a beast',

---

69 Ibn Qayyim al-Jawziyya, *Mukhtaṣar al-Ṣawā'iq* (the abridgement of Ibn al-Mawṣilī), 2:718–720.

70 The editor of *Mukhtaṣar al-Ṣawā'iq* identified this and referred to it in his footnotes; Ibn Qayyim al-Jawziyya, *Mukhtaṣar al-Ṣawā'iq* (the abridgement of Ibn al-Mawṣilī), 2:719. More details on al-Āmidī and his work appear in footnote 36 in this chapter.

71 Sayf al-Dīn al-Āmidī, *Iḥkām al-ḥukm fī uṣūl al-aḥkām*, ed. Sayyid al-Jamīlī, in 4 vols. (Beirut: Dār al-Kitāb al-'Arabī, 1404/1983), 1:55–56.

> 'head of the water' [i.e., the water's origin of spring, a well head], 'head of a matter' [i.e., its beginning], 'head of property' [i.e., capital], 'head of a tribe' [its leader]. Here, the two parts of the annexation (*al-muḍāf wal-muḍāf ilayhⁱ*) form a reality together (*ḥaqīqa*), and when joined to one another they are two subjects. Whoever holds the delusion that the origin (*aṣl*) is the head of a human and it was transferred therefrom to the rest of these expressions, is awfully mistaken, and articulates a saying that they have absolutely no knowledge upon. If another person showed then the opposite of what they had said, there would be no difference between the two. The subject of conflict is the expression of qualified meaning (*al-muqayyad*), whereas the expression of unqualified meaning (*al-muṭlaq*) is not even used [in speech].[72]

The notion of qualification of the expression's meaning is in fact anchored within the common usage of language, for example, in an annexations (*iḍāfa*) such as 'a wing of a bird' (*janāḥ al-ṭā'ir*) or basic figures of speech such as: 'the wing of travel' (*janāḥ al-safar*), meaning a long journey or 'lowering the gentle wing' (*janāḥ al-dhull*), meaning one's submissiveness to their parents.[73] As Ibn al-Qayyim sees it, the expression 'wing' in every one of the above phrases is evenly *ḥaqīqa*. A 'wing' in this respect is not always a wing of feathers, but a semantic wing pertaining to its meaning (*janāḥ ma'nawī*). This is a general rule which applies to all expressions of this kind. In the same vein, the joint particle in a phrase is not a homonym (*mushtarak ishtirāk^{an} lafẓiy^{yan}*), but rather it is acknowledged that there is a certain similarity—or a shared value (*al-qadar al-mushtarak*)—between the expressions, such as the bravery shared by both 'a lion' (*asad*) and a 'heroic person' (*al-rajul al-shajā'*). 'Bravery' itself is of course a description of veridical reality, and is therefore *ḥaqīqa*. Ibn al-Qayyim maintains that considering them to be *ḥaqīqa* just because of that clearly shared value is also an error, since they were both *ḥaqīqa* to begin with. That kind of explanation unfolds a previous separation between the two expressions, which is—as already established by Ibn al-Qayyim—unjust.[74]

Responding to yet another rationalistic claim involving the contextual approach, Ibn al-Qayyim speaks of the context of expression (*al-qarā'in al-lafẓiy-*

---

72 Ibn Qayyim al-Jawziyya, *Mukhtaṣar al-Ṣawā'iq* (the abridgement of Ibn al-Mawṣilī), 2:721–722.

73 Lane, *Arabic-English Lexicon / Book I*, 2:469. The same example is found in Ibn Taymiyya's writing, as can be seen in: Ali, *Medieval Islamic Pragmatics*, 120, 123–124.

74 Ibn Qayyim al-Jawziyya, *Mukhtaṣar al-Ṣawā'iq* (the abridgement of Ibn al-Mawṣilī), 2:723.

ya) and semantic context (*al-qarāʾin al-maʿnawiyya* or *al-qarāʾin al-ʿaqliyya*; also: context of Reason), emphasizing that the latter is the one in relation to which expressions gain their meaning. This clarification arrives in the course of his reply to the rationalistic separation between the context of expression (*al-qarāʾin al-lafẓiyya*) and context of Reason (*al-qarāʾin al-ʿaqliyya*); when the understanding of an expression requires a context of Reason, the expression is *majāz*, and when understanding requires a context of expression, it is *ḥaqīqa*.[75] Ibn al-Qayyim rebukes this view, sustaining that Reason has nothing to do with expressions' assignment of meanings. Expressions are comprehended by their linguistic transference (*naql*)[76] and usage (*istiʿmāl*), when Reason perceives their intention by the means of: 1. the habitual use of an expression in a certain meaning; 2. the knowledge that the speaker intended this meaning to be understood. Context in itself—excluding expressions—does not signify any meaning, be it *ḥaqīqa*, *majāz* or anything else. Several other rationalistic reasoning attempts of corresponding spirit are noted by Ibn al-Qayyim only to be refuted shortly after, leaving the reader well informed of his adherence to the concepts of context-dependency and the literal-veridical understanding of expressions.[77]

Ibn al-Qayyim further conceptualizes his positive hermeneutical approach, maintaining that the entire language is to be taken at face value as *ḥaqīqa* and that there is no such thing as *majāz*. He reaches this generalization as he thoroughly probes and repudiates a number of rationalistic suppositions in the field of linguistics, which were deployed by Ashʿarite scholars in order to justify the theological use of *majāz*. A fascinating example of this can be seen in Ibn al-Qayyim's reprimand of the claims of the philologist and grammarian Ibn Jinnī Abu 'l-Fatḥ ʿUthmān (d. 392/1002), who claimed most of language is *majāz*, therefore is understood as metaphorical speech.[78] This notion was carried forward in Ibn Jinnī's teachings and is also apparent in the works of

75 Noteworthy is that despite the difference of subject, to a certain extent this rationalistic model of dual context reminds one of the Avicennan usage of the word *ḥaqīqa* in that it distinguishes between its ontological meaning (*ḥaqīqat al-shayʾ*) and logical meaning (*al-ḥaqīqa al-ʿaqliyya*); Louis Gardet, "Ḥaḳīḳa," *EI*², 3:75–76. That is to say, there seems to be a significant diffusion of ideas from the general discourse of *falsafa* and the rhetorical/linguistic discourse employed here by Ibn al-Qayyim. The term *ḥaqīqa* will be discussed separately in this chapter.

76 For an explanation on this kind of *naql*, see page 202 above.

77 Ibn Qayyim al-Jawziyya, *Mukhtaṣar al-Ṣawāʿiq* (the abridgement of Ibn al-Mawṣilī), 2:725, 780–781.

78 See further elaboration on Ibn Jinnī in Ibn al-Qayyim's discussion in section 5.4 hereinafter. The editor of *Mukhtaṣar al-Ṣawāʿiq* notes that Ibn al-Qayyim refers here to Ibn

his pupils, who at times stated "all is *majāz*" (i.e., all of the language is to be figuratively understood). As Ibn al-Qayyim explains Ibn Jinnī's ideas, he mentions this includes all verbs (*afʿāl*), for example: "got up" (*qām^{a}*), "sat" (*qaʿad^{a}*), "went away" (*inṭalaq^{a}*) or "arrived" (*jāʾ^{a}*), for a verb imparts a generic quality (*jinsiyya*) to an action. According to Ibn al-Qayyim, the intention in this statement is that the Quranic verses are all metaphorical expressions with no veridical reality, including those in which God described Himself as the source of the divine Message and Islamic faith, such as: (Q 9:33) "It is He who has sent His Messenger with guidance and the religion of truth," (Q 4:79) "We have sent you as a messenger to people," or (Q 2:213) "God sent prophets to bring good news and warning." More so, the perception of all verbs (*afʿāl*) denoting generic actions expands/un-qualifies their meanings as being completely abstract (i.e., to the past, present and all other forms of possible beings). To Ibn al-Qayyim, this does not make any sense; how could it be that ambiguous and illusive action may as well roam around and never in a hundred years meet a single person in a single time? This is absurd and, had it been possible, even the most basic sentence "Zayd got up" (*qām^{a} Zayd^{un}*) would be allegorically understood as a metaphor with no basis in reality. As a matter of fact, Ibn al-Qayyim vigorously turns the discussion towards the divine actions attributed to God (*afʿāl al-Allāh*), thus accusing Ibn Jinnī of stripping God of His honorable acts by regarding them as mere metaphors. The creation of the skies and the earth, sending the divine Message to humankind or God's sitting above on His throne—all of these are reduced into expressions of no veridical reality nor essence, and therefore are ashamed of God and express heresy and madness. "Creating" becomes a generic act that is not performed by God, because it just came into existence (*ḥādith*); it is a mere metaphor used in speech that conveys a non-existential relation (*al-taʿalluq al-ʿadamī*) between that which is created and the Creator.[79]

Ibn al-Qayyim goes further by analytically sketching the trajectory of linguistic reasoning followed by Ibn Jinnī and his supporters, who made wrongful use of *majāz*, while contrasting them to sensible people (*ʿuqalāʾ*; people of common sense). Exploiting the leverage gained by contesting the extreme exam-

---

Jinnī's important work *Al-Khaṣāʾiṣ fī ʿilm uṣūl al-ʿarabiyya* (Particularities in the Science of Arabic Foundations). This work will shortly be referred to as well; Ibn Qayyim al-Jawziyya, *Mukhtaṣar al-Ṣawāʿiq* (the abridgement of Ibn al-Mawṣilī), 2:699, 771–772.

79 Ibid, 2:772–773. Ibn al-Qayyim implicitly responds here to the Muʿtazilite—and afterwards, Ashʿarite—differentiation between "attributes of essence" (*ṣifāt al-dhāt*) and "attributes of act" (*ṣifāt al-fiʿl*), which he clearly finds unnecessary; Claude Gilliot, "Attributes of God," *Encyclopaedia of Islam, THREE*. 1:176–180.

ple of Ibn Jinnī, Ibn al-Qayyim strikes the mainstream Ashʿarite rationalists by assimilating the linguistic elements used in their hermeneutical methodology. Ibn Jinnī's approach in favor of *majāz* first concentrates on the absolute generalization and generic understanding of acts as referring to all individuals and universals (*dalālat al-fiʿl ʿalā jamiʿi ʾl-afrādi wal-jinsi*); when a general act is qualified to an agent/carrier (*al-taqyīd bil-fāʿil*) it becomes a metaphor. In parallel, another classification used to explain a metaphorical understanding of expressions is by specifying a general signification (*takhṣīṣ al-ʿāmm*).[80] Ibn Jinnī used a narrowing mechanism which, according to him, creates a figure of speech, since the expression is removed from its assigned meaning (*ikhrāj ʿan al-mawḍūʿi*):

> Even if Ibn Jinnī and his supporters recognized the veridical reality (*ḥaqīqa*) of God's acts, they would consider them to be metaphors because of [the rule] that they settled regarding the signification (*dalāl*) of the verb onto individuals and universals. Then, when [Ibn Jinnī and his supporters] are ashamed of that in front of the sensible people, they say that [the acts] are *ḥaqīqa* [i.e., describe reality]. Thus, they are compelled to admit the contradiction (*fa-yaltazimuhumu ʾl-tanāquḍu*)—the simplest compeller of all (*aysaru ʾl-lāzimīna*), since verbs signify an unqualified origin, not a general one. So, when they are compelled to admit that [God's acts] are metaphors for their qualification to a carrier—that is the same case as the earlier compelling argument (*iltizām*), that specifying general expressions turns them into *majāz*. As they force [the first part of the Islamic profession of faith] 'there is no God but Allah' to be a metaphor, they force [its second part] "and Muḥammad is His Messenger" to be a metaphor for the qualification of the unqualified [expression] already changed its assignment; like the claim that specifying the general [expression] already changed its assignment. Both of these arguments are wrong and most despicable, because an expression does not change its assigned [meaning] by specification, neither by qualification.

80 In the science of the founding of language, two different classifications were set up for the assignment of meanings to expressions: one classification distinguished a generic assignment (*waḍʿ nawʿī*) from an individualized assignment (*waḍʿ shakhṣī*); another classification distinguished a general assignment (*waḍʿ ʿāmm*) from a specific assignment (*waḍʿ khāṣṣ*), and it reflects more jurisprudential interests; Weiss, "Waḍʿ al-Luġa," *Encyclopedia of Arabic Language and Linguistics*, online source; Aḥmad Māhir al-Baqrī, *Ibn al-Qayyim al-lughawī*, 198, 201–205.

> Even if an expression was changed/removed from its assigned [meaning] by specification or qualification, it would have several assignments in accordance with its various qualifications. Then, it could be announced as (1) *majāz* in all of them, (2) *ḥaqīqa* in all of them or (3) *majāz*/*ḥaqīqa* alternately. The first and third options are false; so that the second one is kept … the expression's signification may vary [in utterances expressing negation, question, passive form, imperative etc.], but it is *ḥaqīqa* in all of them … This is always the case whether you add qualifications [of meaning] in a clear reasonable Arabic language, or decrease the signification of an unqualified expression, and it does not change its essential reality (*ḥaqīqatih*[i]). Whoever claims that [the expression] loses its reality and is changed/removed from its assignment form is mistaken. So, if you say 'we voyaged upon the sea and it gushed with us' (*rakibna 'l-baḥr*[a] *fa-hāj*[a] *binā*), this is *ḥaqīqa*; and if you say 'we came to the sea seeking for its knowledge'—this is *ḥaqīqa*. If you say 'we embarked on a journey and suddenly a lion appeared and interrupted our way', this speech's intention is self-evident; and if you say 'we stayed with the lion and it protected us and welcomed us in' (*nazalnā ʿala 'l-asad*[i] *fa-ḥamānā wa-aqrānā*)—this is self-evident and *ḥaqīqa*. The expression ['lion'] is assigned in these two meanings and is used either as qualified or unqualified evenly. What is the difference between [the utterances] so that the expression to be announced as *majāz* in some cases and *ḥaqīqa* in others? For that understanding of those of "sharp minds", two groups were formed: a group which denied the *majāz* completely and a group which announced that the whole language—apart from rare exceptions—is *majāz*. They saw the fault of those [pro-*majāz*] groups and their contradiction and do not find contentment in it and in their cold judgment.[81]

This passage sheds more light on Ibn al-Qayyim's comprehension of the term *ḥaqīqa* as an expression of essential reality, which therefore must be understood as stated in the text for the assignment of meaning (i.e., in its literal obvious sense together with its surrounding context). Important in relation to his positive conceptualization of hermeneutics, rebuking the opinions that linguistically legitimize *majāz* drives Ibn al-Qayyim to infer here an ontological essentialism concerning the divine attributes having an essential prop-

81 Ibn Qayyim al-Jawziyya, *Mukhtaṣar al-Ṣawāʿiq* (the abridgement of Ibn al-Mawṣilī), 2:773–775.

erty of reality. Such traditionalistic perception of divine attributes had already appeared in the advanced teachings of Ibn Taymiyya,[82] and yet Ibn al-Qayyim endorses it here at a sheer *Kalām*ic level by his rationalization of the familiar argument—most evidently by forcing his ideological adversaries to acknowledge an absurdum. Looking at the dialectical features in the passage above, Ibn al-Qayyim's application of *ilzām* arguments (in the beginning of the citation) is notable as is his use of *taqsīm* exclusive disjunction[83] (listing the three possibilities—language is all *majāz*/ all *ḥaqīqa*/ may mutually alternate). In addition, Ibn al-Qayyim brings up numerous examples of specific linguistic cases as evidence to support his claim and implements a logical deduction. Not unintentional, Ibn al-Qayyim's general contentious and denouncing tone wraps everything up in a speculative envelope which serves the end of his discussion on abolishing the *ḥaqīqa*/*majāz* dichotomy well and proving that most—if not all—language expressions describe and convey veridical reality (*ḥaqīqa*).[84]

Another remarkable reason Ibn al-Qayyim presents to sustain the conceptualization of *ḥaqīqa* as the only possible state of all expressions involves the principle of linguistic qualification of meaning itself (*taqyīd*). The following is an excerpt that illustrates an *a fortiori* argument raised by Ibn al-Qayyim against what he perceives to be extremist assessments of the theological implications of the *ḥaqīqa/majāz* dichotomy:

> These expressions, which are used with respect to the Creator and the created, can be reflected upon in three ways: the first is that they are qualified to the Creator, such as God's hearing, His seeing, His face, His hands, His sitting on the throne, His descent, His knowledge, His ability and His life. The second is that [the expressions] are qualified to the created, such as a hand of a human, his face, and his hands,[85] and his sitting [possibly on a throne]. The third is that [the expressions] are isolated/abstracted from both of the forms of annexations (*tujarrad*^{u} *'an kila 'l-iḍāfatayn*^{i}), and exist unqualified (*wa-tūjad*^{u} *muṭlaqa*^{tun}).
>
> You do affirm that [the expressions] have an essential reality (*ḥaqīqa*) whether we take the first consideration, or the second, or the third, as

82 Hoover, Ibn Taymiyya's *Theodicy of Perpetual Optimism*, 95–96. Also, see section 5.2 above.

83 Also, see footnote 106 in chapter 2 above.

84 Ibn Qayyim al-Jawziyya, *Mukhtaṣar al-Ṣawāʿiq* (the abridgement of Ibn al-Mawṣilī), 2:776–777. Ibn al-Qayyim's depicted approach also appears, with regard to Ibn Taymiyya's view, in: Mohamed M. Yunis Ali in *Medieval Islamic Pragmatics*, 117–119.

85 The repetition of the 'divine hands' appears in the original text.

> there is no forth [possibility] here. Therefore, if you consider them [i.e., the expressions] to be *ḥaqīqa* for its qualification to the Creator, then they are *majāz* when [qualified to] the created. This is the viewpoint held by Abu 'l-ʿAbbās al-Nāshī (d. 293/906)[86] and his group. If you consider them [i.e., the expressions] to be *ḥaqīqa* for its qualification to the created, then they are *majāz* when [qualified to] the Creator. This is the standpoint of the "Imam of the denying-group" (*imam al-muʿaṭṭila*), Jahm ibn Ṣafwān,[87] and his proponents followed him [i.e., the Muʿtazilites]. If you consider them [i.e., the expressions] to be *ḥaqīqa* for the common value (*al-qadr al-mushtarak*) without stating a differentiating value (*al-qadar al-mumayyiz*) instead of it, then they are *ḥaqīqa* both [when qualified to] the Creator and the created. This is the stance of all sensible people (*ʿāmmat al-ʿuqalāʾ*, people of common sense) and it is correct. If you separate some expressions from the others, you create a contradiction and degraded judgment.[88]

Arguing in favor of the absolute essentiality of expressions attributed to God and mankind alike, Ibn al-Qayyim entwines previous—and somewhat opposing—hermeneutical approaches, while reproving them both. Since the *ḥaqīqa*-particle exists in all variations of the rationalistic dichotomy of *ḥaqīqa* and *majāz*, Ibn al-Qayyim sees it as a sufficient "middle term" to confirm the syllogistic argument drawn from the general premise that 'all expressions have an essential meaning of reality'. According to Ibn al-Qayyim, some say this *ḥaqīqa* is confined to created beings alone, others say it refers only to God; either way, expressions entail *ḥaqīqa*. Furthermore, Ibn al-Qayyim finds no supplementary

---

86 ʿAbdallāh ibn Muḥammad ibn Shirshīr al-Anbārī, was a poet and a Muʿtazilite theologian, although he remained an outsider from the Muʿtazilite mainstream of his lifetime. His opinions seem to be closer to the Murjiʾties. Segnificant in this context is the observation made by van Ess that, "He stressed the singularity of God in a way unheard of in the Muʿtazila up to that time, by denying even nominal similarity with creation: God is the absolute Other in contrast to whom man cannot be said to possess positive attributes (like knowing, acting etc.) unless in a metaphorical way. The only exception he made was with respect to the Prophet: when Muḥammad brought forth the revelation he spoke the truth in a veritative, not only in a metaphorical way. Moreover, the metaphorical character of human action did not entail determinism; man has a free will because he possesses a soul which grants him free disposition of his body"; Josef van Ess, "al-Nās͟hiʾ al-Akbar", *EI*², 7:975.

87 See more details on Jahm ibn Ṣafwān in page 46 above.

88 Ibn Qayyim al-Jawziyya, *Mukhtaṣar al-Ṣawāʿiq* (the abridgement of Ibn al-Mawṣilī), 2:749–750.

ground for separating the usage of expressions as it is done in the rationalistic arguments. Thus, for Ibn al-Qayyim, these claims are unconvincing and lead to error. His terminology sounds as if it were an intrinsic part of the *Kalām*ic discourse.[89] Once again, Ibn al-Qayyim exhibits a skillful deployment of logical reasoning tools and methodologies which enables him to detect flaws in his adversaries' reasoning and effectively eliminate them.

In another place, Ibn al-Qayyim goes as far as to distinguish between two kinds of *ḥaqīqa*, contrasting between that of God and that of the creation. This appears in a work Ibn al-Qayyim composed prior to *al-Ṣawāʿiq* titled *Badāʾiʿ al-fawāʾid* (The Amazing Benefits).[90] In fact, the passage cited above was already mentioned in the text of *Badāʾiʿ al-fawāʾid*, with slight alterations and in a simplified fashion. The stylistic difference between *al-Badāʾiʿ* and *al-Ṣawāʿiq* can be a result of the natural refinement process; from an earlier work to a more mature one. Another explanation may be a shift in the audience Ibn al-Qayyim wished to address in each work (several aspects of Ibn al-Qayyim's authorship were inspected in chapter 2 of this study, but currently my main interest is a content analysis based on the two versions of the cited passage rather than a close comparison of them).

In *Badāʾiʿ al-fawāʾid*, Ibn al-Qayyim explains the two *ḥaqīqatayn* utterly differ from one another; however, this dissimilarity does not prevent either of them from being an essential reality in both God and his created beings (*wa-ikhtilāf*[u] *'l-ḥaqīqatayn*[i] *fihimā lā yukhrijuhā ʿan kawnihā ḥaqīqa*[tan] *fihimā*). The condition for a valid expansion of names such as "seeing" or "hearing" is the correct appropriation of their meanings and essential realities to the described object. Those names and attributes are not attached to the described essence. Therefore, there is no danger in ascribing an attribute like "face" to God; but rather God is to be affirmed (by *ithbāt*) as having a "face" that is not similar or likened to His creation. Whoever negates the attribute of "face" concerning God for its expansion to the created human beings deviates from the righteous way in the matter of His names and denies His attributes of perfection. Whoever assimilates the face of God with that of His human creation likens God to the creation and commits heresy. However, whoever affirms the face of God—which is unlike that of His creation, but is appropriate to His majesty and omnipotence—they are free of the waste of anthropomorphism (*tashbīh*)

89 An examination of the *kalām*ic use of argumentations of syllogism and differentiation (*tamyyiz*) is found in: van Ess, "The Logical Structure of Islamic Theology," 27–29, 38.

90 See more details on the work in section 2.1, page 60.

and the blood of negating the divine attributes (*taʿṭīl*);[91] this is the way of the traditionalists (*ahl al-sunna*).[92]

Ibn al-Qayyim continues by sustaining the outright disparity between the *ḥaqīqa* attributes respectively ascribed to God and human beings, in spite of the terminological identity. In his opinion, assigning an attribute to the created human does not always result in an obligation to deny this when it is ascribed to God. Obviously, mundane human traits are to be denied concerning God, such as the limited human 'life' that depends on the need to sleep and eat, or the human will to attain benefit and to avoid harm, or human aboveness that is dependent on whatever it is beneath them; all qualities of this kind must be negated when referring to the God. In a similar vein, assigning an attribute to God does not always result in its specification to Him alone. The creations cannot be described as having His divine face, nor His eternal compelling all-reaching knowledge, His omnipotence, His obliging divine will and so on. These special deity traits are impossible to be affirmed with relation to human beings. Ibn al-Qayyim states, if we embrace this principle and aptly understand it, the two afflictions of the *Kalām* scholars will be eradicated: likening God to His creation (*tashbīh*) and the negation of His attributes (*taʿṭīl*). The divine attributes must be affirmed as conveying the meaning of the essential realities of God.[93]

Positioning the righteous path in between the two extremes of corporealism and rationalism, Ibn al-Qayyim structures a nuanced hermeneutical approach true to the teachings of his mentor Ibn Taymiyya (as discussed in section 5.2 above). The main claim raised by Ibn al-Qayyim—that *majāz* was developed as a Muʿtazilite hermeneutic device—had previously appeared in Ibn Taymiyya's thought. In truth, Ibn Taymiyya drew on preceding traditionalistic views, and even from the terminology used in *al-Radd ʿala 'l-zanādiqa wal-jahmiyya*, which is attributed to Aḥmad ibn Ḥanbal.[94] The text of *al-Ṣawāʿiq* is abundant with additional sources of inspiration for Ibn al-Qayyim's hermeneutical discussion, the core of which will be surveyed in section 5.5 henceforth. Notable is that Ibn al-Qayyim's work *Ijtimāʿ al-juyūsh al-islāmiyya*—which can be considered a premature version of *al-Ṣawāʿiq*—contains complementary information about scholars whose opinions kindled Ibn al-Qayyim's opinions and writing, mostly

91 Ibn al-Qayyim paraphrases here the Quranic text (Q 16:65–66) "[65]It is God who sends water down from the sky and with it revives the earth when it is dead. There truly is a sign for people who listen. [66]In livestock, too, you have a lesson—We give you a drink from the contents of their bellies, between waste matter and blood, pure milk, sweet to the drinker."

92 Ibn Qayyim al-Jawziyya, *Badāʾiʿ al-fawāʾid*, 1:289–291.

93 Ibn Qayyim al-Jawziyya, *Badāʾiʿ al-fawāʾid*, 1:291–292.

94 As presented in pages 209 and 221 above.

among the early traditionalistic circles.[95] In *al-Ṣawāʿiq* Ibn al-Qayyim conceptually cultivates the linguistic discussion on *ḥaqīqa* to become applicable in the theological sphere and, more precisely, in the hermeneutics of the divine attributes, further developing the Taymiyyan approach.

5.4 Attacking the Muʿtazilite Heritage

Throughout the third *ṭāghūt* refutation in *al-Ṣawāʿiq* as well as the attack on *majāz*, Ibn al-Qayyim seems to direct the lion's share of his critique to no other than the Muʿtazilite school. From a historical perspective, the ultra-rationalistic Muʿtazilite perception on the hermeneutics of the divine attributes was developed between the 2nd/8th and 3rd/9th centuries, gradually penetrating the Ashʿarite dogmatic teachings—which were first established in the 4th/10th century—over the course of the following centuries. Bearing in mind Ibn al-Qayyim's immediate reference range in terms of the Ashʿarite scholarly elite in 8th/14th century Mamluk Damascus, it can be said his decision to focus his denunciation on earlier Muʿtazilite ideas points out their substantial and lively presence in that period of time as well. Moreover, Ibn al-Qayyim's attack on the Muʿtazilite heritage in *al-Ṣawāʿiq* indicates his solid understanding that later Ashʿarism absorbed considerable parts from previous Muʿtazilite notions. Proving his competence in identifying the background heritage of his contemporary Ashʿarite opinions, Ibn al-Qayyim shows his familiarity with the Muʿtazilite positions on *majāz*, which is important as his goal is to ultimately refute them. As a matter of fact, he targeted the rejection of the very fundamentals of the later Ashʿarite views by seeking to neutralize their provenances, thereby causing their methodologies to erode. Thus, expressing an intense rage against the Muʿtazilites gained him more intellectual profit than could have been expected in the discourse of the theological debates (*munāẓarāt*) at his time. The following section hence takes a closer look at the text of *al-Ṣawāʿiq* in order to unfold the broader picture which Ibn al-Qayyim is likely to have had in mind during his hermeneutical discussions.

In the view of the gist of subjects constituting the first section of the third *ṭāghūt* refutation in *al-Ṣawāʿiq*, it is apparent Ibn al-Qayyim refers directly to the Muʿtazilite scholar Ibn Jinnī Abu 'l-Fatḥ ʿUthmān (d. 392/1002) more than to any other scholar in his condemnation of *majāz* as a mere hermeneutical device. A grammarian and philologist, Ibn Jinnī was the disciple and succes-

95 See more details on the work in section 2.1 in this study, page 59.

sor of the luminary Abū ʿAli ʾl-Fārisī,[96] who is mentioned in Ibn al-Qayyim's discussion as well. It would be reasonable to assume Ibn al-Qayyim's attack against the two philologists indicates that he perceived them as an authoritative anchor for the Muʿtazilite hermeneutical stance on *majāz*. This is evident since Ibn al-Qayyim univocally recognizes Ibn Jinnī and al-Fārisī as a part of the Muʿtazilites and 'Jahmites', who were the first to introduce the dichotomy of speech between *ḥaqīqa* and *majāz*, which served them in the negation of the divine attributes. After citing a bulky portion of Ibn Jinnī's work *Kitāb al-Khaṣāʾiṣ fī ʿilm uṣūl al-ʿarabiyya* (Special [Features] of the Science of Arabic Foundations), Ibn al-Qayyim asserts:

> You should know that this man [i.e., Ibn Jinnī] and his Shaykh Abū ʿAli [ʾl-Fārisī] are of the greatest men of innovations (*min kibār^{i} ahl^{i} ʾl-bidaʿ*) and secede [lit., *al-iʿtizāl*, the Muʿtazila] who deny the words of God and His speech. According to them, God never spoke to anyone, and He will not call his worshipers to account Himself in the Day of Resurrection. The Quran and the heavenly books are created, and He does not have any attribute that exists in Him essentially (*wa-lays^{a} lah^{u} ṣifa^{tun} taqūm^{u} bih^{i}*). According to them, He has no knowledge, no ability, no life, no will, no hearing and no sight. He does not create the actions of humans; rather, their actions come from themselves (i.e., are created by them) and not through His choice and volition. According to them, when He wishes that they will do the opposite of what they have done, while they want the opposite of what He wants, their volition (i.e., the will of the people as active agents) prevails rather than His. In other words, what they want materializes and what He wants does not. According to this devious deceptive person [i.e., Ibn Jinnī], He creates and knows only metaphorically and not in an essential reality. This is a metaphor that one should negate, because according to this [scholar], God creates and knows only metaphorically.

96 Al-Fārisī lost work "*Kitāb al-tatabbuʿ li-kalām Abī ʿAli ʾl-Jubbāʾī fi ʾl-tafsīr*" may prove that al-Fārisī was an adherent of the Muʿtazila school of thought"; Reinhard Weipert, "al-Fārisī, Abū ʿAlī," *Encyclopaedia of Islam THREE*, Brill online, 2015. URL address http://referenceworks.brillonline.com/entries/encyclopaedia-of-islam-3/al-farisi-abu-ali-COM_26985 last accessed on 14 October 2015. Furthermore, other researchers consider both Al-Fārisī and Ibn Jinnī to be affiliated with the Muʿtazilite school, as can be seen in Mustafa Shah's study "Classical Islamic Discourse on the Origins of Language: Cultural Memory and the Defense of Orthodoxy," 328–329.

> He whose error in the fundamentals of his religion and faith of his Lord is this error, what is to be thought of his error and distorting of the expressions of the Quran and of the language of Arabs? A person that this is the sum of his knowledge and the end of his understanding may announce that the most of the language is to be understood metaphorically and bring up such nonsense. But the way of God assures that whoever mocks His camp and His soldiers will be disgraced. The man [i.e., Ibn Jinnī] and his Shaykh lived in the time of the peak of the Muʿtazilite power, when the caliphal dynasty was governed by Shiʿites and Muʿtazilites [i.e., the Abbāsid state of ca. 4th/10th century Baghdad]. The Sultan was the Buwayhid ʿAḍud al-Dawla [Abū Shujāʿ Fannā Khusraw, reigned 338/944–372/983], to whom Abū ʿAli [ʾl-Fārisī] wrote the book *al-Īḍāḥ* [*fī ʾl-naḥū*; Advanced Grammar]. The Vizier was Ismāʿīl ibn ʿAbbād (d. 385/995) the [Shiʿite-]Muʿtazilite, and the Chief Judge was ʿAbd al-Jabbār ibn Aḥmad (d. 415/1025) the Muʿtazilite. The first to introduce the division of speech into *ḥaqīqa* and *majāz* were the Muʿtazilites and the Jahmites.[97]

As the aim of this section is to survey the wider context of Ibn al-Qayyim's hermeneutical arguments, several matters that appear in the passage above become especially interesting: In terms of historical orientation, Ibn al-Qayyim accurately identifies the main actors who were involved in the inception of the concept of *majāz* as Muʿtazilite scholars, hence pointing out a sensible evaluation of the time period to be examined (i.e., ca. 4th/10th century). He also recognizes a tight interrelation between the linguistic concept of *majāz* and its adaptation by rationalist theologians. The direct reference that Ibn al-Qayyim makes to Ibn Jinnī and Abū ʿAli ʾl-Fārisī—who were scholars of the Arabic language—enhances his claim that the rendering of the Islamic texts' expressions figuratively stemmed from the sciences of grammar, linguistics and philology rather than the scientific fields of Islamic legal theory and methodology (*uṣūl al-fiqh*) or Islamic theology itself (*uṣūl al-dīn*). Therefore, an inquiry of the notion of *majāz* in the mind of Ibn Jinnī is a good place to begin contextualizing Ibn al-Qayyim's antagonistic approach towards the use of *majāz* in the hermeneutics of the textual sources. Following this, I intend to broaden the spectrum of examination to include other notable grammarians associated with the Muʿtazilite period in order to supply a more comprehensive out-

97 Ibn Qayyim al-Jawziyya, *Mukhtaṣar al-Ṣawāʿiq* (the abridgement of Ibn al-Mawṣilī), 2:821–823.

look on the linguistic aspects of the discussion. This allows a more accurate assessment of Ibn al-Qayyim's view concerning the derivation of the concept of *majāz* and its intellectual outcomes.

Immediately after stating his historical observations—or accusations—as depicted in the passage cited above, Ibn al-Qayyim sets forth a detailed retort of 25 facets (*wujūh*) against what he considers the erroneous parts of Ibn Jinnī's ideas on *majāz*.[98] As noted before, in *al-Ṣawāʿiq*, Ibn al-Qayyim also quotes a considerable—yet selective—part of Ibn Jinnī's work titled *al-Khaṣāʾiṣ*, which stands out as being highly valuable for the contextualization of Ibn al-Qayyim's thoughts in the hermeneutical discussion.[99] *Al-Khaṣāʾiṣ* is a vast encyclopedic work that covers much more than predictable grammatical technicalities and entails many theoretical topics which were not often dealt with by grammarians. Amongst these, Ibn Jinnī discusses the linguistic dilemma regarding the origin of language (*aṣl al-lugha*), maintaining that the correct study of language can lead to more accurate theological conceptions.[100] For example, since many laymen think the divine attributes in scriptures are real, tangible and physical, the linguist should assist in asserting that these attributes are to be understood as metaphorical expressions. In this manner, Ibn Jinnī's deliberation on the origin of language falls under the same category as the Muʿtazilite interests, which are of special relevance to the concept of *majāz*.[101] Hence, similar to other scholars of Arabic linguistics, Ibn Jinnī had his share of indirect impact on the Muʿtazilite hermeneutics on the divine attributes. However, as it namely has to do with his grammatical discussion, Ibn Jinnī's notion of *majāz* represents a different perspective. Nonetheless, Ibn Jinnī's interests are considered to have exceeded those of the average grammarians, especially in his book *al-Khaṣāʾiṣ*.

Captivated by the wholesome elegance and excellence of human language, Ibn Jinnī claims to follow the teachings of Abū ʿAli 'l-Fārisī and Abu 'l-Ḥasan

98 This is the section that closes the first part of the third *ṭāghūt* refutation, after which comes the individual treatment of the specific attributes in an effort to prove each of them should be understood as *ḥaqīqa* that describes an essential reality in God.

99 The cited parts are found in: Ibn Jinnī, Abu 'l-Fatḥ ʿUthmān, *al-Khaṣāʾiṣ*, ed. Muḥammad ʿAli 'l-Najjār, in 3 vols. (Cairo: Maṭbaʿat Dār al-Kutub al-Miṣriyya, 1952). The entry (*bāb*) on the origin of language can be found in 1:40–47 and the two entries on *majāz* appear in 2:442–457.

100 According to Weiss, *al-Khaṣāʾiṣ* contains one of the most comprehensive accounts on the origin of language; Weiss, "Waḍʿ al-Luġa," online source.

101 Kees Versteegh, "The Origin of Speech: Ibn Jinnī and the Two Alternatives," in: *Landmarks in Linguistic Thought III: The Arabic Linguistic Tradition* (Routledge: London and New York, 1997), 103–104; idem, "Linguistic Attitudes and the Origin of Speech in the Arab World," 20–25.

al-Akhfash (d. ca. 235–315/849–927)[102] who said that language came from God (i.e., reflecting the theory of *tawqīf*, meaning the origin of language is revelational). They deduced this from the Quranic verse 2:31 "He taught Adam all the names." However, Ibn Jinnī is aware that the verse can also be interpreted as "God enabled Adam to give names," implying the empowering of humankind to create language on its own right (i.e., inferring the theory of *iṣṭilāḥ*). After admitting to have consulted the writings of his fellow linguists and the traditions transmitted from the Prophet, Ibn Jinnī concludes the correct understanding of the verse is the first one, meaning that human language resulted from God's greatest wisdom.[103] The theories of *tawqīf* vs. *iṣṭilāḥ* were raised as highly admissible in the discussion on divine attributes, as can be seen in Ibn al-Qayyim's own reference to the subject, as mentioned above.[104] The doctrine of *iṣṭilāḥ* provided the ultra-rationalists with a powerful linguistic ground on which to establish their devotion to the idea of *majāz*. At times, this was a part of their linguistic legitimizations to deny the divine attributes and allegorically interpret them as *majāzāt*. In fact, the opinion voiced by Ibn Jinnī in favor of *tawqīf* was indeed an exception in the Muʿtazilite landscape of his time. Furthermore, the grammarians were an exception within the Muʿtazilites in their support of the doctrine of *tawqīf*, as they were fascinated by the language and saw it as nothing less than a divine miracle.[105] Albeit, Ibn Jinnī did acknowledge an obligational cogency for the use of metaphors to interpret various divine attributes in order to transcend God beyond the worldly experience.

Moving forward to the passages in *al-Khaṣāʾiṣ* in which Ibn Jinnī investigates more specifically the concept of *majāz*, it is obvious he does not intentionally pay attention to its theological implications; however, his deliberation still reflect his proximity to the Muʿtazilite stances on the divine attributes. This becomes evident when, among many other examples given in his grammatical clarifications, Ibn Jinnī uses particular verses from the Quran which explicitly involve the divine attributes. Ibn Jinnī dedicates two sections to the concept of *majāz*: first he establishes "the difference between *ḥaqīqa* and *majāz*," and

---

102 He is also known as al-Akhfash al-Aṣghar, or al-Ṣaghīr, Abu 'l-Ḥasan ʿAlī ibn Sulaymān. He was an Arab philologist and a man of letters who introduced the grammatical tradition of Baghdad to Egypt; Reinhard Weipert, "al-Akhfash," *Encyclopaedia of Islam* THREE, http://referenceworks.brillonline.com/entries/encyclopaedia-of-islam-3/al-akhfash-COM_22808.

103 Versteegh, "The Origin of Speech: Ibn Jinnī and the Two Alternatives," 101–102.

104 See in page 224 above.

105 Mustafa Shah, "Classical Islamic Discourse on the Origins of Language," 323–324, 328–331, 333.

then analyzes "the *majāz*, that when it increases it becomes *ḥaqīqa*" (*al-majāz idhā kathar*^{a} *laḥiq*^{a} *bil-ḥaqīqa*^{ti}). When dealing with the idea of *majāz* with relation to verbs that, according to Ibn Jinnī, produce a universal generic meaning (*maʿnā al-jinsiyya*), he brings up several interesting examples which include God and his attributes of action, such as:

> This [i.e., generic understanding of verbs] is also the case of the actions of the Eternal exalted (*afʿāl al-qadīm subḥānah*^{u}), such as God's creation of the sky and the earth and alike. Do you not see that this [does not mean] that He creates our actions? Were He a creator in essential reality (*ḥaqīqa*^{tan}) and not a creator metaphorically (*majāz*^{an}), He would have also created heresy, hostility and all such actions. The same goes for God's knowledge of Zayd's getting up—it is also metaphorical, because the state (*ḥāl*) in which God knows of Zayd's getting up is not the same as His knowledge of the sitting of ʿAmr. We do not affirm God's knowledge for He is knowledgeable on His own sake (*li-annah*^{u} *ʿālim*^{un} *bi-nafsih*^{i}).[106]

Further illustrations of the divine attributes in Ibn Jinnī's discussion are quoted directly from the Quran:

> Regarding God's saying [Q 4:164] "To Moses God spoke directly" (*wa-kallam*^{a} *Allāh*^{u} *Mūsā taklīm*^{an}), it is not a case of a metaphor, but rather this is reality. Abu 'l-Ḥasan [al-Akhfash] said: God created a speech in the shrub so that it spoke through it (*bi-h*^{i}) to Moses. When He originated it, He was speaking through it. Whether He originated it in a mouth or a shrub is an entirely different matter, but the speech exists. Do you not see that for us the speaker deserves the attribute [of speech] only as he is indeed the [performer of the action of the] speaker, not anything else; not because he originated it via a vessel (*fī āla*^{tin}, i.e. an object) which he made to speak. If he did so, he would not be speaking until he activated the vessels of his speech.[107]
>
> However, in a case of an emphasis by an infinitive form (*tawkīd bil-maṣdar*), "To Moses God spoke directly" is metaphorical. A metaphor of emphasis (*tawkīd al-majāz*) is as well God's saying [Q 13:16] "God is the Creator of all things." He exalted is a thing that Reason (*ʿaql*) understands

---

106 Ibn Jinnī, *al-Khaṣāʾiṣ*, 2:447–449; Ibn Qayyim al-Jawziyya, *Mukhtaṣar al-Ṣawāʿiq* (the abridgement of Ibn al-Mawṣilī), 2:804–808.

107 Ibn Jinnī, *al-Khaṣāʾiṣ*, 2:454; Ibn Qayyim al-Jawziyya, *Mukhtaṣar al-Ṣawāʿiq* (the abridgement of Ibn al-Mawṣilī), 2:815–816.

> to be exceptional by intuition and there is no need to actively make it such. So, an existing thing does not create itself.[108]
>
> Regarding God's saying [Q 12:76] "Above everyone who has knowledge there is the One who is all knowing" (*wa-fawq*^{q} *kull*^{i} *dhī ʿilm*^{in} *ʿalīm*^{un}), this is essential reality (*ḥaqīqa*) not a metaphor. That is since knowledge [is not attributed] to God, and hence He is the all knowing who is above all of those ascribed with knowledge [i.e., *dhū ʿilm*^{in}; lit., Possessor of knowledge].[109]

The above-mentioned grammatical understanding of Quranic verses which depict certain divine attributes demonstrates Ibn Jinnī's Muʿtazilite view, as he refuses to ascribe God any attributes of essential reality. The concept of *majāz* enables Ibn Jinnī to avoid the assimilation of God with any characterization that he found undesirable. These instances which suggest the divine attributes are freely intertwined within other rather trivial grammatical explanatory remarks along the familiar lines of '*qām*^{a} *Zayd*^{un}' or '*jalas*^{a} *ʿAmr*'. In this perspective, Ibn Jinnī's focus on *majāz* in his work *al-Khaṣāʾiṣ* can be seen as a side-discussion to his foremost commitment to linguistic doctrinal matters. His engagement with *majāz* in *al-Khaṣāʾiṣ* is quite short, but still intriguing when contrasted with Ibn al-Qayyim's refutation of this hermeneutic tool. Interestingly, Ibn al-Qayyim connects Ibn Jinnī's view on the issue of the origin of language and his contemplation concerning the use of *majāz*, as both issues have been raised in the third *ṭāghūt* refutation in *al-Ṣawāʿiq*.

The opposition that Ibn al-Qayyim articulates in *al-Ṣawāʿiq* against Ibn Jinnī's view encompasses more than a mere citation from the work *al-Khaṣāʾiṣ*. As presented in the previous section, Ibn al-Qayyim proves a close acquaintance with the Muʿtazilite ideological stances demonstrated in his reference to Ibn Jinnī and his teacher Abū ʿAli 'l-Fārisī, which are perceived here as the foremost derivation of the later Ashʿarite rationalistic use of *majāz* in his own time.[110] In this regard, it is notable that Ibn al-Qayyim's devaluation of Ibn Jinnī's positions in *al-Ṣawāʿiq* draws heavily from the underlying teachings of

---

108 Ibn Jinnī, *al-Khaṣāʾiṣ*, 2:456; Ibn Qayyim al-Jawziyya, *Mukhtaṣar al-Ṣawāʿiq* (the abridgement of Ibn al-Mawṣilī), 2:818–820.

109 Ibn Jinnī, *al-Khaṣāʾiṣ*, 2:457; Ibn Qayyim al-Jawziyya, *Mukhtaṣar al-Ṣawāʿiq* (the abridgement of Ibn al-Mawṣilī), 2:820.

110 Ibn al-Qayyim knew and mentioned Ibn Jinnī's *al-Khaṣāʾiṣ* in several of his works, including *Badāʾiʿ al-fawāʾid*. He also was well acquainted with the works of al-Fārisī; Ayman ʿAbd al-Razzāq al-Shawwā, *Ibn Qayyim al-Jawziyya wa-ārāʾuh*^{u} *'l-naḥwiyya* (Damascus, Dār al-Bashāʾir lil-Ṭibāʿa wal-Nashr, 1995), 102, 424–427.

Ibn Taymiyya. As has already been discussed, Ibn Taymiyya revived the topic of *tawqīf*—which he gave his own bent—in order to contest the validity of *majāz* according to the theory of *iṣṭilāḥ*.[111] Not only does Ibn al-Qayyim follow the Taymiyyan line of argumentation, he also manifests his contribution to the subject in terms of assembling the larger intellectual picture and arranging the earlier sources available to him.

In *al-Ṣawāʿiq*, Ibn al-Qayyim addresses rather early scholars, who were active in the days when Muʿtazilite activity had diminished, signifying the school's decline. To some extent, this historical period overlapped the dawn of the early Ashʿarite theological school in the 4th/10th century. By and large, the Ashʿarites of that formative time formulized a milder traditionalism which accepted the use of several rationalistic tools. During the 5th/11th century, and by the beginning of the 6th/12th century, Ashʿarite dogma moderately grew and constituted the prevailing attitude of Sunnite Islam, culminating with the appearance of al-Ghazālī who paved the way for a positive interaction between *Kalām* and *falsafa*. A century later, it was Fakhr al-Dīn al-Rāzī who further expanded the Ashʿarite intellectual horizons, allowing a more progressive exchange between *Kalām* and *falsafa* to the level of a profound synthesis of ideas.[112] This historical course of events can be observed in the undercurrents of *al-Ṣawāʿiq*. While reading, it becomes evident Ibn al-Qayyim was indeed aware of the historical and intellectual shifts that occurred within Ashʿarism and its inclination to rationalism, thus he deliberately placed himself in opposition to it. He is accurate in his identification of the most important and relevant scholars and aims a substantial portion of his criticism against them. This observation is also corroborated by modern research on the Muʿtazilite concepts of *ḥaqīqa* and *majāz*, which ascribes the grammarians—including Ibn Jinnī and his *al-Khaṣāʾiṣ*—a prominent role in the formulation of the classical dichotomist theory used in the theological discourse in the 4th/10th century. The following century introduced the important developments of the theory by the scholars of linguistics (*balāgha, bayān*), for example, with the contribution of ʿAbd al-Qāhir al-Jurjānī (d. ca. 471/1078).[113]

111 See page 206 above.

112 George Makdisi, "Ashʿarī and the Ashʿarites in Islamic Religious History I," *Studia Islamica* 17 (1962): 37–40; idem, "Ashʿarī and the Ashʿarites in Islamic Religious History II," *Studia Islamica* 18 (1963), 37–39; Shihadeh, "From al-Ghazālī to al-Rāzī," 141–142, 156, 162–164, 171–172; idem, *The Teleological Ethics of Fakhr al-Dīn al-Rāzī*, 1–2; Griffel, "On Fakhr al-Dīn al-Rāzī's Life," 338–340.

113 Wolfhart Heinrichs, "On the Genesis of the *Ḥaqīqa-Majāz* Dichotomy," *Studia Islamica* 59 (1984): 139–140.

Albeit, several reservations are to be made in this context: with his claim that "nearly all of the language is metaphorical", Ibn Jinnī presents an extremist view among the advocates of the idea of *majāz*. In addition, the lack of focused theological consideration in Ibn Jinnī's work can indicate that the incorporation of the *majāz* within the mass of argumentations on the divine attributes was still incomplete at Ibn Jinnī's time. It is definitely not identical to the Ashʿarite notion of *majāz* formulated after al-Ghazālī and al-Rāzī, which was still present at the time of Ibn al-Qayyim's activity; his Ashʿarites contemporaries rigidly refrained from interpreting the modality of the divine attributes, especially those that could imply of anthropomorphism (via *bi-lā kayf*[a]). Moreover, in the time of Ibn Jinnī the issue of the origin of language was a matter of dispute between Muʿtazilites and Ashʿarites[114]—Ibn al-Qayyim does not explicitly comment on this subtlety of rationalistic-traditionalistic disagreement and its hermeneutical implications on the theological topic of the divine attributes. Instead, he treats Ibn Jinnī as a representative of the so-called "Jahmites", attaching the Muʿtazilite and Ashʿarite approaches to one another merely due to the fact that both employed the device of *majāz*; at first sight, he seems to accuse both parties uniformly and indiscriminately. However, as his declared objective is to eradicate the later Ashʿarite use of *majāz*, it would be more sensible to claim he is actually seeking the background and heritage of the Ashʿarite methodologies and, hence, reaches all the way back to their basic Muʿtazilite hardliner conception. In other words, Ibn al-Qayyim attacks an extremist Muʿtazilite scholar in an effort to ultimately strike down the Ashʿarite position and, more precisely, his later Ashʿarite contemporaries.

5.5 Ibn al-Qayyim's Rational-Traditionalistic Inspiration

Highly notable is the fact that, in his third *ṭāghūt* refutation in *al-Ṣawāʿiq*, Ibn al-Qayyim dedicated a much larger portion of his writing to opposing the rationalistic stances rather than magnifying the significance of the early traditionalists with whom he sees eye to eye on the matter of negating the use of *majāz*; due to the determined dialectic objective of the work, this is understandable. Nonetheless, since attaining a better understanding can help illuminate Ibn al-Qayyim's motives for writing this part of *al-Ṣawāʿiq*, a few words should be said about the highpoints of Ibn al-Qayyim's positive appreciation expressed

114 Shah, "Classical Islamic Discourse on the Origins of Language: Cultural Memory and the Defense of Orthodoxy," 318–319, 323.

towards several earlier scholars and their views. Apart from his proclaimed and much-expected adherence to the legendary righteous ancestors (*salaf*) and his renowned mentor Ibn Taymiyya, it is interesting to follow his pinpointing of scholars and ideas that he found to be aptly authoritative as well as inspiring. In parallel to his critique of *majāz*, Ibn al-Qayyim finds his sources of inspiration in the image of scholarly figures such as the early Ashʿarite luminary of the 5th/11th century Abū Isḥāq al-Isfarāyīnī (d. 418/1027), and the Ḥanbalite scholars from the 6th/12th century Abū Yaʿlā ibn al-Farrāʾ (d. 458/1066) and his disciple Abu ʾl-Wafāʾ ibn ʿAqīl (d. 513/1119).[115] From this perspective, the latter two can be considered early portents of the forthcoming process of rationalization within the Ḥanbalite traditionalistic thought, leading towards the progressed stage of rationalized-traditionalism that Ibn al-Qayyim exemplifies in *al-Ṣawāʿiq*.

First, concerning Abū Isḥāq al-Isfarāyīnī, Ibn al-Qayyim's affirmative assessment of his ideas fits al-Isfarāyīnī's characterization in modern research as a rather unconventional and original representative of Ashʿarite thought, who exhibited an interesting doctrinal flexibility. None of his works have survived, including those on dogmatic theology; however, quotes from his work were often made by the following scholars. With relation to the issue of divine attributes we have been discussing, he expressed a view closer to Muʿtazilite doctrine which supported the idea of an utterly abstract God.[116] Clear evidence of his perception of a completely transcendent God can be found in an anecdote that depicts his brilliant victory in a public debate in the sultan's court against an anonymous Karrāmite, holding the sect's well-known corporealistic view on the meaning of the divine attributes. The Karrāmite asked Abū Isḥāq al-Isfarāyīnī whether it was possible God was on His throne and that the throne was the place of God (*makān^{un} lah^{u}*). Al-Isfarāyīnī refuted the Karrāmite's claim: first, he theatrically spread his arms, put one palm over the other and said: "This is how a thing is above another thing." Then he explained that, unlike his palms, God could not be particularized (*mukhaṣṣaṣ*), because every particular thing (*makhṣūṣ*) was physically limited, and that which was limited could not be a god. Frustrated by their inability to counter this decisive argument, the Karrāmite crowd gathered around Abū Isḥāq al-Isfarāyīnī in a threatening manner until the sultan himself intervened and pushed them

115 See Ibn al-Qayyim's discussion in page 221 above.

116 Angelika Brodersen, "Abū Isḥāq al-Isfarāyīnī," *Encyclopaedia of Islam THREE*, Brill online, URL address http://referenceworks.brillonline.com/entries/encyclopaedia-of-islam-3/abu-ishaq-al-isfarayini-COM_26291 last accessed on 15 October 2015. Also see footnote 28 in this chapter.

aside. When the vizier, whose name was Abu 'l-ʿAbbās al-Isfarāyīnī, entered the court, the irritated sultan exclaimed: "Where have you been? Your townsman hit the god of the Karrāmites on his head!"[117]

Alluding with more detail to the inexistence of metaphors in the Arabic language, Abū Isḥāq al-Isfarāyīnī is reported to have stated that "if *majāz* (metaphor) existed, mutual understanding [between people] would become faulty, since it may conceal the context (*qad yuḥfi 'l-qarīna^ta^*)." Although he was not completely opposed to it, he meant to abstain from using it. He refused to perceive every 'lion' as a metaphor for the brave, nor every 'donkey' as a metaphor for a fool, claiming that perhaps it would be better to put more thought into it instead of redundantly recapping such alleged metaphors. Moreover, since an expression gains its meaning from the power of its context, the entire unit of speech is to be understood as veridical reality (*ḥaqīqa*).[118] Al-Isfarāyīnī's view in the terminological dispute about the dichotomy of *ḥaqīqa*/*majāz* is quite unusual for the Ashʿarite landscape, as he preferred stressing the contextual factor to the use of figurative expressions. In addition, al-Isfarāyīnī is known to have devised a merged version of the theories on *tawqīf* and *iṣṭilāḥ*, presenting yet another solution to the related quandary of the origin of language. To his mind, God revealed the elementarily required portion of the language to mankind by *tawqīf*, which enabled the following process of *iṣṭilāḥ*.[119] As noted before, a similar approach was expressed later by Ibn Taymiyya, hence it is not impossible Ibn al-Qayyim's explicit mentioning of al-Isfarāyīnī might indicate he was one of the sources of Ibn Taymiyya's postulate.

Important in this respect is also Ibn al-Qayyim's favorable evaluation of the Ḥanbalites Abū Yaʿlā ibn al-Farrāʾ and Ibn ʿAqīl, since the two scholars are con-

117 The anecdote appears in the study: Holtzman and Ovadia, "On Divine Aboveness (*al-Fawqiyya*)," 23. Abu 'l-Muẓaffar, Ṭāhir ibn Muḥammad al-Isfarāyīnī (d. 471/1079), *al-Tabṣīr fi 'l-dīn wa-tamyyiz al-firqa al-nājiya ʿan al-firaq al-hālikīn*, ed. Kamāl Yūsuf al-Ḥūt (Beirut: ʿĀlam al-Kutub, 1403/1983), 112; not much is known about Abu 'l-Muẓaffar al-Isfarāyīnī. In his work, he praises Abū Isḥāq al-Isfarāyīnī, his valuable scholarly work and his sincere adherence to *ahl al-sunna wal-jamāʿa*. ibid, 193.

118 Abū Isḥāq al-Isfarāyīnī's approach is briefly quoted in the entry *majāz* in the vast lexical work of the Indian philologist and lexicologist al-Tahanāwī from the 12th/18th century: al-Tahanāwī, Muḥammad Aʿlā ibn ʿAlī ibn Mawlānā, *Mawsūʿat iṣṭilāḥāt al-ʿulūm al-islāmiyya (al-maʿrūf bi-kashshāf iṣṭilāḥāt al-funūn)*, ed. Muḥammad Wajīh ʿAbd al-Ḥaqq, in 6 vols. (Beirut, Khiyāṭ: al-Maktaba al-Islāmiyya, [1385]/1966), 1:223.

119 Shah, "Classical Islamic Discourse on the Origins of Language: Cultural Memory and the Defense of Orthodoxy," 333.

sidered to have a more rationalistic tendency than might be expected from the traditionalists of the 5th/11th–6th/12th centuries. To some degree, both of them came from a Muʿtazilite background. Apart from his noteworthy *Kalām* manual titled *al-Muʿtamad fī uṣūl al-dīn* ([The Book of] Foundation on the Principles of Religion),[120] Abū Yaʿlā also composed an extensive work on the interpretation of God's corporeal attributes in Hadith literature, which titled *Ibṭāl al-taʾwīlāt li-akhbār al-ṣifāt* (Abolishing the [Metaphorical] Interpretations of the Traditions of the Attributes); a section of this work is cited by Ibn al-Qayyim in *al-Ṣawāʿiq* (as will be shortly discussed). In this work he contrasted the obedient faith (*taslīm*) of the Ḥanbalites with the metaphorical interpretation (*taʾwīl*) of the Ashʿarites:[121]

> Those who negate all of the attributes are the Qadarites ... others such as the Christians described God exulted as a substance (*jawhar*), the corporealists described God with a body (*jism*), and the anthropomorphists assimilated His descriptions with those of His creation.
>
> It has been said [Q 42:12] "there is nothing like Him" ... God has already described Himself in His Book, and His Messenger has described Him in the truthful traditions. The righteous ancestors (*salaf*) of this community of believers affirmed what we clarify here, so that it only remains to understand [the traditions] as they were revealed.
>
> You should know that it is not allowed to reject these traditions (*akhbār*) in the way of some of the Muʿtazilites, nor is it to engage in the metaphorical interpretation (*taʾwīl*) in the way of the Ashʿarites. It is obligatory to interpret them literally (*ḥamluhā ʿalā ẓāhirihā*). The divine attributes do not resemble any other created beings which are depicted [in the same manner]. We do not believe in likening [God to His creation; *tashbīh*], but rather we follow what was transmitted by our Shaykh and Imam Abī ʿAbd Allāh Aḥmad ibn Muḥammad ibn Ḥanbal and the other Imams of the traditionalists (*aṣḥāb al-ḥadīth*), who said about these traditions: 'pass them on just as they have come' (*amirrūhā kamā jaʾat*). So,

120 See footnote 3 in chapter 3 above.

121 Laoust, "Ibn al-Farrāʾ," *EI*², 3:766; Much of the work is dedicated to a specific affirmation (*ithbāt*) of particular attributes of God, such as His right hand and grip (*ṣifat al-yad wal-yamīn wal-qabḍ*), His foot and leg (*ṣifat al-rijl wal-qadam*) or His aboveness (*ṣifat al-ʿulū*); Abū Yaʿlā, Muḥammad ibn al-Ḥusayn Ibn al-Farrāʾ (d. 458/1066), *Ibṭāl al-taʾwīlāt li-akhbār al-ṣifāt*, ed. Muḥammad ibn Ḥamd al-Ḥamūd al-Najjdī, in two vols. (Riyadh: Dār Īlāf al-Dawliyya, [1407]/[1987]).

> we understand them as they appear and as the descriptions of God, which do not resemble any other described [creatures].[122]

In Abū Yaʿlā's opinion, it is impossible that God's corporeal descriptions in the texts—strictly stressing the Hadith—can be understood as implying God's corporeality (*tajsīm*); however, he evenly rejected the figurative interpretation (*taʾwīl*) of these expressions. For Abū Yaʿlā these attributes of God truly describe his essence and are to be taken at face value without attempting to grasp their meaning. A more specific example of Abū Yaʿlā's treatment of the divine attributes can be seen with relation to several eschatological Hadith accounts that depict God laughing "until his molars and uvula are shown." This laughter was interpreted by Ashʿarite scholars as a metaphor of God's mercy, grace or astonishment. Abū Yaʿlā discarded such interpretations, while accepting the text literally and somewhat ignoring its problematic parts of the implied similarity between God and the created humans. With respect to the anthropomorphic question, the general approach promoted by Abū Yaʿlā is to reconcile between rationalistic *Kalām* and Ḥanbalite traditionalism.[123]

Already in the introduction of *al-Ṣawāʿiq* Ibn al-Qayyim specifically refers to Abū Yaʿlā's works directed against *taʾwīl*, as one of the supporting sources written by earlier scholars against the undesirable metaphorical interpretation performed by the *mutakallimūn*.[124] Given the context depicted, it is not improbable Ibn al-Qayyim had Abū Yaʿlā's *Ibṭāl al-taʾwīlāt* in mind. After defining the proper act of interpretation (*tafsīr*) for the purpose of attaining an understanding of the Islamic sacred texts, Ibn al-Qayyim convicts the rationalistic method of interpretation, saying:

> As for the Muʿtazilites, the Jahmites and the rest of the scholars of the *Kalām*, their intention [of the word] interpretation [i.e., *taʾwīl*] is to divert an expression from its apparent meaning (*ẓāhir*) and its essential reality (*ḥaqīqa*) into a metaphor (*majāz*) and what contradicts its apparent meaning. This became a widespread practice among the later theologians and legal theoreticians. This is why they say: [figurative] interpretation is contrary to the origin (*ʿalā khilāfⁱ ʾl-aṣlⁱ*), and that it requires indicators (*yaḥtājᵘ ilā dalīlⁱⁿ*). This is the [malice] interpretation about which works

122 Abū Yaʿlā Ibn al-Farrāʾ, *Ibṭāl al-taʾwīlāt li-akhbār al-ṣifāt*, 1:42–44.

123 Hoover, "Ḥanbalī Theology," 7–8; Holtzman, 'Does God Really Laugh?', 186–187.

124 The introduction of *al-Ṣawāʿiq* was elaborately discussed in section 2.5, and more closely in part on *taʾwīl* as Linguistic Phenomenon.

> were written from two [conflicting] sides—for its authorization or invalidation. One group composed works in favor of the metaphorical interpretation of the divine attributes in the Quranic verses and Hadith, like Abū Bakr ibn Fūrak (d. 406/1015),[125] Ibn Mahdi al-Ṭabarī (d. ca. 380/990)[126] and such. Other scholars opposed them, and wrote on the invalidation of such metaphorical interpretation, such as the Qāḍī Abū Yaʿlā and the Shaykh Muwaffaq al-Dīn ibn Qudāma (d. 620/1223),[127] who transmitted the consensus of the righteous ancestors (*salaf*) concerning the lack of [use of *taʾwīl*].[128]

In fact, Ibn al-Qayyim's favorable mentioning of Abū Yaʿlā—and possibly *Ibṭāl al-taʾwīlāt*—emphasizes the traditionalistic attitude of complete loyalty to the Hadith materials. At first glance, it seems only natural for any traditionalistic scholar to defend the sayings of the Prophet, yet in the specific case of *al-Ṣawāʿiq* it also has to do with the rationalized-traditionalistic stance constructed by Ibn al-Qayyim, which envelopes Ibn al-Qayyim rationalized theoretical discussions with a traditionalistic "Hadith binding" (see chapter 6 hereinafter).

Abū Yaʿlā's most prominent disciple Ibn ʿAqīl is also presented as a positive scholastic example by Ibn al-Qayyim. Ibn ʿAqīl is known to have studied and employed parts of the Muʿtazilite doctrines of *Kalām* into his thought, but was compelled to retract this inclination due to the political tensions against rationalism in 5th/11th century Baghdad. In fact, Ibn ʿAqīl was certainly involved in scandalous episode, being a Ḥanbalite scholar who underwent harsh and direct persecution because of his theological conceptions as well as other reasons. At the end of the day he was forced to sign a public retraction (*tawba*), discard

125 Abū Bakr Muḥammad ibn al-Ḥasan ibn Fūrak al-Anṣārī al-Iṣbahānī was an early Ashʿarite theologian and traditionist, who played a significant role in the formalization of the Ashʿarite creed. Notable is his theological treatise *Mushkil al-ḥadīth wa-bayānuhu* (The Book of Ambiguous *ḥadīths* and their Clarification), in which he concentrates on the divine attributes; William Montgomery Watt, "Ibn Fūrak," *EI*², 3:767.

126 ʿAlī ibn Muḥammad al-Mahdī al-Ṭabarī al-Ashʿarī was a pupil of Abū Ḥasan al-Ashʿarī and one of the early scholars of *Kalām*; Ibn al-Qayyim, *al-Ṣawāʿiq al-mursala*, 1:179, footnote 3.

127 Muwaffaq al-Dīn Abū Muḥammad ʿAbdallāh ibn Aḥmad ibn Muḥammd ibn Qudāma al-Maqdisī al-Ḥanbalī was a renowned Damascene Ḥanbalite scholar of jurisprudence and traditionalistic theology. His work against *taʾwīl* is called *Taḥrīm al-naẓar fī kutub al-kalām* (Censure of Speculative Theology) and was translated into English by George Makdisi; George Makdisi, "Ibn Ḳudāma al-Maḳdīsī," *EI*², 3:842–843.

128 Ibn al-Qayyim, *al-Ṣawāʿiq al-mursala*, 1:178–180.

his Muʿtazilite tendencies and prove himself a devoted Ḥanbalite in front of his peers. Nevertheless, the Ḥanbalite approach of Ibn ʿAqīl accentuated the place of Reason and incorporated rationalistic elements into the traditionalistic Ḥanbalite doctrines, such as the science of dialectics (*jadal*) as a means to attain the truth. Mostly prior to his retraction, Ibn ʿAqīl is known to have even permitted a limited use of *taʾwīl*, in other words, a metaphorical interpretation of divine attributes that can imply God's form (*ṣūra*) or acts (such as human anger or dissatisfaction) in order to refrain from anthropomorphism. In the latter part of his life, Ibn ʿAqīl declared that God alone knows His attributes, and they can only be known through Him. Ibn ʿAqīl represents a combined approach in this case, accepting only *taʾwīl* which "conforms to the proofs of Reason and Revelation (*al-taʾwīl^u ʾl-muṭābiq li-adillat^i ʾl-sharʿ^i wal-ʿaql^i*)."[129] Be that as it may, he was definitely a scholar who attracted ambivalent—at times even contradictory—responses from several of the later traditionalists, not all of whom were certain he had ever fully retracted his ideas full retraction.[130]

Unfortunately, the vast majority of the works authored by Ibn ʿAqīl have not survived, including his major theological work titled *al-Irshād fī uṣūl al-dīn* (Guidance on the Principles of Religion); however, a significant number of passages from this text were preserved as they were cited in works of later scholars. In fact, considerable passages of *al-Irshād* can be found verbatim in the works of Ibn Taymiyya, for example, in *Bayān talbīs al-jahmiyya*.[131] These textual excerpts together with the contextual location in which they were cited disclose much about Ibn ʿAqīl's theological notions on the issue of the divine attributes and, equally as important, on the opinions of the scholars who referred to him in their writings. Highly informative for this purpose is George Makdisi's scrutiny of Ibn ʿAqīl's theological conception on the issue of the divine attributes as it appears in Ibn Taymiyya's *Bayān al-talbīs*, the main object of which was the condemnation of logic. Makdisi has also translated into

129 Makdisi, "Ḥanbalite Islam," 238; Hoover, "Ḥanbalī Theology," 8; Holtzman, "The miḥna of Ibn ʿAqīl (d. 513/1119) and the fitnat Ibn al-Qushayrī (d. 514/1120)," *The Oxford Handbook of Islamic Theology*, ed. Sabine Schmidtke (Oxford: Oxford University Press, 2016)—online version, pp. 3–6.

130 For instance, two of his biographers Shams al-Dīn al-Dhahabī (d. 748/1347) and Ibn Rajab (d. 795/1392) highly praised Ibn ʿAqīl in their writing, and yet also showed their displeasure with his early Muʿtazilite tendencies and adoption of metaphorical interpretation of certain divine attributes; Makdisi, *Ibn ʿAqīl: Religion and Culture in Classical Islam* (Edinburgh: Edinburgh University Press, 1997), 49–50, 85–88, 102–107.

131 *Bayān talbīs al-jahmiyya* of Ibn Taymiyya was depicted in sections 3.3 and 3.4 of this study in relation to Ibn al-Qayyim's epistemological discussion.

English large sections relevant to the discussion on Ibn ʿAqīl's views regarding the appropriate understanding of the divine attributes.[132] Ibn Taymiyya's representation of Ibn ʿAqīl's position surely puts forward important insights on Ibn Qayyim's own course of deliberation concerning the hermeneutics of the Islamic texts in *al-Ṣawāʿiq*.

According to Makdisi's close inspection of the scholastic impression Ibn ʿAqīl left on Ibn Taymiyya, it becomes apparent the latter did not always think highly of his predecessor. In different works, Ibn Taymiyya changed his attitude towards Ibn ʿAqīl; however, all in all Ibn Taymiyya pointed out that "although Ibn ʿAqīl had Muʿtazilite tendencies in his early years, he ended by adhering to the pure Sunnite orthodoxy." This is also a strong indication of the shift that occurred in Ibn ʿAqīl's thought and his alternation to "a more moderate intellectualism," as Makdisi puts it. Ibn Taymiyya sees Ibn ʿAqīl as an admirable scholar, who established a firm alternative model of intellectual religious discourse to the Ashʿarism formed by al-Ghazālī:

> Abu 'l-Wafā' Ibn ʿAqīl was of surpassing excellence in his day, and highly respected by all the communities for his brilliance, sagacity and intelligence. He is more learned than Abū Ḥāmid [al-Ghazālī] in positive law (*fiqh*), in *Kalām* theology, in Hadith, and in the meanings of Quranic words and concepts (*maʿāni 'l-qur'ān*). He is in religion among the most pious men. As for Abū Ḥāmid [al-Ghazālī], he became involved with certain philosophical doctrines which are heretical in the opinion of Ibn ʿAqīl, who refuted the metaphorical interpretations of the philosophers which [al-Ghazālī] had taken up.[133]

---

132 Makdisi conducted several comprehensive studies on Ibn ʿAqīl and his historical place in the milieu of 5th/11th century Baghdad, for example, *Ibn 'Aqīl et la résurgence de l'Islām traditionaliste au XIe siècle/Ve siècle de l'Hégire* (Damascus: Institut Français de Damas, 1963). The main currents in the thought of Ibn ʿAqīl stood in the center of a following book: *Ibn ʿAqīl: Religion and Culture in Classical Islam*, in which Makdisi collected and analyzed the quotations of Ibn ʿAqīl as it appears in other works; Makdisi, *Ibn ʿAqīl: Religion and Culture*, xiii.

133 This is a part of the translation offered by Makdisi (the Arabic terms in brackets were inserted by me). The source quoted is Ibn Taymiyya's treatise entitled *al-Ikhnā'iyya* or *al-Radd ʿala 'l-Ikhna'ī*, however it should be noted that in many other cases Ibn Taymiyya cites Ibn ʿAqīl and Abū Yaʿlā as scholars of *Kalām* or as reflective reasoners (*nāẓir*) of Islam; Makdisi, *Ibn ʿAqīl: Religion and Culture*, 48–49, 111.

This passage shows that, to Ibn Taymiyya's mind, the use of Reason represented by Ibn ʿAqīl surpasses the rationalistic utilization of 'foreign logic' such as philosophy. Instead, Ibn Taymiyya beckons Ibn ʿAqīl's use of the science of dialectics (*jadal*) as the adequate propaedeutic to the field of Principles of Religion (*uṣūl al-fiqh*). Once again, Ibn Taymiyya proves here his knowledge of Islamic intellectual-religious history, as well as the doctrines of Ibn ʿAqīl.[134]

As a matter of fact, Makdisi mentions several traditionalists who belonged to the Taymiyyan circle of immediate disciples and shared their master's high esteem of Ibn ʿAqīl, such as Shams al-Dīn al-Dhahabī (d. 748/1347), Ibn Kathīr (d. 774/1373) and Ibn Rajab (d. 795/1392). Each one of these three had recorded Ibn ʿAqīl's biography in their bio-bibliographical works; albeit, they somewhat inconveniently never failed to mention Ibn ʿAqīl's former Muʿtazilite affiliation and his restricted approval of *taʾwīl* concerning the divine attributes. However, Makdisi does not mention Ibn al-Qayyim amid Ibn Taymiyya's followers in this context, most likely because Ibn al-Qayyim did not record Ibn ʿAqīl's life-story as the authors of the biographical dictionaries or historical accounts mentioned above did—this point was Makdisi's main subject of interest in his research.[135] Still, Makdisi's description of the other Taymiyyan scholars makes Ibn al-Qayyim's appreciation towards Ibn ʿAqīl in *al-Ṣawāʿiq* appear in a new light. Not only does Ibn al-Qayyim take up Ibn Taymiyya's positive view concerning Ibn ʿAqīl's thought, he also stands out as the 'disciple' who grasped the teacher's mindset in a very precise manner, which his fellow contemporaries did not. Furthermore, Ibn al-Qayyim referred to Ibn ʿAqīl as a source of inspiration in the course of a work devoted exclusively to the theological issue of the divine attributes; whereas his three contemporaries mentioned above seem to have point out to a biographical detail of Ibn ʿAqīl in a more superficial fashion. In addition, Ibn al-Qayyim is proven to be truly committed to using the science of dialectics (*jadal*), as he de facto applies in his work *al-Ṣawāʿiq*. The observations noted above lead to the conclusion that Ibn al-Qayyim's positive mentioning of Ibn ʿAqīl in *al-Ṣawāʿiq* represents his crystallized comprehension of the heritage of Taymiyyan thought alongside its active implementation in the form of his dialectic discussion on hermeneutics in *al-Ṣawāʿiq*.

To sum up, in this case, the scholars who inspired Ibn al-Qayyim's held a certain rationalistic affiliation in one way or another; both Abū Yaʿlā and Ibn ʿAqīl were Ḥanbalites with a Muʿtazilite background. Active in 5th/11th century Baghdad, the two are considered to have shaped the development of

134 Makdisi, *Ibn ʿAqīl: Religion and Culture*, 51, 102.

135 Makdisi, *Ibn ʿAqīl: Religion and Culture*, 48–51.

traditionalism throughout the classical period of Islam, striving for the infusion of Reason as a vital element of traditionalistic Ḥanbalite thought. Makdisi designated the two scholars' impact as an "intellectualist trend," which could not have occurred without the presence of Ashʿarite rationalism and the traditionalists' counter-attack. Notwithstanding, fideistic Ḥanbalite traditionalism maintained its prestige alongside—at times with some hostility—the intellectualist trend. But Ibn ʿAqīl's role is highly noteworthy as one of the scholars who updated the discipline of Principles of Law (*uṣūl al-fiqh*, theoretical legal methodology) in order to better face the rationalists of his day. Makdisi sustained that "after Abū Yaʿlā and Ibn ʿAqīl, *kalām* was accepted by Hanbali religious intellectuals for use in apologetics, generally against non-Traditionalists."[136] Even if Makdisi's statement might have gone slightly overboard with his inclusive reference to 'all Ḥanbalite intellectuals,' it seems to be suitable for the considerations of the present discussion: such a dynamic model of the scholastic penetration of rationalism into traditionalism extended beyond the classical period, as can be seen some three centuries later with the examples of Ibn Taymiyya and Ibn al-Qayyim. Focusing on Ibn al-Qayyim and the text *al-Ṣawāʿiq* reveals that traditionalism in its duller fideistic version did not suffice for him; Ibn al-Qayyim sought more invigorating reasoning to satisfy his intellect as well as his belief. Thus, he supports his approach through relying on scholars who consider Reason to be an integral part of the roots of knowledge, going hand in hand with Revelation. Moreover, *al-Ṣawāʿiq* illustrates Ibn al-Qayyim's own expansion and adaptation of the "intellectualist trend" to the highly developed discourse of the later Ashʿarite *Kalām* that was widely spread in the scenery of Mamluk Damascus.

5.6 Ibn al-Qayyim's Recruitment of Ibn Rushd against *taʾwīl*

The intellectual torrent of allegations against the device of *majāz* as a central element in the rationalistic hermeneutical method demonstrates Ibn al-Qayyim's high level of discussion in *al-Ṣawāʿiq*. The third *ṭāghūt* refutation directed against *majāz* specifically strives to eliminate its theoretical legitimization and, more so, to establish an appropriate hermeneutical substitute to the use of metaphors in order to explain the descriptions of God which are considered to be problematic. As shown in previous sections, Ibn al-Qayyim's writing on hermeneutics was stimulated by a variety of earlier scholars who

136 Makdisi, *Ibn ʿAqīl: Religion and Culture*, 92–99, 257–260.

opposed rationalism as it was reflected in Muʿtazilite and Ashʿarite thought. However, these scholars cannot be described as completely fideist, as they definitely incorporated their version of rationality into traditionalistic arguments. Alongside the scholars mentioned above (i.e., Abū Isḥāq al-Isfarāyīnī, Abū Yaʿlā ibn al-Farrāʾ, Ibn ʿAqīl and Ibn Taymiyya) another interesting source of inspiration that merits our attention is the great jurist, theologian, and the philosopher of Islam Abu ʾl-Walīd Ibn Rushd (Averroes, d. 595/1198) of Cordova. A distinguished scholar of Quranic sciences and natural sciences alike, Ibn Rushd's oeuvre spreads across a wide range of theoretical topics including his famous Arabic translations of the classical works of Aristotle. In *al-Ṣawāʿiq*, Ibn al-Qayyim cited a considerable section of one of Ibn Rushd's major theological works titled *al-Kashf ʿan manāhij al-adilla fī ʿaqāʾid al-milla wa-taʿrīf mā waqaʿ^{a} fīhā bi-ḥasb^{i} ʾl-taʾwīl min al-shubah^{i} ʾl-muzayyifa wal-bidaʿ al-muḍilla* (Exposition of the Methods of Religious Arguments, and Definition of the Equivocations and Innovations which Appear in them as Methods of Interpretation and which Distort Truth or Lead to Error).[137] The segment cited from this work does not appear in the third *ṭāghūt* refutation in *al-Ṣawāʿiq* but, rather, in the introduction of *al-Ṣawāʿiq* when he discusses *taʾwīl* as a destructive intellectual phenomenon, encompassing all fields of human knowledge.[138] Nevertheless, the subjects discussed in the passages taken from *al-Kashf* are very closely connected to Ibn al-Qayyim's theoretical preoccupation with *majāz*, and deal with the correct manner to understand the divine attributes. Since modern research has begun to identify his mentor Ibn Taymiyya as a scholar of an "Averroistic attitude", especially with regard to philosophical-theological matters,[139] Ibn al-Qayyim's compliance with the great philosopher becomes important. The fol-

137 Roger Arnaldez, "Ibn Rushd," *EI*², 3:913; Ibn Rushd, Abu ʾl-Walīd Muḥammad ibn Aḥmad ibn Muḥammd al-Andalusī al-Mālikī (d. 595/1198), *al-Kashf ʿan manāhij al-adilla fī ʿaqʾid al-milla, aw naqd ʿilm al-kalām ḍidd^{an} ʿala ʾl-tarsīm al-īdiyūlūjī lil-ʿaqīda wa-difāʿ^{an} ʿan al-ʿilm wal-ḥuriyya wal-ikhtiyār fī ʾl-fikr wal-fiʿl*, ed. Muḥammad ʿĀbid al-Jābirī (Beirut: Markaz Dirāsāt al-Waḥda al-ʿArabiyya, [1418]/1998), the editor's introduction, 67.

138 The introduction to *al-Ṣawāʿiq* stood in the center of section 2.5 above; Ibn Rushd is referred to in a somewhat separate segment (*faṣl*) between the 17th and 18th section of the introduction.

139 Georges Tamer, "The Curse of Philosophy: Ibn Taymiyya as a Philosopher in Contemporary Islamic Thought," 341–341. Noteworthy studies in Arabic largely depicted in Tamer's article are: ʿAbd al-Ḥakīm Ajhar, *Ibn Taymiyya wa-istiʾnāf al-qawl al-falsafī fī ʾl-islām* (Beirut: al-Markaz al-Thaqāfī al-ʿArabī, 2004); ʿAbd al-Majīd al-Ṣughayyar, *"Mawāqif "rushdiyya" li-Taqī al-Dīn Ibn Taymiyya?"*, in: *Tajliyāt al-fikr al-ʿarabī: dirasāt wa-murājaʿāt naqdiyya fī taʾrīkh al-falsafa wal-taṣawwuf bil-maghrib* (Casablanca: al-Madāris, 1421/2000), 97–120.

lowing section will hence inspect Ibn Rushd's theological designs as delivered by Ibn al-Qayyim in *al-Ṣawāʿiq* as another means for the work's contextualization and overall evaluation.

A proper point of departure for assessing Ibn al-Qayyim's reference to Ibn Rushd and *al-Kashf* in *al-Ṣawāʿiq* would be by observing the striking affinities discovered in recent research between Ibn Taymiyya and Ibn Rushd. In the course of his rejection of philosophy and Aristotelian logic in works like *al-Radd ʿala 'l-manṭiqiyyīn* or *Darʾ taʿāruḍ al-ʿaql wal-naql* (as discussed in section 3.3), Ibn Taymiyya did not spare his harsh criticism from Ibn Rushd. Yet, at the same time, Ibn Taymiyya absorbed parts of the Peripatetic methods of argumentation and proof, and also expressed his respect for several of the Islamic philosophers, among whom he considered Ibn Rushd to be "the closest philosopher to Islam."[140] The studies of ʿAbd al-Majīd al-Ṣughayyar and Georges Tamer point to meaningful similarities between the leading principles in the thought of the two scholars on theological subjects, such as their conceptions of causality and the creation of the world. Of greater relevance to our current discussion however are the issues of the relationship between Reason and Revelation and the hermeneutics of the divine attributes. First, despite the fact that at least outwardly Ibn Rushd and Ibn Taymiyya represent antithetical approaches regarding the relationship between Reason and Revelation, they in fact equally agree on the idea of the unity of truth and its accessibility to human beings through divine Revelation and by means of Reason. They share the methodological principle according to which human rational thinking ultimately conforms to the texts of the Quran and Hadith, and on which each of them—separately and respectively—based and developed his criticism against other philosophers and the scholars of *Kalām*. Al-Ṣughayyar argues that, in this respect, Ibn Taymiyya mostly extended the already existing reproof of the later Ashʿarites articulated by Ibn Rushd before him. In different times and environments of activity, each of them made use of this fundamental in order to challenge the established traditionalistic thought and stir an intellectual transformation.[141]

Second, Ibn Tayimiyya and Ibn Rushd both principally rejected the rationalistic denial of the corporealistic attributes of God as they appear in the Islamic texts (i.e., *taʿṭīl*). Of course, in general the desired solution proposed by each of the two was different; whereas Ibn Rushd strongly argues for the allegorical

140 Tamer, "The Curse of Philosophy," 329–332, 347; Kügelgen, "The Poison of Philosophy," 256, 289, footnote 152; Najjar, "Ibn Rushd's Theory of Rationality," *Alif: Journal of Comparative Poetics*, 16—Averroës and the Rational Legacy in the East and the West (1996), 191–192.

141 Tamer, "The Curse of Philosophy," 341–343; al-Ṣughayyar, *"Mawāqif "rushdiyya" li-Taqī al-Dīn Ibn Taymiyya?"*, 99–102.

meaning of the divine attributes, Ibn Taymiyya stated they are to be literally understood as ontological realities. Nonetheless, they both accepted all the Prophetic traditions and ascribed no modality to God. An interesting attribute in this context is God's direction (or spatiality, *jiha*), which will be discussed shortly with relation to Ibn al-Qayyim's discussion in *al-Ṣawāʿiq*. By and large, God's attribute of direction was metaphorically interpreted by Muʿtazilite and Ashʿarite scholars (for example, al-Ghazālī and Fakhr al-Dīn al-Rāzī), who preferred the approach of using negative utterances (*lugha salbiyya*) on the matter, as in stating that God is nowhere and also unlimited in space or direction. However, Ibn Rushd affirmed (by *ithbāt*) God's direction, since in his opinion it does not imply a physical place (*makān*) and hence does not convey corporeality concerning God.[142] Reinforcing his stance on the essential reality of divine attributes, Ibn Taymiyya embraced Ibn Rushd's reasoning of setting apart God's direction and His 'place', and connected it with the affirmation of God's direction by the *salaf*. Ibn Taymiyya cited Ibn Rushd's opinion from *al-Kashf* in *al-ʿAqīda al-wasiṭiyya* and *Darʾ al-taʿāruḍ* in order to substantiate his claim against Fakhr al-Dīn al-Rāzī in *Kitāb al-arbaʿīn*.[143] As will be shown shortly, Ibn Rushd's reasoning on God's direction served Ibn Taymiyya as well as Ibn al-Qayyim in his refutation against the rationalistic *taʾwīl*.

In the realm of theology, Ibn Rushd's work *al-Kashf* is dated to 575/1179 and is considered to be the second composition in his theological-philosophic trilogy.[144] *Al-Kashf* is a scholarly piece dedicated to analyzing the proper methodologies for comprehending God's existence (*ithbāt al-ṣāniʿ*), essence (*dhāt*) and unity (*waḥdāniyya*),[145] His attributes (*ṣifāt*) and His actions (*afʿāl*). As convinc-

142 Tamer, "The Curse of Philosophy," 344; al-Ṣughayyar, *"Mawāqif "rushdiyya" li-Taqī al-Dīn Ibn Taymiyya?,"* 111–112.

143 Ajhar, *Ibn Taymiyya wa-istiʾnāf al-qawl al-falsafī fi 'l-islām*, 58–61.

144 The first is the Decisive Treatise on the Relation of Philosophy and Religion (*Faṣl al-Maqāl*, 574/1178) with a short tract commonly referred to as the Appendix (*al-Damima*), and the third is the Incoherence of the Incoherence (*Tahāfut al-Tahāfut*, 576/1180), a rebuttal of al-Ghazālī's own Incoherence of the Philosophers (*Tahāfut al-Falāsifa*); Majid Fakhry, *Averroes (Ibn Rushd): His Life, Works and Influence* (Oxford: Oneworld, 2001), 3–4; Oliver Leaman, *Averroes and His Philosophy* (Richmond, Surrey [England]: Curzon, 1998), 1–14; Watt, *Islamic Philosophy and Theology*, 118–119. Insights on the relations between the works of Ibn Rushd's trilogy appear in: Muhsin Mahdi, "Remarks on Averroes' Decisive Treatise," in: (eds.) Hourani, George Fadlo; Marmura, Michael E., *Islamic Theology and Philosophy: Studies in honor of George F. Hourani* (Albany: State University of New York Press, 1984), 188–202.

145 Further information about this part of the *al-Kashf* is found in the study: Taneli Kukkonen, "Averroes and the Teleological Argument," *Religious Studies* 38/4 (Dec. 2002), 405–428.

ingly suggested by Ibrahim Y. Najjar, who studied *al-Kashf*, the work discloses Ibn Rushd's approach according to which religion and philosophy share an even portion of legitimate authority in the hermeneutical discourse; according to Ibn Rushd's theory of rationality, these two components work in harmony with each other rather than in conflict, with clear lines of demarcation. This point becomes even more pronounced in the issue of the separation between the clear expressions in the Islamic texts and the vague or ambiguous ones. "While no disagreement arises about the clear religious texts and their acceptance is required of all believers upon faith, ambiguous texts call for interpretation and the interference of Reason. One obvious requirement is that interpretations cannot come into conflict with clear and unambiguous texts. Reason is necessary, and without it the understanding of religious texts remains incomplete."[146] In fact, in *al-Kashf* Ibn Rushd criticized the Islamic theological sects which—in his opinion—irresponsibly applied a literal understanding of the Quran and Hadith literature, specifying the Ḥashwiyya (extremist literalists who excluded any use of Reason). According to Ibn Rushd, the Ṣufīs, Muʿtazilites, and most of all the Ashʿarites, with their practice of *Kalām*, are all equally mistaken in their hermeneutics as applied to the Revelation.[147] On the basis of the scientific theoretical knowledge (*al-maʿrifa 'l-ʿilmiyya*) derived from his unique harmonization between Aristotelian teachings and religious thought—and sharply differentiated this way from the rationalistic speculative theology[148]—Ibn Rushd preferred sticking to the literal meanings of the Islamic texts (*al-ḥaml ʿala 'l-ẓāhir*). Thus, it is not of much surprise that in the final part of *al-Kashf* Ibn Rushd rejected al-Ghazālī's "universal rule" and the doctrinal subordination of Revelation to Reason, a stance which had been a result of the teachings of the latter's teacher Imam al-Ḥaramayn Abu 'l-Maʿāli 'l-Juwaynī (d. 478/1085);[149] both scholars were decried by Ibn Rushd.[150]

---

146 Najjar, *Faith and Reason in Islam: Averroes' Exposition of Religious Arguments* (Oxford: Oneworld, 2001), the preface, i–ii; Najjar, "Ibn Rushd's Theory of Rationality," 194–195.

147 Najjar, "Ibn Rushd's Theory of Rationality," 210–211.

148 Arnaldez, "Ibn Rus̲h̲d," 913–915; Ibn Rushd, *al-Kashf*, the editor's introduction, 72–76; Fakhry, *Averroes (Ibn Rushd)*, 74–76, 78–81.

149 Najjar, *Faith and Reason in Islam: Averroes' Exposition of Religious Arguments*, introduction, part II; for more information on al-Juwaynī, see footnote 15 in chapter 4.

150 A far sterner proclamation of the hermeneutical divergence between Ibn Rushd and al-Ghazālī becomes apparent in the latter's famous work *Tahāfut al-falāsifa* (The Incoherence of the Philosophers), where he accused the Neoplatinic philosophers of contradicting the central tenets of Islam. Ibn Rushd composed a retort titled *Tahāfut al-tahāfut* (The Incoherence of the Incoherence), in which he criticized al-Ghazālī on a broad Aristotelian

Prior to quoting Ibn Rushd on God's attribute of direction, Ibn al-Qayyim argues that *ta'wīl* endangers the textual sources that convey the Islamic monotheistic belief (*tawḥīd*), both in terms of theory and practice. In fact, it seems that by doing so Ibn al-Qayyim reflects the first part of *al-Kashf*, where Ibn Rushd discusses God's essence (*dhāt*). Following the lines of Ibn al-Qayyim's claim, there are two kinds of textual utterances regarding *tawḥīd*: the first are informative and contain theoretical knowledge (*al-tawḥīd al-ʿilmī*), such as the Quranic verse 112:1 "Say, 'He is God the One'," whereas the second kind is performative and contains practical knowledge of the intention of worshiping a sole deity (*al-tawḥīd al-ʿamalī*), such as verses 109:1–2 "Say [Prophet], 'Disbelievers:⁽¹⁾ I do not worship what you worship'⁽²⁾" (usually understood as multiple gods). The foundation for the informative monotheism entails the affirmation of God's attributes of perfection together with His transcendence (*ithbāt ṣifāt al-kamāl lil-rabb ... wa-tanzīhih*[i]). The foundation for performative monotheism entails the active and voluntary qualification of worshiping God alone (*tajrīd al-qaṣd bil-ʿubūdiyya li-llāh*[i] *waḥdih*[i]). If figurative interpretation is imposed on the informative textual evidence concerning monotheistic belief, it becomes easier to impose it on the performative ones, leading to the abolishment of monotheism and the raise of notions of denial as well as assigning copartners to God (*maʿālim al-taʿṭīl wal-shirk*). For this reason, Ibn al-Qayyim states a denial of the divine attributes necessarily infers polytheism, hence threatening the Islamic creed.[151]

Sustaining this convoluted claim, Ibn al-Qayyim states that the most skillful philosophers (*ḥudhdhāq*[u] *'l-falāsifa*) have already acknowledged and supported this, pointing directly to Ibn Rushd and his work *al-Kashf*. The sections from *al-Kashf* cited by Ibn al-Qayyim in *al-Ṣawāʿiq* are taken from the second chapter of the work by Ibn Rushd, which intricately deals with the divine attributes. Ibn al-Qayyim's citation begins with Ibn Rushd's specific engagement with the divine attribute of direction (*ṣifat al-jiha*), exactly as addressed

---

or Neoplatinic philosophical basis; Ali Hasan, "Al-Ghazali and Ibn Rushd (Averroes) on Creation and the Divine Attributes," in: J. Diller and A. Kasher (eds.), *Models of God and Alternative Ultimate Realities* (Dordrecht: Springer Netherlands, 2013), 141–143. Notable is the fact that, in *al-Ṣawāʿiq*, Ibn al-Qayyim also briefly referred to Ibn Rushd's work *Tahāfut al-Tahāfut*, dealing with epistemology; Ibn al-Qayyim, *al-Ṣawāʿiq al-mursala*, 3:841.

151 Ibn al-Qayyim, *al-Ṣawāʿiq al-mursala*, 2:401–403. As a matter of fact, Ibn al-Qayyim echoes here the argument on God's unity (*al-waḥda 'l-ilahiyya*) already voiced by Ibn Taymiyya in *Dar' al-taʿāruḍ*, where he refers to the teachings of Ibn Rushd in *al-Kashf*; Ajhar, *Ibn Taymiyya wa-istiʾnāf al-qawl al-falsafī fi 'l-islām*, 84–88.

by Ibn Taymiyya in *Dar᾽ taʿāruḍ al-ʿaql wal-naql*.[152] In his earlier work *Ijtimāʿ al-Juyūsh al-islāmiyya*, Ibn al-Qayyim had already quoted a shortened version of the same part taken from *al-Kashf*.[153] In *al-Ṣawāʿiq*, the first and foremost argument that Ibn al-Qayyim aims to develop is that accepting *ta᾽wīl* exposes the entire corpus of religious texts (*sharʿ*)—and thus religion itself—as being a mere matter of interpretation. In this context, the hermeneutics of Ibn Rushd on the divine attribute of direction are relevant:

> As for the attribute of direction, the people of *sharīʿa* had been affirming it from the beginning, although the Muʿtazilites denied it. Following them, the later Ashʿarites denied it as well, such as Abu ᾿l-Maʿālī [al-Juwaynī] and those who continued his claim. [However,] the entire apparent sacred texts (*wa-ẓawāhir*ᵘ *᾿l-shar*ʿⁱ *kulluhā*) require the affirmation of the direction, such as:
>
> [Q 20:5] "The Lord of Mercy established on His throne"
>
> [Q 69:17] "… on that day, eight of them [i.e., the angels] will bear the throne of your Lord above them"
>
> [Q 32:5] "He runs everything, from the heavens to the earth, and everything will ascend to Him in the end, on a Day that will measure a thousand years in your reckoning"
>
> [Q 70:4] "… The angels and the spirit ascend to Him"
>
> [Q 67:16] "Are you sure that He who is in Heaven will not make the earth swallow you up with a violent shudder?"
>
> And the rest of these verses, which—if the figurative interpretation is imposed—the whole religious texts (*sharʿ*) will become interpreted. If they are regarded as a part of the ambiguous verses (*mutshābihāt*), the whole religious texts will become ambiguous. That is since the entirety of the religious texts rests upon God being in the sky, wherefrom angels descended with Revelation to the prophets, and that from the sky descended the Books, and to the sky the Prophet—peace upon him—ascended [in the Nocturnal Journey, *al-isrā᾽*] until he reached the Lotus Tree [in the seventh heaven]. All of the philosophers (*ḥukamā᾽*) have already agreed that God and His angels are in the sky, as is agreed in all the religions.[154]

---

152 Ibn Taymiyya, *Dar᾽ taʿāruḍ al-ʿaql wal-naql*, 6:212–226.

153 Holtzman and Ovadia, "On Divine Aboveness (*al-Fawqiyya*)," 43–46.

154 Ibn al-Qayyim, *al-Ṣawāʿiq al-mursala*, 2:404–407; Ibn Rushd, *al-Kashf*, 145.

Evidently, Ibn al-Qayyim recruits Ibn Rushd's discussion on the attribute of direction ascribed to God in the Islamic sources, together with the philosopher's argument that negating it or trying to interpret the divine attributes will result in a catastrophe for Islam as a religion. Just like Ibn Taymiyya, Ibn al-Qayyim further cites verbatim the philosophical Aristotelian perception of the divine ontology, diligently following the texts of *al-Kashf*:

> The argument that led them to negate the divine direction is that they opined that the affirmation of a direction requires the affirmation of a spatial place (*makān*), and the affirmation of a spatial place requires the affirmation of physicality (*jismiyya*). But we say: none of this is required. Direction is not a place. Rather, direction is only the surfaces of a body which surround it, and they are six. For animals, there is 'above' and 'under', 'right' and 'left', and 'in front' and 'behind'. Or they are the surfaces of a body surrounded by another body having the above-mentioned six directions. As for the directions, which are the surfaces of the body itself, they are not a place of a body originally; however, the surfaces of bodies which surround [the other body] are its spatial place. Such as the surfaces of air that surround a human being, and the surfaces of the celestial sphere that surround the air so they are the spatial place of the air; and the same goes for all of the celestial spheres that surround each other, and hence are the places of one another. As for the exterior celestial sphere, it is evident that there is no body beyond it; for had it been so, it would be necessary that beyond it be another body to infinity. So that the surface of the exterior body on the world is not a spatial place necessarily, since it cannot contain any other body—for all that is a spatial place must contain a body. Therefore, if there is evidence that something exists in that [exterior] direction, it cannot be a body ... it is also known from the theoretical sciences (*al-ʿulūm al-naẓariyya*) that there cannot be a void [beyond the exterior direction].[155]
>
> But rather, it was established by the ancient opinions and [the evidence of] past religions that this is the dwelling place of the spiritual (*maskan al-rūḥāniyyin*), meaning God and His angels. This is not a spatial place

155 Ibn Rushd accepted the Aristotelian understanding on the external space, including the concepts of place and body, also concerning God: "What lies outside heaven is an infinite void and place in which an infinite body or infinite worlds might exist;" Edward Grant, *Much Ado about Nothing: Theories of Space and Vacuum from the Middle Ages to the Scientific Revolution* (Cambridge [England]; New York: Cambridge University Press, 1981), 17–20, 110, 117–120.

and is not governed by time, because everything governed by time and place can be corrupted. And it is necessary that the things there will be uncorrupted and uncreated (*kāʾin*).

This becomes clear by my saying, that there is nothing there [i.e., in the exterior direction of the universe] except for either an existent that is sensationally perceptible (*al-mawjūd al-maḥsūs*) or inexistence (*ʿadam*). It is self-evident that an existent object is always referred to by its existence; that is, it is said that it exists, or it has an existence. So, if anything exists there, it must be the noblest of all, and it is necessarily referred to as an existent that is sensationally perceptible to the most honorable part, which is Heavens. God said about that: [Q 40:57] "The creation of the heavens and earth is greater by far than the creation of the mankind, though most people do not know it." This is fully acknowledged by the scholars firmly rooted in knowledge [*al-rāsikhīn fī ʾl-ʿilm*, i.e., the natural scientists and the philosophers].

So, it has become clear to you that the affirmation of direction is required by both Religious evidence and Reason (*wājib^{un} bil-sharʿ^{i} wal-ʿaql^{i}*). [Direction] comes in the sacred texts and is set by it. Rejecting this principle is a rejection of religious evidence. It is difficult to make one understand this along with negating physicality (*maʿ^{a} nafī ʾl-jismiyya*), as there is no visible illustration of it, which is for itself the reason that the religious texts do not declare to reject a body for the Creator exalted; as the common people will confirm an invisible object when its existence is known in the visible world, such as the existence of the Maker … [This is known] only by the scholars firmly rooted in knowledge … sacred evidence is given only when the subject is required to be known, like knowledge of the soul … The fear of those rejecting [the divine] direction is that the common people will not be able to comprehend it, because they have not been informed beforehand that God is not a body. Therefore, it is necessary to take examples [for the matter] from the entire religious texts; otherwise, figurative interpretation [will be imposed] on that which religious evidence did not declare to be interpreted.[156]

156 Ibn al-Qayyim, *al-Ṣawāʿiq al-mursala*, 2:407–411; Ibn Rushd, *al-Kashf*, 145–147. In order to achieve a more accurate account of Ibn Rushd's text with relation to Ibn al-Qayyim's writing, I translated the passages myself while consulting two previous translations: Ibrahim Y. Najjar, *Faith and Reason in Islam*, 54–56, and Mohammad Jamil-ur-Rahman, *The Philosophy and Theology of Ibn Rushd: Tractata Translated from Arabic* (Baroda: Manibhai Mathurbhal Gupta, 1921), 172–181.

Supported by Revelation and Reason alike, Ibn Rushd depicts in these passages the cosmological array of the universe and God's unphysical being in the exterior heaven.[157] This perception is confirmed by the verses of the Quran, which are used at times to sustain Ibn Rushd's ontological understanding of the divine attribute of direction. Ibn al-Qayyim's recruitment of the ideas articulated by Ibn Rushd faithfully follows Ibn Taymiyya's teachings denouncing the later Ashʿarite formulation of the allegorical method of interpretation (*taʾwīl*) via the authority of the celebrated philosopher. The Taymiyyan agreement with Ibn Rushd's outlook against Ashʿarite hermeneutics definitely represents their shared belief in the veridical reality of divine attributes.[158] In my opinion, it is also a result of the striking compatibility between Ibn Taymiyya's perceptions of Reason with respect to Revelation and Ibn Rushd's theory of rationality and the unity of truth and existence. This observation meets the argument raised in recent research that the Taymiyyan aspiration of harmonizing Reason and Revelation was possibly even encouraged by the thought of Ibn Rushd.[159] However, unlike the Taymiyyan hermeneutical model—which was further constructed by Ibn al-Qayyim—the fundamental source of authority to Ibn Rushd's claim to affirm the divine direction is the scientific knowledge of the philosophers, being the guardians of Reason, through whom knowledge on the metaphysical is attained.[160]

It can be said that the hostility articulated by Ibn Rushd against Ashʿarite *taʾwīl* stems from a worldview of scholarly hierarchy, which differs from al-Ghazālī's more clearly elitist later Ashʿarite stance, and is also notably more moderate. According to Ibn Rushd, knowledge about God and the metaphysical is accessible to all people; however, it is an asset which requires a qualified

157 Ibn Taymiyya also shared Ibn Rushd's Aristotelian explanation on the movement of the heavenly spheres, which is relevant to God's attribute of direction; Tamer, "The Curse of Philosophy," 346; al-Ṣughayyar, *"Mawāqif "rushdiyya" li-Taqī al-Dīn Ibn Taymiyya?,"* 117; Najjar, "Ibn Rushd's Theory of Rationality," 207–211.

158 Ibn Rushd's ontological view regarding the divine attributes is contrasted with al-Ghazālī's monism in: Hasan, *Al-Ghazali and Ibn Rushd (Averroes) on Creation and the Divine Attributes*, 155.

159 Tamer, "The Curse of Philosophy," 329–332, 347; Kügelgen, "The Poison of Philosophy," 256, 289, footnote 152; Ajhar, *Ibn Taymiyya wa-istiʾnāf al-qawl al-falsafī fi 'l-islām*, 82–84. According to my inspection of the text *Darʾ taʿāruḍ al-ʿaql wal-naql*, Ibn Taymiyya indeed depends on Ibn Rushd in a considerable manner, as he significantly relies there on a quotation from *al-Kashf* and discusses them, for example (on the divine attributes): Ibn Taymiyya, *Darʾ taʿāruḍ al-ʿaql wal-naql*, 6:212–245, 9:84–112, 10:242–284.

160 Najjar, "Ibn Rushd's Theory of Rationality," 199.

treatment. The expertise of the philosophers is needed to transfer the religious tenets and commands to the general public (*jumhūr*) using both Scriptures and Reason.[161] Nonetheless, a portion of the scholars (i.e., the Ashʿarite dialecticians) does not manage to grasp the inherent meanings of the texts, thus expressing doubts on the knowledge derived therefrom; these are the ones who ought to be condemned. Thus, Ibn Rushd describes three levels of proficiency in the acquisition of religious knowledge (*al-taʿlīm al-sharʿī*): the scholars firmly rooted in knowledge (*al-ʿulamāʾ al-rāsikhīn*), who are the fewest in number; the scholars who express doubts about the texts, who cause the ambiguity (*tashābuh*) and are to be condemned; and the laymen who are the majority of people. In this manner, Ibn Rushd indirectly forms an epistemic hierarchy and defines the role of philosophers as the deliverers of religious knowledge to the masses, the quality of which is a result of the competence of the highest scholars. Most significant is Ibn Rushd's observation concerning the 'middle category' of doubtful scholars: religious corpus (*sharʿ*) for them is like bread made of wheat to some people; usually it is nutritious food, but for a small number of people it is harmful. According to Ibn Rushd, those are the ones referred to in verse Q 2:26 "it is only the rebels He makes go astray."[162]

Ibn al-Qayyim's quotation continues in the next two sections from *al-Kashf*, in which Ibn Rushd expresses a harsh criticism against the scholars of *Kalām*. The first passage is titled in the edited text of *al-Kashf* as "The Ambiguous" (*al-mutashābih*), where Ibn Rushd explains that the ambiguous verses of the Quran are merely few in number, and most of them inform on that which is concealed and have no explanatory visible evidence (*ashyāʾ fī 'l-ghāʾib*^i^ *lays*^a^ *lahā mithāl*^un^ *fī 'l-shāhid*^in^). Those who are unable to properly apprehend them assimilate them to the known and visible, which causes them to have a peculiar feeling and doubts. As Ibn Rushd puts it, these are the "ill minority" of the dialecticians and scholars of *Kalām* (*ahl al-jadal wal-kalām*). He states the worse infliction they had upon religious thought was their allegorical interpretation of what they perceived as being opposed to its apparent expression, thereby altering the original intention of the texts. In fact, Ibn Rushd accuses the rationalists of announcing the parts of the Islamic texts they had failed to understand as 'ambiguous' which they then figuratively interpret; viz., the declaration of textual ambiguity is a part of the Ashʿarite hermeneutical methodology. In his

161 Najjar, "Ibn Rushd's Theory of Rationality," 200–201; Hasan, *Al-Ghazali and Ibn Rushd (Averroes) on Creation and the Divine Attributes*, 150–152; Ibn Rushd, *al-Kashf*, the editor's introduction, 73.

162 Ibn al-Qayyim, *al-Ṣawāʿiq al-mursala*, 2:411–412; Ibn Rushd, *al-Kashf*, 147–148; Najjar, "Ibn Rushd's Theory of Rationality," 203–204.

opinion, this is utterly wrongful and has no proof (*burhān*); even more so, it harmfully affects both the theoretical knowledge that is transferred to the public and the religious practices—*al-ʿilm wal-ʿamal* (as previously mentioned by Ibn al-Qayyim).[163]

The last passage cited by Ibn al-Qayyim from the text *al-Kashf* firmly involves the detrimental implications of the rationalistic *taʾwīl* on the religious texts (*sharʿ*). Ibn Rushd illustrates the acts of interpreting a single fraction of the Islamic texts, claiming that this interpretation is grasping the intention in the texts and transferring this intention to the laymen, like the act of a handing out a medicine prescribed and made by a skillful physician in order to safeguard the public's health. If a person of a rare damaged nature finds the highly beneficial medicine unsuitable for himself, therefore announcing an alternative medicine with a far-fetched metaphorical name (other than the first medication's common one), people are attracted to that second false 'interpreted' medicine, and the first powerful medicine loses its prestige as well as its benefit. Moreover, additional falsified re-modeled medicines appear, the use of which harms the people and will even cause further illnesses which were unknown before the synthetically 'interpreted' medicines. As time goes by, the true essence of the first valuable medicine is disastrously dented, so that it may no longer cure people. To the mind of Ibn Rushd, this is the situation religious knowledge has been facing with each group who attempted to interpret the textual sources, slashing it into pieces and distancing it from its original meaning. When the Prophet Muḥammad—referred to as *ṣāḥib al-sharʿ*—learnt of this, he said in a Hadith account: "My community will be parted into 72 groups, all of which will arrive to Hellfire except for one," that is the group that follows the apparent meanings of the religious texts (*ẓāhir al-sharʿ*) and do not interpret it with *taʾwīl*. The first group to 'alter the great of all medicines' was the Khārijites, then the Muʿtazilites, then the Ṣūfīs, and then came Abu 'l-Ḥāmid al-Ghazālī and "the torrent of the valley over-fled the meadows."[164]

All in all, Ibn al-Qayyim utilization of the teachings and works of the philosopher of Islam is striking. It would make sense that it was a shared enemy which inspired Ibn al-Qayyim and made him cite Ibn Rushd, rather than Ibn al-Qayyim's affinity to philosophy; he openly criticized the philosophers in many occasions in *al-Ṣawāʿiq*.[165] Nevertheless, the approach reflected in Ibn

163 Ibn al-Qayyim, *al-Ṣawāʿiq al-mursala*, 2:412–414; Ibn Rushd, *al-Kashf*, 148–149; Najjar, "Ibn Rushd's Theory of Rationality," 209–212.

164 Ibn al-Qayyim, *al-Ṣawāʿiq al-mursala*, 2:414–418; Ibn Rushd, *al-Kashf*, 149–150.

165 For example, see Ibn al-Qayyim's criticism against the Muslim philosophers as it appears in the discussion in chapter 3, page 134.

Rushd's discussion in *al-Kashf* was certainly music to Ibn al-Qayyim's ears, especially the former's conception of the place of Reason as complimenting Revelation rather than being of higher supremacy. In this respect, notable is that Ibn Rushd's anti-Ashʿarite criticism is already evident in the teachings of Ibn Taymiyya, who was well aware of the intellectual trends of his times and the rivalries within Islamic rationalism itself. Ibn Rushd's approach challenged the Ashʿarites of the 6th/12th century, as he revived the Peripatetic tradition in Islamic thought and reproached the Ashʿarites for using superficial methods of argumentation.[166] Ibn Taymiyya's correct historical impressions seem to have been successfully implemented in Ibn al-Qayyim's own thought as it is unfolded in *al-Ṣawāʿiq*.

Furthermore, Ibn al-Qayyim's lengthy engagement with Ibn Rushd's notions on the divine attributes and his denunciation of al-Ghazālī—the conceiver of the 'universal rule of interpretation'—proves the richness of the sources at Ibn al-Qayyim's disposal and his convincing manner of using them. Ibn Rushd's *al-Kashf* is a work of theory and methodology, which deals with subjects similar to those discussed in *al-Ṣawāʿiq*. The hermeneutical view formulated by Ibn Rushd therein does indeed resemble that which Ibn al-Qayyim promoted, in the sense of amplifying the ontological aspect of the divine attributes as having qualities of a perfect essence. Another similarity is, as noted, the mutual discrediting of the rationalistic method of *taʾwīl* taken by the Ashʿarites, which is based upon the Muʿtazilite instrumental concept of *majāz*. However, the motives for which each of the scholars (i.e., Ibn Rushd and Ibn al-Qayyim) opposed later Ashʿarite rationalism must be differentiated. Whereas Ibn Rushd advocated in favor of a hierarchical approach, dividing the intellectual roles of the scholarly elite (*khāṣṣa*) from that of the laymen (*ʿāmma*), Ibn al-Qayyim shared his mentor's pragmatic approach regarding knowledge acquisition. In *al-Ṣawāʿiq* Ibn al-Qayyim explicitly hands readers a practical methodology for Taymiyyan hermeneutics, stressing the element of context-dependent meaning (*qarīna*) which is ingrained in the speaker's habitual use of language (*ʿurf*). The notion leading this practical epistemic approach entails the Taymiyyan conviction that knowledge is accessible for all—not only for the scholarly elite—via the apparent Islamic texts. This has to do with the different political power battles Ibn Taymiyya and Ibn al-Qayyim encountered in the scenery of

166 It was only in the 7th/13th century that Ashʿarite scholars such as Fakhr al-Dīn al-Rāzī and Sayf al-Dīn al-Āmidī developed the Ashʿarite methods and led Ashʿarism to flourish; M. Sait Özervarli, "The Qurʾānic Rational Theology of Ibn Taymiyya and His Criticism of the Mutakallimūn", in: ed. Yossef Rapoport and Shahab Ahmed, *Ibn Taymiyya and His Times*, (Karachi: Oxford University Press, 2010), 78–79.

8th/14th century Mamluk Damascus, in which they were generally considered and treated as the politically weaker party. Be that as it may, Ibn al-Qayyim's harnessing of Ibn Rushd's theological-philosophical work and his citation of this work in *al-Ṣawāʿiq* shows their shared hermeneutical values and most certainly sheds more light on Ibn al-Qayyim's hermeneutical engagement as a whole.

CHAPTER 6

Fourth *ṭāghūt* Refutation: Hadith Literature Produces Certainty

Shifting his discussion back to the subject matter of epistemology and the level of certainty which can be attained from the Islamic canonical scriptures, Ibn al-Qayyim's fourth *ṭāghūt* refutation in *al-Ṣawāʿiq* focuses on specific traditions within the vast literature of Hadith classified as *akhbār al-āḥād*, viz., traditions of a limited number of chains of transmission.[1] This category of Prophetic traditions stems from the formal disciplines of Hadith criticism which developed in the first centuries of Islam in a scholarly attempt to preserve the Prophetic traditions and their authenticity, as well as to prevent potential forgery. The scientific branch called *ʿilm al-jarḥ wal-taʿdīl*, which evaluates the reliability of the traditions according to their narrators and distribution range, commonly identifies three types of *ḥadīth*s: *mutawātir* (i.e., massively transmitted), *manshūr* (i.e., well-known, widely distributed) and *āḥād* (also known as *kabar al-wāḥid*; a tradition of a limited number of transmissions). In the field of Islamic legal methodological theory (*uṣūl al-fiqh*), this classification entailed significant jurisprudential implications. Since the two first degrees of *mutawātir* and *manshūr* were perceived as producers of certain knowledge, they were commonly accepted as the second source of Islamic law, after the Quran. Yet, *akhbār al-āḥād* were mostly regarded as much inferior to the first two types in their epistemic value and the kind of knowledge they might produce for legal rulings.[2]

Therefore, the epistemological status of different *ḥadīth*s is directly connected to their validation and legitimization as producers of religious knowledge. For our discussion in the current chapter, the dilemma which specifically

---

1 Due to the varying terminology which appears in the primary text of *al-Ṣawāʿiq*, henceforth I use the terms *khabar* and *ḥadīth* interchangeably to denote a single Prophetic tradition.

2 Whereas *ḥadīth mutawātir* "has been transmitted throughout the first three centuries of Muslims by such a large number of narrators that the possibility of fabrication must be entirely discarded", a *manshūr* is one "which although transmitted in the first generation by two, three or four transmitters, was later transmitted, on their authority, by a large number in the subsequent two generations," and *āḥād* are "traditions which were transmitted during the first three centuries of Muslims by one (or two, three or four) narrators only;" Siddiqi, *Hadith Literature*, 1–13, 107–110; Zysow, *The Economy of Certainty*, 7–13.

 | DOI: 10.1163/9789004372511_008

refers to *akhbār al-āḥād* is: do they yield knowledge of certainty, and how so? In a prominent study that explores diverse aspects of the topic, Aron Zysow probes relevant mechanisms established in the field of *uṣūl al-fiqh* for the authentication of *ḥadīths*. Zysow examines the dividing line in Islamic legal theory, distinguishing between epistemological formalism and materialism. The formalist jurists considered the leading validating force of the texts to be the general framework of the system of *uṣūl al-fiqh*. In their opinion, the stability of this religious science inferred the high quality of their ruling effort, even if it resulted only in a presumption (and not in certain knowledge). According to the formalists, the validating force of *ḥadīths* was the reliability of their chains of transmission; hence, *ḥadīth al-āḥād* is invalid and produces no trustworthy knowledge. As for the materialist jurists, the validating force of *ḥadīths* was their matter, meaning the contents they convey. Preferring substance to form, the materialists saw the chains of narration as a lesser factor in the validation of *ḥadīths*. *Ḥadīth al-āḥād* is thus authentic and produces certain knowledge. Furthermore, in the eyes of the materialists, a presumption had no room in the formulation of the rules of law, since the religious law must be firmly anchored in certitude. Such certitude exists in the substance of the *ḥadīths*.[3]

As was shown in chapters 2 and 3 before, a comparable discussion on the epistemic certainty of the textual sources was a point of a crucial disagreement between rationalist and the traditionalist theologians in the debate about divine attributes. Originated in legal theory, the idea of authentication of *ḥadīths* and the terminology on their classification permeated the closely connected realm of Islamic theology. Since theology holds the highest rank amongst the Islamic religious sciences—above that of any legal theory—the predicament of 'certainty vs. presumption' increased substantially. For formalists and materialists alike, only certain knowledge is permissible when engaging with the divine, not a presumption. In his fourth *ṭāghūt* refutation in *al-Ṣawāʿiq*, Ibn al-Qayyim seeks to refute the rationalistic claim that *ḥadīth al-āḥād* does not produce certainty and therefore cannot be advanced as an argument on any of the divine attributes (*lā yuḥtajj bi-kalām rasūl Allāh*^{i} *ʿalā shayʾ*^{in} *min ṣifāt*^{i} *dhi ʾl-jalāl*^{i}).[4] Following the lines of the legal classifications for the validation of *ḥadīths*, this rationalistic principal evidently conveys a formalist epistemological approach.

---

3 Aron Zysow, *The Economy of Certainty*, 2–5.

4 Ibn Qayyim al-Jawziyya, *Mukhtaṣar al-Ṣawāʿiq* (the abridgement of Ibn al-Mawṣilī), 4:1400–1401.

Thus, Ibn al-Qayyim's fourth *ṭāghūt* refutation in *al-Ṣawāʿiq* has to do with the differentiated epistemological attitudes each theological school expressed towards *aḥādīth al-ṣifāt*, many of which are classified as *ḥadīth al-āḥād*. *Aḥādīth al-ṣifāt* contain the most challenging anthropomorphic descriptions of God, and therefore were not always easily accepted as producing knowledge, let alone certainty. The ultra-rationalist Muʿtazilites, for example, did not hesitate to discard these anthropomorphic *ḥadīth*s, as they rejected (or simply ignored) the problematic descriptions of God in *aḥādīth al-ṣifāt*. Contrariwise, the Ḥanbalite traditionalists largely accepted the entire corpus of *ḥadīth*s as producers of knowledge about God, irrespective to the classification (relying on their literal understanding "without asking how" they realize). For the innately traditionalistic nature of the Ashʿarite school and its basic commitment to the textual sources, discarding the problematic *ḥadīth*s—as had been done by the Muʿtazilites—was not as simple. Still adhering to the texts, they employed the traditionalistic formula of *bi-lā kayfa* while accommodating the method of *taʾwīl* in order to allegorically interpret *aḥādīth al-ṣifāt* in an appropriate manner to the discourse about God (i.e., without interpreting their modality). The later Ashʿarites presented a more convoluted epistemological approach. Fakhr al-Dīn al-Rāzī, for example, never forbade the use of *aḥādīth al-ṣifāt* in theological debates; however his arguments in favor of their understanding by *taʾwīl* differed from that of his preceding Ashʿarites, taking a far more *Kalām*ic-philosophical slant.[5] In his already mentioned work *Asās al-taqdīs*, al-Rāzī reproved the traditionalistic approval of *akhbār al-āḥād* as part of his general promotion of *taʾwīl*. Articulating a formalist stance, he perceived *akhbār al-āḥād* as invalid for attaining knowledge about God and His attributes, since they only produce presumptions (*inna ahbāra ʾl-āḥādi maẓnūnatun*).[6] That is precisely the allegation Ibn al-Qayyim seeks to counter in his fourth *ṭāghūt* refutation in *al-Ṣawāʿiq*, advocating for epistemological materialism of *akhbār al-āḥād*.

---

5 Holtzman, *Anthropomorphism in Islam*, 301–302, 306–308.

6 Fakhr al-Dīn al-Rāzī, *Asās al-taqdīs*, 215–219; al-Rāzī dedicates an independent section (some 3 pages) to the subject of *akhbār al-āḥād*. In addition, he articulates the same stance in considerably shortened versions (as a single sentence or even a comment) in two of his works already discussed in chapter 3 above: *al-Muḥaṣṣal*, 208 (*wa-riwāyatu ʾl-āḥādi lā tufīdu ʾl-ʿilma*), and in *Kitāb al-Arbaʿīn*, 2:252. In *Kitāb al-Arbaʿīn*, al-Rāzī mentions the *riwāyat al-āḥād* as a producer of mere presumption in his elaboration on the second condition among the 'ten conditions needed for certitude' constituting the first *ṭāghūt* in *al-Ṣawāʿiq* (for the works' description, see section 3.2).

This chapter concentrates on the final chord of *al-Ṣawāʿiq* and therefore comprises Ibn al-Qayyim's fourth *ṭāghūt* refutation and his advancement of the Taymiyyan approach: section 6.1 briefly describes Ibn Taymiyya's initial view on *akhbār al-āḥād*, while section 6.2 thereafter presents Ibn al-Qayyim's singular appropriation thereof in *al-Ṣawāʿiq*'s final refutation. Sealing the engagement with *al-Ṣawāʿiq*'s text, section 6.3 zooms out of the individual *ṭāghūt* refutations, taking a wider look on the structure of the work and its special relation to al-Rāzī's *Asās al-taqdīs*. This section also unravels *al-Ṣawāʿiq*'s functional structure of literary symmetry.

6.1 Ibn Taymiyya on the Validity of *ḥadīth al-āḥād*

Due to his strict adherence to the Islamic texts as providers of instinctive knowledge, Ibn Taymiyya held a materialist approach with respect to *ḥadīth al-āḥād*. Furthermore, belonging to the canonic Hadith literature, he deemed these *ḥadīth*s as producers of certainty. In a short yet instructive section in his immense work *Darʾ taʿāruḍ al-ʿaql wal-naql*, Ibn Taymiyya lists the main approaches of traditionalist theologians concerning the affirmation of divine attributes which convey information about God's essence and actions (*al-ṣifāt al-khabariyya*). Generally, Ibn Taymiyya explains, the traditionalists affirm these divine attributes. Nevertheless, some scholars—such as Ibn ʿAqīl, at times[7]—affirm only the divine attributes which appear in the Quran and the massively transmitted *ḥadīth*s (*al-sunna al-mutawātira*); however they negate attributes which lack a cogent indicator (*dalīl qāṭiʿ*). Other scholars affirm the divine attributes by the force of *akhbār al-āḥād* which are to be accepted. Others only affirm the divine attributes by the power of absolutely sound (*ṣaḥīḥa*) *ḥadīth*s. Lastly, Ibn Taymiyya depicts the technique he perceives as the most correct one. According to him, every piece of indicative evidence has its own power (*ḥaqq*); if it is cogent (*qāṭiʿ*), we can cogently affirm the attributes. If an indicator outweighs another one (*rājiḥ*) but is not cogent, we acknowledge its power. That is to say, we either affirm or negate the attributes only by the power of cogent indicators. In case of an outweighing indicator, we 'tip the scale' to its direction.[8] With specific relation to the epistemic status of different indicators, Ibn Taymiyya's description here still lacks the kind of knowledge produced by *akhbār al-āḥād*, although he definitely accepts their authority as yielders of religious knowledge.

7 See footnotes 3 and 4 in chapter 3.

8 Ibn Taymiyya, *Darʾ taʿāruḍ al-ʿaql wal-naql*, 3:383–384.

Supplementary clarification is found in Ibn Taymiyya's work *Bayān talbīs al-jahmiyya*. Replying back to al-Rāzī's denunciation of "those who affirm [the divine] direction" (*muthbiti 'l-jiha^{ti}*, which in his opinion required ascribing God a physical form and location above the skies, and hence anthropomorphism), Ibn Taymiyya unfolds another part of his positive assessment of *akhbār al-āḥād*. To his mind, since the textual sources are abundant with evidence on the divine aboveness (*al-fawqiyya*), they sustain each other, and therefore, turn into producers of certitude. This applies to other evidence as well: when the apparent expressions in the textual sources (*ẓawāhir*) accumulate and support one another as they point to a single indication, they become cogent. In a similar manner, when numerous presumptions (*ẓunūn*) back each other up, they create certain knowledge. That is also the case of *akhbār al-āḥād*—when they consecutively arrive conveying a single meaning, they gain the status of *tawātur*; that is to say, they must be acknowledged as valid producers of certain knowledge.[9] This is, then, the underlying materialist principle Ibn Taymiyya passed onwards to Ibn al-Qayyim, pertaining to the theological issue of divine attributes.

Before delving into Ibn al-Qayyim's appropriation of the Taymiyyan stance as to *ḥadīth al-āḥād*, an essential remark must be noted. The Taymiyyan succinct reasoning depicted above does not seem to have grown to become a prominent Ḥanbalite epistemological notion as far as it had to do with *uṣūl al-fiqh*. In sharp contrast to Ibn Taymiyya and Ibn al-Qayyim, two earlier important Ḥanbalite scholars of rationalistic inclinations, Ibn ʿAqīl and Abū Yaʿla ibn al-Farra' (who were mentioned in chapter 5), had already stood by the formalist view on *ḥadīth al-āḥād*. They found these *ḥadīth*s to produce meager presumptions which are insufficient evidence for theological debates. In the long run, and despite the bold Taymiyyan attitude, the formalist position became the standard of the Ḥanbalite school (for various reasons which rest beyond the aim of our present discussion). In fact, Ibn Taymiyya shared significant epistemological suppositions about the certitude derived from *ḥadīth al-āḥād* with no other than Ibn Ḥazm of the Ẓāhirite school.[10] As will be shown in the next section, further illustration of the resemblance of their perspectives is found in Ibn al-Qayyim's fourth *ṭāghūt* refutation in *al-Ṣawāʿiq*.

---

9 Ibn Taymiyya, *Bayān talbīs al-jahmiyya*, 5:304–305, 316–317.

10 Zysow, *The Economy of Certainty*, 29–34.

6.2 Ibn al-Qayyim's Ten Arguments on the Value of *ḥadīth al-āḥād*

In the opening of his fourth *ṭāghūt* refutation, Ibn al-Qayyim presents the statement made by "the people of *taʿṭīl*" (i.e., those who 'strip' God from His attributes, the Muʿtazilites and Ashʿarites): Prophetical tradition with a limited number of chains of transmission cannot produce certain knowledge. Even without stating any particular scholar by name, it soon becomes evident that Ibn al-Qayyim refers to al-Rāzī's formalistic stance expressed in *Asās al-taqdīs* against the validity of *akhbār al-āḥād* in any discussion on the divine.[11] For Ibn al-Qayyim, this declaration renounces de facto the entire corpus of Hadith from supplying apodictic and cogent indications in theological deliberations, the issue of divine attributes included. As he scolds the Rāziyyan opinion, Ibn al-Qayyim argues that the rationalists divide the *ḥadīth*s into two types: *mutawātir* and *āḥād*. Within this division, even when the chain of authorities of *ḥadīth mutawātir* is cogent (*qaṭʿi 'l-sanad*), its indication is not cogent (*ghayr*^{u} *qaṭʿi 'l-dalāla*^{ti}); as for *ḥadīth al-āḥād*, it does not produce any knowledge at all (*lā tufīd*^{u} *'l-ʿilm*^{a}). Hence, verbal indicators (*adilla lafẓiyya*) do not produce certain knowledge (*al-yaqīn*).[12] According to Ibn al-Qayyim, this claim slanders the Quranic indications as well as sayings of the Prophet on the divine attributes. Instead of holding onto the textual sources, people turn to imaginary theories and conditionings they designate as rational cogencies (*qawāṭiʿ ʿaqliyya*) and transmitted proofs (*barāhin naqliyya*). In fact, Ibn al-Qayyim maintains, similar to other deeds of disbelieves, the rationalistic thinking method is (Q, 24:39) "like a mirage in a desert: the thirsty person thinks there will be water but, when he gets there, he finds it is nothing. There he finds only God, who pays him his account in full—God is swift in reckoning."[13] Therefore, much like in the case of the first *ṭāghūt* in *al-Ṣawāʿiq*, Ibn al-Qayyim's fourth *ṭāghūt* refutation responds to a particular section on epistemology in al-Rāzī's work *Asās al-taqdīs*.

Ibn al-Qayyim's reply in the fourth refutation includes ten arguments which are aimed to support his opposed postulation, advancing the materialistic obligation to see the text of the Hadith as indicative evidence on the divine

11 See footnote 6 above.

12 This division concerning *ḥadīth al-āḥād* also appears in al-Rāzī's discussion in *Kitāb al-maḥsūl fī ʿilm al-uṣūl*, as he mentions the opinion of the Baghdadi grammarian and philologist Abu 'l-Brrakāt (ibn) al-Anbarī (d. 577/1181; for example, in his work *Lumaʿ al-adilla fī usūl al-nahw*). Once again al-Rāzī's epistemic skepticism prevailed, arguing that even *ḥadīth mutawātir* does not assist in achieving certainty of knowledge; Weiss, "Language and Tradition in Medieval Islam," 93–97.

13 Ibn Qayyim al-Jawziyya, *Mukhtaṣar al-Ṣawāʿiq* (the abridgement of Ibn al-Mawṣilī), 4:1401.

attributes. The first three arguments are rather short and express an overall traditionalistic fideistic approach. First, Ibn al-Qayyim notes *ḥadīth*s produce cogent indication on the speaker's intention, as he has already treated this epistemic concept at length before. Second, the *ḥadīth*s which are dismissed as belonging to the category of *al-āḥād* comply with the Quran; they interpret it, further elaborate and explain its content, and also comply with the massively transmitted traditions. The reasoning of the rationalists on this point is the same as that which was used to discard the Quran from providing certain knowledge (like in the first *ṭāghūt*); if before they rejected it arguing for its kind of indication (as in being verbal indication; *min jiha^ti 'l-dalāla*), now they turn to the formalist aspect of the chains of transmissions (*min jiha^ti 'l-sanad*). One way or another, says Ibn al-Qayyim, the apodictic epistemic status (*manzila*) of *ḥadīth al-āḥād* is equal to that of the stories in the Quran (*qiṣaṣ al-qur'ān*). Pinpointing the origin of the rationalistic claim, Ibn al-Qayyim ascribes it first to the Muʿtazilites, and then to the Ashʿarites and the philosophers.[14] The third argument Ibn al-Qayyim provides has to do with the Islamic obligation to accept the textual sources of Revelation (*wujūb talqīhā bil-qubūl^i*). Abundantly citing the texts of Revelation (*nuṣūṣ al-waḥy*), Ibn al-Qayyim describes the ways in which the righteous early scholars of the *salaf* interpreted the anthropomorphic descriptions of God in the Quran using the Hadith (i.e., *tafsīr bil-ma'thūr*), such as God's form (*ṣūra*), happiness (*faraḥ*) or laughter (*ḍiḥk*).[15] In addition, he recounts that whoever dismisses *aḥādīth al-ṣifāt* for being *akhbār al-āḥād* which 'do not produce knowledge,' betrays the religious command to love the Prophet and to pursue his judgment (*farḍ ḥubb al-rasūl wa-wujūb al-taḥākum ilayh^i*). These are the people referred to in verse Q 4:60 "Do you [Prophet] not see those who claim to believe in what has been sent down to you, and in what was sent down before you, yet still want to turn to unjust tyrants (*ṭawāghīt*) for judgment, although they have been ordered to reject them? Satan wants to lead them far astray."[16]

The following arguments 4–7 comprise the middle part of Ibn al-Qayyim's refutation and reflect his approach in a more interesting rationalized-traditionalistic mode of argumentation. The fourth of Ibn al-Qayyim's arguments is the

14 Ibn Qayyim al-Jawziyya, *Mukhtaṣar al-Ṣawāʿiq* (the abridgement of Ibn al-Mawṣilī), 4:1402–1410.

15 Ibn Qayyim al-Jawziyya, *Mukhtaṣar al-Ṣawāʿiq* (the abridgement of Ibn al-Mawṣilī), 4:1411–1431.

16 The third argument is the only one which is not clearly indicated, however it seems to begin in page 1407; Ibn Qayyim al-Jawziyya, *Mukhtaṣar al-Ṣawāʿiq* (the abridgement of Ibn al-Mawṣilī), 4:1446–1449.

lengthiest one, in which he elaborately attests to the knowledge and certitude produced by *akhbār al-āḥād.* Ibn al-Qayyim starts with presenting four kinds of *ḥadīth*s accepted for theoretical informative issues (*al-umūr al-khabariyya 'l-ʿilmiyya*):

1. Massively transmitted traditions, both in their verbal expressions and meaning.
2. Massively transmitted traditions in their meaning, even if they were expressed in more than one way.
3. Clearly expressed/perspicuous (*mustafīḍa*) traditions which are accepted by the Muslim community.
4. Traditions with a limited number of chains of transmissions told by a righteous one (*al-ʿadal al-ḍābiṭ*) on behalf of another righteous and so on, until they reach God's Messenger.

The first two kinds mostly contain eschatological *ḥadīth*s, including God's attributes of aboveness and his seat on His throne (*aḥādīth ʿulūh*^{u} *fawq*^{a} *samawātih*^{i} *ʿalā ʿarshih*^{i}) and Him being seen and addressing the believers in the Day of Judgment (*ru'yat*^{i} *'l-rabb tabārak*^{a} *wa-taʿālā wa-taklīmih*^{i} *ʿibādah*^{u} *yawm*^{a} *'l-qiyāmat*^{i}). Ibn al-Qayyim states that, since these *ḥadīth*s preserve the Prophet's expressions and intended meaning, they necessarily produce certain, beneficial knowledge that cannot be rebutted. For the traditionalist (*ahl al-ḥadīth*), this knowledge is greater than that of the best physicians, such as Hippocrates (d. 370 BC) or Galen (d. ca. 210 AD), and that of the eminent Arab grammarians, such as Sībawayhi (d. ca. 177/793), al-Khalīl (d. ca. 175/791) or al-Farrā' (d. 207/822); however, the speculating rationalists (*ahl al-kalām*)—the Muʿtazilites and their followers, i.e., the Ashʿarites—are the least knowledgeable of the Hadith, show no interest in it and deny its certitude.[17]

As for *khabar al-wāḥid,* Ibn al-Qayyim admits not all of these *ḥadīth*s produce knowledge or certainty, since that depends of the reliability level of its single narrator. Nevertheless, that does not suffice in order to discredit these *ḥadīth*s altogether. According to Ibn al-Qayyim, *khabar al-wāḥid* produces knowledge under particular conditions. First, in case there is a cogent indicative proof on its correctness; this is a conquering tradition (*khabar*^{u} *'l-wāḥid*^{u} *'l-qahhār*^{u}) whose transmitter was indeed reliable. Another possibility

17 Apparently, Ibn al-Qayyim skips the third kind listed above, although it is plausible that the discussion on the first two kinds apply to the third as well; Ibn Qayyim al-Jawziyya, *Mukhtaṣar al-Ṣawāʿiq* (the abridgement of Ibn al-Mawṣilī), 4:1459–1462.

for *khabar al-wāḥid* to produce knowledge is that in which the tradition was transmitted in the presence of the Prophet himself, thus gaining his direct validation. That is, for example, the case of 'the *ḥadīth* of the divine fingers', which describes God placing the skies, the earths and the trees on his fingers. According to the *ḥadīth*, when the Prophet heard that, he laughed as a sign of admiration and approval of its truthfulness;[18] hence, this *khabar al-wāḥid* produces certain knowledge. The same goes for *ḥadīth*s the Prophet's companions transmitted to one another on behalf of the Prophet, for they are the most knowledgeable, righteous men. Since *aḥādīth al-ṣifāt* were transmitted in a similar manner on behalf of the God's Messenger, Ibn al-Qayyim announces they produce cogent and certain knowledge. Disvaluing these traditions is therefore contrary to the consensus (*ijmāʿ*) of the companions, their followers and the four great Imams (i.e., *al-salaf*). To sustain his claim, Ibn al-Qayyim sets forth numerous citations of previous scholars, including Ibn Taymiyya, who trustfully accepted *akhbār al-wāḥid*. Moreover, Ibn al-Qayyim says, if the many scholars who heard a certain tradition accepted its veracity unanimously, that indicates its knowledge is true, for had it been false, they would not have remained silent and would have announced it to be false. Therefore, the produced knowledge is a result of their speculative contemplation (*wal-ʿilm*^{un}... *wāqiʿ*^{un} *ʿan naẓar*^{in} *wa-istidlāl*^{in}).[19]

Next, Ibn al-Qayyim presents the opinion of his Shaykh, Ibn Taymiyya, who differentiated between massively transmitted *ḥadīth*s (in *tawātur*) and those which had only limited chains of narration (*āḥād*). Referring to the latter kind, Ibn Taymiyya explains that these are *ḥadīth*s told by a single righteous one, whose expressions were not transmitted verbatim and meanings were transmitted only in a general manner. Nevertheless, the Islamic community validates these *ḥadīth*s and believes in them. Thus, they indeed produce certain knowledge for the believers, be them either of the first generations of Islam or their followers. The worthy ancestors (*al-salaf*) had no disagreement about that, and this is also the jurisprudential way of their followers (*al-khalaf*) among the four Imams (*madhhab al-fuqahāʾ al-kibār*). Ibn Taymiyya lists well-known scholars of each of the four legal schools in Islam who approved *akhbār al-āḥād*, and amid them he also mentions rationalist scholars, such as the important early Ashʿarites Abū Isḥāq al-Isfarāyīnī and Ibn

18 For an interesting and very much relevant study on this *ḥadīth* and others, see: Holtzman, *Anthropomorphism in Islam*, 284–285.

19 Ibn Qayyim al-Jawziyya, *Mukhtaṣar al-Ṣawāʿiq* (the abridgement of Ibn al-Mawṣilī), 4:1456–1472, 1484–1485.

Fūrak[20] and the Muʿtazilite Abū Isḥāq al-Naẓẓām.[21] Ibn Taymiyya remarks that the disagreement about *akhbār al-āḥād* occurred within "that sect", viz. rationalism, by the early Ashʿarite Ibn al-Bāqillānī (d. 403/1013) and those who followed his way, such as Abu 'l-Maʿālī,[22] al-Ghazālī and Ibn ʿAqīl. However, the Islamic community accepted *akhbār al-āḥād* in consensus and it is infallible of agreeing upon falsities of *ḥadīths* and opinions (*wal-umma^tu maʿṣūma^tu min^a 'l-khaṭ'^in*). *Al-āḥād* can be of presumptions; when they gain strength they become informative knowledge, but when they weaken they become foul imaginations and fantasies. The context (*al-qarā'in*) in which knowledge appears also assists in verifying the truthfulness of these *ḥadīths*. Therefore, *ḥadīths* which were accepted by Muslim scholars specialized in the science of Hadith, who are well-informed about the Prophet's sayings and actions, convey certain knowledge.[23]

Another important scholar Ibn al-Qayyim quotes is Ẓāhirite scholar Ibn Ḥazm and his work on legal methodology *al-Iḥkām fī uṣūl al-aḥkām*,[24] in which he wished to clarify that the Hadith produces knowledge. Citing verse Q 16:44 "We have sent down the message to you too [Prophet], so that you can explain to people what was sent for them", Ibn Ḥazm aims to show the Prophet was ordered to clarify the religious duties in the Quran, and otherwise we would not have known God's intention. Raising a rhetorical question, Ibn Ḥazm asks those who discredit *akabār al-āḥād* (mostly the Muʿtazilites, in this case): is it possible that the laws, commends and prohibitions brought by the Messenger of God—and are still obligatory to the Muslims after his death—will become

20 See footnote 125 in chapter 5.

21 See footnote 46 in chapter 4. Zysow points to al-Naẓẓām's untypical approach with relation to massively transmitted traditions. As the Muʿtazilite scholar saw it, even *mutawātir* did not always produce certainty. However, a citation brought by Zysow states that "al-Naẓẓām held that it [i.e., *ḥadīth mutawātir*] does not impose certainty by itself but only with external evidence. Equally the unit-report [i.e., *ḥadīth al-āḥād*] can impose certainty with external evidence [i.e., *qarīna*; as in context]. An example of this is the report that someone has died. When there is a crowd at his door, the sound of weeping is heard, and a bier appears, this report imposes certainty;" Zysow, *The Economy of Certainty*, 13–15. Hence, Ibn Taymiyya's somewhat surprising reference to al-Naẓẓām seems sensible here, in that they shared the idea on the importance of the context of meaning in discerning the kind of knowledge a *ḥadīth* produces.

22 See footnote 15 in chapter 4.

23 I tend to agree with the editor of *Mukhtaṣar al-Ṣawāʿiq*, who notes it is not entirely sure which of Ibn Taymiyya's books Ibn al-Qayyim cited here; Ibn Qayyim al-Jawziyya, *Mukhtaṣar al-Ṣawāʿiq* (the abridgement of Ibn al-Mawṣilī), 4:1496–1502, 1511 footnote 2.

24 Ibn al-Qayyim has already quoted from this work in his introduction to *al-Ṣawāʿiq*; see in chapter 2 page 107.

unknown to the point in which not a single Muslim in the world will ever know them with certainty? Is it possible that a wrongful ruling will be approved and incorporated in the religious law (*sharīʿa*) without any Muslin ever detecting it? If they say these two situations are impossible, they are convinced and accept our view that every *ḥadīth* transmitted trustworthily on behalf of the Prophet is the truth as he had said it, which conveys knowledge and certainty, since it is impossible a false statement would ever be incorporated in the texts. If they say the two situations above are indeed possible, they determine that the Islam is corrupted and false; they consider the Prophet's message to be mere presumption, which is a destructive lie that promotes only doubts on God's commands. It is therefore becomes certainly clear, Ibn Ḥazm concludes, that *khabar al-wāḥid* transmitted on behalf of the Prophet conveys cogent truth which is required to be known and practiced.[25]

Ibn al-Qayyim further quotes Ibn Ḥazm's opinion, as the latter accuses the Muʿtazilites of seeking refuge by avoiding the use of *khabar al-wāḥid* in their rulings, deceptively thinking that secures them against error. Moreover, they show open enmity towards what it necessarily known to be correct, and they wrongfully blame all of the Prophet's companions, their followers and the scholars of every generation in a lie (*takdhīb*). All of these scholars transmitted the reports of the Prophet without a doubt, used them as compulsory proves, followed them, and assisted them in the issuing of religious rulings. The denial of *khabar al-wāḥid* is also a rejection of the Islamic consensus on what is certain and what is false, where there is no disagreement. In addition, the dismissal of the Hadith invalidates many of the religious obligations which no one—be they Muslim or not—doubts the fact they were not clarified in the Quran, such as the prayer (*ṣalāt*), alms-giving (*zakāt*), pilgrimage to Mecca (*ḥājj*) and so on; only by the sayings of God's Messenger do we know how these principal Islamic duties are to be practiced. Ibn Ḥazm's concludes that the entirety of Hadith is cogent truth, since God forbade ruling on religious matters based on presumptions (*taḥrīm al-ḥukm fi ʾl-dīn bil-ẓann*). In the Hadith, God distinguished righteousness from sin and err, the right path being what He sent with the sayings and actions of His Prophet.[26]

As he embraces Ibn Ḥazm's view, Ibn al-Qayyim lists some 21 indications (*dalāʾil*) from the Islamic scriptures on the certitude granted by *khabar al-wāḥid*. In a very rich discussion, he cites *ḥadīth*s by which he interprets Quranic

25 Ibn Qayyim al-Jawziyya, *Mukhtaṣar al-Ṣawāʿiq* (the abridgement of Ibn al-Mawṣilī), 4:1511–1516; Zysow, *The Economy of Certainty*, 32–33.

26 Ibn Qayyim al-Jawziyya, *Mukhtaṣar al-Ṣawāʿiq* (the abridgement of Ibn al-Mawṣilī), 4:1531–1534.

verses, explains particular *ḥadīth*s himself, and also endorses ideas of previous scholars. Ibn al-Qayyim's use of the textual sources in this case is, therefore, not limited to offering 'block citations' alone (as can be seen in the above examples of block-quoting Ibn Taymiyya and Ibn Ḥazm); Ibn al-Qayyim does validate his arguments while extensively depending on the Islamic textual sources, yet he uses the raw text for his own authorial benefit as well—he accumulates the proves which he finds sufficiently convincing and hence authoritative. Later, in his conclusion of the fourth argument on the epistemic value of *khabar al-wāḥid*, Ibn al-Qayyim notes it is known that one should learn the customs and the biography of God's Messenger, as well as his guidance. These provide the believer with necessary theoretical knowledge which cannot be gained from any other source, while others who do not pay close attention to the Hadith remain ignorant of that knowledge.[27]

Ibn al-Qayyim's fifth argument moves onwards to the area of overlap between Islamic theology and law. Ibn al-Qayyim dialectically argues that even if *akhbār al-wāḥid* did not produce epistemic certitude, they would stand as a binding overpowering presumption (*fa-inn*^{a} *'l-ẓann*^{a} *'l-ghālib*^{a} *ḥāṣil*^{un} *minhā*; i.e. in legal terms). Consequently, it is allowed to affirm God's names and attributes using these *ḥadīth*s, just as it is allowed to use them to affirm the rulings concerning the religious practices (*ithbāt*^{a} *'l-aḥkām*^{i} *'l-ṭalabiyya*). The Muslim community consensually permits (in *ijmāʿ*) the use of these *ḥadīth*s evenly, either when dealing with informative theoretical knowledge or practical religious knowledge. In fact, knowledge of the Islamic practices includes information about God and the rules of His religion (*sharʿuh*^{u} *wa-dīnuh*^{u}), which eventually reaches His names and attributes. The Prophet's companions, their followers, their followers' followers, the people of Hadith and Sunna (i.e., the traditionalists)—all of them use these *ḥadīth*s as proves both in theological issues, such as the names, attributes and predetermination, as well as in issues of legal rulings. Where did the *salaf* separate between theological and legal discussions? They did not. The ones to separate them were the later *mutakallimīn* who do not take an interest in what came on behalf of God, His Messenger and the companions (viz., the textual sources). Rather, the hearts are diverted from being rightly guided about theological issues by the Quran, the Sunna and the sayings of the companions, as they turn to the opinions of the rationalists. The rationalists divided religion to informative issues, denoting them "roots" (*uṣūl*), and practical issues, denoting them "branches" (*furūʿ*); each of them requires

27 Ibn Qayyim al-Jawziyya, *Mukhtaṣar al-Ṣawāʿiq* (the abridgement of Ibn al-Mawṣilī), 4:1534–1556, 1569–1570.

a different kind of proves. They discerned the one truth on the "roots" issues, whereas on "branches" issues they declared God did not state a specific rule, which makes a mistake almost impossible. Ibn al-Qayyim forcefully opposes this division, asserting it is an arbitrary terminological separation of no justification (*mujarrad*[i] *'l-iṣṭilāḥ*).[28]

In his sixth argument, Ibn al-Qayyim contrasts the kind of knowledge produced from *akhbār al-wāḥid* with that which is allegedly produced by the rationalistic argumentation techniques. According to Ibn al-Qayyim, the so-called presumption produced from the *ḥadīth*s is more powerful than what is derived from the rationalistic delusionary imaginations. The rationalists designate their false convictions as "rational cogencies and certain proves" (*qawāṭiʿ ʿaqliyya wa-barāhīn yaqīniyya*), whereas the texts of the Quran and Sunna are taken as "scriptural apparent expressions which do not produce certain knowledge" (*ẓawāhir samʿiyya lā tufīd*[u] *'l-yaqīn*[a]). But then, whoever delves into the textual sources discovers the exact opposite; the rationalistic arguments contradict the texts and produce neither knowledge nor presumption. The 'uncontaminated Reason' and the natural disposition of the believers (*ṣarīḥ al-ʿuqūl wal-fiṭar*) disclose that these arguments are untruthful fabrications, even though many sects agree upon them. Each rationalistic group announces its own 'reason'; when in reality they even contradict one another, such as the example of the *Kalām* scholars and the philosophers. After expanding this claim by citing a large part of the teachings of the Hadith scholar and jurist Abu 'l-Muẓaffar Manṣūr ibn Muḥammad al-Samʿānī (d. 489/1096), Ibn al-Qayyim depicts basic epistemic differences between the traditionalists (*ahl al-sunna*) and the rationalists (whom he derogatorily designate as *ahl al-bidaʿ*, namely 'the people of undesired religious innovations'). In sum, he accuses the rationalists of independently selecting the *ḥadīth*s which comply with their arbitrary views based on whim, as they leave behind those which don not. When they fail to convincingly explain that, they tangle themselves in undesired figurative interpretations which distort the the already established meanings of the Hadith's text.[29]

---

28 That claim has already been raised by Ibn Taymiyya, who accused the Muʿtazilites of creating this division; Ibn Qayyim al-Jawziyya, *Mukhtaṣar al-Ṣawāʿiq* (the abridgement of Ibn al-Mawṣilī), 4:1570–1574; Zysow also observed Ibn Taymiyya's criticism, and more so Ibn al-Qayyim's, against the Ashʿarite detached epistemological approaches concerning theology on one hand, and legal theory on the other; Zysow, *The Economy of Certainty*, 200–201.

29 Ibn Qayyim al-Jawziyya, *Mukhtaṣar al-Ṣawāʿiq* (the abridgement of Ibn al-Mawṣilī), 4:1591–1607.

The seventh argument Ibn al-Qayyim presents in his epistemological discussion closes the more dialectical middle-section of his ten argumentations for the refutation of the fourth *ṭāghūt*. Theoretically reflecting on the basic character of an indicative proof (*dalīl*), Ibn al-Qayyim argues that qualifying it as being either presumption or cogent is a relative matter (*amr nisbī*) which is dependent on the personal perception of the one who makes an argument while using it. A single indicative proof can be considered cogent for Zayd, but of presumption for ʿAmr. Thus, the rationalistic statement, that sound *ḥadīth*s (*akhbār rasūl Allāh^{i} 'l-ṣaḥīḥa*) which are accepted by the Muslim community do not produce knowledge since they are of presumption, tells us about the rationalistic perception of knowledge attainment. Their statement therefore does not require a complete negation of the *ḥadīth*s. This is similar to the state of a person who feels either pain or pleasure; either love or hatred, when another person comes up with proves that the former is not in pain and suffer, does neither love nor hates. Then, many self-doubts rise in the first person, foremost concerning the gap between the experienced feeling in reality and the one which has come to be "proven", yet is absolutely false. Ibn al-Qayyim hence replies to the rationalists: pay your attention to the message of the Prophet, protect it and follow it. Make its study your ultimate end and highest goal, guarding it like the great Imams of the four *madhāhib*, as they attained the necessary knowledge for their teachings via the textual sources. Then, you will learn whether the *ḥadīth*s produce knowledge or not. If despite your true efforts the texts do not provide you knowledge or even presumption, you will know of your destined share of fortune with them.[30] Advising the reader to seek true knowledge autonomously, the didactic tone Ibn al-Qayyim expresses here is obvious.

The three remaining arguments Ibn al-Qayyim advances, 8–10, return to express a more fideistic mindset. Emphasizing the validating force of Islamic consensus of the *salaf*, in the eighth argument Ibn al-Qayyim declares it is cogently known that not only are *akhbār al-wāḥid* accepted, they are to be used to affirm the divine attributes. Rebutting Islamic groups he finds to be heretic, Ibn al-Qayyim militantly depicts them as crossing swards at the Sunna and the Islamic faith, as they deny their heresy, while removing the protecting garment of Islam off their necks and shoulders (*wa-khalaʿū ribqat^{a} 'l-islām^{i} min aʿnāqihim*). With relation to their rejection (*radd*) of the *ḥadīth*s, Ibn al-Qayyim diligently lists the different early sects he refers to, such as: the Khārijites,

30 Ibn Qayyim al-Jawziyya, *Mukhtaṣar al-Ṣawāʿiq* (the abridgement of Ibn al-Mawṣilī), 4:1607–1609.

those who only accept *ḥadīth*s which comply with—or do not contradict—the Quran, those who only accept the massively transmitted *ḥadīth*s and not *al-āḥād*, the Shiʿites, the Muʿtazilites, those who reject *ḥadīth*s which do not fit their opinions, and those who reject *ḥadīth*s for their lack of knowledge. Thereafter, Ibn al-Qayyim underlines the traditionalistic stance, that none of the *ḥadīth* contradicts either the Quran or human Reason; rejecting Prophetic traditions entails the denial of the divine Revelation. To further sustain this, Ibn al-Qayyim presents the views of the great Imams al-Shāfiʿī and Ibn Ḥanbal, which condemn the rejection of *ḥadīth*s while relying on numerous quotations from the Quran and Sunna. Finally, Ibn al-Qayyim reaches his main target: *ahl al-kalām al-mubtadiʿ al-madhmūm*, namely his contemporary Ashʿarites. As he grasps it, the Ashʿarites castoff specific *ḥadīth*s in their engagement with the divine attributes, yet accept others on topics, like jurisprudence. They misuse verse Q 42:11 "there is nothing like Him" in order to reject sound traditions (*aḥādīth ṣaḥīḥa*), as they distort the established meaning of the verse and understand *aḥādīth al-ṣifāt* in a manner neither God nor His Messenger intended them. Moreover, Ibn al-Qayyim stresses, no one of *ahl al-islām* (viz., the 'real believers') understands *aḥādīth al-ṣifāt* in such way in which their affirmation requires the assimilation (*tamthīl*) of God to His creation.[31]

In a quite succinct manner, Ibn al-Qayyim combines his engagement with the ninth argument together with the tenth one; these two argumrnts are not only the very last part of the fourth *ṭāghūt* refutation, but end the entire work *al-Ṣawāʿiq*. First addressing the later Ashʿarite rationalistic standpoint—that *khabar al-wāḥid* does not produce knowledge—Ibn al-Qayyim maintains that all reasonable people agree it is false (*qaḍiya kādhiba bi-ittifāq^i 'l-ʿuqalā'*). Ibn al-Qayyim also argues that one of the rationalists went as far as lying about the Ḥanbalites, saying they accept *khabar al-wāḥid* as producer of knowledge when it appears without any context.[32] Ibn al-Qayyim replies that whoever dares to spread lies about God and His Messenger, describes God in a way He did not describe Himself, negates the attributes He Himself affirmed, speaks of God without knowledge—of course they maliciously allow themselves to tell lies on a fellow created-being. Then, Ibn al-Qayyim reassures that there is not even the slightest doubt concerning the obligation of professing the belief (*shahāda*)

---

31 Ibn Qayyim al-Jawziyya, *Mukhtaṣar al-Ṣawāʿiq* (the abridgement of Ibn al-Mawṣilī), 4:1609–1645.

32 According to the editor's note, Ibn al-Qayyim might be referring here to Sayf al-Dīn al-Āmidī in his work *Kitāb al-aḥkām*. That assumption seems plausible, since Ibn al-Qayyim had studies this work (see footnote 6 in chapter 1 above); Ibn Qayyim al-Jawziyya, *Mukhtaṣar al-Ṣawāʿiq* (the abridgement of Ibn al-Mawṣilī), 4:1646.

in God, as depicted in *aḥādīth al-ṣifāt*, and in His Messenger who brought them. Concluding his discussion, Ibn al-Qayyim cites verse Q 6:150 "Say, 'Bring your witnesses to testify that God has forbidden all this.' If they do testify, do not bear witness with them;" their testimony is their views of whim, Ibn al-Qayyim says, which God forbade.[33] The verse cited is usually understood as referring to the testimony of the polytheists who denied the Islamic Revelation, adhering to the belief in muptiple deities; this consolidates Ibn al-Qayyim's grand accusation in *al-Ṣawāʿiq* against the false *ṭawāghīt*.

A number of interesting insights can be drawn from Ibn al-Qayyim's concise treatment of the fourth *ṭāghūt* in *al-Ṣawāʿiq*, with regard to both its epistemological contents and their structural form of delivery. As already noted, Ibn al-Qayyim generally aimed to revalidate the epistemic stature of the Hadith literature when dealing with theological issues and with the divine attributes in particular. Doing so, he formed his fourth *ṭāghūt* refutation in a design of ten argumentations (or points of discussion, *maqāmāt*). Bearing in mind Ibn al-Qayyim's main object of attack, i.e. al-Rāzī's ideas concerning theological debates as articulated in his work *Asās al-Taqdīs*, the ground behind the structural choice for the fourth *ṭāghūt* refutation in *al-Ṣawāʿiq* becomes evident: In order to counter al-Rāzī's skepticism formed in the ten conditions for attaining certain knowledge from the Islamic textual sources ("Universal Rule", *al-qānūn al-kullī*),[34] Ibn al-Qayyim offers a traditionalistic epistemic solution—arranged in akin ten arguments—positively emphasizing the certitude produced by the Hadith. Noteworthy is that in comparison to al-Rāzī's succinct, laconic and rather dry 'ten conditions', Ibn al-Qayyim's 'ten arguments' spread out on some 200 pages and contain a more evocative discussion. Hence, it would be more accurate to say Ibn al-Qayyim took al-Rāzī's 'ten conditions' as a model of argumentation, to which the former responded in considerable elaboration. Thematically as well as structurally, Ibn al-Qayyim's first and fourth refutations are therefore tightly connected. Moreover, the far more anthropomorphically challenging divine attributes appear in *aḥādīth al-ṣifāt*, most of which are classified as *al-āḥād*. Ibn al-Qayyim seems to have deliberately focused on this specific portion of *ḥadīth*s while criticizing the Rāziyyan 'ten conditions', ridiculing them to a greater extant. It follows that Ibn al-Qayyim's plausible authorial decision to dedicate the final part of *al-Ṣawāʿiq* to two of

---

33 Ibn Qayyim al-Jawziyya, *Mukhtaṣar al-Ṣawāʿiq* (the abridgement of Ibn al-Mawṣilī), 4:1646–1648.

34 The topic was scrutinized in detail in chapter 3, while exploring the first *ṭāghūt* refutation in *al-Ṣawāʿiq* (especially in section 3.2).

al-Rāzī's chief suppositions in *Asās al-Taqdīs*—(1) on the theme of *ḥadīth al-āḥād* and (2) in a structure parallel to the 'ten conditions'—is indeed remarkable.

Another observation can be made with respect to the inner-construction of the fourth *ṭāghūt* refutation. In my presentation of Ibn al-Qayyim's ten arguments above, I divided his ten arguments into three sections: arguments 1–3, 4–7, and 8–10. Whereas the opening and ending sections reflect a traditionalistic approach of textual fideism, the middle section is comprised of rationalized-traditionalistic ideas, written in a far more rationalized method of thinking. The following table demonstrates the matter:

Opening (arguments 1–3): fideism	**Middle part (arguments 4–7): rationalized-traditionalism**	**Ending (arguments 8–10): fideism**
1. Revelation conveys cogent indicative proves, according to the speaker's intention	4. *aḥādīth al-āḥād* produce certain knowledge on theoretical issues as well as religious practices	8. *aḥādīth al-āḥād* are accepted in *ijmaʿ* and they are to be used to affirm the divine attributes
2. *aḥādīth al-āḥād* comply with the Quran and interpret it	5.even if *ḥadīth al-āḥād* only produces a presumption, it is still overpowers other kinds of indicators	9. all reasonable people accept *aḥādīth al-āḥād* and use them to affirm the divine attributes
3. *aḥādīth al-āḥād* must be accepted as producers of knowledge, as part of Revelation	6. *aḥādīth al-āḥād* overpower rationalistic delusionary imaginations	10. It is permissible to profess the belief (*shahāda*) in God, as depicted in *aḥādīth al-ṣifāt*, and in His Messenger who brought them
	7. *aḥādīth al-āḥād* produce knowledge for those preoccupied with the Hadith	

It becomes evident that the ten arguments constituting the fourth *ṭāghūt* refutation in *al-Ṣawāʿiq* are constructed in thematic symmetry, having a clear opening, middle-part and ending. Ibn al-Qayyim, thus, adeptly organizes his arguments in a symmetrical fashion in order to frame his rationalized-traditionalistic epistemological conceptions. This is but a single representation of Ibn al-Qayyim's sensitivity to literary aesthetics and his appealing authorial command, combining the dialectical with the didactic (complementary aspects of the work's overall structure are surveyed in the next section 6.3). In a similar vein, Ibn al-Qayyim repeats the Islamic profession of faith (*shahada*)—which Muslim authors mention in the beginning of writing—once more in *al-Ṣawāʿiq*'s closure (i.e., tenth argument), including the affirmation of the divine attributes. This creates another interesting, nuanced symmetry between the opening and closing parts of the whole work.

6.3 Structural Aspects of Ibn al-Qayyim's Rationalization: *al-Ṣawāʿiq*'s Literary Symmetry

At first glance, it may seem that the symmetry displayed in the shape of the fourth *ṭāghūt* refutation of *al-Ṣawāʿiq* is but a coincidental particle of the total arrangement of this gigantic work. However, after dedicating much thought to the overall structure of *al-Ṣawāʿiq*, this finding opens the gate for concluding a more comprehensive symmetrical construction of the work in its entirety. As will be demonstrated here, the symmetrical structure of *al-Ṣawāʿiq* manifests Ibn al-Qayyim's functional utilization of this literary stylistic feature in order to corroborate a twofold goal: first, demolishing the fundamentals of the rationalistic ideology he found destructive to Islam, and second, promoting the Taymiyyan alternative via a sophisticated rationalized-traditionalistic mode of discourse. This section, thus, untangles the fashion in which Ibn al-Qayyim authored *al-Ṣawāʿiq*, taking a wide structural perspective.

In the view of the contents constituting *al-Ṣawāʿiq* and its four *ṭawāghīt* refutations, it becomes obvious that Ibn al-Qayyim does not display a typical linear manner of authorship when connecting the different parts of the work. Moreover, Ibn al-Qayyim designed a literary structure of symmetry that highlights the position of the Islamic textual sources, with special consideration given to the literature of Hadith. In fact, he creates a Hadith-binding for his rationalized-traditionalistic alternative to the later Ashʿarite ideas, which to a certain degree depart from the texts and turn to exterior means of religious reasoning. The symmetrical structure of *al-Ṣawāʿiq* can be graphically clarified by Ibn al-Qayyim's conclusions concerning each part of the work, as follows:

First *ṭāghūt* refutation	Second *ṭāghūt* refutation	Third *ṭāghūt* refutation	Fourth *ṭāghūt* refutation
The Islamic Scriptures convey certain knowledge	Revelation (not Reason) is the provenance of knowledge	Disproving the concept of *majāz*	The entire Hadith literature convey certain knowledge

Negative rationalized argumentations

Positive rationalized argumentations of the traditionalistic stance

This sketch of the symmetrical formation of *al-Ṣawāʿiq* shows that Ibn al-Qayyim's traditionalistic adherence to the textual sources is also reflected in his choice of literary aesthetics while composing his monograph.[35] His ability to utilize literary structures of composition in order to clearly express his harsh intellectual disagreement with the later Ashʿarite thought is indeed remarkable. Notable is that Ibn al-Qayyim's calculated editorial approach has already been indicated with relation to another of his major theological works titled: *Shifāʾ al-ʿalīl fī masāʾil al-qaḍāʾ wal-qadar wal-ḥikma wal-taʿlīl* (Healing the Person inflicted by Wrong Concepts about Predetermination and Causality); *Shifāʾ al-ʿalīl* can also be described with a symmetrical connection between its opening and closing parts.[36] This aesthetic principle is established in *al-Ṣawāʿiq* to an even a greater extent—not only does Ibn al-Qayyim envelope his discussion with complimenting sections *Ṣawāʿiq* (i.e., first and fourth *ṭawāghīt* refutations), the aesthetic binding itself is cleverly exploited to accentuate the discussed contents and the rationalized-traditionalistic discourse represented.

35 The importance of symmetry as a symbol of unity, harmony and divine beauty in classical literature as well as during history is the topic of numerous and various studies. Outlining the main conceptions on the matter are, for instance: Rhys Carpenter, *The Esthetic Basis of the Greek Art of the Fifth and Fourth Centuries B.C.* (New York: Longmans, Green and Co., 1921); Harold Osborne, *Theory of Beauty: an Introduction to Aesthetics* (London: Routledge and Kegan Paul, 1952); R.G. Peterson, "Critical Calculations: Measure and Symmetry in Literature," *PMLA* 91/ 3 (May, 1976), 367–375; H. Osborne, "Symmetry as an Aesthetic Factor," *Computers & Mathematics with Applications* 12/1–2 (April 1986): 77–82; Alexander V. Voloshinov, "Symmetry as a Superprinciple of Science and Art," *Leonardo* 29/ 2 (1996), 109–113.

36 Holtzman, "Human Choice, Divine Guidance and the *Fiṭra* Tradition," 165–166, 178–181.

Additionally, the interior parts of *al-Ṣawāʿiq* (i.e., second and third *ṭawāghīt* refutations) are also modeled in accordance with the exterior overarching symmetry.

With respect to the historical depth of the refuted argument in each of its four parts, *al-Ṣawāʿiq*'s symmetric structuring also entails a dimension of temporality. Commencing with the rebuke of al-Rāzī's skepticism in the first *ṭāghūt*, Ibn al-Qayyim predominantly directs his condemnation towards his contemporary Ashʿarite scholars in Mamluk Damascus. Keen advocates and practitioners of the Rāziyyan thought, the Ashʿarite of Damascus were those who prosecuted Ibn Taymiyya as well as himself and placed them on public trials (as depicted in chapter 1). Taking a step back in time, the second *ṭāghūt* refutation is aimed at al-Rāzī along with the originator of his 'universal rule', al-Ghazālī. The third *ṭāghūt* refutation goes further back to the Muʿtazilite period of activity, denouncing their inception of the device of *majāz* (e.g., that of Ibn Jinnī). This *ṭāghūt* is the axis of symmetry, as Ibn al-Qayyim begins moving forwards on the timeline, referring to the early Ashʿarites and Ḥanbalites as authoritative scholars while constructing his alternative hermeneutical design. The fourth and last *ṭāghūt* refutation concludes the historical symmetry, returning to the later Ashʿarite thought of al-Rāzī widespread at Ibn al-Qayyim's time. Therefore, Ibn al-Qayyim presents his wide-ranging historical perspective as well as his momentous ability to express it in an erudite literary form.

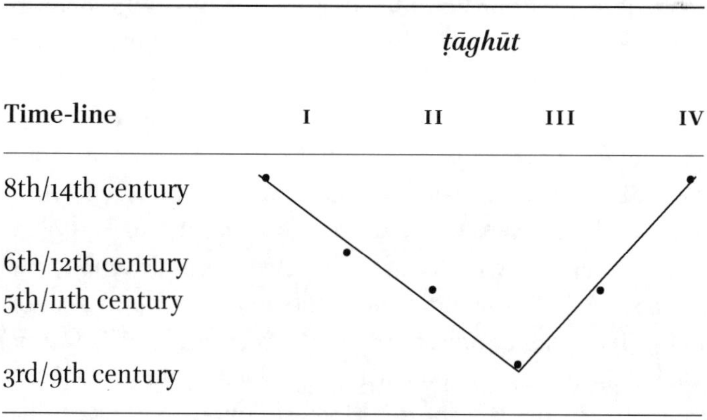

At this point, Ibn al-Qayyim's arrangement of his third *ṭāghūt* refutation—containing the axis of symmetry—merits further attention. As mentioned in the beginning of chapter 5, the third *ṭāghūt* refutation comprises two parts: the first part is dedicated to the theoretical negation of *majāz*, claiming that it was developed as an early Muʿtazilite hermeneutical devise designed for the purpose of addressing problematic anthropomorphic descriptions of God in the Islamic texts. The second part of the refutation is subdivided into ten sections; each of them focuses on a single anthropomorphic attribute. Ibn al-Qayyim mostly opens the discussion on an individual attribute with a description of the wrongful interpretations given to the attribute by the 'heretic' rationalistic groups, (e.g., Muʿtazilites, later Ashʿarites, Karrāmites etc.). Next, Ibn al-Qayyim unfolds a highly organized and hierarchical discussion aiming to prove the meaning of an essential reality concerning God for each and every one of the ten specific attributes. Altogether, the refutation is hence consciously assembled in a didactical manner as a consequence of Ibn al-Qayyim's systematic analysis of the denied argument as well as the promoted alternative.

As for the specific reference to each of the ten anthropomorphic descriptions of God Ibn al-Qayyim addresses, notable is Ibn al-Qayyim's singular selection of the attributes under examination in his discussion after his broad rejection of the theoretical aspect of *majāz*. Ibn al-Qayyim explains that he is moving on to an elaborate discussion on exemplary attributes, which the rationalists perceived as metaphorical;[37] as will be illustrated shortly, it is likely that his selection here is indeed very much intentional. From early times onward, in their theological discussions on the divine attributes, for the most part Muslim theologians concentrated namely on seven thereof: omniscience/knowledge, omnipotence/power, will, life, hearing, sight and speech.[38] In one way or another, these attributes can be considered as acceptable by rationalists and traditionalists alike, despite the differentiated understandings thereof. Interestingly enough, Ibn al-Qayyim's choice of attributes for specific deliberation in his third *ṭāghūt* refutation diverts from the commonly acceptable ones, decisively turning the attention to ten of the most hermeneutically-challenging attributes for the rationalists—attributes which can strongly infer anthropomorphism or the proximity of God to the creation. These divine attributes mostly appear in the literature of Hadith that Ibn al-Qayyim struggles to protect in *al-Ṣawāʿiq*. The ten attributes Ibn al-Qayyim discusses are: God's arrival (*majīʾ*), God's names (*asmāʾ Allāh*), God's sitting on His throne (*istiwāʾ*), God's two hands (*yadaynⁱ*), God's face (*wajh*), God's light (*nūr*), God's aboveness (*fawqiyya*), God's descent (*nuzūl*), God's simultaneity (*maʿiyya*, lit.

37 Ibn Qayyim al-Jawziyya, *Mukhtaṣar al-Ṣawāʿiq* (the abridgement of Ibn al-Mawṣilī), 3:856.

38 Abu 'l-Ḥasan al-Ashʿarī (d. 324/935) is known to have additionally listed an eighth attribute of permanence or enduringness (*baqāʾ*); Gilliot, "Attributes of God," *Encyclopaedia of Islam THREE*, 1:179–180; Watt, *Islamic Philosophy and Theology*, 48–49.

being with His creation) and closeness (*qurb*), God's proclamation and addressing in speech (*al-nidāʾ wal-taklīm*).[39] In effect, instead of following the well-known conformist lines of theological engagement with the seven "permitted" attributes listed above, Ibn al-Qayyim takes up the cudgels and attacks ten prominent cases in which the use of *majāz* was most common. Therefore, the manner in which Ibn al-Qayyim strives to prove the rationalists wrong is highly sophisticated. It seems that he plays with the Ashʿarite intermediary traditionalistic-rationalistic path of referring mainly to the seven more hermeneutically convenient attributes of knowledge, power etc., when in fact he is addressing the more difficult anthropomorphic ones (for the Ashʿarites), proving them to describe actual reality, i.e., *ḥaqīqa*.

Paying close attention to the subject matter and Ibn al-Qayyim's discussion on the ten specific 'anthropomorphic attributes' in the final part of his third *ṭāghūt* refutation, several additional similarities between the contents and structures of *al-Ṣawāʿiq* and Fakr al-Dīn al-Rāzī's theological work *Asās al-taqdīs* become clear. The importance of *Asās al-taqdīs* with relation to the Taymiyyan scholarship and *al-Ṣawāʿiq* has already been detected and examined in the previous chapters, regarding the epistemological deliberations in *al-Ṣawāʿiq*'s first and fourth *ṭāghūt*.[40] Al-Rāzī's leading demonstration of epistemic skepticism in the form of his "ten conditions for certain knowledge" is articulated in the third part of *Asās al-taqdīs*, which was explicitly written in order to sponsor the rationalistic use of figurative interpretation (*taʾwīl*) and counter the traditionalistic hermeneutical approach. In the view of Ibn al-Qayyim's hermeneutical discussion at the end of the third *ṭāghūt*, al-Rāzī's methodology concerning the issue of divine attributes in *Asās al-taqdīs* is especially significant in that it represents his adoption of Muʿtazilite primary conceptions. A critical feature in this respect is surely the implementation of the use of metaphors (*majāzāt*), which Ibn al-Qayyim zealously endeavors to invalidate. Moreover, in terms of structure, it seems that, to some extent, Ibn al-Qayyim imports the arrangement of *Asās al-taqdīs* to his closing discussion of the third *ṭāghūt* refutation in *al-Ṣawāʿiq*. His particular selection of the ten 'anthropomorphic attributes' gives the impression of addressing ten out of some thirty attributes which al-Rāzī specifically notes as metaphors in the second part of *Asās al-taqdīs*. This part of the work is dedicated to "the figurative

39 Thereafter Ibn al-Qayyim concisely addresses "the rest of the attributes," also based on the Hadith; Ibn Qayyim al-Jawziyya, *Mukhtaṣar al-Ṣawāʿiq* (the abridgement of Ibn al-Mawṣilī), 3:856–4:1400.

40 In particular, see sections 1.1, 1.2, 3.2 and 6.2.

interpretation of the ambiguous [expressions in] the Prophetic traditions and Quranic verses" (*fī taʾwīl*[i] *'l-mutashābihāt min*[a] *'l-akhbār wal-āyāt*).[41]

In addition, Ibn al-Qayyim's sturdy affirmation of the divine attribute of direction (*jiha*)—evident in his recruitment of the Averroist-Aristotelian reasoning in its favor—supplies further support of the claim that Ibn al-Qayyim structured his discussion having al-Rāzī's *Asās al-taqdīs* in mind. The first part of al-Rāzī's work opens with a categorical rejection of any corporeality regarding God, under the title of "Indications on God's Transcendence beyond Corporeality and on Him not Being Confined [by any spatial location]" (*al-dalāʾil al-dalla ʿalā annah*[u] *taʿālā munazzah ʿan al-jismiyya wal-ḥayz*). That is, in fact, his definition of anthropomorphism: al-Rāzī maintains that the one God is not present in a direction; He is not a space-occupying entity and is not a body, an assertion for which he provides proofs based on rational and textual evidence. In a speculative manner of argumentation, al-Rāzī raises numerous claims, which he then contradicts with his own opinion. Although al-Rāzī does not explicitly mention any scholar by name, the claims he contradicts are namely those held by the corporealist Karrāmites and the ultra-traditionalists who affirmed God's direction (*jiha*) and its veridical meaning (as *ḥaqīqa*).[42] Comprising a substantial part of his entire work, in his discussion al-Rāzī articulates the Muʿtazilite stance on this matter and explains the proper figurative interpretation, according to his opinion.[43] Ibn al-Qayyim's reference to Ibn Rushd and his teachings on God's direction occupies only a little fragment in his hermeneutical discussion, and is included at the height of *al-Ṣawāʿiq*'s introduction against *taʾwīl* (as demonstrated in section 5.6). Nonetheless, since Ibn al-Qayyim aims his criticism directly at al-Rāzī, it can be simultaneously compared to the opening part of *Asās al-taqdīs*. Likewise, al-Rāzī also lists the divine attribute of direction once more as the 30th attribute in the second part of *Asās al-taqdīs*, also with relation to the attributes of aboveness (*fawqiyya*, *ʿulū*).[44]

---

41 Fakhr al-Dīn al-Rāzī, *Asās al-taqdīs*, 103–193; the Muʿtazilte imprint therein was observed in: Jaffer, "Muʿtazilite Aspects of Fakhr al-Dīn al-Rāzī's Thought," 516.

42 Fakhr al-Dīn al-Rāzī, *Asās al-taqdīs*, 13–101; As Holtzman shows, al-Rāzī actually wrote *Asās al-taqdīs* to counter the book *Kitāb al-tawḥīd* composed by the ultra-traditionalist Ibn Khuzayma in 4th/10th century Nishapur against the prevailing Muʿtazilite dogma. In *Asās al-taqdīs*, al-Rāzī referred to Ibn Khuzayma as 'the corporealist' (*al-mujassim*). During the following few centuries, *Kitāb al-tawḥīd* remained very conspicuous amid the traditionalistic circles, including that of Damascus in Ibn al-Qayyim's times; Holtzman, *Anthropomorphism in Islam*, 278–281, 310–311. Also see footnote 55 in chapter 1.

43 Jaffer, "Muʿtazilite Aspects of Fakhr al-Dīn al-Rāzī's Thought," 516–522.

44 Fakhr al-Dīn al-Rāzī, *Asās al-taqdīs*, 194–214.

The table below concisely illustrates the parallel lines of contents between *al-Ṣawāʿiq* and *Asās al-taqdīs*. The table accents the analogous sections within the relevant sections of each of the works, in accordance with the discussion thus far:[45]

Asās al-taqdīs	*al-Ṣawāʿiq*
1. Evidence that God's Transcendence is above corporeality and spatial location – negation of the divine direction (*jiha*)	Introduction against *taʾwīl* – Averroist discussion on the affirmation of the divine direction (*jiha*)
2. On the [Metaphorical] Interpretation of the ambiguous (*mutashābihāt*) Quranic verses and Prophetic reports (Prologue and 32 sections) – specific reference to 30 anthropomorphic attributes as metaphors (*majāzāt*) – section 30: negating the divine direction – section 31: discrediting Prophetic traditions of a limited number of chains of transmissions (*akhbār al-āḥād*)	Third *ṭāghūt* refutation – invalidation of the Muʿtazilite concept of *majāz* – specific reference to 10 anthropomorphic attributes as essential realities (*ḥaqīqa*) Fourth *ṭāghūt* refutation – asserting the cogent epistemic certitude produced by *akhbār al-āḥād* and the whole corpus of the Hadith—in ten arguments
3. An Account of the way of the Pious Ancestors – the 'general rule' (*al-qānūn al-kullī*) and the ten conditions for certainty of knowledge (pp. 234–235 in *Asās al-taqdīs*)	First *ṭāghūt* refutation – against al-Rāzī's 'ten conditions': verbal indications produce certain knowledge Second *ṭāghūt* refutation – against al-Ghazālī's 'universal rule of interpretation', which is the origin of al-Rāzī's 'general rule'

45 For several of the titles in *Asās al-taqdīs*, I have used Jaffer's paper: "Muʿtazilite Aspects of Fakhr al-Dīn al-Rāzī's Thought," 516. I have omitted the forth section in *Asās al-taqdīs*, titled "Remaining Issues," since it of less relevance to the discussion about the structure of *al-Ṣawāʿiq*.

As can be clearly observed, the thematic tendency represented in Ibn al-Qayyim's *al-Ṣawāʿiq* meticulously responds to al-Rāzī's preceding work, with a stark intention to dispute its arguments. Bearing in mind the arrangement of *al-Ṣawāʿiq* vis-à-vis that of *Asās al-taqdīs*, it appears that Ibn al-Qayyim placed the response to the third part of *Asās al-taqdīs* (i.e., first and second *ṭawāghīt* refutations) prior to the response directed at its second part (i.e., third and fourth *ṭawāghīt* refutations), thereby creating the functional symmetry in *al-Ṣawāʿiq*.

As already established in chapters 1 and 3, *Asās al-taqdīs* is more than a simple Rāziyyan promotion of the hermeneutical methodology of *taʾwīl*; the work expresses al-Rāzī's strife with his contemporary intellectual opponents, most obviously the Ḥanbalite scholars, as he advanced ideas derived from the Muʿtazilite thought. Written for the scholastic elite of that time, the most important contribution of *Asās al-taqdīs* to the polemics on *aḥādīth al-ṣifāt* was providing a concrete definition of *tashbīh* as ascribing God a physical form (that expalins why the attribute of direction was the first to be negated). This definition, which appears in the two last chapters of *Asās al-taqdīs*, was indeed unique, because it relied on logic and was articulated in a straightforward manner.[46] Both in his theological-political treatise *al-Ḥamawiyya 'l-kubrā* and in his voluminous work *Bayān talbīs al-jahmiyya*, Ibn Taymiyya had already voiced a decisive dissent from the Rāziyyan approach commonly accepted by the elite of his surrounding scholars. Taking the Taymiyyan opposition a significant step forward, Ibn al-Qayyim's skillful writing in *al-Ṣawāʿiq* is designed to confront the highpoints in al-Rāzī's *Asās al-taqdīs* and supply alternative models of epistemology and hermeneutics following his mentor's path.[47] When observed against the backdrop of the structure of *Asās al-taqdīs*—one of the works that probably served as a catalyst for writing *al-Ṣawāʿiq*—Ibn al-Qayyim's authorial aptitudes and contributions are impressive. The overall dialectical tone of *al-Ṣawāʿiq* is unmistakable and, hand in hand with the work's symmetrical structure, the theoretical discussions assembled by Ibn al-Qayyim in *al-Ṣawāʿiq* are framed in a rationalized-traditionalistic formulation. This finding is surely confirmed taking into account the high level of sophistication in Ibn al-Qayyim's authorship in *al-Ṣawāʿiq*.

---

46 Jaffer, "Muʿtazilite Aspects of Fakhr al-Dīn al-Rāzī's Thought," 514–517; Holtzman, *Anthropomorphism in Islam*, 310.

47 Ibn Taymiyya wrote his iconic treatise *al-Ḥamawiyya 'l-kubrā*—for which he was persecuted—to discredit the Rāzziyan form of *Kalām* (for further elaboration, see section 1.1). He also composed the work *Bayān talbīs al-jahmiyya* as a furious response to al-Rāzī's *Asās al-taqdīs*. The matter was discussed in section 3.3.

Conclusions

The theological topic of divine attributes as reflected in Ibn al-Qayyim's major dialectical work *al-Ṣawāʿiq* lies at the heart of this study; more than anything, this topic represents the intellectual schism between traditionalism and rationalism in medieval Islamic thought. Within the setting of social and political struggles of powers between religious scholars of various schools in Mamluk Damascus, Ibn al-Qayyim authored *al-Ṣawāʿiq* in hope of abolishing central fundamentals upheld by the later Ashʿarite rational-traditionalists, thereby vouching for traditionalism in its Taymiyyan form. Ibn al-Qayyim's contemporary rationalists namely followed the approach formulated more than a century earlier by Fakhr al-Dīn al-Rāzī who openly expressed epistemic doubts regarding the meanings of the literal expressions used in the textual sources of the Quran and Hadith literature. This resulted in further validation of the figurative hermeneutical approach (*taʾwīl*) on the matter of anthropomorphic descriptions of God in the texts, as practiced formerly by the Muʿtazilites. Al-Rāzī articulated these doctrinal ideas, for example, in his popular work at the time titled *Asās al-taqdīs*. In contrast, Ibn al-Qayyim rigorously maintained the traditionalistic stances of closely adhering to the texts and their full acceptance at face value as describing veridical realities, while considerably restructuring the known Taymiyyan approach as the desired alternative to the later Ashʿarite standpoints. A close reading of *al-Ṣawāʿiq* along with its contextualization with other primary sources of direct significance supports the main premise of this study, which considers the work to be a profound example of rationalized-traditionalistic writing which succeeds time and again in contesting commonly deployed presuppositions of the rationalistic trends in Islamic theology. Furthermore, in *al-Ṣawāʿiq* Ibn al-Qayyim demonstrates an impressive familiarity with the argumentations and methodologies of his rationalist ideological adversaries. This is also represented in his own rationalized—even *Kalām*ic—writing capabilities, which he sharply uses to oppose *Kalām*ic concepts.

The various primary sources read and analyzed throughout this research in addition to the chief text of *al-Ṣawāʿiq* embody Ibn al-Qayyim's intellectual strength and literary intensity. First, with regard to *al-Ṣawāʿiq* itself, nowadays the work *al-Ṣawāʿiq* includes (at least) two available versions which have been critically and individually edited: *al-Ṣawāʿiq*, which contains only the first half of the work, and *Mukhtaṣar al-ṣawāʿiq* (the abridged version), which contains its condensed second half as well. The present study examined selected units of discussion taken from both available parts of the work; the epistemological ones appear in more detail in *al-Ṣawāʿiq* (i.e., first and second *ṭawāghīt* refuta-

 | DOI: 10.1163/9789004372511_009

tions discussed in chapters 3 and 4), and—since they appear only there—the hermeneutical ones are mainly taken from *Mukhtaṣar al-ṣawāʿiq* (i.e., third and fourth *ṭawāghīt* refutations in chapters 5 and 6), but also from *al-Ṣawāʿiq*'s introduction (section 5 in chapter 2). To the best of my knowledge, this study is therefore the first academic analysis to comprehensively delve into the complex theological discussion conveyed by Ibn al-Qayyim in *al-Ṣawāʿiq* as a nearly complete textual unity in a manner that combines its two parts currently available. Second, the primary sources chosen for *al-Ṣawāʿiq*'s contextualization represent writings which were particularly intellectually inspiring for the theological dialectics in the work at hand, as well as offer a glance at Ibn al-Qayyim's wide-ranging spectrum of literary and scholarly reference. By examining the text of *al-Ṣawāʿiq* as a full monograph in relation to other prominent primary sources, we were able to exhibit Ibn al-Qayyim's theological claims while securing them in their proper historical and intellectual contexts. This approach facilitated the drawing of conclusions not only on the interior ideas of *al-Ṣawāʿiq*, but also its outer connections to different time periods, different works and different authors, which contribute to understanding the larger picture surrounding *al-Ṣawāʿiq*. As a whole, the findings of the study also portray a more crystalized image of Ibn al-Qayyim as a scholar with a special emphasis on his theological dialectical authorship concerning the pivotal issue of divine attributes.

Evidently, Ibn al-Qayyim laid out the doctrinal ideas of Ibn Taymiyya on the issue of divine attributes, while at the same time systemizing the master's principal theories of epistemology and hermeneutics. Therefore, his rationalization entailed more than rendered dialectical methodology and stylistic structure; it also involved the conceptualization of key ideas, which were then honed. That, in turn, resulted in *al-Ṣawāʿiq* being constructed as a *Kalām* manual, which brought about a salient exercise of rationalized traditionalism. From this aspect, *al-Ṣawāʿiq* is a work that articulates the principal Taymiyyan theories of knowledge and interpretation, relating to many other fields of knowledge other than theology, such as Islamic legal theory and its various practical applications (*uṣūl al-fiqh* and *furūʿ al-fiqh*). As a result, Ibn al-Qayyim's intellectual pinnacle contributions as presented in *al-Ṣawāʿiq* go far beyond the theological polemics on the issue of divine attributes and his *Kalām*ic writing; they represent a highly valuable means of understanding the Taymiyyan thought, crystalizing its underlying theoretical foundations.

Predominantly, the findings which have arisen in this study strongly suggest Ibn al-Qayyim's construction of hermeneutical principles forms a highly rationalized version of the known Taymiyyan-traditionalistic stances regarding the issue of divine attributes. Such a rendered mode of traditionalistic discourse is evident throughout Ibn al-Qayyim's deliberation also in his basic inclination of citing and using sources of intellectual inspiration, which is reflected in his recasting of the scholarly figures he refers to as both a driving force as well as reliable (as discussed in chapter 5). Ibn al-Qayyim selectively points out earlier Ḥanbalite scholars, but also early Ashʿarites, who shared a rationalistic tendency to a certain extent. Of course, the scholars mentioned do not bear an authoritative status similar to the righteous *salaf*, (i.e., the pious traditionists of the formative Islamic generations, whom Ibn al-Qayyim depicts as 'following Reason');[1] however, the sources of inspirations which had been affected rationalistically are indeed incorporated in Ibn al-Qayyim's discussion as a part of his vast repository of the literary textual sources used in his writing. This development of the Taymiyyan hermeneutical approach on its own already entails a high degree of dialectical engagement and *Kalām*ic features. In addition, Ibn al-Qayyim's embracement of the Aristotelian-based theology expressed in the writings of Ibn Rushd, for example, provides yet another signification of Ibn al-Qayyim's rationalized mode of discussion. However, in this regard, we still remain inconclusive about Ibn al-Qayyim's possible familiarity with philosophy and the Hellenistic scholarship. It is clear he did know parts of it—perhaps only second-handedly—as they were present in the discourse of the rationalist milieu around him, or from his acquaintance with the rationalistic curriculum of his days. Unfortunately, despite his mild engagement with Greek philosophical ideas in *al-Ṣawāʿiq*, it is difficult to discern if Ibn al-Qayyim indeed read such sources himself, and if so, which ones and to what extent. Still, the existence of such intellectual motivators in *al-Ṣawāʿiq* definitely points towards a transformed design of religious authoritativeness for the traditionalistic theological concerns.

Ibn al-Qayyim's rendering of the traditionalistic theological discourse is also structural and can be seen in his argumentation methodology and his employment of a *Kalām*-like line of reasoning. Considerably advancing the Taymiyyan reproach of the later Ashʿarites, Ibn al-Qayyim devalues the paradigms standing in the very basis of their epistemological and hermeneutical theories popular at the time, therefore establishing alternative rationalized-traditionalistic models. Beside his inclination to employ various dialectical techniques, Ibn al-Qayyim's construction of his *ṭawāghīt* refutations in *al-Ṣawāʿiq* is highly systematic and reflects a prearranged logical and (more or less) chronological arrangement. In addition, the symmetrical structure of the work—derived from Ibn al-Qayyim's counter reply to al-Rāzī's *Asās al-taqdīs*—further supports the claim

1 See in page 187.

that *al-Ṣawāʿiq* is a text created in line with *Kalām*ic authorship. *Al-Ṣawāʿiq*'s *Kalām*ic traits become even more entrancing given the inferred meaning of the symmetrical literary structure of the work. Ibn al-Qayyim created a positive connection between the opening (i.e., first *ṭāghūt* refutation) on the certitude produced from the Islamic texts, and the final note (i.e., fourth *ṭāghūt* refutation) on the apodictic value of the entire Hadith literature—where the majority of anthropomorphic depictions of God appear. These two corresponding parts envelope the more rationalized argumentations conveyed in the heart of the work (i.e., second and third refutations) with a sheer traditionalistic binding, which heightens the stature of the Islamic textual sources. Hence, the symmetrical structure of *al-Ṣawāʿiq* demonstrates Ibn al-Qayyim's ability to functionally deploy the aesthetic features and literary formation of the work as a means of accentuating its ideas to a great extant.

Ibn al-Qayyim's polished authorial approach manifested in *al-Ṣawāʿiq* can definitely signify his political ambitions, or at least his spirited political awareness. As he systemized the Taymiyyan theoretical discourse in *al-Ṣawāʿiq*, he did not only attack his powerful ideological rivals who belonged to the sociopolitical elite, but he also met them on their own scholastic turf and successfully employed their dialectical reasoning to prove them wrong. By validating the Taymiyyan doctrine of divine attributes, Ibn al-Qayyim offered more than a mere blunt duplication of ideas (i.e., *taqlīd*): he strived to revolutionize the traditionalistic religious discourse of his time of activity. Indeed, his rationalized-traditionalistic mode of writing served him well while scolding his later Ashʿarite adversaries. Nevertheless, his authorship in *al-Ṣawāʿiq* also articulates a clear defiance against his peer traditionalist scholars who preferred remaining in political latency to perusing public goals and following the activist example formerly set by Ibn Taymiyya. In their theological writing, the traditionalists around Ibn al-Qayyim mostly kept producing somewhat redundant accumulations of previous scholarship, or at times simply refrained from touching on the burning issues at stake. Contrastingly, Ibn al-Qayyim's *al-Ṣawāʿiq* called out for traditionalistic ideological-political resistance and, more so, it declared a traditionalistic triumph. In *al-Ṣawāʿiq*, Ibn al-Qayyim attempted to demonstrate the victory of traditionalism over rationalism, as can be seen for example in his presentation of the alleged religious repentance of Abū Ḥāmid al-Ghazālī and Fakhr al-Dīn al-Rāzī (as discussed in chapter 4). Ibn al-Qayyim thus directed his readers to follow "the footsteps" of these two prominent later Ashʿarites and reevaluate their religious path and the fundamentals standing at the very basis of their faith. In this respect, Ibn al-Qayyim's rationalized-traditionalistic mode of authorship in *al-Ṣawāʿiq* reflects therefore his uncompromising loyalty to the Taymiyyan ideology.

Still to be discerned are the scholarly functions *al-Ṣawāʿiq* fulfilled and the possible impacts it generated. In illustrating Ibn al-Qayyim's *Kalām*ic authorship, the challenging text of *al-Ṣawāʿiq* raises further questions with respect to its magnitude of circulation and reception. A vessel of knowledge transmission, the text conveys a systemized outlook of the Taymiyyan theoretical foundations which could have attracted other scholars in other places and time periods. It is hard to believe *al-Ṣawāʿiq* remained within the bounds of the Taymiyyan circle alone; however, for the time being it is difficult to determine whether it indeed reached its plausible target audience, including the Ashʿarite scholarly elite of Mamluk times (although, the treatises written by the Damascene Chief Judge Taki 'l-Dīn al-Subkī may imply so. This was discussed in chapter 2). At any rate, the full magnitude of *al-Ṣawāʿiq*'s reception and circulation through history goes beyond the scope of this study and surely deserves a separate inquiry. An additional trajectory of feasibly related investigation involves the evolution of traditionalistic thought in the post classical period and its process of rationalization exemplified by Ibn al-Qayyim in *al-Ṣawāʿiq*, while also covering the intellectual endeavors of Ibn Taymiyya: did it continue after their prime time of activity and, if so, then by whom and how? Satisfactory answers to such questions and others are, of course, remote from the declared object of the current research and deserve a separate line of examination. Be that as it may, the fact that the singular authorship Ibn al-Qayyim presented in *al-Ṣawāʿiq* triggers an ongoing scholarly interest—definitely substantiates his importance as a theologian and as a scholar.

Bibliography

Primary Sources

al-Āmidī, ʿAlī ibn Abī ʿAlī Sayf al-Dīn (d. 631/1233), *Iḥkām al-ḥukm fī uṣūl al-aḥkām*, ed. Sayyid al-Jamīlī, in 4 vols. (Beirut: Dār al-Kitāb al-ʿArabī, 1404/1983).

al-Āmidī, ʿAlī ibn Abī ʿAlī Sayf al-Dīn (d. 631/1233), *al-Iḥkām fī uṣūl al-aḥkām*, ed. ʿAbd al-Razzāq ʿAfīfī, in 4 vols. (Riyadh: Dār al-Ṣamīʿī lil-Nashr wal-Tanzīʿ, 1424/2003).

al-Bukhārī, Muḥammad ibn Ismāʿīl Abū ʿAbdallāh al-Juʿfī (d. 256/870), *Ṣaḥīḥ al-Bukhārī*, ed. Muḥammad Zuhayr Nāṣir al-Nāṣir, in 9 vols. (Beirut: Dār Ṭawq al-Najāh, 1422/[2001]).

al-Ghazālī, Abū Ḥāmid Muḥammad ibn Muḥammad al-Ṭūsī (d. 505/1111), *Iḥyāʾ ʿulūm al-dīn: lil-Imām Abī Ḥāmid al-Ghazālī*, no editor mentioned, in 16 vols. (Cairo: Dār al-Shaʿb, [n. d.]).

al-Ghazālī, Abū Ḥāmid Muḥammad ibn Muḥammad al-Ṭūsī (d. 505/1111), *al-Mustaṣfā min ʿulūm al-dīn*, ed. Ḥamza ibn Zuhayr Ḥāfiẓ, in 4 vols. (Medina: Dār al-Nashr Shirkat al-Madīna ʾl-Munawwara lil-Ṭibāʿa, [1413]/[1993]).

al-Ghazālī, Abū Ḥāmid Muḥammad ibn Muḥammad al-Ṭūsī (d. 505/1111), *The Book of Knowledge: Being a Translation of the Kitāb al-ʿIlm of al-Ghazālī's "Iḥyāʾ ʿUlūm al-Dīn."* English trans. Faris, Nabih Amin (Lahore: Sh. Muhammad Ashraf, 1962).

al-Ghazālī, Abū Ḥāmid Muḥammad ibn Muḥammad al-Ṭūsī (d. 505/1111), *The Foundations of the Articles of Faith: Being a Translation of the Kitāb Qawāʿid al-ʿAqāʾid of al-Ghazālī's "Iḥyāʾ ʿUlūm al-Dīn."* English trans. Faris, Nabih Amin, 1st ed. (Lahore: Sh. Muhammad Ashraf, 1963).

al-Ghazālī, Abū Ḥāmid Muḥammad ibn Muḥammad al-Ṭūsī (d. 505/1111), *Ha-podeh min ha-teʾiyyah ve-ha-taʾut* הפודה מן התעייה והטעות*: Modern Hebrew Translation of al-Ghazālī's 'Deliverer from Error' (al-Munqidh min al-dalāl)*, ed. Hava Lazarus-Yafeh (Tel Aviv: Dvir, 1965).

al-Ḥamawī, Shihāb al-Dīn Abū ʿAbdallāh Yāqūt ibn ʿAbdallāh al-Rūmī (d. 626/1229), *Muʿjam al-Buldān*, in 5 vols. (Beirut: Dār Ṣādir, 1397/1977).

Ibn ʿAsākir, Abu ʾl-Qāsim ʿAlī ibn Abī Muḥammad al-Ḥasan (d. 571/1176), *Tāʾrīkh Dimashq*. ed. ʿAmr ibn Gharāma al-ʿAmrawī. 80 vols. (Beirut: Dār al-Fikr lil-Ṭibāʿa wal-Nashr wal-Tawzīʿ, 1415/1995).

Ibn al-Farrāʾ, Abū Yaʿlā Muḥammad ibn al-Ḥusayn (d. 458/1066), *Kitāb al-muʿtamad fī uṣūl al-dīn*, ed. Wadīʿ Nirān Ḥaddād (Beirut: Dār al-Mashriq, [1393]/1974).

Ibn al-Farrāʾ, Abū Yaʿlā Muḥammad ibn al-Ḥusayn (d. 458/1066), *Ibṭāl al-taʾwīlāt li-akhbār al-ṣifāt*, ed. Muḥammad ibn Ḥamd al-Ḥamūd al-Najjdī, in 2 vols. (Riyadh: Dār Īlāf al-Dawliyya, [1407]/[1987]).

Ibn Ḥanbal, Aḥmad (d. 241/855), "*al-Radd ʿala ʾl-zanādiqa wal-jahmiyya*," in: *ʿAqāʾid al-salaf: lil-a'ima Aḥmad ibn Ḥanbal wal-Bukhārī wa-Ibn Qutayba wa-Uthmān al-dārimī*, ed. ʿAlī S. Al-Nashshār and ʿImār J. Al-Ṭālibī (Cairo: Dār al-Salām, 1428/2007), 39–77.

Ibn al-Mawṣilī, Shams al-Dīn Abū ʿAbdallāh Muḥammad ibn Muḥammad (d. 774/1372), *Mukhtaṣar al-Ṣawāʿiq al-mursala ʿala 'l-jahmiyya wal-muʿaṭṭila*, originally written by Ibn Qayyim al-Jawziyya, ed. Al-ʿAlawī, Al-Ḥasan ibn ʿAbd al-Raḥman, in 4 vols. (Riyadh: Aḍwā' al-Salaf, 1425/2004).

Ibn Ḥajar al-ʿAsqalānī, Shihāb al-Dīn Abu 'l-Faḍl Aḥmad ibn ʿAlī (d. 853/1449), *al-Durar al-kāmina fī aʿyān al-mi'a al-thāmina*, ed. Muḥammad ʿAbd al-Muʿīd Ḍān, in 6 vols. (Hyderabad, India: Da'irat al-Maʿārif al-ʿUthmāniyya, 1392/1972).

Ibn Ḥazm, Abū Muḥammad ʿAlī al-Ẓāhirī (d. 456/1064), *al-Faṣl fī 'l-milal wal-ahwā' wal-niḥal*, eds. Muḥammad Ibrāhīm Naṣīr and ʿAbd al-Raḥmān ʿAmīra, second edition in 5 vols. (Beirut: Dār al-Jīl, 1416/1996).

Ibn Jinnī, Abu 'l-Fatḥ ʿUthmān (d. 392/1002), *al-Khaṣā'iṣ*, ed. Muḥammad ʿAli 'l-Najjār, in 3 vols. (Cairo: Maṭbaʿat Dār al-Kutub al-Miṣriyya, 1952).

Ibn Qayyim al-Jawziyya, Shams al-Dīn Abū Bakr Muḥammad (d. 751/1350), *Badā'iʿ al-fawā'id*, ed. Al-ʿImrān, ʿAlī ibn Muḥammad and Abū Zayd, Bakr ibn ʿAbdallāh, in 5 vols. (Mecca: Dār ʿĀlam al-Fawā'id lil-Nashr wal-Tawzīʿ, [1424]/2003).

Ibn Qayyim al-Jawziyya, Shams al-Dīn Abū Bakr Muḥammad (d. 751/1350), *Ijtimāʿ al-juyūsh al-islāmiyya ʿalā ghazw al-muʿaṭṭila wal-jahmiyya*, ed. ʿAwwād ʿAbdallāh al-Muʿtiq, in 2 vols. (Riyadh: Maṭābīʿ al-Farazdaq al-Tijāriyya, 1408/1988).

Ibn Qayyim al-Jawziyya, Shams al-Dīn Abū Bakr Muḥammad (d. 751/1350), *Mukhtaṣar al-ṣawāʿiq al-mursala ʿala 'l-Jahmiyya wal-Muʿaṭṭila: the Abridgement of Muḥammad ibn ʿAbd al-Wahhāb*, ed. Daghash ibn Shabīb al-ʿAjmī (Kuwait: Maktabat Ahl al-Āthār, [2015?]). Accessed June 15, 2016. http://librairie-salafsalih.com/produit/moukhtasar-as-sawaiq-al-moursala-cheikh-mohammed-ibn-abdel-wahhab/ or http://maktabah-sunnah.com/en/uniqueness-and-belief/1710--.html.

Ibn Qayyim al-Jawziyya, Shams al-Dīn Abū Bakr Muḥammad (d. 751/1350), *al-Ṣawāʿiq al-mursala ʿala 'l-Jahmiyya wal-muʿaṭṭila*, ed. ʿAlī al-Dakhīl Allah, third edition in 4 vols. (Riyadh: Dār al-ʿĀṣima, 1418/1998).

Ibn Rajab, Zayn al-Dīn Abū al-Faraj ʿAbd al-Raḥman ibn Aḥmad (d. 795/1392), *al-Dhayl ʿalā ṭabaqāt al-ḥanābila*, ed. M.Ḥ. al-Faqīy in 2 vols. (Cairo: Maṭbaʿat al-Sunna al-Muḥammadiyya, 1372/1952).

Ibn Rushd, Abu 'l-Walīd Muḥammad ibn Aḥmad ibn Muḥammd al-Andalusi 'l-Mālikī (d. 595/1198), *al-Kashf ʿan manāhij al-adilla fī ʿaq'id al-milla: aw naqd ʿilm al-kalām ḍiddan ʿala 'l-tarsīm al-īdiyūlūjī lil-ʿaqīda wa-difāʿan ʿan al-ilm wal-ḥuriyya wal-ikhtiyār fī 'l-fikr wal-fiʿl*, ed. Muḥammad ʿĀbid al-Jābirī (Beirut: Markaz Dirāsāt al-Waḥda 'l-ʿArabiyya, [1418]/1998).

Ibn Taymiyya, Taqi 'l-Dīn Aḥmad (d. 728/1328), *Bayān talbīs al-jahmiyya fī ta'sīs bidaʿihim al-kalāmiyya*, ed. Yaḥyā ibn Muḥammad al-Hindī in 10 vols. (Medina: Majmaʿ al-Malik Fahd li-Ṭibāʿat al-Muṣḥaf al-Sharīf, 1426/[2005]).

Ibn Taymiyya, Taqi 'l-Dīn Aḥmad (d. 728/1328), *Dar' ta'āruḍ al-'aql wal-naql*, ed. M.R. Sālim in 10 vols. (Riyadh: Jāmi'at al-Imām Muḥammad ibn Sa'ūd al-Islāmiyya, 1411/1991).

Ibn Taymiyya, Taqi 'l-Dīn Aḥmad (d. 728/1328), *al-Fatwa 'l-Ḥamawiya 'l-kubrā*, ed. Ḥamad 'Abd al-Muḥsin al-Tuwayjirī (Riyadh: Dār al-Ṣamī'ī, 1425/2004).

Ibn Taymiyya, Taqi 'l-Dīn Aḥmad (d. 728/1328), *Jāmi' al-rasā'il*, ed. M.R. Sālim, in 2 vols. (Riyadh: Dār al-'Aṭā', 1422/2001).

Ibn Taymiyya, Taqi 'l-Dīn Aḥmad (d. 728/1328), *Majmū'at al-fatāwā*, ed. 'Āmir Al-Jazzār and Anwar Al-Bāz, in 37 vols. (Riyadh: Dār al-Wafā' lil-Ṭibā'a wal-Nashr wal-Tawzī', 1419/1998).

al-Jurjānī, Abu 'l-Bakr 'Abd al-Qāhir ibn 'Abd al-Raḥman (d. 471/1078), *Asrar al-balāgha fī 'ilm al-bayān*, ed. Muḥammad 'Abduh and Muḥammad Rashīd Riḍā (Beirut: Dār al-Ma'rifa, [1398]/1978).

al-Rāzī, Fakhr al-Dīn Abū 'Abdallāh Muḥammad ibn 'Umar (d. 606/1209), *Asās al-Taqdīs*, ed. Aḥmad Ḥijāzī al-Saqā (Cairo: Maktabat al-Kulliyyāt al-Azhariyya, 1406/1986).

al-Rāzī, Fakhr al-Dīn Abū 'Abdallāh Muḥammad ibn 'Umar (d. 606/1209), *Kitāb al-arba'īn fī uṣūl al-dīn*, no ed. mentioned (Hyderabad, India: Majlis Dā'irat al-Ma'ārif al-'Uthmāniyya, 1353/[1934]).

al-Rāzī, Fakhr al-Dīn Abū 'Abdallāh Muḥammad ibn 'Umar (d. 606/1209), *Kitāb al-arba'īn fī uṣūl al-dīn*, ed. Aḥmad Ḥijazī al-Saqqā in 2 vols. (Cairo: Maktabat al-Kulliyyāt al-Azhariyya, [1409/1989]).

al-Rāzī, Fakhr al-Dīn Abū 'Abdallāh Muḥammad ibn 'Umar (d. 606/1209), *Muḥaṣṣal afkār al-mutaqaddimīn wal-muta'akhkhirīn min al-'ulamā' wal-ḥukamā' wal-mutakallimīn*, ed. al-Ṭūsī, Nṣīr al-Dīn Abū Ja'far Muḥammad ibn Muḥammad ibn al-Ḥasan and Sa'd, Ṭaha 'Abd al-Ru'ūf, with the commentary *Talkhīṣ al-muḥaṣṣal* by al-Ṭūsī (Cairo: Maktabat al-Kulliyyāt al-Azhariyya, [n.d.]).

al-Ṣafadī, Ṣalāḥ al-Dīn Khalīl ibn Aybak (d. 764/1362), *A'yān al-'aṣr wa-a'wān al-naṣr*, ed, 'Alī Abū Zayd et al. in 5 vols. (Beirut: Dār al-Fikr al-Mu'āṣir, 1418/1998).

al-Ṣafadī, Ṣalāḥ al-Dīn Khalīl ibn Aybak (d. 764/1362), *al-Wāfī bil-wafayāt*. eds. Aḥmad al-Arnā'ūṭ and Turkī Muṣṭafā in 29 vols. (Beirut: Dār Iḥyā' al-Turāth, 1420/2000).

al-Subkī, Taqī al-Dīn Abū al-Ḥasan 'Alī ibn 'Abd al-Kāfī (d. 756/1355), *Fatāwa 'l-Subkī* (Beirut: Dār al-Ma'rifa, [1410]/[1990]).

al-Subkī, Taqī al-Dīn Abū al-Ḥasan 'Alī ibn 'Abd al-Kāfī (d. 756/1355), *al-Rasā'il al-Subkiyya fī al-radd 'alā Ibn Taymiyya wa-tilmidhihi Ibn Qayyim al-Jawziyya*. ed. Abū al-Munā, Kamāl (Beirut: 'Ālam al-Kutub, 1403/1983).

al-Tahanāwī, Muḥammad A'lā ibn 'Alī, *Mawsū'at iṣṭilāḥāt al-'ulūm al-islāmiyya* (*al-ma'rūf bi-kashshāf iṣṭilāḥāt al-funūn*), ed. Muḥammad Wajīh 'Abd 'l-Ḥaqq in 6 vols. (Beirut, Khiyāṭ: al-Maktaba al-Islāmiyya, [1385]/1966).

Translation of the Quran

Abdel Haleem, M.A.S., *The Qur'an: A new translation*, Oxford World's Classics (Oxford: Oxford University Press, 2008).

Secondary Literature

Abrahamov, Binyamin, *Anthropomorphism and Interpretation of the Qur'ān in the Theology of al-Qāsim ibn Ibrāhīm: Kitab al-Mustarshid* (Leiden: Brill, 1996).

Abrahamov, Binyamin, "Ibn Taymiyya on the Agreement of Reason with Tradition," *The Muslim World* 82 (3–4), 1992: 256–272.

Abrahamov, Binyamin, *Islamic Theology: Traditionalism and Rationalism* (Edinburgh: Edinburgh University Press, 1998).

Abrahamov, Binyamin, "Necessary Knowledge in Islamic Theology," *British Journal of Middle Eastern Studies* 20/1, 1993: 20–32.

Abrahamov, Binyamin, "The "Bi-lā Kayfa" Doctrine and Its Foundations in Islamic Theology," *Arabica* 42/1–3, 1995: 365–379.

Abrahamov, Binyamin, "The Creation and Duration of Paradise and Hell in Islamic Theology," Der Islam 79/1, 2002: 87–102.

Abrahamov, Binyamin, "Scripturalist and Traditionalist Theology." In: *Oxford Handbook of Islamic Theology*, ed. Sabine Schmidtke (Oxford: Oxford University Press, 2016).

Abū Zayd, Bakr ʿAbdullah, *Al-taqrib li-ʿulūm Ibn al-Qayyim* (Mecca: Dār al-ʿĀṣima lil-Nashr wa-Tawzīʿ, [1417]/1996).

Abū Zayd, Bakr ʿAbdullah, *Ibn Qayyim al-Jawziyya: ḥayātuhu, athāruhu, mawāriduhu*, 2nd ed. (Riyadh: Dār al-ʿĀṣima lil-Nashr wa-Tawzīʿ, [1422]/[2002]).

Ajhar, ʿAbd al-Ḥakīm, *Ibn Taymiyya wa-istiʾnāf al-qawl al-falsafī fī 'l-islām* (Beirut: al-Markaz al-Thaqāfī al-ʿArabī, 2004).

Ali, Mohamed Mohamed Yunis, *Medieval Islamic Pragmatics: Sunni Legal Theorists' Models of Textual Communication* (Richmond, Surrey: Routledge, 2000).

Anjum, Ovamir, *Politics, Law and Community in Islamic Thought: The Taymiyyan Moment*, Cambridge studies in Islamic civilization (Cambridge, New York: Cambridge University Press, 2012).

Arberry, Arthur J., *Revelation and Reason in Islam*, The Forward Lectures for 1956 Delivered in University of Liverpool (London: Allen and Urwin Ltd., 1965).

Arnaldez, Roger, "Ibn Ḥazm," *EI*², 3:790–799.

Arnaldez, Roger, "Ibn Rushd," *EI*², 3:909–920.

Averroës, and Ibrahim Y. Najjar, *Faith and Reason in Islam: Averroes' Exposition of Religious Arguments*, Great Islamic writings (Oxford: Oneworld, 2001).

Badi, Jamal Ahmed, "*Qawāʿid wa-ḍawābiṭ wa-fawāʾid min kitāb al-Ṣawāʿiq al-mursala li-Ibn al-Qayyim*," *Majalat al-Hikma* 24 (2008?): 461–506. http://www.alhikma59.com/R1.htm.

Baltzly, Dirk, "Stoicism", *The Stanford Encyclopedia of Philosophy Online*. Accessed July 17, 2015. http://plato.stanford.edu/archives/spr2014/entries/stoicism.

al-Baqrī, Aḥmad M., *Ibn al-Qayyim al-lughawī* (Cairo: al-Maʿārif, 1989).

Bauer, Thomas, "Mamluk Literature: Misunderstandings and New Approaches," *Mamlūk Studies Review* 9/2 (2005): 105–132.

Bauer, Thomas, "Mamluk Literature as a Means of Communication", in: *Ubi sumus? Quo vademus? Mamluk Studies—State of the Art*, ed. Stephan Conermann, Mamluk studies 3 (Göttingen: Vandenhoeck & Ruprecht, 2013), 23–56.

Bavaj, Riccardo, "Intellectual History," *Docupedia-Zeitgeschichte* (2010), http://docupedia.de/zg/Intellectual_History?oldid=106434.

Bazzano, Elliott A., "Ibn Taymiyya, Radical Polymath, Part 1: Scholarly Perceptions," *Religion Compass* 9/4 (2015): 100–116. doi:10.1111/rec3.12114.

Bazzano, Elliott A., "Ibn Taymiyya, Radical Polymath, Part 2: Intellectual Contributions," *Religion Compass* 9/4 (2015): 117–139. doi:10.1111/rec3.12115.

Belhaj, Abdessamad, *Argumentation et dialectique en islam: Formes et séquences de la munazara* (Brussels: Presses universitaires de Louvain, 2010).

Belhaj, Abdessamad, "Disputation is a Fighting Sport: *munāẓara* according to Ibn Qayyim al-Jawziyya," *Mamlūk Studies Review* 18/1 (2016): 1–13.

Belhaj, Abdessamad, "Ibn Qayyim al-Ğawziyyah et sa contribution à la rhétorique arabe," in: *A Scholar in the Shadow: Essays in the Legal and Theological Thought of Ibn Qayyim al-Ğawziyyah*, eds. Caterina Bori and Livnat Holtzman, Oriente Moderno XC/1. (Rome: Istituto per l'Oriente C.A. Nallino, 2010), 151–160.

Belhaj, Abdessamad, "Ibn Taimiyya et la négation de la métaphore," in: *Continuity and Change in the Realms of Islam: Studies in Honour of Professor Urbain Vermeulen*, Orientalia Lovaniensia Analecta 171 (Leuven: Uitgeverij Peeters, 2008), 65–75.

Bell, Joseph N., *Love theory in later Hanbalite Islam*, Studies in Islamic philosophy and science (Albany: State University of New York Press, 1979).

Berkey, Jonathan P., "Popular Culture under the Mamluks: A Historiographical Survey," *Mamlūk Studies Review* 9/2 (2005): 133–146.

Berkey, Jonathan P., *Popular Preaching & Religious Authority in Medieval Islamic Near* East (Seattle and London: University of Washington Press, 2001).

Bonnell, Victoria E., Lynn Hunt, and Richard Biernacki, *Beyond the Cultural Turn: New Directions in the Study of Society and Culture*, Studies on the history of society and culture 34 (Berkeley: University of California Press, 1999).

Bori, Caterina, "A New Source for the Biography of Ibn Taymiyya", *Bulletin of the School of Oriental and African Studies, University of London* 67/3 (2004): 321–348.

Bori, Caterina, *Ibn Taymiyya: una vita esemplare: Analisi delle fonti classiche della sua biografia*, Supplemento monografico n. 1 alla Rivista di Studi Orientali, LXXVI (Pisa-Roma: Istituti Poligrafici Internazionali, 2003).

Bori, Caterina, "Ibn Taymiyya *wa-jamāʿatuhu*: Authority, Conflict and Consensus in Ibn Taymiyya's Circle," in: *Ibn Taymiyya and His Times*, ed. Yossef Rapoport and Shahab Ahmed, Studies in Islamic philosophy iv. (Karachi: Oxford University Press, 2010), 23–52.

Bori, Caterina, "The Collection and Edition of Ibn Taymīyah's Works: Concerns of a Disciple," *Mamlūk Studies Review* 13/2 (2009): 47–68.

Bori, Caterina, "Theology, Politics, Society: the missing link: Studying Religion in the Mamluk Period," in: *Ubi sumus? Quo vademus? Mamluk Studies—State of the Art*, ed. Stephan Conermann, Mamluk studies 3 (Göttingen: Vandenhoeck & Ruprecht, 2013), 57–94.

Bosworth, Clifford E., "Karrāmiyya," *EI*², 4:667–669.

Bowen, H., "ʿAḍud al-Dawla," *EI*², 1:211–212.

Brockelmann, C.; Gardet, Louis, "al-Djuwaynī," *EI*², 2:605–606.

Brodersen, Angelika, "Abū Isḥāq al-Isfarāyīnī," *EI THREE* Online. Accessed October 15, 2015. http://referenceworks.brillonline.com/entries/encyclopaedia-of-islam-3/abu-ishaq-al-isfarayini-COM_26291.

Calder, N.; Hooker, M.B., "Sharīʿa," *EI*², 9:321–328.

Carpenter, Rhys, *the Esthetic Basis of the Greek Art of the Fifth and Fourth Centuries B.C.* (New York: Longmans, Green and Co., 1921).

Chamberlain, Michael, *Knowledge and Social Practice in Medieval Damascus, 1190–1350* (Cambridge: Cambridge University Press, 1994).

Chittick, William C., "Microcosm, Macrocosm, and Perfect Man in the View of Ibn al-ʾArabī," *Islamic Culture* 63/1–2 (January–April 1989): 1–12.

Chittick, William C., *The Sufi Path of Knowledge: Ibn al-ʿArabi's Metaphysics of Imagination* (Albany, N.Y.: State University of New York Press, 1989).

Cohen, Avivit, "Between "the Garden of Lovers" and "the Censure of Profance Love": A Comparative Study of Ibn Qayyim al-Jawziyya and Ibn al-Jawzi's Theory of Love," unpublished MA thesis, Bar-Ilan University, Ramat Gan, 2010.

Commins, David, "From Wahhabi to Salafi," in: *Saudi Arabia in Transition: Insights on Social, Political, Economic and Religious Change*, eds. Bernard Haykel, Thomas Hegghammer, and Stéphane Lacroix (New York: Cambridge University Press, 2015), 151–166.

Cook, Michael, "On the Origins of Wahhābism," *Journal of the Royal Asiatic Society* 2/2 (Third Series, 1992): 191–202.

Cooperson, Michael, *Classical Arabic Biography: The Heirs of the Prophets in the Age of al-Maʾmūn. Cambridge studies in Islamic civilization* (Cambridge: Cambridge University Press, 2000).

Daiber, H.; Ragep, F.J., "al-Ṭūsī, Naṣīr al-Dīn," *EI*², 10: 746–752.

De Blois, François C., "Zindīḳ," *EI*², 11: 510–513.

El-Bizri, Nader, "God: Essence and Attributes," in: *The Cambridge Companion to Classical Islamic Theology*, ed. Tim Winter (Cambridge: Cambridge University Press, 2008), 121–140.

Elqayam, Avraham, "al-Fatihah: The Mystery of Opening in Jewish and Islamic Mysticism," in: *The East Write Itself*, ed. Haviva Pedaya (Tel Aviv: Gama, 2015), 157–249.

Ernst, C., "S͟haṭḥ," *EI*², 9: 361–362.

Fakhry, Majid, *Averroes (Ibn Rushd): His life, works and influence*, Great Islamic Thinkers (Oxford: Oneworld, 2001).

al-Fiqī, Muḥammad Ḥāmid, *Athar al-daʿwa al-wahhābiyya fi 'l-islāḥ al-dīnī wal-ʿumrānī fī jazirat al-ʿarab wa-ghayrihā* (Cairo: Matbaʿat al-Nahda, 1354/[1935]).

Frank, Richard M., "Ḥāll," *EI*², 12: 343–348.

Frank, Richard M., "Knowledge and Taqlîd: The Foundations of Religious Belief in Classical Ashʿarism," *Journal of the American Oriental Society* 109/1 (1989): 37–62. doi:10.2307/604336.

Frank, Richard M., "The Science of Kalām," *Arabic Sciences and Philosophy* 2 (1992): 7–37.

Friedman, Yaron, *the Nuṣayrī-ʿAlawīs: An Introduction to the Religion, History, and Identity of the Leading Minority in Syria*, Islamic history and civilization 77 (Leiden, Boston: Brill, 2010).

Gardet, Louis, "ʿAḳliyyāt," *EI*², 1:342–343.

Gardet, Louis, "Allāh," *EI*², 1:406–417.

Gardet, Louis, "al-Asmāʾ al-Ḥusnā," *EI*², 1:714–717.

Gardet, Louis, "al-D͟jubbāʾī," *EI*², 2: 569–570.

Gardet, Louis, "Ḥaḳīḳa," *EI*², 3:75–76.

Gardet, Louis, "Kas͟hf," *EI*², 4: 696–698.

Genette, Gerard, and Marie Maclean, "Introduction to the Paratext," *New Literary History* 22/2 (1991): 261–272. doi:10.2307/469037.

Geoffroy, E., "al-Suyūṭī," *EI*², 9:913–916.

Gharaibeh, Mohammad, "The Buldāniyyāt of as-Saḫāwī (d. 902/1496): A Case Study on Knowledge Specialization and Knowledge Brokerage in the Field of Ḥadīṯ Collections," *Annemarie Schimmel Kolleg Working Paper* 18 (2014): 1–16. https://www.mamluk.uni-bonn.de/publications/working-paper/ask-wp-18-gharaibeh.pdf.

Ghazzal, Zuhair, "The ʿUlamāʾ: Status and Function," in: *A Companion to the History of the Middle East*, ed. Youssef M. Choueiri, (Malden, MA: Blackwell Pub., 2005), 71–86.

Gibb, H.A.R., "Abū ʿUbayda," *EI*², 1:158.

Gilliot, Claude, "Attributes of God," *EI THREE*, 1:179–182.

Gilliot, Claude, "Exegesis of the Qurʾān: Classical and Medieval," *Encyclopaedia of the Qurʾān*. 2:99–124.

Gimaret, Daniel, "al-Shaḥḥām," *EI*², 9:202–203.

Gimaret, Daniel, "Ṣifa," *EI*², 9:551–552.

Gimaret, Daniel, "Théories de l'acte humain dans l'école hanbalite," *Bulletin d'études orientales* 29 (1977): 156–178.

Gimaret, Daniel, *Théories de l'acte humain en théologie musulmane* (Paris: Vrin, 1980).

Ginzburg, Carlo, "High and Low: The Theme of Forbidden Knowledge in the Sixteenth and Seventeenth Centuries," *Past and Present* 73 (1976): 28–41.

Goichon, A.M., "Ibn Sīnā," *EI*², 3:941–948.

Goldstein, Miriam, "Abū l-Faraj Hārūn (Jerusalem, 11th c.) on *majāz*, between *uṣūl al-naḥw, uṣūl al-fiqh* and *iʿjāz al-Qurʾān*," *Der Islam* 90/2 (2013): 376–411. doi:10.1515/islam-2013-0012.

Goldziher, Ignaz, *Vorlesungen über den Islam*, Hebrew transl. M.M. Plessner and Y.Y. Rivlin (Jerusalem: Bialik Institute, 1951).

Goldziher, Ignaz, *Vorlesungen über den Islam*, second edition (Heidelberg, Germany: C. Winter, 1925).

Gordon, Peter E., "What Is Intellectual History? A Frankly Partisan Introduction to a Frequently Misunderstood Field" (Harvard University, spring, 2012). http://projects.iq.harvard.edu/files/history/files/what_is_intell_history_pgordon_mar2012.pdf

Grant, Edward, *Much ado about Nothing: Theories of Space and Vacuum from the Middle Ages to the Scientific Revolution* (Cambridge, New York: Cambridge University Press, 1981).

Griffel, Frank, "Fakhr al-Dīn al-Rāzī", *Encyclopedia of Medieval Philosophy*, ed. Henrik Lagerlund (Springer: Dordrecht, 2011), 1:341–345.

Griffel, Frank, "Al-Ghazālī at His Most Rationalist: The Universal Rule for Allegorically Interpreting Revelation (*al-Qānūn al-Kullī fī t-Taʾwīl*)," in: *Islam and Rationality: The Impact of al-Ghazālī. Papers Collected on His 900th Anniversary*. Vol. 1, ed. Georges Tamer (Leiden, Brill, 2015), 89–120.

Griffel, Frank, "Al-Ghazālī's Concept of Prophecy: The Introduction of Avicennan Psychology into Ašʿarite Theology," *Arabic Sciences and Philosophy* 14/1 (2004): 101–144. doi: 10.1017/S0957423904000025.

Griffel, Frank, *Al-Ghazālī's Philosophical Theology* (New York: Oxford University Press, 2009).

Griffel, Frank, "On Fakhr al-Din al-Razi's Life and the Patronage He received," *Journal of Islamic Studies* 18/3 (2007): 313–344. doi:10.1093/jis/etm029.

Gutas, Dimitri, "Classical Arabic Wisdom Literature: Nature and Scope," *Journal of the American Oriental Society* 101/1 (1981): Oriental Wisdom, 49–86.

Gutas, Dimitri, *Greek thought, Arabic culture: The Graeco-Arabic translation movement in Baghdad and early ʿAbbāsid society (2nd–4th/8th–10th centuries)* (London, New York: Routledge, 1998).

al-Ḥaddād, Yāsīn Ḥ., *Ibn Qayyim al-Jawziyya: minhajuhu, wa-marwīyātuhu al-taʾrikhīya fi ʾl-sīra al-nabawiyya al-sharīfa* (Cairo: Dār al-Fajr lil-Nashr wa-Tawzīʿ, [1421]/2001).

Halkin, A.S., "The Ḥashwiyya," *Journal of the American Oriental Society* 1 (Mar., 1934): 1–28.

Hallaq, Wael B., *A history of Islamic legal theories: An introduction to Sunnī uṣūl al-fiqh* (Cambridge, New York: Cambridge University Press, 1997).

Hallaq, Wael B., *Ibn Taymiyya against the Greek Logicians* (Oxford: Oxford University Press, 1993).

Hallaq, Wael B., *the Origins and Evolution of Islamic Law*, Themes in Islamic law 1 (Cambridge, New York: Cambridge University Press, 2005).

Halldén, Philip, "What Is Arab Islamic Rhetoric? Rethinking the History of Muslim Oratory Art and Homiletics," *International Journal of Middle East Studies* 37/1 (2005): 19–38. http://dx.doi.org/10.1017/S0020743805050038.

Hammam, Belgacem, "*Jadaliyyat al-taʾwīl wal-majāz ʿind[a] Ibn Qayyim al-Jawziyya min khilāl[i] kitābih[i] al-Ṣawāʿiq al-mursala*," *Fikr wa-Ibdāʿ* (before 2010?): 245–276.

Ḥamūda, Ṭāhir Sulaymān, *Ibn Qayyim al-Jawziyya: juhūduh[u] fī 'l-dars al-lughawī* (Alexandria: Dār al-Jāmiʿāt al-Miṣriyya, 1976).

Hardy, Paul-A., "Epistemology and Divine Discourse," in: *The Cambridge Companion to Classical Islamic Theology*, ed. Tim Winter (Cambridge: Cambridge University Press, 2008), 288–307.

Harris, Roy, Talbot J. Taylor, and Versteegh, C.H.M., *Landmarks in linguistic thought: Volume III: The Arabic Linguistic Tradition (History of Linguistic Thought)*, Routledge history of linguistic thought series in 3 vols. (London, New York: Routledge, 1997).

Hasan, Ali, "Al-Ghazali and Ibn Rushd (Averroes) on Creation and the Divine Attributes," in: *Models of God and Alternative Ultimate Realities*, eds. Jeanine Diller and Asa Kasher (Dordrecht: Springer Netherlands, 2013), 141–156.

Heinrichs, Wolfhart, "Contacts between Scriptural Hermeneutics and Literary Theory in Islam: The Case of Majāz," *Zeitschrift für Geschichte der arabisch islamischen Wissenschaften* 7 (1991/92): 253–284.

Heinrichs, Wolfhart, "On the Genesis of the Ḥaqīqa-Majāz Dichotomy," *Studia Islamica* 59 (1984): 111–140.

Ḥijāzī, Awḍallah, *Ibn al-Qayyim wa-mawqifuh[u] min al-tafkīr al-islāmī* ([Cairo]: Majmaʿ al-Buḥūth al-Islāmiyya, 1392/1972).

Hirschler, Konrad, *Medieval Arabic historiography: Authors as actors*, SOAS/Routledge studies on the Middle East 5 (London, New York: Routledge, 2006).

Hodgson, M.G.S., "Bāṭiniyya," *EI*², 1:1099–1100.

Holtzman, Livnat, "Accused of Anthropomorphism: Ibn Taymiyya's *Miḥan* as Reflected in Ibn Qayyim al-Jawziyya's *al-Kāfiya al-Shāfiya*," *The Muslim World* 106:3 (July, 2016), 561–587.

Holtzman, Livnat, "Aḥmad b. Ḥanbal," *EI THREE*, 1:15–23.

Holtzman, Livnat, "Anthropomorphism," *EI THREE*, 1:46–55.

Holtzman, Livnat, *Anthropomorphism in Islam: The Challenge of Traditionalism, 700–1550* (Edinburgh: Edinburgh University Press, forthcoming March 2018).

Holtzman, Livnat, "Debating the Doctrine of Jabr (Compulsion): Ibn Qayyim al-Jawziyya Reads Fakhr al-Dīn al-Rāzī," in: *Islamic Theology, Philosophy and Law: Debating Ibn Taymiyya and Ibn Qayyim al-Jawziyya*, eds. Birgit Krawietz and Georges Tamer, Studien zur Geschichte und Kultur des islamischen Orients Neue Folge 27 (Berlin, Boston: De Gruyter, 2013), 62–93.

Holtzman, Livnat, "'Does God Really Laugh?': Appropriate and Inappropriate Descriptions of God in Islamic Traditionalist Theology," in: *Laughter in the Middle Ages and Early Modern Times*, ed. Albrecht Classen (Berlin, New York: Degruyter, 2010), 165–200.

Holtzman, Livnat, "The Dhimmi's Question on Predetermination and the Ulama's Six Responses: The Dynamics of Composing Polemical Didactic Poems in Mamluk Cairo and Damascus," *Mamlūk Studies Review* XVI (2012): 1–54.

Holtzman, Livnat, "The Politics of Fiṭra: On Ibn Taymiyya's Epistemological Optimism," An Essay Review on Politics, Law, and Community in Islamic Thought: The Taymiyyan Moment, by Ovamir Anjum, *Ilahiyat Studies: A Journal on Islamic and Religious Studies* 5 (2), 239–247. https://doi.org/10.12730/13091719.2014.52.110

Holtzman, Livnat, "Elements of Acceptance and Rejection in Ibn Qayyim al-Jawziyya's Systematic Reading of Ibn Ḥazm," in: *Ibn Ḥazm of Cordoba: The Life and Works of a Controversial Thinker*, eds. Camilla Adang, Ma. Isabel Fierro, and Sabine Schmidtke, Handbook of Oriental studies. Section 1, the Near and Middle East v. 103 (Leiden, Boston: Brill, 2013), 601–644.

Holtzman, Livnat, "Ḥanbalīs," in: *Oxford Bibliographies Online*, accessed March 13, 2015. doi: 10.1093/OBO/9780195390155-0210

Holtzman, Livnat, "Human Choice, Divine Guidance and the Fiṭra Tradition: The Use of Ḥadīth in Theological Treatises by Ibn Taymiyya and Ibn Qayyim al-Jawziyya," in: *Ibn Taymiyya and His Times*, ed. Yossef Rapoport and Shahab Ahmed, Studies in Islamic philosophy iv. (Karachi: Oxford University Press, 2010), 163–188.

Holtzman, Livnat, "Ibn Qayyim al-Jawziyya (1292–1350)," in: *Essays in Arabic Literary Biography*, eds. Roger Allen and Joseph E. Lowry, Mîzân 17 (Wiesbaden: Harrassowitz, 2009), 201–222.

Holtzman, Livnat, "Insult, Fury, and Frustration: The Martyrological Narrative of Ibn Qayyim al-Jawzīyah's al-Kāfiyah al-Shāfiyah," *Mamlūk Studies Review* 17/1 (2013): 155–198.

Holtzman, Livnat, "Islamic Theology," in: *Handbook of medieval studies, Vol. 1*, ed. Albrecht Classen. in 3 vols. (Berlin, New York: De Gruyter, 2010), 56–68.

Holtzman, Livnat, "The miḥna of Ibn ʿAqīl (d. 513/1119) and the fitnat Ibn al-Qushayrī (d. 514/1120)," in: *Oxford Handbook of Islamic Theology*, ed. Sabine Schmidtke (Oxford: Oxford University Press, 2016), 660–678.

Holtzman, Livnat, "Predestination (*al-Qaḍā' wa-l-Qadar*) and Free Will (*al-Ikhtiyār*) as Reflected in the Works of the Neo-Ḥanbalites in the Fourteenth Century," PhD Dissertation, Bar-Ilan University, 2003.

Holtzman, Livant and Ovadia, Miriam, "On Divine Aboveness (*al-Fawqiyya*): The Development of Rationalized Ḥadīth-Based Argumentations in Islamic Theology," in: *Rationalization in Religions*, eds. Yohanan Friedmann and Christoph Markschies (Berlin: De Gruyter, forthcoming 2018).

Hoover, Jon, "Ḥanbalī Theology," in: *Oxford handbook of Islamic Theology*, ed. Sabine Schmidtke (Oxford: Oxford University Press, 2016), 625–646.

Hoover, Jon, *Ibn Taymiyya's Theodicy of Perpetual Optimism*, Islamic philosophy, theology, and science 73 (Leiden, Boston: Brill, 2007).

Hoover, Jon, "Islamic Universalism: Ibn Qayyim al-Jawziyya's Salafī Deliberations on the Duration of Hell-Fire," *The Muslim World* 99 (2009): 181–201.

Horkheimer, Max, and Theodor W. Adorno, *Dialectic of Enlightenment: Philosophical Fragments*, ed. Schmid Noerr, Gunzelin, transl. Edmund Jephcott. Cultural memory in the present (Palo Alto: Stanford University Press, 2002).

Ibn Qayyim al-Jawziyya, Yasrā al-Sayyid Muḥammad and Ṣāliḥ Aḥmad al-Shāmī, *Badā'i' al-tafsīr: al-jāmi' limā fassarah*[u] *al-imām Ibn Qayyim al-Jawziyya*, 2nd ed. in 3 vols. (Riyadh: Dār Ibn al-Jawzī lil-nashr wal-tawzī', 1427/[2005]).

Ibn Taymiyya, Taqi 'l-Dīn Aḥmad (d. 728/1328), Yahya Michot, and Bruce B. Lawrence, *Against extremisms: Texts Translated & Introduction* ([Beirut]: Albouraq Editions, 2012).

Irwin, Robert, "Mamluk Literature", *Mamlūk Studies Review* 7/1 (2003): 1–29.

al-Isfarā'inī, 'Iṣām al-Dīn Ibrāhīm ibn Muḥammad, *Sharḥ al-'aqā'id* ([Istanbul]: [n.p.], [1833]/1249).

Jackson, Sherman A., "Ibn Taymiyyah on Trial in Damascus," *Journal of Semitic Studies* XXXIX-1 (1994): 41–85. doi:10.1093/jss/XXXIX.1.41.

Jaffer, Tariq, "Mu'tazilite Aspects of Faḫr al-Dīn al-Rāzī's Thought," *Arabica* 59/5 (2012): 510–535. doi:10.1163/157005812X618943.

al-Jamil, Tariq, "Ibn Taymiyya and Ibn al-Muṭahhar al-Ḥillī: Shi'ī Polemics and the Struggle for Religious Authority in Medieval Islam," in: *Ibn Taymiyya and His Times*, ed. Yossef Rapoport and Shahab Ahmed, (Karachi: Oxford University Press, 2010), 229–246.

Johanson, Baber, "Signs as Evidence: The Doctrine of Ibn Taymiyya (1263–1328) and Ibn Qayyim al-Jawziyya (d. 1351) on Proof," *Islamic Law and Society* 9/2 (2002): 168–193.

Jones, Linda G., *the Power of Oratory in the Medieval Muslim World*. Cambridge studies in Islamic civilization (New York: Cambridge University Press, 2012).

Juynboll, G.H.A., "Ṣafwān ibn al-Mu'aṭṭal," *EI*[2], 8:820.

Juynboll, G.H.A., "Tawātur," *EI*[2], 10:381–382.

Kerferd, G.B., *The Sophistic Movement* (Cambridge, New York: Cambridge University Press, 1981).

Khalil, Esam N., "Cohesion," *Encyclopedia of Arabic Language and Linguistics*, Brill Online. Accessed March 2016.

http://referenceworks.brillonline.com.proxy1.athensams.net/entries/encyclopedia-ofarabic-language-and-linguistics/cohesion-EALL_SIM_0017.

Kinberg, Leah, "Ambiguous," *Encyclopaedia of the Qur'ān*, ed. Jane D. McAuliffe, 1:70–77.

Kouloughli, Djamel E., "Maʿnā," Encyclopedia of Arabic Language and Linguistics, Brill Online. Accessed March 2016. http://referenceworks.brillonline.com.proxy1.athensams.net/entries/encyclopedia-ofarabic-language-and-linguistics/mana-EALL_COM_vol3_0204.

Kraus, Paul, "Les 'Conreverses' de Fakhr al-Dīn al-Rāzī," *Bulletin d'Institut d'Egypte* 19 (1937): 187–214.

Krawietz, Birgit, "Ibn Qayyim al-Jawzīyah: His Life and Works," *Mamlūk Studies Review* 10/2 (2006): 19–64.

von Kügelgen, Anke, "Ibn Taymīyas Kritik an der Aristotelischen Logik und sein Gegenentwurf", in: *Logik und Theologie: das Organon im arabischen und im lateinischen Mittelalter*, eds. Dominik Perler and Ulrich Rudolph, Studien und Texte zur Geistesgeschichte des Mittelalters 84 (Leiden: Brill, 2005), 167–226.

von Kügelgen, Anke, "The Poison of Philosophy: Ibn Taymiyya's Struggle For and Against Reason," in: *Islamic Theology, Philosophy and Law: Debating Ibn Taymiyya and Ibn Qayyim al-Jawziyya*, eds. Birgit Krawietz and Georges Tamer, Studien zur Geschichte und Kultur des islamischen Orients Neue Folge 27 (Berlin, Boston: De Gruyter, 2013), 253–328.

Kukkonen, Taneli, "Averroes and the Teleological Argument," *Religious Studies* 38/4 (2002): 405–428.

Landau, Rom, *The Philosophy of Ibn al-ʿArabī* (London: George Allen & Unwin Ltd, 1959).

Lane, Edward W., *Arabic-English Lexicon: Book I*. 8 vols. (New York: F. Ungar Pub. Co., [1955–1956]).

Langermann, Y. Tzvi, "The Naturalization of Science in Ibn Qayyim al-Jawziyya's Kitāb al-rūḥ," in: *A Scholar in the Shadow: Essays in the Legal and Theological Thought of Ibn Qayyim al-Ǧawziyyah*, eds. Caterina Bori and Livnat Holtzman, Oriente Moderno XC/1 (Rome: Istituto per l'Oriente C.A. Nallino, 2010), 211–228.

Laoust, Henri, "Aḥmad b. Ḥanbal," *EI*², 1:272–277.

Laoust, Henri, *Essai sur les doctrines sociales et politiques d'Ibn Taimîya (661/1262–728/1328)*, (Le Caire: Imprimerie de l'Institut Français d'Archéologie Orientale, 1939).

Laoust, Henri, "Ibn al-Djawzī," *EI*², 3:751–752.

Laoust, Henri, "Ibn al-Farrā'," *EI*², 3:765–766.

Laoust, Henri, "Ibn Taymiyya," *EI*², 3:951–955.

Laoust, Henri, "Ibn Ḳayyim al-Djawziyya," *EI*², 3:821–822.

Laoust, Henri, "al-Khiraḳī," *EI*², 5:9–10.

Laoust, Henri, "Les premiere professions de foi Ḥanbalites," *Melanges Louis Massignion* 3 (1956): 7–35.

Laoust, Henri, *La profession de foi d'Ibn Taymiyya: texte, traduction et commentaire de la Wāsiṭiyya*, Bibliothèque d'études islamiques 10 (Paris: Geuther, 1986).

Lav, Daniel, *Radical Islam and the Revival of Medieval Theology* (New York: Cambridge University Press. 2012).

Law, Vivien, "Language and its Students: the History of Linguistics," in: *An Encyclopaedia of Language*, ed. N.E. Collinge (London, New York: Routledge, 1990), 784–842.

Lazarus-Yafeh, Hava, the preface to *The Majlis: Interreligious Encounters in Medieval Islam*, eds. Hava Lazarus-Yafeh, Mark R. Cohen, Sasson Somekh, and Sydney H. Griffith, Studies in Arabic language and literature v. 4 (Wiesbaden: Harrassowitz, 1999), 7–11.

Leaman, Oliver, *Averroes and his philosophy* (Richmond, Surrey [England]: Curzon, 1998).

Levanoni, Amalia, "Who Were the 'Salt of the Earth' in Fifteenth-Century Egypt?", *Mamlūk Studies Review* 14/1 (2010): 63–83.

Livingston, John W., "Ibn Qayyim al-Jawziyyah: A Fourteenth Century Defense against Astrological Divination and Alchemical Transmutation," *Journal of the American Oriental Society* 91/1 (1971): 96–103. doi:10.2307/600445.

Maclean, Marie, "Pretexts and Paratexts: The Art of the Peripheral," *New Literary History* 22/2 (1991): 273–279. doi:10.2307/469038.

Madelung, Wilferd F., "Abū 'l-Ḥusayn al-Baṣrī," *EI THREE—Brill Online*, Accessed July 25, 2015. http://referenceworks.brillonline.com/entries/encyclopaedia-of-islam-3/abu-l-husayn-al-basri-COM_0011.

Madelung, Wilferd F., "al-Isfarāyīnī," *EI*², 4:108.

Madelung, Wilferd F., "Ḳarmaṭī," *EI*², 4:660–665.

Mahdi, Muhsin, "Remarks on Averroes' Decisive Treatise," in: *Islamic Theology and Philosophy: Studies in honor of George F. Hourani*, eds. George F. Hourani and Michael E. Marmura (Albany: State University of New York Press, 1984), 188–202.

Makdisi, George, "Ashʿarī and the Ashʿarites in Islamic Religious History, parts I and II," *Studia Islamica* 17, 18 (1962–1963): 37–80; 19–39.

Makdisi, George, "Ḥanbalite Islam," in: *Studies on Islam*, ed. M.L. Swartz (New York: Oxford University Press, 1981), 216–275.

Makdisi, George, "Ibn ʿAqīl," *EI*², 3:699–700.

Makdisi, George, *Ibn ʿAqīl et la résurgence de l'islam traditionaliste au XIe siècle (Ve siècle de l'Hégire)*, (Damascus: Institut Français de Damas, 1963).

Makdisi, George, *Ibn ʿAqil: Religion and Culture in Classical Islam* (Edinburgh: Edinburgh University Press, 1997).

Makdisi, George, "Ibn Ḳudāma al-Maḳdīsī," *EI*², 3:842–843.

Makdisi, George, "The Significance of the Sunni Schools of Law in Islamic Religious History," *International Journal of Middle East Studies* 10/1 (1979): 1–8.

Mark, Joshua J., "Protagoras," *Ancient History Encyclopedia* (2009). Accessed June 10, 2015. http://www.ancient.eu/protagoras/

Meisami, Julie S., and Paul Starkey, *The Routledge Encyclopedia of Arabic Literature* (London: Routledge, 2010).

Merquior, José G., *Foucault* (Berkeley: University of California Press, 1987).

Monnot, G., "Ṣalāt," *EI*², 8:925–934.

Mouline, Muḥammad Nabīl, *'Ulamā' al-islām: ja'rīkh wa-bunyat al-mu'asassa al-dīniyya fi 'l-sa'ūdiyya bayna 'l-qarnayni 'l-thāmin 'ashar wal-ḥādī wal-'ishrīn*, transl. Muḥammad al-Ḥājj Sālim and 'Ādil ibn 'Abdallāh, 2nd ed. (Beirut: al-Shabka 'l-'Arabiyya lil-Abḥāth wal-Nashr, 2013).

al-Musawi, Muhsin, "Pre-modern Belletristic Prose," in: *The Cambridge History of Arabic Literature*, eds. Roger Allen and D.S. Richards (Cambridge: Cambridge University Press, 2006), 99–133.

Najjar, Ibrahim Y., "Ibn Rushd's Theory of Rationality," *Alif: Journal of Comparative Poetics* 16, Averroës and the Rational Legacy in the East and the West (1996): 191–216.

Najjar, Ibrahim Y., *Faith and Reason in Islam: Averroes' Exposition of Religious Arguments* (Oxford: Oneworld, 2001).

Netton, I.R., "al-Sūfisṭā'iyyūn," *EI*², 8:765.

[not-specified], "Lafḏ", *Encyclopedia of Arabic Language and Linguistics*. Brill Online. Accessed March 2016. http://referenceworks.brillonline.com.proxy1.athensams.net/entries/encyclopedia-of-arabiclanguage-and-linguistics/lafd-EALL_COM_vol2_0080

Nyberg, H.S., "Abu 'l-Hudhayl al-'Allāf," *EI*², 1:128–129.

Osborne, Harold, *Theory of Beauty: an Introduction to Aesthetics* (London: Routledge and Kegan Paul, 1952).

Osborne, Harold, "Symmetry as an Aesthetic Factor," *Computers & Mathematics with Applications* 12/1–2 (1986): 77–82.

Ovadia (Ben Moshe), Miriam, "Ibn Qayyim al-Jawziyya's Hermeneutical Approach to God's Attributes and the Anthropomorphic Expressions in the Quran and the Hadith Literature," unpublished MA thesis, Bar Ilan University, Ramat Gan, 2012.

Özervarli, M.S., "The Qur'ānic Rational Theology of Ibn Taymiyya and His Criticism of the Mutakallimūn," in: *Ibn Taymiyya and His Times*, eds. Yossef Rapoport and Shahab Ahmed, Studies in Islamic philosophy iv. (Karachi: Oxford University Press, 2010), 78–100.

Pedersen, J., "Ibn D̲j̲innī," *EI*², 3:755.

Peña, Salvador, "Which Curiousity? Ibn Ḥazm's Suspicion of Grammarians," in: *Ibn Ḥazm of Cordoba: The Life and Works of a Controversial Thinker*, eds. Camilla Adang,

Ma. Isabel Fierro, and Sabine Schmidtke, Handbook of Oriental studies. Section 1, the Near and Middle East v. 103 (Leiden, Boston: Brill, 2013), 233–250.

Perho, Irmeli, "Ibn Qayyim al-Ǧawziyyah's contribution to the Prophet Medicine," in: *A Scholar in the Shadow: Essays in the Legal and Theological Thought of Ibn Qayyim al-Ǧawziyyah*, eds. Caterina Bori and Livnat Holtzman, Oriente Moderno XC/1 (Rome: Istituto per l'Oriente C.A. Nallino, 2010), 191–210.

Perho, Irmeli, "Man Chooses his Destiny: Ibn Qayyim al-Jawziyya's views on predestination," *Islam and Christian–Muslim Relations* 12/1 (2010): 61–70. doi:10.1080/09596410124404.

Perler, Dominik and Ulrich Rudolph, eds., *Logik und Theologie: das Organon im arabischen und im lateinischen Mittelalter*. Studien und Texte zur Geistesgeschichte des Mittelalters 84 (Leiden: Brill, 2005).

Peterson, R.G., "Critical Calculations: Measure and Symmetry in Literature," *PMLA* 91/3 (1976): 367–375.

Puerta Vílchez, José M., "Abū Muḥammad ʿAlī Ibn Ḥazm: A biographical Sketch," in: *Ibn Ḥazm of Cordoba: The Life and Works of a Controversial Thinker*, eds. Camilla Adang, Ma. Isabel Fierro, and Sabine Schmidtke, Handbook of Oriental studies. Section 1, the Near and Middle East v. 103 (Leiden, Boston: Brill, 2013), 3–24.

Qadhi, Yasir. "'The Unleashed Thunderbolts' of Ibn Qayyim al-Jawziyya: An Introductory Essay," in: *A Scholar in the Shadow: Essays in the Legal and Theological Thought of Ibn Qayyim al-Ǧawziyyah*, eds. Caterina Bori and Livnat Holtzman. Oriente Moderno XC/1 (Rome: Istituto per l'Oriente C.A. Nallino, 2010), 135–149.

Raddatz, H.P., "Sufyān al-T͟hawrī," *EI*², 9:771–772.

Rapoport, Yossef, "Ibn Taymiyya on Divorce Oaths," in: *The Mamluks in Egyptian and Syrian Politics and Society*, eds. Michael Winter and Amalia Levanoni, The medieval Mediterranean v. 51 (Leiden, Boston, MA: Brill, 2004), 191–217.

Rosenthal, Franz, *Knowledge Triumphant: The concept of Knowledge in medieval Islam*, Brill classics in Islam v. 2 (Boston, Leiden: Brill, 2007).

Sabra, Abdelhanid I., "The Appropriation and Subsequent Naturalization of Greek Science in Medieval Islam: A Preliminary Statement," *History of Science* 25 (1987): 223–243.

Saleh, Walid A., "Ibn Taymiyya and the Rise of Radical Hermeneutics: An Analysis of An Introduction to the Foundations of Qurʾāic Exgesis," in: *Ibn Taymiyya and His Times*, eds. Yossef Rapoport and Shahab Ahmed, Studies in Islamic philosophy iv (Karachi: Oxford University Press, 2010), 123–162.

al-Sarhan, Saud S., "Early Muslim Traditionalism: A Critical Study of the Works and Political Theology of Aḥmad Ibn Ḥanbal," doctoral dissertation (University of Exeter, 2011). https://ore.exeter.ac.uk/repository/handle/10036/3374.

Schacht, J.; Carra de Vaux, B.; Nader, A.N., "Bishr b. G͟hiyāt͟h b. Abī Karīma Abū ʿAbd al-Raḥān al-Marīsī," *EI*², 1:1242.

Seale, Morris S., *Muslim Theology: A Study of Origins with Reference to the Church Fathers* (London: Luzac, 1964).

Sellheim, R., "al-Tahānawī," *EI*², 10:98.

Shah, Mustafa, "Classical Islamic Discourse on the Origins of Language: Cultural Memory and the Defense of Orthodoxy," *Numen* (Brill) 58/2 (2011): 314–343. doi:10.1163/156852711X562335.

Shah, Mustafa, "Trajectories in the Development of Islamic Theological Thought: the Synthesis of *Kalām*," *Religion Compass* 1/4 (2007): 430–454. doi:10.1111/j.1749–8171.2007.00026.x

Sharaf al-Dīn, ʿAbd al-ʿAẓīm ʿAbd al-Salām, *Ibn Qayyim al-Jawziyya: ʿaṣruhᵘ wa-manhaguhᵘ wa-ārāʾuhᵘ fī ʾl-fiqh wal-ʿaqāʾid wal-taṣawwūf*, 3rd ed. (Kuwait: Dār al-Qalam, 1405/1984).

al-Shawwā, Ayman ʿAbd al-Razzāq, *Ibn Qayyim al-Jawziyya wa-ārāʾuhᵘ ʾl-naḥwiyya* (Damascus: Dār al-Bashāʾir lil-Ṭibāʿa wal-Nashr, 1995).

Shihadeh, Ayman, "From al-Ghazālī to al-Rāzī: 6th/12th Century Developments in Muslim Philosophical Theology," *Arabic Sciences and Philosophy* 15/1 (1999): 141–179.

Shihadeh, Ayman, "The Mystic and the Sceptic in Fakhr al-Dīn al-Rāzī" in: *Sufism and Theology*, ed. Ayman Shihadeh (Edinburgh: Edinburgh University Press, 2007), 101–122.

Shihadeh, Ayman, *the Teleological Ethics of Fakhr Al-Dīn Al-Rāzī*. Islamic philosophy, theology and science 64 (Leiden, Boston: Brill, 2006).

Shoshan, Boaz, "High Culture and Popular Culture in Medieval Islam," *Studia Islamica* 73 (1991): 67–107.

Siddiqi, Muḥammad Z., and Abdal H. Murad, *Ḥadīth Literature: Its Origin, Development and Special Features*, 2nd ed. (Cambridge: Islamic Texts Society, 1993).

Simon, Udo, "Majāz," *Encyclopedia of Arabic Language and Linguistics*, Brill Online. Accessed March 2016. http://referenceworks.brillonline.com.proxy1.athensams.net/entries/encyclopedia-of-arabiclanguage-arabiclanguage-and-linguistics/majaz-EALL_SIM_vol3_0082

Sourdel, Dominique, "al-Āmidī," *EI*², 1:434.

Stroumsa, Sarah, "Ibn al-Rānādī's *sūʾ adab al-mujadāla*: the Role of Bad Manners in Medieval Disputations," in: *The Majlis: Interreligious Encounters in Medieval Islam*, eds. Hava Lazarus-Yafeh, Mark R. Cohen, Sasson Somekh, and Sydney H. Griffith. Studies in Arabic language and literature v. 4 (Wiesbaden: Harrassowitz, 1999), 66–85.

al-Ṣughayyar, ʿAbd al-Majīd, "Mawāqif "rushdiyya" li-Taqi ʾl-Dīn Ibn Taymiyya?", in: *Tajliyāt al-fikr al-ʿarabī: dirasāt wa-murājaʿāt naqdiyya fī taʾrīkh al-falsafa wal-taṣawwuf bil-maghrib* (Casablanca: al-Madāris, 1421/2000), 97–120.

Takeshita, Masataka, "Ibn ʾArabi's Theory of the Perfect Man and its Place in the History of Islamic Thought," PhD dissertation, Institute for the study of Languages and Cultures of Asia and Africa, Tokyo University of Foreign Studies, 1987.

Tamer, Georges, "The Curse of Philosophy," in: *Islamic Theology, Philosophy and Law: Debating Ibn Taymiyya and Ibn Qayyim al-Jawziyya*, eds. Birgit Krawietz and Georges Tamer, Studien zur Geschichte und Kultur des islamischen Orients Neue Folge 27 (Berlin, Boston: De Gruyter, 2013), 329–376.

Taylor, Christopher S., *In the Vicinity of the Righteous: Ziyāra and the Veneration of Muslim Saints in Late Medieval Egypt*. Islamic history and civilization. Studies and texts v. 22 (Leiden, Boston: Brill, 1999).

Turki, Abdel-Magid, "al-Ẓāhiriyya," *EI*², 11:394–397.

Turkī, Ibrāhīm ibn Manṣūr, *Inkār al-majāz ʿind^a Ibn Taymiyya bayn^a ʾl-dars al-balāghī wal-lughawī* (Riyadh: Dār al-Miʿrāj al-Dawliyya, 1999).

van den Bergh, S., "Dalīl," *EI*², 2:101–102.

van Ess, Josef, *Die Erkenntnislehre des ʿAḍuddadīn al-Īcī: Übersetzung und Kommentar des ersten Buches seiner Mawaqif* (Weisbaden: Steiner, 1966).

van Ess, Josef, *Der Eine und das Andere: Beobachtungen an islamischen häresiographischen Texten*, in 2 vols. (Berlin: De Gruyter, 2010).

van Ess, Josef, *the Flowering of Muslim Theology*, transl. J.M. Todd. (Cambridge: Harvard University Press, 2006).

van Ess, Josef, "The Logical Structure of Islamic Theology," in: *Classical Islamic Culture*, ed. Gustav E. von Grunebaum (Wiesbaden: Harrassowitz, 1970), 21–50.

van Ess, Josef, "al-Naẓẓām," *EI*², 7:1057–1058.

van Ess, Josef, *Theologie und Gesellschaft im 2. und 3. Jahrhundert Hidschra: eine Geschichte des religiosen Denkens im fruhen Islam*, in 6 vols. (Berlin: De Gruyter, 1990).

Veccia Vaglieri, L., "Ibn Abi ʾl-Ḥadīd," *EI*², 3: 684–686.

Versteegh, Kess, *Arabic Grammar and Qurʾanic Exegesis in Early Islam* (Leiden: Brill, 1993).

Versteegh, Kess, *The Arabic Linguistic Tradition*, Routledge history of linguistic thought series 3, Landmarks in Linguistic Thought Volume III (London, New York: Routledge, 1997).

Versteegh, Kess, "Linguistic Attitudes and the Origin of Speech in the Arab World," in: *Understanding Arabic: Essays in Contemporary Arabic Linguistics in Honor of El-Said Badawi* (Cairo: American University in Cairo Press, 1996), 15–31.

Vishanoff, David R., *The Formation of Islamic Hermeneutics: How Sunni Legal Theorists imagined a Revealed Law*. American oriental series vol. 93 (New Haven, Conn: American Oriental Society, 2011).

Voloshinov, Alexander V., "Symmetry as a Superprinciple of Science and Art," *Leonardo* 29/2 (1996): 109–113.

Von Grunebaum, Gustave E., *Medieval Islam: A Study in Cultural Orientation*, 2nd ed. (Chicago, London: The University of Chicago Press, 1969).

Wagner, E., "Munāẓara," *EI*², 7:565–569.

Walker, Paul E., "Bāṭiniyya," *EI THREE*, Brill Online. Accessed July 8, 2013. http://

referenceworks.brillonline.com/entries/encyclopaedia-of-islam-3/batiniyya-COM_22745

Walzer, R., "al-Fārābī," *EI*², 2:778–781.

Watt, William Montgomery, "Abu 'l-Ḥasan al-Ashʿarī," *EI*², 1:694.

Watt, William Montgomery, "Djahm b. Ṣafwān," *EI*², 2:388.

Watt, William Montgomery, "Djahmiyya," *EI*², 2:388.

Watt, William Montgomery, *The Formative Period of Islamic Thought* (Edinburgh: Edinburgh University Press. 1973).

Watt, William Montgomery, "al-Ghazālī," *EI*², 2:1038–1041.

Watt, William Montgomery, "Ibn Fūrak," *EI*², 3:767.

Watt, William Montgomery, *Islamic Philosophy and Theology: An Extended Survey*, 2nd ed. Islamic Surveys (Edinburgh: Edinburgh University Press, 1985).

Wehr, Hans, *A Dictionary of Modern Written Arabic*, with the assistance of J.M. Cowan. 3rd ed. (Beirut: Librairie du Liban, 1980).

Weiss, Bernard G., "al-Āmidī, Sayf al-Dīn," *EI THREE*, Brill Online: http://referenceworks.brillonline.com/entries/encyclopaedia-of-islam-3/al-amidi-sayf-al-din-COM_24214.

Weiss, Bernard G., "Language and Tradition in Medieval Islam: The Question of *al-Ṭarīq ilā maʿrifat al-lugha*", *Miszellen* 61 (1984): 91–99.

Weiss, Bernard G., "Medieval Muslim Discussions of the Origin of Language," *Zeitschrift der Deutschen Morgenländischen Gesellschaft* 124/1 (1974): 33–41.

Weiss, Bernard G., *The search for God's law: Islamic jurisprudence in the writings of Sayf al-Dīn al-Āmidī*, revised ed. (Salt Lake City, Herndon, Va: University of Utah Press; International Institute of Islamic Thought, 2010).

Weiss, Bernard G., "Waḍʿ al-Luġa," *Encyclopedia of Arabic Language and Linguistics*, Brill Online. Accessed March 2016. http://referenceworks.brillonline.com.proxy1.athensams.net/entries/encyclopedia-ofarabic-language-and-linguistics/wad-al-luga-EALL_SIM_0141.

Wensinck, Arent J., *the Muslim Creed: Its Genesis and Historical Development* (Cambridge, London: Frank Cass, 1932).

Wensinck, Arent J., [Heinrichs, W.F.], "Mutawātir," *EI*², 7:781–782.

Winter, Michael, "ʿUlamāʾ between the State and the Society in Pre-Modern Sunni Islam," in: *Guardians of Faith in Modern Times: ʿUlamāʾ in the Middle East*, ed. Meir Hatina, Social, economic and political studies of the Middle East and Asia v. 105 (Leiden, Boston: Brill, 2009), 21–45.

Wolfson, Harry Austryn, "Albinus and Plotinus on Divine Attributes," *Studies in the History of Philosophy and Religion*, eds. Twersky, Isadore; Williams, George H. (Cambridge: Harvard University Press, 1973–1977), 1:115–130.

Wolfson, Harry Austryn, *The Philosophy of the Kalam*, Structure and Growth of Philosophic Systems from Plato to Spinoza 4 (Cambridge, Mass: Harvard University Press, 1976).

Zouggar, Nadjet, "Interprétation autorisée et interprétation proscrite: selon le 'Livre du rejet de la contradiction entre raison et Écriture' de Taqī al-Dīn Aḥmad b. Taymiyya," *Annales Islamologiques* 44 (2010):195–206.

Zysow, Aron, *The Economy of Certainty: An Introduction to the Typology of Islamic Legal Theory*, Resources in Arabic and Islamic Studies (Atlanta, Georgia: Lockwood Press, 2013).

Index of Names

Abrahamov, Binyamin 11n24, 13n31, 35n36, 56n8, 94n93, 100n108, 114n1, 175n1
Abu 'l-Ma'ālī (d. 478/1085) 180–182
Abū 'Ubayda ibn al-Muthannā (d. 209/824–825) 203
Majāz al-qur'ān 209, 220–221
Abū Zayd, Bakr 14n33, 145n78
Ajhar, 'Abd al-Ḥakīm 253n139
al-'Alawī, al-Ḥasan ibn 'Abd al-Raḥman 9
Ali, Mohamed M. Yunis 37n42, 118–119n15, 121n21
al-Āmidī, 'Alī Sayf al-Dīn (d. 631/1233) 56, 115
Al-aḥkām fī uṣūl al-aḥkām 25, 280n32
Iḥkām al-ḥukm fī uṣūl al-aḥkām 213–214, 225
Anjum, Ovamir 75, 80, 120n18, 156, 184n22, 187–188
al-Ash'arī, Abu 'l-Ḥasan (d. 324/935) 88n79, 286n38
Maqālāt al-islāmiyyīn 171–172

Bauer, Thomas 62
Belhaj, Abdessamad 38n43, 64–65, 116n10, 204n11
Bell, Joseph N. 14n32
Berkey, Jonathan P. 23n3, 40n47
Bori, Caterina 15n35, 36, 40n46, 53–54, 159n107
al-Bukhārī (d. 256/870) 123n25

Chamberlain, Michael 63
Chittick, William C. 123n24, 180n13
Cook, Michael 7n13

al-Dakhīl Allāh, 'Alī ibn Muḥammad 8
al-Dhahabī, Shams al-Dīn (d. 748/1347) 74, 249n130, 251

al-Fārābī (d. 339/950) 195
al-Farrā' (d. 207/822) 220, 273
Frank, Richard M. 84n71, 87–88

Galen (d. ca. 210 AD) 273
al-Ghazālī, Abū Ḥāmid (d. 505/1111) 5, 17, 53, 56, 70, 75, 79, 103, 115–117, 137, 173, 176, 202, 217n46, 242–243, 250, 255–256, 261–264, 275, 285, 289, 294
Iḥyā' 'ulūm al-dīn 182–189
al-Munqidh min al-dalāl 185n26
al-Mustaṣfā min 'ulūm al-dīn 115n5
al-Qānūn al-kullī fī 'l-ta'wīl 178–179, 189
Tahāfut al-falāsifa 179n8, 188–189, 255n144, 256–257n150
Gilliot, Claude 3n4, 13n31, 47n65, 286n38
Gimaret, Daniel 13n31, 37n42
Goldziher, Ignaz 12
Griffel, Frank 5n9, 44n57, 112n134, 140–141n68, 146, 179n8
Gutas, Dimitri 173n147

Halkin, A.S. 184n22
Hallaq, Wael B. 76–77, 80, 153n96
Hasan, Ali 261n158
Heinrichs, Wolfhart 202, 208, 220n52
Ḥijāzī, Awḍallah 81–82
Hippocrates (d. 370 BC) 273
Holtzman, Livnat 4n7, 13n31, 15n35, 36, 40n45, 41–43, 55n5, 62n21, 68–69, 77–78, 82, 104n120, 209n23, 274n18, 288n42
Hoover, Jon 9n20, 35n36, 35n37, 42, 77n57

Ibn 'Abd al-Wahhāb, Muḥammad (d. 1206/1792) 7–8
Ibn Abu 'l-Ḥadīd (d. 655/1257 or 656/1258) 180–181
Ibn 'Aqīl, Abu 'l-Wafā' (d. 513/1119) 71, 114–115, 221, 244–245, 248–253, 269–270, 275
al-Irshād fī uṣūl al-dīn 249
Ibn 'Asākir, 'Alī (d. 571/1176) 165n124, 185–186n27
Ibn Abi 'l-Ḥadīd (d. 655/1257 or 656/1258) 180–181
Ibn al-Farrā', Abū Ya'lā (d. 458/1066) 88n79, 121, 244–248, 252–253, 270
al-mu'tamad fī uṣūl al-dīn 114, 246
Ibṭāl al-ta'wīlāt li-akhbār al-ṣifāt 246–248
Ibn Fūrak (d. 406/1015) 42–43, 248, 275
Ibn Ḥanbal, Aḥmad (d. 241/855) 24, 49–51, 125n29, 162, 183, 246, 280

al-Radd ʿala 'l-zanādiqa wal-jahmiyya (attributed work) 49, 50n75, 92, 209, 221, 234
Ibn al-Mawṣilī, Shams al-Dīn (d. 774/1372) 6–7, 9
Mukhtaṣar al-Ṣawāʿiq al-mursala 55, 57, 136
Ibn Ḥajar al-ʿAsqalānī (d. 853/1449)
al-Durar al-kāmina 6
Ibn Ḥazm (d. 456/1064) 17, 106–107, 130n45, 135n56, 270
al-Faṣl fi 'l-milal wal-ahwāʾ wal-niḥal 121n22, 138
al-Iḥkām fī uṣūl al-aḥkām 275–277
Ibn Jinnī (d. 392/1002) 227–229, 285
al-Khaṣāʾiṣ fī ʿilm uṣūl al-ʿarabiyya 235–243
Ibn Kathīr (d. 774/1373) 74, 249n130, 251
Ibn Qayyim al-Jawziyya (d. 751/1350)
Aḥkām ahl al-dhimma 16n37
Badāʾiʿ al-fawāʾid 60–61, 233–234, 241n110
Ighathat al-lahfān 16n37
Ijtimāʿ al-juyūsh al-islāmiyya 51n77, 59, 61, 36n26, 80–81, 234, 258
Iʿlām al-muwaqqiʿīn 34n32, 37, 67
al-Kāfiya al-shāfiya 36, 59–61, 62n21, 67, 69, 71, 80, 138n63
Kitāb al-rūḥ 25, 110n132, 116n9, 138n63, 174, 216n44
al-Ṣawāʿiq al-mursala 2–5, 8–10, 34–35
Shifāʾ al-ʿalīl 34, 55n5, 209n23, 284
Zād al-maʿād (including *al-Tibb al-nabawī*) 25, 174
Ibn Qutayba (d. 276/889) 42, 203
Ibn Rajab (d. 795/1392) 14n33, 32, 56, 74, 249n130, 251
Ibn Rushd (Averroes, d. 595/1198) 17, 56, 71, 252, 288, 293
al-Kashf ʿan manāhij al-adilla 81n65, 200, 253–265
Ibn Sīnā (Avicenna, d. 428/1037) 56, 195
Ibn Taymiyya (d. 728/1328)
al-ʿAqīda 'l-wāsiṭiyya 30–31, 217, 255
Bayān talbīs al-jahmiyya 5, 24, 44–52, 146–156, 217n46, 249, 270, 290
Darʾ taʿāruḍ al-ʿaql wal-naql 4, 56, 93, 153n95, 177, 254, 258, 261n159, 269
al-Ḥamawiyya 'l-kubrā 24, 30–31, 41–45, 51, 90, 211, 216–217, 290
Kitāb al-imān 206, 208–210
al-Radd ʿala 'l-manṭiqiyyīn 76, 85, 153–156, 158, 170, 222n60, 254
al-Risāla 'l-madaniyya 210–213
Risālat al-ḥaqīqa wal-majāz 210, 213–215
Sharḥ awwal al-muḥaṣṣal lil-imām Fakhr al-Dīn (extinct) 145, 164, 157
Sharḥ biḍʿat ʿashr masʾala min al-arbaʿīn lil-Rāzī (extinct) 145, 157
Irwin, Robert 61
al-Isfarāyīnī, Abū Isḥāq (d. 418/1027) 71, 210, 221, 244–245, 274

Jackson, Sherman 31n26
Jaffer, Tariq 143, 147, 288n41
al-Jāḥiẓ (d. 255/868–869) 203
Jahm ibn Ṣafwān 46n62, 232
See also Jahmiyya
al-Jurjānī, ʿAbd al-Qāhir (d. 471/1078) 242
Asrar al-balāgha 203–204
al-Juwaynī, Abu 'l-Maʿālī (Imam al-Ḥaramayn; d. 478/1085) 181–182, 256, 258, 275

al-Khalīl (d. 173/789) 220, 273
Kokoschka, Alina 15, 18
Kraus, Paul 140n68
Krawietz, Birgit 15, 18, 82
von Kügelgen, Anke 85, 154–156

Langermann, Y. Tzvi 116n6, 158, 183
Laoust, Henri 12, 37n42, 38n43
Lav, Daniel 7n13

Makdisi, George 12, 84n72, 85–86, 87–88n79, 249–252
Mouline, Muḥammad Nabīl 7n13

al-Nawbakhtī, al-Ḥasan ibn Mūsa (d. ca. 300/912) 172
Najjar, Ibrahim Y. 256, 260n156
al-Nāshī, Abu 'l-ʿAbbās (d. 293/906) 232
al-Naẓẓām, Abū Isḥāq (d. 220/835–230/845) 195, 275

Özervarli, M.S. 246n166

Perho, Irmeli 74–75n53, 77, 174n149

Qadhi, Yasir 9n20, 82

Rapoport, Yossef 29n17
al-Rāzī, Fakhr al-Dīn (d. 606/1209) 5, 17, 39, 41, 53, 56, 115, 117–118, 138–139, 157, 176, 189–190, 242–243, 285, 294
Asās al-Taqdīs (also entitled *Taʾsīs al-taqdīs*) 43–47, 51, 110, 140–141, 146–147, 157, 178, 268–271, 281–282, 287–291, 293
Kitāb al-arbaʿīn fī uṣūl al-dīn 25, 140–146, 157, 255, 268n6
al-Maḥṣūl fī ʿilm al-uṣūl 24, 204
Muḥaṣṣal afkār al-mutaqaddimīn wal-mutaʾakhkhirīn 25, 140–146, 157, 178, 268n6
Nihāyat al-ījāz fī dirāyat al-iʿjāz 204
Rosenthal, Franz 114n2

Sabra, Abdelhanid I. 116n9
Seale, Morris S. 12n30
Shah, Mustafa 87–88n79
Shihadeh, Ayman 112n134, 141, 143
Sibawayh (d. 180/796) 220, 273
al-Subkī, Taqī al-Dīn (d. 756/1355) 33–34, 38, 160n109, 295
al-Iʿtibār bi-baqāʾ al-janna wal-nār 35
al-Sayf al-ṣaqīl fī ʾl-radd ʿalā Ibn Zafīl 36, 64n27
al-Ṣughayyar, ʿAbd al-Majīd 253n139, 254

Tamer, Georges 254
Taylor, Christopher S. 14n34

van Ess, Josef 13n31, 72, 114n1
Versteegh, Kess 202, 205n15

Watt, William Montgomery 12n30
Weiss, Bernard G. 116n11, 205n15
Wensinck, Arent J. 84n72
Zysow, Aron 267

General Index

acts, of God (*afʿāl al-Allāh*) 30n20, 98, 228, 240, 255
abrogation (*naskh*) 107, 140
abstract speech (*tajrīd*) 214, 217, 225, 228, 231
affirmation (*ithbāt*) 13, 167, 277
 of divine attributes (*al-ṣifāt*) 30n21, 41n49, 191, 212, 233, 246n121, 255, 257
ambiguous, verses or traditions (*mutashābihāt*) 45, 94, 104, 262, 288–289
annihilation, of Hell and Heaven (*fanāʾ*) 9n20, 35n36, 100
anthropomorphism (*tashbīh*; also likening) 2, 29, 96–97, 104, 212, 233–234, 246, 290
 see also corporealism
apparent (*ẓāhir*) *see in either* meaning *or* expression
argument
 a fortiori (*qiyās al-awlā*) 155, 231
 analogical, syllogism (*qiyās*) 67, 116, 133, 153, 155, 179–180, 216
 compelling (*ilzām*) 167, 229, 231
 dialectical (*jadalī*) 89, 117, 135, 159–160
 of exclusive disjunction (*taqsīm, qisma*) 99–100, 193, 218–219, 231
associationism (*shirk, mushrikūn*) 35n36, 66, 91, 183, 257
attribute(s) (*ṣifa*, pl. *ṣifāt*) [of God] 1–2, 30n20, 4–44, 94, 199, 212, 255, 296
 as descriptive (*waṣf, naʿt*) 96, 212
 derived from an "agent" (*bil-fāʿil*) 229, 236
 of aboveness (*fawqiyya, ʿulū*) 81, 119, 199, 212, 234, 270, 273, 286, 288
 of action(s) (*al-fiʿl*) 95, 98, 106, 120, 152, 162, 187, 208, 212, 228n79, 255, 269
 of arrival (*majīʾ*) 286
 of descent (*al-nuzūl*) 96, 199, 231, 286
 of direction (or spatiality, *jiha*) 43, 255, 257–261, 269–270, 288–290
 of essence (*al-dhāt*) 93, 208, 212, 247, 257, 274, 269
 of eyes (*al-ʿayn*) 2
 of sitting on His throne (*istiwāʾ*) 286
 of face (*al-wajh*) 2, 96, 199, 212, 231, 233–234, 286
 of two hands (*al-yadayn*) 96, 199, 231, 286
 of hearing 95, 98, 207, 212, 221, 231, 233, 236, 286
 of knowing/knowledge 100, 207, 241
 of light (*nūr*) 286
 of living/life 207
 of perfection (*al-kamāl*) 1, 3, 42, 51, 96, 120, 233, 257
 of power/omnipotence 100, 109, 152, 283–284, 286–287
 of proclamation (*al-nidāʾ wal-taklīm*) 287
 of God's seat on His throne (*al-istiwāʾ*; *ʿarsh*) 2, 41, 96–97, 100, 199, 212, 228, 231, 244, 258, 273, 268
 of seeing/sight 95, 98, 207, 221, 231, 233, 236, 286
 of simultaneity (*maʿiyya*) and closeness (*qurb*) 286–287
 of volition, will (*mashīʾa*) 152, 236, 234
Ashʿarites *see in ʿulamāʾ*
assimilating (*tamthīl*) 30, 103n115, 104, 217, 233, 241, 246, 280

bi-lā kayfa 41–43, 50n72, 51, 100, 168, 212, 218, 243, 268
body(ies) (*jism*, pl. *ajsām*) 212, 216–217, 232n86, 246, 259–260, 288
brain (*ʿaql*) 119, 122–123

Christians 66, 102, 181, 196, 216, 246
civil strife (*fitna*) 165n124
clarity (*bayān*) 98–99, 102, 104, 119, 125, 131–132, 201, 203, 242
clear, verses (*muḥkamāt*) 45n61
command (*amr*) 98n102, 99, 148, 184, 211, 262, 272, 276
companions, of the Prophet (*ṣaḥāba*) 30n20, 94, 106–107, 163, 184, 196, 209, 216, 220, 274, 276–277
compulsion (*jabr*) 110n132, 139n64, 143n74
consensus (*ijmāʿ*) 11, 28, 36, 47, 212–213, 248, 274–276, 279
context (*qarina, qarāʾin*) 48, 125–126, 128–132, 164, 211, 214–216, 224–227, 230, 245, 264, 275, 280
contemplating (*taʾammul*; cogitating) 87

corporealism (*tajsīm, mujassima*) 30, 43, 96, 104n118, 208n20, 217, 234, 244, 246–247, 254–255, 288–289
creation (*khalq, makhlūq*) 2, 97, 99, 119–120, 122, 203, 212, 223, 228, 233–234, 240, 254, 260, 286–287
of Paradise and Hell 35n36
of the Quran 103n115
signs of (*al-āyāt al-makhlūqa*) 152, 155
creator (*ṣāniʿ*; maker) [i.e., God] 167, 189, 194, 255

debates (*munāẓarāt*) 19, 38–40, 59, 63, 72, 87–89, 118, 174, 187, 235
definition (*ḥadd*) 153, 217
differentiation (*tamyyiz*) 233n89
disputation, dialectics (*jadal*) 38, 87–88, 115–117, 134–135n54, 138, 183, 195, 249–251, 262, 292–294
disagreement (*ikhtilāf*) 94, 106–107, 129, 166, 195, 256, 274–276
divorce (*ṭalāq*) 29, 33–34, 37
duplication of ideas (*taqlīd*; imitation) 20, 67, 103, 107, 158, 294

elite/elitism (*khāṣṣa; aʿyān*) 20, 22, 23n3, 28, 32–33, 38–41, 45, 68, 70–75, 112, 143n74, 151, 160, 174, 185n25, 253, 261, 264, 290, 294–295
epistemology 20–21, 82–89, 118–138, 152–159, 175–190, 201, 266–283
of formalism 267–268, 270–272
of materialism 267–271
of optimism 75, 118, 135, 159–174, 191–197
of skepticism/pessimism 75, 83, 118, 120–122, 130, 135, 138–148, 155–159, 164, 176, 271n12, 281, 285, 287
essence (*dhāt*) 2, 92–93, 96–97, 212, 214, 218, 233, 255, 257
etymological derivative (*ishtiqāq, mushtaqq*) 129, 215
expansion (*iṭlāq*; loosening of meaning) 214, 224–225
expression (*lafẓ*) 58, 64, 83, 97–104, 118, 122, 125–133, 140, 148–150, 162–164, 167, 202–207, 213–238, 254, 291
apparent (*ẓāhir*; literal) 46n63, 47–51, 92–94, 97–99, 128, 166, 216, 246–247, 256, 262, 270, 273–274, 278
technical (*iṣṭilāḥī*; terminological) 47, 186, 222, 219, 278, 286

falāsifa see philosophers
falsification (*taḥrīf*) 30, 50, 93–95
fideism 91, 122, 125, 135, 151, 194, 197, 223, 252–253, 272, 279, 282
fiṭra see natural disposition
free choice (*ikhtiyār*) 15n35, 139n64, 143n74

grammar (*naḥū*; syntax) 59–60, 125n30, 128–130, 148, 171, 199–209, 214, 219, 222, 227, 237–243

ḥadīth(s) (pl. *aḥādīth*; *khabar*, pl. *akhbār*; prophetic reports)
criticism of (*ʿilm uṣūl al-ḥadīth*) 21, 266–267
massively transmitted (*mutawātir, tawātur*) 128, 143–144, 148–149, 162, 164, 169, 266, 269–275
of a limited number of narrators (*al-āḥād, al-wāḥid*) 58, 83, 266–282, 289
of the attributes 2–3, 41–44, 211, 247–248, 268–269, 273–274, 280–282, 286, 290
reference to specific *ḥadīths* 123n25, 166n128, 263
sound (*ṣaḥīḥ*) 108, 269, 279–280
transmitters *see* traditionists
Ḥanbalites *see in ʿulamāʾ*
ḥaqīqa see reality
Ḥashwiyya (sing. *ḥashwī*) 43, 184, 208, 256
heavens, skies 35, 65, 96, 124, 129, 228, 258, 260–261, 270, 274
hellfire 9n20, 35, 191n36, 263
hermeneutics 12–13, 41n49, 51, 83–89, 110, 132, 199–265, 285–288
homonym (*ishtirāk*) 131, 140, 215, 226
hysteron proteron (*al-taqdīm wal-taʾkhīr*) 140

idolatry *see* associationism
ignorance (*jahl*) 50, 104, 105, 203
ijtihād see in law, independent ruling
implication (*iḍmār*) 131, 140
Indians 91

indicator(s) (*dalīl*, pl. *adilla*, *dalāʾil*) 114, 118n15, 119, 247, 269, 282
contradictory (*muʿāriḍ*) 140, 149, 170–173, 177, 186, 193
'informative', scriptural (*samʿī*/*ḍarūrī*) 98, 105, 132–135, 142–143, 149–152, 162, 170, 179, 187, 192
rational (*ʿaqlī*, *ʿaqaliyyāt*) 98, 105, 132–135, 142–143, 149–153, 170, 192
verbal (*lafẓī*) 58, 83, 108, 118–129, 135, 140, 143–144, 146–147, 160–162, 170, 173, 271
infallibility (*ʿiṣma*) 140, 151, 161, 171, 275
inflection (*iʿrāb*; grammatical) 128, 140
innovation(s) (*bidʿa*) 51, 102, 104, 183–185, 206, 236, 278
intention (*murād*; *qaṣd*)
of the speaker (*al-mutakallim*) 49, 92–94, 100, 106, 126–133, 147–151, 160–170, 211–215, 230, 247, 262–263, 272, 275, 282
interpretation 47n65
figurative (*taʾwīl*; allegorical) 19, 32, 43–47, 50–51, 57, 90, 95–112, 146, 167–168, 176, 197, 211–216, 246–249, 253, 257–264, 278, 286–289
explanatory (*tafsīr*; literal) 47, 51, 92–95, 99, 220–221, 246–249, 272
of the Quran; exegesis 47n65, 61, 123–124, 132
the 'universal rule of interpretation', al-Ghazālī's 79, 178–182, 250, 264, 289
intuitive instincts (*badīhiyyāt*; *ḥissiyāt*) 120–121, 132, 154
iṣṭilāḥ see in either expression *or* language

Jahmites 36, 46, 49n71, 55n5, 63, 97, 134, 222, 236–237, 247
Jews 66, 102, 181, 196, 216
jihad see struggle, religious
jurisprudence, theoretical and practical (*uṣūl al-fiqh*, *furūʿ al-fiqh*) 21, 24, 60–61, 85, 116, 201–204, 214, 237, 250–252, 266–267, 292

Kalām see in theology, speculative
khalaf (*tābiʿūn*; devout follower Muslim scholars) 90, 107, 188, 196, 212–213, 274
Khārijites 263, 279
Karrāmites 45n59, 104n118, 244–245, 286, 288
knowledge (*ʿilm* pl. *ʿulūm*; *maʿrifa*)
acquired (*kasbī*) / speculative (*naẓarī*) 154
certain (*yaqīn*) / cogent (*qaṭʿī*) 58, 83, 108, 114, 119, 122, 127–129, 140, 142, 146–148, 154, 158, 161, 271, 278
informative (*khabarī*) 93, 135, 263, 273
necessary (*ḍarūrī*, *iḍṭirārī*) / intuitive (*badīhī*) 114, 154, 169
practical, preformative (*ṭalabī*) 93

language (*lugha*)
assigned by God (*tawqīf*; revelational) 101, 205–206, 223–224, 239, 242–245
assigned by humans (*iṣṭilāḥ*; conventionalist) 101, 205–209, 223, 239, 242–245
habitual (*ʿalā ʾl-ʿādāt*; *fī ʾl-ʿurf*) 127–128, 130, 186, 221–223, 264
imposition of (*waḍʿ*) 48, 93, 101, 129, 205, 223–224, 229n80
origin of (*aṣl*; *mabdaʾ*) 201, 204, 226, 238, 247
use of (*isitiʿmāl*) 224
law (*sharʿ*, *sharīʿa*) [as derived from the scriptures] 27, 67, 102, 131, 183, 194, 201, 213, 219, 223, 249, 258–263, 276–277
independent ruling (*ijtihād*, *mujtahid*) 25, 106, 213–214
laypeople (*ʿāmma*, *ʿāmmī*, *al-ʿawām*) 26, 40, 44, 69–70, 74, 105, 160, 184, 238, 262–264
legal theory *see* jurisprudence
linguistics, Arabic 21, 42, 48, 51, 60–61, 91–100, 124–128, 130–131, 148–149, 164, 199–209, 219–235, 241
literal *see* apparent
literalism 119, 138, 256
logic, Aristotelian *see in* philosophy

manuals, of *Kalām* 81–88, 114, 175, 246, 292
meaning (*maʿnā*; *murād*) 95, 148, 162, 218
apparent, literal (*ẓāhir al-naṣṣ*, *al kalām*) 47–48, 106–107n126, 130, 180n11, 211–212, 246, 256, 263
esoteric (*bāṭin*) 43n63, 163, 180
generic (*jinsī*; *nawʿī*) 228–229, 240
intended [by illocutionary force] 130, 133, 149–151, 161, 187, 211, 215, 224, 227, 273, 280

metaphor (*majāz; istiʿāra*) 48, 58, 78, 83, 90, 93, 100, 108, 130, 140, 198, 199–265, 284–289
modality (*takyīf*) 30, 41–42n49, 212, 216, 218, 243, 255, 268
monism (*ittiḥād*) 180
monotheism (*tawḥīd*; God's unity) 257, 288n42
morphology (*taṣrīf*) 21, 128, 140, 201
Moses 100, 134, 221, 240
munāẓarāt see debates
mutafalsifa see philosophers
mutakallimūn see in ʿulamāʾ
Muʿtazilites *see in ʿulamāʾ*

naql see either Revelation *or* polysemy
natural disposition (*fiṭra*) 75, 77–78, 104–105, 119–122, 153–156, 176, 187, 196, 205, 278
naẓar see rationalistic inquiry
negation [of the divine attributes] *see* stripping

optimism *see in* epistemology
ordeals (*miḥna*, pl. *miḥan*) 69, 103, 165n124

Persians 165n124, 216
philosophy
  Aristotelian (Peripatetic) 85, 105n122, 115, 133, 153–155, 158, 171, 254, 256–257, 259, 261n157, 264, 288, 293
  Greek 25–26, 76, 90–91, 104n117, 105n122, 112, 115–116, 157–159, 166–167n128, 172–173, 196, 205n16, 293
  Sophistic 119–121, 135
  Stoic 115, 121n21, 134–135n54
philosophers (*falāsifa, mutafalsifa*; *ḥukamāʾ*) 66, 91, 133, 153, 171, 188–189, 257–258
pilgrimage (*ḥajj*) 32, 149–150, 276
place (*makān*; ascribed to God) 97, 244, 255, 259–260
polysemy (*naql*) 126, 140
polytheism *see* associationism
preponderance (*tarjīḥ*) 122–123, 192
presumption(s) (*ẓann*, pl. *ẓunūn*) 108, 142–144, 149–150, 154, 158, 169, 192, 267–270, 275–279, 282
poetry (*qaṣīda*) 222n62
  didactic 26, 39–40, 59–62, 67–71
prophecy (*nubuwwa*) 87, 98n102, 104, 133, 150, 171, 179n8, 194
profession of faith (*shahāda*) 1–3, 229, 280–283
proof (*burhān*; *ḥujja*) 65, 120, 125–126, 165, 171, 196, 263, 278
prose, rhymed (*sajʿ*) 40, 62, 64, 69–70, 77

qualification (*qayd, taqyīd*) 224–226, 229–232

rationalists 30, 39, 42–48, 56–57, 64–66, 71, 74, 86, 90, 95, 98, 103–104, 111–117, 135, 139, 165–166, 171–174, 177, 202–204, 219, 239, 243, 267, 278, 286, 291–293
  ultra-rationalistic *see in ʿulamāʾ*, Muʿtazilites
rationalistic inquiry (*naẓar*; *istidlāl*) 93, 102, 154, 169, 179–180, 187, 259, 274
reality (*ḥaqīqa*, pl. *ḥaqāʾiq*; actual, veridical, essential, ontological) 44, 47, 58, 83, 92–100, 108, 131, 199–248, 287–289
Reason (*ʿaql*) 5, 11, 58, 66–67, 83, 90, 96–98, 105, 109, 117–124, 140, 142–143, 151–156, 170–172, 175–197, 207–208, 220–222, 227, 240, 249–256, 260–261, 278, 280, 284, 293
  clear (*ṣarīḥ*; pure) 154, 158, 172, 183, 278
  conceptual (*maʿqūl*) 67, 204
reasonable person (*ʿāqil*, pl. *ʿuqalāʾ*) 152–153, 163, 192–193, 195–197, 216, 228, 232, 280, 282
relativism 121, 154, 170
Revelation (*naql*; *nuṣūṣ al-waḥy*; transmitted textual sources) 51, 58, 71, 81, 83, 98, 102, 105, 109, 117–124, 130–134, 139–140, 142, 151–158, 162–163, 173, 175–197, 199–201, 216–222, 249, 252, 254–264, 272, 280–282, 284
repentance (*tawba*; retraction) 73, 181–182, 248–249, 294

salaf (the pious early Muslim) 7, 32, 47, 59, 86, 90, 94, 105, 182–183, 186–188, 212–214, 244–248, 255, 272–274, 277, 279, 293
sciences (*ʿulūm*)
  Hellenistic 115–116n9, 173–174, 216, 293
  theoretical (*al-ʿulūm al-naẓariyya*) 165, 202, 259

scripturalism 138
seen/visible world (*shāhid* vs. unseen, *ghā'ib*) 260, 262
semantics 97–101, 204, 222
sensations (*ḥissiyāt, maḥsūsāt*) 120–121, 134n54, 154, 165, 204, 260
sharʿ, *sharīʿa see* law, religious
Shīʿites 50, 163, 172, 237, 280
Ismāʿilites 46, 163, 180n11, 181
shirk see associationism
skepticism *see in* epistemology
skies *see* heavens
sophistic *see in* philosophy
speech (*khiṭāb*; *kalām*; message, discourse) 11, 48–49, 66–68, 98–101, 106, 108, 126–134, 148, 161, 165, 168–172, 187, 211–215, 226, 230, 236–238, 240
specification (*takhṣīṣ*) 131, 140, 225, 229, 230, 234
stoicism *see in* philosophy
stripping (*taʿṭīl*; God from His attributes) 30, 63, 97, 167, 197, 217, 228, 232, 234, 254, 257, 271
struggle, religious (*jihad*) 7, 64
substance (*jawhar*) 45n59, 246
Ṣūfīs 32, 180n11, 181, 211n32, 256, 263

tafsīr see interpretation
ṭāghūt (pl. *ṭawāghīt*; false idol or conviction) 5, 7, 20, 55, 57–58, 62, 65–68, 83, 108–109, 114, 118, 136–138, 175, 177–178, 189–192, 199–200, 218, 266–267, 282–285, 289
taḥrīf see falsification
takyīf see modality
tamthīl see assimilating
tanzīh see transcendence
tarjīḥ see preponderance
tashbīh see anthropomorphism
taʿṭīl see stripping
tawqīf see in language
technical terminology (*iṣṭilāḥ*) *see in* expression
theology (*ʿilm uṣūl al-dīn*) 8, 10–13, 20–21, 25, 53, 56, 114–117, 201–202, 237, 267
rationalized-traditionalistic 54, 56, 59, 70–75, 81–89, 111–113, 135–137, 158–159, 231–233, 291–295
speculative (*Kalām*) 5, 25, 39–41, 53, 56, 84–87, 102, 112, 114–117, 141–143, 181–185, 201–203, 242–243, 250
throne, of God *see in* attribute, of God's seat on His throne
traditionists (*muḥaddithūn*; *mukhbirūn; ruwāh*; transmitters of Hadith) 140, 158, 163, 169, 184, 266, 273
traditionalists (*aṣḥāb al-ḥadīth, ahl al-sunna wal-ḥadīth*) 4, 11–12, 41, 56, 72–74, 86, 103n115, 104, 134, 183, 196–197, 207, 211, 234, 246, 249, 251–252, 268, 277–278, 294
ultra-traditionalist *see in ʿulamā'*, Ḥanbalites
transcendence (*tanzīh, munazzah* referring to God) 1, 3, 30n21, 97, 168, 207, 244, 257, 288–289
transmission (*tawātur*; of Hadith traditions) 47, 58, 83, 128, 143–144, 149, 158, 162, 164, 266–267, 270–274, 289
trials, of Ibn Taymiyya 29–31, 37–39, 43, 111, 285
trickeries, judicial (*ḥiyāl*) 34

ʿulamā' (religious scholars) 5, 7, 15, 20, 22–45, 62–63, 70–75, 79, 87, 101, 262
Ashʿarites 4–5, 38–43, 55–56, 60, 68, 70–79, 87, 101, 105–106, 110, 134, 151, 158, 173, 176, 179, 182, 212–214, 242–243, 246–245, 264, 268, 271–247, 281, 285–287, 293–294
Ḥanbalites 4–5, 28–30, 39, 45, 74, 85–86, 245–246, 251, 280, 285
Karrāmites 104n118, 245, 286, 288
mutakallimūn 32, 46–47, 50, 56, 66, 88, 92, 99, 127, 140, 158, 182–184, 247, 277
Muʿtazīlites 11n26, 30–33, 43–44, 46, 49–51, 60, 68, 70, 85, 87, 96, 101–103, 110–111, 115, 125n30, 143–148, 168, 176, 181, 196, 203–223, 232–258, 263–268, 271–276, 285–291
Ẓāhirites 138, 210, 270, 275
unity, divine (*tawḥīd*) *see* monotheism

Wahhābi, movement 7–8

Zanādiqa (sing. *zindīq*) 49n71, 109, 134, 182
Ẓāhirites *see in ʿulamā'*
Zoroastrians 66, 91, 196

Printed in the United States
By Bookmasters